Introduction To
Social Psychology
A European Perspective

BPS TEXTBOOKS IN PSYCHOLOGY

BPS Blackwell presents a comprehensive and authoritative series covering everything a student needs in order to complete an undergraduate degree in psychology. Refreshingly written to consider more than North American research, this series is the first to give a truly international perspective. Written by the very best names in the field, the series offers an extensive range of titles from introductory level through to final year optional modules, and every text fully complies with the BPS syllabus in that topic. No other series bears the BPS seal of approval!

Each book is supported by a companion website, featuring additional resource materials for both instructors and students, designed to encourage critical thinking, and providing for all your course lecturing and testing needs.

Published

Psychology Edited by Miles Hewstone, Frank Fincham and Jonathan Foster

Personality and Individual Differences Tomas Chamorro-Premuzic

Introduction to Social Psychology, 4th edition Edited by Miles Hewstone, Wolfgang Stroebe and Klaus Jonas

Forthcoming

Judgment and Decision-Making David Hardman

Psychopathology Graham Davey

An Introduction to Reading Development and Reading Difficulties Kate Cain and Yvonne Griffiths

Memory Chris Moulin and Martin Conway

Cognition John Groeger and Benjamin Clegg

Miles Hewstone, Wolfgang Stroebe and Klaus Jonas

Introduction To
Social Psychology
A European Perspective
Fourth Edition

BPS TEXTBOOKS  **IN PSYCHOLOGY**

The British Psychological Society

BPS Blackwell

BLACKWELL PUBLISHING
350 Main Street, Malden, MA 02148-5020, USA
9600 Garsington Road, Oxford OX4 2DQ, UK
550 Swanston Street, Carlton, Victoria 3053, Australia

First published 2008 by the British Psychological Society and Blackwell Publishing Ltd

1   2008

Library of Congress Cataloging-in-Publication Data

Introduction to social psychology / edited by Miles Hewstone, Wolfgang Stroebe and Klaus Jonas. — 4th ed.
      p. cm. — (BPS textbooks in psychology)
   Includes bibliographical references and index.
      ISBN 978-1-4051-2400-3 (pbk. : alk. paper)   1. Social psychology.   2. Social psychology—Europe.
I. Hewstone, Miles.   II. Stroebe, Wolfgang.   III. Jonas, Klaus.

   HM1033.I59 2008
   302—dc22   2007030473

A catalogue record for this title is available from the British Library.

Set in 9.5/11.5pt Dante by Graphicraft Limited, Hong Kong
Printed and bound in Singapore by Utopia Press Pte Ltd

The publisher's policy is to use permanent paper from mills that operate a sustainable forestry policy, and which has been manufactured from pulp processed using acid-free and elementary chlorine-free practices. Furthermore, the publisher ensures that the text paper and cover board used have met acceptable environmental accreditation standards.

For further information on
BPS Blackwell, visit our website at
www.bpsblackwell.com

The British Psychological Society's free Research Digest email service rounds up the latest research and relates it to your syllabus in a user-friendly way. To subscribe go to www.researchdigest.org.uk or send a blank email to subscribe-rd@lists.bps.org.uk

Commissioning Editor:	Andrew McAleer
Development Editor:	Elizabeth-Ann Johnston
Marketing Managers:	Darren Reed and Leann Fowler
Production Editors:	Jenny Phillips and Simon Eckley
Project Manager:	Brigitte Lee
Copy-editor:	Brigitte Lee
Proofreader:	Caroline Morris
Indexer:	Ann Dean
Picture Editor:	Leanda Shrimpton
Picture Researcher:	Kitty Bocking

To

Claudia, Rebecca and William Hewstone

Maggie and Katherine Stroebe

and

Jessie and Julie Jonas

....

Brief Contents

Contents

9 Prosocial Behaviour   176

Hans W. Bierhoff

10 Affiliation, Attraction and Close Relationships   196

Abraham P. Buunk and Pieternel Dijkstra

11 Social Influence   216

Miles Hewstone and Robin Martin

12 The Psychology of Groups: Basic Principles   244

Bernard A. Nijstad and Daan van Knippenberg

13 Group Performance and Leadership   264

Stefan Schulz-Hardt and Felix C. Brodbeck

14 Prejudice and Intergroup Relations   290

Thomas Kessler and Amélie Mummendey

15 Social Psychology in Action   316

Klaus Jonas and Carmen Lebherz

Notes on Contributors

Hans W. Bierhoff is Professor of Social Psychology at the Ruhr-University Bochum. He is currently chairman of the board of the Institute of Psychology Information (ZPID) at the University of Trier. He was previously vice-president of the German Psychological Association. He is author of *Prosocial Behaviour* and has written many scholarly books, chapters and articles on topics in social psychology.

Felix C. Brodbeck is Chair of Industrial and Organizational Psychology at Aston Business School, Aston University, and future Chair of Industrial and Organizational Psychology at Ludwig-Maximilians University, Munich. His main research interests are leadership, group performance, collective information processing, diversity and cross-cultural psychology. He has edited or authored several books, including *Culture and Leadership Across the World*, and numerous research papers.

Abraham (Bram) P. Buunk is Academy Professor of Evolutionary Social Psychology on behalf of the Royal Netherlands Academy of Arts and Sciences at the University of Groningen. He has published widely on the role of social comparison and social exchange processes in applied settings. His current research focuses on the evolutionary and biological background of social behaviour, in particular intrasexual competition and mate selection.

Dr. Pieternel Dijkstra is a freelance psychologist, researcher and writer. She has published widely on the topics of jealousy and relationship satisfaction. Her current research focuses on relationship quality and the role of humour and physical attractiveness in intimate relationships.

Geoffrey Haddock is a Reader in Social Psychology at Cardiff University. He has published widely on the topics of attitudes and social cognition. His current research focuses on affective processes of evaluation.

Miles Hewstone is Professor in Social Psychology and Fellow of New College, Oxford University. His main research topic is intergroup relations and the reduction of intergroup conflict, especially via intergroup contact, and he has edited or authored many books, including *Psychology* (Blackwell, 2006).

Klaus Jonas is Professor of Social and Business Psychology at the University of Zürich. He has published on attitudes, stereotypes and human resource management. His current interests concern the influence of leadership on performance and satisfaction of subordinates.

Thomas Kessler is Professor of Social Psychology at the School of Psychology, University of Exeter. His main research interests are in intergroup relations and the explicit negative treatment of outgroups, as well as evolutionary approaches to intergroup phenomena. He has published several articles and book chapters.

Barbara Krahé is Professor of Social Psychology at the University of Potsdam, Germany. Her research focuses on aggression and social cognition applied to legal decision-making. She is a council member of the International Society for Research on Aggression and co-editor of its journal, *Aggressive Behavior*.

Carmen Lebherz is Assistant Professor at the Psychology Department of the University of Zurich. She is currently interested in person perception, particularly in the effectiveness of impression management tactics.

Gregory R. Maio is a Professor of Social Psychology at Cardiff University. He has published widely on the topics of attitudes and social cognition. His current research focuses on the mental structure of social values.

Antony S.R. Manstead is Professor of Psychology at Cardiff University, having held positions at the Universities of Sussex, Manchester, Amsterdam and Cambridge. He has been president of the European Association of Experimental Social Psychology and editor of the *British Journal of Social Psychology*. He is currently associate editor of the *Journal of Personality and Social Psychology*. His research focuses on emotion.

Robin Martin is Professor of Social and Organizational Psychology at Aston Business School, Aston University, Birmingham. He has served on the faculties of the Universities of Sheffield, Swansea, Cardiff and Queensland (Brisbane, Australia). He conducts research in the area of social influence processes (especially majority and minority influence), workplace leadership, innovation and team working.

Amélie Mummendey is Professor of Social Psychology in the Institute of Psychology, Friedrich Schiller University Jena. Her key research topic is group conflict and cooperation.

Bernard A. Nijstad is Associate Professor of Organizational Psychology at the University of Amsterdam. His main research interests are group creativity and group decision-making.

Brian Parkinson lectures at Oxford University. His research focuses on the interpersonal causes, effects and functions of emotion. His books include *Ideas and Realities of Emotion* (1995) and (with Fischer and Manstead) *Emotion in Social Relations* (2005).

Louise Pendry is Senior Lecturer in Psychology at Exeter University. She has published articles on stereotyping and social cognition. More recently, her research focuses on some applications of social cognition and stereotype activation/use (e.g., within the field of diversity training.)

Stefan Schulz-Hardt is Professor of Industrial, Economic and Social Psychology at Georg-August-University Göttingen. He has published on group decision-making, selective exposure to information, price trend perception and other topics. One of his current research interests is the facilitation of process gains in group performance.

Bernd Simon is Professor of Social Psychology and Evaluation Research at the University of Kiel (Germany). He has published widely on the topics of self, identity and group processes. His current research focuses on the role of identity in respect, power and collective action.

Wolfgang Stroebe has taught social psychology at universities in Germany, England, the USA and the Netherlands. At present he is Professor of Social Psychology at Utrecht University (the Netherlands). He has authored numerous books, chapters and articles in scientific journals on social and health psychology and is co-editor (with Miles Hewstone) of the *European Review of Social Psychology*.

Roman Trötschel is lecturer at the University of Trier, Germany. His main research interest is in intergroup behaviour, self-regulation in negotiations and social conflict.

Daan van Knippenberg is a Professor of Organizational Behaviour at RSM Erasmus University, The Netherlands. His main research interests are group diversity, group decision-making, leadership (in particular the role of self-concept and emotions) and social identity processes in organizations.

Preface to the Fourth Edition

This is the fourth, and completely revised, edition of this widely selling textbook, designed to teach social psychology to an audience of students at universities throughout Europe and many other parts of the world. When, in 1986, we set out with the aim of publishing such a book, we certainly did not imagine either that it would end up being translated into a host of foreign editions (ranging from Croatian to Japanese) or that we would be publishing this new edition more than 20 years later.

In that period of time, of course, the world has changed quite dramatically, and we have tried to reflect those changes in the material we cover and the examples used to illustrate social psychological phenomena. The European Community, for example, has enlarged significantly, and there is continuing debate about the relationship between national and superordinate ('European') identity; there have also been appalling genocides in the heart of Europe (in ex-Yugoslavia) and a long way away from it, in Rwanda (see Chapter 14). The terrifying scourge of AIDS threatens the health of millions across the globe, and a significant part of the fight against this disease is built on social psychological principles of changing health-related behaviours (see Chapter 15). And the response to the Indian Ocean tsunami, which dominated the news in late December 2004, challenged existing conceptions of altruism and helping behaviour (see Chapter 9). These are just some of the real-life examples the chapters in this volume address, and just a few of the ways in which one can demonstrate that social psychology is a discipline that has an important role to play in contemporary society.

Notwithstanding the success of previous editions, this new volume represents the most thorough revision, in terms of topics covered and pedagogical aids. The volume contains chapters dealing with all the core topics one would expect to find in an introduction to social psychology (methods, social cognition, attitudes, aggression, prosocial behaviour, relationships, social influence, group processes and intergroup relations). We have also added three new chapters to this edition. First, there is an Introduction (Chapter 1), which will help orient all new readers to the field of social psychology as a whole; it covers how we address research questions, how social psychology is defined and distinguished from related disciplines, what are the main historical developments, and what are the most notable emerging theoretical perspectives. We strongly recommend that all students read this chapter before launching into the specific core topics of social psychology, covered in the remaining chapters. Second, there is a chapter on the self (Chapter 5), which considers the meaning and role of self and identity as social psychological concepts and deals with fascinating phenomena such as the self-concept and self-knowledge, self-esteem, and the cultural impact on self and identity. Third, there is a chapter on social psychology in action (Chapter 15), which addresses how social psychology can be applied to the 'real world' and describes the application of social psychology to the topics of advertising, the workplace and health.

There are many didactic improvements and pedagogical aids in this new edition. Each chapter focuses on the central *theories*, *concepts*, *paradigms*, *results* and *conclusions*. In terms of structure, each chapter contains the following specific features, designed to improve learning and enhance the enjoyment of the task:

- A short outline written in clear English, providing an overview of the chapter.

- A list of key concepts, consisting of the main terms which a student should know about each topic area; the definitions of each key concept are provided in the text of each chapter and gathered together in an alphabetical glossary at the end of the book.

- The body of the text in each chapter is broken down into clear sections, and the reader is guided by subheadings throughout the chapter to prevent long, uninterrupted passages of text. Text is also broken up by figures, tables and occasional photographs.

- Each main section or subsection of the chapter begins with 'learning questions': these are the major questions that the student should be able to answer having read the chapter.

- Each major section of the chapter ends with a summary, and each chapter ends with a summary and conclusions in the form of bullet points.

- A list of suggestions for further reading, with a sentence indicating what the student will find in each source, concludes each chapter.

- Each chapter includes brief biographies of 'pioneers' in the field.

- Each chapter contains two to three boxes of three different types:
  - *Research close-ups*: Brief summaries of classic and contemporary research studies, explaining clearly why and how the research was done, what it found and what its implications are.
  - *Individual differences measure*: Illustrative items from scales used to measure variables discussed in the text.
  - *Everyday social psychology*: The description of a 'real-life' application of theory and research described in the chapter.

Features designed to aid learning and help both instructors and students do not end with the material *inside* the book. Extensive material is also provided on the web (www.blackwellpublishing. com/socialpsych), including learning objectives, and a large bank of multiple choice, true or false, and fill-in-the-blank questions, as well as links to other useful websites.

As always when we come to the end of an edition, we are grateful that we are such poor predictors of how much work is involved. Had we known this at the outset, we might not have succumbed yet again to the temptation to initiate a new edition. As always in such a major enterprise, there are many others to whom we owe thanks. First and foremost, we thank our authors for their excellent manuscripts and their willingness to go through repeated revisions in response to our editorial feedback. We would also like to thank the editorial team at Blackwell for their support in this endeavour. Last and certainly not least, we owe thanks to our families, who have patiently lived with, and through, this new edition.

Miles Hewstone, Oxford
Wolfgang Stroebe, Utrecht
Klaus Jonas, Zürich

1 Introducing Social Psychology

Wolfgang Stroebe, Miles Hewstone and Klaus Jonas

CHAPTER OUTLINE

....

We introduce social psychology with a few examples of classic studies to give an impression of the research questions social psychologists address and of the methods they use to tackle these questions. We then present a formal definition of social psychology and discuss the differences between social psychology and related areas. The main part of the chapter is devoted to the history of social psychology, which we trace from the starting years around 1900 until today. Most of this history took place in the USA, but this development was strongly influenced by European researchers, even before the establishment of a European social psychology following World War II.

Introduction: Some Classic Studies

....

How do social psychologists go about addressing research questions?

In 1954, Muzafer Sherif (see Pioneer box, Chapter 14, p. 295), who was then professor of social psychology at the University of Oklahoma (USA), conducted one of a series of classic studies with 11-year-old boys, who had been sent to a remote summer camp at Robbers Cave State Park, Oklahoma. None of the boys knew each other before the study. They were divided into two groups, who stayed in cabins far apart from each other and did not know of each other's existence. For one week, each of the groups enjoyed the typical summer camp life, engaging in fun activities like camping out, transporting canoes over rough terrain to the water and playing various games. They had a great time. It is therefore not surprising that at the end of the week, group members had grown very fond of one another and that the groups developed strong group identities. Each chose a name for itself (the 'Rattlers' and the 'Eagles'), which they proudly displayed on shirts and flags.

At the end of the week, each of the groups was told that there was another group in the vicinity. As though acceding to the boys' requests, the staff arranged tournaments of games (e.g., touch football, baseball, tug of war) between the groups. The winning team would receive a cup and members of the winning team would each be given a new penknife. The tournament started in the spirit of good sportsmanship, but as it progressed, hostilities between the groups began to develop. 'Soon members of each group began to call their rivals "stinkers", "sneaks" and "cheats" . . . Near the end of this stage, the members of each group found the other group and its members so distasteful that they expressed strong preferences to have no further contact with them at all' (Sherif, 1967, p. 82).

What was the point of all of this? What can tales about boys in a summer camp tell us about real life? The answer is: a great deal. These studies actually mark a turning point in the study of prejudice (i.e., dislike for members of an outgroup), because they challenged the then dominant view of prejudice as either an outflow of a prejudiced personality disposition (authoritarian personality) or as the result of displaced frustration (scapegoat theory). There was no indication that these boys had prejudiced personalities or needed scapegoats to displace their aggression. And yet, they developed strong dislikes for the members of the other group (the 'stinkers' and 'sneaks'), because they were competing with them for some valued good which only one of the two groups could attain. Sherif interpreted these findings as support for his realistic conflict theory, which assumed that intergroup hostility and intergroup prejudice are usually the result of a conflict of interest between groups over valued commodities or opportunities. Goals were the central concept in Sherif's theory: he argued that when two groups were competing for the same goal, which only one could achieve, then there would be intergroup hostility.

Not surprising, you might say. After all, this is the reason why football supporters beat each other up every so often before and after games between their clubs. And yet, this is not the full story. Nearly two decades later, Henri Tajfel (see Pioneer box, Chapter 14, p. 297), then professor of social psychology at Bristol University (UK), and colleagues conducted a series of studies, which called into question the assumption that competitive goals are a *necessary* condition for the development of intergroup hostility (Tajfel, Billig, Bundy & Flament, 1971). Participants in these studies were 14- to 15-year-old schoolboys, who all knew each other well and came to the psychology laboratory in groups of eight, to participate in an experiment on visual perception. Their task was to estimate the number of dots that were flashed on a screen. After completion of this task, they were told that they would also participate in a second experiment and, for the ease of coding, would be divided on the basis of the dot estimates they had just made. Half the boys were then (randomly) assigned to the 'under-estimators' group, the other half to the 'over-estimators' group. (In later studies, boys were often divided on the basis of their alleged preference for paintings by Klee or Kandinsky, an equally irrelevant criterion for boys of that age.) The boys then had to assign rewards to other individuals in real money. They did not know the identity of the other individuals, but only their code numbers and their group membership. Tajfel and colleagues were especially interested in how the boys would divide money up between a member of their own group and a member of the other group. The results were quite surprising: in making their intergroup choices, most boys gave consistently more money to members of their own group than to members of the other group. These studies were again quite innovative, because they showed that intergroup conflict was *not* an essential cause of intergroup discrimination (or at least ingroup favouritism). Apparently, the mere fact of division into groups was sufficient to trigger discriminatory behaviour.

You may now believe that you have some idea of what social psychology is all about and how social psychologists conduct their research. You might also think that the approach of Sherif was more in line with what you had expected but that the studies by Tajfel, despite their artificiality, led to some interesting results. However, you will be somewhat premature in your confidence, as you may realize when we describe two more studies that have become classics in social psychology.

In 1994, Neil Macrae (then at Cardiff University) and colleagues studied people's ability to suppress their prejudicial thoughts (Macrae, Bodenhausen, Milne & Jetten, 1994). After all, there is a great deal of evidence that people acquire their prejudices quite early and may not be able to get rid of them later in life, even if these prejudicial thoughts have become inconsistent with their egalitarian values (Wilson, Lindzey & Schooler, 2000). Thus, if people cannot forget their prejudicial thoughts, it would be good if, at least, they could inhibit them and prevent them from affecting their actions. As the studies by Macrae, Bodenhausen et al. (1994) show, this may be more difficult than one would think.

Participants in these studies were students. When they arrived at the laboratory, they were told that they were to participate in an investigation of people's ability to construct life event details from visual information. They were then presented with a colour photograph of a skinhead and were asked to write a short essay about a typical day in the life of a skinhead. Skinheads were chosen here not only because there is widespread prejudice against them, but also because, unlike prejudice towards other minority groups, expressing prejudice towards skinheads is not (yet) politically incorrect. Half of the participants were asked to suppress their prejudice against skinheads in writing this essay. They were told to try to write this essay without being influenced by their stereotypes about skinheads, that is, the beliefs they might have about the characteristics of skinheads in general. The other half (i.e., the control group) were not given this instruction.

After participants had finished the first essay, they were given a photo of another skinhead and asked to write another essay. This time, however, they were not given any instructions about suppressing stereotypes. Both essays were then rated by independent raters, who did not know whether a given essay had been written by a participant from either the experimental or the control group, and who evaluated the extent to which writers expressed stereotypes about skinheads. With regard to the first essay, results were not very surprising. As one would expect of 'good' (i.e., obedient) participants, individuals who had been instructed to suppress their stereotypes in their first essay did so quite successfully. Their

Plate 1.1 *How easy is it for people to suppress their prejudice towards skinheads?*

essays were much less stereotypic than the essays of the control group. However, the analysis of their second essays provided a striking finding: *there was a rebound effect*. The second essay of these 'suppressors' was more stereotypic than that of the control group. Thus, when people no longer tried to suppress their stereotypes, they showed a higher level of stereotypical thinking than if they had never tried to suppress their thoughts in the first place.

Although these are fascinating results, Macrae (see Chapter 4, this volume) and colleagues were not satisfied with merely showing a rebound effect of stereotype suppression on *thinking*. They also wanted to know whether attempts to suppress one's stereotype would affect people's *action*. They therefore conducted a second study. The first part of this study was identical to that of their first experiment. However, after having written an essay under either stereotype suppression or no-suppression instructions, participants were told that they would now go next door to meet the person depicted on the photograph (i.e., the skinhead). When they entered the room next door, there was a row of chairs standing next to each other, but no skinhead. However, on the first chair there was a denim jacket and bag. The experimenter told the participant that the other person must just have gone to the toilet and would return shortly and that the participant should sit down on one of the chairs in the meantime. The measure of interest in this case was the seating position, that is, how far the participant would choose to sit away from the skinhead he or she was supposed to meet. We would all acknowledge that the distance we keep from someone is an indication of our liking for that person (Macrae, Bodenhausen et al., 1994). And in line with the findings of the previous study, participants who had (successfully) suppressed their stereotype on writing the essay now chose a chair that was significantly further away from the skinhead than did individuals in the control group. Thus, the rebound effect of stereotype suppression affected not only thoughts but also behaviour (but for some constraints on the general effect, see Monteith, Sherman & Devine, 1998).

As surprising as these findings were, the impact of stereotypes on behaviour was still restricted to the way the individual behaved towards a member of the group towards whom the stereotype was held. As we will see in the next experiment, the impact of stereotypes can be even more pervasive. This study was conducted by John Bargh (see Pioneer box, Chapter 4, p. 75) and his colleagues (Bargh, Chen & Burrows, 1996) at New York University (USA). In the first part of this experiment, participants had to complete a scrambled sentence test in which they had to form sentences from scrambled sets of words. For participants in the experimental group, these sentences contained words that were part of the (American) stereotype of the elderly such as 'Florida', 'Bingo' and 'grey'. This procedure is known as 'priming', because these words will bring the elderly stereotype to participants' minds (i.e., make it more accessible), including characteristics of elderly people that were not even mentioned in the priming procedure.

One such characteristic that is typically attributed to the elderly, but was not mentioned in the priming procedure, is that elderly people move rather slowly. The researchers assumed that participants who were primed with the stereotype of the elderly would also think of 'moving slowly' as another salient characteristic of the elderly. It was further assumed that this thought would affect *the participants' own behaviour*. The researchers predicted that participants primed with the elderly stereotype would move more slowly than participants in the control condition who had been exposed to neutral primes. The experimenters then measured the time it took participants to walk from the experimental room to the nearest lift. In line with the hypothesis, participants who were primed with the elderly stereotype took significantly longer to reach the lift than did participants who had been primed with neutral words. It appears that thinking of the concept 'slow' influenced behaviour, and that consciousness did not play any part in this process, because participants were aware neither that they had been primed nor that they had been led to walk more slowly (see Research close-up 4.1, p. 74).

We hope that reading about these studies has stimulated your interest in social psychology. If it has, you can read more about the first two studies in Chapter 14 (Prejudice and intergroup relations). The last two studies are discussed in Chapter 4 (Social cognition). Given that the research we have discussed so far is quite varied in its research questions, scope and methods, we now turn to a more general discussion of the nature of social psychology.

WHAT IS SOCIAL PSYCHOLOGY?

How do social psychologists define their discipline?

When social psychologists are called upon to define their discipline, they usually refer to the definition given by Gordon Allport (1954a) (see Pioneer box, Chapter 14, p. 309) in his classic chapter on the history of social psychology, published in the second edition of the *Handbook of Social Psychology*: 'Social psychology is the attempt to understand and explain how the thoughts, feelings, and behaviors of individuals are influenced by the actual, imagined, or implied presence of other human beings' (p. 5). This is quite a good definition, which can accommodate the studies that we have described earlier.

One characteristic of social psychology, which Allport implied but did not mention specifically, is the use of *scientific methods*. The scientific method of choice used in the studies we just described was the experiment. We will discuss this method only briefly, because you will learn more about the experimental method in the chapter on methods (Chapter 2). Experiments are a method in which the researcher deliberately introduces some change into a setting to examine the consequences of that change. The typical procedure used in experiments is that conditions in which a change has been introduced (i.e., an independent variable manipulated) are compared to conditions in which this has not been the case, the so-called control group. By randomly assigning participants to either experimental or control group, the researcher can be reasonably certain that any difference between the two groups was due to the manipulation of the independent variable. Thus, Macrae and colleagues asked half their participants to suppress their stereotype of skinheads, and compared their thoughts and behaviour to those of a control group of individuals who had not been asked to suppress their stereotype. Bargh and colleagues compared the walking speed of participants who had been primed with the elderly stereotype with that of (control) participants, who had not been primed. The study by Sherif is somewhat deficient in this respect, because he did not really have a proper control group. He compared the impact of the introduction of intergroup competition on group members' behaviour over time. The control conditions in the Tajfel experiment are difficult to explain without a more detailed description of the study. You may remember that Tajfel and colleagues assessed how the boys would divide money between a member of their own group and a member of the other group. As a control for ingroup bias, they simply reversed the alleged group membership of the two individuals between whom the money had to be divided.

Another methodological difference between the study by Sherif and those of the other researchers is that Sherif's study was a field rather than a laboratory experiment: he used a natural setting (summer camp) to test his hypotheses. The other studies were all laboratory experiments which used settings that were specially created by the experimenter. For example, Macrae and colleagues led their participants to believe that they were in a study of people's ability to construct life event details from visual information. This is also an example of a darker aspect of social psychology, namely, that we often have to use deception to test our predictions. But if the participants in the study by Macrae and colleagues (1994) had known the real purpose of the study, this would have influenced their thoughts and behaviour and the results of such a study would have been meaningless. (We therefore often disregard the data of participants who guess the purpose of our experiments.) Field and laboratory experiments are not the only scientific methods used by social psychologists to test their hypotheses. You can read about other methods in Chapter 2 (Research methods in social psychology).

Obviously, the use of scientific methods is not a characteristic that allows one to distinguish social psychology from other social sciences. By definition, all sciences use scientific methods and for many of them, experiments are the method of choice. A more distinctive characteristic introduced by Allport is the fact that social psychology is concerned with social influence and that it studies the impact of others on individuals' thoughts, feelings and behaviours. All of the studies we described earlier tried to understand and explain how thoughts, feelings and behaviours of their participants were influenced by the presence of other human beings. In the case of the study by Sherif, these human beings were mainly the members of the other group with whom the boys competed, although the members of their own groups also influenced the behaviour of these boys. In contrast to the Sherif study, where the others were actually present, the presence of others was imagined rather than real in the Tajfel study (recall that Allport's careful definition allowed for the impact of the *imagined* presence of others). Finally, in the studies by Macrae and by Bargh and colleagues, it was not really the presence of others that influenced participants' thoughts or behaviour but the suppression or activation of their beliefs about other groups.

The studies by Macrae and Bargh are also good examples of an aspect of social psychological research that is less clearly emphasized in Allport's definition, namely, the fact that we are interested not only in the impact others have on our thoughts, feelings and behaviour but also in the *cognitive processes* by which our thoughts, emotions and goals guide our understanding of the world around us and our actions. You can read more about this in Chapter 4 (Social cognition).

A final characteristic of social psychology emphasized in Allport's definition is that social psychologists study the impact that the implied or actual presence of others has on the thoughts, feelings and behaviours of *individuals*. Thus, even when we study social groups, we examine the impact groups have on the individual group members. For example, in the classic study of conformity with group majorities, Asch (1956) examined the impact of the majority opinion on the judgements of individual participants (see Chapter 11, this volume). Similarly, Tajfel and colleagues (1971) studied the impact of the mere categorization of others into ingroup and outgroup on the way individuals distributed money between them. This emphasis on the individual is actually a very important point which had already been made by the elder brother of Gordon Allport, Floyd Allport, in his classic textbook of social psychology: 'There is no psychology of groups which is not essentially and entirely a psychology of individuals. Social psychology must not be placed in contradistinction to the psychology of the individual; it is a part of the psychology of the individual, whose behaviour it studies in relation to that sector of his environment comprised by his fellows' (F. Allport, 1924, p. 4). The emphasis on the individual does not deny the importance of the social context as a determinant of individual behaviour, but it rejects the existence of a group consciousness or a collective mind as separate from the minds of the individuals who comprise the group.

HOW DOES SOCIAL PSYCHOLOGY DIFFER FROM OTHER DISCIPLINES?

What differentiates social psychology from related disciplines such as personality psychology and sociology?

In addition to using examples of studies as well as a definition to illuminate the nature of social psychology, it might be helpful to contrast social psychological research to that of research in related disciplines. As in the previous section, we will use the example of

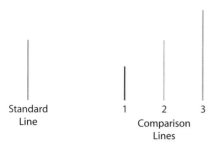

Figure 1.1 *Example of the stimulus pattern used in the conformity studies of Asch (1955).*

an experimental study to clarify these differences. This study was conducted at a small elite college in the United States and was announced as an experiment on perception. The experimental sessions were held in a small classroom and eight participants attended each of the sessions. The participants, who were seated in two rows of four, were presented with sets of four lines of different length, a standard line and three comparison lines. Their task consisted of the comparison of the standard line with the three other lines, one of which was equal to the standard line. The comparison lines were numbered from 1 to 3, and the participants stated their judgements by calling out one of the numbers (see Figure 1.1).

Obviously, this was a simple experiment in visual discrimination in which the experimenter probably wanted to find out how accurately participants could differentiate between lines of different lengths and where the threshold lay at which people would begin to make mistakes. However, there is one feature of the experiment which does not fit with standard procedures in perception experiments, namely, that participants judged these lines in groups. This would not have been a problem had the experimenter ensured that judgements were written down, to exclude the possibility that participants would be aware of each other's judgements. But in the present experiment, participants were asked to *call out* their judgements to the experimenter. This appears to be a serious methodological fault. Any determination of a difference threshold based on such data would be flawed, because participants might have been influenced by the earlier judgements that they overheard. Let us assume that the first participant calling out his judgements committed an error. The second participant, who might normally have given a correct response, might now have become uncertain and given the same erroneous response as the first participant. In this way, an experiment on perception might, in fact, have become a study of social influence.

Since we are concerned here with social psychology, it will not come as a surprise that the experimenter, a professor of social psychology at Swarthmore College, Pennsylvania, was not really interested in measuring perceptual thresholds but in the extent to which individuals would be influenced by a discrepant majority judgement. In fact, only one of the eight participants in each session was a 'naïve' participant; all the others were confederates of the experimenter and were instructed to give unanimous but wrong judgements on 12 out of the 18 trials. These judgements were so easy that participants who judged the stimuli in individual

sessions made practically no incorrect judgements. And yet, when participants were exposed to the incorrect judgements of a unanimous majority, 36.8 per cent of their judgements were incorrect (Asch, 1955).

With this experimental setting, Asch created a situation which is familiar to most of us from everyday life. We have probably all had the experience of members of our group disagreeing with us on some issue, and then having to decide whether we should go with the group or stick to our own position at the risk of becoming disliked or of looking foolish. Naturally, we do not usually disagree about the length of lines but about some issue of greater importance, and often the disagreeing majority is not unanimous. However, the setting that was developed by Asch would allow us to manipulate all these variables, and most of them have indeed been investigated in subsequent research (for a review, see Allen, 1965). Our decision to stick to our guns or go with the group will depend very much on how confident we are of the correctness of our own opinion, on how important a correct decision is for us and for the group, and on how well we know the other group members. We are probably also more willing to conform to a majority if we are confronted with a majority that is unanimous rather than divided. If we return to Gordon Allport's definition of social psychology, it is easy to see that the Asch experiment fits all of the characteristics: Asch used a laboratory experiment to study the social influence which a (false) majority judgement would have on the thoughts and behaviours (i.e., judgements) of individuals.

The Asch experiment also allows us to demonstrate the difference between social psychology and 'asocial' *general psychology*. If Asch had been interested in studying perceptual thresholds, he would have systematically varied the difference in the lengths of his standard and comparison stimuli to assess the extent to which such variations affected perceptual judgements. The (perceptual) judgements would have remained the same, but they would now be investigated in relation to variations in the physical aspects of the stimuli, while keeping the social context constant. In contrast, Asch kept the physical stimulus constellation relatively constant and was interested in the effect that varying the social context (i.e., majority size and unanimity) had on perceptual judgements.

The Asch situation is also useful for demonstrating the difference between social and personality psychology. As a social psychologist, Asch was interested in the impact that characteristics of the social situation had on the thoughts and behaviours of his participants. Does the rate of conformity increase if we increase the number of majority members who give erroneous judgements? Does the conformity rate decrease if participants are allowed to give their judgements anonymously? Asch's approach is typical of social psychological research, which usually *manipulates* important aspects of the social context in order to assess the impact these changes have on the thoughts, feelings and behaviour of the target person.

Personality psychologists, on the other hand, might be less interested in the impact of the social context on behaviour and, instead, ask themselves why some participants are influenced by the erroneous judgements of the majority while others remain unaffected. Thus, the personality psychologist would be interested in the personality traits that are responsible for the fact that different individuals act differently in what is essentially the same social situation. The personality psychologist might test whether intelligent individuals are less likely than unintelligent ones to conform to majorities, or whether conformity is more prevalent among authoritarian rather than non-authoritarian personalities (see the discussion of the authoritarian personality in Chapter 14, this volume; Adorno et al., 1950).

Personality psychologists would not, however, only address the question of individual differences as determinants of conformity; they would also want to know how these individual differences came about. Is it possible to relate differences in authoritarianism to differences in the way parents brought up their children, and what aspects of a person's upbringing determine his or her self-esteem? Thus, one could try to separate the disciplines of social and personality psychology as follows: individual behaviour is determined by three factors: (1) the biological constitution of individuals, (2) their acquired traits and (3) the social and physical context. Whereas personality psychologists are mainly interested in studying how particular traits are acquired and how these traits influence the individual's behaviour, social psychologists study the impact of the social situation on individual behaviour.

Unfortunately, such a distinction would oversimplify the differences between social and personality psychology (for more details, see Krahé, 1992) because one of the central concepts of social psychology, namely social attitudes, is defined by many social psychologists (e.g., Eagly & Chaiken, 1993) as a tendency (i.e., individual disposition) to evaluate an attitude object positively or negatively (see Chapter 6, this volume). Even though social psychologists are mainly interested in studying how attitudes change in response to social influence attempts (see Chapters 7 and 11, this volume), they also use attitudes to predict individual behaviour (see Chapter 6, this volume). Furthermore, within social psychology, researchers have often been interested in studying individual difference variables, such as the degree to which individuals are prone to prejudice and susceptible to fascist ideologies ('authoritarianism'; Adorno et al., 1950; see Chapter 14, this volume), or the degree to which individuals are oriented to situational cues or reactions of others ('self-monitoring'; Snyder, 1974).

Since there is a great deal of agreement that individual behaviour is influenced by personality traits (see Chapter 8, this volume, on aggression) as well as the social context, the two fields of personality psychology and social psychology are, in fact, difficult to separate. It is therefore not surprising that the leading social psychological journal is the *Journal of Personality and Social Psychology* and that most American social psychologists are members of the Society of Personality and Social Psychology. However, there are subtle differences in focus. Social psychologists are typically interested in personality variables as *moderators*. They look for the extent to which the impact of an independent variable on a dependent variable is qualified by, or depends on, the level of an individual's score on a personality measure. For example, there is a higher correlation between attitudes and behaviour for 'low' than for 'high' self-monitors (Snyder & Kendzierski, 1982). Many of the chapters in this volume refer to such personality influences on social behaviour. Social psychologists also tend to emphasize that the impact of personality variables on social behaviour is weaker in 'strong' compared to 'weak' social situations

(Mischel, 1977). Thus social psychologists emphasize the power of strong social situations to relegate personality influences to the background. This occurs, for example, in experiments investigating helping in emergencies (Latané & Darley, 1976; see Chapter 9, this volume) and obeying an authority figure's orders to behave in immoral ways (Milgram, 1974; see Chapter 11, this volume).

After the difficulties we experienced in distinguishing social psychology from personality psychology, distinguishing it from neighbouring social sciences such as sociology might seem easy. It would appear that sociology differs from social psychology both in the issues it studies and in the level of analysis at which it addresses these issues. Unfortunately, things are again not that simple. First, there is quite a bit of overlap between the issues studied by social psychologists and those that interest sociologists. Thus, social groups and group norms are topics that are of equal interest to sociologists and social psychologists. The sociologist George Homans wrote one of the classic monographs on social groups (Homans, 1950) and the sociologists Hechter and Opp (2001) recently edited a volume that summarizes the important work of sociologists in the area of social norms.

Although there are sociological approaches which, influenced by the work of Talcott Parsons and Emile Durkheim, emphasize that sociological facts should not be explained through psychological processes (Vanberg, 1975), most sociologists would no longer accept this position. In fact, sociologists have made major contributions to the development of individualistic social psychological theories. Thus, the sociologists Homans (1964) and Blau (1964) have written monographs on exchange theory, a theory that has become central in social psychology through the classic *Social Psychology of Groups* written by the social psychologists Thibaut and Kelley (1959). The central tenet of exchange theory is that individuals interact with those others who provide the greatest rewards for the least costs (the social exchange view is covered in Chapters 10, 12 and 13, this volume). Thus, most sociologists agree with social psychologists in espousing what has been called 'methodological individualism', namely the idea that even collective behaviour is essentially behaviour of the individuals who form the collective and therefore has to be explained in terms of rewards and costs of this behaviour to the individual (e.g., Klandermans, 1997).

Even though there is a great deal of overlap between sociology and social psychology, there are also major differences in the way these areas approach social behaviour. Sociologists are more likely to trace social behaviour upwards to structural variables such as norms, roles or social class, whereas social psychologists will trace it downwards to the individual's goals, motives and cognitions. For example, both sociologists and social psychologists are interested in aggression and violence. Social psychologists have studied the cognitive and affective processes through which anger can, given the right contextual cues, explode in aggressive behaviour, that is, behaviour performed with the express intention of hurting another person (Chapter 8, this volume). Sociologists, on the other hand, have been more interested in why levels of aggression are higher in some societies or groups than in others. Why is the murder rate in the USA so much higher than in Canada, even though guns are widely available in both countries? Since a possible difference could be the type of guns that are available in the

Plate 1.2 *How is the way social psychologists study aggression and violence different from the approach of sociologists?*

two countries, with hunting rifles being more prevalent in Canada and hand guns or assault weapons more frequently held in the United States, the potential answer might lie in the aggressive images that will be activated by different types of weapons, leading us back to individual psychological processes. Thus, even though sociologists are more likely to link individual behaviour to social structural variables, while social psychologists are more likely to study individual processes, a combination of the two approaches might often provide a fuller explanation than either discipline can offer on its own.

A BRIEF HISTORY OF SOCIAL PSYCHOLOGY

The beginning

Who conducted the first experiment?
Who wrote the first textbook?

Authors who write about the history of a scientific discipline usually like to report dates marking the official beginning of that discipline. Often these are the years in which the first textbooks or handbooks bearing the name of the discipline were published. In social psychology, 1908 is usually noted as the year when the first two textbooks of social psychology were published, one by a

sociologist (Ross, 1908), the other by a psychologist (McDougall, 1908). However, since both texts cover very little material that we would consider social psychological these days, 1908 may not be the best choice for the birth year of social psychology.

One could also argue that using the date of the first textbook to mark the beginning of a discipline is questionable anyway, because it would be difficult to write a textbook about a discipline that does not already exist. There must first be relevant theorizing and research available with which to fill the pages of a textbook. It is probably for this reason that another date has become quite prominent in chapters on the history of social psychology, namely the date of (presumably) the first social psychological experiment, a study published in 1898 by Norman Triplett. Triplett appeared to have been a fan of bicycle races. He was interested in the phenomenon that racing cyclists go faster when racing with others or when being paced than when riding alone, racing against the clock. Since there are records of the average speed of the different kinds of races, he could have used these records rather than doing his own study. However, the problem with using records is that different racers participate in different kinds of races, so that the differences in speed could have been due to self-selection. Triplett therefore had young boys and girls pull in a fishing reel as fast as possible and they had to perform this task either in pairs or alone. Rather than randomly assigning his participants to the two conditions, he had each participant do three trials alone and three in pairs, alternating these conditions (i.e., a within-subject design). A few children were slower in competition, some were unaffected, but the majority were faster and the experiment is usually cited as demonstrating the effects of what later became known as social facilitation, the phenomenon that the performance of simple tasks is facilitated by the presence of an audience or of others working on the same task (see Chapter 11, this volume).

Although the study by Triplett (1898) had all the artificiality that became the hallmark of experimentation in social psychology, its historical significance has been challenged by scholars who doubted whether it really was the *first* social psychological experiment. For example, Haines and Vaughan (1979) have argued that there were other experiments before 1898 deserving to be called social psychological, such as studies on suggestibility (e.g., Binet & Henri, 1894). But social psychological experiments may have been performed even earlier by the French agricultural engineer Max Ringelmann, who between 1882 and 1887 conducted investigations into the maximum performance of workers pulling a load under different conditions (Kravitz & Martin, 1986). Although the comparison of individual and group performance was of only secondary interest to Ringelmann, he found the first evidence of productivity loss in groups, a phenomenon that was later named 'social loafing' (see Chapter 13, this volume). Ringelmann found that eight men who pull at a rope together achieve only about 50 per cent of the pulling power that could be expected on the basis of their pulling measured individually. However, since Ringelmann only published this research in 1913, Triplett predates him, certainly as far as publication is concerned.

It is interesting to note that these early experiments were studies of an applied nature in areas which later became known as sports psychology and psychology of work performance. There were other studies of this nature available in other applied areas

Plate 1.3 *Do the men pull to their potential? If not, why not?*

Floyd Henry Allport (1890–1978), the elder brother of Gordon Allport, received both his undergraduate degree (1914) and his PhD (1919) from Harvard University. His dissertation was based on his studies on social facilitation, a research area that had been suggested to him by Hugo Münsterberg, then professor of psychology at Harvard. In 1922 Allport found a position as Associate Professor of Social Psychology at the University of North Carolina at Chapel Hill. It was here that he began writing his *Social Psychology*, which was widely praised and adopted as a text. This book and his studies on the impact of the group on individual cognitive performance are his major contribution to social psychology. He retired from Syracuse University in 1956.

(e.g., Mayer, 1903; Moede, 1920) and it needed somebody to recognize that the study of the impact of the social context on performance was really a discipline by itself, namely, social psychology. It may then be justifiable to choose the date of the first textbook or handbook about a discipline as its 'origin' insofar as a discipline is characterized not only by its content but also by its disciplinary identity. Thus, it is not sufficient that research that is vaguely social psychological has been conducted in the area of sports psychology or even agriculture. There needs to be somebody who pulls all of this research together and declares the emergence of a new area (in which, incidentally, this applied research then becomes fundamental).

In our view, this was first achieved by Floyd Allport (1924), who in his textbook made several major contributions towards defining the field of social psychology. He declared the study of social behaviour as the subject of social psychology. He defined social behaviour as 'behavior in which the responses either serve as social stimuli or are evoked by social stimuli' (p. 148). As mentioned above, he postulated that social psychology 'is part of the psychology of the individual, whose behavior it studies in relation to that sector of the environment comprised by his fellows' (p. 4). 'For . . . only within the individual can we find the behavioural mechanisms and the consciousness which are fundamental in the interactions between individuals' (p. vi). A third contribution, which may be less embraced today, was his emphasis on the experimental method. Although the experimental method is still one of the major research tools of social psychologists, other research methods have become equally accepted these days. However, in Allport's time, the emphasis on experiments was probably essential for establishing the scientific respectability of social psychology. It would also have helped to distinguish it further from sociology, a discipline that still prefers surveys and field studies to conducting experiments. It is interesting, though, that with the exception of his chapter on the 'Response to social stimulation in groups', Allport (1924) reviewed very little experimental evidence of a social psychological nature.

The early years

What were the key contributions to social psychology during the first half of the twentieth century?

It would be an exaggeration to claim that the publication of Floyd Allport's textbook immediately stimulated an exponential growth in social psychological research. In fact, not that many milestones are to be reported for the period before World War II. A rather doubtful one is the publication of the first *Handbook of Social Psychology* by Carl Murchison (1935). We call it doubtful because this handbook is an odd collection of chapters on topics that nobody would consider social psychological these days, from the 'Population behavior of bacteria' to the 'Social history of the yellow man'. There are really only two chapters included in this volume that are truly social psychological: the chapter by Gordon Allport on attitudes and that by Dashiell on 'Experimental studies of the influence of social situation on the behaviour of individual human adults'. While the attitude chapter achieved lasting fame through its widely cited first sentence ('The concept of attitude is probably the most distinctive and indispensable concept in contemporary American social psychology', p. 798), the chapter by Dashiell reports an extensive series of experimental studies on social facilitation and inhibition.

Three other significant events during this early period were the publication by Thurstone (1928) of a paper with the provocative title 'Attitudes can be measured', *The Psychology of Social Norms* by Sherif in 1936, and Newcomb's (1943) *Personality and Social Change*, a study of attitude formation in the student community of Bennington College. Thurstone's article was remarkable because

PIONEER

Theodore Newcomb (1903–1984) received his undergraduate degree from Oberlin College in 1924 and entered Union Theological Seminary in New York intending to become a Christian Missionary (Converse, 1994). However, more attracted by the psychology courses taught at Columbia University across the road, he switched to psychology and received his PhD from Columbia in 1929. He joined Bennington College in 1934, a newly founded women's college that drew its students from the politically conservative 'upper crust' of Vermont's society but had a famously liberal atmosphere. His Bennington study of the change in attitudes that these young women underwent during their studies became a classic. Not only was the longitudinal design innovative at that time, but the study captured the interplay between individual and group processes and thus supported one of the central assumptions of social psychology. After a stint of wartime research, he became director of a joint doctoral program of the departments of sociology and social psychology at the University of Michigan, where he stayed for the remainder of his career. Intrigued by the work of Fritz Heider, Newcomb developed his own interpersonal version of balance theory.

he described the first psychometrically sound method for the measurement of attitudes. Sherif's study became a classic, because he devised an experimental paradigm which allowed him to study the development of group norms in a laboratory situation (see Chapter 11, this volume). Participants in his study were repeatedly exposed to a stationary light source in a darkened room. Sherif made use of the fact that participants perceive this light source as moving (autokinetic effect) and that, if asked to judge the movement over repeated trials, they establish relatively stable individual norms. By putting individuals who had developed widely differing individual estimates into a group situation, Sherif could demonstrate that individuals in groups develop a joint and stable group norm, which they then maintain even when they continue to make their estimates again in individual situations.

Finally, Newcomb's Bennington study became a classic, because it is an ingenious longitudinal field study of social influence on a college campus. It maps out the way in which the political attitudes of students, all women who came from conservative homes, changed over time towards the liberal attitudes that were predominant on this college campus. Thus, it illustrates how individual beliefs and attitudes can be shaped by the group context and thus supports one of the basic assumptions of social psychology. The study is particularly interesting because these students were followed up for 50 years, allowing researchers to demonstrate the stability of their attitude change over a lifetime (Alwin, Cohen & Newcomb, 1991).

The years of expansion

How did Adolf Hitler further the development of social psychology in the USA?

Who were the key figures in social psychology in the post-war period?

Somewhat tongue in cheek, Cartwright once wrote that the one person who most furthered the development of social psychology in North America was Adolf Hitler (Cartwright, 1979). This observation is correct, though indirectly, insofar as Hitler's actions had an important impact on the development of social psychology in the USA. World War II greatly stimulated interest in social psychological research. The Information and Education Branch of the US Army initiated surveys and experiments to assess the impact of army propaganda films on the morale of their soldiers. One social psychologist who became heavily involved in this work was Carl Hovland. Originally a learning theorist, Hovland became fascinated by the experimental study of the determinants of attitude change. The work he directed during his army years on experiments in mass communication was eventually published as one of

Plate 1.4 *How did Hitler's actions affect the development of social psychology?*

 **PIONEER**

Carl Iver Hovland (1912–1961) received his bachelor's and master's degrees from Northwestern University in 1932 and 1933. He then moved to Yale to work for his PhD under the prominent learning theorist Clark Hull. In his dissertation, Hovland provided the first evidence for a law of generalization, according to which the learned tendency to make a response to a particular stimulus falls off exponentially with the distance separating that stimulus from the original training stimulus along some sensory continuum. After finishing his dissertation in 1936, Hovland was invited to join the Yale faculty, of which he remained a member for the rest of his life. Hovland never abandoned his interest in learning theory. Even when he became fascinated by persuasion and attitude change during his wartime leave from Yale in the period from 1942 to 1945, he used learning theory principles as a theoretical perspective. His wartime research was published (with Lumsdaine and Sheffield) in 1949 in *Experiments in Mass Communication*. After returning to Yale, Hovland established the Yale Communication and Attitude Change program, which he directed until his premature death in 1961. The research conducted there by Hovland and 30 students and co-workers over a 15-year period established the field of attitude change research as we know it today (Shepard, undated).

the volumes of the *American Soldier* series under the editorship of the sociologist Stouffer (Hovland, Lumsdaine & Sheffield, 1949).

After the war, Hovland returned to his academic career and founded the Yale Communication and Attitude Change program. This program attracted young researchers from a variety of universities and generated a stream of collaborative studies that defined attitude change research for decades to come (see Chapter 7, this volume). The program resulted in the publication of four highly influential volumes on studies of the determinants of persuasion and attitude change. In the first of these volumes, Hovland, Janis and Kelley (1953) explored the impact of communicator variables (e.g., prestige, credibility and expertise), communication variables (e.g., fear appeals) and context variables (e.g., salience of reference groups). Although the theoretical perspective of the program was eclectic, Hovland himself was most comfortable with the view that attitude change was a special form of human learning (Jones, 1998).

Following this classic volume, members of the program published a number of more specialized but also highly influential monographs dealing with order effects (Hovland, 1957), personality (Hovland & Janis, 1959), cognitive consistency factors (Rosenberg, Hovland, McGuire, Abelson & Brehm, 1960) and the role of social judgement, in particular assimilation and contrast, in attitude

change (Sherif & Hovland, 1961). William McGuire, one of the members of the Yale Communication and Attitude Change program, returned to Yale and, with his information-processing paradigm (see Chapter 7, this volume), essentially continued the Yale research program well into the 1980s (e.g., McGuire, 1969, 1985).

A second action of the Hitler regime that advanced the development of social psychology in the USA was the forced emigration of Jewish academics from Germany (e.g., Köhler, Koffka, Lewin, Wertheimer). The most important of these émigrés from Germany for social psychology was undoubtedly Kurt Lewin, considered by many to be the most charismatic psychologist of his generation (Marrow, 1969). Lewin left the Berlin Psychological Institute in 1933 for the Department of Home Economics at Cornell University, to move in 1935 to the Iowa Child Research Station. In 1945 he established the Research Center for Group Dynamics at the Massachusetts Institute of Technology, which after his premature death in 1947 (aged 57 years) was moved to the University of Michigan.

 **PIONEER**

Kurt Lewin (1890–1947) studied psychology and philosophy in Berlin. After fulfilling the formal requirements for a PhD in 1914 (a degree he received only in 1916), he volunteered for the army and spent the next four years fighting World War I (Marrow, 1969). He then returned to the University of Berlin to join the Gestalt psychologists Köhler and Wertheimer at the Institute of Psychology, where he stayed until his (permanent) move to the United States in 1933. The time at Berlin University was probably Lewin's most productive period. He attracted an international group of students, developed his field theory, which argued that behaviour is a function of both the person and the environment, and supervised a series of classic studies, mainly conducted by his students as part of their dissertation. These studies addressed fundamental issues of the psychology of motivation. Lewin's interest in social psychology developed only after his move to the United States (Marrow, 1969). In the USA he first worked at Cornell University, and then moved to the University of Iowa. During his ten years at the University of Iowa (1935–1945) Lewin conducted some classic experimental studies in social psychology, such as the experiment on the impact of authoritarian and democratic leadership styles on group atmosphere and performance (Lewin et al., 1939), which later stimulated research on participative leadership to overcome resistance to change (Coch & French, 1948). Lewin became more and more interested in social processes, and in 1944 he moved to Massachusetts Institute of Technology where he founded the Research Center for Group Dynamics.

It is difficult to understand today how and why Lewin became such a key figure in social psychology. As is the case today, the impact of a researcher in those days was mainly determined by three factors: (1) the development of a theory, which stimulated a great deal of research; (2) publication of numerous studies that supported that theory, preferably involving intriguing new research paradigms; and (3) training of a stream of outstanding graduate students, who would later continue the work. Lewin did not score all that well on the first two criteria. The field theory he developed, though monumental and impressive, was more of a heuristic framework and did not lend itself easily to the derivation of testable hypotheses. Even his own empirical work was only very loosely related to that theory. He only published a few studies in social psychology, the most well known being the study of autocratic and democratic leadership (Lewin, Lippitt & White, 1939), which initiated interest in the impact of leadership styles on group atmosphere and performance. However, Lewin's approach to social psychology has two characteristics which were novel at the time. For him, a problem was only worth studying if addressing it would make a difference with regard to actual problems in the world (Festinger, 1980). Second, and more importantly, he insisted on studying such problems experimentally and on creating in the laboratory powerful situations that made a big difference (Festinger, 1980). Lewin instilled these ideas in his graduate students, and his impact on social psychology was mainly due to these graduate students, who nearly all became leaders of the field during the second half of the twentieth century. Among his graduate students during his US years were Kurt Back, Dorwin Cartwright, Morton Deutsch, Leon Festinger, Harold Kelley, Stanley Schachter, and John Thibaut.

All these individuals shaped the field of experimental psychology in the post-war period, but the most illustrious among them was undoubtedly Leon Festinger, whose theory of cognitive dissonance dictated the research agenda in social psychology during the 1960s and 1970s (Festinger, 1957; see Chapter 7, this volume). The theory of social comparison processes, which he had developed earlier (Festinger, 1954), had less of an immediate impact but is still influential today (see, e.g., Chapters 5, 10, 11 and 12, this volume).

Another important émigré was the Austrian Fritz Heider (see Pioneer box, Chapter 3, p. 47), although in this case Hitler cannot be blamed for his emigration. Heider came to the USA in 1930 to work with Kurt Koffka, who was then at Smith College in Northampton, Massachusetts. He had initially planned to stay for only one year, but decided to remain when he fell in love with Grace Moore, whom he later married. He moved to the University of Kansas in 1947 where he remained until his retirement. His impact on the field is intriguing, because he was not a prolific writer, attracted few graduate students, and published no experimental research in social psychology. And yet, he stimulated two of the theoretical traditions which dominated social psychology during the second half of the last century, namely consistency theory and attribution theory.

With his paper on balance theory in 1946, Heider developed the notion central to consistency theories that inconsistency between our attitudes and beliefs creates tension in our cognitive system and a tendency to establish consistency. Although only a

PIONEER

Leon Festinger (1919–1990) completed his undergraduate studies at City College in New York, and his graduate research at the University of Iowa, with the German psychologist Kurt Lewin. After receiving his PhD in 1942, and a stint of wartime research, he rejoined Lewin and the newly formed Center for Group Dynamics at the Massachusetts Institute of Technology in 1945. In 1948, he moved with the Center to the University of Michigan, from there to the University of Minnesota in 1951, on to Stanford in 1955, and finally, in 1968, to the New School for Social Research in New York, where he stayed until his retirement (Schachter, 1994). During his period at MIT, Festinger, Schachter and Back (1950) conducted their classic study of friendship patterns and residential proximity (see Chapter 10, this volume). This study showed that students were most likely to form friendships with those who lived close to them, that students who appeared close together in social networks had similar attitudes, and that those who had deviant attitudes were social isolates (see Chapter 11, this volume). Festinger (1950) published his first theoretical paper in social psychology on informal social communication and the process, via social comparison, of establishing the correctness of one's beliefs. These ideas were later elaborated in his paper on social comparison processes (Festinger, 1954). Soon afterwards, Festinger (1957) published the work for which he is best known, his theory of cognitive dissonance (see Chapter 7, this volume). The key hypothesis of this theory – that when we hold two or more incompatible ideas, there will be pressure to reduce this inconsistency – bears close relationship to his earlier work as well as to balance theory. It is more the research he conducted to test these ideas, rather than the theory itself, which turned it into arguably the most impressive body of research in social psychology to date. But it also marked the end of his interest in social psychology, which shifted, first, to the visual system and perception, and then to archaeology and the history of religion.

limited amount of research has been conducted to test Heider's balance theory, the theory stimulated the development of other consistency theories, most importantly the theory of cognitive dissonance.

With his paper on phenomenal causality, published in 1944, and his monograph *The Psychology of Interpersonal Relations*, published in 1958, Heider initiated another important theoretical perspective, namely attribution theory (see Chapter 3, this volume). Attribution theory is a social psychological theory about how individuals manage to infer the 'causes' underlying the behaviour of others or even their own behaviour. In trying to interpret behaviour, we will typically attempt to disentangle the contribution of internal causes (e.g., personality traits, motivation) from external causes (e.g., situational factors). For example, if a mother learns that her son has received a poor grade in his first maths test, she will wonder whether this poor result is due to lack of ability, lack of motivation or to an overly zealous maths teacher who gave too tough a test. Deciding between these alternatives will be important for her because it will suggest different strategies to prevent this situation from happening again.

The impact of attribution theory in stimulating a great deal of research in the 1960s and 1970s is intriguing, because neither Heider's (1958) monograph nor his 1944 article was written in a way that would make it accessible or appealing to the average researcher in North America. There was also very little research to back up Heider's ideas. It is generally accepted that attribution theory became influential because three major figures in the field of social psychology – Edward Jones, Harold Kelley and Bernard Weiner – adopted it and translated it into a language that was more accessible to social psychologists and yielded clear, testable hypotheses (Jones & Davis, 1965; Kelley, 1967; Weiner, 1986). Probably most influential was Kelley's (1967) covariation model of attribution. This model was appealing because Kelley argued that, in inferring causes of behaviour, our inference process would be analogous to conducting an analysis of variance, a statistical procedure highly familiar to social psychologists. Other influential adaptations of attribution theory were Jones and Davis's (1965) correspondent inference theory and Weiner's (1986) application of attribution theory to achievement motivation and emotion.

A final way in which Hitler influenced the development of social psychology is by stimulating interest in particular topics. For example, the questions of how the German people could accept such an authoritarian regime and how people could execute commands they must have perceived as criminal, even at the time, stimulated some of the most influential research in social psychology. Thus, researchers studied the authoritarian personality (Adorno et al., 1950), the determinants of conformity (Asch, 1955) and obedience (Milgram, 1963). Lewin's interest in the effects of authoritarian and democratic leadership styles can be seen as an attempt to demonstrate the superiority of the democratic style, an attempt that was only partly effective because autocratically led groups outperformed the democratic groups with regard to quantity of production, although democratic leadership produced more creative groups whose performance did not deteriorate so dramatically when the leader was removed (White & Lippitt, 1976).

The crisis years

How and why did the crisis in social psychology develop?

So far the history of social psychology appears to have been one of unmitigated success. Stimulated by World War II, social psychological research expanded enormously and there was soon no single psychology department at a top university that did not also have a strong social psychology unit. But just when social psychology was on the up and up, it ran into a crisis of confidence that led to years of infighting about the right course it should follow. This crisis was probably initiated by two critical papers published in 1967 and 1973.

The first of this duo was a paper by Kenneth Ring entitled 'Experimental social psychology: Some sober questions about some frivolous values', published in the highly respected *Journal of Experimental Social Psychology*. In this paper, Ring contrasted the vision of Kurt Lewin of a social psychology that would contribute to the solution of important social problems with what he called the 'fun and games' attitude of the social psychology of his days. He argued that: 'Experimental social psychology today seems dominated by values that suggest the following slogan: "Social psychology ought to be and is a lot of fun" . . . Clever experimentation on exotic topics with zany manipulations seems to be the guaranteed formula for success . . . One sometimes gets the impression that an ever-growing coterie of social psychologists is playing (largely for another's benefit) a game of "can you top this?"' (pp. 116–17). Although Ring did not refer to any specific examples of this fun and games approach, his criticism was probably directed at some of the work conducted in tests of dissonance theory. Since Ring, although a respected researcher, was not a very central figure in the social psychology of his days, the paper stimulated some discussion but did not really have a serious impact on the field. However, in 1973, one of the golden boys of experimental social psychology, Kenneth Gergen, published a paper entitled 'Social psychology as history' in the top journal of our discipline, the *Journal of Personality and Social Psychology*. As the title already suggests, Gergen's paper was not an attack on the values directing social psychological research. Much more seriously, he questioned its scientific value. His two most important arguments were (1) that knowledge of social psychological principles could change our behaviour in ways which would negate these principles, and (2) that since the basic motives assumed by many of our theories are unlikely to be genetically determined, they might be affected by cultural change.

As an example of the first principle, Gergen argued that once groups were aware of their tendency to make extreme decisions (i.e., group polarization; see Chapter 11, this volume), they might consciously counteract this tendency in their decision-making. As an example of the second principle, Gergen used social comparison and dissonance theory. Social comparison theory assumes that people have a desire to evaluate themselves accurately and do this by comparing themselves to others. Gergen argued that one could easily imagine societies where such a desire would not exist. Similarly, dissonance theory assumes a need for consistency, which not everybody might share. Gergen saw these problems as the main reason why, as he claimed, social psychological research often failed to be replicable, and hence did not result in a body of cumulative knowledge.

Most researchers these days would accept these arguments without questioning the scientific status of social psychology. With regard to Gergen's first point, we would argue that it would be difficult, even for a trained social psychologist, to keep in mind all situations where our behaviour might be affected by others, to recognize all the relevant cues signalling such situations, and then to counteract the situational pressures. Furthermore, people might not be very motivated to engage in such effortful processing, because these context effects are often minimal and sometimes contribute positively to the functioning of the group. Second, since the evaluation of one's own abilities through social comparison is highly functional, and essential for effective action, it is hard to imagine societies where people do not engage in social comparison. However, we do know that there are individual differences in the need for social comparison (Gibbons & Buunk, 1999), as there are in individual need for consistency (Cialdini, Trost & Newsom, 1995). Thus, if we want to correct for such differences, we simply add a measure of these needs to our experimental procedure.

Gergen's (1973) critique would probably have been less effective had it not come at a time when the collective self-esteem of social psychologists had been undermined by other developments. For one, there was an attack on the usefulness of a concept that Allport (1935) had hailed as the most central concept of social psychology. In a review of studies that empirically assessed the value of social attitudes in predicting behaviour, the sociologist Alan Wicker (1969) drew the following conclusion: 'Taken as a whole, these studies suggest that it is considerably more likely that attitudes will be unrelated or only slightly related to overt behavior than that attitudes will be closely related to actions' (p. 65). This conclusion was highly damaging, since social psychologists were interested in attitudes mainly because they expected them to predict behaviour. Since attitude change in most studies is assessed through an individual's self-rated position on some attitude dimension, the news that such ratings might be unrelated to behaviour was devastating.

A second development with a negative impact on the collective self-esteem of the scientific community of social psychologists was the publication of a series of papers that were highly critical of the experimental method. Thus, Martin Orne (1962) had suggested that most experimental situations contained 'demand characteristics', which would help research participants to guess the hypothesis to be tested in a given study. Since participants typically tried to be 'good subjects', Orne argued, they would then do their best to support these hypotheses.[1] Even more damaging was the suggestion of Robert Rosenthal (Rosenthal & Fode, 1963) that the expectations of the experimenter might influence the behaviour of research participants, even without their knowledge. The impact of these expectations on the behaviour of research participants could, for example, be mediated by experimenters' reacting positively to responses that supported their hypotheses and negatively to responses that were inconsistent with expectations.

The reaction to these critical voices was the organization of numerous conferences in which the crisis was discussed, sometimes in rather heated language. Although these conferences resulted in a number of crisis books (e.g., Strickland, Aboud & Gergen, 1976), they failed to bridge the theoretical and methodological chasm that separated the critics from mainstream social psychology. The critics finally founded their own social psychological schools, such as social constructionism in the United States (e.g., Gergen, 1999) and discourse analysis in the United Kingdom (e.g., Potter & Wetherell, 1987), which developed their own methodologies in an attempt to address these problems.

Overcoming the crisis

How was the crisis overcome?

In mainstream social psychology a number of developments were initiated, which over the years helped to alleviate some of the problems highlighted by these critics:

- Social psychologists began to demonstrate their ability to contribute to the solution of real-life problems by developing several applied areas, which contributed to resolving important societal problems. To mention only one such area, health psychology is an application of social psychology. One of the major research areas in health psychology is aimed at changing health-impairing behaviour patterns in our society (e.g., smoking, eating too much, drinking too much alcohol, practising unsafe sex). Social psychologists have helped to understand the reasons why people engage in these behaviours as well as to develop interventions aimed at changing them (Stroebe, 2001; see Chapter 15, this volume).

- The impression that social psychological research did not result in cumulative knowledge may have been the result of improper strategies of reviewing, a problem that was mostly resolved with the development of meta-analytic procedures (see Chapter 2, this volume). When reviewing research areas, researchers often erroneously concluded that support for a theory was missing or inconsistent, because few studies supported the theory by yielding significant results, whereas the majority of studies failed to find significant results. In the meantime, we have realized as a discipline that the failure to find significant results may simply have been due to conducting a study with an insufficiently large number of participants. If the effects we were looking for were small, this might have resulted in insignificant findings, even though the differences between conditions might all have been in the predicted direction. Since then, meta-analytic procedures have been developed which allow us to integrate statistically the results of independent studies of a given phenomenon, with a view to establishing whether the findings exhibit a pattern of relationships that is reliable across studies (Cooper & Hedges, 1994).

- We now know that attitudes are predictive of behaviour but that this relationship is often obscured in studies which employ inappropriate procedures in measuring the two components (see Chapter 6, this volume). As Ajzen and Fishbein (1977) demonstrated in their classic review, attitudes are related to behaviour if both components are assessed with measures that are both reliable and compatible. To be reliable, measures have to consist of multiple items rather than a single item. To be compatible, attitude and behaviour have to be assessed at the same level of specificity. Thus, if we want to predict whether people are likely to engage in physical exercise to improve their health, we should not measure their attitude towards their health but their attitude towards engaging in physical exercise. The latter attitude is likely to be highly correlated with an aggregate measure of a variety of exercise behaviours (such as jogging, walking, going to the gym). If one wanted to predict specific exercise behaviour, such as whether an individual is likely to jog, one should measure his or her attitude towards jogging rather than towards physical exercise in general.

● Finally, social psychologists have tried to design their experimental manipulations in ways that would minimize the threat of demand characteristics and experimenter expectancy effects. Furthermore, the fact that many research participants do not even meet experimenters any more, because experiments are often run on the computer by computer programs, should certainly rule out experimenter expectancy effects. The depressing fact that most experiments do not work out the way they were expected to by the experimenter who designed them also appears to suggest that these effects cannot be all that powerful. Festinger (1980) most aptly expressed these feelings when he wrote: 'I've always wondered why, if these spurious experimenter effects were so strong, so many of my own experiments did not show the expected results' (p. 252).

SOCIAL PSYCHOLOGY IN EUROPE

How did social psychology develop in Europe?
Why and in what way was the foundation of the European Association of Experimental Social Psychology important for the development of European social psychology?

Until the end of World War II, the development of social psychology as a discipline was restricted to the USA. However, even before the influx of academic refugees in the 1930s, there had been a great deal of European influence on this development. For example, F. Allport's (1924) work on social facilitation had been stimulated by one of his academic teachers at Harvard, the German Hugo Münsterberg, whom Allport explicitly thanks in the preface to his book (Allport, 1924, p. vii). Münsterberg, in turn, was familiar with similar work that had been done in Germany by Moede (1920). The experimental work of Bartlett (1932) in Britain on remembering can be viewed as a major precursor of contemporary research on social cognition. And finally, the theorizing underlying Sherif's (1936) studies of norm development is heavily influenced by Gestalt psychology.

However, even though there were individuals in Europe who conducted research that could be considered social psychological, there was no unitary social psychology. This situation continued into the 1960s, even though social psychology groups had been established at a number of European universities. But while there *was* social psychology in Europe, there was no *European social psychology*: there was no European collaboration and most European researchers had not met each other, nor were they even aware of each other's work.

Obviously, a European network was not necessary for the development of a strong social psychology in some of the European countries where effective social psychology research groups already existed (e.g., Belgium, Britain, the Netherlands and Germany). However, in some other countries it would probably have taken many decades for social psychology to develop. Furthermore, since most of the European researchers met each other, if at all, only at conferences held in the USA, without the foundation of a European association European social psychology would probably have remained a minor appendix of North American social psychology rather than developing its own theoretical perspective. Thus the foundation of the European Association of Experimental Social Psychology was critical.

Given the dominance of North American social psychology at that time, even in Europe, it is no coincidence that it was again an American, John Lanzetta, who set things in motion in 1963. During a sabbatical year in London, Lanzetta, then Professor of Social Psychology at the University of Delaware, visited various social psychology groups in Europe. He was struck by the fact that many of these colleagues, though well informed about US social psychology, were not really aware of what was going on in the social psychology departments of neighbouring European countries. He decided to change this and raised funds for a first European Conference on Experimental Social Psychology, held in Sorrento, Italy, in 1963 (Nuttin, 1990). One of the main initiatives which emerged from this and two follow-up conferences was the foundation of the European Association of Experimental Social Psychology (EAESP) in 1966. The European Association engaged in a number of regular activities, which had great impact on the development of social psychology in Europe. These included:

● Summer schools for advanced students, taught by outstanding researchers.

● Publication of the *European Journal of Social Psychology* in 1970, which included most of the early research thought of (then at least) as typically 'European' (e.g., studies of intergroup relations or minority influence). Other key European publications were the *European Monographs* series and the *European Review of Social Psychology*. The first edition of the textbook you are reading now was published in 1988, in part to counteract the tendency of American textbooks to under-report the work of European social psychologists.

● The regular organization of conferences, including plenary meetings of the whole membership, and special East–West meetings (the latter were particularly effective forums at a time when travel and currency restrictions made it extremely difficult for social psychologists from Eastern and Western Europe to meet).

Membership in the EAESP has grown at a phenomenal rate, from less than 30 in 1970 to more than 1,000 members in 2005. During this period, scientific development in social psychology also changed from being a one-sided enterprise, with American ideas being adopted in Europe, to a mutual development, with European ideas being taken up enthusiastically in the United States and ever-increasing collaboration leading to scientific growth. It is now accepted practice for prominent North American journals (*Journal of Personality and Social Psychology*, *Journal of Experimental Social Psychology* and *Personality and Social Psychology Bulletin*) to have at least one European editor, and likewise for the *European Journal of Social Psychology* to have non-European editors.

Probably the two most important examples of European ideas influencing social psychology in the United States are research on intergroup behaviour and on minority influence. Although Tajfel was not the first to conduct experimental research on intergroup behaviour (that honour goes to Sherif), he developed the paradigm (the 'minimal group paradigm') that turned intergroup behaviour into a major research area (see Chapter 14, this volume). The minimal group paradigm offered an easy and very economical procedure for the study of intergroup behaviour, but Tajfel and Turner (1979, 1986) developed from it a theoretical framework that could account for these findings, social identity theory.

The second theoretical innovation that was started in Europe and then accepted in the United States is research on minority influence. Social influence research in North America focused exclusively on conformity, that is, on explaining how majorities influence minorities. It was Moscovici who first pointed out that this type of theorizing could hardly explain social or religious innovations, where powerless minorities influenced powerful majorities (e.g., women's rights, Christianity). After Moscovici and his colleagues in Paris (e.g., Moscovici, Lage & Naffrechoux, 1969) had published a number of studies demonstrating minority influence, and again with the development of a theory that could account for these effects, research on minority influence became a major research area both in the USA and in Europe (Moscovici, 1976; see Chapter 11, this volume).

SOCIAL PSYCHOLOGY TODAY

What new theoretical perspectives have emerged during the last few decades?

In the 1980s most of the researchers who had contributed to modern social psychology, and who, as often as not, had come from the research centres directed by either Lewin or Hovland, were still alive and active (Cartwright, 1979). In the meantime, not only have many of these pioneers retired or died, but so also have most of the students whom they, in turn, had trained. The field has grown at an exponential rate. There are now chairs in social psychology at practically all major universities in the United States, in Northern Europe, and in some countries of Southern Europe, and social psychologists number in the thousands rather than a few

hundreds. Social psychology has also become an essential part of the psychology curriculum in these countries.

Not surprisingly, social psychology has also changed over these decades. Major scientific perspectives, such as consistency theory or attribution theory, have faded and new perspectives, such as *social cognition*, *evolutionary social psychology* and *social neuroscience*, have emerged. Jones (1998) colourfully described these changing trends in research as 'band wagons and sinking ships' (p. 54).

Social cognition research is an application of principles of cognitive psychology to the area of social psychology (see Devine, Hamilton & Ostrom, 1994). Unlike other psychological disciplines, social psychology has always placed a strong emphasis on how individuals internally represent their environment. Many of our theories have been labelled 'cognitive' (e.g., cognitive dissonance), and central concepts of social psychology (e.g., attitudes, beliefs, intentions) are cognitive constructs. It would thus appear a small step for social psychologists to borrow methods from cognitive psychology to study how social information is encoded and how the information is stored and retrieved from memory. This perspective has had a widespread influence across the field of social psychology, but is seen perhaps most clearly in changes to the way we theorize and do research in person perception (see Chapters 3 and 4, this volume), attitude change (Chapter 7) and prejudice and intergroup relations (Chapter 14).

Evolutionary social psychology (e.g., Burnstein & Branigan, 2001; Buss & Kenrick, 1998) is an application of evolutionary theory to social psychology. Evolutionary theory explains human behaviours, including differences in partner preference according to gender, from their reproductive value, that is, their value in producing offspring in our evolutionary past. Evolutionary psychology makes the basic assumption that if a given behaviour is (1) at least partly genetically determined and (2) increases the probability that an individual will produce offspring, the gene that determines this behaviour will become more prevalent in the gene pool of future generations. Evolutionary social psychologists have made important contributions to the study of interpersonal attraction (Chapter 10, this volume), helping and cooperation (Chapter 9) and aggression (Chapter 8). The development of evolutionary social psychology as an accepted research area in social psychology is surprising, as talking about genetic determinants of social behaviour was considered heresy in the decades following World War II and the defeat of the race ideology of the Hitler regime. However, modern applications of evolutionary social psychology are less deterministic, less ideological and, most importantly, more solidly based on evolutionary theory than such earlier approaches.

Social neuroscience is the study of the neural correlates of social psychological phenomena (Cacioppo & Berntson, 2005; Ochsner & Lieberman, 2001). Building on huge recent advances in the use of non-invasive techniques for examining the functioning of the human brain, social neuroscience studies participants' brains while they are engaged in processing social information. Already studies have used such techniques to further our understanding of prejudice (see Chapter 14, this volume). Some studies, for example, have examined changes in blood flow within the brain (using functional magnetic resonance imaging, fMRI) while people are shown race-relevant stimuli under different conditions. Such research has shown that there is a link between social categorization and the

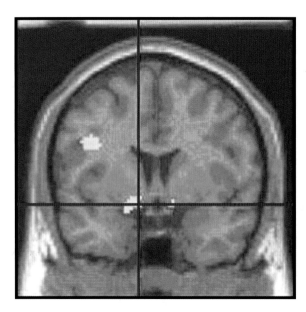

Plate 1.5 *An fMRI scan shows activation of the amygdala processing social, fear-related information.*

amygdala, a structure in the limbic system which has a role in response to stimuli that signal danger or threat. Phelps et al. (2000) showed, for example, that white participants' greater amygdala activation in response to black versus white faces was significantly correlated with their implicit racial prejudice only when the faces were of unknown black people, but not when they were of famous and well-liked black and white individuals. These findings suggest that amygdala activation and behavioural responses of race evaluation are heavily shaped by social learning, and that personal experience with members of these groups can modulate bias. Thus, involvement of biological processes does not imply something fundamental and unchangeable. In fact, social neuroscience emphasizes that *social* variables can *influence* biological processes (Eberhardt, 2005; Phelps & Thomas, 2003). In our view, this new direction is less a theoretical than an empirical approach, but none the less exciting. We anticipate that, during the lifetime of this book, there will be many new developments in social neuroscience.

Social psychology today is an exhilarating and thriving enterprise. Living up to Lewin's motto that nothing is as practical as a good theory, social psychologists are applying the understanding they have gained from their study of fundamental cognitive, emotional and motivational processes to the solution of real-life problems. They have contributed importantly to the development of applied areas such as health and organizational psychology (see Chapter 15, this volume), and social psychological theories and research on intergroup conflict and prejudice can provide important guidelines for avoiding or resolving conflicts in European societies which are becoming increasingly multicultural (see Chapter 14, this volume). In the absence of systematic and controlled social psychological research in most areas, Allport (1924) had to rely heavily on speculation in his ambitious road map for social psychology as an empirical science. We hope that the readers of this textbook will appreciate the progress social psychologists have made in less than a century in replacing speculation with theory-guided empirical research.

SUMMARY AND CONCLUSIONS

- Social psychology is often defined as the scientific attempt to understand and explain how thoughts, feelings and behaviours of individuals are influenced by the actual, imagined or implied presence of other human beings.

- There are several candidates that could claim to have been the first experiment in social psychology, but all were conducted just before 1900.

- The first textbook that covered topics which would still be considered social psychology today was written by Floyd Allport (1924).

- Allport (1924) defined social psychology as part of the psychology of the individual and as based on experimental methods.

- Although there was some important research conducted before World War II, most theorizing and research considered part of modern social psychology has been published since 1945.

- World War II stimulated interest in social influence and attitude change. Carl Hovland, who during his army years directed a section concerned with experimental work on mass communication, later founded and directed the highly influential Yale Communication and Attitude Change program. This laid the foundation for modern research on attitude change.

- The development of social psychology in the USA was strongly influenced by two academic émigrés from Europe, Kurt Lewin from Germany and Fritz Heider from Austria.

- Kurt Lewin's influence was mainly through his students, an illustrious group who shaped social psychology in the decades following World War II.

- Fritz Heider stimulated two theoretical traditions, consistency and attribution theory, which influenced the research agenda of social psychology for the post-war period.

- Although there were researchers conducting social psychological research in Europe, European social psychology developed only in the mid-1960s.

- The development of European social psychology was greatly stimulated by the foundation of the European Association of Experimental Social Psychology in 1966.

Note

1   Early research reports referred to those who took part in psychological research as 'subjects'. It is now standard practice to refer to them as 'participants'.

Suggestions for further reading

Berscheid, E. (1992). A glance back at a quarter century of social psychology. *Journal of Personality and Social Psychology, 63,* 525–533. A personal reflection by a leading scholar on developments in North America in the 25 years up to its publication.

Cartwright, D. (1979). Contemporary social psychology in social perspective. *Social Psychology Quarterly, 42,* 82–93. A lively attempt to put social psychology into historical perspective, famous for highlighting the 'influence' of Adolf Hitler.

Farr, R.M. (1996). *The roots of modern social psychology 1872–1954.* Oxford: Blackwell. Scholarly treatment of the background to the modern era, with special reference to the relationship between social psychology and other social sciences.

Gilbert, D.T., Fiske, S.T. & Lindzey, G. (Eds.) (1998). *The handbook of social psychology* (4th edn, Vol. 1, pp. 3–95). New York: McGraw-Hill. Two chapters deal with different aspects of modern history, those by E.E. Jones and S.E. Taylor.

Goethals, G.R. (2003). A century of social psychology: Individuals, ideas, and investigations. In M. Hogg & J. Cooper (Eds.), *Sage handbook of social psychology* (pp. 3–23). London: Sage. A short and approachable historical overview.

2

Research Methods in Social Psychology

Antony S.R. Manstead

CHAPTER OUTLINE

....

This chapter provides an overview of research methods in social psychology, from the development of theory to the collection of data. After describing three quantitative research strategies (survey research, experiments and quasi-experiments), the chapter briefly discusses qualitative approaches, focusing on discourse analysis. There follows a description of the key elements of experiments and of threats to validity in experimental research, and a discussion of problems with experimental research in social psychology. The final section of the chapter contains a description of three methods of data collection (observation, self-report and implicit measures).

Introduction

....

How do social psychologists develop their theories?
How do social psychologists go about testing their theories?

Methods provide a means of translating a researcher's ideas into actions. These ideas usually revolve around one or more questions about a phenomenon. An example of such a question in social psychology would be: 'How can a group of capable people make a decision that is stupid and could moreover have been shown to be so at the time the decision was taken?' (see Chapter 11). A researcher might have a hunch about how to explain this phenomenon. For example, the poor decision might have arisen from the fact that the group had a powerful leader who expressed a preference early in the decision-making process and thereby stifled proper evaluation of superior options. To assess the correctness of this hunch the researcher would have to collect information about styles of leadership in groups making poor decisions. Research methods are the procedures the researcher would follow in gathering such information, and *methodology* is a term used to refer to all aspects of the implementation of methods.

Although this chapter is primarily concerned with the methods used by social psychologists to test the validity of their ideas, it is worth considering where these ideas originate. In the typical case, the researcher begins with a *theory* about the phenomenon under investigation. Where does such a theory come from? An obvious source is observation of real-life events. Consider Janis's (1982) theory concerning the poor quality of decision-making that is apparent even in groups of competent and experienced persons. This theory arose from his reading of accounts of how the United States government took the decision to invade Cuba in 1961 (see Research close-up 2.1, pp. 23–24). A second important element of theory building in social psychology is existing theory. The fact that Janis was already conversant with theory and research on group processes and social influence in groups provided him with ideas that he could use to explain defective decision-making by groups.

theory a set of abstract concepts (i.e., constructs) together with propositions about how those constructs are related to one another

Another version of this process of theory building begins with a set of apparently conflicting findings from previous research. An example is Zajonc's (1965) attempt to reconcile conflicting findings in previous studies of the effects on individual task performance of being observed by others (see Chapter 11). Some researchers had found that being observed by others had beneficial effects on task performance, but others had found that it resulted in poorer performance. To reconcile these findings, Zajonc drew on principles derived from learning theory. Once again, the theorist began with a phenomenon that required an explanation, and drew on existing theoretical concepts and processes to make sense of that phenomenon.

In what sense does a theory 'explain' a phenomenon such as the defective decision-making of high-calibre groups, or the divergent effects of being observed on task performance? Social psychological theories usually consist of a set of concepts and statements about the relationships among these concepts. For example, Janis's (1982) theory consists of one set of concepts representing the antecedent conditions of poor group decision-making, another set representing the symptoms of groupthink, a third set representing symptoms of poor decision-making, and a final set representing the process linking antecedent conditions to the symptoms of groupthink and poor decision-making (see Figure 2.1). One of the *antecedent conditions* is a 'cohesive group', a group whose members are psychologically dependent on the group. Because they are dependent on their group membership, they are more likely to conform to what they believe to be the consensual position in the group. An example *symptom* of groupthink is the presence of 'mind guards', a term Janis used to describe group members who take it upon themselves to protect the group from information that questions the correctness or morality of the emerging decision. An example symptom of defective decision-making is failure to examine the risks of the preferred decision. The *mediating process* specified by Janis is a 'concurrence-seeking tendency', a powerful preference for agreement with fellow group members. Thus antecedent conditions are linked to symptoms via a mediating process (see p. 34, below).

Three concepts need to be introduced at this point. *Construct* is the term used to refer to abstract concepts in a theory. In Janis's theory concepts such as group cohesiveness and concurrence-seeking tendency are theoretical *constructs*. *Variable* is a term used to refer to a measurable representation of a construct. To represent the construct of group cohesiveness, for example, we might assess one or more of the following: how long the group has been in existence; the extent to which group members nominate each other as personal friends; and how much group members say they value their membership of the group. So there are various ways in which the researcher can represent the

> **construct** an abstract theoretical concept (such as social influence)
>
> **variable** the term used to refer to the measurable representation of a construct

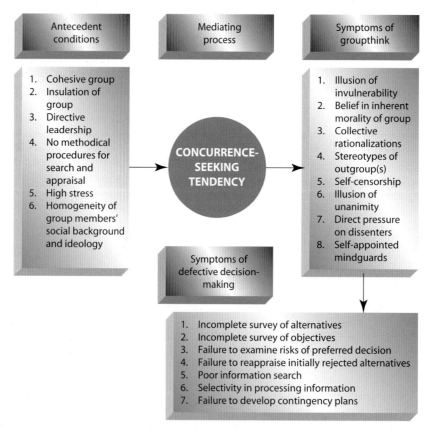

Figure 2.1 *Antecedent conditions, mediating process and symptoms of groupthink in Janis's (1982) theoretical model (based on Figure 10.1 in Janis, 1982).*

operationalization the way in which a theoretical construct is turned into a measurable dependent variable or a manipulable independent variable in a particular study

construct of cohesiveness as a variable. *Operationalization* refers to the way in which a construct is turned into a measurable variable. If group cohesiveness is measured in terms of how much group members value their membership of the group, this is a different operationalization of cohesiveness than if it is measured in terms of the extent to which group members nominate each other as personal friends.

We can derive predictions from a theory. In the case of Janis's theory, a prediction that we can logically derive from the theory is that groups that are more cohesive should be more prone to making poor-quality decisions than groups that are less

hypothesis a prediction derived from a theory concerning the relationship between variables

cohesive. Armed with such a prediction (or *hypothesis*), the researcher tries to find evidence to support the prediction (see Research close-up 2.1).

To the extent that the evidence is consistent with the prediction, confidence in the theory from which the prediction was derived is enhanced. Correspondingly, if the evidence is inconsistent with the prediction, confidence in the underlying theory is weakened. So methods are the means by which researchers put their ideas to the test.

SUMMARY

Methods are the tools researchers use to test their theoretical ideas. These ideas can come from a variety of sources, but two that are quite common in social psychology are observations of real-life events and conflicts in previous research findings. A theory consists of a set of constructs linked together in a system, and specifies when particular phenomena should occur.

RESEARCH CLOSE-UP 2.1

Archival analyses of 'groupthink'

Janis, I.L. (1972). *Victims of groupthink: A psychological study of foreign-policy decisions and fiascoes*. Boston: Houghton Mifflin.

Introduction

Janis's research on groupthink provides an excellent example of 'archival research', a research strategy that is not described or discussed elsewhere in the present chapter. In archival research the data come from archives, that is, from stored records of facts. 'Archival data may include such items as personal documents (letters or diaries), creative products (poems, paintings, essays), biographies or autobiographies, and histories or governmental records' (Simonton, 1981, p. 218). Janis (1972) decided to study in detail archival material relating to four major US foreign policy fiascoes: the Bay of Pigs invasion of Cuba in 1961; the decision to escalate the Korean War in 1950; the failure to be prepared for the attack on Pearl Harbour in 1941; and the decision to escalate the Vietnam War in 1964. Janis argues that in the case of each of these disastrous decisions, information was potentially or actually available to the policy-making groups that should have led them to different decisions.

Method

Janis's research took the form of careful scouring of all the documentary sources of information on the circumstances in which these faulty decisions were made. In his 1972 book *Victims of Groupthink*, Janis attempted to show how the archival data on

each of these decisions can be regarded as forming a consistent social psychological pattern, the essence of which is shown in Figure 2.1. Janis (1982) published a second edition of his book in which he applied the notion of groupthink to the Watergate incident that ultimately led to US President Richard Nixon's resignation in 1974.

Later research

Tetlock (1979) conducted a more quantitative analysis of archival materials. He applied standardized procedures for analysing the content of public statements made by key decision-makers involved in the 'groupthink' and 'non-groupthink' decisions examined by Janis (1972). Tetlock was particularly interested in assessing the extent to which public statements made by key decision-makers reflected 'a tendency to process policy-relevant information in simplistic and biased ways' (p. 1317), and the extent to which these statements reflected 'a tendency to evaluate one's own group highly positively and to evaluate one's . . . opponents highly negatively' (p. 1317). To assess these two aspects of groupthink, Tetlock identified six key decision-makers who were intimately involved in five different foreign policy decisions, two of which were classified by Janis as 'non-groupthink', while the other three were classified by Janis as 'groupthink' decisions. He then randomly selected 12 paragraph-sized passages from the public statements made by each decision-maker at the time of each crisis for content analysis. He found that the public statements of decision-makers in groupthink crises were characterized by significantly lower levels of 'integrative complexity' – a measure of complexity of information processing – than were the public statements of decision-makers in non-groupthink crises. He also found evidence that decision-makers in the groupthink crises gave more positive evaluations of their own political groups than did decision-makers in crises not characterized by groupthink. However, contrary to predictions, there was no difference between groupthink and non-groupthink decision-makers in terms of the intensity of negative evaluations of their political opponents. With the exception of this last finding, the results of Tetlock's study are consistent with Janis's conclusions, which were based on a more qualitative analysis of historical documents.

Discussion

A key advantage of the archival research strategy is that the evidence gleaned from archives is not distorted by participants' knowledge that their behaviour is being investigated by researchers. The behaviour took place in natural settings at an earlier time than that at which the behaviour was studied. There is, therefore, little or no chance that the behaviour could have been 'contaminated' by the research process. As Simonton (1981) put it, 'Because archival research exploits data already collected by others for purposes often very different from the intentions of the researcher, this methodology constitutes a class of "unobtrusive measures" ' (p. 218).

RESEARCH STRATEGIES

What are the principal research strategies available to the social psychologist?
What are the strengths and weaknesses of each strategy?

Researchers who want to test their ideas and predictions have different research strategies available to them. It is worth pointing out that although some research strategies will be better suited than others to studying a given phenomenon, each and every strategy, however sophisticated its implementation, has its limitations. It is for this reason that one of the great pioneers of research methodology in the social sciences, Donald Campbell (see Pioneer box, opposite), argued for *triangulation*. By this he meant that the use of multiple methods to study a given issue would provide a better basis for drawing conclusions than would any single method. The term triangulation comes from navigation: an accurate way to determine the position of a fixed point is by calculating the angles to it from two fixed points that are a known distance apart. Because each method has its own strengths and weaknesses, the use of different methods will help the strengths of one method to compensate for the weaknesses of another, and vice versa.

Many research strategies are available to the social psychologist. Here we will consider three quantitative strategies before briefly considering qualitative research.

> **triangulation** the use of multiple methods and measures to research a given issue

| | **PIONEER** |

Donald T. Campbell (1917–1996) is regarded as having been a master research methodologist. Campbell completed his undergraduate education at the University of California, Berkeley. After serving in the US Naval Reserve during World War II, he earned his doctorate from Berkeley and subsequently served on the faculties at Ohio State, the University of Chicago, Northwestern, and Lehigh. He made lasting contributions in a wide range of disciplines, including psychology, sociology, anthropology, biology and philosophy. In social psychology he is best known for co-authoring two of the most influential research methodology texts ever published, *Experimentation and Quasi-Experimental Designs for Research* (1966, with Julian C. Stanley) and *Quasi-Experimentation: Design and Analysis Issues for Field Settings* (1979, with Thomas D. Cook). Campbell argued that the sophisticated use of many approaches, each with its own distinct but measurable flaws, was required to design reliable research projects. The paper he wrote with Donald W. Fiske to present this thesis, 'Convergent and discriminant validation by the multitrait–multimethod matrix' (1959), is one of the most frequently cited papers in the social science literature.

Survey research

One strategy for gathering research evidence is to survey public opinion and / or behaviour, by interview or by questionnaire. This strategy is known as *survey research* (Schwarz, Groves & Schuman, 1998) and is well known in the form of opinion polls. The main

> **survey research** a research strategy that involves interviewing (or administering a questionnaire to) a sample of respondents who are selected so as to be representative of the population from which they are drawn

Plate 2.1 *One strategy for gathering research evidence is to survey public opinion by interview.*

objective is to describe the characteristics of one or more groups of people. Such descriptions can range from the simple (e.g., describing the percentage of persons eligible to vote in a particular constituency who say that they intend to vote for a particular political candidate) to the more complex (e.g., describing the personal and social characteristics associated with illegal use of drugs among school-age children and teenagers). Note that the first type of description is 'pure' description, while the second describes relationships between variables – such as those between drug use, on the one hand, and age, sex, socioeconomic status and educational achievement, on the other.

The survey researcher's primary concern is with the extent to which the respondents are *representative* of a population (such as all adults living in a particular community, region or country). One way of addressing this issue would be to interview or collect completed questionnaires from the entire population in question (as is done in a census). If you are able to describe the entire population, the findings are by definition 'representative' of that population. In most cases, however, collecting data from all members of a population is simply not practicable. Then the researcher has to choose which members of that population to survey. The process of selecting a subset of members is known as *sampling*.

Two main types of sampling are used in survey research: probabilistic and non-probabilistic. The most basic form of probabilistic sampling is the *simple random sample*. A simple random sample is one which satisfies two conditions: first, each member of the population has an equal chance of being selected; second, the selection of every possible combination of the desired number of members is equally likely. To explain the second condition, imagine that the population size is 10 (consisting of persons labelled A to J) and the

> **sampling** the process of selecting a subset of members of a population with a view to describing the population from which they are taken

> **simple random sample** a sample in which each member of the population has an equal chance of being selected and in which the selection of every possible combination of the desired number of members is equally likely

sample size is 2. There are 45 possible combinations of 2 members of the population (A + B, A + C, A + D and so on to I + J). In simple random sampling each of these 45 possible combinations of 2 members has to be equally likely. In practice researchers achieve this by allocating numbers to each member of the population and using computer-generated random numbers to select a sample of the required size (see www.randomizer.org/). So the first randomly generated number defines the first member of the population to be sampled, and so on, until the sample is full.

Because probability sampling is expensive and time-consuming, non-probability sampling is frequently used. The most common form of non-probability sample is the *quota sample*. Here the objective is to select a sample that reflects basic attributes of the population. Such attributes might be age and sex. If you know the age and sex composition of the population concerned, you then ensure that the age and sex composition of the sample reflects that of the population. The term 'quota' refers to the number of persons of a given type (e.g., females between the ages of 55 and 60) who have to be interviewed. The major advantage of quota sampling is that the interviewer can approach potential respondents until the quotas are filled, without needing to recruit a specifically identified respondent.

> **quota sample** a sample that fills certain pre-specified quotas and thereby reflects certain attributes of the population (such as age and sex) that are thought to be important to the issue being researched

Experiments and quasi-experiments

Experimental research is designed to yield causal information. The goal of an *experiment* is to see what happens to a phenomenon when the researcher deliberately modifies some feature of the environment in which the phenomenon occurs ('If I change variable *B*, will there be resulting changes in variable *A*?'). By controlling the variation in *B*, the researcher who finds that there are changes in *A* can draw causal conclusions. Instead of just knowing that more of variable *A* is associated with more of variable *B*, the experimental researcher discovers whether *A* increases when *B* is increased, decreases when *B* is reduced, remains stable when *B* is left unchanged, and so on. Such a pattern of results would suggest that changes in *B cause* the changes in *A*.

> **experiment** a method in which the researcher deliberately introduces some change into a setting to examine the consequences of that change

The experimental method is a theme with many variations. Two common variations are the *quasi-experiment* and the *true randomized experiment*. They differ with respect to the realism of the setting in which the data are collected and the degree of control that the researcher has over that setting. A quasi-experiment is typically conducted in a

> **quasi-experiment** an experiment in which participants are not randomly allocated to the different experimental conditions (typically because of factors beyond the control of the researcher)

> **true randomized experiment** an experiment in which participants are allocated to the different conditions of the experiment on a random basis

RESEARCH CLOSE-UP 2.2

A field experiment to study helping behaviour

Darley, J.M. & Batson, C.D. (1973). From Jerusalem to Jericho: A study of situational and dispositional variables in helping behavior. *Journal of Personality and Social Psychology, 27*, 100–108.

....

Introduction

The researchers were interested in testing the idea that one reason why bystanders do not come to the assistance of others, even when these others clearly need help, is that helping is costly. The particular 'cost' they studied in their research was time. To come to a stranger's assistance often involves a departure from your original plan. Such a departure can throw you off your schedule. The researchers also wanted to examine whether reminding people of the parable of the Good Samaritan, in which a passer-by does come to the assistance of a stranger in need of help, would influence willingness to give help. They tested these notions in a field experiment (see also Chapter 9, this volume).

Method

The participants in their study were male seminary students (i.e., trainee priests) who believed that they were taking part in a study on 'religious education and vocations'. Each participant began the study in one building and was then asked to proceed to a second building to complete the study. Before leaving the first building, the participant was led to believe one of three things about the speed with which he should go to the other building: that there was no special hurry, that there was an intermediate degree of hurry, or that he was late for the second part of the study and should hurry up. This was the manipulation of the first variable, time pressure. In the second part of the study, the participant expected to do one of two things: either talk about the parable of the Good Samaritan or talk about job prospects for seminary students. This constituted the second manipulation: either having or not having the parable of the Good Samaritan made psychologically salient.

On his way to the other building, the participant passed through an alley in which a person (the 'victim', but actually an accomplice of the experimenters) was sitting slumped in doorway, head down, eyes closed. As the participant passed the victim, the latter coughed twice and groaned. The dependent variable in this field experiment was the extent to which the participant did anything to help this person apparently in distress. The extent of the participant's helping behaviour was observed and coded.

Results

Helping was significantly influenced by the time pressure manipulation. Those in the 'no hurry' condition were more helpful than those in the 'intermediate hurry' condition, who in turn were more helpful than those in the 'hurry' condition. There was also a tendency for being reminded about the parable to have an influence. Those who were reminded were more helpful than those who were not.

Discussion

Even those who have chosen to be trained in a vocation in which helping others is supposed to play a central role were affected by the time pressure variable. When they were in a hurry, even those trainee priests who thought that they were on their way to a discussion of the parable of the Good Samaritan were less likely to offer help to a stranger in need than were their counterparts who were in less of a hurry. From a methodological perspective, the neat thing about this experiment is that it was conducted in a natural, everyday setting. Participants were randomly allocated to one of the six conditions of the experiment, so any differences found between these six conditions resulted in principle from the experimental manipulations, so internal validity was high (i.e., the researchers could be confident that changes in the independent variable *caused* changes in the dependent variable). But the fact that the setting of the experiment was such an everyday one means that this study also scores quite highly on realism. It is a good example of a field experiment.

Plate 2.2 *Would you be more likely to help someone in need after hearing a sermon on the parable of the Good Samaritan?*

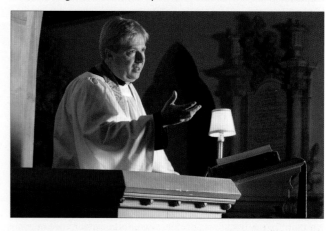

natural, everyday setting, one over which the researcher does not have complete control. The true randomized experiment, by contrast, is one in which the researcher has complete control over key features of the setting; however, this often involves a loss of realism. It is worth emphasizing that it *is* possible to conduct true experiments in field settings, in which case they are referred to as ***field experiments***, which attempt to combine the control of a laboratory experiment with the realism of a quasi-experiment. An example of such a field experiment is given in Research close-up 2.2.

field experiment a true randomized experiment conducted in a natural setting

To grasp the key difference between a quasi-experiment and a true experiment, we need to consider further what is meant by the term experiment. Experiments are studies in which the researcher examines the effects of one class of variables (independent, or manipulated, variables) on another class of variables (dependent, or measured, variables). In a true randomized experiment the researcher has control over the independent variable *and* over who is exposed to this variable. Most importantly, the researcher is able to allocate research participants randomly to different conditions of the experiment (***random allocation***). In a quasi-experiment the researcher usually cannot control who is exposed to the independent variable. In a typical quasi-experiment, pre-existing groups of people are either exposed or not exposed to the independent variable. Examples of each method may help to bring out the points of difference.

random allocation (sometimes called random assignment) the process of allocating participants to groups (or conditions) in such a way that each participant has an equal chance of being assigned to each group

Social psychologists interested in aggression have studied whether exposure to violent film and television material has an impact on the subsequent behaviour of the viewer (see Chapter 8). This can be done using true randomized experiments or quasi-experiments. An example of a true experiment on this issue is the study reported by Liebert and Baron (1972). Male and female children in each of two age groups were randomly allocated to one of two experimental conditions, one in which they viewed an excerpt from a violent television programme and another in which they viewed an exciting athletics race. Later both groups of children were ostensibly given the opportunity to hurt another child. Those who had seen the violent material were more likely to use this opportunity than were those who had seen the non-violent material. Because children had been allocated to the violent and non-violent conditions randomly, the observed difference can be attributed to the difference in type of material seen, rather than any difference in the type of children who saw the material.

An example of a quasi-experimental study of the same issue is the study reported by Black and Bevan (1992). They asked people to complete a questionnaire measure of tendency to engage in aggressive behaviour under one of four conditions: while waiting in line outside a cinema to see a violent movie; while waiting in line to see a non-violent movie; having just seen a violent movie; and

Plate 2.3 *What research method might be used to study the impact of viewing violent television on subsequent behaviour?*

having just seen a non-violent movie. As can be seen in Figure 2.2, the researchers found that those waiting to see the violent film had higher aggression scores than those waiting to see the non-violent film; and also that those who had just seen the violent film scored higher than those waiting to see the violent film, although there was no difference in aggression scores between those who had just seen a non-violent movie and those waiting to see a non-violent movie. These findings are consistent with the notion that viewing a violent movie increases the tendency to aggress, but the fact that participants were not allocated at random to the different conditions makes it impossible to rule out alternative explanations. For example, it may be that violent movies only increase aggressive tendencies among those who are attracted to view such movies in the first place.

Often the only way in which to conduct an experimental study of a social phenomenon is via a quasi-experiment. Ethical and practical considerations frequently make it impossible to allocate people randomly to different experimental conditions. If, like

Plate 2.4 *Are those who choose to see violent films more aggressive?*

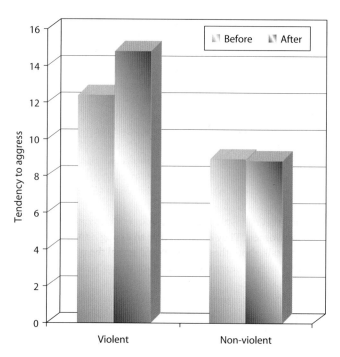

Figure 2.2 *Self-reported tendency to aggress, as a function of type of film, and whether or not the respondent was waiting to see the film or had just seen the film (based on data reported by Black & Bevan, 1992).*

Stroebe, Stroebe and Domittner (1988), you wish to study the effects of bereavement, for example, you obviously cannot randomly allocate research participants to a 'bereaved' and 'non-bereaved' condition. The same applies in many other fields of research. Thus the choice of research strategy is often a compromise between what is optimal and what is practicable. Fortunately, the sophistication of some quasi-experimental designs is such that it is possible to draw conclusions about causality with some confidence (Judd & Kenny, 1981a; West, Biesanz & Pitts, 2000).

Qualitative approaches

Traditionally, social psychological research has been quantitative and the overwhelming majority of the research discussed in this book is quantitative in nature. That is, it seeks to operationalize constructs in ways that make them quantifiable, and thereby allow the researcher to describe a variable, or the relationship between two or more variables, in quantitative terms. By contrast, research in other social science disciplines, such as social anthropology, is typically qualitative in nature, meaning that constructs and relationships between constructs are described and discussed using ordinary language. A fundamental assumption shared by qualitative researchers is that we should try to understand the meanings of social behaviours and social experiences from the perspectives of the participants concerned, and that to do this properly we need to pay due regard to the contexts in which these behaviours or experiences naturally occur (see Henwood, 1996).

Although it is common practice for social psychologists to use qualitative methods (such as participant observation or semi-structured interviewing, both described later) in the early stages of their research (for example, to develop and refine the questions to be posed in a questionnaire), there are also social psychologists who exclusively use qualitative methods. They do so in the belief that a quantitative approach provides at best a partial and at worst a distorted view of the phenomenon they want to study. In the context of the present chapter we can do little more than sketch the range of qualitative research methods that can be deployed in social psychological research. Henwood (1996) provides a good overview of the different possibilities within qualitative enquiry. Here we limit ourselves to a brief description of one prominent example of qualitative enquiry, namely *discourse analysis*. Although this sounds like a single method, it is a term used to describe a family of methods for analysing talk and texts. Discourse analysis starts from the observation that everyday talk is orderly and can be systematically studied through the

discourse analysis a family of methods for analysing talk and texts, with the goal of revealing how people make sense of their everyday worlds

transcription and analysis of audiovisual recordings. By recording and analysing everyday interaction and discourse, it is argued, we can gain a better insight into the ways that people conduct their lives and account for themselves.

The discourse analyst seeks to show how, for example, racist or sexist attitudes arise not because of the beliefs or biases of the individual who expresses them, but rather as evaluations that emerge in the context of particular social interactions. Rather than being relatively fixed products of individual cognitive systems, such evaluations arise in the context of conversations and vary according to the particular cultural setting. An example of the use of discourse analysis is the study reported by Wetherell, Stiven and Potter (1987). These researchers were interested in male and female university students' views about employment opportunities for women. They reasoned that analysing how a group of 17 students talk about these issues would reveal the practical ideologies that are used to reproduce gender inequalities. The students were interviewed in a semi-structured way and their responses were transcribed and analysed. A benefit of this approach is that it enabled the researchers to identify contradictions in the way ordinary people talk about issues like gender inequality. Rather than having a single attitude, the students tended to endorse different positions at different points during the interview, and some of these positions were inconsistent with each other.

This sort of qualitative approach is not represented in the present volume, where the emphasis is on the strengths of a realist, quantifiable social psychology. This is not to say that qualitative methods play no role in the research that is represented in this book. It is more that, as noted above, qualitative methods are used in the early stages of such research, rather than being the sole research method. The role played by qualitative research methods in social psychology largely reflects differences in philosophical belief about the causation of social behaviour. For realist social psychologists, social behaviour has causes, and the goal of research is to shed light on those causes. For many qualitative researchers, social behaviour does not have causes in the same way that, say, an earthquake has causes. Such researchers use qualitative research methods to identify how people construct their own and others' behaviours. From the standpoint of the research represented in the present volume, qualitative research seems to be more focused on description than explanation, and more concerned with how behaviour is constructed than with how it is caused.

SUMMARY

Research strategies are broad categories of research methods that are available to study social psychological phenomena. We began by noting that it often makes sense to study a phenomenon using more than one strategy. Here we identified three quantitative strategies (survey research, experiments and quasi-experiments) before discussing qualitative research strategies.

A CLOSER LOOK AT EXPERIMENTATION IN SOCIAL PSYCHOLOGY

What are the main elements of a social psychological experiment?

Experimentation has been the dominant research method in social psychology, mainly because it is unrivalled as a method for testing theories that predict causal relationships between variables. Standard guides to research in social psychology (e.g., Aronson, Ellsworth, Carlsmith & Gonzales, 1990; Aronson, Wilson & Brewer, 1998) treat experimentation as the preferred research method. In fact there are grounds for questioning the extent to which experimental studies provide unambiguous evidence about causation, as we shall see later.

We will first describe the principal features of the experimental approach to social psychological research. To assist this process of description, we will use Milgram's (1965; see Chapter 11) well-known study of obedience as an illustrative example.

Features of the social psychological experiment

The **experimental scenario** is the context in which the study is presented. In laboratory settings it is important to devise a scenario for which there is a convincing and well-integrated rationale, because the situation should strike participants as realistic and involving, and the experimental manipulations and the measurement process should not 'leap out' at the participant. In Milgram's study, participants were told that the study was an investigation of the effects of punishment on learning. The participant was given, apparently at random, the role of 'teacher', while an accomplice of the experimenter posing as another participant (known as a **confederate**) took the role of 'learner'. The learner's task was to memorize a list of word pairs. The teacher's task was to read out the first word of each pair, to see whether the learner could correctly remember the second word, and to administer a graded series of punishments, in the form of electric shocks of increasing severity, if the learner failed to recall the correct word (which he had been instructed to do from time to time). This scenario was devised with a view to convincing the participant that the shocks were genuine (which they were not), and that the learner was actually receiving the shocks.

> **experimental scenario** the 'package' within which an experiment is presented to participants. In field experiments it is, ideally, something that happens naturally. In laboratory experiments it is important to devise a scenario that strikes the participant as realistic and involving

> **confederate** an accomplice or assistant of the experimenter who is ostensibly another participant but who in fact plays a prescribed role in the experiment

independent variable the variable that an experimenter manipulates or modifies in order to examine the effect on one or more dependent variables

The *independent variable* is the one that is deliberately manipulated by the experimenter. All other aspects of the scenario are held constant, and the independent variable is changed systematically. Each change produces a new 'condition' of the experiment: one change yields two conditions, two changes yield three conditions, and so on. In Milgram's research a key independent variable was the proximity of the 'learner' to the 'teacher'. In one condition, learner and teacher were in separate rooms; in a second condition, the teacher could hear the learner but could not see him; in a third condition, the teacher could both see and hear the learner's reactions; in a fourth condition, the teacher had to hold the learner's hand down on a metal plate in order for the shock to be delivered (the touch-proximity condition). All other aspects of the experimental setting were held constant, so that variations in the teachers' behaviour in these four conditions were attributable to the change in proximity between teacher and learner.

The success of an experiment often hinges on the effectiveness of manipulations of the independent variable. By *effectiveness* we mean (1) the extent to which changes in the independent variable capture the essential qualities of the construct that is theoretically expected to have a causal influence on behaviour, and (2) the size of the changes that are introduced. For example, in Milgram's study, we should consider how well the four proximity conditions capture the construct of proximity. What is being manipulated, clearly, is *physical* proximity. Then there is the question of whether the changes between the four conditions are sufficiently large to produce an effect. In this case it is hard to see how the proximity variable could have been manipulated more powerfully; an investigator who adopts weaker manipulations runs the risk of failing to find the predicted effects simply because the variations across levels of the independent variable are too subtle to have an impact. It has become standard practice in social psychological experiments to include among the measured variables one or more measures of the effectiveness of the manipulation: these are known as *manipulation checks*.

manipulation checks a measure of the effectiveness of the independent variable

dependent variable the variable that is expected to change as a function of changes in the independent variable. Measured changes in the dependent variable are seen as 'dependent on' manipulated changes in the independent variable

Assessing whether an independent variable has had an effect requires the measurement of the participant's behaviour or internal state. This measured variable is known as the *dependent variable*, so called because systematic changes in this measured variable *depend upon* the impact of the independent variable. In Milgram's study, the dependent variable was the intensity of shocks in a 30-step sequence that the teacher was prepared to deliver. The results of Milgram's experiments are often expressed in terms of the percentage of participants who gave the maximum shock level (corresponding to 450 volts). The results of the Milgram (1965) study are shown in these terms in Figure 2.3. A key question to ask of any dependent variable is the extent to which it is a good measure of the

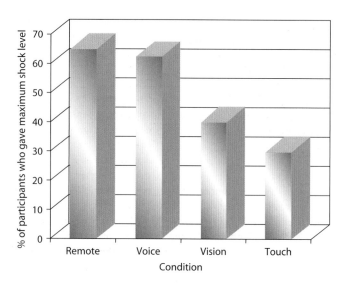

Figure 2.3 *Percentage of participants who administered the maximum shock level, and who were therefore deemed to be fully obedient (based on data reported by Milgram, 1965).*

underlying theoretical construct. In addition to this question of the 'fit' between a theoretical construct and the measured or dependent variable, the most important issue involved in designing dependent variables is what type of measure to use. We will discuss this in more detail below.

Laboratory experiments often involve deception, in the sense that the participant is misled about some aspect of the research. The extent of this deception can range from withholding information about the purpose of the research to misleading participants into thinking that the research is concerned with something other than its real purpose. The main reason for using deception is that participants would act differently if they were aware of the true objective of the study. If Milgram's participants had known that his was a study of obedience, we can be sure that the rate of disobedience would have been higher: the participants would have wanted to demonstrate their ability to resist orders to harm a fellow human. Attitudes to the use of deception in social psychological research have changed during the past 40 years: misleading participants about the nature of an experiment is now viewed more negatively. The reason for this change is partly moral (i.e., where possible one should avoid deceiving someone else, whether or not in the context of an experiment) and partly practical (if participants are routinely misled about research, they will enter any future participation in the expectation that they are going to be misled, which may influence their behaviour). Striking an appropriate balance between being completely honest with participants and wanting to study them free of the influence of their knowledge of the nature of the experiment is difficult. Most universities in Europe, North America and Australasia have some form of ethics committee that monitors research involving human participants, and national bodies such as the American Psychological Association (APA) and the British Psychological Society (BPS) have published guidelines concerning research using human participants that have to be followed by their members.

debriefing the practice of explaining to participants the purpose of the experiment in which they have just participated, and answering any questions the participant may have. It is especially important to debrief participants when the experimental procedure involved deception – in which case the debriefing should also explain why the deception was considered to be necessary

One way to address ethical issues entailed in using deception is by careful use of **debriefing**. This takes place at the end of the experimental session and involves informing the participant as fully as possible about the nature and purpose of the experiment, and the reason for any deception. In Milgram's study, for example, care was taken to assure participants that the 'shocks' they had administered were in fact bogus, and that the learner had not been harmed in any way; the reason for the deception was also carefully explained. Ideally, the debriefing process should leave participants understanding the purpose of the research, satisfied with their role in the experiment, and with as much self-respect as they had before participating in the study.

Experimental designs

Why is it important to have a control condition in an experiment? What is an interaction effect?

As we have seen, it is important that participants are allocated randomly to the different conditions of an experiment. Failure to achieve this goal hinders the researcher's ability to conclude that observed differences between conditions in the dependent variable result from changes in the independent variable. We shall now examine more closely the question of designing experiments in order to rule out alternative inferences as far as possible.

one-shot case study a research design in which observations are made on a group after some event has occurred or some manipulation has been introduced. The problem is that there is nothing with which these observations may be compared, so one has no way of knowing whether the event or manipulation had an effect

First, consider a study that may *appear* to be an experiment but cannot properly be described as experimental. This is the **one-shot case study**. Following Cook and Campbell (1979), we shall use the symbols X to stand for a manipulation (i.e., of the independent variable) and O to stand for observation (i.e., the dependent variable). In these terms the one-shot design looks like this:

$$X \qquad\qquad O$$
$$\xrightarrow{\hspace{3cm}}$$
$$\text{time}$$

To take an example, imagine that an educational researcher wanted to know the effect of a new teaching method on learning. The researcher takes a class of students, introduces the new method (X) and measures the students' comprehension of the taught material (O). What conclusions can be drawn from such a design? Strictly speaking, none, for there is nothing with which O can be compared, so the researcher cannot infer whether the observed comprehension is good, poor or indifferent.

A simple extension of the one-shot design provides the *minimum* requirements for a true experimental study and is known as the **post-test only control group design**. Let R stand for random assignment of participants to conditions, and X and O stand for manipulation and observation, as before. This design looks like this:

Experimental group	R	X	O_1
Control group	R		O_2

$$\xrightarrow{\hspace{4cm}}$$
$$\text{time}$$

post-test only control group design a minimal design for a true experiment. Participants are randomly allocated to one of two groups. One group is exposed to the independent variable; another (the control group) is not. Both groups are assessed on the dependent variable, and comparison of the two groups on this measure indicates whether or not the independent variable had an effect

Here there are two conditions. In the experimental condition participants are exposed to the manipulation (participants in this condition are known as the **experimental group**), and possible effects of the manipulation are measured. In the control condition there is no manipulation (here the participants are known as the **control group**), but these participants are also assessed on the same dependent variable and at the same time point as the experimental group. Now the observation made in the experimental condition (O_1) *can* be compared with something: the observation made in the control condition (O_2). So the researcher might compare one group of students who have been exposed to the new teaching method with another group who continued to receive the normal method, with respect to their comprehension of the course material. An important point is that participants are randomly allocated to the two conditions, ruling out the possibility that differences between O_1 and O_2 are due to differences between the two groups of participants that were present before X was implemented. It follows that if O_1 and O_2 differ markedly it is reasonable to infer that X causes this difference.

experimental group a group of participants allocated to the 'experimental' condition of the experiment, i.e., the condition in which participants are exposed to that level of the independent variable that is predicted to influence their thoughts, feelings or behaviour

control group a group of participants who are typically not exposed to the independent variable(s) used in experimental research. Measures of the dependent variable derived from these participants are compared with those derived from participants who are exposed to the independent variable (i.e., the experimental group), providing a basis for inferring whether the independent variable determines scores on the dependent variable

There are several other more sophisticated and complex designs, each representing a more complete attempt to rule out the possibility that observed differences between conditions result from something other than the manipulation of the independent variable (see Cook & Campbell, 1979). A common design in social psychological experiments is the **factorial experiment**, in which two or more independent variables are manipulated within the same study. The

factorial experiment an experiment in which two or more independent variables are manipulated within the same design

simplest case can be represented as follows, where R stands for random assignment of participants to conditions, X stands for a variable with two levels (X_1 and X_2) and Y stands for another variable with two levels (Y_1 and Y_2):

$$
\begin{array}{lll}
R & X_1Y_1 & O_1 \\
R & X_1Y_2 & O_2 \\
R & X_2Y_1 & O_3 \\
R & X_2Y_2 & O_4
\end{array}
$$

time

A factorial design contains all possible combinations of the independent variables. In the design shown above, each independent variable has two levels, resulting in four conditions. The main benefit of a factorial design is that it allows the researcher to examine the separate *and combined* effects of two or more independent variables. The separate effects of each independent variable are known as **main effects**. If the combined effect of two independent variables differs from the sum of their two main effects, this is known as an **interaction effect**.

main effect a term used to refer to the separate effects of each independent variable in a factorial experiment

interaction effect a term used when the combined effects of two (or more) independent variables in a factorial experiment yield a pattern that differs from the sum of the main effects

To illustrate an interaction effect, let us consider a study of the effects of persuasive communications on attitude change, reported by Petty, Cacioppo and Goldman (1981). To test Petty and Cacioppo's (1986a) elaboration likelihood model of persuasion (see Chapter 7), these researchers manipulated two variables. The first was argument quality, i.e., whether the persuasive communication the participants read consisted of strong or weak

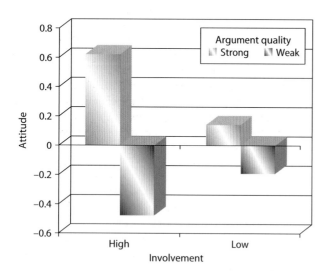

Figure 2.4 *Interaction between argument quality and involvement, showing that argument quality had a much stronger effect on attitudes when involvement was high (based on data reported by Petty, Cacioppo & Goldman, 1981).*

arguments in favour of making the university examination system tougher. The second variable was involvement, i.e., whether the participants, who were students, thought that the university would introduce the tougher exam system next year, such that it would affect them personally (high involvement), or in the next decade, such that it would not affect them personally (low involvement). According to the elaboration likelihood model, argument quality should have a stronger impact on attitudes when participants are involved with the message topic than when they are not. Figure 2.4 shows some of the key findings from Petty et al.'s (1981) study. It can be seen that the effect of argument quality on attitudes was much greater when involvement was high than when it was low, just as the theory predicts. Because the predicted effect is an interaction, testing this prediction requires a factorial design.

Threats to validity in experimental research

What is the difference between internal and external validity? What is meant by the term 'confounding' in the context of experimental research?

In a research context, **validity** refers to the extent to which one is justified in drawing inferences from one's findings. Experimental research attempts to maximize each of three types of validity: internal validity, construct validity and external validity.

validity a measure is valid to the extent that it measures precisely what it is supposed to measure

internal validity refers to the validity of the inference that changes in the independent variable result in changes in the dependent variable

Internal validity refers to the validity of the conclusion that an observed relationship between independent and dependent variables reflects a *causal* relationship, and is promoted by the use of a sound experimental design. We have already seen that the use of a control group greatly enhances internal validity, but even if one uses a control group there remain many potential threats to internal validity (Brewer, 2000; Cook & Campbell, 1979). Prime among these is the possibility that the groups being compared differ with respect to more than the independent variable of interest.

For example, let's assume that in Milgram's obedience research a different experimenter had been used for each of the four conditions described earlier, such that experimenter 1 ran all participants in one condition, experimenter 2 ran all participants in another condition, and so on. It might seem sensible to divide the work among different experimenters, but to do so in this way poses a major threat to the internal validity of the experiment. This is because the four conditions would no longer differ *solely* in terms of the physical proximity of the 'victim'; they would also differ in that different experimenters conducted them. Thus the differing amounts of obedience observed in the four conditions *might* reflect the impact of the physical proximity variable, *or* the influence of the different experimenters (or, indeed, some combination of these two factors). The problem is that the physical

confounding a variable that incorporates two or more potentially separable components is a confounded variable. When an independent variable is confounded, the researcher's ability to draw unambiguous causal inferences is seriously constrained

construct validity the validity of the assumption that independent and dependent variables adequately capture the abstract variables (constructs) they are supposed to represent

proximity variable would be *confounded* with a second variable, namely experimenter identity. It is impossible to disentangle the effects of confounded variables.

Even when we are confident that the relationship between X and O is a causal one, in the sense that internal validity is high, we need to consider carefully the nature of the constructs involved in this relationship. *Construct validity* refers to the validity of the assumption that independent or dependent variables adequately capture the variables (or 'constructs') they are supposed to represent. Even if the researcher has reason to feel satisfied with the construct validity of the independent variable, there remains the question of whether the dependent variables actually assess what they were intended to assess. There are three main types of threat to the construct validity of dependent variables in social psychological experimentation: social desirability, demand characteristics and experimenter expectancy.

social desirability refers to the fact that research participants are likely to want to be seen in a positive light and may therefore adjust their responses or behaviour in order to avoid being negatively evaluated

Social desirability refers to the fact that participants are usually keen to be seen in a positive light, and may therefore be reluctant to provide honest reports of anything which they think would be regarded negatively. Equally, participants may 'censor' some of their behaviours so as to avoid being evaluated negatively. To the extent that a researcher's measures are affected by social desirability, they fail to capture the theoretical construct of interest. An obvious way to reduce social desirability effects is to make the measurement process unobtrusive: if participants do not know what it is that is being measured, they will be unable to modify their behaviour.

Demand characteristics are cues that convey the experimenter's hypothesis to the participant. Individuals who know that they are being studied will often have hunches about what the experimenter is expecting to find. They may then attempt to provide the expected responses. When behaviour is enacted with the intention of fulfilling the experimenter's hypotheses, it is said to be a response to the demand characteristics of the experiment. Orne (1962, 1969) conducted much research on demand characteristics and suggested ways of pinpointing the role they play in any given experimental situation. For example, he advocated the use of *post-experimental enquiry*, in the form of an interview, preferably conducted by someone other than the experimenter, the object being to elicit from participants what they believed to be the aim of the experiment and the extent to

demand characteristics cues that are perceived as telling participants how they are expected to behave or respond in a research setting, i.e., cues that 'demand' a certain sort of response

post-experimental enquiry a technique advocated by Orne for detecting the operation of demand characteristics. The participant is carefully interviewed after participation in an experiment, the object being to assess perceptions of the purpose of the experiment

which this affected their behaviour. Clearly, researchers should do all they can to minimize the operation of demand characteristics, for example by using *unobtrusive measures*, that is, measures that are so unobtrusive that participants are unaware of the fact that they are being taken, or by telling participants that the purpose of the experiment cannot be revealed until the end of the study and that in the meantime it is important that they do *not* attempt to guess the hypothesis. A *cover story* that leads participants to believe that the purpose of the study is something other than the real purpose is a widely used means of lessening the impact of demand characteristics.

unobtrusive measures (also called non-reactive measures) measures that the participant is not aware of, and which therefore cannot influence his or her behaviour

cover story a false but supposedly plausible explanation of the purpose of an experiment. The intention is to limit the operation of demand characteristics

Experimenter expectancy refers to the experimenter's own hypothesis or expectations about the outcome of the research. This expectancy can unintentionally influence the experimenter's behaviour towards participants in such a way as to enhance the likelihood that they will confirm his or her hypothesis. Rosenthal (1966) called this type of influence the *experimenter expectancy effect*. The processes mediating experimenter expectancy effects are complex, but nonverbal communication is centrally involved. An obvious strategy for reducing these effects is to keep experimenters 'blind' to the hypothesis under test, or at least blind to the condition to

experimenter expectancy effects effects unintentionally produced by the experimenter in the course of his or her interaction with the participant. These effects result from the experimenter's knowledge of the hypothesis under test, and they increase the likelihood that the participants will behave in such a way as to confirm the hypothesis

which a given participant has been allocated; other possibilities include minimizing the interaction between experimenter and participant, and automating the experiment as far as possible. Indeed, in much current social psychological research, the entire experiment, including all instructions to the participants, is presented via a computer. This obviously limits the opportunity for experimenters to communicate their expectancies.

Even if the experimenter manages to avoid all these threats to internal and construct validity, an important question remains: to what extent can the causal relationship between X and O be generalized beyond the circumstances of the experiment? *External validity* refers to the generalizability of a finding beyond the circumstances in which it was observed by the researcher. One important feature of the experimental

external validity refers to the generalizability of research findings to settings and populations other than those involved in the research

circumstances, of course, is the type of person who participates in the experiment. In many cases participants volunteer their participation, and to establish external validity it is important to consider whether results obtained using volunteers can be generalized to other populations. There is a good deal of research on differences between volunteers and non-volunteers in psychological studies (see Rosenthal & Rosnow, 1975). The general conclusion is that there *are* systematic personality differences between volunteers and non-volunteers. Such findings are explained in terms of volunteers' supposedly greater sensitivity to and willingness to comply with demand characteristics. The external validity of studies based only on volunteers' behaviour is therefore open to question, and the solution to this problem is to use a 'captive' population, preferably in a field setting.

Another criticism of social (and indeed other) psychological experiments is that the participants are often university students. Sears (1986) examined research articles published in major social psychology journals in 1985 and found that 74 per cent were conducted with student participants. Although students are certainly unrepresentative of the general population, being younger, more intelligent and more highly educated than the average citizen, this in itself is *not* a threat to the validity of the research. This is because the goal of much social psychological research is to understand the process(es) underlying a phenomenon (such as attitude change or stereotyping), rather than to describe the general population (a goal for which survey research is much better suited). In any case, there is often little reason to suppose that the processes underlying a phenomenon such as attitude change or stereotyping differ in some fundamental way between students and non-students.

Social psychological experiments on the Internet

What are the advantages and disadvantages of web-based experiments?

A relatively new development in psychological research is the use of the Internet to recruit and conduct experiments (**Internet experiments**). People are invited to participate in the research by visiting a website where the server runs the whole study, from allocating participants to an experimental condition to debriefing them about the nature and purpose of the study once they have completed the experimental task. Birnbaum (2000) noted that the number of experiments listed on sites such as the one maintained by the American Psychological Society (psych.hanover.edu/Research/exponnet.html) has grown very rapidly, by around 100 per cent per year, and that many of these studies are social psychological.

What are the primary advantages and disadvantages of such web-based experiments? A major advantage is the ease with which quite large amounts of data can be collected in a relatively short time. Other advantages are that participants are recruited from different countries, from different age groups and – to the extent that access to the Internet becomes more widespread – from different socioeconomic backgrounds. Obvious disadvantages are that the researcher loses a degree of control over the running of the experiment. Participants complete the study in different physical settings, at different times of the day and night, and probably with differing levels of motivation and seriousness. There are also issues to do with the representativeness of those who choose to

Internet experiments experiments that are run on a server which participants access via the Internet

participate in an Internet study (they tend to be white, from the USA or from Europe, and to be relatively young – but not as young as those who take part in laboratory experiments) and with the effect of linguistic competence on the reliability and validity of responses (most studies posted on the web are in English, and although the majority of respondents tend to be from the USA or other English-speaking countries, some are not).

Despite the potential problems associated with running experiments on the web, the evidence suggests that Internet studies yield results that parallel those of conventional experiments (see Krantz & Dalal, 2000). It is clear that this way of conducting experiments is going to continue to expand very rapidly. Before embarking on such research it is important to consult sources such as Nosek, Banaji and Greenwald (2002) and Reips (2002), who offer advice about how best to avoid the potential pitfalls.

Problems with experimentation

What are the main criticisms that have been levelled at the use of experiments in social psychology?
What is meant by the term 'mediation' in the context of psychological research?

It is widely assumed that the experimental method provides the 'royal road' to causal inference (Aronson et al., 1998). In fact causal inference from the results of experiments is more problematic than some commentators allow. One problem concerns what Gergen (1978) has called the *cultural embeddedness* of social events, by which he means that a laboratory experimental demonstration that independent variable X has an impact on dependent variable O needs to be qualified by adding that the circumstances in which X was manipulated may have played a role in producing the observed effects on O. Smith and Bond (1998) review many social psychological experiments, including the Milgram obedience experiment, that have been conducted in different countries. It is not unusual for these experiments to produce different findings as a function of the cultural setting.

A related problem noted by Gergen is that although the experimental method supposedly allows us to trace the causal sequence from antecedent conditions to the behaviour of interest, its capacity to do so depends on the assumption that external events are related in a one-to-one fashion with particular states or processes in the individual. The result is that what one experimenter believes to be a demonstration of the effect of X on O via the mediating process Z, another will prefer to explain in terms of a different process. Social psychology abounds with such debates between rival accounts for findings (for examples, see Tetlock & Levi, 1982; Tetlock & Manstead, 1985), and some have come to the view that experimentation is not a suitable way to settle such between-theory disputes.

The heart of the problem identified by Gergen is that phenomena of interest to social psychologists often entail *chains* of events. If we strip this issue down to its bare essentials, we can ask whether variable X influences variable O *directly*, or whether the relation between X and O is mediated by another variable, Z. By conducting an experiment we may establish that there is a causal relation between X and O; but had we also measured Z, we might have found that the relation between X and Z is also very high, as is the relation between Z and O. Indeed, we might find that once the X–Z and Z–O relationships are statistically taken into account, the originally established relationship between X and O disappears. This is the type of situation in which one can infer that the relationship between X and O is *mediated* by Z (Baron & Kenny, 1986).

> **mediating variable** a variable that mediates the relation between two other variables. Assume that independent variable X and dependent variable O are related. If a third variable Z is related to both X and O, and if the X–O relation disappears when we take the role of Z into account, then Z is said to mediate the relation between X and O

Indeed, one strategy that helps to overcome the problem of alternative explanations identified by Gergen is to design experiments that include the assessment of possible *mediating variables*. In modern social psychological research, researchers often attempt to measure such variables and then to conduct mediational analysis, for which there are well-established procedures (see Judd & Kenny, 1981b; Kenny, Kashy & Bolger, 1998).

A final problem worth mentioning is that although the ostensible goal of social psychological experimentation is the accumulation of scientific knowledge, in the form of laws or principles of social behaviour that are valid across time, there is some reason to doubt whether experimentation (or, indeed, any other method) is capable of generating evidence that could be the basis of such laws. To understand why this is the case in social sciences but not in natural sciences, bear in mind that the relationship between researcher and the object of study is radically different in these two types of science. Testing of theories in the natural sciences is concerned with the analysis and explanation of the *object world*, a world that does not engage in the construction and interpretation of the meaning of its own activity. The objects of investigation in social sciences are people, who do of course attribute meaning and significance to their own actions. Social psychology cannot therefore be neatly separated from what it studies. Laypersons are able to acquire social psychological knowledge and use it to modify their actions in a way that atoms, elements and particles cannot.

One implication of this is that even well-supported social psychological theories should not be regarded as embodying 'laws' that hold good across time: if learning about a theory leads people to modify the behaviour that the theory tries to explain, the theory has limited temporal validity. Gergen (1973, 1978) has been the leading advocate of this sobering view, although others, including Schlenker (1974), have challenged his arguments. It is also worth noting that some of the problems of accumulation of knowledge in social psychology can be addressed through the use of *meta-analysis*. This is a technique for statistically integrating the results of independent studies of the same phenomenon in order to establish whether findings are reliable across a number of independent investigations (see Cooper, 1990; Hedges & Olkin, 1985; Johnson & Eagly, 2000). The increasing use of meta-analysis in social psychology (where relevant, one is cited in every chapter of this book) has shown, without doubt, that many social psychological claims have, in fact, been confirmed

> **meta-analysis** a set of techniques for statistically integrating the results of independent studies of a given phenomenon, with a view to establishing whether the findings exhibit a pattern of relationships that is reliable across studies

over multiple experiments, often conducted over many decades. This accumulation of evidence does not support Gergen's claim.

What are the implications of these problems for the status of experimentation in social psychological research? Even some of the harshest critics of the experimental approach do not advocate the abandonment of experimentation. For example, Gergen acknowledged that experiments would continue to play an important role in the explication of the relationship between biological processes (such as physiological arousal) and social behaviour; that studies such as the Milgram experiment are useful for raising consciousness about the insidious nature of social influence; that experiments can increase the impact of theories by providing vivid demonstrations of conditions under which a theory makes successful predictions; and that experimentation can be useful to evaluate social reforms, such as the effectiveness of measures designed to conserve energy. Thus the debate about the utility of experimentation revolves around the types of inference that can reasonably be made on the basis of experimental evidence, with 'traditionalists' such as Aronson et al. (1998) sticking to the view that experimentation provides a firm basis on which to build knowledge, and critics such as Gergen questioning this assumption. Given that over 30 years have now elapsed since Gergen's critique, and experimental social psychology continues to grow and flourish, we can conclude in any case that experiments have *not* been abandoned.

SUMMARY

We examined different aspects of the use of experimentation in social psychology. We began by describing the principal features of the social psychological experiment, before going on to discuss some common experimental designs. We then considered the main threats to validity in experimental research, such as demand characteristics and experimenter expectancy effects, before going on to describe how researchers are making increasing use of the Internet to conduct experiments. Finally, we considered some possible problems with the use of experiments in social psychological research.

DATA COLLECTION TECHNIQUES

What are the principal data collection techniques used in social psychological research?
What are the strengths and weaknesses of each of these techniques?

Assuming that an investigator is conducting quantitative research, he or she will need to measure one or more variables, regardless of which research strategy has been adopted. In correlational designs the researcher has to measure each of the variables that are expected to correlate. In experimental designs the researcher needs to measure the dependent variable. In either case, the investigator is confronted with the task of translating a theoretical construct (for example, aggression) into a measurable variable (for example, willingness to harm someone). Any psychological measure should be both reliable and valid. *Reliability* here refers to the stability of the measure. If you measure an adult's height, the measurement will be highly stable from one day to the next and will also be independent of who is doing the measuring.

reliability the degree to which a measure is free from measurement error; a measure is reliable if it yields the same result on more than one occasion or when used by different individuals

A reliable measure is one that is not dependent on the time of measurement or on the person taking the measurement. A measure can be highly reliable and yet be low in validity. To pursue the height example, let us imagine that what you *really* want to measure is a person's weight. In the absence of a proper weighing scale you decide to measure height instead, because you do have a tape-measure. Of course, height and weight are correlated with each other, so height may be a better estimate of weight than simple guesswork. But clearly, height is not especially valid as a measure of weight. So validity in this context refers to the extent to which the measured variable really captures the underlying construct.

In social psychological research the investigator typically chooses to measure a variable using one or more of the following: observational measures, self-report measures or (a more recent development) implicit measures.

Observational measures

If the object of one's research is to collect information about social *behaviour*, an obvious means of doing so is by observation. Many behaviours of interest to social psychologists are detectable without sophisticated equipment and take place in public settings, which makes them suitable for observation. Although observational methods vary in kind from the informal and unstructured to the highly formal and structured, the object in each case is the same: to abstract from the complex flux of social behaviour those actions that are of potential significance to the research question, and to record each instance of such actions over some period (Weick, 1985).

Sometimes the nature of the research setting or topic dictates that observation is conducted in a relatively informal and unstructured manner, with the researcher posing as a member of the group being observed. A classic example of research employing this method is Festinger, Riecken and Schachter's (1956) study of the consequences of blatant disconfirmation of strongly held beliefs. The investigators identified a religious sect that predicted that the northern hemisphere would be destroyed by flood on a certain date. By joining that sect, members of the research team were able to observe what happened when the predicted events failed to materialize. Under such circumstances, observation clearly has to be covert and informal: if other sect members suspected that the researchers were not *bona fide* believers, the opportunity for observation would be removed. This type of observation is known as *participant observation*, and typically yields qualitative data.

participant observation a method of observation in which the researcher studies the target group or community from within, making careful records of what he or she observes

More formal methods of observation can be used when it is possible to record actions relevant to the research question without disrupting the occurrence of the behaviour. An example is Carey's (1978) series of studies investigating the hypothesis that when one pedestrian approaches another on the street, a rule of 'civil inattention' applies, whereby each looks at the other up to the point where they are approximately 8 feet apart, after which their gaze is averted. Goffman (1963) first advanced this hypothesis on the basis of informal observation. Carey's purpose was to verify, using more formal methods, the existence of this rule, and to establish parameters such as the distance between pedestrians when gaze is first averted. He covertly photographed pairs of pedestrians as they approached and passed each other on a street, taking the photographs from upper storeys of buildings overlooking the street. The resulting photographs were coded for variables such as distance between the pair, whether their heads and eyelids were level or lowered, and whether gaze direction was towards or away from the approaching person.

The two examples cited above have in common the fact that the targets of the researchers' observations were unaware that they were being observed. Although such failure to inform persons of their involuntary participation in a research project raises ethical questions, it does overcome a problem peculiar to any research that uses humans as participants, namely the tendency for the measurement process itself to have an impact on participants' behaviour, a phenomenon known as *reactivity*. It is well established that the knowledge that one is being observed can influence behaviour. A well-known instance of such an effect is a study of worker productivity conducted at the Hawthorne plant of the Western Electric Company (Roethlisberger & Dickson, 1939), where it was found that merely observing workers raised their motivation and thereby increased productivity. Instances of such influence have come to be known as *Hawthorne effects*. Awareness of this problem has led many researchers to develop unobtrusive methods of observing and measuring behaviour. Webb, Campbell, Schwartz and Sechrest (2000) compiled a useful sourcebook of methods of unobtrusive measurement.

reactivity a measurement procedure is reactive if it alters the nature of what is being measured (i.e., if the behaviour observed or the verbal response recorded is partly or wholly determined by the participant's awareness that some aspect of his or her behaviour is being measured)

Hawthorne effect a term used to describe the effect of participants' awareness that they are being observed on their behaviour

The most formal type of observational method is one in which the researcher uses a predetermined category system for scoring social behaviour. A well-known example of such a system is Bales's (1950) *interaction process analysis (IPA)*,

interaction process analysis (IPA) a formal observational measurement system devised by Bales for coding the interactions of members of small social groups. It consists of categories and procedures for coding interaction in terms of these categories

developed to study interaction in small social groups. Here the verbal exchanges between group members are coded in terms of 12 predetermined categories (e.g., 'requests information'; see Chapter 12, this volume). The scores of group members can then be used to determine (among other things) who is the leader of the group (see Bales & Slater, 1955). Further examples of observational coding schemes can be found in Bakeman (2000).

Observational methods of data collection have two main advantages over the self-report methods we shall consider below: first, they can often be made unobtrusively; second, even where the participant knows that his or her behaviour is being observed, enacting the behaviour is typically quite engrossing, with the result that participants have less opportunity to modify their behaviour than they would when completing a questionnaire. Nevertheless, there are some types of behaviour that are either difficult to observe directly (because they are normally enacted in private) or impossible to observe directly (because they took place in the past). Moreover, social psychologists are often interested in measuring *people's perceptions, cognitions* or *evaluations*, none of which can be directly assessed simply through observation. For these reasons, researchers often make use of self-report measures.

Self-report measures

The essential feature of data collection using self-report measures is that questions about the participant's beliefs, attitudes and behaviour are put directly to the participant. The responses are self-report data. Self-report measurement is usually quicker, cheaper and easier to use than observational measurement. The researcher does not have to contrive a laboratory setting or find a natural setting in which to observe a behavioural response; furthermore, there is typically no need to train observers or to use recording equipment, for self-reports are usually recorded by the participant. Finally, as noted above, some of the variables that are of most significance to social psychologists are not directly observable. For these reasons, self-report measurement is very common in social psychological research, and it is not unusual for studies to depend exclusively on self-report data.

There are two principal methods of collecting self-report data: the questionnaire and the interview. In the *questionnaire* method, participants are handed a set of questions, along with instructions on how to record their answers. In the *interview* method, questions are put to the participant by an interviewer, who then records the participant's responses. Interviewing is particularly useful when there is reason to believe that the questions might be difficult to understand without clarification. A tactful and sensitive interviewer should be able to establish rapport and ensure that the respondent fully comprehends a question before answering. Another advantage of interviewing is that interviews can be 'semi-structured', meaning that although the interviewer has a set series of topics to be covered in the interview, he or she is able to vary the specific questions that are asked so that they are relevant to the unfolding discussion. However, interviewing is costly in terms of time and money, and a poorly trained interviewer can easily bias the respondent's answers by hinting at a desired or socially acceptable response. Questionnaires are especially useful for gathering data from large numbers of participants with minimal expense, and the comparative anonymity of the process is preferable when the questions touch on sensitive issues. On the other hand, many people who are given questionnaires fail to complete and/or return them. Response rates for questionnaires sent by mail to randomly selected names and addresses vary between 10 and 50 per cent. Because there is always the danger that non-respondents differ systematically from respondents in some respect, low response rates are undesirable.

Devising a good questionnaire or interview schedule is a harder task than one might imagine. As with any psychological measure, the goal is to produce questions that are reliable and valid. Although there are many potential sources of unreliability in the construction of questionnaires, the most serious threat to reliability is *ambiguity*: if a question is ambiguous, different respondents may interpret it differently and therefore provide answers to what is in effect a different question. The most serious threat to question validity is failure on the part of the investigator to have *specific objectives* for each question: the hazier the intent of the researcher in posing a particular question, the greater are the chances that it will fail to elicit information relevant to his or her objectives. However, there are other sources of unreliability and invalidity that cannot easily be controlled. A simple rule-of-thumb is never to assume that answers to a single question will reliably or validly measure a construct. If two or more items are used to measure that construct, the factors that decrease reliability and validity of responses to any single question should cancel each other out, so a measure based on the average of the responses to the different items will be a more reliable measure of the underlying construct.

Because it is difficult to envisage all the potential pitfalls in questionnaire construction, there is no substitute for pilot work in which drafts of the final questionnaire are administered to participants whose answers and comments provide a basis for revision. Constructing an entirely fresh questionnaire can therefore be a time-consuming and painstaking process. Fortunately, there are collections of previously developed and pre-tested questionnaires, such as the one edited by Robinson, Shaver and Wrightsman (1991). It is worth checking such a source before setting out to construct an original questionnaire. If no suitable questionnaire already exists, the researcher should consult a text on questionnaire design such as the one by Oppenheim (1992) before devising a fresh questionnaire.

Self-report measures have several advantages. What are their drawbacks? Obviously, it is not possible to collect self-report data completely unobtrusively: participants are aware that they are under investigation, and may modify their responses as a result of this awareness. In particular, there is ample opportunity for the respondent's answers to be influenced by motivational factors, such as social desirability. There is no simple solution to this difficulty, although there are steps that can be taken which reduce the scale of the problem. First, it is worth emphasizing to participants whenever possible that their responses are anonymous. Second, it is worth stressing the point that there are no right or wrong answers. Third, it is often possible to increase participants' motivation to respond truthfully by treating them as research accomplices rather than 'guinea-pigs'.

Implicit measures

A recent development in social psychological research methods has been the increasing use of techniques for measuring perceptions, cognitions and evaluations that do not rely on the usual type of self-report measure, thereby avoiding the disadvantages of the latter. These techniques are often referred to as *implicit measures* (Greenwald & Banaji, 1995). The use of such measures has quite a long history in social psychology: Campbell (1950) published a classic paper on the indirect assessment of attitudes more than half a century ago. What is different about the modern use of implicit measures is that they usually take advantage of computer technology. Here computers are used not only for the presentation of experimental materials but also (and more importantly) for the precise measurement of various aspects of the participants' responses to these materials. An example of an implicit measure is the use of response latencies (i.e., how long it takes a participant to answer a particular question). Such measures can provide fresh insights into cognitive structures and processes. For instance, in the study reported by Gaertner and McLaughlin (1983), the automatic operation of stereotypes was assessed by the speed (response latency) with which participants made judgements about pairs of words. The participants' task was to say 'yes' if there was an association between each pair of words. White participants responded significantly faster to white-positive word pairs (e.g., white–smart) than black-positive word pairs (e.g., black–smart), thereby suggesting that they engaged in automatic stereotyping of racial groups. Examples of the use of implicit measures to assess attitudes can be found in Chapter 6.

A major advantage of implicit measures is that they are not reactive. That is, implicit measures are not subject to biases such as social desirability and demand characteristics, because they tap processes that operate outside awareness. However, it is by no means certain that such measures have high validity. How does one know, for example, whether a fast reaction time reflects automatic stereotyping as opposed to individual differences in lexical knowledge? To address questions such as this, one ideally needs to have other measures (e.g., observational) that provide evidence that converges with the evidence provided by implicit measures. In principle such evidence helps to establish the *convergent validity* of both types of measure. Convergent validity is established when different operationalizations of the same construct produce the same results. However, the argument that implicit measures tap processes in a way that is less subject to the influence of self-presentational concerns than

> **implicit measures** measures of constructs such as attitudes and stereotypes that are derived from the way respondents behave (such as how long they take to make a decision or to answer a question) rather than from the content of their answers to explicit questions about these constructs. They are a class of unobtrusive measures

> **convergent validity** established by showing that different measures of the same construct (e.g., self-report, implicit, observation) are significantly associated with each other

Plate 2.5 *Implicit measures usually take advantage of computer technology.*

are other measures (especially self-report) obviously raises some tricky issues with regard to cross-validating one measure by means of another.

Another key advantage of implicit measures is that they can assess constructs and processes that may be outside the awareness of the individual. If people are not aware of having certain thoughts or feelings, they will by definition be unable to report them, even if they are highly motivated to be honest. The study of 'automatic' processes has become a central theme in social cognition research (see Bargh & Chartrand, 2000). Given that one of the attributes of an automatic process is that the individual is unaware of it, studying such a process requires the use of implicit measurement.

Choosing a measure

All three types of measure considered here have certain advantages and disadvantages. Although there are no hard-and-fast rules for choosing one type of measure rather than the other, two points should be borne in mind when judging the appropriateness of a measure. First, the three types of measure – observational, self-report and implicit – can be used in conjunction with each other in many types of research. Second, the three types of measure differ in terms of the type of information they yield. If observational, self-report and implicit measures of the same conceptual variable point to the same conclusion, this clearly enhances confidence in that conclusion. Furthermore, self-report measures often assess the outcome of a process; by using observational and implicit measures as well, the researcher can gain insight into the processes responsible for that outcome. A special quality of implicit measures is that they enable researchers to capture aspects of the individual's thoughts, feelings and behaviour that are outside awareness and therefore not susceptible to feigning.

SUMMARY

We examined the main data collection techniques available to the social psychological researcher. Three such techniques were identified: observational, self-report and implicit measurement. We noted that each technique has its own advantages and disadvantages, and that there is often a case for using more than one type of measure in a piece of research.

SUMMARY AND CONCLUSIONS

- Research methods are the procedures a researcher uses to gather information, and *methodology* is a term used to refer to all aspects of the implementation of methods.

- The information gathered using research methods is used to test the researcher's theoretical predictions. These predictions are derived from a theory. The theory is often generated through observation of real-life events or by trying to make sense of puzzling findings from previous research.

- We drew a distinction between research strategies and data collection techniques. We described three quantitative research strategies: survey research, quasi-experiments and true randomized experiments. Two key ways in which these strategies differ are in terms of (1) the degree to which one is able to generalize to a population and (2) the degree to which one can draw inferences about causality.

- We briefly discussed qualitative research methods, noting that these are often used by researchers who believe that quantitative methods are unsuited to studying the phenomenon under investigation. Discourse analysis was identified as a popular qualitative approach. Discourse analysis emphasizes the importance of how social phenomena are constructed through discourse.

- Experimentation was singled out for more detailed discussion because of its prominence as a research strategy in social psychology during the last six decades. The main features of experimentation were identified as: the experimental scenario; the independent variable; the dependent variable; the manipulation check; and debriefing.

- A true experimental design is one that enables the researcher to infer that changes in the independent variable produce changes in the dependent variable. Such a design must therefore incorporate more than one condition, allowing the researcher to compare observations made under different conditions.

- The minimal true experimental design is the post-test only control group design, in which participants are randomly allocated to one of two conditions, only one of which involves being exposed to the manipulation. Several more complex designs are available, and of these the factorial design is very commonly used, mainly because of its ability to test predictions concerning interaction effects.

- Drawing strong inferences from social psychological research depends on three types of validity: internal, construct and external. We identified confounding as a threat to internal validity; social desirability effects, demand characteristics and experimenter effects as threats to construct validity; and volunteer/non-volunteer differences as a threat to external validity.

- The Internet has provided social (and other) psychologists with a new arena in which to conduct experiments, enabling them to reach larger and more diverse groups of participants. The evidence to date suggests that despite the potential problems of web-based experiments, their results tend to parallel those obtained using conventional methods.

- We noted that some social psychologists have questioned the utility of experiments. The cultural embeddedness of social behaviour, the fact that social behaviour is determined by multiple factors, and the ability of humans to modify their behaviour in the light of social psychological theories were identified as grounds for questioning the assumption that experimentation generates cumulative knowledge of the laws governing social behaviour.

- We identified three principal methods of collecting data in social psychological research: observational measurement, self-report measurement and implicit measures. Observational and implicit measures have the advantage of being less susceptible to social desirability effects, and can be made completely unobtrusive. However, observational measures are obviously limited to phenomena that can be observed and are not suited to the assessment of covert cognitive phenomena such as attitudes, causal attributions and stereotypes (see Chapters 3, 6, 7 and 14, this volume).

- To study these more covert phenomena researchers have traditionally relied on self-report measures, although there has been an increasing tendency to make use of implicit measures, the goal of which is to reveal phenomena that may either be outside the awareness of the individual or are likely to be misreported in conventional self-report measures due to social desirability concerns.

- There are obvious advantages in using these different types of measure in conjunction with each other.

Suggestions for further reading

Aronson, E., Ellsworth, P.C., Carlsmith, J.M. & Gonzales, M.H. (1990). *Methods of research in social psychology* (2nd edn). New York: McGraw-Hill. A comprehensive introduction to research methods in social psychology, with an emphasis on experimentation.

Cook, T.D. & Campbell, D.T. (1979). *Quasi-experimentation: Design and analysis issues for field settings.* Chicago: Rand McNally. An authoritative account of how to minimize threats to validity by careful research design.

Gilbert, D.T., Fiske, S.T. & Lindzey, G. (Eds.) (1998). *Handbook of social psychology* (4th edn, Vol. 1). New York: McGraw-Hill. The most recent edition of this essential handbook, containing contributions on experimentation (Chapter 3), survey methods (Chapter 4), measurement (Chapter 5) and data analysis (Chapter 6).

Greenberg, J. & Folger, R. (1988). *Controversial issues in social research methods.* New York: Springer. This book does a good job of presenting the debates surrounding key issues in research.

Greenwood, J.D. (1989). *Explanation and experiment in social psychological science: Realism and the social constitution of action.* New York: Springer. An interesting, critical treatment of the philosophical background to research methods.

Reis, H.T. & Judd, C.M. (Eds.) (2000). *Handbook of research methods in social and personality psychology.* New York: Cambridge University Press. State-of-the-art coverage of the key methodological issues in social and personality psychology.

3

Social Perception and Attribution

Brian Parkinson

CHAPTER OUTLINE

How can we tell what other people are like? How do we explain their actions and experiences (and our own)? This chapter introduces research intended to answer these questions. Studies of *social perception* show that impressions of others depend on what information is presented, how it is presented, and on prior assumptions about how it fits together. Research into *attribution* demonstrates that perceivers consistently favour certain kinds of explanation over others. Our impressions and explanations are also shaped by our specific reasons for constructing them. In particular, we present social events in different ways to different people under different circumstances. Both social perception and attribution therefore involve communication in combination with private interpretation.

Introduction

Can you remember when you first met your closest friend? How quickly did you get a sense of what he or she was like, and of how well you would get on together? Did your impression turn out to be correct, and if not, where and why did you go wrong?

Now imagine that instead of meeting another person face to face, you are told about them by someone else. When we describe other people, we often refer to their traits (relatively consistent personality characteristics or abilities) or dispositions. Peculiar as it might seem, let's suppose that the only information you are given is the following list of traits:

intelligent – skilful – industrious – warm – determined – practical – cautious

How easily did you form an impression this time? Did you reach your conclusions in the same way as when you first met your friend? Are you as certain that your judgement is correct?

It is unusual to meet someone without knowing anything about them. Even if you haven't been told what to expect, the specific location for your meeting (a bar, concert or supermarket) can be revealing. You can already tell that they must be the sort of person who goes to a place like this, and this *category information* may provide sufficient evidence for your purposes (see Chapter 4, this volume, and Fiske & Neuberg, 1990). However, we sometimes start with very few clues and need to construct impressions from scratch. And we often make up our minds about whom we like and dislike before any conversation begins.

But people we dislike at first can later turn out to be excellent company, and people we think we will like may ultimately prove less congenial. In any extended relationship, we get to see how the other person acts in different situations and use these observations to draw conclusions about their feelings and personality. It is rare indeed that all this subsequent information perfectly matches first impressions.

This chapter is about how we make sense of other people. Because we draw inferences about someone else's personality so readily and usually have little trouble understanding the meaning of their actions, it may seem that our social perceptions are straightforward and direct. However, the fact that we often have to correct initial impressions suggests that things may be more complicated. Most social psychologists believe that we piece together and weigh up available information before arriving at any conclusion, even when we are not explicitly aware of going through the various stages of such a process. And each additional stage brings another opportunity for bias to creep in.

The next section of this chapter will review research into social perception, focusing on how information is combined when forming impressions of others, and on how the nature of the presented information may also make a difference. The rest of the chapter concerns attribution theory – the study of people's causal explanations. We present two general models of how information is processed in order to infer the causes of behaviour. We then consider how attributions can influence our motivations and emotions, and examine evidence for various biases in attribution. Next we consider the role of language and conversation in determining attributions and apparent attributional biases. Finally, we raise the question of how basic data-driven perceptual processes might combine with conversational processes in social perception and attribution.

SOCIAL PERCEPTION

How do we form impressions of people?

The contemporary approach to social perception derives from pioneering research conducted by Asch (1946). What struck Asch was how rapidly we seem to arrive at impressions, despite the diversity of information that has to be combined. How, then, do we construct a unified picture of someone's personality from different pieces of information?

To investigate this process, Asch read out personality adjectives to students and asked them to form an impression of the person (*target*) described by these words (just as you were asked to do at the beginning of this chapter). Participants wrote a brief description of the target and then ticked any relevant traits on a personality checklist (e.g., they had to say whether the target was generous or ungenerous, humorous or humourless, and so on).

One of Asch's first studies compared two lists of adjectives that were identical except for a single word. The first list contained the same words that you read earlier (intelligent, skilful, industrious, warm, determined, practical, cautious). Think about these words again. Which do you think had the greatest influence on your impression?

The second list simply replaced the word 'warm' with the word 'cold'. Asch found that this single change made a big difference. Participants hearing the 'warm' list were far more likely to describe the target as generous, wise, good-natured, etc. (see Figure 3.1). A typical description was: 'A person who believes certain things to be right, wants others to see his point, would be sincere in an argument and would like to see his point won' (Asch, 1946, p. 263). By contrast, a typical description of the 'cold personality' was: 'A rather snobbish person who feels that his success and intelligence set him apart from the run-of-the-mill individual. Calculating and unsympathetic' (p. 263).

In the next experiment, Asch replaced 'polite' with 'blunt' instead of 'warm' with 'cold' and found that this change made much less difference. This suggests that warmth is seen as a *central trait* that reconfigures the meaning of the target's whole personality, whereas politeness is a more *peripheral trait* that has only specific and delimited effects. However, Asch found that trait centrality also depends on what other words are presented, and that no word is central across all possible contexts (see Zanna & Hamilton, 1972).

> **central trait** a dispositional characteristic viewed by social perceivers as integral to the organization of personality

> **peripheral trait** within impression formation, a trait whose perceived presence does not significantly change the overall interpretation of a person's personality

Other experiments showed that the order in which adjectives are presented also made a difference. In particular, earlier information seemed to exert a disproportionate impact on impressions. For example, a target described as intelligent, industrious, impulsive, critical, stubborn and envious was seen as competent and ambitious, but when exactly the same words were presented in reverse order (so that 'envious' came first), the target was thought to be overly emotional and socially maladjusted. This greater influence of initial information is generally known as a *primacy effect*. Evidently, people do not wait until all evidence is in before starting to integrate it.

> **primacy effect** the tendency for information presented earlier to be more influential in social perception and interpretation

Kelley (1950) found similar effects on judgements of someone with whom participants actually had direct contact. A guest lecturer was introduced to students either as 'cold' or 'warm' and students rated him only after he had taught them. Not only was the lecturer rated less positively when he had been described as 'cold' but also students interacted with him less and asked fewer questions. Since the first thing that students learned about this lecturer was that he was either warm or cold, these effects could depend on either primacy or trait centrality. Further, because most introductions focus on a speaker's positive rather than negative qualities, describing a lecturer as 'cold' may have had more impact on ratings and behaviour than under other circumstances.

The results presented so far suggest that people do not simply add together the bits of information they receive about a target,

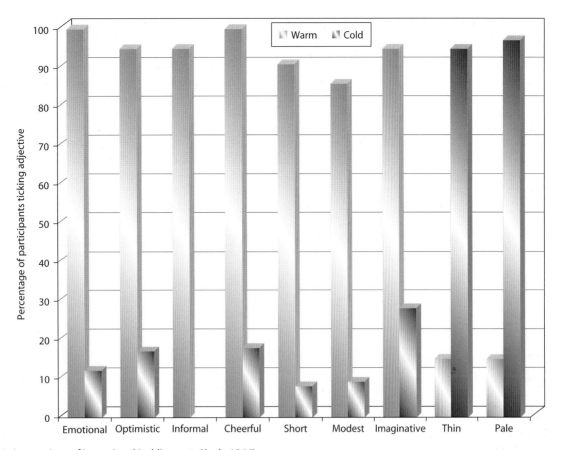

Figure 3.1 *Impressions of 'warm' and 'cold' targets (Asch, 1946).*

but rather actively construct meaning based on their ideas about how different personality characteristics tend to go together. As later theorists concluded, people have their own ***implicit personality theories*** that help to make sense of other people (e.g., Bruner & Tagiuri, 1954). More generally, people seem to integrate social information by trying to infer its holistic pattern (***configural model***).

The alternative ***cognitive algebra*** model suggests that separate pieces of information are simply added together or averaged (e.g., Anderson, 1981). For example, if a person is described as 'warm' but 'boring', the overall impression would be less positive than if she were described as 'warm' but 'interesting', but more positive than if she were described as 'cold' and 'boring'. According to this view, the disproportionate effect of 'central' adjectives depends on them conveying comparatively more evaluative information than the other words that are presented. Further, the impact of a word may depend on its relevance to the judgement being made. For example, we care more about whether someone is 'warm' when selecting a potential friend than a plumber, and

implicit personality theory an integrated set of ideas held by social perceivers about how different traits tend to be organized within a person

configural model a holistic approach to impression formation, implying that social perceivers actively construct deeper meanings out of the bits of information that they receive about other people

cognitive algebra a proposed process for averaging or summing trait information when forming impressions of other people

therefore attach more weight to its connotations. Asch's configural model, by contrast, implies that central adjectives change the meaning of other words rather than simply attracting greater emphasis.

But do social perceivers always make sense of personality information in either of these ways? In Asch's (1946) experiments, participants heard a list of separate personality adjectives and were explicitly told to construct an impression based on these words (as in the task at the start of this chapter). As Asch acknowledged, this is unlike what normally happens when we meet someone face to face (e.g., getting to know your best friend for the first time). How then might this particular way of presenting information have affected the process of impression formation?

Some people get acquainted by email before ever physically meeting (see Chapter 10, this volume). It may take months or even years before they so much as exchange photographs (not necessarily genuine ones: see Ben-Ze'ev, 2004), assuming that they ever do (see Joinson, 2003). What happens when these people finally confront one another in the flesh? Are they surprised by what they see?

Examples such as this suggest that transmitting information in words rather than raw sensory data (sights, sounds and smells) can make a difference to the content of our impressions. Indeed, sensory information can carry direct implications about personality. For example, people with large, round eyes, short noses, high

Plate 3.1 *People with large, round eyes, short noses, high foreheads and/or small chins are typically perceived as less dominant, more naïve and warmer than people with mature-seeming features.*

them and keep it to yourself. Instead, you adjust how you behave to what you think they are like, and they correspondingly adjust their conduct to their impression of you (which is partly based on how you are responding to them, and so on). For example, if you think someone is friendly, you may be more friendly back, leading them in turn to reciprocate your friendly response (and so on). Thus, our impressions of others can lead to *self-fulfilling prophecies* (e.g., Snyder, 1984). However, people are also able to adjust their impressions when expectations are disconfirmed. Indeed, if you know that someone has the wrong idea about you, you may deliberately act in ways that show them that they are mistaken (a *self-verification effect*, Swann, 1984).

> **self-fulfilling prophecy** when an originally false social belief leads to its own fulfilment. Social belief refers to people's expectations regarding another group of people. When a self-fulfilling prophecy occurs, the perceiver's initially false beliefs cause targets to act in ways that objectively confirm those beliefs

SUMMARY

The study of social perception focuses on how we as social perceivers form impressions of other people, and how we combine information about them into a coherent overall picture. Pioneering studies showed how important the nature and order of presented information are, and how perceivers actively construct meaning, rather than simply sum information. But how specific pieces of information are weighted, integrated and used depends on a variety of factors including the situation we find ourselves in, and how much we care about making the right judgement.

ATTRIBUTION THEORY

What are the main theories of causal attribution, and how do they envisage that lay perceivers process causal information?

In one of Pixar™ animation studio's earliest short films, the movements of two anglepoise desk lamps – one large, one small – are accompanied by voice-like sounds. Although items of office furniture do not usually have social relationships, viewers quickly conclude that the larger lamp is the smaller lamp's parent, and that the smaller lamp is a rather boisterous child. The lamps' contractions and extensions soon appear to be actions, and the noises start sounding like communications or expressions of emotion. A little drama of conflicting desires and thwarted impulses seems to unfold on the screen, even though we know that every movement has been computer-generated. How is this impression of human personality and intention achieved? Part of the answer is that our tendency to see motives and dispositions behind human actions may be so automatic that we sometimes find it hard to override it even in situations where motives and dispositions don't really

foreheads and/or small chins (*baby-faced* individuals) are typically perceived as less dominant, more naïve and warmer than people with mature-seeming features (e.g., Berry & McArthur, 1986), and people with louder or higher-pitched voices are often perceived as more extraverted (e.g., Scherer & Scherer, 1981). The way that patterns of sensory information change over time can also carry important information. For example, we are quite accurate at judging which of two people is older by observing the way that they both walk, even when all other evidence is removed. Adults with a younger-seeming gait are also perceived as more energetic (Montepare & Zebrowitz-McArthur, 1988).

Asch's procedure also differs from most everyday interactions because it provides no opportunity for the other person to respond to participants' judgements of them (or for participants to respond to these responses). Interactivity of this kind may make a big difference to the process of impression formation. For example, when you meet someone, you don't simply draw a conclusion about

apply. Attribution theory (e.g., Försterling, 2001; Heider, 1958; Kelley, 1972) provides a set of ideas about how these kinds of inferences about the causes of action are made in the more usual situation of observing or hearing about a human being's actions (rather than those of a desk lamp). It addresses our explanations of our own as well as other people's behaviour.

Most of the phenomena investigated by attribution researchers involve an *observer* explaining an *actor*'s behaviour towards a human or non-human object (or *entity*), but sometimes the actor and observer can be the same person (*self-attribution*). Unlike much of psychology, attribution research is not directly concerned with why actors do what they do, but focuses instead on what observers conclude about why actors do what they do (e.g., whether they *attribute* behaviour to an actor's or object's characteristics or 'attributes'). In the parlance of the theory, to make an *attribution* is to assign causality to some person, object or situation. According to attribution theory, we are all amateur psychologists trying to explain each other's behaviour and our own.

For example, imagine a friend (*actor*) has just spent a substantial proportion of her student loan on an expensive digital camera with all the latest features (*entity*). This might lead you (as *observer*) to think about what provoked such a purchase. Was it an 'impulse buy' reflecting a failure of your friend's self-control? Was she talked into it by a canny sales assistant? Or did her deep-seated interest in photography motivate her spending? Was the camera so special that she just had to have it? Or had other friends persuaded her that she couldn't do without it? Our answers to these questions shape our reactions and our expectations about her future behaviour.

Heider (1958) is usually credited with inventing attribution theory. He argued that people are most concerned with identifying the personal *dispositions* (enduring characteristics such as ability and personality traits) that account for other people's behaviour. In other words, observers want to know what it is about actors that leads them to act the way they do. Drawing dispositional inferences carries two basic advantages. First, it

allows us to integrate a variety of otherwise disorganized information about others, just as knowing that a larger lamp has a maternal attitude to a smaller lamp makes sense of an otherwise baffling piece of animation (see also Heider & Simmel, 1944). Second, it permits prediction (and, to some extent, control) of future behaviour. For example, knowing that you are a friendly person means that I can expect a friendly reaction from you when we meet again.

Correspondent inference theory

How do perceivers decide why one action, rather than others, is performed?

Jones and Davis (1965) tried to make Heider's ideas about dispositional attribution more systematic. Like Heider, they argued that observers learn most from actors' behaviour when it provided information concerning their personal characteristics. For example, you would probably attribute your friend's camera purchase to her specific intention (buying the camera did not just happen to your friend, she decided to do it), and may in turn attribute this intention to an underlying disposition, such as enthusiasm for photography. Jones and Davis called this process of inferring dispositions from behaviour **correspondent inference** because observers infer intentions and dispositions that *correspond* to the behaviour's characteristics.

> **correspondent inference theory** proposes that observers infer correspondent intentions and dispositions for observed intentional behaviour under certain circumstances

Correspondent inference theory proposes that observers consider the range of behaviours available at the time of making a decision in order to work out the actor's intention. Each of these behaviours would have brought a number of different effects if selected. Some of these effects are desirable (your friend's camera has lots of useful features) and some undesirable (the camera cost a great deal of money). According to Jones and Davis, observers work out *why* actions are performed by comparing the effects of the selected action with those of alternative unselected actions (taking into account their perceived desirability). In particular, actors are assumed to have selected their action on the basis of the effects that this action alone produced (effects that would not have happened if another action had been selected).

For example, think back to when you chose to go to the particular university or college where you are currently studying instead of a different one. The theory suggests that we could infer your original intention by comparing the features of these two universities and working out what distinguishes them. For example, the chosen university might be located in a large city and the other one in a quieter, more rural setting. If the rejected university also had several advantages over the one you chose (e.g., a higher reputation, a stronger psychology department, better accommodation), then we might well conclude that living in a city is important enough to you to outweigh all these other considerations. More generally, correspondent inference theory argues that people try to work out what it was about a chosen course of action that made it seem preferable to alternative courses of action. Jones and Davis call this

PIONEER

Fritz Heider (1896–1988), the 'founding father' of attribution theory, was born in Vienna, Austria. He was invited to the USA in 1930 to join the Gestalt psychologist Koffka's laboratory at Smith College, then worked at the University of Kansas from 1947, where his most influential work on attribution was conducted. Heider is famous for two theories in different areas of social psychology: attribution theory and 'balance theory' (a consistency theory about how relationships between more than two people are kept in equilibrium). He was awarded the American Psychological Association's Distinguished Scientific Contribution Award in 1965.

Table 3.1 *Analysis of non-common effects after observed selection of University X*

Features of University X (chosen)	Features of University Y (not chosen)	Are features common or non-common?	Implication about intention
Comfortable accommodation	Comfortable accommodation	Common	None
Sports facilities	Sports facilities	Common	None
Good reputation	Good reputation	Common	None
Friends applying	Friends applying	Common	None
Urban location	Rural location	Non-common	University X chosen because candidate wanted to live in an urban location

analysis of non-common effects
observers infer intentions behind actions by comparing the consequences of the behavioural options that were open to the actor and identifying distinctive outcomes

process the **analysis of non-common effects** (see Table 3.1).

In reality, our analysis may be more complex than implied by this example. For instance, we might focus on why you chose to go to university at all rather than why you selected this particular one. How then do observers know what alternatives to compare when trying to explain a course of action? Research suggests that people are more interested in explaining unusual than predictable events, and that they explain them by comparing what actually happened with what they think would *normally* have happened (Hilton & Slugoski, 1986, and p. 51 below). For example, if a close friend walks past us in the street without saying hello, we think about what is different this time from the usual times when she stops to chat. Perhaps she forgot to put on her glasses this morning, or perhaps you have had such a radical change of hairstyle that you are now almost unrecognizable.

Although correspondent inference theory was only intended to apply when actors are free to *choose* their behaviour, an experiment conducted by Jones and Harris (1967) casts doubt on this assumption. Students at an American university were asked to assess another student's opinion about Fidel Castro's communist regime in Cuba after reading a pro-Castro essay that the other student had supposedly written (see Figure 3.2). One group of participants was told that the writer had *freely chosen* what position to adopt in the essay, whereas another group was told that the essay title had *explicitly requested* pro-Castro arguments. According to correspondent inference theory, participants in the latter condition should have ignored the essay's content when estimating the writer's attitudes. However, participants tended to conclude that the essay-writer had pro-Castro attitudes even when the situational constraint was evident. Given that most American students were strongly anti-Castro when the study was conducted, this conclusion seemed an unlikely one. The investigators concluded that people tend to overestimate personal causes of behaviour but underestimate situational ones, an important phenomenon later termed the **correspondence bias** (see p. 55 below).

correspondence bias the proposed tendency to infer a personal disposition corresponding to observed behaviour even when the behaviour was determined by the situation

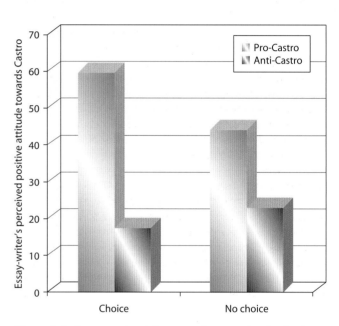

Figure 3.2 *Correspondent inferences of essay-writers' attitudes (Jones & Harris, 1967).*

Covariation theory

How do perceivers weigh up different possible causes of behaviour and decide on an explanation?

Imagine that you know a very conscientious student (Hermione) who always goes through everything on reading lists well in advance of classes. Before you had a chance to look at this chapter, she already told you what it was about and expressed the opinion that attribution theory was a really boring topic. Clearly, you want to know why she said this. Is it because attribution theory actually is tedious? Is it because Hermione is rarely excited by anything? Or is it because her showy lack of enthusiasm was designed to impress your jaundiced room-mate (Ron) who happened to be listening in on this particular conversation? Jones and Davis's model would say that you need to compare the consequences of saying that the material was boring with the consequences of saying or doing something else. However, even if we knew about all the relevant alternatives, this would only allow us to narrow down Hermione's possible intentions, not to say which aspects of the event exerted causal influence. Further, even though analysis of non-common effects might have some use in this particular example, it cannot easily be applied to attributions about non-deliberate behaviours or feelings.

Kelley's (1967) *covariation theory* provides a more general account of how people weigh up different possible causes of an observed action or experience. Its assumption is that an actor (e.g., Hermione) has responded in some way to an object (e.g., attribution theory) in a particular situation (e.g., while Ron was listening). The observer then wants to know whether what happened was caused by something about the actor, something about the object, or something about the situation (or some combination of these three factors). According to Kelley, observers work this out by systematically collecting and processing additional data. The aim is to discover what factors need to be in place for the effect to happen.

> **covariation theory** proposes that observers work out the causes of behaviour by collecting data about comparison cases. Causality is attributed to the person, entity or situation depending on which of these factors covaries with the observed effect

As its name suggests, Kelley's covariation theory argues that observers make their judgements on the basis of covariations or correlations between effects and their possible causes. In other words, 'the effect is attributed to that condition which is present when the effect is present and which is absent when the effect is absent' (Kelley, 1967, p. 194). Inferences of causality thus depend on finding out that the effect's occurrence relates to the presence of one or more of the possible causal factors, but not to the presence of other factors.

Why then did Hermione say that attribution theory was boring? Kelley argues that you need to consider three kinds of evidence, each corresponding to one of the possible causes (the object, situation or person). First, you need to know whether Hermione expresses boredom only about attribution theory (high distinctiveness) or whether she says that a lot of things are boring (low distinctiveness). In other words, you collect *distinctiveness information* by sampling across objects. Second, you need to know whether your friend only says attribution theory is boring in front of Ron (low consistency) or makes similar comments across a range of situations regardless of who might be listening (high consistency). In other words, you collect *consistency information* by sampling across situations. Third, you need to know whether it is only Hermione who finds attribution theory boring (low consensus) or if other students on your course say the same thing (high consensus). In other words, you collect *consensus information* by sampling across actors.

> **distinctiveness information** evidence relating to how an actor responds to different entities under similar circumstances
>
> **consistency information** evidence relating to how an actor's behaviour towards an entity varies across different situations
>
> **consensus information** evidence relating to how different actors behave towards the same entity

Having collected all the relevant data, you are now in a position to make your attribution. For example, if Hermione says lots of things are boring (low distinctiveness), says that attribution theory is boring regardless of circumstances (high consistency) and none of your other friends says it is boring (low consensus), you may conclude that it is something about Hermione that makes her bored (a 'person attribution'). You infer this from the close correlation between the presence of Hermione and statements that something is boring (whenever she is included in a sampled episode, something is described as boring, but whenever she is absent, nothing is described as boring). The causal implications of some other possible combinations of consensus, consistency and distinctiveness (CCD) information are presented in Table 3.2.

One limitation of the covariation model is that the pattern of information supposed to indicate various attributions is incomplete (see Försterling, 2001; Hilton, 1988). For example, knowing that Hermione only says attribution theory is boring in front of Ron does not definitively establish the causal role of this situation because you have not collected data about how different people react to Ron's presence. In fact, there is good evidence that people can *infer* many of the predicted implications of other patterns of CCD information when evidence is provided in this particular form (e.g., McArthur, 1972; see Hewstone, 1989, and Kassin, 1979, for reviews).

Although Kelley's theory provides a logical basis for attribution, it is difficult to imagine that people collect evidence so systematically and engage in such detached processes of analysis every time they make sense of an event's causes. *That* certainly *would* get boring. Many subsequent developments in attribution theory have therefore involved correcting this limitation of the covariation approach.

PIONEER

Along with Bernard Weiner, **Harold Kelley** (1921–2003) was one of two pioneering attribution theorists working at the University of California at Los Angeles. His covariation theory of attribution stands as the most influential general approach to lay causation, although from the start he acknowledged that it did not apply across all possible situations. His second, causal schema theory was specifically intended to explain how people arrive at causal explanations when they are unable to carry out the systematic collection of data implied by covariation theory. In addition to these two influential theories, Kelley also worked on person perception, attitude change and relationships.

Table 3.2 *Four patterns of consensus, consistency and distinctiveness information, and their perceived implications (after Kelley, 1967)*

Consensus (across persons)	Consistency (across situations)	Distinctiveness (across objects)	Attribution
Low (No one else says that attribution theory is boring)	**High** (Hermione says attribution theory is boring in many different contexts)	**Low** (Hermione says that lots of things are boring)	**Person attribution** Effect covaries with person: something about Hermione causes her to say that attribution theory is boring
Low (No one else says that attribution theory is boring)	**Low** (Hermione only says attribution theory is boring in front of Ron)	**High** (Hermione doesn't say that other things are boring)	**Context attribution** Effect covaries with situation: something about the presence of Ron causes Hermione to say that attribution theory is boring
High (Everyone else says attribution theory is boring)	**High** (Hermione says attribution theory is boring in many different contexts)	**High** (Hermione doesn't say that other things are boring)	**Entity attribution** Effect covaries with object: something about attribution theory makes Hermione say that it is boring
Low (No one else says that attribution theory is boring)	**High** (Hermione says attribution theory is boring in many different contexts)	**High** (Hermione doesn't say that other things are boring)	**Person–entity interaction** Effect covaries with Hermione together with attribution theory: something about their combination causes her to say attribution theory is boring

Access to covariation information

How do we make causal attributions when information is incomplete?

One obvious problem for the covariation approach was soon recognized by Kelley (1972) himself: often we want to make causal inferences about events under circumstances when CCD information is either unavailable or too time-consuming to collect. On these occasions, Kelley argued that we fill in missing information by reference to our existing ideas about how effects are produced (*causal schemas*).

causal schema a knowledge structure shaping attributions. Causal schemas may be either abstract representations of general causal principles (e.g., multiple necessary and multiple sufficient causes schemas) or domain-specific ideas about how particular causes determine particular effects

For example, when Hermione says that attribution theory is boring in front of someone else she knows will be impressed by such talk, this already tells you about an important factor potentially causing this behaviour (i.e., a desire to impress this person). Her statement need not reflect a strong personal dislike for attribution theory since this situational factor already partly explains what she said. More generally, Kelley argued that observers discount possible causes when they know of other factors working towards an observed effect (the *discounting principle*) as long as this effect can be produced by a range of alternative factors (*multiple sufficient causes schema*). In other cases, more than one condition must be present for the effect to occur (*multiple*

discounting principle the presence of a causal factor working towards an observed effect implies that other potential factors are less influential. The converse of the augmenting principle

necessary causes schema). Knowledge of factors working *against* an effect leads people to conclude that plausible causes must be stronger than otherwise (the *augmentation principle*). For example, if Hermione wanted to impress someone who was enthusiastic about attribution theory, but *still* told them it was boring, then you would probably conclude that she had a sufficiently strong negative opinion to override her desire to please.

augmentation principle the assumption that causal factors need to be stronger if an inhibitory influence on an observed effect is present. The converse of the discounting principle

Knowledge, expectation and covariation

How do we use our general knowledge to guide our attributions?

Kelley's causal schema theory implies that people take shortcuts to inferential conclusions when information or resources are limited (as in other contemporary dual-process models of social cognition: see Chapter 4). However, Kelley still believed that observers engaged in more systematic analysis of covariation whenever possible. In fact, there is little evidence that people spontaneously collect CCD information even when it is readily available. Lalljee, Lamb, Furnham, and Jaspars (1984) presented participants with descriptions of events that required explanation (e.g., 'John did well on his history essay'). Participants were asked to write down the questions that they wanted to ask in order to explain these events. Fewer than 20 per cent of their questions were specifically related to CCD. Instead, most were designed to evaluate participants' specific hypotheses about why the events had occurred (e.g., 'Did John try especially hard on this occasion?').

On reflection, this is not particularly surprising. A problem with CCD information is that it only tells us whether the actor, object or situation (or some combination of these) caused the event, but not what it is about the actor, object or situation that caused it. As Lalljee and Abelson (1983) point out, knowing that John lied to Mary because of something about Mary begs the question of what this something might be that makes people want to lie to her. To work this out, we would need to refer to our prior knowledge about why people might deceive one another. But then why not just start by consulting this useful knowledge instead of first conducting a time-consuming covariation analysis? If we need to rely on ready-made explanations anyway, and these can tell us what we really want to know, then there is little point in going through the preliminary step of collecting and sifting through all possible combinations of CCD information.

It is now generally accepted that people don't usually engage in a thorough data-driven process every time they make an attribution. Because we already have expectations that events will unfold in a certain way, these can be used as a reference point for our attributions. Indeed, Hilton and Slugoski (1986) argue that people rarely need to ask themselves the causal question implied by covariation theory: 'why did this happen instead of not happening?' (a question that would lead them to weigh up all possible factors that might have led to the event). Instead, they usually want to know 'why did this happen *instead of what usually happens* (under these circumstances)?' Thus, people look for causes among the differences between actual and anticipated event sequences (*abnormal condition focus*) rather than exhaustively sifting through all available evidence. Observers know where to look for relevant causes not only because they understand general principles of causality (as implied by Kelley's causal schema model), but also because they have access to cognitive scripts telling them how particular kinds of event (e.g., conversations, parties, restaurant visits) ordinarily unfold in the social world (e.g., Cheng & Novick, 1990; Read, 1987).

Covariation and causal power

How do we use more specific causal knowledge to guide our causal explanations?

A final limitation of covariation theory is captured by a slogan familiar from statistics classes: 'correlation is not causation'. Establishing that factor X covaries with effect Y can never prove that X caused Y, because a correlated third variable may have exerted the real influence (or indeed Y might have caused X). For example, a covariation between revision and fine weather does not mean that studying hard can make the sun shine.

Again, prior knowledge can help us untangle causal relations of this kind. Because we are already aware of what kinds of factor are possible causes of particular effects, we can reject certain factors as irrelevant and focus down our causal search. We know, for instance, that energy is required to induce movement, pressure to produce deformation of objects, that people sometimes say

things in order to impress others, and that people's actions don't immediately change the weather. However, because much of this specific knowledge needs to be learned from observation, knowledge-based theories of attribution still need to explain how people acquire their knowledge about what typically causes what in the first place.

According to Cheng (1997), covariation information alone cannot answer this question because it is insufficient to imply causation. Perceivers typically supplement covariation analysis with their own innate implicit theory that certain events carry unobservable **causal powers** (see also White, 1989). For example, the fact that a magnet consistently attracts or is attracted to metal objects

> **causal power** an intrinsic property of an object or event that enables it to exert influence on some other object or event

leads us to conclude it has an invisible quality ('magnetism') that brings about these effects. Because our predisposition is to uncover causal powers rather than to record observable regularities for their own sake, our sampling of covariation data can be more principled and focused. In particular, covariations between competing potential causes and the observed effect are *compared* (*probabilistic contrast*) in order to determine the nature of the underlying causal process. For example, a child might find out that audible distress brings about parental attention by repeatedly crying in similar situations (so that all other plausible causes remain constant) and registering any consistent effects on Mum or Dad. The child might also compare this strategy with throwing toys around. Thus, even small infants may conduct informal experiments based on an innate theory that effects are caused by events with intrinsic causal powers. Cheng argues that the more specific causal knowledge guiding our subsequent attributions is originally acquired by making probabilistic contrasts of this kind.

Attributions for success and failure

What are the implications of attributing success and failure in different ways?

Some of the events that we are most motivated to explain are successes and failures. For example, if you get a better than usual grade in an exam, you may wonder whether this was due to your particular affinity for the topics covered, your thorough exam revision or the fact that exactly the right questions happened to come up. Your conclusion will help you work out how likely it is that you will be able to maintain this level of performance and how you might go about achieving this.

The most influential theory of achievement-related attribution was developed by Weiner (1979, 1985), who argued that our conclusions about the causes of success and failure directly affect future expectations, motivations and emotions. One of Weiner's main contributions was his classification of the perceived causes of success and failure (see Table 3.3). According to this classification, perceived causal factors may be: (1) internal or external (*locus*); (2) stable or variable (*stability*); and (3) controllable or uncontrollable (*controllability*).

Attributing your exam success to an internal factor means that you believe that something relating to you as a person determined

Plate 3.2 *Do our conclusions about the causes of success and failure, e.g. in an exam, directly affect future expectations, motivations and emotions?*

PIONEER

Bernard Weiner (b. 1935) is currently Professor of Psychology at the University of California, Los Angeles, where he has worked since 1965. He received his undergraduate degree from the University of Chicago and his doctorate from the University of Michigan in 1963. In 1965, following two years at the University of Minnesota, he went to UCLA. He is most famous for his influential research into attributions for success and failure, identifying the main types of attribution, their underlying dimensions and their effects on motivation and emotion. His classification of perceived causes of behaviour has had an even greater impact.

the outcome, whereas attributing performance to an external factor means that something to do with the situation was responsible. Both internal and external factors can be either variable or stable. For example, attributing your performance to intelligence means that you think something internal and relatively unchanging about you led you to do well.

Weiner also argued that causal factors are perceived as either controllable or uncontrollable, and that this distinction too makes a difference to your reaction to achievement outcomes. For example, if you believe that your exam success was due to an internal, stable and uncontrollable factor (your innate aptitude for this kind of material), then you may feel that there is no need to try hard in order to repeat your success. On the other hand, if you think that your good grade was due to an internal, variable and controllable factor (e.g., effort), you will probably conclude that you need to stay motivated in order to succeed in future. Thus, attributions about success and failure are not simply intellectual conclusions about performance, they also make a real difference to our expectations and motivation.

Attributional reformulation of learned helplessness theory

Are certain patterns of attribution symptoms, or causes, of depression?

Weiner's conclusions about the motivational consequences of attributions for success and failure have broader implications for understanding clinical disorders. One influential application has been the attributional reformulation of **learned helplessness theory** of depression. Learned helplessness theory (Seligman, 1975) originally argued that depression results from learning that nothing you do makes any difference to outcomes. The idea was that if rewards and punishments have no relation to your actions, you soon learn to give up trying to attain the former and avoid the latter. However, there are many uncontrollable situations in everyday life that don't make people depressed. For example, many people enjoy betting on games of chance, where the outcomes are

> **learned helplessness theory** the proposal that depression results from learning that outcomes are not contingent on one's behaviour

Table 3.3 *Possible causes of success and failure (after Weiner, 1979, 1985)*

	Internal		**External**	
	Stable	*Unstable*	*Stable*	*Unstable*
Controllable	Mastery (e.g., knowledge, skill)	Effort	Enduring situational and social resources (e.g., contacts, wealth)	Temporarily available situational and social resources (e.g., advice, assistance)
Uncontrollable	Aptitude (e.g., intelligence, coordination)	Energy	Task ease or difficulty	Luck/chance

Figure 3.3 *Five steps to depression: the attributional reformulation of learned helplessness theory (Abramson et al., 1978).*

completely beyond their influence. Gambling does not always make people depressed even if money is lost.

This observation suggests that helplessness alone does not automatically lead to depression; other factors must also be present. One clue to what these other factors might be comes from another key clinical feature of depression that learned helplessness theory cannot explain, namely an exaggerated sense of personal responsibility for negative outcomes. If uncontrollable events cause depression, why should depressed people think that they have caused these events to happen? Abramson, Seligman and Teasdale's (1978) answer is that helplessness only makes people feel chronically depressed if it is attributed to intrinsic features of the self. In other words, a specific pattern of attribution for uncontrollability may determine clinical depression (see Figure 3.3).

In defining this pattern, Abramson and colleagues extended Weiner's classification to include another distinction between specific and global causes. Global causes apply to a wide variety of situations, whereas specific factors relate only to the particular situation at hand. The quality and persistence of depression depends on whether the cause of uncontrollability is perceived as internal or external, stable or variable, and global or specific.

To illustrate this classification, Abramson and colleagues used the example of a woman who has been rejected by a man in whom she is romantically interested. Nothing she does makes any difference to the way he feels about her. According to the model, the way this woman reacts to this experience of helplessness depends on what she thinks the causes of rejection might be (see Table 3.4).

The least-threatening interpretation would be that her rejection was caused by something external, unstable and specific. This man in particular was not attracted to her at this moment and in this particular situation (e.g., he may simply not have been in the mood for romance at the time). The consequences of this conclusion are not too serious for the woman, because she is still able to anticipate greater success with this man or other men in future.

Consider, however, the contrasting attribution to internal, stable and global causes: the man finds her unattractive not out of any passing whim but because of the kind of person she is. His dislike is permanent and applies across all situations. Because being disliked is seen as reflecting something about her, other men will probably dislike her too and her future chances of romantic happiness are slim indeed. Further, because the factors are global they apply not only to romantic attraction but to other areas of her life as well. She can only look forward to consistent and universal bad outcomes which she can do nothing about. These negative expectations unsurprisingly lead to depression.

The theory thus argues that people who have developed a tendency to attribute uncontrollable events to internal, stable and global attributions have a greater risk of subsequently developing chronic depression. However, there is little evidence that attributions made prior to the onset of depression are distorted in this way (Lewinsohn, Steinmetz, Larson & Franklin, 1981), so it seems equally plausible that self-focused explanations are symptoms rather than causes of depression (but see Rude, Valdez, Odom & Ebrahimi, 2003).

Although depressed and non-depressed people evidently interpret negative events in different ways, who is more accurate? Some theorists have argued that it is not depressed people who are unduly pessimistic and unable to see the glass as half-full rather than half-empty, but rather non-depressed people who protect themselves from unpleasant realities by seeing everything in an unrealistically positive light (the 'illusory glow', Taylor & Brown, 1988). According to this view, termed ***depressive realism***, depressed people are 'sadder but wiser'. In support of this idea, Lewinsohn and colleagues (1980) found that depressed participants' ratings of their social functioning during a

> **depressive realism** the idea that depressed people's interpretations of reality are more accurate than those of non-depressed people

Table 3.4 *Possible causes of romantic rejection (from Abramson et al., 1978)*

	Internal		External	
	Stable	**Unstable**	**Stable**	**Unstable**
Global	I'm unattractive to men	My conversation sometimes bores men	Men are overly competitive with intelligent women	Men get into rejecting moods
Specific	I'm unattractive to him	My conversation sometimes bores him	He's overly competitive with intelligent women	He was in a rejecting mood

group discussion were closer to those of observers than were non-depressed participants' ratings. Although observers rated the performance of non-depressed participants more positively than that of depressed participants, they did not rate it as positively as the non-depressed participants themselves did.

However, Campbell and Fehr (1990) found that participants with low self-esteem (a typical feature of depression) were more accurate only when their judgements were compared against those of an observer who did not participate in the interaction. Indeed, evidence suggests that outside observers may be unduly harsh judges because they think that their task is to be critical. When participants' own ratings were compared with those of the person they were having the conversation with, participants with *high* rather than low self-esteem came out as more accurate. It seems then that depressives' judgements are probably only more accurate when circumstances match their negative outlook. However, it is also worth bearing in mind that depressives' negative judgements can easily turn into self-fulfilling prophecies. If someone doesn't even try because they are sure they will fail regardless of effort, this makes it more likely that they will in fact fail.

Whether the attributional pattern associated with depression is a symptom or cause of depression, and whether it is realistic or unrealistic, reformulated learned helplessness theory suggests that therapy should focus on changing it in order to alleviate the symptoms of depression. In practice, current cognitive and psychodynamic therapies for depression attempt to modify a wide range of negative interpretations, but correcting maladaptive attributions for failure may explain part of their apparent effectiveness (e.g., Barber et al., 2005).

Misattribution of arousal

How do we ascertain what we are feeling and why?

The attributional reformulation of learned helplessness theory suggests that we feel more depressed about unpleasant events if we conclude that their causes are internal, stable and global. But how do we recognize our reaction to this attributional pattern as depression rather than something else? This may sound a silly question because it usually seems that the nature of our current emotional state is self-evident. By contrast, misattribution theories imply that we sometimes need to work out what it is we are feeling and that this inference process is susceptible to social influence.

One of the earliest psychological theories of emotion was devised by William James (1884). He argued that each emotion has its own distinctive profile of bodily changes and that we can directly sense our emotion by registering these changes. However, Cannon (1927) pointed out that the patterns of internal physiological activity associated with very different emotions are actually rather similar. For example, both fear and anger involve increases in heart rate, blood pressure and other kinds of metabolic activity (physiological arousal in the autonomic nervous system, ANS) designed to release energy to the muscles in preparation for vigorous activity. This means that we cannot tell these emotions apart simply by checking what is happening inside our bodies.

PIONEER

Stanley Schachter (1922–1997) is best known for his two-factor theory which inspired the cognitive approach to emotion, and for his clever experiment with Jerome Singer which remains a classic despite the apparent inconclusiveness of its results. His earlier work on affiliation also provided a forerunner of contemporary interpersonal approaches to emotion, showing that people seek out other people in order to make sense of their own feelings. Throughout his career, Schachter pursued the important idea that external cues (including social cues) can shape the interpretation of supposedly internal states such as emotions and feelings of pain and hunger. Such an approach provides a valuable counterargument to the more usual assumption that emotion, sensation and motivation are primarily biological and individual processes.

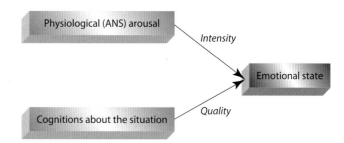

Figure 3.4 *Schachter's two-factor theory of emotion.*

Schachter (1964) therefore argued that emotions depend upon the attributions we make for our internal feelings, rather than directly reflecting these feelings themselves. Thus, perceptions of arousal (the physiological factor) tell us *that* we may be experiencing an emotion, but not *what* emotion it is. We therefore try to work out why our bodies are aroused (the cognitive factor) in order to answer this second question (see Figure 3.4). If we conclude that our arousal is caused by the attractive person we are having coffee with, we may interpret it as a symptom of love (or at least lust: see Chapter 10, this volume). However, if we think our arousal is due to the fact that someone else keeps butting into our private conversation, we may conclude that it reflects anger. Finally, if we attribute our symptoms to the caffeine in the strong cup of coffee we are drinking, we may conclude that our arousal is non-emotional.

In a famous experiment, Schachter and Singer (1962) tried to determine whether an identical physiological state could be perceived as anger, euphoria or non-emotionally depending on participants' interpretations of its causes. Autonomic arousal was manipulated by administering an adrenaline injection to one group of participants and a placebo injection to others under the guise that the syringe contained a new vitamin compound (*Suproxin*) that the experimenters were testing.

Adrenaline-injected participants in one group were told that Suproxin might lead them to experience side effects such as a pounding heart and shaking hands (genuine arousal symptoms). These participants were therefore able to interpret their bodily symptoms correctly as non-emotional responses to the injection. However, participants in another group were given incorrect information about the adrenaline injection's effects (i.e., that there would be no side effects or arousal-irrelevant side effects). Participants in this condition should therefore experience arousal symptoms without knowing their cause, and consequently seek an emotional explanation.

Schachter and Singer stage-managed the situation to encourage specific attributions for any unexplained arousal. Each participant was left in a waiting room with an accomplice of the experimenter posing as another participant who behaved in one of two ways. In one condition, the accomplice improvised a basketball game using scrap paper and a wastebasket, and encouraged the other participant to join in. In the other condition, the accomplice became progressively more irate while working through an increasingly insulting questionnaire that the participant also had to complete. Its final item read: 'With how many men (other than your father) has your mother had extra-marital relationships?' The only response alternatives provided were: '10 and over', '5–9' and '4 and under'.

According to Schachter's theory, emotion should only occur when autonomic arousal is attributed to an emotional cause. In other words, emotion should not have been experienced by either placebo-injected participants (because they were not aroused) or participants who had been correctly informed about the adrenaline injection's effects (because they did not attribute their arousal to the emotional situation). However, adrenaline-injected participants who were unaware that their symptoms were caused by this injection should have explained their arousal in terms of the plausibly euphoric situation when with the playful confederate, but in terms of the plausibly irritating situation when completing the insulting questionnaire. These two groups, therefore, should have experienced widely divergent emotional reactions of euphoria and anger, respectively.

In fact, results were less clear-cut (see Reisenzein, 1983). For example, placebo-injected participants did not report significantly less emotion than participants who were injected with adrenaline but not informed about the injection's genuine side effects. Further, emotion reports of misinformed adrenaline-injected participants did not differ substantially between euphoria and anger conditions (participants reported themselves to be mildly happy in both conditions; see Zimbardo, Ebbesen & Maslach, 1977).

One significant result obtained by Schachter and Singer clearly did accord with predictions, however. Participants injected with adrenaline and correctly warned of the effects consistently reported less positive emotion in the euphoria condition, and less negative emotion in the anger condition than participants misled about side effects. Schachter's explanation was that the informed group correctly *attributed* their arousal to the injection and labelled it in non-emotional terms.

Subsequent experiments have suggested that genuinely emotional arousal may also be misattributed to non-emotional sources,

allowing clinicians to minimize otherwise maladaptive reactions (e.g., Ross, Rodin & Zimbardo, 1969). For example, Storms and Nisbett (1970) reported that students with mild insomnia fell asleep more quickly after being told that they had taken an arousal-inducing pill (*reverse placebo effect*). The investigators argued that misattribution of arousal symptoms to the pill neutralized the mild-insomniac participants' usual interpretation in terms of anxiety. However, Calvert-Boyanowsky and Leventhal (1975) demonstrated that such effects may be explained by the correct anticipations set up by symptom warnings rather than misattribution per se. For example, knowing what is about to happen to your body means that symptoms are less surprising and less emotionally upsetting when they arrive. However, it is less clear whether this explanation can explain the reduced happiness of participants in Schachter and Singer's informed euphoria condition.

In sum, Schachter and Singer's clever experiment does not offer conclusive support for all aspects of two-factor theory. This may be partly because it is difficult to manipulate arousal and emotional cognitions independently when the two usually go hand in hand. Subsequent studies have been similarly inconclusive (e.g., Erdmann & Janke, 1978; Marshall & Zimbardo, 1979; Maslach, 1979), and many theorists now believe that Schachter overstated how easy it was to influence emotional interpretations. Because our attributions about, and appraisals of, emotional situations usually determine our autonomic as well as emotional reactions in the first place (e.g., Lazarus, 1991), we often know in advance what we are going to feel.

Attributional bias

What are the main types of attributional bias, and how can they be explained?

Covariation theory and the correspondent inference model both tended to view attribution as a data-driven process wherein all potentially relevant information is systematically processed. However, as we have seen, subsequent research suggests that causal inferences are shaped by prior knowledge and expectations (e.g., Hilton & Slugoski, 1986; Read, 1987), or by learned attributional styles (e.g., Abramson et al., 1978), and that they may be extraneously influenced by contextual variables (e.g., Schachter & Singer, 1962). Thus, people seem to attach more weight to some causes at the expense of others when drawing causal conclusions. Precisely what kinds of causes are typically favoured under different circumstances has been the focus of research into various **attributional biases**.

> **attributional bias** systematic distortions in the sampling or processing of information about the causes of behaviour

The correspondence bias In their professional lives, psychologists of different persuasions sometimes disagree about whether internal or external explanations of human behaviour deserve more emphasis. For example, most experimental social psychologists focus on situational influences and often ignore people's characteristic dispositions. By contrast, personality psychologists attach more weight to personal traits, usually without giving much

RESEARCH CLOSE-UP 3.1

The correspondence bias in attributing knowledge to the quiz master or the contestant

Ross, L.D., Amabile, T.M. & Steinmetz, J.L. (1977). Social roles, social control, and biases in social-perception processes. *Journal of Personality and Social Psychology, 35*, 483–494.

....

Introduction

People's social roles shape the way that they interact with one another. These influences are most obvious in situations when one person has relatively greater control over an interaction. An oral examination, for example, permits examiners to decide what topics should be discussed while the examinee has relatively less influence. One consequence is that examiners have greater opportunity to display their specialized knowledge. In accordance with the correspondence bias, Ross and colleagues argue that people take insufficient account of these role-conferred advantages when arriving at attributions for behaviour. As a consequence, people with relatively greater social control appear wiser and more able than they really are (and their social position therefore seems more justified). To test this hypothesis, the investigators simulated a quiz game in which participants were allocated the role of either questioner or contestant. Questioners were given the opportunity to devise their own questions, thereby permitting an unrepresentative demonstration of their idiosyncratic expertise. The prediction was that questioners would be viewed as higher in general knowledge.

Method

Participants

Eighteen pairs of male students and 18 pairs of female students from an introductory psychology class were recruited for a study into processes whereby 'people form impressions about general knowledge'. Twelve pairs of participants of each gender were assigned to the experimental condition and six pairs of each gender were assigned to the control condition. For the observer condition, another 24 pairs of participants subsequently watched individual simulations of the quizzes originally conducted by female pairs.

Design and procedure

In the experimental condition, the role of questioner or contestant was allocated to one person in each pair using an explicitly random procedure. Questioners were told to devise 10 'challenging but not impossible' general knowledge questions, which they then asked contestants in a quiz. For example, one question was: 'What is the longest glacier in the world?' In the control condition, contestants were asked questions devised by earlier participants from the experimental condition. In the observer condition, the quizzes conducted by female

participants from the experimental condition were individually simulated by confederates posing as participants. Each simulated quiz was watched by a pair of observer participants who did not know that it was a simulation. As soon as the quiz was over, questioners, contestants and observers all separately rated the general knowledge of the questioner and contestant compared to the average student at the same university, using a 100-point scale.

Results

On average, contestants got only 4 out of 10 questions right in the quiz. General knowledge ratings of questioners and contestants were analysed. Contestants in the experimental condition rated their own general knowledge as significantly worse than that of questioners, and observer participants also rated contestants' general knowledge as significantly inferior. However, questioners did not rate their own general knowledge as higher than that of contestants (see Figure 3.5 for the mean ratings for these conditions). Further, control participants showed significantly smaller differences between their ratings of questioners and participants than did experimental participants. Although no integrated analysis of the results was presented by the investigators, the pattern of findings clearly accords with predictions.

Discussion

The findings demonstrate that the situational advantage conferred by being allowed to devise your own questions led to higher general knowledge ratings from both contestants and observers (who probably attempted to answer the questions

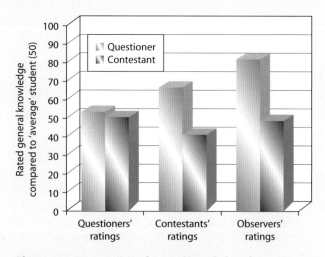

Figure 3.5 *Mean ratings of general knowledge after quiz game (adapted from Ross et al., 1977).*

privately to themselves too). This seems to provide a clear example of the correspondence bias. Because participants' roles were allocated randomly in this study, it is statistically unlikely that one group (the questioners) should happen to be genuinely higher in general knowledge. Indeed, Ross and colleagues administered brief tests of general knowledge to all participants after the quiz and found no differences in performance.

The study also carries implications about the limits of the correspondence bias. Questioners in the experimental condition did not conclude that contestants' inability to answer

their questions meant that they must be inferior in general knowledge, presumably because their own role-conferred advantage was extremely salient to them. Thus questioners apparently recognized their own relatively advantaged position, and were able to correct any attributional bias.

Subsequent studies have shown that observers are aware of limitations to the apparent superiority of the questioners (Johnson, Jemmott & Pettigrew, 1984; Sumpton & Gregson, 1981), and that bias in this setting depends partly on what questions are asked (e.g., Schwarz, 1994).

attention to the impact of the environment (see Chapter 1, this volume). The correspondence bias suggests that the naïve psychology practised by laypeople is closer to personality psychology than to experimental social psychology. Behaviour is often seen as a reflection of an actor's corresponding internal disposition (e.g., aggressive behaviour reflects aggressive personality) even when it was actually caused by situational factors (e.g., severe provocation). Research close-up 3.1 presents a famous example of this effect (see also Jones & Harris, 1967, described earlier).

Why do people underestimate situational influences? According to Gilbert and Malone (1995), a number of different processes may be involved. First, some situational forces are subtle and difficult to detect. If observers are not aware of these influences in the first place, they can hardly be expected to factor them into their explanations. Second, our *expectations* about how other people will behave may distort our interpretations. For example, we may mistakenly assume that the prospect of public speaking terrifies others just as much as it terrifies us (an example of the *false consensus bias*). Therefore, when someone appears calm before their turn to speak, we may

false consensus bias the assumption that other people generally share one's own personal attitudes and opinions

conclude that their confident personality must be over-riding an otherwise anxiety-provoking situation.

Finally, Gilbert and Malone suggest that people sometimes fail to correct their initial inferences about the causes of behaviour, especially when processing demands are high. The idea here is that people's automatic reaction to observed behaviour is to conclude that it reflects an actor's disposition. Any relevant situational influences are then factored in using a more deliberate reasoning process. Because the initial dispositional inference is effortless,

it happens regardless of current circumstances. However, other demands on cognitive resources may interfere with the situational correction process, leading us to underestimate the power of external factors. (The different stages at which these sources of bias may intrude are shown in Figure 3.6.)

An experiment conducted by Gilbert, Pelham and Krull (1988) provides support for this last explanation. Participants observed a silent videotape of a woman talking nervously to a stranger and then rated how anxious she was as a person. Subtitles indicating current conversation topics informed some participants that the woman was discussing her sexual fantasies (offering a situational explanation for her nervousness) but told others that she was talking about gardening. Further, some participants were told to memorize the subtitles, imposing an additional cognitive demand that should interfere with any situational correction process. As predicted, participants under higher cognitive demand tended to believe that the woman had an anxious personality regardless of conversation topic, whereas low-demand participants rated her as less dispositionally anxious when they believed she was discussing sex rather than gardening. Presumably the low-demand participants had sufficient cognitive resources remaining to correct for their initial automatic dispositional inference.

Gilbert and colleagues' theory suggests that attribution *always* involves automatic processes but only *sometimes* involves controlled processes as well (e.g., Shiffrin & Schneider, 1977). It is therefore another example of the dual-process models that are currently popular in research on social perception and cognition (see Chapter 4, this volume). The argument that we spontaneously and automatically make inferences about people's traits is supported by research conducted by Smith and Miller (1983). In two studies, these investigators demonstrated that participants

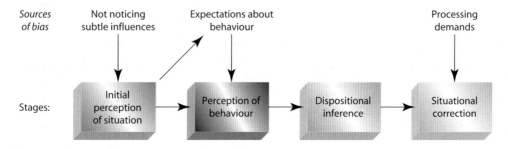

Figure 3.6 *Processes leading to correspondence biases (adapted from Gilbert & Malone, 1985).*

presented with sentences describing an actor's behaviour (e.g., 'Ted breaks a friend's expensive camera that he borrowed') made judgements about the actor's traits more quickly than they made inferences about the specific causes of the action. Indeed, it may be that we only go to the effort of engaging in a deliberate causal analysis and check the validity of our automatic trait attributions when we are specifically motivated to think about why a particular behaviour occurred (e.g., when the behaviour affects us negatively, or when it is unexpected), and when we have sufficient cognitive resources to engage in the necessary controlled processing.

Variability in correspondence biases The correspondence bias was once believed to be so pervasive and inescapable that it was dubbed 'the fundamental attribution error' (Ross, 1977). However, subsequent research suggests that it is more context-dependent than such a description implies (see Gawronski, 2005, for a review). For example, a study by Krull (1993) showed that asking people to diagnose the situation rather than the person led them to make automatic situational rather than dispositional inferences. Participants were again exposed to a silent videotape showing a woman talking, and were told that she was discussing sensitive topics with her therapist. Those whose task was to assess how anxiety-provoking the conversation was rated the woman as less dispositionally anxious, but the situation as more anxiety-provoking, when cognitive load was high than when it was low. By contrast, those whose task was to assess how dispositionally anxious the woman was rated the woman as more dispositionally anxious, but the situation as less anxiety-provoking, when cognitive load was high. It therefore seems that automatic dispositional inferences only occur if the inferential goal is to understand the person rather than the situation that person is in.

Many attribution studies have implicitly encouraged such inferential goals by orienting participants to actors rather than circumstances. For example, like all other sentences presented in Smith and Miller's (1983) study, 'Ted breaks a friend's expensive camera that he borrowed' begins with, and uses as subject of the sentence, the name of the actor performing the behaviour. Perhaps such sentences convey trait information more directly than they convey situational information (see also Brown & Fish, 1983, discussed below).

Operation of the correspondence bias also varies across cultures. For example, Miller (1984) compared explanations offered for deviant and prosocial behaviours by children (aged 8, 11 and 15) and adults from the USA and Southern India. She found that US adults attributed events to dispositional causes significantly more than Indian adults or children from either country, suggesting that North Americans but not Indian Hindus learn over the course of development to favour dispositional explanations (see Figure 3.7).

Why should members of some societies develop a stronger preference for dispositional explanations? Many western societies such as the USA and many European countries are said to be characterized by a culture of *individualism* in which personal effort and ability combine to produce deserved outcomes. People socialized into such cultures may learn to adopt the inferential goal of understanding actors rather than their circumstances in most contexts. However, in some other societies (e.g., India, Japan),

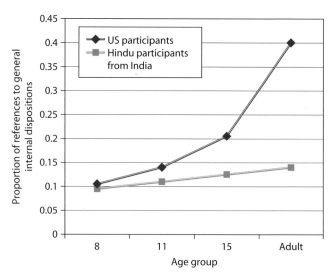

Figure 3.7 *Dispositional attributions in two cultural settings across four age groups (Miller, 1984).*

Plate 3.3 *Members of collectivistic cultures are more sensitive than members of individualistic cultures to the power of situations.*

children are socialized to see themselves more as part of groups that must work together to attain valued goals (*collectivistic culture*). This cultural emphasis is likely to lead to more frequent applicability of inferential goals directed at situations (especially social situations) rather than individual actors.

Despite their relatively higher preference for situational explanations, even collectivists frequently assume that actors have dispositions corresponding to their behaviour. For example, Korean participants (like US participants) assumed that a controversial essay reflected the writer's opinions even when they believed that the writer had been told what point of view to defend (Choi & Nisbett, 1998). However, when the situational constraint was made more **salient**, Korean participants were better able to take its influence into account. Choi and colleagues (1999) argue that members of

salience a property of stimuli in relation to perceivers that causes them to attract attention

collectivistic cultures are more sensitive to the power of situations than are members of individualistic cultures, enabling them to correct their initial dispositional inferences under some circumstances.

The actor–observer difference The *actor-observer difference* compares attributions people make about others with those that they make about themselves. Although westerners' default assumption is often that other people's behaviour reflects a corresponding disposition, it seems that we tend to emphasize external, situational factors when explaining our own behaviour. This difference was first identified by Jones and Nisbett (1972) and has received qualified support since then (e.g., see Watson, 1982).

> **actor–observer difference** general tendency for people to explain their own behaviour in more situational terms but other people's behaviour in more dispositional terms

Why don't explanations of our own conduct follow identical principles to our explanation of other people's conduct? Two main explanations have been proposed, and both probably play some role in accounting for actor–observer differences. First, actors have access to a wider range of information about the factors leading to their own actions (Jones & Nisbett, 1972). For example, when explaining your liveliness at a party, you are able to consider other situations in which you have acted in a less extroverted manner (e.g., when meeting someone for the first time, or being interviewed), and may therefore conclude that you are not a consistently lively person. By contrast, most other people only know

Plate 3.4 *Your behaviour, e.g. being lively at a party, may appear more consistent to others than it really is.*

how you have acted in a restricted set of contexts. Thus, your behaviour may appear more consistent to them than it really is.

The second factor contributing to actor–observer differences concerns direction of attention. When observing someone else's behaviour, we tend to focus on that person rather than their situation. Conversely, when we ourselves are acting, our attention tends to be directed outwards. Perhaps then we simply assume that whatever is occupying our attention is exerting the most causal influence (e.g., Taylor & Fiske, 1978; see Research close-up 3.2 on Storms, 1973).

RESEARCH CLOSE-UP 3.2

Reversing the actor–observer effect by manipulating perspective

Storms, M.D. (1973). Videotape and the attribution process: Reversing actors' and observers' points of view. *Journal of Personality and Social Psychology, 27,* 165–175.

Introduction

Storms (1973) proposed that differences between actors' and observers' attribution depend partly on their different physical points of view: actors' attention is typically directed outwards towards the situation (including other actors), whereas observers' attention focuses on the observed person (i.e., the actor). Indeed, one explanation for the correspondence bias is that actors are often the most dynamic and interesting objects in the environment and therefore attract observers' attention (and deflect it from other aspects of the situation; see Heider, 1958; Taylor & Fiske, 1978). The increasing availability of video technology in the early 1970s allowed Storms to manipulate actors' and observers' perspectives in order to assess the influence of this factor on situational and dispositional attributions.

Method

Participants
Thirty groups of four male students took part in this study. Two members of each group were randomly assigned the role of observer and the other two were assigned the role of actor.

Design and procedure
Stage 1. Actors were told to have a conversation to get to know each other, while facing each other across a table. Each observer was seated next to one of the actors and told to observe the actor across the table from him. Two video cameras were also set up, each trained on one of the actors (see Figure 3.8, Stage 1).

Stage 2. Participants in the video condition were told that they would now see the videotape of the interaction played back, but because only one camera had worked they would only see the tape of one of the actors. Thus, one actor and one observer from each group saw a replay of the conversation from the same perspective as before, while the other actor and observer saw a video replay from the reversed perspective (i.e., the actor now

Stage 1 Bird's-eye view of get acquainted session (arrows indicate direction of attention)

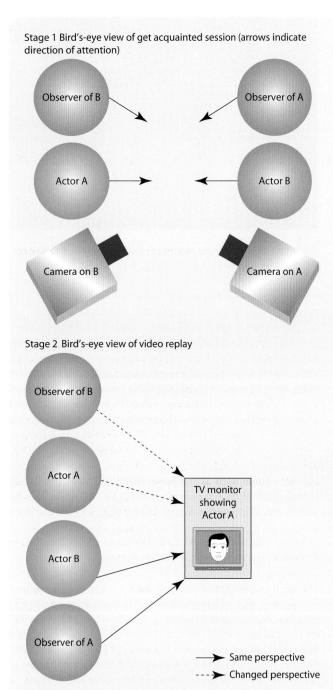

Stage 2 Bird's-eye view of video replay

→ Same perspective

---→ Changed perspective

Figure 3.8 *The two stages of Storms's (1973) procedure.*

saw his own face, and the observer saw the face of the actor that he had not originally observed; see Figure 3.8, Stage 2). In the no-video condition, participants were told that none of the video equipment had worked and that the planned video replay would therefore not take place.

Measures
After Stage 2, actors rated their own friendliness, nervousness, talkativeness and dominance during the conversation, then rated the extent to which each of these behaviours had been caused

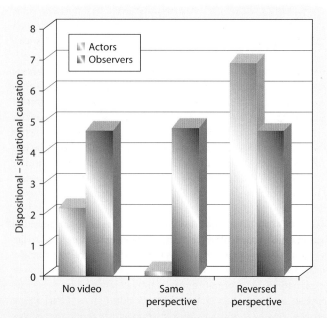

Figure 3.9 *Reversing the actor–observer difference following video replay (adapted from Storms, 1973).*

by personal characteristics and by characteristics of the situation. Observers rated their respective actors from Stage 1.

Results

Storms calculated difference scores by subtracting summed ratings of situational attribution for the four key behaviours from summed ratings of dispositional attribution. These difference scores were then analysed. In the no-video and same-perspective conditions, actors' attributions were less dispositional (more situational) than observers' (see Figure 3.9). But in the reversed-perspective condition, observers' attributions were less dispositional (more situational) than actors'.

Discussion

This study demonstrates that actor–observer differences can be reversed by showing actors their own behaviour and showing observers the situation that actors are responding to (in this case, the other actor). A more general conclusion may also be possible: that actors and observers tend to attribute greater causality wherever they pay attention. Indeed, later studies (e.g., Taylor & Fiske, 1978) have shown that salient (attention-grabbing) factors tend to be seen as exerting more causal influence than non-salient factors.

One criticism of this study is that the usual actor–observer difference was not demonstrated (e.g., Gilbert & Malone, 1995). For example, analysis of direct ratings rather than difference scores shows that actors were rated in equally dispositional terms by themselves and their observers across all conditions. However, the reported effect on situational attribution is theoretically interesting even if dispositional attribution is unaffected. The general implication is that we can correct for inattention to situational factors by manipulating attention.

Of course, direction of attention can only explain preferences for dispositional explanations of other people's behaviour when the other person is physically present. However, observers also tend to say that the actor was the cause of behaviour when it is described to them in words. For example, when told that 'John went to the cinema', most people will tend to think that this reflects something about John rather than something about the cinema. According to Brown and Fish (1983), the reason is that the English language implies that subjects of action verbs are responsible for the action described. By contrast, the *objects* of *experience* verbs are usually seen as causal (e.g., we tend to interpret the sentence *John liked Angela* as John's liking for Angela being caused by something about Angela).

Self-serving attributional biases What pushes or pulls our attributions in particular directions? The examples presented so far suggest either that we are drawn towards salient factors or that we are following generally valid rules of explanation (e.g., persons cause effects) in circumstances where they happen to be less appropriate (see Nisbett & Ross, 1980). The basic idea is that people's attributions are occasionally imperfect approximations of the causal structure of reality, but at least aim to represent that reality accurately. However, some kinds of bias are harder to explain in these terms. *Self-serving attributional biases* are those that seem to represent a *motivated* distortion of what has happened in order to serve personal interests. Instead of being neutral observers of social events, we may sometimes interpret them in ways that suit us (or ways that suit our ingroup more generally; Islam & Hewstone, 1993, and see Chapter 14, this volume), allowing us to feel better about what has happened.

self-serving biases motivated distortions of attributional conclusions that function to preserve or increase self-esteem

Let's assume that you have just done well in an exam. Your tendency may be to conclude that this reflects your innate ability (*self-enhancing bias*). However, if you do badly, perhaps you will decide that the questions were unfair or unusually difficult, or that the person sitting next to you in the examination hall was distracting you by sharpening his pencils so noisily (*self-protective bias*). More generally, you may be inclined to arrive at conclusions that maintain your positive self-image.

One of the earliest demonstrations of self-serving bias was an experiment by Johnson, Feigenbaum and Weiby (1964). Participants were educational psychology students and their task was to teach two children how to multiply numbers via a one-way intercom system, which meant that they never actually saw or heard the children. The first phase involved explaining how to multiply by 10 and the second phase involved explaining how to multiply by 20. After each phase, the pupils' worksheets were returned to participants, allowing them to assess how successfully the concepts had been conveyed. In fact, the worksheets were concocted by the experimenters to manipulate whether or not the answers were correct. In both conditions, pupil A answered the questions on both worksheets correctly. However, pupil B either did badly on both tasks or did badly on the first but improved on the second. In other words, the students either failed or succeeded in teaching pupil B how to multiply. In the condition where pupil

Plate 3.5 *Teacher's explanations of pupils' success and failure can show self-serving bias.*

B's performance improved, the students explained this improvement in terms of their own abilities as a teacher. But when pupil B failed to improve, they attributed this to his lack of ability rather than their ineffective teaching methods.

Zuckerman (1979) reviewed a number of apparent demonstrations of self-serving bias, and concluded that the effect depends on a desire to maintain self-esteem. The extent to which the current context makes self-esteem concerns salient should therefore determine the strength of the reported effect. However, competing motivations such as self-presentation can also reduce self-serving attributions. For example, we may be less inclined to take credit for positive outcomes in public settings, either because we don't want to be seen to show off, or in order to avoid any embarrassment at failing to live up to the unduly favourable image that this would imply (e.g., Weary et al., 1982).

Abramson and colleagues' (1978) attributional reformulation of learned helplessness theory (see above) implies that depressed people adopt an attributional style that is the precise opposite of the self-serving pattern (they take rather than disown responsibility for failure). Indeed, research suggests that simply being in a bad mood can reverse self-serving biases (e.g., Forgas, Bower & Moylan, 1990), perhaps by removing the illusory glow that ordinarily preserves our sense of well-being in happier states (Taylor & Brown, 1988, and see above).

Motivational or cognitive effect? In the 1970s, a debate arose about whether self-serving biases were genuinely self-serving. Miller and Ross (1975) proposed that some personally advantageous attributions were entirely rational, while others simply reflected the application of principles of explanation that would normally be valid. According to this view, people do not distort their thinking to protect self-esteem (*motivational* explanation) but rather use rules of thumb that happen to lead to faulty conclusions on some occasions (*cognitive* explanation). Take the educational psychology students in Johnson and colleagues' research. It would be illogical for them to attribute pupil B's improvement on the second exercise to the pupil's abilities, because the pupil had done badly on the first sheet. Further, improvement followed the teacher's careful attempt to explain 20 times multiplication after the pupil had done badly in 10 times multiplication. Under these circumstances, it makes perfect sense to conclude that the application of the participant's teaching skills led to success. In the failure condition, by contrast, the pupil did not improve *despite* renewed efforts at explanation, and was consistently worse than pupil A on both exercise sheets. Thus, failure covaries with pupil B but not with pupil A, or with the person doing the teaching. According to Kelley's covariation principle, even a detached observer should attribute bad performance to pupil B rather than the teacher when these conditions hold.

More generally, Miller and Ross argued that apparently self-serving biases arise because effort covaries with success but not with failure. If trying harder does not improve performance, then it is reasonable to conclude that something about the task is presenting an obstacle. However, if trying harder does improve performance, then success is logically attributable to your trying.

Although these are valid points, few contemporary psychologists would deny that thinking can also be distorted by motivations and emotions. Indeed, the idea that we adjust our inferences to match existing positive expectations already sounds rather like an acknowledgement that we want to make ourselves look good under certain circumstances (Tetlock & Levi, 1982). Thus, many apparently cognitive explanations can be translated into motivational terms, and many apparently motivational explanations can be translated into cognitive terms. Under these circumstances, trying to tease apart cognitive and motivational processes is practically impossible.

The naïve scientist metaphor

Do lay perceivers behave as scientists when making causal attributions, or do they have more practical concerns?

Most of the theory and research considered above assumes that people seek to understand the social world in a detached, scientific manner, but sometimes get it wrong. This assumption is generally known as the **naïve scientist model** (e.g., Fiske & Taylor, 1991), and, like all metaphors, it has its limits. Perhaps some of our explanations are not designed to provide a neutral characterization of reality in the first place. In this case, evaluating attributions against abstract rules of inference such as Kelley's covariation principle is rather like complaining that someone playing draughts is not correctly following the rules of chess.

> **naïve scientist model** a metaphor for how social information is processed that likens social perceivers to academic researchers who attempt to develop theories and explanations for the purposes of prediction and control of behaviour

If people are not trying to be scientific when making attributions, what are they trying to do? One possibility is that explanations are generated to solve specific practical problems (White, 1989). For example, if you have to explain why you have done well in an examination, you probably don't weigh up all possible contributory factors. Instead, you look specifically for those causes that will further your ends in the current situation. If the explanation is formulated while talking with a friend who is disappointed by her own performance, you might search your memory for any bits of good luck that aided your success. If, on the other hand, you are trying to score a point against the other person, you might try to think of some particularly clever things that you wrote.

Hilton (1990) argues that the explanations we provide in conversations are specifically designed to meet the information requirements of the person we are talking to. For example, when discussing with my local greengrocer how I got sick after trying kiwi fruit for the first time, I will tend to attribute the sickness to the fruit, because I assume that she is interested in possible reactions to different fruits. However, when explaining my kiwi-induced sickness to the doctor, her focus will be on what distinguishes me from other patients and what my particular complaint may be. In this context, therefore, I am more likely to attribute the sickness to my own apparent allergy to kiwi fruit.

Note that these two explanations are mutually compatible and may both be true, despite the fact that one refers to an external cause (the kiwi fruit) and the other to an internal cause (my allergy). Typically, a number of factors need to be in place to cause a given event, and attribution involves selecting which of these factors to emphasize in a particular context. To look at this another way, a number of changes in prior events could have averted the effect of getting sick (I could have eaten a different fruit, not had a kiwi fruit allergy, not liked the taste and refused to eat the fruit, and so on) and each of these possible changes reflects one of the causes contributing to my sickness (the fruit, my allergy, my liking of the taste, etc.). Deciding which of these causes to emphasize depends on what you think the person to whom you are explaining the event already knows about its causes, and what you think they expected to happen.

On some occasions, of course, another person's expectations about what would normally happen are not entirely obvious, leading to ambiguity about how to approach the explanatory task. However, the precise phrasing of the causal question often helps to clarify matters. For example, if someone asks you 'Does kiwi fruit make you sick?' the question's implicit emphasis (i.e., kiwi fruit as the subject of the action verb) may suggest that the questioner wants to know about the fruit's effects. According to Hilton (1990), some apparent cases of bias can be explained by applying these conversational principles. For example, Nisbett and colleagues (1973) found that students explained their own choice of course in more situational terms than their best friend's choice of course, consistent with the actor–observer difference. However, the emphasis of the question 'why did you choose this university course?' naturally falls on the course as the topic about which information is required. By contrast, the question 'why did your best friend choose this course?' implies that the investigators want to know about the friend rather than the course (otherwise, why not directly ask for the participant's own reasons?). In this study, then, the reported actor–observer difference may simply reflect a rationally motivated attempt to provide the kind of information that was implicitly requested.

An experiment by McGill (1989) supports this reasoning. She found that a simple change in wording reversed the effect found by Nisbett et al. When participants were asked 'why did you *in particular* choose this course?' they tended to offer less situational explanations than when they were asked 'why did your friend choose this course *in particular*?'

More generally, attribution experiments may be viewed as conversations taking place between experimenters and participants in which the participants are trying to work out what information the experimenter is seeking (Schwarz, 1994). Making sense of questionnaire items often depends on thinking about who is asking these questions and for what purposes. Adopting this kind of conversational approach also allows a reinterpretation of other supposed illustrations of attributional bias. For example, in Jones and Harris's (1967) original demonstration of the correspondence bias (discussed earlier), participants were told to work out another student's attitudes towards Castro. In order to do this, they were provided with an excerpt from an essay that this other student had (supposedly) written. Should participants simply ignore this essay if its writer had been told what position to take on this issue? Surely the experimenter wouldn't have gone to the trouble of showing it to them if it provided no information about the writer's opinions. Participants probably assume, therefore, that the experimenter believes that the essay is relevant and conclude that they are meant to infer the writer's opinion on the basis of its content. Indeed, when participants are explicitly warned that some of the material they will see may not be relevant, the correspondence bias is reduced (Wright & Wells, 1988).

Attributions as discourse

Do attributions always function as part of a cooperative process between people?

Hilton's working assumption is that people try to provide other people with information that helps to complete their understanding of events (Grice, 1975). However, conversations are not always cooperative processes in which information is generously exchanged. Often, our aim is not to help someone else understand what has happened, but rather to argue against them or defend our own point of view against their attack. According to Edwards and Potter (1993), attributions may be formulated rather differently in these more antagonistic contexts. For example, they present a transcript of a court case in which an allegation of rape is being contested. The defence barrister is questioning the victim of the alleged rape and apparently trying to suggest that she is partly culpable. The interchange ran as follows:

> Barrister: (*referring to a club where the defendant and the victim met*) It's where girls and fellas meet isn't it?
> Victim: People go there. (Edwards & Potter, 1993, p. 30)

Note that the way the barrister describes what happened on the night in question implies certain motives and intentions on the part of the victim, i.e., that she had gone to this place specifically to meet with members of the opposite sex. Her response in turn is designed specifically to neutralize this inference. Although neither party to this exchange is explicitly presenting explanations, the

Plate 3.6 *Attributions do not always function as part of a cooperative process between people.*

way that events are formulated already carries implications for what caused what and who is to blame. Clearly, this isn't a cooperative process, but rather one in which attributions are actively contested.

Like White (1984), Edwards and Potter (1993) believe that attributions are formulated for particular purposes, but these purposes specifically reflect conversational goals such as persuading, undermining, blaming or accusing. Conversational maxims are often explicitly flouted when explanations are presented. Further, a range of alternative tactics and strategies may be improvised online in response to the other person's formulations. In this view, attributions do not function as attempts to explain a separately existing social reality, but instead to *construct* a version of reality suited to the current conversational business. Attributions are not descriptive representations but rhetorical moves in an ongoing dialogue.

SUMMARY

In this central part of the chapter we have covered a huge amount of ground. We reviewed the major theories of attribution and identified some of their limitations, including the need to explain how general and specific knowledge is used as part of the attribution process. We also considered applications of attribution theory, notably to clinical depression. Next we considered the key role of attributions in emotion and the misattribution of arousal, and summarized the evidence for the main types of attributional bias and their underlying causes. Finally, we evaluated whether lay perceivers do, in fact, function as naïve scientists, and the role of causal attributions within the study of conversations and everyday discourse.

SOCIAL PERCEPTION AND SOCIAL REALITY

....

What are the main constraints on how social perceivers understand other people and explain their actions?

Conversational and discursive models of attribution take us some distance from Asch's and Heider's project of finding out how people privately make sense of other people and what they do. More generally, they unsettle the notion that people are simply naïve scientists trying to uncover the structure of an independent social reality. Subsequent models have seen social perceivers as lawyers (Hamilton, 1980), pragmatists (White, 1984), tacticians (Fiske & Taylor, 1991) or politicians (Tetlock, 2002). Although there is some truth in all of these characterizations, the bottom line seems to be that a variety of strategies are available for dealing with social information, which may be deployed selectively depending on circumstances.

But does this mean that social perceivers are free to construct whatever formulation suits their current purposes? There are three reasons why this is not the case. The first is that biology and culture do not equip people with infinitely flexible conceptual resources for understanding other people. On the one hand, we are innately attuned to certain kinds of social information at the expense of others (e.g., Fantz, 1963; Johnson & Morton, 1991). On the other hand, we are socialized into particular ways of thinking about the social world (e.g., social representations; Farr & Moscovici, 1984). Attribution and social perception always take place against the backdrop of norms of understanding that make some inferences more likely than others.

A second and related point is that other people will contest any formulation of social reality that doesn't match their own (just as their own formulation may be contested in turn). The upshot is that some consensus tends to emerge among people who have regular contact with one another. However, social reality may also be influenced by the representations that are applied to it. For example, our judgements about others can lead us to behave in ways that bring out the very characteristics that we expected (via self-fulfilling prophecies; see Snyder, 1984, and Chapter 10, this volume).

The final constraint on representations is the content of the social information itself. Although social perception research tends to focus on the interpretation of verbally represented information or static, sensory stimuli, when people confront each other in everyday life they often have access to a dynamic multimodal presentation that is responsive to their own conduct. Some characteristics of others can be read directly from the available information (Baron & Boudreau, 1987; Gibson, 1979). For example, we register where someone else's attention is focused from the orientation of their sensory organs. It seems therefore that some kinds of social perception and attribution are not explicit verbally mediated processes but instead involve direct registration of sensory information. The challenge facing future research is to specify how these two kinds of process – verbal representation as shaped by conversational pragmatics and rhetoric, and direct perception determined by active pick-up of social information – might relate to one another.

SUMMARY AND CONCLUSIONS

- *Person perception* is influenced by the form as well as the content of information, and not all information is equally weighted.

- Some kinds of information (e.g., facial configuration) are perceived as direct indicators of personality, and some kinds of information are weighted highly (e.g., first-presented information and 'central' traits) but rarely in all situations.

- *Causal attribution* is shaped by prior general knowledge, as in correspondent inference theory and covariation theory. But we do not always have access to this information and specific knowledge is also used.

- Inferences about the causes of achievement influence motivation and, relatedly, internal, stable and global attributions for helplessness may exacerbate depression.

- Attributions for internal symptoms may alter interpretations of emotional experience.

- As with person perception, not all information is equally weighted when making attributions about the causes of behaviour; causal information that is salient is especially influential.

- Various biases have been identified, which qualify the general theories and bring them more into line with how attributions operate in everday life.

- People in individualistic societies tend to overestimate personal causes of behaviour (the correspondence bias), but this correspondence bias is neither inevitable nor uncontrollable.

- Differences in actors' and observers' attributions depend partly, but not entirely, on their different perceptual perspectives.

- Motivational factors are implicated in some instances of self-serving bias.

- Attribution typically operates within a conversational context and is responsive to conversational demands.

- Although people sometimes act like naïve scientists, they make attributions in ways that are strategic for the goals of social interaction, serving a variety of rhetorical purposes.

Suggestions for further reading

Fiske, S.T. & Taylor, S.E. (1991). *Social cognition* (2nd edn). New York: McGraw-Hill. Includes treatment of attribution theory (Chapters 2 and 3) within an overarching perspective on social cognition.

Försterling, F. (2001). *Attribution: An introduction to theories, research, and applications*. Hove: Psychology Press. An accessible overview of attribution models and findings from Heider to the early twenty-first century.

Hewstone, M. (1989). *Causal attribution: From cognitive processes to collective beliefs*. Oxford: Blackwell. A wide-ranging view of the field, including intrapersonal, interpersonal, intergroup and societal aspects of attribution.

Ross, L. & Nisbett, R.E. (1991). *The person and the situation: Perspectives of social psychology*. Boston: McGraw-Hill. Highly readable introduction to the cognitive perspective on attributional bias and other aspects of social perception and inference.

Zebrowitz, L.A. (1990). *Social perception*. Buckingham: Open University Press. A thorough review of research into social perception that attempts to integrate ecological and cognitive approaches.

4 | Social Cognition

Louise Pendry

CHAPTER OUTLINE

....

This chapter introduces the topic of social cognition: the study of how we make sense of others and ourselves. It focuses especially on the distinction between social processes and judgements that are often rapid and automatic, such as categorization and stereotype activation, and those which may require more effort, deliberation and control (for example, stereotype suppression and individuated impression formation).

Introduction

....

What is social cognition?
What kinds of processes can social cognition research help to explain?

We inhabit a hectic social world. In any one day we can expect to deal with many other people. We may meet people for the first time, we may go out with old friends, we may find ourselves in a job interview trying to make a good impression on our prospective employer, queuing in a supermarket to pay for groceries, waiting for a train on a busy platform. Even for those of us professing to live ordinary lives, no two days are exactly alike. So, precisely how do we navigate this complex social life? What social information do we attend to, organize, remember and use? These are some of the questions that interest social cognition researchers, and providing answers to them strikes at the very heart of understanding human mental life.

As we go about our daily schedules, we are busy 'doing' social cognition for real. So, just what is it? Essentially, the study of social cognition promotes a deeper understanding of the mental processes that underlie human social behaviour (Fiske & Taylor, 1991). As Fiske (2004, p. 122) puts it, 'Social cognition analyzes the steps in people's train of thought about other people'. If we think about it for just a moment, it has implications for a very broad range of human social phenomena and domains. What is especially intriguing about social cognition is that it taps into the kinds of questions we find ourselves asking. Questions such as:

- Why did I assume that the man at the coffee machine in the boardroom was the company director when he was in fact the secretary?
- Why did I assume that Dr Alex James would be male/white?
- Why is it that I expected Albert to be elderly?

- Why did it surprise me to discover that Hilda, my elderly neighbour, had a passion for car maintenance?

- Why did I take the time to talk to my new black work colleague and find myself subsequently re-evaluating my initially stereotypic impression of her?

The aim of this chapter is to pass on to you a little of what we have learned thus far about some of the main theoretical issues in the field (for more detail see Bless, Fiedler & Strack, 2004; Fiske & Taylor, 1991; Kunda, 1999; Moskowitz, 2005). This chapter will give you a flavour of some of the more established theories in the field, and consider both the classic and more contemporary research that such theories have generated in their quest to understand better the workings of the social mind.

Although the field of social cognition is extremely broad and vibrant, few researchers would deny that one recurring, overarching theme is the distinction between social thinking that is *fast and furious* and social thinking that is more *measured and precise*. Since the 1970s, significant developments in theory and methodology have meant it is possible for us to now focus independently on these different types of thinking, that is, the influence of *unintentional* (i.e., unconscious) and *intentional* (i.e., conscious) processes in human thought and behaviour (Posner & Snyder, 1975).

automatic process a process that occurs without intention, effort or awareness and does not interfere with other concurrent cognitive processes

controlled process a process that is intentional, under the individual's volitional control, effortful and entailing conscious awareness

You might see this distinction encompassed in the term *dual-processing theories*. Or, to put it yet another way (and the way we will mainly refer to it hereafter), it refers to the contrast between *automatic* and *controlled processes*.

In this chapter, we focus primarily upon this distinction as it applies to *stereotyping* (e.g., Bargh, 1999; Devine, 1989). Do we process information about members of social groups carefully and rationally, or do we instead make rash judgements on the spur of the moment? Understanding when and why we engage in automatic or controlled processing can tell us a lot about how we view our social world.

To make this kind of distinction a little clearer, consider the following passage:

Simon tried to put nationalities to faces, according to stereotype. The group of brawny, over-tanned and over-jewelled men and women who had ordered Bordeaux rather than local wine should be German – prosperous, large and loud. Any table giving off a cloud of cigarette smoke should be French, just as a table of non-smokers, with more water than wine being drunk, should be Americans. The English loaded butter onto their bread and ordered the heaviest desserts. The Swiss ate neatly and kept their elbows off the table, alternating sips of wine and sips of water like clockwork. (Mayle, 1993, p. 234)

Simon's observations may not strike us as particularly unusual. We may not endorse the national stereotypes conveyed in the above quotation, or at least question their accuracy, but somehow, we know exactly what he is talking about. Despite the perils of stereotypical thinking, it is something that we are apt to find irresistible (e.g., Brewer, 1988; Devine, 1989; Fiske & Neuberg, 1990).

Did Simon pause for even a moment to consider if his snap decisions were accurate? Did he stop to consider that in fact several of the French contingent were not actually smoking? Or that at least two of the English group were nibbling abstemiously on fruit salad (no cream)? No. The questions for social cognition researchers are: how and why did he respond in this manner? What processes led him to these conclusions? In social cognitive terms, the above illustration demonstrates several steps in a process that will be the focus of the next section. Simon has:

- *categorized* each of the persons in the restaurant in terms of nationality (grouped them into discrete sets – here, nationalities – based upon perceived shared characteristics);

- *activated* the *content* of these categories (what we term *schemas*: our expectancies about people belonging to such groups);

schema a cognitive structure or mental representation comprising pre-digested information about objects or people from specific categories; our expectancies about objects or groups; what defines them

- applied these schemas in such a way that *confirms the stereotypes* of the groups (looked only for information that is consistent with his expectancies).

Much of this occurred fairly spontaneously. Simon did not stop to deliberate more carefully. As we shall see, it is a fundamental tenet of social cognition research that we often process information in precisely this way, only moving beyond the obvious stereotype if motivated and able to do so (e.g., Fiske & Neuberg, 1990). Stereotypes such as those outlined above have a functional role to play in facilitating person perception. They are, as Bodenhausen (1990) has noted, a kind of cognitive shortcut, a simplifying rule of thumb or *heuristic* that serves us well a lot of the time, but not always (for more on heuristics, see also Chapter 7, this volume).

heuristic a well-used, non-optimal rule of thumb used to arrive at a judgement that is effective in many but not all cases; stereotypes are often said to function as heuristics

In this chapter, we will consider some of the research that speaks to the automatic and controlled distinction: when, why and how do we engage in automatic versus controlled processing in person perception and stereotyping? By the end of this chapter you will be well equipped to provide preliminary answers to these questions.

JUMPING TO CONCLUSIONS: THE AUTOMATIC PILOT WITHIN

What makes a process automatic?
Are stereotypes activated automatically?
What part do categories and schemas play in the process of judging and understanding others?
How does stereotype activation impact upon behaviour?

Read the following passage:

> A father and his son were involved in a car accident in which the father was killed and the son was seriously injured. The father was pronounced dead at the scene of the accident and his body taken to a local morgue. The son was taken by ambulance to a nearby hospital and was immediately wheeled into an emergency operating room. A surgeon was called. Upon arrival, and seeing the patient, the attending surgeon exclaimed, 'Oh my God, it's my son!'
>
> Can you explain this?

So, how did you do? Many people find this question impossible to answer (based on lab class demonstrations over a number of years, often more than 40 per cent of students simply cannot do it). Moreover, they are apt to generate a wide range of convoluted explanations (for example, the 'father' who was killed is a Catholic priest and the term 'son' is therefore being used rather loosely) other than the most obvious one (the surgeon is the boy's mother). Why do people have so much trouble and why do they generate such complex rationalizations? Essentially, they find it hard to overcome the automatically activated *stereotype* (i.e., surgeons are generally men). As we shall see, this tendency to activate stereotypes automatically happens an awful lot. We will now pay some closer attention to why this occurs.

> **stereotype** a cognitive structure that contains our knowledge, beliefs and expectancies about some human social group

What makes a process automatic?

For a process to be considered automatic, several criteria are deemed necessary (e.g., Posner & Snyder, 1975): the process needs to occur without *intention*, *effort* or *awareness* and is *not expected to interfere with other concurrent cognitive processes*. For those of us who have been behind the wheel of a car for a few years, the act of changing gear would possibly meet these criteria. A controlled process, on the other hand, is one that is: *intentional, under the individual's volitional control, effortful* and *entails conscious awareness*. To continue the driving analogy, deciding whether it is safe to

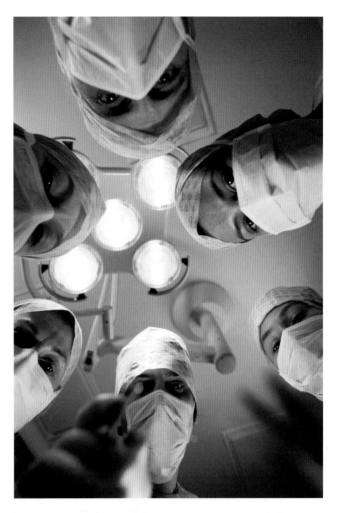

Plate 4.1 *Did you assume that these surgeons were men?*

overtake on a busy motorway should (one would hope!) fulfil these criteria. Let us now consider how this automatic versus controlled distinction contributes to our understanding of the process of stereotyping. We will start by looking at social categorization.

The pervasive nature of social categorization

Almost every doctor who saw and examined me, labelled me a very interesting but also a hopeless case. Many told my mother very gently that I was mentally defective and would remain so . . . nothing could be done for me.

(Christy Brown, 1954/1990, p. 10)

Christy Brown suffered from cerebral palsy and was considered mentally disabled until one day he snatched a piece of chalk from his sister and wrote some words with it. He went on to astound and defy the medical profession by becoming a widely acclaimed

categorization the tendency to group objects (including people) into discrete groups, based upon shared characteristics common to them

author, whose autobiography was made into a successful film, *My Left Foot*. Branded from birth as 'retarded and useless', he fought to overcome prejudice and ignorance. The consequences of *categorization* can, then, sometimes be rather unpalatable. Once we assign others to particular social categories, associated stereotypic information can dominate our judgements to a worrying degree. Nonetheless, it does seem unlikely that we can view others in total isolation from their obvious physical and social categories. This is the view adopted by many theorists who work in the area (e.g., Brewer, 1988; Fiske & Neuberg, 1990; Macrae & Bodenhausen, 2000), and we will now turn our attention to why they endorse such a position.

Categorization refers to the tendency we have to group objects (including people) into discrete groups, based upon shared characteristics. There are object categories for furniture, takeaway food and musical instruments, but also social categories for women, refuse collectors, children, rock stars and so on. It is a fundamental premise of the social cognition approach that such categories serve a very useful function (e.g., Allport, 1954; Macrae, Milne & Bodenhausen, 1994). Why do you think this is?

Consider the following thought experiment. Imagine a far-off planet, Zygon, a place where perceptual mechanisms and inferential strategies have evolved in a decidedly unearthly manner. One day, an inhabitant from Zygon lands her spaceship somewhere on planet Earth and begins her journey into the unknown. She will doubtless be faced with many new objects and life forms that we human beings would, effortlessly, be able to sort into people, buildings, animals, trees and so on. Not so the Zygonian. Devoid of the cognitive know-how to parse this new and complex social landscape into something more intelligible, she would eventually experience information overload. There would simply be too many stimuli to process, at least in any meaningful manner.

This ability to separate our social world into discrete social categories is therefore a vital adaptation that ensures we don't find ourselves in a similarly daunting position. Without it, each person we met (or each object) would be unique and need be treated accordingly. Imagine how much time and effort that would take. Stated simply, *categorization favours simplification*, which in turn renders the world a more orderly, predictable and controllable place.

So, having established why categorization is so useful, let's look in more detail at the evidence that it is an *automatic* process. In 1989, Devine published an influential article in which she argued that (1) knowledge about racial stereotypes is culturally shared, even by people who do not endorse such stereotypes, and (2) activation of this knowledge (i.e., stereotype activation) is an automatic process. Recall that the criteria for a process to be automatic include that it is unconscious and does not require intention, attention or effort. If stereotype activation is truly automatic, this should mean that any time the appropriate cues are present (e.g., age, race or gender), stereotype activation should *invariably* result. So, how might this be tested empirically? Devine

PIONEER

Patricia Devine (b. 1959) spent her undergraduate years at the State University of New York, graduating in 1981, *summa cum laude*. This was followed by an MA (in 1983) and a PhD (in 1986) from Ohio State University. Devine's research centres around the intrapersonal and interpersonal challenges associated with prejudice in contemporary society. Her early work on the automatic and controlled components of stereotyping (1989) has been extremely influential in the field. Recent research concerns include the relation between explicit and implicit prejudice and the processes that regulate the use of stereotypes.

(1989, Study 2) used what is known as a *priming* paradigm (see Bargh & Pietromonaco, 1982). We need to dwell a moment on what priming is

priming activating one stimulus (e.g., bird) facilitates the subsequent processing of another related stimulus (e.g., wing, feather)

and why the priming paradigm is such a useful research tool to enable us to test Devine's hypothesis (and indeed, many other related research questions).

When a construct is triggered in memory and made *temporarily accessible*, this is called priming and the stimulus that leads to this construct being triggered is called the prime (Moskowitz, 2005). In concrete terms, priming or activating one stimulus (e.g., bird) facilitates the subsequent processing of another related stimulus (e.g., wing, feather) via a process known as *spreading activation* (e.g., Neely, 1977). Once a construct is activated, associated concepts are also triggered and attain a state of heightened *accessibility*, even if they were not directly primed initially. Such concepts therefore re-

accessibility the extent to which information is easily located and retrieved

quire some kind of cue to render them momentarily accessible. To use an analogy proposed by Higgins, Bargh and Lombardi (1985), these concepts are like a battery that is running low but can be recharged in certain circumstances (i.e., when the appropriate environmental trigger is present). It should be noted that other concepts, such as strongly held political beliefs, are often perpetually well charged (aided, for example, by repeated exposure to political arguments in the press, or political debates with like-minded friends). Being in a state of permanently high charge, they are routinely more accessible. These are termed *chronically accessible* concepts (for a detailed review see Moskowitz, 2005). Here, though, we focus primarily on how priming makes concepts temporarily accessible.

In one measure of accessibility, known as a *lexical decision task*, priming stimuli (e.g., words or pictures) are often presented on a computer, usually very quickly. Participants are then shown a letter string that may or may not be associated with the prime (and may or may not be a real word), and asked to decide if it is a real word or a non-word by pressing a computer key. A priming effect is obtained when participants are shown to respond significantly faster to real words preceded by an associated prime (i.e., are quicker to respond to *wing* after being primed with *bird*). The advantage of priming paradigms is that they usually indicate uncontrolled automatic processing. Participants' subsequent reaction times are not prey to intentional self-presentational strategies (i.e., wanting to show themselves in a certain, often socially desirable, light), as might be the case, say, with paper and pencil measures of stereotyping.

Now that we are clearer about how priming paradigms work and why they are so suited to the study of automatic processes, let's return to Devine's work. In her experiment, primes related to a stereotype were presented outside of participants' conscious awareness. In order to do this, she presented the primes outside of participants' parafoveal field (i.e., out of their direct line of vision). The primes Devine used were terms related to the black stereotype (i.e., labels such as *blacks*, *niggers*, and physical or trait characteristics including *poor*, *lazy*). The participants had been pre-tested for prejudice level: half were high in prejudice towards black people, whereas half were low. This distinction forms an important part of Devine's experimental hypotheses, as we shall see later. Devine presented some participants with a high proportion (80 per cent) of ethnically associated words, and other participants with a much lower proportion (20 per cent).

Following the prime, in an ostensibly unrelated second experiment, participants read a brief scenario and were asked to form an impression of a target person who engaged in ambiguously hostile behaviours (after a paradigm originally developed by Srull & Wyer, 1979). Why hostile? Because pre-testing had indicated that hostility was a very strong feature of the black stereotype (see also Duncan, 1976). None of the words used in the priming phase, however, was directly related to hostility. This is important because it suggests that if the prime exerts the predicted effects upon interpretation of the ambiguous behaviour, it is due to automatic stereotype activation rather than simple priming of the hostile construct (but see Research close-up 4.3, below, for discussion of this point).

Let's consider what Devine predicted and found. Devine reported that those participants who received the high proportion of ethnic primes rated the target person in the story significantly more negatively (e.g., as more hostile and unfriendly) than did participants who received the low proportion of ethnic primes. Recall that Devine's view is that stereotypes are activated automatically. If this is so, then we should find that participants activate the black stereotype in the priming phase of the study (unconsciously) and go on to use it (without awareness) in the second part of the study (when forming an impression of the target). This should translate into higher ratings of the target as hostile, following a black prime. What about the differing levels of prejudice among participants? This was a very neat twist: if these results are found in both high- and low-prejudice individuals, it is stronger evidence still that stereotype knowledge is culturally shared and that activation is indeed automatic. If the priming effect can be demonstrated even among individuals who do not endorse the stereotype, this is pretty good evidence that it happened automatically. If low-prejudice participants could have found some way of controlling

this rather undesired response, they surely would have done so, since it is clearly at odds with their beliefs. In fact, Devine found that participants' prior level of prejudice made little difference to how susceptible they were to the ethnic primes (but see Lepore & Brown, 1997, and the discussion in Research close-up 4.3).

This study is one of a number that have investigated the so-called automaticity of stereotype activation (see also Banaji & Hardin, 1996; Perdue & Gurtman, 1990). The results seem to provide quite compelling evidence. Moreover, during the 1990s research in this area blossomed and the literature is now replete with evidence of the seeming automaticity of stereotype activation (for recent reviews see Bargh, 1999; Devine & Monteith, 1999).

So should we conclude that the case for the automaticity of stereotype activation is established beyond question? Perhaps not just yet. The situation regarding automaticity is actually rather complex and researchers themselves are divided in terms of how it is best interpreted (see Bargh, 1999; Devine & Monteith, 1999). Moreover, recent research has provided some important qualifications to the debate, as we shall see later in this chapter. For now, we will note that stereotypes are often automatically activated. The question we now consider is this: once a stereotype has been activated, what can happen next?

Schemas: The next step in the process?

Several years ago a British national daily paper ran an advertising campaign on television. The advertisements featured a skinhead running at speed towards a businessman. Plates 4.2a and 4.2b show two shots in the sequence; what do you think happened next?

Most people, when asked, assumed the next shot showed the skinhead mugging the businessman. Turn to Plate 4.2c, p. 73, to see what actually happened. The newspaper used this example to illustrate its commitment to impartial reporting – the need to get the full picture. Here it serves a useful educational purpose: it potently depicts what can happen once a category has been activated. Why did people jump to this conclusion? The answer lies in the spontaneous **encoding** of the situation. People see the skinhead, readily activate the pertinent skinhead schema (e.g., anarchic, violent) and arrive

> **encoding** the way in which we translate what we see into a digestible format to be stored in the mind

at the mistaken conclusion that he is probably about to behave aggressively. Encoding refers to the way in which we translate what we see into a digestible format to be stored in the mind (Fiske & Taylor, 1991).

This example illustrates that whilst it may be a useful strategy to leap to the first obvious conclusions when perceiving others, it is not always a sound one. The behaviour was somewhat *ambiguous*: there are many reasons why a person may be running in the direction of another. The important point is that, in this case, the activated schema *biased the interpretation of the behaviour* in line with the skinhead stereotype.

This tendency has been demonstrated in a number of laboratory experiments. Duncan (1976) showed white students a video

(a)

(b)

Plates 4.2a and b *Two stills of a skinhead in the* Guardian *advertising campaign.*

Table 4.1 *When do we rely upon schemas? (from Fiske & Taylor, 1991)*

Role schemas may dominate over traits (role schemas more informative)
Subtype schemas (business woman) may be used more than superordinate ones (woman)
Information presented early on can cue schemas (primacy)
We use schemas that attract our attention (salience)
We use schemas that have previously been primed (accessibility)
We use schemas consistent with our current feelings (mood)
We use schemas relevant to controlling outcomes (power)

featuring a quarrel between two protagonists, culminating in one shoving the other. The race of the person performing the shove and being shoved was varied. Half the participants saw a white person push either a black or a white person, whereas the other half saw a black person doing the pushing of either a black or white person. Later, participants were asked to describe what they had seen. Irrespective of the race of the 'victim', when the protagonist was black, 73 per cent of participants said he had acted in an aggressive manner, compared to only 13 per cent when the protagonist was white. Thus, exactly the same behaviour was encoded differently depending upon (and in line with the stereotype of) the race of the aggressor. Such studies reveal how schemas can bias the interpretation given to social events. Let's now consider the schema topic in more detail.

Once we have activated a category stereotype, we bring into play the *knowledge* contained within these structures: our schemas or stereotypes (Brewer, 1988; Fiske & Neuberg, 1990). Schemas are – stated simply – packets of pre-digested information we hold in our heads about objects or people from specific categories: our expectancies about objects or groups. As an illustration, consider the kinds of information that come to mind when the category 'class swot' or 'teacher's pet' is activated (e.g., the studious pupil in the class who does nothing but work and is readily described as *boring, shy, introverted, socially unskilled, never goes out, bookish, unpopular, generally disliked*). Clearly, several different types of information may be discerned, including, for example, knowledge about 'class swots' (what they typically do and don't do) and value judgements about them (their likeability, popularity, etc.) However, a schema should not be misconstrued as a long list of separate, unrelated items and attributes. Rather, it is a cognitive structure within which attributes are organized and relations between them perceived. Thus, we might perceive a relationship between the fact that 'class swots' are socially unskilled and don't go out much, or perhaps between the observation that they are boring and not very well liked.

So, a schema contains many different kinds of knowledge about a particular category. Armed with this knowledge, the process of impression formation is greatly facilitated, because schemas affect how quickly we perceive, notice and interpret available information (Fiske & Taylor, 1991; Kunda, 1999). We are apt to rely upon schemas for a number of reasons. Table 4.1 summarizes some of the main ones (from Fiske & Taylor, 1991).

So far, we have seen how schemas can influence what we pay attention to and the way in which information is encoded. Allied to this, schemas play an important role in the process of what we subsequently remember about others.

Schemas and person memory

Schema theory in social cognition draws heavily upon associated work in cognitive psychology suggesting that schematic representations aid the organization, **retrieval** and recognition of material in memory (Bransford & Johnson, 1972). Once a schematic expectancy

retrieval the process of recovering information from memory once it has been encoded

Plate 4.2c *Final still of the skinhead in the* Guardian *campaign.*

(a)

(b)

Plates 4.3a and b *What kind of music do you guess the stereotypical librarian and waitress listen to? Do they drink beer or wine?*

(stereotype) is activated, research has shown that we are often better able to recall information that is consistent, as opposed to inconsistent, with this schema (for a review, see Stangor & McMillan, 1992). A study by Cohen (1981) demonstrates this well. Participants were shown a video of a woman interacting with her husband. Before viewing the video, half were told the woman was a librarian, half that she was a waitress. Some behaviours were consistent with the stereotype of librarians but inconsistent with the stereotype of waitresses. For example, she wore glasses and listened to classical music (librarian stereotype). Other information was instead consistent with the waitress stereotype, but inconsistent with the librarian stereotype (drinks beer, affectionate towards husband).

In a later recall task, participants showed better memory for information that was consistent with the stereotype expectancy. According to researchers, this tendency is explained by the fact that consistent information fits better with what we expect to be true about a person (Hamilton, Sherman & Ruvolo, 1990). Our prior knowledge structures (schemas) help us to tie several pieces of new information together and link them to existing beliefs. Macrae, Milne and Bodenhausen (1994), for example, showed that memory for a series of traits associated with the doctor stereotype (e.g., *caring*, *upstanding*) was significantly improved when participants were given a stereotypic label (i.e., doctor) than when it was not provided.

However, research has not always found preferential recall for stereotype-consistent information. Stereotype-inconsistent information can also predominate in our recollections of others. Nonetheless, the schema is still playing a part. For example, if we have a very strong expectation that a colleague, Jim, is a kind, cheery sort, we will be rather taken aback if he one day seems to be acting in an aloof and serious manner. That is not the Jim we know, and we will be apt to remember this out-of-character (schema-inconsistent) behaviour as a result.

Many laboratory studies testify to this tendency. Hastie and Kumar (1979) gave participants a list of behaviours performed by a person whom they were led to believe was intelligent. Some of the behavioural descriptions fitted with this label (i.e., were stereo-type consistent), some did not (i.e., were stereotype inconsistent) and some were simply neutral with respect to the stereotype. When later probed for their memory, participants recalled more inconsistent than consistent information. So, what is driving this effect? Certainly, it seems plausible that information that violates our expectancies will grab our attention, but there is probably more to it than that. Precisely because this information is so out of step with what we expect, we face something of a cognitive struggle to reconcile it with what we already believe to be true (our pre-existing schema).

Hastie and Kumar (1979) argued that information that does not correspond to a prior expectancy is harder to comprehend. As a result, it is processed more deeply and it is ultimately more memorable. Later research does suggest that the process of *inconsistency resolution*, as it is called, is one that does demand attention. Pendry and Macrae (1999) asked particip-

inconsistency resolution the way in which we reconcile inconsistent information with a pre-established schema

ants to form an impression of a target. Half did so with no distrac-tions, but the other half were required to do so at the same time as memorizing a long string of digits (known as a digit rehearsal task). This extra task meant that they were unable to devote all their attention to the impression formation task. Hence, particip-ants' ability to recall more inconsistent information was signific-antly diminished when they formed an impression of the target under such cognitive load.

How do we reconcile these findings? Stangor and McMillan (1992) conclude their review by saying that inconsistent informa-tion will be preferentially recalled when participants are motiv-ated to be accurate and attend to all presented information. Under these conditions, participants will make considerable effort to re-concile inconsistent information, and will be more likely to recall it. However, when participants are not motivated to be accurate, or else are preoccupied with a distracting concurrent mental task, they are probably more likely to recall consistent information.

Whilst the picture appears complex, for our present purposes we need really only note one important point. When it comes to person memory, be it for information that is consistent or in-consistent with a prior expectancy, and whether the expectancy is provided at the encoding (information presentation) or retrieval (memory) stage, *schemas definitely matter*.

Schema activation and behaviour

In the late 1990s, a number of articles appeared that demonstrated a very intriguing phenomenon: behavioural responses (e.g., walk-ing slowly) can be automatically activated in response to an activ-ated stereotype-relevant word (e.g., 'wrinkle'). (See Research close-up 4.1.)

This same basic effect was subsequently demonstrated using a range of category stereotypes and trait concepts, and several behavioural consequences (e.g., intelligence tasks, interpersonal behaviour, memory performance: for a review, see Dijksterhuis

RESEARCH CLOSE-UP 4.1

The effect of priming on behaviour

Bargh, J.A., Chen, M. & Burrows, L. (1996). Automaticity of social behavior: Direct effects of trait construct and stereotype activation on action. *Journal of Personality and Social Psychology, 71*, 230–244.

....

Introduction

This set of studies builds upon past priming research that demonstrates how a recently activated trait construct or stereo-type, in an apparently unrelated context, can persist and exert an unintended effect upon the *interpretation of behaviour*. Here, the authors argue that *behavioural responses* to situations can also occur in response to an activated trait or stereotype prime. This rather disquieting suggestion is somewhat at odds with the prevailing assumption that behavioural responses to the social world are under conscious control. However, the authors rea-son that behavioural responses can be represented internally, just as are trait concepts and attitudes, and as such they should be capable of being automatically activated when triggering re-sponses from the environment are present.

In three studies, the authors set out to put this hypothesis to the test. Here we focus on Study 2a: Behavioural effects of activating the elderly stereotype, in which participants were primed either with the elderly stereotype or with a neutral prime, and their subsequent walking speed was assessed. The authors hypothesized that elderly-primed participants would demonstrate significantly slower walking speeds in comparison to neutral-primed participants.

Method

Participants
Thirty male and female students participated in the study.

Design and procedure
Participants were first asked to work on a scrambled sentence task under the guise of a language proficiency experiment. For each of 30 items, participants had to use the five words listed to construct a grammatically correct four-word sentence as quickly as possible. This task formed the priming phase, serving to activate (or not) the appropriate stereotype. Hidden within

the scrambled sentences were words either relevant to the elderly stereotype (e.g., *grey*, *bingo*, *wrinkle*) or neutral, non-age-specific words. Participants were randomly assigned to either the elderly or neutral prime condition. Importantly, elderly words associated with slowness (a common elderly stereotypic trait) were excluded from the elderly prime condition. After completing the task, participants were partially debriefed. A second experimenter then covertly recorded the amount of time participants took to walk down the corridor after leaving the laboratory. Finally, participants were fully debriefed.

Results

After the conclusion of the experiment, participants in the elderly priming condition walked down a hallway more slowly than neutral prime control participants (see Figure 4.1).

Discussion

These results, together with data from other studies reported in this article, provided compelling initial evidence in support of the authors' hypothesis. After participants were exposed to an elderly prime, they demonstrated motor behaviour in line with the activated stereotype (i.e., slower walking speeds). Importantly, the authors took care to exclude any references to time or speed in the stimulus materials, so the effect is not simply a result of trait priming. This suggests that the elderly-prime stimulus words instead activated the elderly stereotype in memory.

The take-home message is that social behaviour can be triggered automatically by relevant features of the stimulus environment and can occur without awareness. This finding is qualified somewhat by the authors' observation that it may only

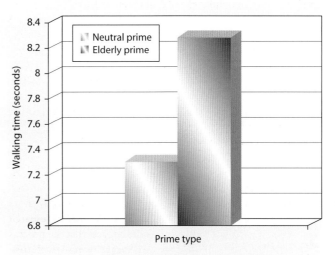

Figure 4.1 *Mean time (in seconds) needed to walk down a hallway as a function of prime type (from Bargh et al., 1996, Study 2a).*

occur if the behavioural representation activated by the prime is already associated with that situation, and that the motivation to act thus is part of the person's behavioural repertoire. As they note (Bargh et al., 1996, p. 240), 'It is doubtful, for example, that the participants in Experiment 2 left our building to go buy condos in Florida' (Florida being a popular spot for retired persons in the USA).

This paper spawned a great deal of interest and subsequent research. As an initial demonstration of what is termed 'automatic social behaviour', it remains a classic.

PIONEER

John Bargh (b. 1955) attended the University of Illinois as an undergraduate. He attended graduate school at the University of Michigan, with Robert Zajonc as his adviser. In 1981 he was awarded his PhD, and he then worked for several years at New York University. Currently he is at Yale University. He has received many prestigious awards, including the SESP Dissertation Award in 1982 and the APA Early Career Award for contributions to psychology in 1989. His research interests centre on the topic of automaticity and analysis of the unconscious nature of a wide range of psychological phenomena such as attitudes, emotions, motivations and social behaviour.

& Bargh, 2001). So, why does it happen? Again, automatic stereotype activation is thought to play a part. Think back to the work we reviewed earlier. Recall that once a social category (e.g., black) is activated, associated stereotypic traits (e.g., musical, hostile) are also activated (e.g., Devine, 1989). Likewise, trait words strongly linked to a particular category can act to cue the activation of the category. In the Bargh et al. (1996) study, for example, the trait primes associated with the elderly appeared to cue the activation of the elderly stereotype and lead participants to walk away from the experiment more slowly than non-primed participants.

Other studies have shown that category primes (e.g., professor) can cue the activation of associated traits and behaviours (e.g., intelligent, hard-working), leading to superior performance on an intelligence-related quiz (Dijksterhuis & van Knippenberg, 1998). So, when participants are primed with 'professor', this seemingly activates traits and behaviours associated with the category. Participants are therefore assumed to approach the subsequent quiz task with these traits unwittingly at the forefront of their minds, and the one that is relevant here (intelligence) exerts an influence upon performance.

Plate 4.4 *Primes associated with the elderly appear to cue the activation of the elderly stereotype (e.g., walking more slowly).*

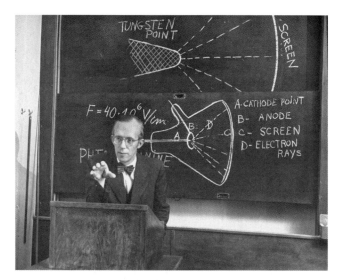

Plate 4.5 *Could being primed with a photo of a 'professor' make you perform better at a quiz?*

Research of this kind provides more evidence for the idea that stereotypes can be automatically activated and, in this case, lead to some rather unexpected consequences. Later on in this chapter, though, we shall see that such effects are not inevitable.

SUMMARY

Thus far, we have considered how stereotypes can be activated automatically and explored some of the consequences of this. Taken to an extreme conclusion, such research can generate some seemingly pessimistic conclusions about how much in control we are of our person-perception faculties. If so much goes on without our awareness, are we forever at the mercy of our processing frailties? That is certainly one interpretation of this literature (and for a spirited and compelling defence of this view, see Bargh, 1999). Many researchers, though, would argue that just because social information can be automatically activated, it does not necessarily follow that we will act in line with this information (Devine, 1989; Fiske, 2004; Monteith, Sherman & Devine, 1998; Monteith, Spicer & Tooman, 1998).

So, what factors cause us to look beyond our first schema-driven impressions and instead engage in a more systematic appraisal of the data? In the next section we shall consider a number of interlinked theoretical approaches that will provide some answers to this question.

These findings may at first seem somewhat implausible, but there is quite a lot of evidence accumulating in support of these results. In a recent review article, Dijksterhuis and Bargh (2001) provide a possible process explanation for their findings (see Figure 4.2).

They argue that the effects of stereotype activation on memory are mediated by trait activation. In other words, these effects are only shown when participants do activate the traits implied by the stereotype. Dijksterhuis, Aarts, Bargh and van Knippenberg (2000) showed that activating the elderly stereotype made participants more forgetful, but only if they actually associated the elderly with forgetfulness in the first place. Dijksterhuis and Bargh (2001) further note that trait concepts can activate behaviour representations. For example, activating the trait 'slow' results in activation of concrete behaviours such as 'linger' or 'dawdle'.

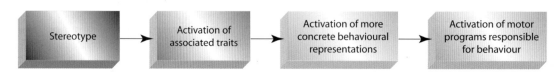

Figure 4.2 *A possible process explanation for the automatic social behaviour effect (from Dijksterhuis & Bargh, 2001).*

GOING THE EXTRA MILE: REGAINING COGNITIVE CONTROL

When are stereotypes not automatically activated?
Under what conditions does stereotype activation not lead to a stereotypic response?

Recently a colleague recounted the following story. He had been introduced at a party to a staff member from another department, computer science. He recounted his tale thus: 'When I first saw him I thought, computer nerd! The geeky 70s clothes, the old-fashioned specs, the terrible hairstyle. The kind of guy who drives a Skoda and watches endless episodes of *Star Trek*. But after a few minutes of talking to him, I had to think again. This guy was wild. A real party animal, who drove an Audi TT and enjoyed bungee jumping in his spare time. I couldn't have been more wrong.' This illustration hints at the yawning gap that can exist between our initial category-driven impressions and the reality of what lies beyond. The colleague took the time to get beyond his initial impression. In this section we'll look at when and why, like this colleague, we may go this extra mile.

Stereotype? What stereotype? Stopping the stereotype being activated in the first place

In the wake of early research implying the inevitability of stereotype activation, researchers have documented a number of qualifications to this view. Let's consider two indicative illustrations. Macrae and colleagues (1997) showed that stereotypes are not inevitably activated. Rather, perceivers have to process target information in a semantic manner in order to activate the stereotype (see Research close-up 4.2).

RESEARCH CLOSE-UP 4.2

The goal-dependent nature of stereotype activation

Macrae, C.N., Bodenhausen, G.V., Milne, A.B., Thorn, T.M.J. & Castelli, L. (1997). On the activation of social stereotypes: The moderating role of processing objectives. *Journal of Experimental Social Psychology, 33*, 471–489.

Introduction

This article challenged the classic view that mere exposure to a member of a stereotyped group is sufficient to activate the associated stereotype. The authors reason that the degree to which stereotypes may be automatically activated may relate to the extent to which we are interested in the social meaning of the stimuli we encounter. It is possible that in some situations (for example, when you are in a busy lecture hall trying to locate your friend) you are more concerned with navigating your way through the throng than with forming impressions of the individuals who comprise it. In such situations, where people are simply objects to be navigated around en route to your desired destination, perhaps you do not activate any stereotypes at all. This situation was one that was modelled in a study by Macrae et al. (1997, Study 1).

Method

Participants
Forty-eight students took part in the study.

Design and procedure
The study had a 3 (processing set: feature detection or semantic judgement or exposure) × 2 (trait type: stereotypic or counterstereotypic) mixed-design with repeated measures on the second factor. Participants were shown faces of female undergraduates and pictures of common household objects. One group of participants was asked to detect, by means of a key press, whether a white dot appeared on each picture (feature detection condition). A second group was told just to press a key once each picture appeared on screen (exposure condition). A third group (semantic condition) was directed to process the pictures in a semantic manner: to decide whether each picture was of an animate or inanimate object (this is a semantic task because, in order to reach this decision, participants need first to process the object in terms of what it is and what it is called – this is semantic processing).

Participants also completed a lexical decision task (LDT). Each time they responded to a picture, a letter string would appear on screen and participants had to decide if it represented a real word (e.g., emotional) or a non-word (e.g., ingrac). The logic is that participants are quicker to respond to words if the construct associated with the words has previously been activated. So, if the construct 'woman' is activated in the first phase of the study, participants should be quicker to respond to words associated with this category (e.g., emotional) than if the construct has not been activated.

Results

The dependent measures of interest were latencies of response on the LDT task (see Figure 4.3). The results suggested that on trials where a photo of a woman had been presented, responses to stereotypically female word strings were much faster than to counterstereotypical words. It seemed that the picture of a woman had indeed activated the female category. However, this effect was only found for participants who had been instructed to process the photographs in a semantic fashion. So the simple feature detection goal (i.e., check stimuli for spots) served to eliminate stereotype activation. For activation to occur, then, some basic level of interest in the target had to be present.

Discussion

This study provides evidence that stereotype activation is not always a spontaneous by-product of a triggering stimulus. Rather, activation only occurred when participants processed the target in a semantic manner. The authors assert that the activation (and indeed, application) of stereotypes is likely governed by pragmatic concerns, here related to the particular processing goals in place. In sum, and in line with a growing research literature, this study highlights the goal-dependent nature of stereotype activation.

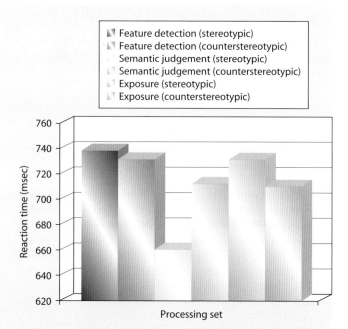

Figure 4.3 *Mean LDT (lexical decision task) latencies in msecs as a function of processing set and trait stereotypicality (from Macrae et al., 1997, Study 1).*
Note: Latencies for pictures of women (not objects) shown.

Stereotype activation is also affected by the extent to which participants endorse egalitarian world views. Moskowitz, Gollwitzer, Wasel and Schaal (1999) suggest there may be an effortless, preconscious form of cognitive control that in certain individuals prevents stereotype activation. Consider two people, Jack and Joe. Both would say they are low-prejudice, but whereas Jack would experience a feeling of incompleteness and self-disappointment upon learning that he had inadvertently acted in a stereotypic manner (and may want to do something about it), for Joe this realization would not be too troubling. Moskowitz et al. (1999) would view Jack as a 'chronic egalitarian': committed to being egalitarian, fair, tolerant and open-minded. Joe, on the other hand, would be more of a 'non-chronic egalitarian' in this respect. Do such differences impact upon stereotype activation? Moskowitz et al. (1999, Study 3) investigated this very question.

Participants were classified as chronic or non-chronic based upon responses to measures designed to assess commitment to egalitarian goals (here, with respect to fair treatment for women). In a second phase, participants saw photographs of men or women followed by an attribute, and were asked to pronounce this attribute as fast as possible. The attributes were either consistent with or irrelevant to the stereotype of women, and they were presented either 200 ms or 1,500 ms after the prime. Stereotype activation was demonstrated if participants were quicker to respond to stereotype-relevant attributes (e.g., kind) following stereotype-relevant primes (woman). Importantly, only non-chronics showed evidence of such stereotype activation. Participants with chronic goals failed to show this effect. This lack of activation could not, however, be due to conscious goals

exerted on the part of chronics, because the difference between chronics and non-chronics was found even when attributes were presented 200 ms after the prime (conscious control is possible only after 600 ms have elapsed between the presentation of a prime and a stimulus). This led Moskowitz et al. (1999) to conclude that stereotype activation is not inevitable.

These and several other studies temper the initially extreme conclusions reached about the inevitability and automaticity of stereotype activation. In a review article, Macrae and Bodenhausen (2000) argued that two factors seem to play a prominent role in the regulation of category activation: perceivers' temporary processing goals and their general attitudes (i.e., prejudice level). The research outlined above is in accord with this view. Hence, category activation would appear to be ***goal dependent*** (Bargh, 1994), arising from the interplay of cognitive and motivational factors. In sum, evidence is accumulating that suggests it is sometimes possible to prevent stereotype activation (for more detail see Bargh, 1999; Devine & Monteith, 1999; Moskowitz, 2005; see Research close-up 4.3, p. 82).

> **goal dependent** where an outcome is conditional upon a specific goal being in place (e.g., goal-dependent automatic stereotype activation)

Quashing the effects of stereotype activation once it has occurred

What happens, though, in those situations in which it is not possible to prevent activation? If stereotype activation happens, and we would really rather it hadn't, what can we do? Most researchers agree that perceivers are able to exercise some degree of choice in their responses towards others (Fiske, 1989), provided they are *aware* of the potential influence of the stereotype, have sufficient *cognitive resources* available to exert control, and are in some way *motivated* not to respond in a stereotypic fashion (Devine & Monteith, 1999). If we fulfil these important criteria, then there are a number of strategies at our disposal.

In this section we consider several theoretical approaches that have furthered our understanding of the processes that may intervene following stereotype activation: Fiske and Neuberg's (1990) continuum model of impression formation; Devine's (1989) dissociation model of stereotyping; research on stereotype suppression (e.g., Macrae, Bodenhausen, Milne & Jetten, 1994); and moderators of the perception–behaviour link (Dijksterhuis & Bargh, 2001).

Impression formation: The rocky road from category-based to individuated processing

When forming impressions of others, we commonly rely upon two sources of information: (1) knowledge of a person's category membership (e.g., female, elderly, as we saw in the work reviewed earlier) and (2) details of his or her personal or *individuating* characteristics (e.g., honest, forgetful). The persistent problem facing researchers has been to determine which of these contrasting sources of information contribute to the impressions derived (e.g., Brewer, 1988; Fiske & Neuberg, 1990).

Fiske and Neuberg's (1990) *continuum model of impression formation* provides one detailed answer to this puzzle. This model proposes that perceivers' evaluations of others fall somewhere along a continuum of impression formation, with category-based evaluations anchoring one end of the continuum and individuated responses the other. Constructed upon a number of theoretical premises, the model asserts that: (1) category-based responses have priority, and (2) movement along the continuum, from category-based to individuated responses, is a function of interpretational, motivational and attentional factors.

According to the model (and in line with much of the work we have already considered in this chapter), perceivers initially encounter a target and readily categorize him as a member of a particular social group. They then consider the personal relevance of the categorized target in the context of currently active concerns and goals. If the target is of little interest (e.g., the perceiver is merely passing a person in a street), then the impression formation process is short-circuited and resulting evaluations are predominantly category-based. If, however, the target is of at least minimal relevance (e.g., the target is an interviewer and the perceiver an interviewee hopeful of securing a new job), attentional resources are allocated to an appraisal of his or her personal attributes, and the protracted journey towards a more individuated

> **individuating information** information about a person's personal characteristics (not normally derived from a particular category membership)
>
> **continuum model of impression formation** a theoretical model advanced by Fiske and Neuberg (1990) that views impression formation as a process going from category-based evaluations at one end of the continuum to individuated responses at the other. Progress along the continuum is thought to depend upon the interplay of motivational and attentional factors

PIONEER

Susan Fiske (b. 1952) obtained her PhD from Harvard in 1978. After a number of years at the University of Massachussetts (Amherst) she moved to Princeton. In the course of her career she has amassed many prestigious awards, including (with Shelley Taylor) the 2003 Thomas Ostrom Award from the Person Memory Interest Group for work in social cognition. A past president of the American Psychological Society (2002–2003), she has published numerous articles, book chapters and books. Her current research focuses upon how stereotyping, prejudice and discrimination are encouraged or discouraged by social relationships, such as cooperation, competition and power.

impression begins. There are several stages at which processing can stop. An illustration of how this might work in practice in different situations is provided in Figure 4.4.

Thus, initial categorization is relatively spontaneous, but the social perceiver will only stop here if the motivation to go further is lacking or if there are pressures (e.g., scarcity of time) conspiring against a more systematic appraisal of the evidence. Research on perceiver motivation and its effects on the impression formation process has resulted in the identification of several goals and task objectives that reliably elicit more individuated processing. Among the most important are: (1) *outcome dependency* on a target (participants believe they will later meet the target and work together on a jointly judged task; Neuberg & Fiske, 1987; Pendry & Macrae, 1994); (2) perceiver *accountability* (perceivers believe they will have to justify their responses to a third party and be held responsible for their impressions; Pendry, 1998; Tetlock, 1983); and (3) accuracy-set instructions (perceivers are instructed to be as accurate as possible; Kruglanski & Freund, 1983).

> **outcome dependency** a motivational objective in which participants believe they will later meet a target and work together on a jointly judged task; shown to lead to less stereotypical target impressions
>
> **accountability** a processing goal whereby perceivers believe they will have to justify their responses to a third party and be held responsible for their impressions; this typically leads to less stereotypical impressions

While differing on a number of counts, these motivational factors all share a common feature: they increase perceiver involvement with the target and encourage more individuated impressions. However, motivation to engage in controlled processing may on its own be insufficient if cognitive resources are depleted. For example, Pendry and Macrae (1994, Study 1) led participants to believe they would meet and interact with Hilda, an elderly female. Half the participants were also made outcome dependent: they stood to gain £20 for their joint performance with Hilda on a word-puzzle task. The remaining participants would work with

	Example	Example	Example
Initial categorization	Woman encountered in busy supermarket with a clutch of kids trailing behind: probably a mother *Processing stops here*, target is of no further interest/perceiver is in a hurry	Person overheard in next office, has high-pitched voice: probably female Perceiver needs to know more (could be new work colleague), looks for more clues	Elderly person who is female called Hilda. Perceiver needs to know more (it's his prospective mother-in-law)
Confirmatory categorization		Person is applying make-up: definitely female Perceiver still not satisfied, processing continues	Hilda enjoys listening to *The Darkness* and visiting her grandchildren: not your average elderly woman; hard to confirm initial categorization as sufficient, perceiver carries on
Recategorization		Wait a minute, she is also carrying a briefcase and a palmtop organizer, so actually she is probably a *business* woman *Processing stops here*, perceiver is satisfied (realizes he will not be working with this business woman); recategorization will suffice	Hilda services her own car and likes spicy curries and flower arranging: defies an obvious recategorization, perceiver probes deeper
Piecemeal integration			This family-loving, elderly woman called Hilda enjoys loud modern music, calmer creative activities, is mechanically minded and thrives on a diet of chicken vindaloo and Bombay potatoes *Processing stops here*: target is not amenable to a categorical impression; perceiver satisfied with impression, although he has an extremely atypical mother-in-law

Figure 4.4 *Fiske & Neuberg's (1990) continuum model of impression formation: an illustration of how processing can stop at different stages.*

Hilda, but their outcome would not depend on her performance. All participants received the same information about Hilda, half of which (12 items) was stereotypic, half of which was counterstereotypic.

Whilst reading the profile, half the participants performed a resource-depleting concurrent mental task (digit rehearsal), the others simply read the profile. To assess their impressions, all participants were asked to rate six personality traits (three pretested as stereotypic and three as counterstereotypic with respect to elderly females) for how characteristic they were of Hilda. Pendry and Macrae predicted and found that the formation of an individuated impression was contingent upon participants being both motivated (here, by being outcome dependent) and having full processing capacity (i.e., not being required to rehearse the digit whilst forming the impression).

In a second study, Pendry and Macrae (1994) sought to establish whether participants who are outcome dependent rather than outcome independent devote a greater proportion of their attentional capacity when forming an impression of a target. The idea that motivated perceivers allocate more attention to processing information is a fundamental premise of Fiske and Neuberg's model, although support for it at that time was somewhat limited.

To test this hypothesis, Pendry and Macrae (1994, Study 2) used what is called a *probe reaction task* (PRT; see Bargh, 1982). Participants were instructed to optimize their performance on the impression formation task and to use their remaining attentional capacity to respond to a subsidiary probe stimulus (i.e., turning off a randomly illuminated light bulb that appeared several times on a computer screen whilst the impression task was being performed). Importantly, this probe reaction task was not a method of resource depletion (like the digit rehearsal task). That is, its purpose was not to divert attentional resources away from the primary impression formation task and make the process harder. Rather, it assessed what attention was not being used in the primary task (how much attention was left over). If more involving motivational goals do entail greater attention to the target, then we should expect that participants under these conditions would have less attention left over to switch off the light bulb quickly. This translates into slower reaction times on this measure for outcome-dependent participants. This is indeed what the study found (see Figure 4.5).

This research provides evidence for the view that motivated involvement with a target can lead to more controlled processing (and hence less stereotypic impressions; Neuberg & Fiske, 1987). More than this, it suggests that the extent to which we are able to go beyond initial, category-based impressions will be dependent upon the interplay between motivational and attentional factors. In sum, once attention is depleted, our ability to systematically process information about others, even if we are motivated to do so, may be diminished.

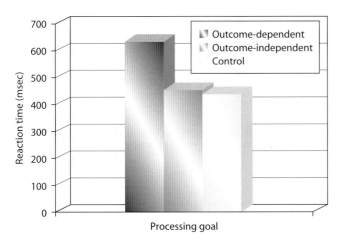

Figure 4.5 *Participants' mean probe reaction times (PRTs) in msecs as a function of processing goal (from Pendry & Macrae, 1994, Study 2).*

Replacing stereotypic thoughts with egalitarian responses As we saw earlier, Devine's (1989) paper provided some initial evidence for the automaticity of stereotype activation. Devine's thesis did not, however, stop there. In her *dissociation model* of stereotyping, she argued that automatic and controlled processes may be dissociated. What this means is that automatic activation of a stereotype does not inevitably lead to stereotypic responding.

> **dissociation model** a model that proposes that two different processes can occur independently, and that one does not inevitably follow from the other (e.g., Devine's theoretical model that proposes a dissociation between automatic and controlled processes in stereotyping)

Later research echoes this general sentiment. For example, Monteith (1993) has shown that when people are committed to being non-prejudiced and their behaviour appears to violate these standards, they feel guilty, become self-focused (direct attention towards the self) and direct their efforts at reducing this discrepancy to ensure it does not happen again. Hence, Monteith (1993) found that low-prejudice participants provided unfavourable (i.e., non-stereotypic) evaluations of jokes about gays, but only if they had been made to realize that in an earlier phase of the experiment they had (without realizing it) acted in a prejudiced fashion.

What research of this kind demonstrates is that it is possible to regulate stereotypic responding if (1) we are aware of the possibility of unconscious prejudicial influence, (2) we are sufficiently motivated (here, by virtue of a desire to appear unprejudiced) and (3) we have the required time available to do so (see Macrae & Bodenhausen, 2000). There are several issues of note here. For example, we may not always be aware of the unfelt influence of the stereotype (Bargh, 1999; Wilson & Brekke, 1994). Also, as we have seen, time or processing capacity limitations can impede even the most motivated perceiver (Pendry & Macrae, 1994). It is possible, too, that even if we are motivated to control stereotypic reactions, attempts at control can backfire for an altogether different reason, as we shall now see.

Stereotype suppression: Pushing the unwanted thought out of mind (if not always out of sight) Imagine you have just encountered an elderly woman in the supermarket. She looms large as you enter the fruit and veg aisle, thwarting your speedy passage to secure an aubergine by inconveniently standing right in front of you, consulting her shopping list. 'Dithery old biddy, it must be pension day!' you catch yourself thinking, and then you chastise yourself. You think, 'I really must stop this, she is no more in my way than anyone else, she is just rather older than most'. You try to banish such stereotypic thoughts and proceed to the dairy aisle. There, you encounter another elderly female. She is also in your way, but this time she's carefully weighing up the prices of different cheeses as you wait to extricate the last packet of Parmesan from the depleted shelf above her. How do you react to this second elderly female? Are you successfully able to suppress the elderly stereotype?

There has been a great deal of interest in precisely this topic: does *stereotype suppression* work? The research was stimulated by Wegner's (1994) ironic processes of mental control model. According to Wegner, when we try to suppress unwanted thoughts, two mental processes result. First, the intentional operating process (IOP) begins to search for thoughts that can serve as distractors (to distract us from thinking about the thing we don't want to think about). At the same time, a second, ironic monitoring process (IMP) kicks in, searching for evidence of the unwanted thoughts. In order to identify these unwanted thoughts, the IMP has to hold at some preconscious level the very thoughts one wants to suppress. Here's the important point: the IOP is a cognitively demanding process. To use the terminology we employed earlier, it entails controlled thinking. However, the IMP is thought to operate in an automatic manner.

> **stereotype suppression** the act of trying to prevent an activated stereotype from impacting upon one's judgements about a person from a stereotyped group

So what happens next? Because the IMP (the process that spots signs of suppression failure) can operate in the absence of cognitive resources, it is free to run mental riot even when resources are depleted, constantly searching for signs of failure (i.e., of the unwanted thought itself). Recall earlier we learned that constructs that were frequently activated (primed) become more accessible. Well, that is pretty much what is hypothesized to happen here. The unwanted thoughts on which IMP is focusing receive a healthy dose of priming and, without the IOP, become even more accessible. In other words, a *rebound effect* is demonstrated. The implication for stereotype suppression is that, under certain circumstances, the more people try to suppress stereotypes, the less successful they will be.

> **rebound effect** where suppression attempts fail; used here to demonstrate how a suppressed stereotype returns to have an even greater impact upon one's judgements about a person from a stereotyped group

Macrae, Bodenhausen, Milne and Jetten (1994) reported a series of experiments that demonstrate this rebound effect. In their first study, participants were asked to write about a day in the life of a skinhead, with a photo as a prompt (the study purportedly investigated people's ability to construct life event details from visual information). Half were told to avoid stereotypic thoughts about skinheads (i.e., suppress stereotype) while writing the passage, half were not. Later, they were shown another skinhead photograph

Automatic and controlled components of stereotypes and prejudice

Devine, P.G. (1989, Study 3). Stereotypes and prejudice: Their automatic and controlled components. *Journal of Personality and Social Psychology*, 56, 5–18.

Introduction

In her first study in this series, Devine demonstrated that all participants, whether high or low in prejudice, were equally knowledgeable of the cultural stereotype of blacks. The second study demonstrated that when participants' ability to consciously monitor stereotype activation was prevented, all participants responded in line with the activated stereotype (as we saw earlier). Devine's thesis did not, however, stop there. In her theoretical model, she argues that automatic and controlled processes may be dissociated. What this means is that automatic activation of a stereotype does not inevitably lead to stereotypic responding. When participants have time and motivation to correct for initially stereotypic thoughts, they will do so. Later on in the paper (Study 3), she set out to demonstrate this.

Method

Participants
Sixty-seven white students took part in the study. Participants were divided into high-prejudice (*N* = 34) and low-prejudice (*N* = 33) groups based on a median split of scores on the Modern Racism Scale (MRS; McConahay, Hardee & Batts, 1981).

Design and procedure
The design involved a simple one-way comparison between participants low vs. high on prejudice. Participants were run in small groups. First, they were asked to list as many alternate labels as possible for the social group black Americans (to include slang terms). This served to activate participants' cognitive representations of blacks. Following the label-generation task, they were asked to list their honest thoughts about the racial group blacks, under anonymous conditions. Afterwards, they completed the seven-item MRS.

Results

The proportion of pejorative and non-pejorative labels arising from the label-generation task was computed for each participant. A comparison between high- and low-prejudice participants revealed no significant differences in terms of the proportion of pejorative labels generated in the first phase. Then participants' responses to the thought-listing task were coded in terms of valence (positive or negative) and whether the thought concerned a belief about the group or was instead a trait description. Thus, there were four different kinds of thoughts coded (positive trait, negative trait, positive belief, negative belief).

Analyses of the frequencies of different types of thoughts listed by participants revealed that high-prejudice participants more often listed negative traits than each of the other three types of thoughts (which did not differ from each other). However, low-prejudice participants listed positive belief thoughts more often than the other three types of thoughts (which did not differ from each other).

Discussion

This study demonstrated that low-prejudice participants were able to provide non-stereotypic and egalitarian descriptions about blacks *provided they were given sufficient time to generate these descriptions*. As such, it appears to qualify the rather pessimistic conclusions highlighted by the first two studies in the paper.

It should be noted, though, that there are a few methodological issues associated with this paper. For example, although the first study appeared to show no differences in activation as a function of prejudice level, we cannot be sure activation differences do not exist (perhaps future research using a different method might still detect differences in activation). Allied to this, the MRS measure used in these studies may not be the most sensitive (or indeed the only) way to look at individual differences (as we saw with the Moskowitz et al., 1999, study). Second, the primes used were both category (e.g., *nigger*) and negatively valenced trait (e.g., *lazy*) types, so it is difficult to be sure that it is category priming and not simply semantic priming that is driving the effects. Later research focusing just on category labels (e.g., *blacks*) and neutral semantic associates (e.g., *ethnic*) showed that low-prejudice participants displayed less negative reactions to outgroup-related primes than did high-prejudice participants (e.g., Lepore & Brown, 1997). Finally, the stimulus materials were words, not pictures or real-life interactions. It may be unwise to assume effects will inevitably be similar irrespective of the nature of the prime (e.g., Gilbert & Hixon, 1991). Whilst later research has qualified some of these findings, this remains an extremely influential and widely cited paper in the field.

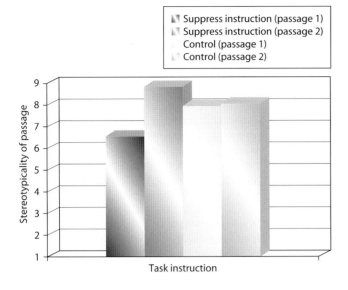

Figure 4.6 *Ratings of passage stereotypicality as a function of task instruction (from Macrae et al., 1994, Study 1).*

and asked to write a second passage. This time no 'skinhead suppression' instructions were given. The researchers hypothesized that if the 'suppression' participants experienced repeated stereotype priming in the first phase, then they might show evidence of a rebound effect in the second phase. As a result, their passages should be more stereotypic in the second phase. This is indeed what Macrae et al. found (see Figure 4.6).

Two additional studies provide further support for this finding. In a second study, the rebound effect was demonstrated in a different way (behavioural reactions). Participants initially suppressing a stereotype in the first phase elected to sit further away from a skinhead's belongings (i.e., where he would presumably return to sit down) in the second phase than participants who were not instructed to suppress. The final study used a lexical decision task to demonstrate that participants who were suppressing a stereotype about a skinhead later showed faster responses to traits related to the skinhead stereotype. This finding suggests that the initial suppression phase resulted in the stereotype becoming hyperaccessible. Later research developed these preliminary findings, in particular by showing that heightened self-focus can cause suppression to occur in a spontaneous fashion (e.g., Macrae, Bodenhausen & Milne, 1998).

Although these results paint a fairly convincing picture, several years and a handful of studies later some caveats are in order that pertain to methodological issues and concerns about external validity (for a review, see Monteith, Sherman & Devine, 1998). Consider the stereotypes used in these early studies. Skinheads (and in other studies, hairdressers, supermodels and construction workers) may not be groups for whom we feel a great need to suppress stereotypes (in comparison to, say, blacks, gays or women). Stereotyping certain groups may not carry the same potential penalties or condemnation. Also, people differ in terms of the extent to which they endorse or avoid stereotyping. Where

stereotypes of arguably more sensitive groups such as gays are studied, rebound effects are weakened among participants low in prejudice towards this group (e.g., Monteith, Spicer & Tooman, 1998). However, participants high in prejudice demonstrate the same rebound effects we saw earlier.

Several reasons are advanced for these differences (see Monteith, Sherman & Devine, 1998). It may be that people low in prejudice are more motivated to avoid prejudiced reactions (Fazio & Dunton, 1997); or that they are more practised in trying to rid themselves of stereotypic thoughts. Perhaps they have faster access to replacement (i.e., non-stereotypic) thoughts (e.g., Blair & Banaji, 1996); or they may be more motivated to form individuated impressions of others (e.g., Fiske & Neuberg's, 1990, continuum model mentioned previously). Finally, they may possess a goal state that encourages them to create a particular desirable state of mind (e.g., chronic egalitarian goals, as in the research by Moskowitz et al., 1999, we saw earlier) as opposed to suppressing an unfavourable one (stereotypes). Monteith, Sherman and Devine (1998) suggest that an important goal for future research will be to identify the part such factors play in stereotype regulation. For now, though, the initially gloomy picture about the consequences of suppressing stereotypes seems unwarranted.

The link between social perception and social behaviour is not inevitable Earlier, we saw some intriguing demonstrations of the link between stereotype activation (e.g., priming participants with elderly traits) and behaviour (e.g., participants walking more slowly). This seems quite compelling evidence for the inevitability of stereotype activation. Subsequent research has, however, enabled us to build a more balanced picture. It appears that whilst this effect does often happen, there are several factors which, when present, modify the typical pattern of results.

Many of the studies demonstrating the automatic effects of schema activation upon behaviour fail to take into account the potentially moderating effect of both factors inside the person (perceivers' motivations and goals) and factors outside the person (characteristics of the environment). Macrae and Johnston's (1998) paper neatly fills this gap. In the first study, participants were primed (here, with a trait construct: helping or not helping). As they were preparing to leave the experimental room to move to an adjacent laboratory, the experimenter dropped her belongings upon the floor, including a number of pens. Importantly, in one condition the pens were leaking badly, but in the other condition they were not. What Macrae and Johnston predicted and found was that participants were more likely overall to help following the helpful prime, but only when the pens were normal (helping was high in both help prime and control prime conditions: 93.7 per cent and 68.7 per cent, respectively). But the prime had no effect when the pens were leaky. Apparently, the thought of helping to pick up the pens and getting covered in ink was a strong disincentive to help in both priming conditions (help prime: 6.2 per cent and control prime: 12.5 per cent). In the second study, participants were again primed with the construct of helpfulness. In addition, they were told they were either on time or late. Again, as they got up to leave, the experimenter dropped her belongings, including some pens (none of which was leaking). Whilst participants primed with helpful were more inclined to help, this tendency was notably decreased for participants led to believe they were running late.

These findings imply that the typical effects of perception upon behaviour are dominated by current processing goals, when the behaviours needed to attain the goals are at odds with those implied perceptually (i.e., even though primed with helpful, the costs of being helpful in terms of getting covered in ink or being late serve to override the effects of the prime). Hence, behavioural control is viewed as a battle between activated schemas and various environmental cues and internal goal states either promoting or inhibiting the occurrence of certain action patterns (Shallice, 1988).

The effects of priming on automatic social behaviour seem also to be eliminated when participants' self-focus is increased (for more on effects of self-focus, see Chapter 5, this volume). Dijksterhuis, Bargh and Miedema (2000) primed participants with the politician stereotype (or did not). Half were seated in front of a mirror (high self-focus), half were not. Later they were all asked to write an essay about nuclear testing. Pre-testing had established that an aspect of the politician stereotype is that they are notoriously long-winded. Hence, the researchers hypothesized that the politician prime would result in longer essays. This was true, but only for participants in the low self-focus condition. Participants seated in front of a mirror did not show the effect.

So why does self-focus diminish the effects of the prime? The researchers argue that self-focus has been shown to activate what are termed *action tendencies* (Carver & Scheier, 1981). The action tendencies that self-focus can make more salient and accessible are certain norms, behavioural standards and goals. Here self-focus effectively serves to prevent the execution of an undesirable behaviour (being long-winded). Under conditions of self-focus, usual effects of perception on behaviour can be eliminated.

So, the situation regarding the seemingly automatic effects of schema activation upon behaviour is rather more elaborate than was first thought. In many cases, though, the effects of stereotypes and other schemas are far from inevitable.

Can schemas change?

So far we have discussed how it is possible for schema-based processing to be overridden by a more considered appraisal of available data. For example, how it is possible for us, once a stereotype has been activated (e.g., blacks are athletic and into gangsta rap; see Johnson, Trawalter & Dovidio, 2000), to avoid its effects in favour of judging a target in a more individuated fashion (this black person is a kind, gentle, classical music-loving person who adores his family). What we have not yet tackled is the extent to which schemas (in the form of stereotypes) can change. So, rather than having to overcome the activated stereotype, is it possible for the schema itself to be modified? It is possible, but that is not to say it is easy.

Recall that schemas, acting as cognitive shortcuts, are a functional way of parsing our social environment. They provide order and predictability. The benefits of having schemas ultimately mean there are often pressures to maintain them (Fiske & Taylor, 1991). Some of these pressures include our desire not to change schemas

even in the face of disconfirming evidence; the fact that thinking about a schema strengthens and commits us to holding it even more; and a seeming inability to reconsider if our old schematic beliefs are still applicable in the face of new information (see Fiske & Taylor, 1991). So why bother? As Fiske (2004, p. 156) neatly sums it up: 'the cost of constructing a new schema seems psychologically prohibitive'.

And yet, in certain circumstances, schemas *can* and *do* change. It is, after all, only worth relying upon our schemas when we have reason to believe they are serving us well. Having a schema that is incorrect or inaccurate can lead to errors in judgement and memory. Research suggests that schemas change when they are clearly disconfirmed, when people come across alternative schemas and take the time and trouble to scrutinize unique, individual instances (Fiske, 2004).

Within social cognition, several models of schema (stereotype) change have been proposed (Hewstone, 1994; Weber & Crocker, 1983). In the *bookkeeping* model, schema revision is viewed as a very steady process, whereby each new piece of disconfirming information is logged, leading to a very gradual modification of the original schema. The *conversion* model, however, predicts rather rapid and wholesale change of a schema in response to a large amount of disconfirming information. Finally, the *subtyping* model suggests that subcategories develop when faced with individuals from a category who strongly disconfirm it. This last model is better termed a model of maintenance, as opposed to change, since the formation of such subtypes effectively insulates the pre-existing stereotype from change.

A programme of research by Hewstone and his colleagues has focused closely upon specifying the conditions leading to schema change via the above routes (for a review see Hewstone, 1994; for alternative interventions to reduce prejudice, see Chapter 14, this volume, on intergroup relations). For example, in one study (Johnston & Hewstone, 1992, Study 1) participants (psychology students) received information about a group of physics students. Some of the information was consistent with the stereotype (dress in rather nerdy clothes), some was inconsistent (likes to go out) and some was neutral. Importantly, the pattern of inconsistent information was systematically varied. For some participants, the inconsistent information was concentrated in two out of the eight physics students (so they were really rather atypical); for others, this same information was dispersed across six members (who each only slightly disconfirmed the stereotype). A final intermediate condition distributed inconsistent information across four targets.

What these researchers found was that participants in the concentrated condition rated inconsistent traits as significantly less characteristic of the group than did participants in either the intermediate or dispersed conditions. It is likely, then, that participants in the concentrated condition lumped the two wildly inconsistent individuals into a single atypical subtype and did not incorporate them in their subsequent evaluations of the group. Where there were several examples of individuals who each disconfirmed the stereotype, even if only slightly (as in the dispersed and, to some extent, the intermediate conditions), this inconsistent information was rated as more characteristic of the group.

The take-home message here is that for schemas to change, it is not enough simply to encounter disconfirming information.

Schema change may be more likely when we encounter several people who seem to be just a bit unlike the stereotype, as opposed to encountering just one or two who really seem to disconfirm it greatly. The fit between target members and group is so weak that little or no effort is made to integrate the inconsistent information. It is hence easier to discount these extreme individuals as too atypical to be taken seriously. In sum, stereotypes can change in response to disconfirming information, but an important moderating factor is the manner in which the disconfirming information that should promote change is presented to us.

SUMMARY

In this section, we have seen how it is sometimes possible to exert control over stereotype activation. Moreover, we may still be able to rescue the situation even if stereotypes have been activated, provided we are aware of the potential influence of the activated stereotype, are motivated not to stereotype and are cognitively able to do so. Finally, we have seen how, under certain conditions, it is possible for stereotypes to change. So, the picture may be less bleak than we might have feared.

SUMMARY AND CONCLUSIONS

Now that you have reached the end of this chapter, you are in a better position to provide answers to some of the questions posed at the beginning. Let's revisit them and then recap on what we have covered.

- Why did I assume that the man at the coffee machine in the boardroom was the company director when he was in fact the secretary?

- Why did I assume that Dr Alex James would be male/white?

- Why is it that I expected Albert to be elderly?

Answer: automatic stereotype activation. Categories like gender, race and age are readily activated in the presence of a person from or a name associated with these groups.

- Why did it surprise me to discover that Hilda, my elderly neighbour, had a passion for car maintenance?

Answer: we expect, and often seek out, information that is consistent with our stereotypes. An elderly female's penchant for wielding the spanner violates our well-established expectancies of what little old ladies typically do.

- Why did I take the time to talk to my new black work colleague and find myself subsequently re-evaluating my initially stereotypic impression of her?

Answer: when we are motivated – for example by virtue of needing to get along with someone or because we are low in prejudice towards members of that group – and have the cognitive resources available, we are able to move beyond initial category-based impressions to form more individuated ones.

- Social cognition research has provided us with some important theoretical clues about when and why we engage in automatic versus controlled processing of social information.

- Automatic processes are those that occur without intention, effort or awareness and are not expected to interfere with other concurrent cognitive processes. Controlled processes are intentional, under an individual's volitional control, effortful and entail conscious awareness.

- Often, stereotype activation can occur automatically. Once a category is activated, we can bring into play the knowledge contained within these structures (schemas). Schemas affect how quickly we perceive and interpret available information, and impact on subsequent processes of judgement and memory. They can also impact upon our behaviour, as shown by research into the perception–behaviour link.

- Sometimes we process social information more systematically. We may, under certain circumstances, not activate stereotypes at all. If we do activate them, we may engage in several strategies to avoid responding in a stereotypic way. For example, we may engage in a more complex appraisal of the available information (individuated impression formation), replace stereotypic thoughts with more egalitarian ones or attempt to suppress the stereotype. Under certain conditions, too, stereotypes can change.

- Some researchers, such as Bargh (1999), consider that stereotype activation is more inevitable than we might like. Others, like Devine and Monteith (1999), take a more cautious view, arguing that control appears to be possible, at least some of the time.

- This chapter has used the automatic/controlled distinction as a focus to introduce you to some of the fascinating theoretical questions and research methodologies that typify social cognition research. The research conducted in this area speaks to issues of considerable social importance. Researchers will continue to pose intriguing questions and develop yet more sophisticated ways in which to assess the complex processes that underlie our daily mental life.

Suggestions for further reading

Bargh, J.A. (1999). The cognitive monster: Evidence against the controllability of automatic stereotype effects. In S. Chaiken & Y. Trope (Eds.), *Dual process theories in social psychology* (pp. 361–382). New York: Guilford. A spirited and utterly engaging defence of the inevitability of stereotype activation.

Devine, P.G. & Monteith, M.J. (1999). Automaticity and control in stereotyping. In S. Chaiken & Y. Trope (Eds.), *Dual process theories in social psychology* (pp. 339–360). New York: Guilford. A slightly more even-handed debate on the same topic.

Dijksterhuis, A. & Bargh, J.A. (2001). The perception–behavior expressway: Automatic effects of social perception on social behaviour. In M. Zanna (Ed.), *Advances in experimental social psychology* (Vol. 33, pp. 1–40). San Diego, CA: Academic Press. This chapter brings together much of the recent literature on this topic and attempts to provide a better understanding of the mechanisms that may underlie the effects.

Fiske, S.T. & Taylor, S.T. (1991). *Social cognition* (2nd edn). New York: McGraw-Hill. This is the classic text on the topic, with extensive coverage of a wide range of issues within the discipline.

Macrae, C.N. & Bodenhausen, G.V. (2000). Social cognition: Thinking categorically about others. *Annual Review of Psychology*, *51*, 93–120. A thorough, readable overview of the literature.

Monteith, M.J., Sherman, J.W. & Devine, P.G. (1998). Suppression as a stereotype control strategy. *Personality and Social Psychology Review*, *2*, 63–82. A clear, considered and interesting review of the literature.

Moskowitz, G.B. (2005). *Social cognition: Understanding self and others*. New York: Guilford. A welcome new addition, bang-up-to-date, engagingly written and comprehensive in scope.

5 Self and Social Identity

Bernd Simon and Roman Trötschel

CHAPTER OUTLINE

....

This chapter reviews social psychological theory and research on self and social identity. We start with an explanation of the meaning and role of self and identity as social psychological concepts. The remaining part of the chapter is organized around seven prominent themes of the self: self-concept and self-knowledge, continuity of self over time, self-awareness, self as agent and regulatory process, self-evaluation and self-esteem, self-extension and levels of identity, and finally, cultural impact on self and identity.

Introduction

....

A taste of self

Think first of swallowing the saliva in your mouth, or do so. Then imagine expectorating it into a tumbler and drinking it! What seemed natural and 'mine' suddenly becomes disgusting and alien . . . What I perceive as belonging intimately to my body is warm and welcome, what I perceive as separate from my body becomes, in the twinkling of an eye, cold and foreign.

This juicy thought experiment was suggested by Gordon Allport (1968, p. 28) – a pioneer of social psychology (see Pioneer box, Chapter 14, p. 309) – many decades ago to illustrate the experiential reality of our sense of self. What is associated with or included in our selves obviously acquires a distinct psychological quality very different from that of things dissociated or excluded from the self. Although Allport's (1968) illustration draws on the role of our physical bodies as an anchor of our sense of self, it will soon become clear that a bodily sense is by no means the only, and possibly not even a necessary, anchor of the self. However, the thought experiment nicely illustrates that the notion of self or identity is indispensable as an explanatory concept in order to make sense of otherwise unintelligible variations or even qualitative shifts in human experiences.

Admittedly, the shift from an accepting attitude towards saliva inside our mouth (self) to a rather negative attitude towards saliva outside our mouth (non-self) is a relatively innocuous phenomenon. But remember how you felt about yourself the last time you failed an exam in school, or when you were praised for an excellent performance in class. Also, how do you feel when you go to the stadium to support your favourite football team? Or when you listen to your favourite singer, who always finds the right words to express what you are thinking about life? These are important experiences that can dramatically influence how you see yourself (e.g., you may be ashamed or proud of yourself) and how you behave towards other people (e.g., you ridicule or even attack the

self and identity from a social psychological point of view, self and identity are shorthand expressions for an ensemble of psychological experiences (thoughts, feelings, motives, etc.) that reflect and contribute to a person's understanding of his or her place in the social world

supporters of the rival team). In social psychological terms, your *self* or *identity* is implicated in such situations. The terms 'self' and 'identity' are used here as shorthand expressions for an ensemble of psychological experiences (thoughts, feelings, motives, etc.) that both reflect and influence a person's understanding and enactment of his or her place in the social world.

It is noteworthy that our subsequent discussion of self and identity reflects two influential traditions in social psychology, one of which is primarily of North American origin while the other started as a distinctly European endeavour. Within the North American tradition, the term 'self' is usually preferred to the term 'identity', and the self is typically conceptualized in rather individualistic terms. This is especially true for the social cognition (or social information processing) perspective, which has served as the leading paradigm of this tradition since the 1970s (see Chapter 4, this volume). To be sure, the social cognition perspective does not deny the social dimension of the self, but it sees the roots of the social self primarily in interpersonal relations, while intergroup relations play a minor role. To the extent that a person's group membership is taken into account, it is usually construed as just another individual feature that, together with the person's numerous other individual features, makes up her unique cognitive self-representation which, in turn, feeds into social information processing. The European tradition, with the social identity perspective as its leading paradigm (Tajfel & Turner, 1979, 1986; Turner, Hogg, Oakes, Reicher & Wetherell, 1987) and its preference for the term 'identity', emphasizes the pivotal role of group memberships and intergroup relations. It adds another distinct social dimension to identity (or self) in that it focuses on the antecedents and consequences of collectively shared identities (or selves).

The coexistence of these different though not necessarily mutually exclusive traditions with their respective terminologies is

the reason why we often use the composite expression 'self and identity', although, where possible, we use either the term 'self' or the term 'identity' depending on the traditional background of the theoretical approaches and research under discussion.

The remainder of the chapter is divided into eight sections. First, we clarify the meaning and role of self and identity as social psychological concepts. The remaining sections deal in turn with the following themes: self-concept and self-knowledge, continuity of self over time, self-awareness, self as agent and regulatory process, self-evaluation and self-esteem, self-extension and levels of identity, and cultural impact on self and identity. We thus review the core classic self-themes (G. Allport, 1955, 1968), but also include more recent research trends (e.g., cultural impact). While an overarching theoretical framework that integrates all of these themes into a single coherent whole has yet to be developed, it may be helpful to read the major sections of this chapter while using the metaphor of the self as a system. That is, a person's self or identity may be likened to an *open system*, with the different self-themes capturing important characteristics of open systems. For example, open systems show patterns of activities of exchange with their external environment, tend towards a dynamic equilibrium, have inbuilt (negative) feedback and self-correction mechanisms, and they develop more components or levels as they expand (for a fuller discussion, see Pettigrew, 1996).

Analogously, the self-concept and related self-knowledge can be viewed as a pattern of recurring cognitive activities such as processing of self-related information or stimulation received from one's social environment. This also makes the cultural impact on self and identity possible. Continuity of self over time can be understood as an instance of dynamic equilibrium, while self-awareness and self-evaluation can function as important feedback mechanisms. These mechanisms, in combination with the self as agent and regulatory process, make self-correction and self-improvement possible. Finally, self-extension and the differentiation of various levels of identity resemble system expansion and the ensuing structural differentiation.

SELF AND IDENTITY AS SOCIAL PSYCHOLOGICAL CONCEPTS

Is the self the thinker or the thought?
Are self and identity antecedents or consequences of social interaction?

The notions of self and identity suggest that each of us has an answer to the basic question 'Who am I?' What is more, this reflective process seems to require both a subject and an object of

knowledge – a complication that has kept philosophers busy for centuries (Viney, 1969). Thus Immanuel Kant (1781/1997) introduced the distinction between self as object (the empirical self) and self as subject (the pure ego), which was further pursued by Arthur Schopenhauer (1819/1995) as the distinction between 'the known' and 'the knower' and later by the philosopher and psychologist William James (1890/1950) as the distinction between 'Me' and 'I'.

Building on these distinctions, the psychologist Gordon Allport (1961, 1968) argued that the 'I' should be sharply segregated from the 'Me' because, unlike the 'Me', the 'I' cannot be an object of direct knowledge (see also Markus & Wurf, 1987, p. 314). Accordingly, Allport claimed the problem of the 'Me' for psychology while consigning the problem of the 'I' to philosophy. Note, however, that James (1890/1950) originally argued against such a strict separation of the 'I' and 'Me', though not necessarily against an analytic distinction between the two. For James, the words 'I' and 'Me' are grammatical constructions designed to indicate and emphasize different interpretations of the same *stream of consciousness*, namely interpretations either as *thinker* ('I') or as *thought about oneself* ('Me'). In the final analysis, these interpretations would then be inseparable because 'thought is itself the thinker' (James, 1890/1950, p. 401) – just as the river is inseparable from the water.

The distinction and relation between 'I' and 'Me' (knower and known, thinker and thought) is obviously a complex matter, a fuller discussion of which is beyond the scope of this introductory text. As a general guideline, we opt for the view that there is no need to postulate a separate 'I' that presides over or stands behind the objective person experienced as 'Me' (Flanagan, 1994). Rather, it is the whole human organism with its functional nervous system and active involvement with the external world that enables and guides a stream of experience and consciousness. This stream includes the capacity for self and identity, both in the active subject or agent mode (i.e., as thinker or knower) and in the passive object mode (i.e., as thought or known). This is a compelling view for social psychologists because it fits in with the more general assumption, widely shared in the field, that psychological phenomena can be understood as a joint or interactive function of the personal organism's mind and its environment.

Social psychology as a scientific discipline is concerned with human experience (thoughts, feelings, etc.) and behaviour as they unfold in the context of social interaction. As depicted in Figure 5.1, the relation of self and identity processes to social interaction is twofold. On the one hand, self and identity can be viewed as outcomes or consequences of social interaction. On the other hand, they can be viewed as antecedents that guide subsequent social interaction. In more technical terms, self and identity play a dual role as social psychological concepts in that they can be construed both as a dependent variable or phenomenon to be explained and as an independent variable or phenomenon that explains some other phenomenon.

Acknowledging this dual role, social psychologists have come to conceptualize self and identity as a social psychological mediator – that is, as a variable process that takes shape during social interaction and then guides subsequent interaction. For example, during a discussion with fellow students on some political issue such as abortion, gay marriage or genetic cloning, you may come to see yourself (and others) as either pro or con, or even more generally, as either liberal or conservative. This self-view then impacts on your subsequent behaviour in that it influences how you interact with your fellow students as the discussion continues and possibly also how you relate to them in the future (e.g., whom you invite to your next birthday party). Note that this dynamic, process-oriented approach does away with more static beliefs that view the self or identity as a thing or even as a person-like little creature inside the real person (for further discussion, see Simon, 2004).

SUMMARY

The social psychological analysis of self and identity is concerned with people's answers to the fundamental question: 'Who am I?' In accordance with recent philosophical thinking, the notions of self and identity are used here as shorthand expressions for the variable process of self-understanding which results from the complex interplay between personal mind and social environment. Moreover, this process is viewed as a social psychological mediator which both reflects and guides social interaction.

SELF-CONCEPT AND SELF-KNOWLEDGE

How is knowledge about ourselves cognitively represented?
What are the consequences of different degrees of self-complexity?
How do we know about ourselves?

Most, if not all, of us would claim to have some idea of who we are. Accordingly, psychologists assume that people possess a *self-concept*. A self-concept is a cognitive representation of oneself that gives coherence and meaning to one's experience, including one's relations to other people. It organizes past experience and helps us to recognize and interpret relevant stimuli in the social environment. We will illustrate these processes with reference to *self-schema*, *self-complexity* and sources of *self-knowledge*.

> **self-concept** a cognitive representation of oneself that gives coherence and meaning to one's experience, including one's relations to other people. It organizes past experience and helps us to recognize and interpret relevant stimuli in the social environment

Self-schema

Markus (1977) introduced the social cognition perspective on the self and suggested *self-schemas* as the key components of the self-concept. She defined self-schemas as 'cognitive generalizations about the self, derived from past experience, that organize and guide the processing of self-related information

> **self-schema** a cognitive generalization about the self, derived from past experience, that organizes and guides the processing of self-related information contained in the individual's social experiences

Figure 5.1 *Self and identity as a social psychological mediator.*

contained in the individual's social experiences' (Markus, 1977, p. 64). For example, someone is said to possess an independence self-schema when she considers the feature 'independent' highly self-descriptive and at the same time regards this feature as an important component of her self-description. Such self-schemas can affect how we process information about the self in important ways. More specifically, Markus (1977, Study 1) observed that self-schemas increased both the likelihood that schema-congruent trait adjectives were judged as self-descriptive and the speed with which such judgements were made (see Research close-up 5.1). Markus (1977, Study 2) also found that self-schemas strengthened resistance to schema-incongruent information. That is, people seem

rather unwilling to accept information as self-descriptive that contradicts their self-schemas.

Subsequent research by Markus and colleagues (Markus, Smith & Moreland, 1985) revealed that self-schemas also play a role in the processing of information about other people. People with a self-schema in a particular domain seem to have acquired a domain-specific expertise which provides them with an interpretative framework for understanding the thoughts, feelings and behaviours of others. For example, if you have a masculinity self-schema (i.e., you see yourself as very masculine and this attribute is very important to your self-concept), you will be particularly ready to attribute much of other men's behaviour to their

RESEARCH CLOSE-UP 5.1

Self-schemata and how we process information about the self

Markus, H. (1977). Self-schemata and processing information about the self. *Journal of Personality and Social Psychology, 35*, 63–78.

....

Introduction

Markus (1977) proposed that attempts to organize, summarize or explain one's own behaviour in a particular domain will result in the formation of cognitive structures about the self. For such cognitive structures she then coined the term 'self-schema'. Markus further suggested that, once established, self-schemas have important consequences for subsequent information processing about the self. In her first experiment, she predicted that people who have developed a self-schema in a particular domain (e.g., independence) should process information about the self concerning this domain with relative ease. For example, they should judge a greater number of adjectives that are congruent with the self-schema (e.g., individualistic or ambitious in the case of an independence self-schema) as self-descriptive than should people who have not developed such a self-schema. People with a self-schema should also make such judgements faster (i.e., evince shorter response latencies) for schema-congruent adjectives than for schema-incongruent adjectives. Additional predictions were that self-schemas would make it easier to retrieve evidence for past schema-congruent behaviour of oneself and that self-schemas would increase the perceived likelihood of future schema-congruent behaviour.

Method

Participants
One hundred and one female students took part in an initial questionnaire phase, of whom 48 students qualified for a subsequent laboratory phase of the experiment.

Design and procedure
In the initial questionnaire phase, 101 respondents provided a number of self-ratings related to the independence–dependence dimension. From these respondents, three groups of 16 students each were selected to participate in the experimental sessions three to four weeks later. The three groups were (1) students with an independence self-schema (*Independents*), (2) students with a dependence self-schema (*Dependents*) and (3) students with neither an independence nor a dependence self-schema (*Aschematics*). Independents had indicated in the initial questionnaire that they were highly independent and that this attribute was very important to their self-description. The same was true for Dependents with respect to the attribute dependent. Finally, Aschematics had indicated that they were neither independent nor dependent and that these attributes were not important to their self-description.

In the experimental phase, participants were then presented with a number of trait adjectives. In addition to several practice and control adjectives, they were presented with 15 trait adjectives congruent with an independence self-schema (e.g., individualistic, ambitious, self-confident) and 15 trait adjectives congruent with a dependence self-schema (e.g., conforming, submissive, cautious). Following the presentation of each adjective, participants were required to respond by pushing a *me* button if the adjective was self-descriptive, or a *not me* button if the adjective was not self-descriptive. The response latency was recorded by an electronic clock beginning with the presentation of the stimulus. The experimenter thus obtained information concerning both the content and the speed of participants' self-descriptions. In addition, participants were asked to supply specific evidence from their own past behaviour to indicate why they felt a particular trait adjective was self-descriptive, and they were provided with a number of schema-congruent and schema-incongruent behavioural descriptions for which they had to indicate 'how likely or how probable it is that you would behave or react in this way?'

Results

As shown in the top two panels of Figure 5.2, participants with an independence self-schema judged a greater number of adjectives associated with independence as self-descriptive (*me* judgements) than did participants with a dependence self-schema, and vice versa for adjectives associated with dependence. Furthermore, as shown in the bottom two panels of Figure 5.2, Independents were also much faster at making *me* judgements for independent adjectives than for dependent adjectives whereas the opposite was somewhat true for Dependents. Aschematics (people with neither an independence nor a dependence self-schema) judged both types of adjective at an intermediate level and did not differ in response latency for *me* judgements concerning the two types of adjectives. In addition to such content and speed effects, Markus reported that self-schemas facilitated the retrieval from memory of schema-congruent behavioural episodes and increased the perceived likelihood of future schema-congruent behaviours.

Discussion

The experiment provided empirical support for the concept of self-schema and its role in information processing about the self. Self-schemas obviously facilitate self-judgements on schema-congruent dimensions and provide a basis for schema-congruent retrieval of one's past behaviour and schema-congruent prediction of one's future behaviour. In addition, a second study demonstrated that self-schemas can strengthen resistance to schema-incongruent information. That is, both Independents and Dependents were more unwilling to accept schema-incongruent information than were Aschematics. Markus concluded that her findings have important implications also for research on personality. In particular, she suggested that it is people with self-schemas in a particular domain who are most likely to display a correspondence between self-description and behaviour and to exhibit cross-situational consistency in the respective domain.

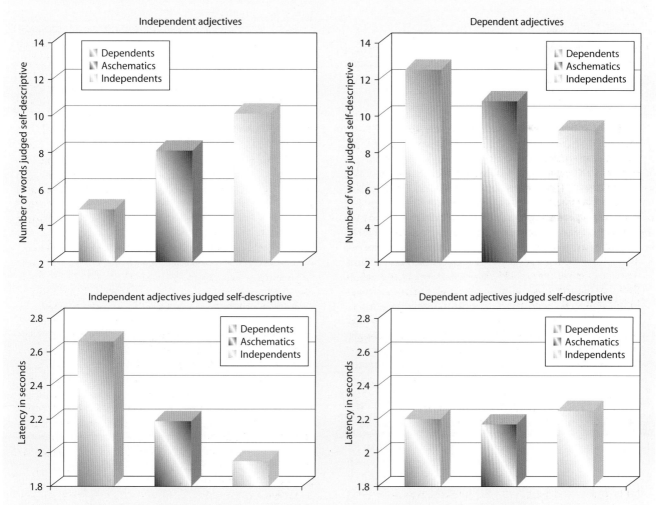

Figure 5.2 *Top panels: Mean number of independent and dependent adjectives judged self-descriptive. Bottom panels: Mean response latency for independent and dependent adjectives judged self-descriptive (Markus, 1977, Figure 1).*

PIONEER

Hazel R. Markus (b. 1949) received her BA from California State University at San Diego and her PhD from the University of Michigan. She has written highly influential articles on self-schemas, possible selves, the influence of the self on the perception of others and on the constructive role of the self in adult development. Her most recent work is in the area of cultural psychology and explores the interdependence between psychological structures, processes and sociocultural environments. She was elected to the American Academy of Arts and Sciences in 1994 and was then named the Davis-Brack Professor in the Behavioral Sciences at Stanford University. Currently Hazel Markus is a Professor of Psychology at Stanford University. She serves as the co-director of Stanford's Research Center for Comparative Studies in Race and Ethnicity.

masculinity. In other words, self-schemas provide us with wider pigeonholes when it comes to making sense of other people's behaviour.

Self-complexity

So far our focus has been on the *content* of the self-concept. However, the *structure* of the self-concept also deserves attention. For example, according to Linville (1985, 1987), people differ in the number of independent components or self-aspects that make up their self-concepts and are used for processing self-related information. In short, people differ in **self-complexity**, which is defined

> **self-complexity** a joint function of the number of self-aspects and the degree of their relatedness. High self-complexity occurs with a large number of independent self-aspects, whereas low self-complexity occurs with a small number of highly interrelated self-aspects

as a joint function of the number of self-aspects and the degree of their relatedness. High self-complexity thus occurs with a large number of independent self-aspects, whereas low self-complexity occurs with a small number of highly interrelated self-aspects. Self-aspects can concern, among other things, physical features, roles, abilities, preferences, attitudes, traits or explicit group or category memberships. Note that the notion of self-aspect is broader than that of self-schema. Whereas self-schemas are viewed as rather stable core components of one's self-concept, the notion of self-aspect also includes less central cognitive categories. For example, I may be well aware of my preference for rock music (self-aspect) without, however, considering it a very important component of my self-concept (self-schema).

Self-complexity as a structural feature of the self-concept has primarily been examined with respect to its implications for

mental and physical well-being. Think of a bad event that recently happened to you, perhaps when you failed an exam or when you were rejected by someone you really felt attracted to. How sad or even depressed did you feel? Now, think of a good event. Perhaps you were praised for a good piece of work or you had a great game in your favourite sport. How happy did you feel then? And how different were your feelings after the good event from your feelings after the bad event?

Research suggests that the extremity of good and bad feelings after pleasant and unpleasant events, respectively, depends on self-complexity. For example, when Linville (1985) confronted research participants either with a success or a failure experience, she found that participants with low self-complexity responded with more positive feelings to the success experience and with more negative feelings to the failure experience than did participants with high self-complexity. In short, low self-complexity was generally associated with more extreme emotional reactions than was high self-complexity, most likely because the self-aspects affected by success or failure (e.g., the self-aspect as a competent student) represented a larger portion of the overall self-concept for people with low self-complexity than for people with high self-complexity.

Research thus indicates that a complex self-structure can protect the individual from emotional turmoil. Just as it may be wise 'not to put all one's eggs in one basket', a more complex self-structure can serve as a healthy buffer against unpleasant experiences and frequent swings in mood – especially when high self-complexity is due to possession of many different positive self-aspects (Morgan & Janoff-Bulman, 1994; Woolfolk, Novalany, Gara, Allen & Polino, 1995).

Sources of self-knowledge

Both self-schemas and self-complexity derive from what we (seem to) know about ourselves. But where does our **self-knowledge** come from? A common answer with much intuitive appeal is that people gain self-knowledge through the careful examination of their own thoughts, feelings, motives and reasons for behaving in a particular way. Such **introspection** helps to reveal some of the contents of one's consciousness, such as

> **self-knowledge** knowledge about one's own characteristics, abilities, opinions, thoughts, feelings, motives, etc. Introspection seems to be a rather limited source of self-knowledge. Better sources are observation of one's own behaviour, careful examination of other people's perceptions of us and self–other comparisons.

> **introspection** the examination of one's own thoughts, feelings, motives and reasons for behaving in a particular way. It does not guarantee valid knowledge about oneself, but involves a constructive process of putting together a coherent and acceptable narrative of one's self and identity

one's *current* thoughts and feelings, but it also has serious limitations and even drawbacks (Wilson & Dunn, 2004). For example, people are commonly motivated to keep unwanted thoughts, feelings or memories out of consciousness. At the same time, the suppressed material continues to influence people even without their awareness. Introspection is therefore at best an imperfect source of effective self-knowledge. Moreover, introspection may even reduce accurate self-knowledge. Wilson and LaFleur (1995) asked university students to make a number of predictions about their future behaviour during the semester (e.g., going to a movie with a particular fellow student). Before making the predictions, half of the students were required to analyse why they might or might not perform each behaviour. The remaining students were in a control condition and made the predictions without the instruction to analyse reasons. The researchers found that analysing reasons increased the likelihood that students would say they would perform the critical behaviour, but analysing reasons did not alter people's actual behaviour during the semester. This sort of introspection thus reduced the accuracy of students' self-predictions (i.e., increased the discrepancy between self-prediction and reality). People can obviously be misguided by illusionary self-knowledge. Taken together, introspection may be less a matter of excavating valid knowledge about oneself and more a constructive process of putting together a coherent and acceptable narrative of one's self and identity.

A more promising source of self-knowledge may be the observation of one's own behaviour as suggested by self-perception theory (Bem, 1972; see also Chapter 7, this volume). Rather than attempting to gain direct, introspective access to one's thoughts, feelings, motives, etc., people often infer their internal states from their overt behaviours. For example, if I notice that I usually avoid going to big parties and would rather stay at home and read a book or listen to classical music, I might rightly infer that I am introverted. This self-perception or inference process may often correctly reveal internal states of which one was not fully aware before, but it can also go awry in that the existence of an internal state that did not exist before is mistakenly inferred or fabricated. To return to our example, I may actually avoid parties not because I am introverted but because I always like to be the centre of attention. This is pretty difficult to achieve, however, at large parties where so many other people are around. To disentangle genuine self-revelation from self-fabrication is an important task for future research on self-perception as a route to self-knowledge (Wilson & Dunn, 2004).

The people around us can also be a source of self-knowledge. We can learn about ourselves by carefully observing how other people view us. To the extent that others agree among themselves about their perception of us they are likely picking up on something valid about us. Moreover, discrepancies between their shared perceptions and our self-perception may point to traits or motives on our part that we are otherwise unable or unwilling to see.

Direct comparisons with others also contribute to our self-knowledge. According to social comparison theory (Festinger, 1954), we compare our opinions with the opinions of others, usually people with whom we share a relevant group membership, because such comparisons tell us what opinions are considered correct or valid and should therefore be incorporated or retained as our own opinions. Similarly, social comparisons with respect to achievements or performances (e.g., in our favourite sport) are sought out in order to define and gauge our abilities (e.g., as a football player). As discussed in more detail below (in the section on self-evaluation and self-esteem), the outcome of such comparisons can also have serious consequences for self-evaluation and self-esteem.

SUMMARY

The self-concept and related self-knowledge can be viewed as the patterned activity of processing self-related information or stimulation received from one's social environment. A person's self-concept is characterized both by its specific content, as captured by the notions of self-schemas and self-aspects, and by its specific structure, as captured by the notion of self-complexity. Introspection, observation of one's own behaviour, careful examination of other people's perceptions of us and self–other comparisons are all possible sources of self-knowledge, although introspection seems to be a rather limited, and sometimes even misleading, route to self-knowledge.

CONTINUITY OF SELF OVER TIME

What is the role of memory in self-continuity?
What is the difference between semantic and episodic memory?

Most of us are pretty certain that the person we see in the bathroom mirror in the morning is the same person we saw in the mirror the night before (although, depending on nocturnal happenings, we might not particularly like our image in the mirror the day after). Without this experience of uninterrupted existence or self-continuity, our sense of self would be seriously shattered (Baumeister, 1986).

An important prerequisite for a continuous sense of self is memory. In order to experience self-continuity, I need to remember today what I experienced and did yesterday, and tomorrow I need to remember important experiences and behaviours of both yesterday and today. In fact, the experience of self-continuity and memory are highly interdependent and not completely separable from each other (Klein, 2001). Self-continuity builds on memories of one's past, while memory for one's past is, in turn, dependent on a continuous sense of self because the past must be identified as one's own past.

To further illuminate the special relationship between such a sense of self and memory, Klein (2001) draws on two important distinctions that have been suggested in the memory literature. The first is the distinction between procedural memory and declarative memory (Schacter & Tulving, 1994). While procedural memory makes possible the acquisition and retention of motor, perceptual and cognitive skills, declarative memory has to do with facts and beliefs about the world. Declarative memory is then further divided into semantic and episodic memory. While semantic memory contains general knowledge (e.g., the knowledge that birds have feathers), episodic memory is concerned with experienced events (e.g., your first day at school). Unlike the contents of

Plate 5.1 *Is the person we see in the mirror each morning the same person we saw in the mirror the night before?*

Plate 5.2 *A continuous sense of self requires memory and vice versa: the experience of self-continuity builds on memories of one's past, but the memorized past must also be identified as one's own past.*

semantic memory, the contents of episodic memory include a reference to the self in subjective space and time (Tulving, 1993). Episodic memory thus enables conscious recollection of personal happenings from the past. It should therefore be closely linked to the sense of self-continuity.

Reviewing evidence from developmental, clinical and neuropsychology, Klein (2001) indeed concludes that a breakdown of the sense of self-continuity is usually accompanied by serious disruptions in episodic memory. However, although a loss of episodic memory typically diminishes the capacity to recollect one's personal past, people stricken with a loss of episodic memory, say as a result of brain injury (amnesia) or developmental disorder (autism), are still able to know things about themselves (e.g., who they are and what they are like). This ability is most likely due to an undamaged semantic memory which may after all enable people to know things about themselves without having to consciously recollect the specific episodes from which that knowledge stems. Nevertheless, it appears that episodic memory, though normally in interaction with semantic memory, is chiefly responsible for the ability to construct a personal narrative and to experience oneself as existing through time.

Note that the sense of self-continuity also spreads to the future. Humans seem to be endowed with an inherent tendency to develop, grow and improve themselves (Maslow, 1970; Rogers, 1959) and can envisage future or possible selves along a trajectory of becoming what they have the potential to become (Markus & Nurius, 1986).

SUMMARY

The experience of self over time resembles a dynamic equilibrium – ever-changing, but continuous. This sense of self-continuity is dependent on and not completely separable from memory of one's past, especially episodic memory. It also has a future dimension in that people can conceive of how they may develop.

SELF-AWARENESS

When do we become self-aware?
How does self-awareness affect our behaviour?

Although most of the time our attention is directed outwards towards our environment (Csikszentmihalyi & Figurski, 1982; Duval & Wicklund, 1972), a variety of external and internal stimuli can turn the spotlight of our consciousness away from the environment towards ourselves: hearing one's own voice played on a tape recorder or seeing oneself in a mirror can lead one to observe oneself and become aware of oneself as an object. A similar state can be created by internal factors such as transitory emotions (e.g., negative mood). More generally, *self-awareness* is a psychological state in which one is aware of oneself as an object, in much the same way as one is aware of other objects such as buildings or other persons.

self-awareness a psychological state in which one is aware of oneself as an object, just as one is aware of other objects such as buildings or other people

Plate 5.3 *Seeing oneself in a mirror can lead one to become aware of oneself as an object.*

According to Duval and Wicklund's (1972) self-awareness theory, people in a state of self-awareness tend to evaluate their ongoing behaviours, their physical appearance or other personal attributes against internalized standards or social norms. When people perceive a negative discrepancy between the standard or norm and their own attributes, appearance or behaviour, they are likely to experience a feeling of discomfort. Self-awareness theory suggests that there are two ways to reduce such discomfort: (1) 'ship out' by withdrawing from self-awareness (if you can; see Everyday Social Psychology 5.1), or (2) 'shape up' by behaving in ways that reduce the perceived discrepancy (see Figure 5.3). For example, imagine Peter sitting in a café bar at a table in front of his date Caroline, who is sitting with her back to a mirror. During the conversation Peter is constantly forced to look directly into the mirror, thereby viewing himself. In such a situation, one that is quite familiar to most of us, most people either 'ship out' from the state of self-awareness (e.g., they change their seating position so that they no longer face the mirror) or 'shape up' by continually comparing and adapting their appearance and behaviour to relevant social norms or internalized standards (e.g., they act very politely or present their best qualities).

Several studies have shown that heightened self-awareness increases the extent to which people conform to standards. For instance, Macrae, Bodenhausen and Milne (1998) examined the effect of self-awareness on conformity to the standard of suppressing stereotypic thoughts about outgroup members. In a series of experiments, female participants were first put into a state of low or high self-awareness (e.g., by the absence or presence of a visible mirror on the wall in the laboratory). They were then asked to rate different target groups (e.g., male construction workers or male yuppies) on stereotype-relevant dimensions. Heightened self-awareness increased participants' conformity to the social (and most likely also internalized) norm that one should not stereotype others.

Carver and Scheier (1981; Scheier & Carver, 1980; see also Fenigstein, Scheier & Buss, 1975) introduced a further qualification to self-awareness theory. They distinguished between two types of self that one can be aware of: private or public self. The private self derives from internal bodily sensations, emotions, feelings, thoughts and other internal stimulations that cannot be observed by other people. In contrast, the public self is reflected in one's behaviour, speech, physical appearance and other attributes visible to others. People differ in the degree to which they attend to aspects of the private and public self. This dimension has been labelled public vs. private *self-consciousness*. Individual Differences 5.1 (p. 99)

> **self-consciousness** people differ in the degree to which they attend to private (e.g., emotions, feelings, thoughts) or public (e.g., behaviour, speech, physical appearance) aspects of the self. This dimension is known as public vs. private self-consciousness

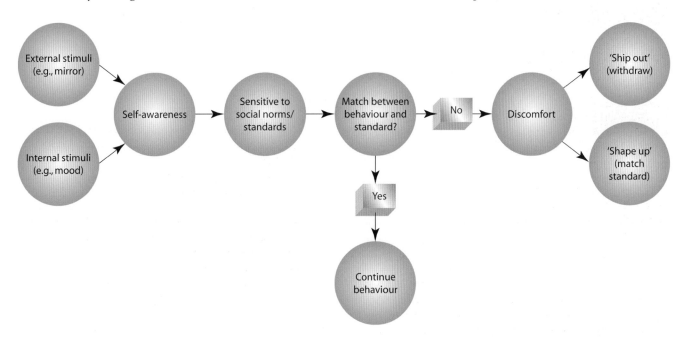

Figure 5.3 *Causes and effects of self-awareness.*

EVERYDAY SOCIAL PSYCHOLOGY 5.1

Big Brother: Self-awareness and social comparison

In the reality TV show *Big Brother*, several contestants move to a communal house and live there over a period of several weeks. Every single point in the house is within view of a video camera. The contestants are not permitted any contact with the outside world: no TV, radio, telephone or Internet are available. At weekly intervals, the public is invited to vote to evict one of the contestants. The last remaining is the winner. The reality TV show takes its title from George Orwell's book *Nineteen Eighty-Four*, in which two-way television screens are fitted in every room so that people's actions are monitored at all times.

Such reality TV shows provide lively illustrations of several of the themes discussed in this chapter. Although the contestants in *Big Brother* may sometimes stop thinking about the presence of the cameras, the whole setting of reality TV repeatedly puts them into a state of self-awareness from which they can hardly

escape. They cannot simply 'ship out' by withdrawing from the cameras. Instead contestants are permanently forced to present themselves to the audience in a way that reduces the risk of being evicted. That is, they have to 'shape up' and behave in ways that correspond to the expectations of the audience.

However, not only the contestants' behaviour but also that of the viewers of reality TV shows can be analysed, and thus better understood, in terms of self and identity processes. In particular, the wish to make self–other comparisons appears to be an important motive for watching reality television. Viewers of reality TV shows obviously make comparisons between themselves and 'the stars' of the show. People like to see that there are others who are going through the same life experiences and are making the same (or even worse) mistakes as they do. Such comparisons can improve viewers' mood and possibly also self-esteem. People's need to compare themselves with and to relate to others thus seems to provide a market for TV shows such as *Big Brother*.

SOURCE: C.M. FRISBY, GETTING REAL WITH REALITY TV, USA TODAY – SOCIETY FOR THE ADVANCEMENT OF EDUCATION (2004). WWW.FINDARTICLES.COM/P/ARTICLES/MI_M1272/IS_2712_133/AI_N6198026

presents example items for the scale developed to measure differences between people on this dimension.

There is strong evidence that type of self-consciousness has important implications for people's feelings and behaviour. People high in private self-consciousness try to align their behaviour with internalized standards (e.g., personal attitudes) in order to maintain or achieve a consistent self-image. People high in public self-consciousness are oriented towards presenting themselves to others in a favourable light. Note that private and public self-consciousness are not mutually exclusive. People can be high in both, low in both or high in one and low in the other.

A related personality variable is the tendency towards *self-monitoring* (Snyder, 1987). This refers to the tendency to regulate one's behaviour either on the basis of external cues such as the reaction of others or on the basis of internal cues such as one's own beliefs and attitudes. Individuals high in self-monitoring are ready and able to modify their behaviour as they move from one social situation to another (see Chapter 6, this volume). There appears to be an empirical relationship between (high and low) self-monitoring and (public and private) self-consciousness. People high in self-monitoring also tend to be high in public self-consciousness, whereas people low in self-monitoring tend to be high in private self-consciousness. Conceptually, however, self-monitoring and self-consciousness emphasize somewhat different aspects of self-awareness. Self-monitoring places particular emphasis on self-presentation skills, whereas self-consciousness emphasizes the focus of a person's attention (see also Fiske & Taylor, 1991; Hoyle, Kernis, Leary & Baldwin, 1999).

SUMMARY

A variety of external and internal stimuli turn our attention inwards towards ourselves so that we become aware of ourselves as an object. Such self-awareness can function as a feedback mechanism which helps us to (re)align our appearance and behaviour with important standards and norms. People differ in the degree to which they attend to aspects of their private or public self and to which they monitor and regulate their appearance and behaviour on the basis of either external or internal cues.

SELF AS AGENT AND REGULATORY PROCESS

How does the understanding of what we are or what we would like to be affect our behaviour?
What are the limits to self-regulation?

People must continually regulate their behaviour in order to survive or, less dramatically, in order to reach desired goals.

INDIVIDUAL DIFFERENCES 5.1

Public vs. Private Self-Consciousness

Please indicate how well or poorly each of the following statements describes your personal style. Use the scale presented below the items.

____ 1 I'm always trying to figure myself out.

____ 2 I'm often the subject of my own fantasies.

____ 3 I'm concerned about the way I present myself.

____ 4 I usually worry about making a good impression.

____ 5 I'm constantly examining my own motives.

____ 6 One of the last things I do before I leave my house is look in the mirror.

____ 7 I'm aware of the way my mind works when I work through a problem.

____ 8 I'm usually aware of my appearance.

1 = Extremely uncharacteristic
2 = Slightly uncharacteristic
3 = Slightly characteristic
4 = Extremely characteristic

These items are taken from a scale developed by Fenigstein et al. (1975) to measure differences between people on the dimension of public vs. private self-consciousness. High scores on items 1, 2, 5 and 7 indicate high *private* self-consciousness, whereas high scores on items 3, 4, 6 and 8 indicate high *public* self-consciousness. Note that the full scale consists of 17 items.

self-regulation the process of controlling and directing one's behaviour in order to achieve desired goals. It involves goal setting, cognitive preparations for behaving in a goal-directed manner as well as the ongoing monitoring, evaluation and correction of goal-directed activities

Self-regulation refers to the process of controlling and directing one's behaviour in order to achieve desired goals. It involves goal setting, cognitive preparations for behaving in a goal-directed manner as well as the ongoing monitoring, evaluation and correction of goal-directed activities.

The self is implicated in this process because the understanding of what one is or wants to become is an important determinant of one's striving for goals. Although we often think of goals primarily in terms of material (e.g., goods, services) or interpersonal outcomes (e.g., esteem, love), many, if not most, goals are also instrumental in maintaining or attaining a desired self or avoiding an undesired self. For example, the goal of graduating from university is instrumental in becoming a psychologist.

Self-discrepancy theory (Higgins, 1987, 1989) proposes that people's ideas of what they ideally would like to be (ideal self-guides) or what they ought to be (ought self-guides) fulfil an important self-regulatory function. Ideal self-guides comprise our own or significant others' hopes, wishes and aspirations and define what we ideally want to be. In contrast, ought self-guides comprise our own or significant others' beliefs concerning our duties, obligations and responsibilities and define what we ought to be. Ideal self-guides operate in such a way that perceived discrepancies between one's personal qualities and what one would ideally like to be lead to approach as the dominant self-regulatory strategy (i.e., moving closer towards one's ideal self). Failure to resolve such perceived discrepancies produces dejection-related emotions such as disappointment, dissatisfaction or sadness. In contrast, when ought self-guides are in operation, perceived discrepancies between one's personal qualities and what one thinks one ought to be lead to avoidance as the dominant self-regulatory strategy (i.e., staying away from incriminating activities). Failure to resolve these discrepancies produces agitation-related emotions such as fear or anxiety.

In his more recent regulatory focus theory, Higgins (1999) further developed and expanded this perspective on self-regulation. More specifically, he elaborated on two broader motivational orientations – promotion vs. prevention focus. Ideal and ought self-guides are important antecedents of the promotion or prevention focus, respectively, but they are not the only antecedents. Individual needs and situational demands and opportunities also play a role. For example, when you already have a secure job, but come across an attractive job ad that promises better pay, it is very likely that you adopt a promotion focus. You would then be concerned primarily with advancement, growth and accomplishment worth approaching or striving for ('Let's go for it!'). In contrast, your potential new employer, who had just fired your incompetent or lazy predecessor, would very likely adopt a prevention focus. With such a focus, people are concerned with security, safety and responsibility and are motivated to act particularly prudently ('Don't make a mistake!').

The extent to which people engage in self-regulation, and thus emerge as influential social agents (Bruner, 1994; DeCharms, 1968), is strongly related to their beliefs or expectations about their ability to control their environment and achieve important goals (Bandura, 1997). Whether or not people strive for particular goals largely depends on such *self-efficacy* expectations. The same is true for effort mobilization. The higher is perceived self-efficacy, the stronger one's effort to attain a desired goal even in the face of obstacles. It is also important to note that self-efficacy expectations are not general beliefs about control. Rather, they are *domain-specific* perceptions of one's own ability to perform behaviours that lead to the attainment of a desired end-state. Hence, in order to predict whether or not a student will work hard to prepare for an exam one needs to know her self-efficacy expectations concerning the academic domain (e.g., 'I can get things organized to do well in this exam') rather than her general beliefs about her ability to control her environment and achieve her goals ('I believe that I have control over my life').

self-efficacy beliefs in one's ability to carry out certain actions required to attain a specific goal (e.g., that one is capable of giving up smoking or doing well in an exam)

Self-regulation is an important human facility, but, as with so many other good things in life, it is not for free. Recent research suggests that active self-regulation is costly in the sense that it depletes some inner resource, leading to a state of ***ego depletion*** (Baumeister, 2002). More specifically, self-regulation seems to depend on a limited inner resource, akin to

ego depletion a temporary reduction in the self's regulatory capacity

energy or strength, that is consumed when the self actively regulates its responses. As a result, the amount of resources the self has available to use for further acts of self-regulation is reduced.

For example, Baumeister, Bratslavsky, Muraven and Tice (1998, Experiment 1) found that an initial act of impulse control impaired subsequent persistence at a puzzle task. Research participants were first seated in a room in which chocolate chip cookies were baked in a small oven so that the room was filled with the delicious aroma of fresh chocolate and baking. Participants were then either allowed to follow their impulse and eat two or three cookies or other sweets (no impulse control) or they had to resist the sweet temptation and eat two or three radishes instead (impulse control). Afterwards, participants in both groups attempted to solve a puzzle which was actually unsolvable. As can be seen in Figure 5.4, participants showed less persistence at the puzzle task (i.e., they spent less time on it and made fewer attempts to solve it) when they had used up regulatory energy through prior impulse control (i.e., when they had to stay away from the sweets). There was also a control group who went directly to the puzzle task without the food part. They showed the same persistence as the participants without prior impulse control.

At first blush, these findings seem to suggest that our stock of self-regulatory energy is alarmingly small. However, following Baumeister's (2002) more optimistic reading, such depletion phenomena may actually be indicative of a useful conservation process. Reduced self-regulation after some self-control exercise may not entirely be due to an actual lack of self-regulatory energy but may also be a clever tactic through which the self saves residual resources for later and possibly more important use. Finally, rest and positive affect usually help to replenish the self.

Plate 5.4 *How long would you work at a puzzle if you were told to stay away from the cookies?*

SUMMARY

The self's function as an agent and regulatory process is vital for our physical survival and social existence. Perceived discrepancies between what we presently are and what we ideally want or ought to be help us to direct, and if necessary to correct, our behaviour. Domain-specific perceptions of ourselves as efficacious social agents affect our self-regulatory efforts. Self-regulation taxes a limited inner resource, but the self seems to pursue a circumspect conservation strategy and can also be replenished.

SELF-EVALUATION AND SELF-ESTEEM

Why do people strive for high self-esteem?
How is our self-esteem affected when we are outperformed by a close friend?
What strategies do we use to achieve or maintain a positive self-evaluation?

By evaluating our behaviours, physical appearance and other attributes we acquire an attitude towards ourselves and develop

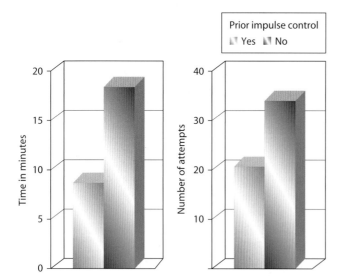

Figure 5.4 *Persistence at a puzzle task as a function of prior impulse control (Baumeister et al., 1998, Table 1).*

self-esteem attitude towards oneself along a positive–negative dimension

self-evaluation evaluation of one's own behaviours, physical appearance, abilities or other personal attributes against internalized standards or social norms

a feeling of *self-esteem* which varies along a positive–negative dimension. It seems that people generally strive for high self-esteem. This need for high self-esteem most likely has evolutionary roots. A propensity to high self-esteem or self-love is likely to be selected in evolution because it fosters self-care, which in turn increases the likelihood of survival and reproductive success (Greenwald & Pratkanis, 1984). Interestingly, positive *self-evaluation* or high self-esteem seems to foster mental health and successful life adjustment, even if it is a 'positive illusion' that does not conform to reality (Taylor & Brown, 1988). Furthermore, because humans evolved in groups and needed each other to survive and reproduce, it is assumed that self-esteem came to function as an important feedback mechanism or 'sociometer' of social relationships – a subjective gauge of interpersonal or intragroup connection (Leary & Baumeister, 2000; Leary, Tambor, Terdal & Downs, 1995). According to this view, an increase in self-esteem signals or reflects an increase in the degree to which one is socially included and accepted by others. In contrast, a loss of self-esteem signals or reflects (the danger of) social rejection or exclusion by others and may thus assist self-correction and social (re)integration.

Moreover, people actively use various strategies to achieve and maintain high self-esteem. In his self-evaluation maintenance model, Tesser (1988) identifies several antecedent conditions and corresponding strategies, with an emphasis on self–other comparisons. As to antecedent conditions, three variables play a key role: the relative performance of self and other people, the closeness of self–other relationships and the degree to which other people's

performance is relevant to one's self-definition. Certain combinations of these variables have a positive effect on one's self-esteem, whereas others constitute a threat to one's self-esteem (Figure 5.5).

For example, when you are outperformed by a close friend on a dimension that is relevant to your self-definition, threat to your self-esteem is imminent. Remember the last time a close friend outperformed you in your favourite subject or sport? It probably didn't feel good. In such situations, people typically resort to one of three strategies: they try to improve their own performance, they distance themselves from the person who outperformed them, or they reduce the subjective importance of the comparison dimension. However, when outperformed by a close friend on a dimension that is irrelevant to your self-definition, your self-esteem is likely to get a boost. Wouldn't it feel great if you had a friend who was a world-class pianist (provided piano playing was beyond your own ambition)? This strategy of associating oneself with successful or otherwise attractive people is also referred to as 'basking in reflected glory' (BIRGing; Cialdini & Richardson, 1980). Thus, in addition to striving for actual success and self-improvement, there are many other strategies that people can use to achieve or maintain a high level of self-esteem. They are called *self-enhancement* (or self-protective) strategies (see Table 5.1 for additional examples).

self-enhancement tendency to achieve or maintain a high level of self-esteem by way of different strategies (e.g., self-serving attributions or basking in reflected glory)

As already mentioned in Tesser's (1988) model, the consequences of negative self–other comparisons for one's self-esteem critically depend on the personal relevance of the comparison dimension. In fact, people seem to be particularly vulnerable to unfavourable feedback in domains on which they have staked their self-esteem. Such contingencies of self-esteem (i.e., domain-specific vulnerability of self-esteem) have recently been demonstrated by

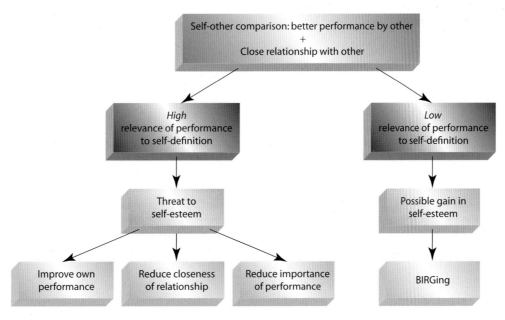

Figure 5.5 *Maintenance of positive self-evaluation: exemplary antecedents and strategies according to Tesser's (1988) self-evaluation maintenance model (BIRGing = basking in reflected glory).*

Table 5.1 *Self-enhancement strategies*

- **Self-serving attributions** (e.g., Miller & Ross, 1975)
  People create attributions that allow them to take credit for success ('I passed the exam because I worked hard') and to deny responsibility for failure ('I failed because the teacher is incompetent').

- **Self-handicapping** (e.g., Berglas & Jones, 1978)
  Sometimes when people anticipate future failure, they actively sabotage their own performance in order to have an excuse (e.g., by partying all night before an exam).

- **Self-affirmation** (Steele, 1988)
  When experiencing a threat to one particular self-aspect, people emphasize other positive self-aspects and thus restore the integrity of their overall self ('I may not be a very good student, but I am a reliable friend').

- **Downward social comparison** (e.g., Wills, 1981)
  People compare themselves with others who are worse off or inferior on a particular comparison dimension ('I may not have done that well in the exam, but look at him, he is an absolute disaster').

Crocker and colleagues for a domain which should be of particular interest to our readers (and the authors of this chapter alike), namely, the domain of academic competence (Crocker, Karpinski, Quinn & Chase, 2003). They examined the impact of grades on daily self-esteem in a sample of male and female students majoring in engineering and psychology. Academic contingency (i.e., the extent to which research participants staked their self-esteem on academic competence) was measured at a pre-test with items such as 'When I do poorly on an exam or paper, my self-esteem suffers' or 'Whether or not I am a good student is unrelated to my overall opinion of myself' (reverse scored). During the main phase of the study, research participants then reported their grades and current self-esteem on a web page at least three times per week for three weeks. The critical results are depicted in Figure 5.6.

As expected, the negative effect of bad grades on daily self-esteem was greater the more students based their self-esteem on academic competence (high academic contingency; see bottom panel of Figure 5.6). The biggest drop in self-esteem was actually observed for female students in engineering who were highly contingent on academic competence. Fear of confirming negative stereotypes about women's ability in the domain of engineering may have been responsible for this amplification. Crocker et al. (2003) also examined the effects of good grades, but this analysis revealed a less consistent pattern. Analogous to the findings for bad grades, there was some evidence that students with high academic contingency were more able to gain a self-esteem boost from good grades. But this was true only if students were in gender-congruent or stereotypical majors (female students in psychology and male students in engineering). In gender-incongruent or counterstereotypical majors (female students in engineering and male students in psychology), however, it was the students with low academic

contingency that tended to reap the greater boost from good grades. Perhaps success was so unexpected for those students that it had a particularly powerful surprise effect.

SUMMARY

Self-evaluation and self-esteem, and the associated need for positive self-evaluation and high self-esteem, likely have evolutionary roots. Self-evaluation and self-esteem function as important feedback mechanisms that assist social integration and can spur performance and self-improvement. People also use various self-enhancement strategies to achieve and maintain high self-esteem and are particularly vulnerable to negative feedback in domains on which they have staked their self-esteem.

SELF-EXTENSION AND LEVELS OF IDENTITY

What are the consequences of including others in one's self or identity?
How do personal and social identity differ from each other?
What determines which of our multiple identities is psychologically active in a particular moment?

This self-theme revolves around the *variable* 'range and extent of one's feeling of self-involvement' (Allport, 1968, p. 29). Allport actually considered it a mark of maturity that the self can be extended to include concrete objects, other people or abstract ideals which then become matters of high personal importance and are valued as 'mine' (see also Kohlberg, 1976).

A growing body of research indicates that participants in a close relationship include each other in their psychological selves with important consequences for information processing and behaviour (Aron, Aron & Norman, 2001; Aron, Aron, Tudor & Nelson, 1991). For example, these researchers observed that married graduate students had more difficulty deciding whether a particular trait was self-descriptive or not when they differed from their spouse in the critical trait than when self and spouse were similar in this respect. A possible explanation for this finding is that the spouse was actually included in the psychological self so that self–spouse dissimilarities created cognitive confusion which interfered with self-related information processing (see Chapter 10, this volume).

More generally, self-extension reflects the human capacity to identify with others at different levels of social inclusiveness (family, neighbourhood, university, political party, nation, etc.). Think for a minute about the groups you identify with. How important

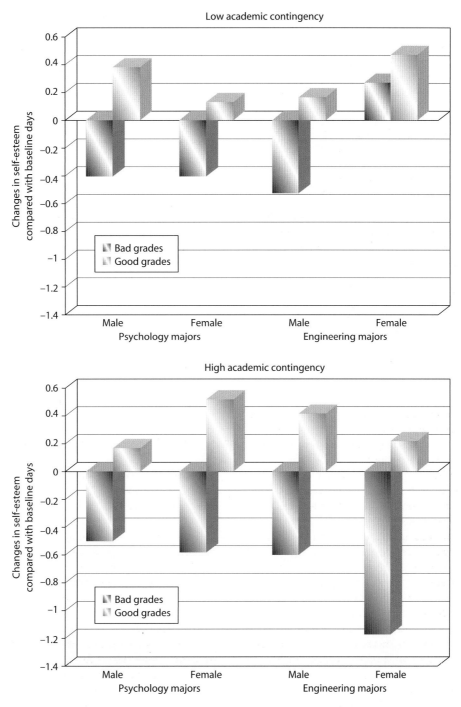

Figure 5.6 *Change in daily self-esteem in response to bad and good grades for students high or low in academic contingency by gender and major (Crocker et al., 2003, Figure 1).*

are these groups to you? For example, how do you feel when your national football team wins a game? What are your feelings when your preferred political party loses an election? Do you feel offended when your university is unfairly evaluated?

The major theoretical and empirical contributions to the study of such social or group identifications have been made or were critically inspired by European social psychologists. Most notably, these contributions crystallized into the social identity theory of intergroup relations (Tajfel & Turner, 1979, 1986) and self-categorization theory (Turner et al., 1987). These two highly influential theories are referred to collectively as the social identity perspective.

The social identity theory of intergroup relations

Social identity theory (SIT) is a theoretical framework for the social psychological analysis of intergroup relations and social change in socially stratified societies (Tajfel & Turner, 1979, 1986; Turner & Reynolds, 2001). At the theory's heart lies the idea that categorization into ingroup (a group to which one belongs) and outgroup (a group to which one does not belong) provides the germ for the development of a group-based social identity. *Social identity* is defined as that part of a person's self-concept which derives from the knowledge of his or her membership in a social group (or groups) together with the value and emotional significance attached to that membership. Social identity can spur intergroup discrimination and other forms of intergroup conflict. More specifically, SIT proposes that, when acting as group members, people have a need for positive social identity and are therefore motivated to positively differentiate their ingroup from relevant outgroups ('We are better than they are!'). Intergroup discrimination can then be a means, though not the only one, to establish such positive ingroup distinctiveness ('The fact that we have and deserve more than they do just shows that we are superior!').

social identity that part of a person's self-concept which derives from the knowledge of his or her membership in a social group (or groups) together with the value and emotional significance attached to that membership

A typical application of SIT can be found in the analysis of the social psychology of low-status minorities or otherwise disadvantaged groups (e.g., immigrants, blue-collar workers, women or gays and lesbians). According to SIT, the disadvantaged social position of such groups confers an unsatisfactory social identity on the respective group members (e.g., Lücken & Simon, 2005; see Research close-up 5.2). This predicament then motivates group members to search for appropriate problem-solving strategies which help them to achieve a more satisfactory social identity. These strategies can range from individualistic strategies of social mobility, such as leaving the disadvantaged minority and joining the advantaged majority (where that is possible), to collective or group strategies of social change, such as collective protest or even revolutionary reversals of status and power relations (Tajfel, 1981; see Chapter 14, this volume).

RESEARCH CLOSE-UP 5.2

Cognitive and affective responses to being in minority versus majority groups

Lücken, M. & Simon, B. (2005). Cognitive and affective experiences of minority and majority members: The role of group size, status, and power. *Journal of Experimental Social Psychology, 41,* 396–413.

Introduction

Many, if not most, real-life intergroup contexts consist of groups that hold minority or majority positions vis-à-vis each other. Lücken and Simon (2005) proposed that knowledge of one's membership in a minority or majority group has important effects on one's thinking and feeling. Their first experiment dealt with minorities and majorities defined in purely numerical terms. The authors made two major predictions. First, because membership in a minority group is a rare self-aspect with particular attention-grabbing power, members of minority groups should display a stronger tendency to be cognitively preoccupied with (constantly thinking of) their group membership than members of majority groups. Second, because numerical inferiority is typically associated with error and deviance or weakness and powerlessness (at least in western democratic societies), people should react with more negative (or less positive) affect when they find themselves in a minority as opposed to a majority group.

Method

Participants

Sixty-one students (28 men and 33 women) participated in the study. Each participant received 5 euros for his or her participation.

Design and procedure

The design consisted of one independent variable with two experimental conditions: minority vs. majority membership. The experiment allegedly examined the relationship between artistic preferences and personality. Participants were paced through a series of paintings presented on a computer monitor and indicated how much they liked each painting on a 50-step scroll bar with endpoints labelled *not at all* and *very much*. Following this task, participants were informed that the paintings they had just rated were paintings by two different painters who remained anonymous and were referred to as Painter X and Painter Y throughout the experiment. The computer then allegedly determined each participant's artistic preference. In reality, all participants were told that they preferred Painter X over Painter Y. They were also told that prior research had discovered that these preferences were correlated with different personality styles. Participants also received a bogus personality profile of a typical ingroup member which was written in an ambiguous manner so that every participant found him- or herself adequately described at least to some degree.

Participants in the minority condition were told that usually only 10 per cent of people would prefer Painter X, but about 80 per cent would prefer Painter Y (allowing for the possibility that some people may not have a clear preference). Percentages were reversed in the majority condition. To further strengthen the minority–majority manipulation, participants were provided with an alleged update of the preference statistics from the current research project. In the minority condition, they were informed that only 15.7 per cent of the participants preferred Painter X, but 84.3 per cent preferred Painter Y. Again, percentages were reversed in the majority condition.

The main dependent measures, administered after the manipulation of the independent variable (minority vs. majority membership), were: measures of cognitive preoccupation with one's group membership (e.g., 'Since I have learned that I am a member of this group, this thought enters my mind time and again'), affect (e.g., 'At the moment I feel cheerful', 'At the moment I feel sad') and collective identification (e.g., 'I feel strong ties to other ingroup members'). Ratings were made on seven-point scales ranging from *not true* (0) to *very true* (6).

Results

Both predictions were confirmed. As shown in the top panel of Figure 5.7, cognitive preoccupation with one's group membership was stronger for minority members than for majority members. At the same time, minority members reported less positive affect (averaged over positive and negative items) than did majority members (bottom panel of Figure 5.7). Replicating prior research findings, minority members also showed stronger collective identification than did majority members. Finally, additional analyses revealed that minority members' increased cognitive preoccupation with their group membership, but not their affective reaction, was responsible for (mediated) their increased collective identification.

Discussion

The experiment confirmed that minority membership and majority membership have differential implications for group members' thinking and feeling. First, unlike majority membership, minority membership preoccupies group members' minds, thus keeping them focused on their collective identity. Second,

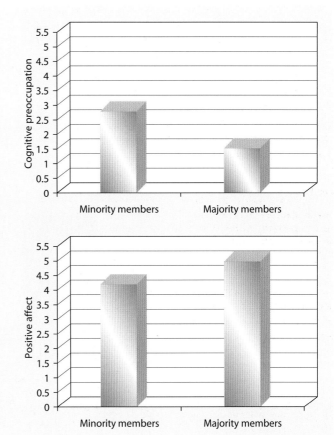

Figure 5.7 *Cognitive preoccupation with one's group membership and affect as a function of minority and majority membership (Lücken & Simon, 2005).*

compared with majority members, minority members experience less positive (or more negative) affect as a result of their group membership. Taken together, minority members likely experience an internal conflict in that cognitive forces pull them towards their group, whereas affective forces push them away from it. Three additional studies substantiated these results and revealed that (implicit as well as explicit) power differences between minority and majority groups play an important role in the differential cognitive and affective experiences of minority and majority members.

Self-categorization theory

Turner's (1982) distinction between personal identity and social identity marks the beginning of self-categorization theory (SCT; see also Chapter 11, this volume). *Personal identity* means self-definition as a unique individual in terms of

personal identity self-definition as a unique individual in terms of interpersonal or intragroup differentiations ('I' or 'me' versus 'you')

interpersonal or intragroup differentiations ('I' or 'me' versus 'you'), whereas social identity now means self-definition as an interchangeable group member in terms of ingroup–outgroup differentiations ('we' or 'us' versus 'they' or 'them'). The theory was then elaborated in greater detail by Turner et al. (1987). It is a more general theoretical framework than SIT. Whereas SIT is not, and was probably never intended to be, a general theory of self or identity, SCT specifies the antecedents and consequences of both personal and social identity. It can thus provide explanations for

PIONEER

John C. Turner (b. 1947), co-author of *social identity theory* and author of *self-categorization theory*, was born in London, England. He received his PhD at the University of Bristol, where he also taught and co-directed the first research program on social identity theory. In self-categorization theory he reconceptualized the nature of the psychological group in terms of his now widely accepted distinction between personal and social identity; he showed that group processes are an emergent product of a change in the level of self-categorization rather than an amalgam of interpersonal relationships. This extremely influential theory has transformed our understanding of many fundamental social psychological phenomena. John Turner moved to Australia in 1983 and is currently a professor of psychology and an Australian Professorial Fellow at the Australian National University, Canberra.

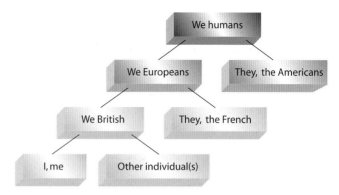

Figure 5.8 *Levels of self-categorization and identity.*

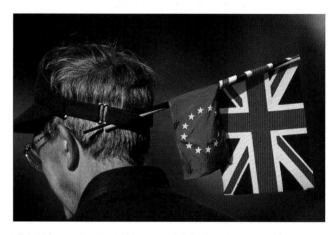

Plate 5.5 *One's social identity as a European citizen is more inclusive than one's national identity.*

both individual behaviour as guided by personal identity (e.g., individual careerism) and group behaviour as guided by social identity (e.g., collective protest).

> **self-categorization** the formation of cognitive groupings of oneself and other people as the same in contrast to some other class of people

According to SCT, both personal (individual) and social (collective) identity derive from **self-categorizations**, which are 'cognitive groupings of oneself and some class of stimuli as the same . . . in contrast to some other class of stimuli' (Turner et al., 1987, p. 44). The theory revolves around three major tenets:

1 Identities can be construed at different levels of social inclusiveness.

2 Identities are comparative constructs.

3 Identity salience is a joint function of the person's readiness to adopt a particular identity and the identity's social contextual fit.

We shall explore each tenet in more detail.

First, despite the key status of the distinction between personal and social identity, there are additional layers of hierarchically organized identities. For example, one's social identity as a British or French citizen is more abstract than, and thus includes, one's personal identity as a unique individual. At the same time, one's social identity as a European citizen or even a human being is more abstract and includes one's lower-level social and personal identities (Figure 5.8).

Second, identities are relative constructs that are compared with, and evaluated relative to, contrasting identities at the same level of abstraction, but in terms of the next more inclusive identity.

For instance, one's personal identity as a unique individual is compared with, and evaluated relative to, the identity of another individual with respect to attributes that (allegedly) characterize the common ingroup in general (e.g., polite for a British ingroup and efficient for a German ingroup). By the same token, one's social identity as a British or German citizen can be compared with, and evaluated relative to, say, Italian citizens with respect to attributes that characterize Europeans in general (e.g., wealthy).

Third, identities vary not only along the dimension of abstraction or social inclusiveness. Another source of variation is the multiplicity of a given person's group memberships even on similar levels of abstraction (e.g., groupings based on gender, sexual orientation, profession or political orientation). People are usually members of many different groups, but not all group memberships are salient (psychologically active) at the same time. Sometimes the authors of this chapter see themselves primarily as males, at other times as scientists, and at still other times as members of a political party. Similarly, the readers of this chapter may see themselves sometimes as men or women, at other times primarily as hardworking students, and at still other times as fans of particular sports clubs or music bands.

According to SCT, identity salience is a joint function of people's readiness to adopt a particular identity and the extent to which that identity fits as a meaningful self-definition within a given social context. Readiness to adopt a particular identity depends on people's general values, changing motives, current goals, prior experiences and so forth. For example, prior experiences of being mistreated because of a particular group membership likely reduce one's readiness to define oneself in terms of the corresponding social identity, if one wishes to escape further mistreatment. However, if one's current goal were to draw public attention to one's mistreatment, readiness for such self-definition should increase. Also, readiness to adopt a particular identity may be influenced by the relative strengths of one's needs for assimilation or differentiation (Brewer, 1991). For example, students at a large anonymous university may wish to join a fraternity or sorority in order to achieve a noticeable identity, whereas in class especially new students may wish to assimilate and blend in with the rest in order not to become an outsider.

The fit of a particular identity as a meaningful self-definition increases with the degree to which observed similarities and differences between people (including oneself) reflect one's expectations and beliefs about 'us' and 'them' (or 'me' and 'you'). For example, gender identity fits well and is meaningful in a situation in which women and men discuss issues of sexual harassment and most women plead for harsh punishment of sexual offenders whereas most men disagree with them and plead for more lenient measures (typical male!).

Although SCT has so far focused primarily on the antecedents and consequences of the salience of social identity, it also contends that the salience of personal identity is governed by the same general principles, but with opposite consequences. The salience of personal identity is similarly construed as a joint function of readiness (e.g., a high need for individuality) and fit (e.g., many perceived differences between people, with each person being relatively consistent over time). But the key difference lies in the consequences of personal vs. social identity salience. A salient personal identity should accentuate the perception of interindividual differences and intraindividual similarity or consistency (e.g., when your personal identity is salient, you might think of the fact that you are a better player than your team-mates, and that you have been all season long). A salient social identity, however, is assumed to enhance the perception of self as similar to, or even interchangeable with, other ingroup members and as different from outgroup members, who are perceived as highly similar to each other. For example, striking workers on a picket line might see each other as very similar, but distinctly different from 'managers',

depersonalization the shift from personal to social identity, entailing the accentuation of intragroup similarities and intergroup differences

who are all seen as alike. It is this mechanism of *depersonalization*, associated with a salient social identity, or personalization, associated with a salient personal identity, that is responsible for group behaviour or individualistic behaviour, respectively. Note that depersonalization indicates a shift from personal to social identity which should not be confused with a *loss* of identity – a state other researchers have referred to as *deindividuation* (Zimbardo, 1970).

Plate 5.6 *Striking workers on a picket line might see each other as very similar, but distinctly different from 'managers', who are all seen as alike.*

Implications SCT offers a distinctive, and often provocative, view of self and identity as a dynamic process. An important implication of this view is that the self is not represented in terms of fixed, absolute properties such as self-schemas (Markus, 1977) or self-aspects (Linville, 1985), but in terms of relational, varying self-categories or identities. Such fluidity in the self-concept has recently been demonstrated by Onorato and Turner (2004) with a modified version of the research paradigm introduced by Markus (1977) and described in Research close-up 5.1. The critical modification concerns the salience of research participants' social as opposed to personal identity. More specifically, Onorato and Turner (2004) made participants' gender identity highly salient (i.e., social identity as either women or men) and predicted that self-descriptions would then reflect this identity and the associated (self-)stereotypes. Because independence and dependence are a part of the gender stereotype for men and women, respectively, men should generally describe themselves as independent and women should generally describe themselves as dependent. Conversely, individual independence and dependence self-schemas should have no effect because they are more closely tied to personal identity.

Like Markus (1977), Onorato and Turner divided their research participants into Independents, Dependents and Aschematics, depending on whether they possessed an independence or dependence self-schema or neither. The subsequent self-description task included several adjectives associated with either independence or dependence. However, instead of 'me/not me' judgements, the self-description task now required 'us/them' judgements where 'us' referred to the more inclusive category 'women' for female participants and 'men' for male participants. Onorato and Turner (2004, Study 1) found that, as predicted, once gender identity was salient, males endorsed more independent adjectives than dependent adjectives, while the opposite was true for females. Response latencies also supported SCT. Males were significantly faster to respond in an independent than in a dependent manner, and the opposite was again true for females. There

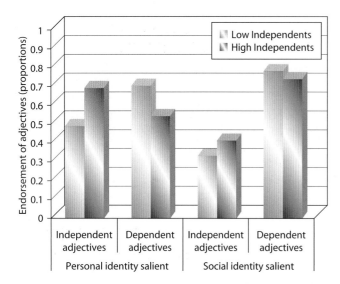

Figure 5.9 *Effects of self-schemas as a function of the salience of personal identity or social identity as women (Onorato & Turner, 2004, Table 1).*

was no effect of individual self-schemas, either on schema-relevant 'us/them' judgements or on the corresponding response latencies. Social identity obviously wiped out the effects of personal identity. In a second study with an all-female sample, Onorato and Turner (2004, Study 2) also included a base-line condition similar to that in Markus (1977) in which personal identity was salient and 'me/not me' judgements were required. In this condition, they found an effect of individual self-schemas, with consistent differences between Low and High Independents. However, this effect was again wiped out when social identity (as women) was made salient (Figure 5.9).

These results should caution us against equating the self-concept or its core with self-schemas or any other type of *fixed* self-aspect. Instead, they make out a strong case for the distinction between personal and social identity and the resulting fluidity of the self-concept. This is not to deny that the self and identity can be experienced as stable. However, SCT suggests that such self-continuity reflects more the stability in the parameters of the dynamic self-categorization process than a fixed underlying cognitive structure. In other words, the experience of self-continuity is a sign that the self-categorization process receives rather stable input (e.g., from the social environment) and therefore produces a stable output. If everybody continually treats me as a professor, no wonder I keep seeing myself as a professor.

Finally, the social identity perspective in general and SCT, with its distinction between personal identity and social identity, in particular have important implications also for the other self-themes discussed so far. Thus self-awareness can no longer be limited to a self defined primarily in terms of personal identity, with the bodily sense as a lifelong anchor (Allport, 1968). Social identity can also be the object or focus of self-awareness, and such self-awareness can involve both private and public aspects of one's social identity (e.g., one's private feelings and thoughts as a group member or one's public appearance and behaviour as a group member). Moreover, social identity plays a critical role as agent and

regulatory process, especially in group contexts, and the analysis of self-evaluation and self-esteem can fruitfully be extended from the level of personal to social identity. Just as *I* as an individual person behave in terms of my *personal* identity and want to be seen in a positive light, so *we* as a group enact our *social* identity and strive for positive collective self-esteem (see Chapter 14, this volume). In fact, in extreme cases of intergroup conflict, self-sacrificial death can be sought out as the highest form of self-fulfilment (Taarnby, 2002), earning one esteem and the admiration of one's fellow in-group members – or condemnation as a terrorist when outgroup members are making the judgement.

SUMMARY

Self and identity expand by extending their psychological range. Close others or even entire groups and categories of people then become integral parts of one's self and identity, with important consequences for information processing and behaviour. Self-categorization theory further specifies different levels of identity that vary in social inclusiveness and form a hierarchical structure. Its central distinction between personal and social identity greatly enriched the traditional analysis of self and identity.

CULTURAL IMPACT ON SELF AND IDENTITY

How does culture shape our self and identity?
How do self and identity contribute to cross-cultural differences?

In a sense, culture functions like a broad social group that provides its members with a set of often implicit normative tasks one has to fulfil to be a good person. At a very general level, individualistic western cultures are distinguished from collectivistic eastern cultures (Triandis, 1995), although the classification of entire nations or even transnational regions on a simple collectivism–individualism dimension is becoming increasingly difficult owing to the entities' internal complexity and general globalization processes. Nevertheless, key elements that are typical of collectivistic cultures are subordination of individual goals to group goals and achievement aimed at improving the position of one's group. Conversely, primacy of individual goals and achievement aimed at improving one's own position as an individual are usually considered key elements of individualistic cultures.

Cultural differences have also been suggested with regard to the content and structure of people's selves and identities (Kashima, Kashima & Aldridge, 2001). A prominent distinction is that between independent self-construal in individualistic cultures and interdependent self-construal in collectivistic cultures

independent self self as an autonomous entity defined predominantly in terms of abstract, internal attributes like traits, abilities and attitudes

interdependent self self construed as socially embedded and defined predominantly in terms of relationships with others, group memberships and social roles

(Markus & Kitayama, 1991; also Rhee, Uleman, Lee & Roman, 1995). According to this approach, the *independent self* is construed as an autonomous entity defined predominantly in terms of abstract, internal attributes like traits, abilities and attitudes. The *interdependent self*, in contrast, is construed as socially embedded and defined predominantly in terms of relationships with others, group memberships and social roles.

Note that the distinction between independent and interdependent selves is not exactly the same as the distinction between independence and dependence self-schemas as suggested by Markus (1977). First, the interdependent self stands for mutual dependence of self and other, whereas a dependence self-schema points to a more unilateral dependence of oneself on others. Second, the distinction between independent and interdependent selves revolves around the extent to which the overall self reflects independence or interdependence, whereas the distinction between independence and dependence self-schemas revolves around the extent to which the specific content of some components of one's self-concept signifies independence or dependence.

Research suggests a number of important cultural differences in cognition, emotion and motivation that may be accounted for by the distinction between independent and interdependent self-construals (Markus & Kitayama, 1991). For example, the tendency to perceive behaviour as the consequence of internal attributes of the person – a tendency that appears to be particularly characteristic of individualistic cultures – may be linked to the prominent role of internal attributes in independent self-construal so prevalent in individualistic cultures (see Chapter 3, this volume). Markus and Kitayama (1991) also discuss evidence that independent self-construal underlies the motivation to confidently display and express one's strengths in individualistic cultures, whereas, in collectivistic cultures, interdependent self-construal promotes the appreciation of modesty and self-restraint. Obviously, these cross-cultural differences are due to culture-specific socialization, for children increasingly incorporate the respective cultural ideals of their society as they grow older (Yoshida, Kojo & Kaku, 1982).

More recently, an innovative line of research has emerged that demonstrated that independent and interdependent self-construals can also be primed *within* a culture with consequences that mirror those found between cultures. For example, Gardner, Gabriel and Lee (1999, Experiment 1) primed European-American students with either independence or interdependence and then presented them with a values inventory including both individualistic values (e.g., freedom and living an exciting life) and collectivistic values (e.g., family safety and respect for elders). The researchers used two different methods of priming. One method required research participants to read a story that described an army general behaving either in an independent or interdependent way. The other method required participants to circle either independent pronouns ('I' or 'mine') or interdependent pronouns

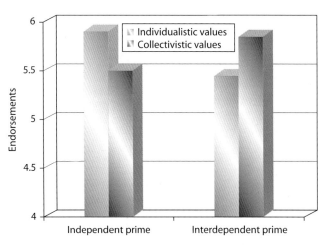

Figure 5.10 *Endorsements of individualistic and collectivistic values as a function of prime in a sample of European-American students (Gardner et al., 1999, Figure 1).*

('we' or 'ours'). Both priming methods were equally effective. More importantly, it was predicted and found that participants who were primed with interdependence gave higher endorsements to collectivistic than individualistic values, whereas the opposite was true for participants primed with independence (see Figure 5.10). Similarly, Kühnen, Hannover and Schubert (2001) showed that participants from individualistic cultures shifted towards more context-dependent thinking when primed with interdependence. For example, these participants then needed more time to discern smaller geometrical figures embedded in complex visual patterns.

Taken together, it appears that cultural differences in cognition, emotion, motivation and behaviour may ultimately be explainable in terms of more general self-processes. According to this view, culture-specific social conditions first activate different self-construals or identities which then mediate differential modes of thinking, feeling and acting. To the extent that a particular self-construal or identity is deeply ingrained in us as the result of our socialization in a particular culture, it will be chronically active resulting in characteristic habits of thinking, feeling and acting.

SUMMARY

As an open system that is amenable to external influences, one's self or identity is shaped by the surrounding culture. A prominent distinction is that between independent self-construal prevalent in individualistic cultures and interdependent self-construal prevalent in collectivistic cultures. Both types of self-construal have been linked to characteristic modes of thinking, feeling and acting. They are typically the result of socialization in a given culture, but shifts from one type to the other can also be effected within a single culture.

SUMMARY AND CONCLUSIONS

- Social psychologists conceptualize self and identity as a social psychological mediator – a variable process that takes shape during social interaction and then guides subsequent interaction.

- A self-concept is a cognitive representation of oneself that gives coherence and meaning to one's experiences, including one's relations to other people. People's self-concepts differ in content (self-schemas) and structure (self-complexity). We gain self-knowledge through observation of our own behaviour, careful examination of other people's perceptions of us and self–other comparisons.

- We usually experience uninterrupted existence or continuity of self over time. The experience of self-continuity is closely linked to episodic memory, which includes knowledge of personal happenings in the past.

- Through a variety of stimuli we can become aware of ourselves as an object. In such a state of self-awareness, we tend to evaluate our behaviour or personal attributes against social norms or internalized standards.

- We must continuously regulate our behaviour in order to reach desired goals. Self-regulation involves goal setting, cognitive preparations for behaving in a goal-directed manner as well as the ongoing monitoring and evaluation of goal-directed activities.

- Through evaluating our behaviour and attributes we develop self-esteem. People try to achieve or maintain high self-esteem by way of different self-enhancement strategies, such as self-serving attribution or downward social comparison.

- Two major levels of self or identity can be distinguished: personal identity as an individual defined in terms of interpersonal or intragroup differentiations, and social identity as a group member defined in terms of ingroup–outgroup differentiations.

- Self-categorization theory (SCT) offers a comprehensive framework for the analysis of identity that specifies the antecedents and consequences of both personal and social identity.

- Self and identity are shaped by the surrounding culture. Important cross-cultural differences in cognition, emotion, motivation and behaviour can be linked to the distinction between independent self-construal in individualistic cultures and interdependent self-construal in collectivistic cultures.

Suggestions for further reading

Baumeister, R.F. (1998). The self. In D.T. Gilbert, S.T. Fiske & G. Lindzey (Eds.), *Handbook of social psychology* (4th edn, Vol. 1, pp. 680–740). New York: McGraw-Hill. Comprehensive overview of social psychological research on the self from the North American perspective.

Brewer, M.B. & Hewstone, M. (Eds.) (2004). *Self and social identity*. Oxford: Blackwell. An edited collection of chapters with contributions from leading researchers representing the diversity of approaches to self and identity.

Simon, B. (2004). *Identity in modern society: A social psychological perspective*. Oxford: Blackwell. An integrative approach to individual and collective identity and their antecedents and consequences.

Turner, J.C., Hogg, M.A., Oakes, P.J., Reicher, S.D. & Wetherell, M.S. (1987). *Rediscovering the social group: A self-categorization theory*. Oxford: Blackwell. A classic which shaped the agenda for generations of scholarly inquiry on social identity processes.

6 Attitudes: Content, Structure and Functions

Geoffrey Haddock and Gregory R. Maio

KEY CONCEPTS

affective component of
    attitude
attitude
attitude–behaviour relation
attitude function
attitudinal ambivalence
behavioural component of
    attitude
cognitive component of
    attitude
explicit measures of attitude
implicit measures of
    attitude
mere exposure effect
MODE model
multicomponent model of
    attitude
one-dimensional
    perspective of attitudes
self-monitoring
self-perception theory
socially desirable
    responding
theory of planned
    behaviour
theory of reasoned action
two-dimensional
    perspective of attitudes

CHAPTER OUTLINE

The study of attitudes is at the core of social psychology. Attitudes refer to our evaluations of people, groups and other types of objects in our social world. Attitudes are an important area of study because they impact both the way we perceive the world and how we behave. In this chapter, we introduce the attitude concept. We consider how attitudes are formed and organized and discuss theories explaining why we hold attitudes. We also address how social psychologists measure attitudes, as well as examining how our attitudes help predict our behaviour.

Introduction

All of us like some things and dislike others. For instance, we both like the Welsh national rugby team and dislike liver. A social psychologist would say that we possess a positive *attitude* towards the Welsh rugby team and a negative *attitude* towards liver. Understanding differences in attitudes across people and uncovering the reasons why people like and dislike different things has long interested social psychologists. Indeed, almost 70 years ago, Gordon Allport (1935, p. 798) asserted that the attitude concept is 'the most distinctive and indispensable concept in . . . social psychology'. That statement remains equally valid today; the study of attitudes remains at the forefront of social psychological research and theory.

attitude an overall evaluation of a stimulus object

In this chapter, we introduce a number of important issues regarding the attitude concept. First, we define the term 'attitude'. We will show that expressing an attitude involves making an evaluative judgement about an attitude object. Second, we devote attention to the content of attitudes. We will show that attitudes have affective, cognitive and behavioural components. Third, we consider the structure of attitudes. We will show that attitudes can be organized and structured in different ways. Fourth, we consider the psychological functions or needs that are served by attitudes. We will show that people hold attitudes for a number of reasons. Fifth, we introduce how attitudes are measured, concentrating on direct and indirect strategies that psychologists have developed to measure attitudes. We will show that attitudes can be measured in many different ways. Finally, we review research that has addressed a key question for attitude researchers: under what circumstances do attitudes predict behaviour? We will show that our attitudes and opinions are quite effective in predicting how we behave.

WHAT IS AN ATTITUDE?

How can we best define an attitude?
Can we have attitudes about anything?

In their influential book *The Psychology of Attitudes*, Eagly and Chaiken (1993, p. 1) define an attitude as 'a psychological tendency that is expressed by evaluating a particular entity with some degree of favor or disfavor'. Inherent in this definition is the idea that reporting an attitude involves the expression of an *evaluative judgement* about a stimulus object. In other words, reporting an attitude involves making a decision concerning liking vs. disliking, approving vs. disapproving or favouring vs. disfavouring a particular issue, object or person.

An attitude, when conceptualized as an evaluative judgement, can vary in two important ways. First, attitudes can differ in *valence*, or direction. Some attitudes that a person possesses are positive (like our attitudes towards the Welsh rugby team), others are negative (like our attitudes towards liver), and yet others are neutral (like our attitudes towards eating fried foods). Second, attitudes can differ in *strength*. For example, while one person might feel very strongly about the Euro, a second person might feel much less strongly about the same topic. You will learn more about different aspects of attitude strength later in this chapter.

Until now, we have used different examples when describing our own attitudes. This leads to an important question – can *anything* be the object of an attitude? Basically, any stimulus that can be evaluated along a dimension of favourability can be conceptualized as an attitude object. As noted by Eagly and Chaiken (1993), some attitude objects are abstract concepts (e.g., 'liberalism'), others are concrete (e.g., a computer). Furthermore, one's own self (e.g., self-esteem) and other individuals (e.g., a particular politician) can serve as attitude objects, as can social policy issues (e.g., capital punishment) and social groups (e.g., people from Canada).

PIONEER

Alice Eagly (b. 1938) completed her undergraduate degree at Radcliffe College before pursuing a PhD at the University of Michigan (1965). Her research on attitude change (with Shelly Chaiken) led to the development of the heuristic-systematic model of persuasion. Together, Eagly and Chaiken (1993) wrote *The Psychology of Attitudes*, arguably the most comprehensive volume written on the attitude concept. In addition to her research on the psychology of attitudes, Eagly has made enormous contributions to our understanding of the psychology of gender.

SUMMARY

Reporting an attitude involves the expression of an evaluative judgement about a stimulus object. Attitudes differ in strength and valence, and any stimulus that can be evaluated along a dimension of favourability can be conceptualized as an attitude object.

THE CONTENT OF ATTITUDES

Can attitudes be influenced by unconsciously learned emotional responses to an object?
How do beliefs shape attitudes?
When do people infer (or perceive) their attitudes from their behaviour?

So far, we have seen that attitudes can be thought of as an overall evaluation (e.g., like–dislike) of an attitude object. This definitional perspective has generated a number of conceptual models of the attitude concept. Historically, one of the most influential models of attitude has been the **multicomponent model** (see Eagly & Chaiken, 1993; Zanna & Rempel, 1988). According to this perspective (see Figure 6.1), attitudes are summary evaluations of an object that have *affective, cognitive* and *behavioural* components. A number of researchers have considered how these three components contribute to the formation and expression of attitudes.

> **multicomponent model of attitude** a model of attitude that conceptualizes attitudes as summary evaluations that have affective, cognitive and behavioural components

Plate 6.1 *How strong is your attitude towards the Euro?*

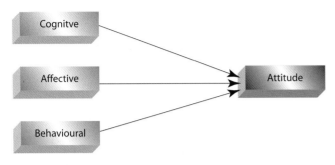

Figure 6.1 *The multicomponent model of attitude.*

The affective component of attitudes

affective component of attitude the feelings or emotions associated with an attitude object.

The *affective component of attitudes* refers to feelings or emotions associated with an attitude object. Affective responses influence attitudes in a number of ways. A primary way in which feelings affect attitudes is due to affective reactions that are aroused in the individual after exposure to the attitude object. For instance, many people indicate that spiders make them feel scared. These negative affective responses are likely to produce a negative attitude towards spiders.

Feelings can become associated with attitude objects in several ways. A number of researchers have used classical conditioning paradigms to assess how pairing affective information with an attitude object can produce a positive or negative attitude. For example, Krosnick, Betz, Jussim and Lynn (1992) conducted a study in which participants were presented with a series of pictures of an unfamiliar person. Importantly, each picture was preceded by an affect-arousing image that was presented at a subliminal level, that is, at very brief exposure below the threshold necessary for conscious encoding (see Chapter 4, this volume). For some participants, these images were negative (e.g., a bucket of snakes, a bloody shark), while for other participants these images were positive (e.g., a pair of kittens, a couple getting married). After seeing the pictures of the unfamiliar person, participants were asked to evaluate this individual. As can be seen in Figure 6.2, Krosnick et al. found that participants who were subliminally presented with the positive images liked the individual more compared with participants who were subliminally presented with the negative images. Not only were participants' attitudes affected by the subliminal presentations, so too were their perceptions of the target person's personality characteristics and physical attractiveness.

In addition to classical conditioning and subliminal priming, another way in which affect guides attitudes comes from research by Zajonc and colleagues (e.g., Kunst-Wilson & Zajonc, 1980; Murphy & Zajonc, 1993; Zajonc, 1968). These researchers argue that attitudes are formed on the basis of affective responses that precede conscious thought. To test this hypothesis, studies have examined how the *mere exposure* of stimuli can influence an attitude. In these

mere exposure effect increase in liking for an object as a result of being repeatedly exposed to it.

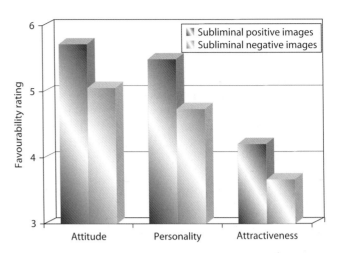

Figure 6.2 *The influence of subliminal priming on social perceptions (adapted from Krosnick et al., 1992).*

studies, different types of unfamiliar stimuli (e.g., various Chinese characters) are presented to participants a certain number of times. They are then shown again to participants along with other, novel stimuli (e.g., new characters), and participants' attitudes towards the familiar and unfamiliar characters are measured. A large number of studies have revealed that stimuli that have been presented many times are liked more than stimuli that have not been seen before. For instance, in one study by Zajonc (1968), participants were initially shown 12 different Chinese characters. During this exposure phase, each character was shown either 25 times, 10 times, 5 times, twice, once or not at all. Later, participants were asked to indicate how much they liked each character. The results of this study are presented in Figure 6.3. As can be seen, participants' attitudes towards the characters became more positive the more times the character had been seen at the exposure phase. The mere exposure phenomenon helps explain why we sometimes come to like classical music melodies that we hear repeatedly, even when we are unable to recall the artist who composed the music or any details of our prior experiences hearing it.

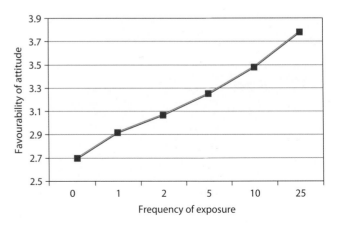

Figure 6.3 *The influence of repeated exposure on attitudes (adapted from Zajonc, 1968).*

PIONEER

Born in Poland, **Robert Zajonc** (b. 1923) completed his PhD at the University of Michigan (1955). He remained at the University of Michigan until 1994. Zajonc's research covered many areas relevant to the psychology of attitudes. His work on the mere exposure effect led to the development of an influential program of study exploring how affective processes influence attitudes and actions. This research led Zajonc to consider the role of unconscious processes in determining preferences and behaviour.

The cognitive component of attitudes

cognitive component of attitude
thoughts, beliefs and attributes associated with an attitude object

The *cognitive component of attitudes* refers to beliefs, thoughts and attributes we associate with a particular object. In many cases, a person's attitude might be based primarily upon a consideration of the positive and negative attributes about the attitude object. For example, when one of us recently bought a new car, he devoted considerable attention to factors such as different vehicles' safety records, petrol mileage, resale value and repair costs. In this example, attitudes towards the different cars were formed via a conscious consideration of the positive and negative characteristics of each car. Cognitions have an impact on many types of attitudes.

Plate 6.2 *Attitudes toward different cars might be based on the positive and negative characteristics of each car.*

Within the study of intergroup attitudes (see Chapters 3 and 14, this volume), stereotypes are usually considered as beliefs about the attributes possessed by a particular social group. Further, many studies have revealed that possessing negative stereotypes about a group of people is associated with having a prejudicial attitude towards the group (e.g., Esses, Haddock & Zanna, 1993; Kawakami, Dion & Dovidio, 1998).

Cognitions, in the form of beliefs, are a key part of one approach to attitudes, which argues that attitudes are derived from more elementary cognitions about the attitude object. Specifically, Fishbein and Ajzen's (1975) expectancy–value approach describes an attitude towards an object as the sum of 'expectancy × value' products. Expectancies are beliefs or subjective probabilities that the object possesses a certain attribute; these beliefs may range from 0 to 1 in strength. Values, or evaluations, are ratings of the attributes, normally from −3 to +3. An attitude object will be evaluated positively if it is seen as leading to, or associated with, positive things and avoiding negative things. Only salient beliefs count towards the overall attitudes; these are beliefs that a person considers most relevant. We can illustrate the model by computing a person's attitude towards the game of golf. This person might think that golf is (1) a valuable form of exercise, (2) a good way to see friends and (3) frustrating. Each of these beliefs will have both an expectancy and a value. For example, exercise might have a high expectancy (.9) and positive evaluation (+3); seeing friends might be perceived as having a lower expected outcome (.7) that is somewhat positive (+2); while frustration is (thankfully!) somewhat infrequent (.3) but very negative (−3). The individual's overall attitude towards golf is computed by summing the belief–evaluation products (e.g., 2.7 + 1.4 − .9 = 3.2).

The behavioural component of attitudes

The *behavioural component of attitudes* refers to past behaviours with respect to an attitude object. For instance, people might infer that they have a negative attitude towards nuclear power plants if they recall having previously signed a petition against having a nuclear power plant built

behavioural component of attitude past behaviours associated with an attitude object

self-perception theory a theory which assumes that individuals often do not know their own attitudes and, like outside observers, have to engage in attributional reasoning to infer their attitudes from their own behaviour

near their neighbourhood. The idea that people might infer their attitudes on the basis of their previous actions was developed by Bem. According to Bem's (1972) *self-perception theory*, individuals do not always have access to their opinions about different objects (see also Nisbett & Wilson, 1977). Bem argued that this is especially likely when the person's attitude is particularly weak or ambiguous. Many studies have shown results consistent with this reasoning. For example, Chaiken and Baldwin (1981) asked participants to complete a questionnaire containing items that were framed in a way to remind people of either their pro-environment behaviours (e.g., picking up the garbage of others) or their anti-environment behaviours (e.g., leaving on lights in unattended rooms). After completing this task, participants indicated their attitude towards the environment. The results were consistent with self-perception theory. When participants had been reminded of their positive behaviours, they reported more favourable attitudes than participants who had been reminded of their negative behaviours. Furthermore, this effect was obtained only among those individuals who, prior to the experiment, had weak attitudes about environmental matters.

Behaviours may also influence strongly held attitudes, but in a different way. Festinger (1954) proposed that people can change their attitudes in order to be consistent with behaviours that they have performed. For example, people might convince themselves that they like several boring tasks if they have just been given a small payment to tell others that the tasks are great (Festinger & Carlsmith, 1959). Many experiments support Festinger's hypothesis that this effect occurs because the counterattitudinal behaviour induces an aversive arousal, which participants are motivated to reduce (Zanna & Cooper, 1974; Zanna, Higgins & Taves, 1976). Additional evidence suggests that this effect is particularly likely to occur when the behaviour is threatening to the self-concept (Holland, Meertens & van Vugt, 2002; see Chapter 7, this volume).

Behaviours also influence attitudes in a more direct way. Research has demonstrated that performing a behaviour that has evaluative implications or connotations influences the favourability of attitudes. For example, Briñol and Petty (2003) conducted a study in which participants believed they were participating in a consumer research study on the quality of headphones. Participants were informed that a headphone manufacturer was interested in determining how headphones performed when listeners were engaged in various movements such as dancing and jogging. Briñol and Petty (2003) had participants move their heads in *either* an up-and-down motion (nodding the head) or a side-to-side motion (shaking the head) as they listened to an editorial played over the headphones. When the arguments contained in the editorial were strong, it was expected that moving one's head in an up-and-down motion would lead participants to be more positive about the position being advocated in the message, because nodding is a motion that is commonly associated with agreement. The results revealed that participants were more likely to agree with the content of a highly persuasive appeal when they moved their heads up and down as compared to side to side (see also Wells & Petty, 1980).

The enactment of other types of behaviour also affects the favourability of individuals' attitudes. For example, Cacioppo, Priester and Berntson (1993) asked participants to engage in either arm flexion (moving one's hand towards the body – a behaviour associated with approach) or arm extension (moving one's hand away from the body – a behaviour associated with avoidance) while viewing a variety of unfamiliar Chinese characters. Later in the experiment, when asked to rate the characters, Cacioppo et al. (1993) found that characters viewed during arm flexion were rated more positively than those viewed during arm extension. Taken together, in both the Briñol and Petty (2003) and Cacioppo et al. (1993) studies, a direct physical behaviour initiated by individuals influenced the favourability of their attitude.

SUMMARY

Attitudes have affective, cognitive and behavioural components. The affective component refers to feelings or emotions associated with an attitude object. The cognitive component refers to beliefs, thoughts and attributes associated with an attitude object. The behavioural component refers to past behaviours with respect to an attitude object.

THE STRUCTURE OF ATTITUDES

What are the two basic perspectives on attitude structure?
What is the evidence supporting a one-dimensional attitude structure?
What are some potential effects of attitudinal ambivalence?

In addition to considering the content of attitudes, another important issue concerns how positive and negative evaluations are organized within and among the affective, cognitive and behavioural components of attitudes. It is typically assumed that the existence of positive feelings, beliefs and behaviours inhibits the occurrence of negative feelings, beliefs and behaviours. For example, this framework suggests that an individual with positive feelings, beliefs and behaviours about the Welsh rugby team is unlikely to have negative feelings, beliefs and behaviours about this team. In other words, according to this *one-dimensional perspective of attitudes*, the positive and negative elements are stored in memory at opposite ends of a single dimension, and people tend to experience either end of the dimension or a location in between.

This one-dimensional view is opposed by a *two-dimensional perspective of attitudes*, which suggests that positive and negative elements are stored along two separate dimensions (Cacioppo, Gardner & Berntson, 1997). One dimension reflects whether the attitude has few or many positive elements, and the other dimension reflects whether the attitude has few or many negative elements. This view proposes that people can possess any combination of positivity or negativity in their attitudes. Consistent with the one-dimensional view, attitudes may consist of few positive and many negative elements, few negative and many positive, or few positive and few negative (i.e., a neutral position). Inconsistent with the one-dimensional view, attitudes might occasionally subsume many positive *and* many negative elements, leading to

> **one-dimensional perspective of attitudes**
> a perspective that perceives positive and negative elements as stored along a single dimension
>
> **two-dimensional perspective of attitudes**
> a perspective that perceives positive and negative elements as stored along separate dimensions

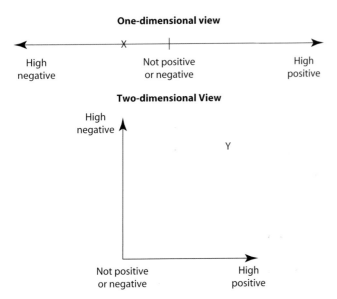

Figure 6.4 *The one-dimensional and two-dimensional perspectives of attitude.*

representing variability in negative evaluations and the other axis (from middle to right) depicting variability in positive evaluations. From this perspective, a person can possess high amounts of negativity and positivity towards an object. For example, Person Y in the figure could be considered highly ambivalent.

Which perspective is superior? At first glance, the two-dimensional perspective seems as though it should be superior because it allows for the same patterns of positivity and negativity as the one-dimensional view, while also allowing for ambivalence. For instance, it is difficult to interpret the meaning of the neutral point in one-dimensional scales for assessing attitudes (Kaplan, 1972). Imagine that people were asked to report their attitude towards eating fried foods on a nine-point scale that ranged from '1 – extremely unfavourable' to '9 – extremely favourable' as the end points, with '5 – neither unfavourable nor favourable' in the middle. If someone indicated that his or her attitude was neutral (e.g., 'neither favourable nor unfavourable'), it is half-way between the most extreme positive response option (e.g., 'extremely favourable') and the most extreme negative response option (e.g., 'extremely unfavourable'). People could choose this option because it is a compromise between many positive and negative elements of their attitude (e.g., they have many positive and negative feelings, thoughts and behaviours regarding eating fried foods) *or* because they have no positive or negative elements whatsoever (e.g., they have never eaten fried foods).

The failure to distinguish between these two reasons for the neutral selection is important, because measures that directly assess ambivalence predict a variety of outcomes. The best known outcome is *response polarization* (Bell & Esses, 2002; MacDonald & Zanna, 1998; see Research close-up 6.1). People who are highly ambivalent towards an object are more strongly influenced by features of their environment that make salient its positive or negative attributes. This causes them to behave more favourably towards the object when the positive elements are salient than when the negative elements are salient. In contrast, non-ambivalent people are less strongly influenced by the acute salience of the positive or negative attributes.

attitudinal ambivalence an instance where an individual both likes and dislikes an attitude object

attitudinal ambivalence. The two-dimensional perspective explicitly allows for this ambivalence to occur, whereas the one-dimensional perspective does not.

The one-dimensional and two-dimensional perspectives are presented in Figure 6.4. The top panel depicts the one-dimensional view of attitudes. Person X, who is plotted on an axis depicting the one-dimensional view, would be slightly negative. The single axis does not permit one to mark Person X as being both negative and positive. The bottom panel of Figure 6.4 depicts the two-dimensional view of attitudes, with one axis (from middle to top)

RESEARCH CLOSE-UP 6.1

Consequences of ambivalent attitudes

MacDonald, T.K. & Zanna, M.P. (1998). Cross-dimension ambivalence toward social groups: Can ambivalence affect intentions to hire feminists? *Personality and Social Psychology Bulletin, 24,* 427–441.

....

Introduction

One of the reasons for the emergence of attitudinal ambivalence as an important construct is its potential to explain why people

sometimes react in very polarized ways to controversial groups or issues. This notion was illustrated nicely in MacDonald and Zanna's (1998) research, which examined consequences of students' ambivalence towards feminists. In an initial set of data, these investigators found that some students tended to both admire feminists *and* dislike them. This pattern can be labelled as cognitive-affective ambivalence, because it represents conflict between how the individuals think (e.g., admire feminists for their perceived courage) and feel (e.g., dislike feminists because of their perceived stridency). The investigators' second study, which is the focus of this close-up, examined an important potential consequence of this ambivalence: polarized evaluations of a feminist's suitability for employment. The researchers expected that ambivalent people would be more strongly influenced by a prior event, which was whether a prior candidate who was admirable-but-dislikeable succeeded or failed in an interview.

Method

Participants
One hundred and two students (76 women and 26 men) took part for psychology course credit.

Design and procedure
The basic design included two factors: cognitive-affective ambivalence (high or low) and prime (either positive or negative). Ambivalence was measured using a questionnaire that was presented before the main study. This questionnaire asked the participants to use several scales to rate the extent to which they admired feminists (e.g., worthy of respect) and liked them (e.g., likeable). Participants who reported admiring feminists while disliking them (or liking but not admiring them) were classified as ambivalent, whereas participants who were similar in their levels of liking and admiration of feminists (either similarly high or similarly low) were classified as non-ambivalent.

These ambivalent and non-ambivalent participants were informed in a subsequent experimental session that they were taking part in a study of how people make hiring decisions. They listened to a 10-minute audio recording of a job interview, which featured an admirable but dislikeable man who was to be successful (positive prime condition) or unsuccessful with his application (negative prime condition). Participants then completed questions about the candidate's admirable qualities (positive prime condition) or dislikeable qualities (negative prime condition).

Finally, participants received, read and evaluated the applications of several women, including one who had completed a thesis and jobs that suggested a feminist political perspective. As part of this final task, participants rated the likelihood that they would hire each woman for a job (e.g., magazine editorial assistant, ombudsman). These ratings were made using different types of scales (e.g., 0% to 100%). To interpret these ratings, the responses were converted to standardized scores, such that very low values (e.g., −2) indicated low likelihood of hiring the candidate and very high values (e.g., +2) indicated high likelihood of hiring the candidate.

Results

The primary dependent measure was the rated likelihood of hiring the feminist applicant. As shown in Figure 6.5, participants

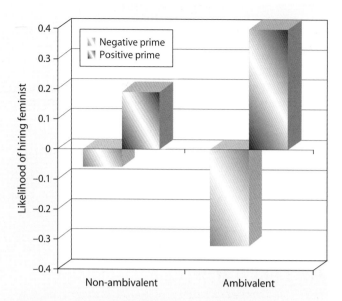

Figure 6.5 *Intentions to hire feminists as a function of cognitive-affective ambivalence and type of prime.*

who exhibited a high degree of ambivalence towards feminists reported stronger intentions to hire the feminist candidate after seeing the admirable-but-dislikeable male candidate succeed than after seeing him fail. In contrast, participants who exhibited a low degree of ambivalence towards feminists were less affected by the success or failure of the admirable-but-dislikeable male candidate. Thus, only the ambivalent participants' intentions were affected by the prime.

Discussion

MacDonald and Zanna (1998) concluded that cognitive-affective ambivalence has important consequences for behaviour. When people possess this ambivalence, making them mindful of either the cognitive (e.g., admiration) or affective (e.g., dislike) elements of their attitudes causes their behaviour to reflect the salient elements. As a result, ambivalent people might appear to strongly favour a person who is a target of their ambivalence (e.g., a feminist) in some situations (e.g., after a positive event), but strongly disfavour the individual in other situations (e.g., after a negative event). Thus, behaviour that may seem quizzical and contradictory on the surface may be explicable by considering the extent to which there is ambivalence in the underlying attitude.

SUMMARY

An important issue related to attitudes concerns how positive and negative evaluations are organized within and among the affective, cognitive and behavioural components of attitude. The one-dimensional view postulates that the positive and negative elements are stored as opposite ends of a single dimension. The two-dimensional view postulates that positive and negative elements are stored along two separate dimensions.

WHY DO WE HOLD ATTITUDES?

What is the most basic psychological need served by attitudes? How might knowledge of attitude functions influence choice of persuasive messages in advertising campaigns? Do people vary in the functions of their attitudes?

Individuals hold attitudes for a variety of reasons. For example, our attitudes towards the Welsh rugby team developed from many of our friends and colleagues supporting the same team. In contrast, our attitudes towards abortion are based on the value we place on an individual's freedom of choice and the sanctity of human life. Over the years, attitude researchers have devoted considerable attention to understanding the needs or functions that are fulfilled by attitudes.

attitude function the psychological need fulfilled by an attitude

The most prominent models of *attitude functions* were developed almost 50 years ago (Katz, 1960; Smith,

Plate 6.3 *Attitudes towards, e.g., the Welsh rugby team may be developed from friends supporting the same team.*

Bruner & White, 1956). Smith et al. (1956) suggested that attitudes serve three primary functions or needs: object appraisal, social adjustment and externalization. *Object appraisal* refers to the ability of attitudes to summarize the positive and negative attributes of objects in our social world. For example, attitudes can help people to approach things that are beneficial for them and avoid things that are harmful to them (Maio, Esses, Arnold & Olson, 2004). *Social adjustment* is fulfilled by attitudes that help us to identify with people we like and to dissociate from people we dislike. For example, individuals may buy a certain soft drink because it is endorsed by their favourite singer. *Externalization* is fulfilled by attitudes that defend the self against internal conflict. For example, bad golfers might develop an intense dislike for the game because their poor performance threatens their self-esteem.

In his own program of research, Katz (1960) proposed four attitude functions, some of which relate to those proposed by Smith et al. (1956): knowledge, utility, ego defence and value expression. The *knowledge* function represents the ability of attitudes to organize information about attitude objects, while the *utilitarian* function exists in attitudes that maximize rewards and minimize punishments obtained from attitude objects. These functions are similar to Smith et al.'s (1956) object-appraisal function. Katz's *ego-defensive* function exists in attitudes that serve to protect an individual's self-esteem and is similar to Smith et al.'s (1956) externalization function. Finally, Katz proposed that attitudes may serve a *value-expressive* function, such that an attitude may express an individual's self-concept and central values. For example, a person might cycle to work because she values health and wishes to preserve the environment.

A number of themes have developed from research on attitude functions since the development of these theoretical perspectives. Here, we focus on two important developments. First, evidence implies that strongly held attitudes fulfil an object-appraisal function. Second, a distinction between instrumental attitudes (those that serve a utilitarian function) and symbolic attitudes (those that serve a value-expressive function) appears to be useful. In the following sections, we describe evidence regarding these observations.

Object appraisal = utilitarian

Smith et al.'s (1956) object-appraisal function (which combines aspects of Katz's utilitarian and knowledge functions) perhaps best explains why people form attitudes in the first place. This function suggests that attitudes classify objects in the environment for the purposes of action. In their description of the object-appraisal function, Smith et al. suggested that attitudes are *energy-saving devices*, because attitudes make attitude-relevant judgements faster and easier to perform. Two programs of research have directly supported this line of reasoning, while suggesting important caveats. First, Fazio (1995, 2000) argued that the object-appraisal function should be more strongly served by attitudes that are high in accessibility. This prediction is based on the assumption that strong attitudes guide relevant judgements and behaviour, whereas weak attitudes will have little effect during judgement and behaviour processes. Consistent with this hypothesis, research has shown that

(a)

(b)

Plates 6.4a and b *Attitudes toward abortion might be based on freedom of choice and sanctity of human life.*

highly accessible attitudes increase the ease with which people make attitude-relevant judgements. For example, people who have accessible attitudes towards an abstract painting have been shown to be subsequently faster at deciding whether they prefer the painting over another painting (see Fazio, 2000).

Another program of research has revealed that the strength of the object-appraisal motivation is influenced by differences across people in the need for closure, which is a 'desire for a definite answer on some topic, any answer as opposed to confusion and ambiguity' (Kruglanski, 1989, p. 14). As applied to the study of attitudes, object appraisal reflects the notion that attitudes can provide such 'answers', because attitudes help people to make decisions about attitude objects. As a result, a high need for closure should increase the desire to form and maintain attitudes. Kruglanski and colleagues have tested this hypothesis in a number of studies. In one study by Kruglanski, Webster and Klem (1993), some participants (who were either high or low in the need for closure) were initially given sufficient information that allowed them to form an attitude about a legal case, whereas other participants were not given this information (and were unable to form

an initial attitude). Later, all participants were given additional information about the case. The results of the study revealed that the impact of the later information on participants' final attitudes depended upon *both* participants' level of need for closure and whether they had already formed an attitude towards the case. As can be seen in Figure 6.6, among participants who had already formed an attitude based on the initial information, those who were high in need for closure were less persuaded by new information than participants who were low in need for closure. In contrast, if participants had not yet formed an attitude, those who were high in need for closure were more persuaded by new information than participants who were low in need for closure.

Instrumental versus value-expressive attitudes

Several researchers have argued for a distinction between instrumental (or utilitarian) and value-expressive attitudes (e.g., Herek,

Plate 6.5 *A person might cycle to work because she values health and wishes to preserve the environment.*

Plate 6.6 *How accessible is your attitude towards Queen Elizabeth II?*

1986; Prentice, 1987; Sears, 1988). Instrumental attitudes classify attitude objects according to their ability to promote self-interest, whereas value-expressive attitudes express concerns about self-image and personal values. Many lines of research support the distinction between instrumental and value-expressive attitudes. First, some attitude *objects* elicit attitudes that are associated primarily with one or the other of these functions. For example, Shavitt (1990) found that people's thoughts about air conditioners and coffee focus on the utility of the objects, whereas thoughts about greeting cards and national flags tend to focus on the objects' capacity to symbolize the self and social values.

Second, evidence indicates that people are more persuaded by messages containing arguments that match the primary function of their attitudes than by messages containing arguments that do not match the primary function of their attitudes. For example, Shavitt (1990) found that instrumental advertisements for products about which people held instrumental attitudes (e.g., an air conditioner) were more persuasive than symbolic advertisements for instrumental products. Similarly, Snyder and DeBono

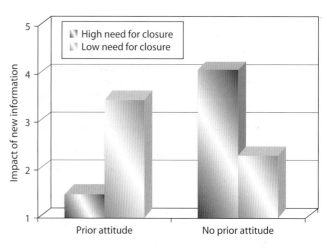

Figure 6.6 *The impact of new information by prior attitude and need for closure (adapted from Kruglanski et al., 1993).*

self-monitoring an individual difference construct concerning differences in how people vary their behaviour across social situations

(1985) found that individual differences in self-monitoring affected the persuasiveness of different types of advertisements. *Self-monitoring* (Snyder, 1974, 1987) refers to differences in how people vary their behaviour across social situations. While high self-monitors are oriented to situational cues and finely tune their behaviour to the situation in which they find themselves, low self-monitors tend to behave in ways that are consistent with their core values and tend not to adapt their behaviour to the situation in which they find themselves (see Individual Differences 6.1). As applied to advertising, Snyder and DeBono predicted that high self-monitors might be more influenced by advertisements that convey the positive images associated with using a particular product, while low self-monitors might be more influenced by advertisements that feature the quality of a product.

To test this hypothesis, Snyder and DeBono (1985) presented participants with one of two versions of an advertisement for a particular brand of whisky. In both versions of the advertisement,

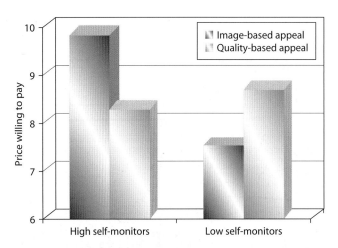

Figure 6.7 *The influence of self-monitoring and appeal type on willingness to pay for a consumer product (adapted from Snyder & DeBono, 1985).*

there was a picture of a whisky bottle resting on a set of architects' plans for a house. In one version of the advertisement, the picture was accompanied by the phrase 'You're not just moving in, you're moving up'. In the second version of the advertisement, the same photo was accompanied by the phrase 'When it comes to great taste, everyone draws the same conclusion'. It was predicted that high self-monitors would be more persuaded by the image-based appeal, while low self-monitors would be more persuaded by the quality-based appeal. The results of the study are shown in Figure 6.7. As predicted, Snyder and DeBono (1985) found that high self-monitors were willing to pay more for the whisky when presented with the image-based appeal, whereas low self-monitors were willing to pay more when presented with the quality-based appeal. Further research has demonstrated that these 'match the message to the function' effects occur because people devote more attention to convincing arguments that match the function of their attitude than to convincing arguments that do not match the function of their attitude (Petty & Wegener, 1998b).

INDIVIDUAL DIFFERENCES 6.1

Self-monitoring

Self-monitoring refers to differences in how people vary their behaviour across social situations (Snyder, 1974). High self-monitors are oriented to situational cues and tune their behaviour to the social situation, whereas low self-monitors tend to behave in ways that are consistent with their values and tend not to mould their behaviour to the social situation. Self-monitoring is assessed by a scale developed by Snyder (1974). Sample items are listed below. For each item, respondents are asked whether the statement is true or false as applied to them.

1 I can make impromptu speeches even on topics about which I have almost no information.
2 I can only argue for ideas which I already believe.
3 When I am uncertain how to act in a social situation, I look to the behaviour of others for cues.
4 My behaviour is usually an expression of my true inner feelings, attitudes and beliefs.
5 In different situations and with different people, I often act like very different persons.
6 I would not change my opinions (or the way I do things) in order to please someone else or win their favour.

High self-monitors would be more likely to judge statements 1, 3 and 5 as true of themselves, whereas low self-monitors would be more likely to judge statements 2, 4 and 6 as true of themselves.

SUMMARY

Individuals hold attitudes for a variety of reasons. The most prominent models of attitude functions were developed almost 50 years ago by Smith et al. (1956) and Katz (1960). Among the functions, the object-appraisal function is especially important as it suggests that attitudes serve as energy-saving devices that make judgements easier and faster to perform. There is also an important distinction between instrumental and value-expressive attitudes. Knowing the primary function of an attitude is important, because attempts at attitude change are more likely to be successful when the persuasive appeal matches the function of the attitude.

LINKING ATTITUDE CONTENT, STRUCTURE AND FUNCTION

What features of attitudes can make them strong?
What are some potential consequences of strong attitudes?

Attitude content, attitude structure and attitude function are inexorably linked. Indeed, we consider them to be analogous to three witches who make a better brew together than alone (Maio & Haddock, 2004). For example, although it is possible to partly disentangle the effects of attitude structure and attitude function (Maio & Olson, 2000; Murray, Haddock & Zanna, 1996), it is apparent that they are often related. This relation can be illustrated by considering attitudes towards a brand of car that are based on a need to conserve fuel. These attitudes should be based on beliefs about the extent to which the car obtains good fuel economy. Similarly, if attitudes towards a style of clothing fulfil a psychological need to enhance social relations, then these attitudes should be based on beliefs about the extent to which the style is preferred among one's friends. In other words, attitudes that serve different functions should often differ in the content of the beliefs that support them (see also Haddock & Maio, 2004).

A question of content, structure and function: How stable are attitudes?

One important question that is relevant to the content, structure and function of attitudes is the extent to which attitudes are stable over time. This question is relevant to efforts to quantify the strength of an attitude. As mentioned at the beginning of the chapter, we feel more strongly about some topics than about others. For over 75 years, the topic of *attitude strength* has been of considerable interest to attitude researchers. During this time, the strength of an attitude has been conceptualized in many different ways. For example, individuals can simply be asked how *certain* they are of their attitude, as well as how *important* their attitude is to them personally (see Haddock, Rothman, Reber & Schwarz, 1999). The strength of an attitude can also be measured by assessing its distance from the middle of a scale. This type of index, known as attitude *extremity*, has been found to have many important outcomes (see Abelson, 1995). Similarly, some attitudes can be retrieved from memory more quickly than others; such easily retrievable attitudes are referred to as being highly *accessible* (Fazio, 1995).

Strong attitudes differ from weak attitudes in a number of ways. Krosnick and Petty (1995) argue that there are four key manifestations of strong attitudes. First, strong attitudes are *more persistent*. That is, they are more temporally stable over the passage of time (Visser & Krosnick, 1998). Second, strong attitudes are *more resistant to change*. When faced with a persuasive appeal, strong attitudes are less likely to change than weak attitudes (Petty, Haugtvedt & Smith, 1995). Third, strong attitudes are *more likely to influence information processing*. Research has revealed that people devote greater attention to information that is relevant to strong versus weak attitudes (Houston & Fazio, 1989). Finally, strong attitudes are *more likely to guide behaviour*. Put simply, we are more likely to act upon strong versus weak attitudes (Holland, Verplanken & van Knippenberg, 2002; see Research close-up 6.2). We return to this last issue later in the chapter.

SUMMARY

Attitude content, attitude structure and attitude function are inexorably linked. Centrally relevant to these concepts is attitude strength. Attitudes vary in the degree to which they are persistent over time, resistant to change, influential in guiding information processing and influential in predicting behaviour.

THE MEASUREMENT OF ATTITUDES

What do we mean by explicit and implicit attitudes?
Do they measure the same thing?
Have social psychologists developed reliable and valid measures of attitudes?

Attitudes, like most constructs in psychology, are not directly observable. For instance, we can not see that a person holds a positive attitude towards red sports cars. Rather, attitudes have to be inferred from the individual's responses to questions about these vehicles (Fazio & Olson, 2003). As a result, social psychologists have needed to develop different methods to measure attitudes. In this section of the chapter, we describe some of the most commonly used techniques that have been developed. For forms of attitude measurement other than those discussed here (e.g., psychophysical measures, behavioural measures), see Bohner and Wänke (2002) and Fazio and Olson (2003).

In introducing different types of attitude measures, we have differentiated them on the basis of whether they are *explicit* (i.e., direct) or *implicit* (i.e., indirect). The distinction between explicit and implicit measures and processes has a long history

explicit measures of attitude attitude measures that directly ask respondents to think about and report an attitude

implicit measures of attitude attitude measures that assess attitudes without directly asking respondents for a verbal report of an attitude

RESEARCH CLOSE-UP 6.2

Attitudes can predict and follow behaviour

Holland, R.W., Verplanken, B. & van Knippenberg, A. (2002). On the nature of attitude–behavior relations: The strong guide, the weak follow. *European Journal of Social Psychology, 32,* 869–876.

Introduction

The experiment considers the circumstances under which (1) attitudes predict behaviour and (2) behaviour predicts attitudes. The authors review evidence demonstrating both causal pathways. First, they review a number of studies demonstrating that attitudes influence behaviour (some of these studies are discussed in this chapter). Second, they review a number of studies (derived from self-perception theory and dissonance theory) demonstrating that attitudes can sometimes be inferred from past behaviour. Holland et al. suggest that the concept of attitude strength is crucial to understanding when attitudes predict behaviour (as opposed to behaviour predicting attitudes). Specifically, Holland et al. postulate that strong attitudes are more likely than weak attitudes to predict behaviour, whereas weak attitudes are more likely than strong attitudes to follow from behaviour.

Method

Participants
One hundred and six students participated in the study.

Design and procedure
The experiment was split into two sessions, with an interval of one week. In session 1, participants completed measures assessing the favourability and the strength of their attitudes towards Greenpeace. Attitude favourability was measured by the question 'How positive or negative is your attitude towards Greenpeace?'; one of the attitude strength items was 'How certain are you about your attitude towards Greenpeace?' One week later, participants returned for an unrelated study. At the

end of this unrelated study, they were paid the equivalent of about £3 (in various coins and bills). Immediately after being paid, participants were told that the experimenter was also conducting a small study for Greenpeace. Importantly, participants were also informed that they could choose to donate money to Greenpeace. After making their decision whether or not to donate money, the experimenter asked participants to complete a short questionnaire, which included an assessment of their attitude towards Greenpeace.

The *attitude–behaviour* relation was derived by comparing the favourability of participants' attitude at time 1 with the amount of money they donated at time 2. The *behaviour–attitude* relation was derived by comparing the amount of money participants donated at time 2 with the measure of attitude that was taken immediately after the donation behaviour.

Results

As expected, the researchers found that attitude strength was crucial for understanding when attitudes predict behaviour as opposed to when behaviour predicts attitudes. First, with respect to the *attitude–behaviour* relation, strong attitudes at time 1 predicted behaviour at time 2; weak attitudes did not. On the other hand, with respect to the *behaviour–attitude* relation, weak attitudes were greatly influenced by behaviour; strong attitudes were not.

Discussion

Holland et al.'s (2002) findings provided support for their main hypotheses. When participants held strong opinions about Greenpeace, the favourability of their attitude predicted the amount of money they subsequently donated to the organization. When participants held weak attitudes about Greenpeace, their attitude was shaped by (i.e., inferred from) their donation behaviour. This study makes an important contribution to our understanding of the bi-dimensional causal relations between attitudes and behaviour.

within psychology. Psychologists usually think of explicit measures as those that require respondents' conscious attention to the construct being measured, whereas implicit measures are those that do not require this conscious attention. Within the context of attitude measurement, these terms can be used to distinguish between attitude measures in which the respondent is either aware *or* unaware that an attitude is being assessed (or how the attitude is being assessed). At a basic level, explicit measures of attitude are those that directly ask respondents to think about and report their attitude, whereas implicit measures of attitude are those that assess

attitudes without *directly* asking respondents for a verbal report of their attitude (Fazio & Olson, 2003).

Explicit measures of attitudes

The majority of attitude measures that have been developed can be conceptualized as explicit indicators. Most often, these measures have been self-report questionnaires, in which participants are asked to respond to direct questions about their opinions towards the object in question. For example, if a group of researchers was interested in knowing a respondent's attitude towards abortion, they might ask the question 'What is your attitude towards abortion?' In the following section, we describe two explicit measures of attitude: Likert scales and the semantic differential.

Likert scales   Likert (1932) introduced a measure of attitude based upon summated ratings. In this approach, statements are written in such a way that responses indicate either a favourable or unfavourable attitude. An example of a Likert scale to assess attitudes towards euthanasia is presented in Figure 6.8. For each item, respondents are asked to indicate their degree of agreement or disagreement. As you read the items presented in Figure 6.8, you will notice that items can be written such that a strong positive attitude towards euthanasia will produce either a 'strongly agree' response (e.g., to item 1) or a 'strongly disagree' response (e.g., to item 3). Researchers create items that are worded in opposite directions in order to help avoid response sets (i.e., the tendency for a respondent to agree or disagree with all items on a scale).

How are Likert scales scored? In a questionnaire like the one in Figure 6.8, each response alternative is allocated a score (in this case from 1 to 5). Usually, a low score is taken to indicate a strong negative attitude and a high score is taken to indicate a strong positive attitude. Thus, for item 1, an individual who strongly disagrees with the statement would be allocated a score of 1, while a person who strongly agrees would be given a score of 5. For item 3 the procedure is reversed because the item is worded in the opposite direction to item 1. Scores for this item are recoded such that an individual who strongly disagrees with the statement is expressing a positive attitude (and hence is allocated a score of 5 for that item), whereas an individual who strongly agrees with that item is expressing a negative attitude (and thus is allocated a score of 1). To the extent that the items assess the same construct (i.e., a respondent's attitude), correlations among responses to each

Please respond to each scale by placing an 'X' in the
space that best represents your opinion.

EUTHANASIA

BAD:__:__:__:__:__:__:__:GOOD
NEGATIVE:__:__:__:__:__:__:__:POSITIVE
DISLIKE:__:__:__:__:__:__:__:LIKE

Figure 6.9   *A semantic differential scale to measure attitudes towards euthanasia.*

item should be high. If they are sufficiently high, scores on the individual items are averaged to form a single attitude score.

Semantic differential scales   A large amount of research is interested in demonstrating how people might hold more positive attitudes towards some attitude objects (e.g., movies directed by Clint Eastwood) than others (e.g., movies directed by Martin Scorsese). To address questions concerning the attitudes that people hold about a variety of attitude objects, it was necessary to develop methodologies that would allow researchers to measure attitudes towards many attitude objects along a common scale. Among the efforts to develop such a technique, the method that has been the most influential is the semantic differential approach (Osgood, Suci & Tannenbaum, 1957). An example of a semantic differential scale is presented in Figure 6.9. In this technique, participants are given a set of bipolar adjective scales, each of which is separated into a number of categories. Participants are asked to rate the attitude object by indicating the response that best represents their opinion. The bipolar adjectives typically include general evaluative terms such as favourable–unfavourable, good–bad and like–dislike. Similar to Likert scales, correlations among the items should be positive (to the extent that they measure the same attitude). If they are sufficiently high, they can be combined to form a single attitude score.

Issues relevant to the explicit measurement of attitudes

Historically, explicit measures of attitudes have dominated empirical research on the psychology of attitudes. Despite their wide appeal, however, a number of concerns have been raised over their use. For example, individuals might sometimes be unaware of their attitude towards an object (Fazio, Jackson, Dunton & Williams, 1995; Greenwald & Banaji, 1995; Nisbett & Wilson, 1977). Further, research has demonstrated that subtle differences in the way in which items are presented can influence responses to direct measures of attitude (see Haddock & Carrick, 1999; Schwarz, 1999).

Probably the most important criticism about direct measures of attitude is that they are affected by people's motivation to give *socially desirable responses*. This refers

socially desirable responding a deliberative attempt to misrepresent responses so as to present oneself in a favourable way

The following statements are part of a survey on public attitudes. There are no right or wrong answers, only opinions. For each statement, indicate the number that best represents your personal opinion by using the following scale:

If you strongly disagree with the statement, indicate 1
If you disagree with the statement, indicate 2
If you neither disagree nor agree with the statement, indicate 3
If you agree with the statement, indicate 4
If you strongly agree with the statement, indicate 5

(1) I think euthanasia should be made legal.   _____

(2) I would support a referendum for the institution of euthanasia. _____

(3) Euthanasia should never be used.   _____

(4) Euthanasia is appropriate when someone wants to die.   _____

(5) I am against the use of euthanasia in all circumstances.   _____

Figure 6.8   *An example of a Likert scale to assess attitudes towards euthanasia.*

to deliberate attempts to misrepresent (or fake) responses in a way that allows respondents to present themselves in a favourable way (Paulhus & John, 1998). To the extent that the researcher is interested in studying attitudes towards sensitive issues and/or issues that highlight norms of political or social appropriateness, people's responses might not necessarily reflect their true opinion, but instead may reflect a desire to present themselves in a positive manner. For example, in many cultures, it is considered socially inappropriate to express a prejudicial attitude towards ethnic minorities. The use of explicit, direct measures of attitude in such contexts may not provide an accurate report of attitude, as respondents may be reluctant to be perceived as prejudiced.

Implicit measures of attitudes

In an attempt to minimize problems associated with direct measures of attitude, social psychologists have developed a number of indirect or implicit response strategies. We describe here two of the most common measures, the evaluative priming technique (see Fazio et al., 1995) and the Implicit Association Test (IAT; Greenwald, McGhee & Schwartz, 1998).

Evaluative priming Fazio (1995) defines an attitude as an association in memory between an attitude object and a summary evaluation. According to Fazio and colleagues, these associations vary in strength, and the strength of the association determines the accessibility of an attitude. Let us describe this perspective more concretely by using an example. One of us *really* hates Brussels sprouts. Even thinking about Brussels sprouts sets off an immediate and strong negative reaction within him. He also dislikes rice cakes, but his reaction is not as aversive. Fazio's model would suggest that the negative attitude towards Brussels sprouts is more accessible than the negative attitude towards rice cakes, because the association in memory between 'Brussels sprouts' and 'dislike' is stronger than the association between 'rice cakes' and 'dislike'.

According to Fazio and colleagues, the strength of these associations should affect how quickly an individual responds to an evaluative word after having been briefly presented with the attitude object. In a typical study of this process, a participant is seated in front of a computer. The attitude object is briefly presented on the computer screen (e.g., the term 'Brussels sprouts') and then replaced by an evaluative adjective (e.g., 'disgusting'). The participant's task is to indicate the valence of the adjective as quickly as possible. That is, the participant indicates whether the *adjective* means something positive or negative, *not* whether the attitude object itself is good or bad. Of primary interest is the speed with which the participant makes this response. In our example, the presentation of 'Brussels sprouts' should produce faster responses to negative adjectives and slower responses to positive adjectives. Furthermore, if the person hates Brussels sprouts more than rice cakes, this facilitation/inhibition should be more pronounced when presented with Brussels sprouts than when presented with rice cakes.

This approach has been used in studies of numerous attitude objects, including attitude objects that might elicit social

desirability concerns on explicit measures. For example, Fazio et al. (1995) adapted the evaluative priming paradigm to study prejudicial attitudes. In this study, white participants were instructed that their task was to indicate the meaning of positive and negative adjectives. However, prior to the presentation of each individual adjective, participants were briefly shown a photo of a black or white person. Fazio et al. (1995) found that, among white participants, the presentation of a black face produced faster responding to negative adjectives and slower responses to positive adjectives (relative to what was found in response to the presentation of white faces). Thus, in this study, a negative attitude towards black people was represented by differences in the time required by white participants to categorize positive and negative adjectives after the presentation of black versus white faces (black participants did not show this tendency). Further, white participants who showed the pattern most strongly were more likely to show more negative behaviour towards a black experimenter in the study. Thus, these differences in response times were easily interpretable as reflecting a negative attitude towards blacks.

The Implicit Association Test Another important indirect procedure is the Implicit Association Test (IAT; Greenwald et al., 1998). For ease of presentation, we will work through an example of procedures that would use the IAT to assess gender attitudes. This example is depicted in Figure 6.10. In a typical IAT study, participants are seated at a computer and asked to classify attitude objects and adjectives. An IAT study generally involves five separate blocks. In *block 1* of a gender IAT, participants are presented

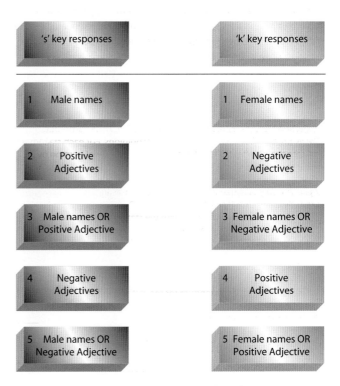

Figure 6.10 *The procedure of the five block Implicit Association Test.*

with a variety of male and female names. Participants would be instructed to make one response (e.g., press the 's' key on a keyboard) when they see a male name and make a different response (e.g., press the 'k' key) when they see a female name. They are asked to perform this task (and all others in the test) as quickly as possible. There might be anywhere from 20–40 trials within this (and subsequent) blocks. In *block 2*, participants are presented with a variety of positive and negative adjectives. Again, they would be asked to make one response (press the 's' key) when a positive adjective appears on the screen and a different response (press the 'k' key) when a negative adjective appears on the screen. In *block 3*, participants are instructed that they will see names or adjectives and that they are to press the 's' key when they see a male name *or* positive adjective, and press the 'k' key when they see a female name *or* negative adjective. *Block 4* is similar to block 2, but this time the responses are reversed, such that a participant now presses the 's' key when a negative word appears and the 'k' key when a positive word appears. *Block 5* is similar to block 3, but this time participants are to press the 's' key when a male name or negative adjective appears, and the 'k' key when a female name or positive adjective appears. The key blocks are 3 and 5 – they measure the strength of association between an attitude object (in this case gender categories) and evaluations.

How does the IAT use these blocks to compute an attitude score? Imagine an individual who is more negative about women compared to men. For this individual, the task in block 3 should be quite simple. If the person favours men to women, trials in which men are associated with positive adjectives and women are associated with negative adjectives should produce fast responses, because the links between these categories and the evaluations are congruent. Let's imagine that our participant's mean response time to trials in this block is 700 ms. In contrast, responses in block 5 should take longer for this participant. Given the person's inherent preference for men over women, trials that associate women with positivity and men with negativity should require more time to elicit a response. Let's imagine that the individual's mean response time for this block is 1200 ms. Thus, our participant's mean response time for block 3 is shorter than that for block 5 by 500 ms. This difference is referred to as the IAT effect (see Greenwald, Nosek & Banaji, 2003; Greenwald et al., 1998, for additional details about computing IAT effects).

The IAT and other implicit measures have become increasingly popular among attitude researchers (see Fazio & Olson, 2003). These types of measures have gained popularity because they assess attitudes without the necessity of asking the participant for a direct verbal report. As noted earlier, part of their appeal is due to the belief that responses on these measures are less likely to be affected by socially desirable responding (see Fazio & Olson, 2003). That said, despite (or perhaps due to) their popularity, implicit measures of attitude have also been the source of criticism.

For example, a number of researchers have argued that the (sometimes) low correlation found between implicit and explicit measures of attitude implies that they assess different constructs (see Karpinski & Hilton, 2001). Other criticisms have focused on *how* implicit measures assess attitudes. For instance, Olson and Fazio (2004) have claimed that the IAT can be contaminated by extrapersonal associations with the attitude object. These authors argue that a personalized version of the IAT (one in which the positive and negative judgements are personalized; e.g., using 'I like' and 'I don't like' versus 'pleasant' and 'unpleasant') is more effective. As research continues to progress on implicit measures of attitude, the debate around implicit measures will surely continue. Our own view is that implicit measures of attitude have much to offer, in that they have allowed social psychologists to generate novel and important questions about the underlying causes of human behaviour.

Are attitude measures reliable and valid?

A sound measure must be both reliable and valid. *Reliability* refers to 'the degree to which test scores are free from errors in measurement' (American Psychological Association, 1985, p. 19). In the context of attitude measurement, reliability has two important meanings. First, internal consistency refers to whether the individual items are assessing the same psychological construct. Items that assess the same construct should be positively correlated. Second, test–retest reliability refers to consistency in scores across time. A sound attitude measure should produce similar scores across repeated testing (in the absence of any true attitude change).

A number of studies have investigated the reliability of explicit and implicit measures of attitude. Explicit measures have been shown to exhibit high reliability. For example, semantic differential scales using the evaluative dimensions of good–bad, positive–negative and favourable–unfavourable exhibit high internal consistency (Huskinson & Haddock, 2004). Given their more recent introduction, less research has been conducted assessing the reliability of implicit measures of attitude. However, a paper by Cunningham, Preacher and Banaji (2001) found that several implicit measures possessed reasonably high internal consistency and test–retest correlations.

The *validity* of a measure refers to the degree to which it assesses the construct it is designed to assess. A number of studies have investigated the validity of explicit and implicit measures of attitude. Explicit measures of attitude have been shown to be valid. For example, Haddock, Zanna and Esses (1993) demonstrated that a semantic differential measure of attitudes towards gay men was highly predictive of a subsequent measure of anti-gay discrimination (see Eagly & Chaiken, 1993, for more examples). Regarding implicit measures, Cunningham et al. (2001) and Fazio and Olson (2003) have found that implicit measures possess convergent and predictive validity. One particularly compelling study used functional magnetic resonance imaging (fMRI) technology to assess brain activity in response to different stimuli. Phelps et al. (2000) found that an IAT measure of racial prejudice was highly predictive of amygdala activation when presented with pictures of unknown black individuals (the amygdala is an area of the brain associated with fearful evaluations). In this research, pronounced amygdala activation in response to black faces was associated with strong implicit prejudice towards African Americans.

SUMMARY

Attitudes can be measured in a number of ways. Attitude measures can be distinguished on the basis of whether they are *explicit* (i.e., direct) or *implicit* (i.e., indirect). Explicit measures of attitude directly ask respondents to think about and report an attitude, whereas implicit measures of attitude are those that assess attitudes *without* directly asking respondents for a verbal report of their attitude. Explicit and implicit measures are both useful tools in attempts to understand and predict human behaviour.

DO ATTITUDES PREDICT BEHAVIOUR?

How do measurement issues affect whether attitudes predict behaviour?

What factors affect relatively deliberative and contemplative attitude–behaviour sequences?

How does the MODE model explain relatively spontaneous attitude–behaviour sequences?

Common sense would dictate that attitudes should predict behaviour. For example, one would expect that an individual who possesses a positive attitude towards the environment would engage in recycling behaviour. Similarly, it seems sensible to predict that a student who strongly supports saving endangered animals will make an annual donation to the World Wildlife Fund. However, is the link between attitudes and behaviour this simple?

In addressing this question, we wish to start by turning back time and visiting the United States of America in the early 1930s. A college professor named Richard LaPiere was travelling across America with a young Chinese couple. At the time, there was widespread anti-Asian prejudice in the United States. As a result of this prejudice, LaPiere was concerned whether he and his travelling companions would be refused service in hotels and restaurants. Much to his surprise, only once (in over 250 establishments) were they not served. A few months after the completion of the journey, LaPiere sent a letter to each of the visited establishments and asked whether they would serve Chinese visitors. Of the establishments that replied, only one indicated that it would serve such a customer, with over 90 per cent stating that they definitely would not (the rest were undecided). While there are a number of methodological problems with LaPiere's (1934) study (e.g., there was no way of ensuring that the individual who answered the letter was the same person who served LaPiere and his friends), it is a reminder that people's behaviour might not necessarily follow from their attitudes.

Let us now move ahead 30 years on from this study. By the late 1960s, a number of studies had examined the relation between attitudes and behaviour. In 1969, Wicker reviewed the findings of these studies. He reached a rather sobering conclusion: attitudes were a relatively poor predictor of behaviour. Across almost 40 studies that were conducted before 1969, Wicker found that the average correlation between attitudes and behaviour was a modest .15. These conclusions led a number of social psychologists to question the value of the attitude concept. It was argued that if attitudes do not guide actions, then the construct is of limited use.

Attitude researchers responded to this criticism by devoting greater attention to the study of *when* and *how* attitudes predict behaviour. In the last 30 years, research findings have led to a more optimistic conclusion – attitudes do predict behaviour, under certain conditions. In a meta-analytic review of the literature, Kraus (1995) compared the results of over 100 studies on the **attitude–behaviour relation**. He found that the average correlation between opinions and actions was .38, a value much higher than that obtained by Wicker

> **attitude–behaviour relation** the degree to which an attitude predicts behaviour

(1969). This difference in correlations could be explained in various ways. First, more modern research might be using better measures of attitudes and/or behaviours. Second, modern researchers might be using better techniques for testing their predictions. Third, contemporary researchers might be doing a better job of examining situations *when* attitudes are highly predictive of behaviour. In this section of the chapter, we consider a number of variables that influence the attitude–behaviour relation and introduce models that have been developed to understand how attitudes predict behaviour.

When do attitudes predict behaviour?

(1) When there is correspondence between attitudinal and behavioural measures A number of early attempts to assess the attitude–behaviour relation (included in Wicker's, 1969, review) were plagued by methodological problems. Specifically, in many of these studies there was a low degree of *correspondence* between the measures of attitude and behaviour. Returning to LaPiere's (1934) research, his measure of attitude asked respondents to indicate whether they would serve 'members of the Chinese race'. This statement is quite broad in comparison to the measure of behaviour, which involved service being offered to a highly educated, well-dressed Chinese couple accompanied by an American college professor. Had the attitude measure been more specific (e.g., 'would you serve a highly educated, well-dressed Chinese couple accompanied by an American college professor?'), the relation between attitudes and behaviour in LaPiere's (1934) study might have been more pronounced.

The idea that there needs to be high correspondence between measures of attitude and behaviour was articulated by Ajzen and Fishbein (1977). They stated that measures of attitude and behaviour need to correspond in four key ways: action, target, context and time. The *action* element refers to the behaviour being performed (e.g., recycling glass). The *target* element refers to the target of the behaviour (e.g., a particular brand of coffee, a political candidate). The *context* element refers to the environment in which the behaviour is performed (e.g., whether the behaviour is performed alone or in the presence of others). Finally, the *time element* refers to the time frame in which the behaviour is performed (e.g., whether the behaviour is to be performed immediately or in one year's time). Ajzen and Fishbein (1977) argued that a measure of attitude will be most effective in predicting behaviour when both measures correspond on these four elements. Further, they conducted a review of the literature that supported this conclusion.

The importance of correspondence between measures of attitude and behaviour was also demonstrated in a study by Davidson and Jaccard (1979). These researchers were interested in predicting women's use of birth control pills. In this study, women were asked a number of questions about their attitudes, ranging from questions that were very general (their attitude towards birth control) to somewhat specific (their attitude towards birth control pills) to very specific (their attitude towards using birth control pills during the next two years). Two years after participants responded to these attitude questions, they were contacted by the researchers and asked to indicate if they had used birth control pills in the previous two years. It was predicted that the correlation between attitudes and behaviour would increase as the measures became more correspondent. The results of this study confirmed the authors' predictions. To start, the general attitude measure did not predict behaviour ($r = .08$), probably because this measure was too general in relation to the measure of behaviour. The question that was somewhat specific did a better job of predicting behaviour ($r = .32$); this item had the advantage of matching the behavioural measure with respect to the target. Finally, the most specific question was very effective in predicting behaviour ($r = .57$), because the attitude measure was highly correspondent with the measure of behaviour with respect to two key elements: target and time.

(2) It depends upon the domain of behaviour Research has also demonstrated that the relation between attitudes and behaviour differs as a function of the topic under investigation. In his review of the literature, Kraus (1995) found that topics varied in the degree to which opinions predicted actions. At one extreme, the relation between political party attitudes and voting behaviour tends to be very high. For example, in an investigation conducted during the 1984 American presidential election, Fazio and Williams (1986) measured attitudes towards the then United States President Ronald Reagan (see Plate 6.7). Approximately five months later, they measured whether participants voted for Reagan or his opponent. Despite the time lag between measures, the correlation between voters' initial attitude towards Reagan and their subsequent voting behaviour was an impressive .78. At the other extreme, Kraus (1995) noted that there is a low correlation between individuals' attitudes towards blood donation and the act of donating blood. At first glance, it is perhaps not surprising that this is a behavioural domain where one might expect a low attitude–behaviour relation. It may be that a low relation arises because the behaviour of donating blood is much more difficult to enact than the simple expression of one's attitude through a behaviour like voting.

(3) It depends upon the strength of the attitude As mentioned earlier in the chapter, attitudes differ in their strength. For

Plate 6.7 *Do attitudes towards politicians predict voting behaviour?*

instance, one of us absolutely loves the music of Bruce Springsteen, the other feels less strongly. As we already know, attitude researchers would say that one author has a very strong positive attitude towards the music of Bruce Springsteen, while the other has a weak attitude. Which author recently drove all night to see Bruce Springsteen perform live . . . for the eighth time? Not surprisingly, it is the one with the strong attitude.

A number of studies have demonstrated that strong attitudes are more likely than weak attitudes to predict behaviour. For instance, returning to the study of Fazio and Williams (1986), recall that they found a very high correlation between political attitudes and voting behaviour. This study also contained a measure of attitude strength – the accessibility of the participants' initial attitude. Some participants had very accessible (i.e., strong) attitudes towards Reagan, whereas other participants' attitudes were less accessible (i.e., weak). Fazio and Williams (1986) found that the correlation between attitudes and behaviour was significantly greater among those individuals whose attitudes towards Reagan were high in accessibility. Similar results have been found in many other studies using different operationalizations of attitude strength (see Eagly & Chaiken, 1993; Kraus, 1995), leading to the conclusion that strong attitudes are more likely than weak attitudes to predict behaviour.

(4) The role of personal variables The final set of variables we wish to consider concerns differences across people in the tendency to behave in line with their actions. In addition to examining how situations influence behaviour, social psychologists are interested in understanding how personality differences help account for our actions. With respect to the attitude–behaviour relation, a number of researchers have examined how various personality constructs moderate the degree to which opinions influence actions.

The personality construct most frequently tested as a moderator of the attitude–behaviour relation is *self-monitoring* (Snyder, 1974, 1987). As discussed earlier in the chapter, self-monitoring refers to differences across people in how they vary their behaviour across social situations. A number of studies have investigated whether the relation between attitudes and behaviour is more pronounced for low self-monitors than for high self-monitors. In one study testing this proposal, Snyder and Kendzierski (1982) investigated attitudes towards affirmative action (policies that give special advantages to members of ethnic minority groups). These researchers gave students who favoured or opposed affirmative action the opportunity to participate in a social situation that supported the behavioural expression of a positive attitude towards this issue. The results revealed that, among low self-monitors, decisions on whether to participate were predicted by their attitude towards affirmative action. However, among high self-monitors the behavioural decision was unrelated to the favourability of their attitude.

Another relevant variable that affects the size of the attitude–behaviour relation is the nature of the participants involved in the research. Research has found that students show lower attitude–behaviour relations compared to non-students. For example, Kraus (1995) observed that the average correlation between attitudes and behaviour was .34 in studies that used student samples; the correlation was .48 in studies with non-student samples. This difference might be attributable to the observation that university students tend to have less crystallized attitudes compared to older individuals (see Sears, 1986; Visser & Krosnick, 1998).

Models of attitude–behaviour relations

In addition to understanding *when* attitudes predict behaviour, social psychologists have developed a number of models to explain *how* attitudes predict behaviour. In this section of the chapter, we describe some of the most prominent models: Fishbein and Azjen's (1975) *theory of reasoned action* (as well as its extension), Fazio's (1990) *MODE model* and Eagly and Chaiken's (1993, 1998) *composite model*.

The theory of reasoned action and theory of planned behaviour
As its name suggests, the *theory of reasoned action* is a model that was developed to predict deliberative (i.e., planned) behaviour. According to this model (see Figure 6.11), the immediate predictor (or determinant) of individuals' behaviour is their *intention*. Put simply, if you intend to

> **theory of reasoned action** a model in which behaviour is predicted by behavioural intentions, which are determined by attitudes and subjective norms

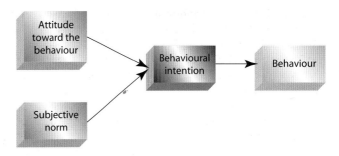

Figure 6.11 *The theory of reasoned action.*

recycle glass bottles, you are likely to engage in this behaviour. Within the original conceptualization of the model, intentions were determined by two factors, attitudes and subjective norms. The *attitude* component refers to the individual's attitude towards the behaviour – whether the person thinks that performing the behaviour is good or bad. A person's attitude towards a behaviour (e.g., recycling glass) is a function of the expectancy that the behaviour will produce a desired consequence (helping the environment) *and* the value attached to this consequence (it is good to help the environment). According to the model, an individual's attitude is derived by multiplying the expectancy and value for each consequence and summing these values.

Subjective norms refer to an individual's beliefs about how significant others view the relevant behaviour. Like the attitude component, subjective norms are perceived to be derived from two factors that are multiplied and then summed. Specifically, the subjective norm component is a function of normative beliefs (how important others expect the individual to act) and the individual's motivation to comply with these expectations. Returning to our example, subjective norms will be high if your family and close friends have positive expectations towards recycling glass and you are motivated to comply with these expectations.

While the theory of reasoned action did a commendable job in predicting behaviour, it soon became clear that individuals' actions were also influenced by whether or not they felt they could perform the relevant behaviour. For example, if an individual wanted to change his dietary habits by eating a healthier diet, a positive attitude and positive subjective norms are unlikely to produce the desired behaviour change if he is unable to restrain himself from eating sweets, chocolates and fish and chips. As a result, the theory of reasoned action was revised to include the notion that behavioural prediction is affected by whether people believe that they can perform the relevant behaviour. This revision is captured by the concept of *perceived behavioural control*. The inclusion of this concept led Ajzen (1991; see also Ajzen & Madden, 1986) to name the revised model the ***theory of planned behaviour***. According to this model (see Figure 6.12), perceived behavioural control is determined by control beliefs – individuals' perceptions about whether they possess the resources and opportunities required to perform the behaviour.

> **theory of planned behaviour** an extension to the theory of reasoned action that includes the concept of perceived behavioural control

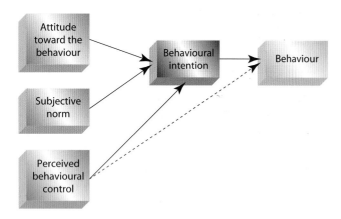

Figure 6.12 *The theory of planned behaviour.*

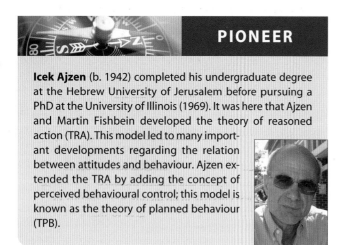

PIONEER

Icek Ajzen (b. 1942) completed his undergraduate degree at the Hebrew University of Jerusalem before pursuing a PhD at the University of Illinois (1969). It was here that Ajzen and Martin Fishbein developed the theory of reasoned action (TRA). This model led to many important developments regarding the relation between attitudes and behaviour. Ajzen extended the TRA by adding the concept of perceived behavioural control; this model is known as the theory of planned behaviour (TPB).

Perceived behavioural control influences behaviour in two ways. First, it is postulated to have a direct causal influence on behavioural intentions. This implies that an individual's intention to engage in a particular behaviour is affected by his or her perceived confidence in their ability to perform the action. Second, perceived behavioural control also has a direct effect on behaviour. This relationship is dependent upon actual control of the relevant action, that is, whether the behaviour can, in reality, be performed. Put simply, while individuals may believe that they can perform the relevant behaviour, their perception may not be accurate.

The theory of reasoned action and theory of planned behaviour are the most frequently tested models of attitude–behaviour relations. Overall, the predictions derived from the models have received strong empirical support. For example, a review by Albarracin, Johnson, Fishbein and Muellerleile (2001) compared the results of over 90 studies assessing whether the theories of reasoned action and planned behaviour do an effective job in predicting condom use. Consistent with the theory of reasoned action, behavioural intentions were predicted by both attitudes and subjective norms, while behavioural intentions predicted condom use. Consistent with the theory of planned behaviour, perceived behavioural control predicted behaviour independently of behavioural intentions. Similar findings supporting the models

have been found in reviews of other behavioural domains (see, e.g., Armitage & Conner, 2001).

One issue pertinent to the reasoned action/planned behaviour approach that has received considerable attention concerns *how* behavioural intentions are translated into behaviour. An important development relevant to this issue is the concept of *implementation intentions* (Gollwitzer, 1999). Implementation intentions are conceptualized as 'if–then' plans that specify a behaviour that one will need to perform in order to achieve a goal and the context in which the behaviour will occur (Sheeran, 2002). That is, implementation intentions take the form of mindsets in which an individual attempts to specify where and when a behaviour will be enacted, in the form of 'When I encounter the situational context A, I will perform behaviour B' (Gollwitzer & Brandstätter, 1997). For example, a student might say to himself, 'when I return from Easter holidays, I will start revising for my exams'. Numerous studies have demonstrated that forming an implementation intention increases the likelihood that an individual will perform a desired behaviour. In one study, Orbell, Hodgkins and Sheeran (1997) considered whether the formation of an implementation intention would increase the likelihood that women would perform breast self-examination (BSE). Participants in an intervention group were asked to indicate where and when they would perform BSE, whereas participants in a control group did not receive these instructions. The results of the study revealed that the formation of an implementation intention was effective in eliciting the desired behaviour. For example, one month after the intervention, 64 per cent of participants in the intervention group reported having performed BSE, compared to 14 per cent in the control group (see Sheeran, Milne, Webb & Gollwitzer, 2005, for a review of implementation intentions and health behaviours).

The MODE model Not all behaviour is deliberative and planned. Quite often we act spontaneously, without consciously thinking of what we intend to do. When our behaviour is spontaneous, the theory of planned behaviour may not provide a proper conceptualization of behavioural prediction (see Fazio, 1990). In an attempt to uncover how attitudes influence spontaneous behaviour, Fazio (1990) developed the *MODE model* of attitude–behaviour relations. MODE refers to Motivation and Opportunity as DEterminants of behaviour.

> **MODE model** a model of attitude–behaviour relations in which motivation and opportunity are necessary to make a deliberative consideration of available information

At a basic level, the MODE model suggests that, if individuals have *both* sufficient motivation and opportunity, they may base their behaviour on a deliberative consideration of the available information. However, when either the motivation or the opportunity to make a reasoned decision is low, only attitudes that are highly accessible will predict spontaneous behaviour. A number of studies by Fazio and colleagues have supported the MODE model (see, e.g., Sanbonmatsu & Fazio, 1990; Schuette & Fazio, 1995). For example, Sanbonmatsu and Fazio (1990) gave participants information about two department stores that included camera departments. Brown's store was described favourably, but its camera department was described negatively. In contrast,

Smith's store was described unfavourably, but its camera department was described positively. After a delay, participants were asked where they would shop for a camera. The results of the study indicated that participants were likely to base their decisions on the description of the camera department when they had received prior instructions asking them to form opinions of the stores *and* their camera departments. Participants were less likely to base their decisions on the description of the camera departments when the instructions encouraged them merely to form an opinion about the stores. More important, when the evaluations were not requested, the information about the camera departments was used *only* when participants were motivated to form an accurate decision and had abundant time to reach their decision.

The composite model   The final model we wish to address is Eagly and Chaiken's (1993, 1998) composite model of attitude–behaviour relations. Like the theories of reasoned action and planned behaviour, the composite model suggests a link between attitudes, intentions and behaviour. The model proposes a number of factors that affect attitudes towards behaviours: habits (relevant past behaviour), attitudes towards targets (the target of the behaviour), utilitarian outcomes (rewards and punishments associated with performing the behaviour), normative outcomes (approval and disapproval from others that might occur from performing the behaviour) and self-identity outcomes (how performing the behaviour might influence the self-concept). Eagly and Chaiken suggested that some of these factors can affect either intentions or behaviour directly. The inclusion of habits is a particularly noteworthy aspect of Eagly and Chaiken's model, as many researchers have suggested that past behaviours are effective in predicting future behaviour (see Aarts, Verplanken & van Knippenberg, 1998; Ouellette & Wood, 1998).

SUMMARY

On the whole, attitudes do a reasonable job of predicting behaviour. The degree to which attitudes predict behaviour depends upon factors such as the level of correspondence across measures, the domain of behaviour, attitude strength and personality factors. The theory of reasoned action and its extension, the theory of planned behaviour, have received strong support as models for predicting deliberate behaviour. The MODE model suggests that motivation and opportunity are necessary to make a deliberative consideration of available information. The composite model proposes a number of variables that affect the attitude–behaviour relation.

SUMMARY AND CONCLUSIONS

- Expressing an attitude involves making an evaluative judgement about an attitude object.

- Attitudes have affective, cognitive and behavioural components. All three components contribute to overall attitudes.

- Positive and negative elements of attitudes contribute to how they are structured and organized.

- Attitudes can serve a number of psychological functions or needs. People hold attitudes for a number of reasons.

- Attitudes differ in their strength. These differences have important consequences.

- Attitudes can be measured in a number of ways. It is important to distinguish between direct (explicit) and indirect (implicit) measures of attitude.

- Attitudes are relatively effective in predicting behaviour.

- While numerous advances have been made regarding attitudes, many issues remain to be studied, including how and where attitudes are represented within the structure of the brain (e.g., via neuropsychological techniques such as fMRI), whether implicit and explicit measures of attitude are more or less effective in predicting spontaneous vs. deliberative behaviours, and the degree to which attitudes are conscious vs. unconscious.

Suggestions for further reading

Eagly, A.H. & Chaiken, S. (1993). *The psychology of attitudes*. Fort Worth, TX: Harcourt Brace Jovanovich. This volume provides a comprehensive review of all aspects of research on the psychology of attitudes.

Fazio, R.H. & Olson, M.A. (2003). Implicit measures in social cognition research: Their meaning and use. *Annual Review of Psychology*, *54*, 297–327. This paper reviews advances that have been made concerning implicit measures of attitude.

Fazio, R.H. & Petty, R.E. (Eds.) (2007). *Attitudes*. Vol. 1: *Structure, function, and consequences*. Hove: Psychology Press. This volume comprises a collection of important published papers on attitude structure, attitude content and the attitude–behaviour relation.

Haddock, G. & Maio, G.R. (Eds.) (2004). *Contemporary perspectives on the psychology of attitudes*. Hove: Psychology Press. This volume reviews a number of contemporary research programs on the psychology of attitudes.

Maio, G.R. & Olson, J.M. (Eds.) (2000). *Why we evaluate: Functions of attitudes*. Mahwah, NJ: Lawrence Erlbaum. This volume is a comprehensive examination of research on attitude functions.

7 Strategies of Attitude and Behaviour Change

Wolfgang Stroebe

KEY CONCEPTS

central route to persuasion
cognitive response model
counterattitudinal
    behaviour
dissonance theory
distraction
dual-process theories of
    persuasion
elaboration
elaboration likelihood
    model (ELM)
habits
heuristic processing
heuristic-systematic model
    (HSM)
intrinsic motivation
need for cognition
over-justification effect
peripheral route to
    persuasion
reactance theory
sufficiency principle
systematic processing
thought-listing

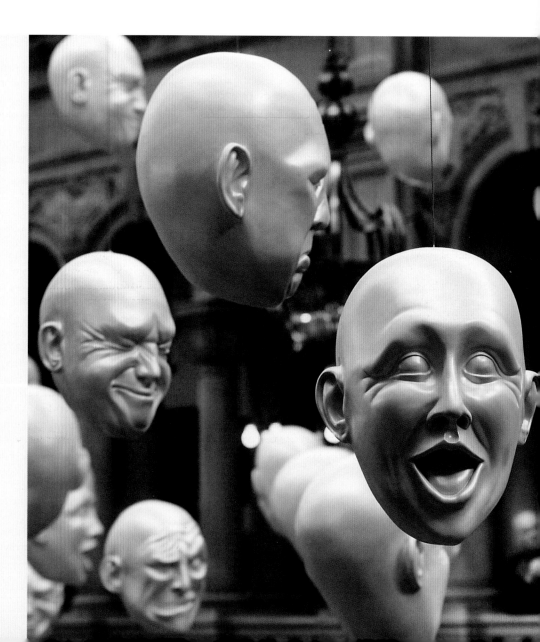

CHAPTER OUTLINE

....

This chapter discusses two strategies of attitude and behaviour change, namely persuasion and the use of incentives (e.g., taxation, legal sanctions). We will discuss when, how and why persuasion results in attitude and behaviour change and review empirical studies that have been conducted to assess the validity of these theoretical interpretations. Finally, we will apply these theories to the area of advertising. The second part of the chapter will focus on the use of incentives. Instead of relying on the uncertain effects of persuasion to induce people to use seatbelts or give up smoking, governments often employ legal sanctions or taxation to influence behaviour directly. These strategies are quite effective in influencing behaviour, but it is much less clear whether they can also result in attitude change.

Introduction

....

The notion of using social psychological knowledge to change attitudes and to influence behaviour conjures up visions of advertising executives planning mass media campaigns to sell cars, refrigerators, alcoholic drinks or margarine. And this vision is certainly not incorrect. However, social psychology is equally useful in persuading people to change unhealthy behaviour patterns such as smoking, drinking or engaging in unsafe sex. In fact, one of the most effective campaigns in recent times, achieving substantial changes in attitudes and behaviour, has probably been the war against smoking. It began in 1964 with the publication of the report of the United States Surgeon General's Advisory Committee on Smoking and Health (USDHEW, 1964). The persuasive information on the substantial health impairment suffered by smokers was quickly adopted by the news media and thus reached a wide audience. The material not only persuaded many smokers to stop, it also convinced politicians that it was time to act and, some years later, compulsory health warnings were introduced on tobacco advertisements and cigarette packets. Finally, in the 1980s, Federal cigarette tax was doubled and various states introduced additional excise taxes on cigarettes. Largely as a result of this anti-smoking campaign, smoking is now generally recognized as a health risk and an addiction. Moreover, especially in the USA, smoking has declined substantially (see Figure 7.1).

This chapter focuses on the two major strategies of attitude and behaviour change, namely (1) the use of *persuasion* and (2) the use of *incentives* or *sanctions*. In each section, we will discuss the effectiveness of these strategies and theoretically analyse the psychological processes which are responsible for their impact.

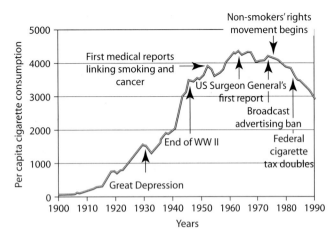

Figure 7.1 *Per capita cigarette consumption per year among adults and major smoking and health events in the USA, 1900–1990 (based on Novotny, Romano, Davis, & Mills, 1992).*

Plate 7.1 *Thanks to effective anti-tobacco campaigns, smoking is now generally recognized as a health risk and an addiction.*

PERSUASION

Persuasion involves the use of communications to change the beliefs, attitudes and behaviour of others. Research on persuasion received a big boost during World War II when the American army looked for strategies to counteract enemy propaganda and to boost the morale of their own troops (Hovland, Lumsdaine & Sheffield, 1949). After the war, Carl Hovland, the director of the mass communication program within the US Army's information and education division, assembled a group of eminent researchers at Yale University (e.g., Abelson, Janis, Kelley, McGuire, Rosenberg) and this group was instrumental in making the study of persuasion and attitude change one of the central areas of social psychology.

Theories of systematic processing

What are the cognitive processes which mediate the impact of persuasive communications on attitudes and behaviour?

Is attitude change determined by our comprehension of persuasive arguments or by the favourable and/or unfavourable thoughts stimulated by these arguments?

What determines whether persuasive arguments stimulate favourable or unfavourable thoughts?

> **systematic processing** thorough, detailed processing of information (e.g., attention to the arguments contained in a persuasive communication); this kind of processing relies on ability and effort

Before 1980, most of the theories of persuasion and attitude change emphasized *systematic processing*. They assumed that attitude change was mediated by the message recipient's detailed processing of the persuasive arguments contained in the communication. The two most influential theories of systematic processing have been the information processing model (McGuire, 1969, 1985) and the cognitive response model (e.g., Greenwald, 1968; Petty, Ostrom & Brock, 1981).

The information processing model of persuasion The paradigm proposed by McGuire (1969, 1985) provides a useful framework for thinking about the stages involved in the processing of persuasive communications. According to this model, the persuasive impact of a message is the product of at least five steps: (1) attention, (2) comprehension, (3) yielding, (4) retention and (5) behaviour. For example, the ultimate objective of speeches given on television by politicians is to get the members of the audience to vote for their party. If viewers use the break between programmes to go to the bathroom (failure to attend), the appeal will not result in attitude change. Even if viewers attend to the communication, it will have little impact if they find the arguments too complex (failure to comprehend) or if they do not accept the communicator's conclusions (failure to yield). But even if the candidate manages to persuade the audience, this will be of no use if viewers change their attitudes again before election day (failure to retain) or if bad weather keeps them away from the ballot box (failure to act). Since the message receiver must go through each of these steps if the communication is to have the ultimate persuasive impact, and since it is unlikely that the probability of any given step will be maximal, McGuire's framework offers one explanation of why it is often difficult to induce behaviour change through information campaigns.

In social psychological studies, the impact of a communication is typically assessed immediately following exposure to the message. Thus, our analysis is restricted to the first three steps of the chain. Moreover, attention and comprehension have usually been combined into a single step of reception of the message content in

PIONEER

William J. McGuire (b. 1925) was born in New York, USA. After a brief stint in the army, he studied psychology at Fordham University, where he received his BA (1949) and MA (1950). He then spent a year as a Research Fellow at the University of Minnesota at the time Festinger was there (see Chapter 1, this volume). In 1951 he went to Yale University for his PhD, which he received in 1954. He stayed on at Yale for four more years, and after holding positions at various other universities (Illinois, Columbia and San Diego) he returned to Yale as Professor of Psychology in 1971, remaining there until his retirement in 1999. Bill McGuire dominated research on attitude and attitude change until the 1980s. During his early time at Yale, he was a member of the famous Yale Communication and Attitude Change Program headed by Carl Hovland (see Chapter 1, this volume). When he returned to Yale ten years after the death of Hovland, he continued the research tradition of the Yale program. He made numerous empirical and theoretical contributions to the area and also authored the highly influential chapters on attitude and attitude change in the second and third edition of the *Handbook of Social Psychology* (McGuire, 1969, 1985).

order to simplify measurement. Thus McGuire's model can be reduced to a two-step version, which states that the probability of a communication resulting in attitude and opinion change is the joint product of reception and acceptance (yielding).

Few studies have supported the claim that the reception of message arguments determines attitude change. In general, message reception, when measured by the recall of message arguments, is not found to correlate significantly with attitude change (see Eagly & Chaiken, 1993). This failure to find correlations between argument recall and attitude change raised doubts about McGuire's two-stage model, in particular the role of attention to and comprehension of the arguments presented in persuasive communications. Even more critical for the model was the fact that it lacked specific theoretical principles that would allow one to predict the factors which affect acceptance and to understand the processes which mediate the relationship between acceptance and attitude change. The cognitive response model provides such a theory.

cognitive response model assumes that attitude change is mediated by the thoughts, or 'cognitive responses', which recipients generate as they receive and reflect upon persuasive communications, and that the magnitude and direction of attitude change obtained by a persuasive communication are functions of the extent of message-relevant thinking as well as its favourability

The cognitive response model: A theory of yielding The *cognitive response model* of persuasion was developed by Greenwald and

his colleagues at Ohio State University partly to explain the absence of a correlation between argument recall and attitude change (Greenwald, 1968; Petty, Ostrom & Brock, 1981). According to this model, it is not the reception of arguments which mediates attitude change but the thoughts (cognitive responses) stimulated in the recipient by those arguments. Listening to a communication is like a mental discussion. Listeners are active participants, who relate the communication to their own knowledge. In doing this, the person may consider much cognitive material that is not contained in the communication itself to generate thoughts for or against the arguments presented in the communication. It is these self-generated thoughts and not the presented arguments *per se* which mediate attitude change. Messages persuade if they evoke predominantly favourable thoughts, and they fail to persuade if they evoke predominantly unfavourable thoughts. Thus, the impact of persuasion variables on attitude change depends not on the extent to which they facilitate argument reception but on the extent to which they stimulate individuals to generate their own favourable or unfavourable thoughts about the information presented.

On first reading, this does not appear to be a very impressive theory. It is also not terribly new. Writing in 1949, Hovland, Lumsdaine and Sheffield had already suggested that audiences may resist persuasion by going over their own arguments against the position during exposure to the communication. Hovland (1951) later emphasized that the best way to study internal processes of attitude change was to have respondents verbalize their thoughts as they responded to the communication. However, although cognitive responses were everybody's favourite concept to be invoked when non-obvious findings of persuasion studies had to be explained (e.g., Festinger & Maccoby, 1964), research on the role of cognitive responses as mediators of persuasion had been hampered by the absence of accepted measures.

One major methodological contribution of the Ohio State researchers to the study of persuasion was therefore the development of a measure of cognitive responses: *thought-listing* (Greenwald, 1968; Osterhouse & Brock, 1970). This enabled them to assess the processes assumed to mediate attitude change. With this thought-listing task recipients of a message are asked to list the thoughts they had whilst listening. These thoughts are later categorized into those which are favourable or unfavourable to the position advocated by the message. Thoughts which do not fit either of these categories (e.g., neutral or irrelevant thoughts) are not considered.

thought-listing a measure of cognitive responses. Message recipients are asked to list all the thoughts that occurred to them while being exposed to a persuasive message. These thoughts are categorized as favourable or unfavourable to the position advocated by the message. Neutral or irrelevant thoughts are not considered

The second major contribution of the Ohio State researchers was theoretical. Previous conceptualizations of cognitive responses had focused only on the production of counterarguments which *reduce* persuasion (e.g., Festinger & Maccoby, 1964). In an important theoretical contribution, Petty, Wells and Brock (1976) broadened the concept of cognitive responses by arguing that strong and well-argued messages are likely to produce predominantly favourable thoughts which should *enhance* persuasion.

This extended cognitive response model accounts for a number of inconsistent findings in the attitude change literature. Thus, it helps to explain why there is often no correlation between argument recall and attitude change. If it is the thoughts stimulated by arguments and not the arguments themselves which are responsible for attitude change, then the message arguments that a recipient remembers could not be expected to be related to attitude change. What one would expect, however, is a correlation between the extent to which these thoughts are favourable or unfavourable towards the arguments presented by the communicator and the amount of attitude change. The newly developed thought-listing measure enabled researchers to test (and to support) this assumption (e.g., Osterhouse & Brock, 1970).

distraction while listening to a persuasive communication, individuals are distracted by having to perform an irrelevant activity or by experiencing sensory stimulation irrelevant to the message

Another inconsistency resolved by the cognitive response approach related to findings of research on the impact of *distraction* on attitude change. We have probably all had the experience of being distracted while listening to some communication. The station on our car radio might have faded in the middle of a broadcast or the people next to us might have started a loud conversation. Since being distracted whilst listening to a communication should impair reception, one would expect distraction to reduce the persuasive impact of a communication. Although some studies reported findings consistent with this prediction (e.g., Haaland & Venkatesan, 1968), others found distraction to strengthen the persuasive impact of a communication (e.g., Festinger & Maccoby, 1964).

According to the cognitive response model, such discrepant results are to be expected. Distraction reduces the recipient's ability to generate cognitive responses to a message. The impact of distraction on attitude change should therefore depend on the favourability of the thoughts produced by a message (Petty et al., 1976). If these dominant thoughts are mainly unfavourable, distraction should enhance persuasion. However, for messages which elicit predominantly favourable thoughts, distraction should work to inhibit persuasion.

But how can we manipulate the favourability of a listener's dominant thoughts? Since we have put so much emphasis on self-generated thoughts as a mediator of persuasion in this section, it is easy to forget that these thoughts are cognitive responses to persuasive arguments and are therefore likely to be influenced by the quality of these arguments. Thus, communications which present several strong arguments (e.g., arguments which are coherent, logical and compelling) are likely to elicit cognitive responses which are predominantly favourable to the position argued, whereas messages consisting mainly of weak arguments should elicit predominantly unfavourable responses. This process is depicted in Figure 7.2.

Petty and colleagues (1976, Experiment 1) exposed students to messages which argued for an increase in tuition fees at their university. These communications consisted of either very strong or very weak arguments. Distraction was manipulated by having participants record visual stimuli (briefly flashed on a screen at a rate of 0, 4, 12 or 20 flashes per minute) while listening to the

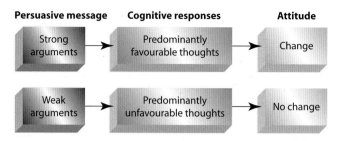

Figure 7.2 *The cognitive response model of persuasion.*

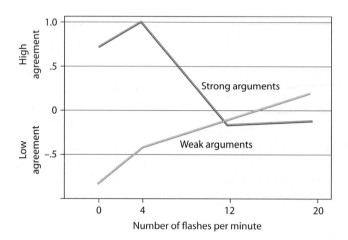

Figure 7.3 *Mean attitudes (shown as z-scores) in relation to message and level of distraction (adapted from Petty et al., 1976).*

message. In line with predictions, increases in distraction enhanced persuasion for the message which consisted of weak arguments, but reduced persuasion for the message containing strong arguments (Figure 7.3). The participants' thought-listing data provided support for the assumption that both the increase and the decrease in persuasion were due to thought disruption. The distraction manipulation decreased recipients' ability to generate counter-arguments for the weak message but reduced the number of favourable thoughts they were able to generate for the strong version of the message.

Dual-process theories of persuasion

Do people sometimes change their attitudes without systematic processing of persuasive arguments?

What factors determine whether people process messages systematically or superficially?

How can we explain attitude change which is not based on systematic processing of arguments?

That attitude change is mediated by detailed processing of the arguments may strike one as a plausible way to analyse the psychological processes that mediate persuasion. After all, is there any other way to be persuaded, if not through the arguments contained in a persuasive communication? However, if we think of the hundreds of advertisements we are exposed to every day, we might become doubtful. Does anybody really think about the arguments contained in advertisements about soft drinks or toothpaste? Do these advertisements even contain arguments? And yet if people were not influenced by them, these companies would not spend millions on their advertising budgets.

The answer to these questions is that advertisements often work through processes of classical conditioning or mere exposure, which we discussed in the previous chapter. But how are classical conditioning and mere exposure related to systematic processing? Under which conditions does each of these processes operate? These are the types of questions which we will address in our discussion of *dual-process theories of persuasion*. Dual-process theories integrate both theories of systematic processing and persuasion processes that are not based on systematic analysis of message arguments (e.g., classical conditioning, self-persuasion, heuristic processing). Dual-process theories also specify the conditions under which people will engage in each of these processes. There are two dual-process theories of persuasion, the *elaboration likelihood model* (Petty & Cacioppo, 1986a; Petty & Wegener, 1999) and the *heuristic-systematic model* (e.g., Chaiken, Liberman & Eagly, 1989; Chen & Chaiken, 1999). There is, however, so much overlap between these theories in their core assumptions that we will focus mainly on the elaboration likelihood model. After having presented the elaboration likelihood model, we will briefly discuss the major aspects in which this theory differs from the heuristic-systematic model of Chaiken and her colleagues.

dual-process theories of persuasion
theories of persuasion postulating two modes of information processing, systematic and non-systematic. Modes differ in the extent to which individuals engage in content-relevant thoughts and critical evaluation of the arguments contained in a message in order to accept or reject the position advocated. The mode used is assumed to depend on processing motivation and ability

elaboration likelihood model (ELM)
assumes that attitude change in response to persuasive communications can be mediated by two different modes of information processing (central and peripheral). Elaboration denotes the extent to which a person thinks about the issue-relevant arguments contained in a message. The probability that a recipient will critically evaluate arguments (the elaboration likelihood) is determined by both processing motivation and ability

heuristic-systematic model (HSM)
assumes that attitude change in response to persuasive communications can be mediated by two different modes of information processing, heuristic and systematic processing, which can operate concurrently. When motivation and ability are high, systematic processing is likely; when they are low, individuals rely on heuristic cues to accept or reject the attitudinal position recommended

The elaboration likelihood model (ELM) When people receive a communication and are faced with the decision whether to accept or reject the position advocated, they will try to form an opinion of its validity. This assessment may be arrived at by two routes of information processing, namely a *central* and a *peripheral* route to persuasion. These two routes mark the endpoints of a continuum that ranges from thoughtful to very non-thoughtful strategies (i.e., the elaboration likelihood continuum). Petty and

Shelly Chaiken (b. 1949) studied mathematics at the University of Maryland (College Park) and received her BA in 1971. She then became a graduate student in social psychology at the University of Massachusetts (Amherst), where she received her MS in 1975 and her PhD in 1978. After brief spells at the University of Toronto and Vanderbilt University, she moved to New York University as Professor of Psychology in 1985, where she stayed until 2005. She is now associated with the University of Wisconsin (Madison). At the University of Massachusetts, she did her graduate studies with Alice Eagly (see Chapter 6) and developed the idea for the heuristic-systematic model during her work for her PhD. She continued her close collaboration with Eagly even after her PhD and co-authored with her the *Psychology of Attitudes* in 1993, which has been the defining book on that topic for many years. She has published numerous empirical articles testing and extending her heuristic-systematic model. In 1999 she also edited (jointly with Yaacov Trope) an important volume on *Dual-process theories in social psychology*.

Richard E. Petty (b. 1951) received his BA in political science and psychology from the University of Virginia in 1973. He then moved to Ohio State University for his graduate studies, where he received his PhD in 1977. He began his academic career the same year at the University of Missouri, from where, after a sabbatical at Yale in 1986, he returned to Ohio State in 1987. Since 1998 he has been Distinguished University Professor at Ohio State University. At Ohio State he began a fruitful collaboration with fellow PhD student John Cacioppo. At that time persuasion research was plagued by inconsistency in empirical findings, which could not be explained by available theoretical models. In their attempt to reconcile these conflicting findings and to integrate different theoretical approaches ranging from cognitive response theory to theories based on classical conditioning, Petty and Cacioppo developed the idea of the two routes to persuasion which formed the basis for their general theory of attitude change, the elaboration likelihood model (ELM). It is probably fair to say that Petty has taken over the mantle of Bill McGuire as the dominant figure in the area of attitude and attitude change research.

elaboration refers to the extent to which a person thinks about the issue-relevant arguments contained in a message

Cacioppo (1986a) use the term *elaboration* to denote the extent to which a person thinks about the issue-relevant arguments contained in a message.

The probability that a recipient will critically evaluate arguments contained in a message (i.e., elaboration likelihood) is determined by both *processing motivation* and *processing ability*. Processing motivation is important because such elaboration requires time and effort. Processing ability is important because, in order to be able to scrutinize arguments, a person needs both issue-relevant knowledge and sufficient time. For example, if a computer salesperson gives us a highly technical speech about the advantages of a computer he or she is trying to sell us, we will not be able to evaluate these arguments if we lack the necessary computer knowledge. But even if we have the necessary knowledge, we might not be able to think about these arguments if we have no time to do so, because we have to come to a decision immediately. If, however, individuals are motivated and able to think about the arguments contained in a communication, they will engage in systematic processing and follow the *central route to persuasion* (Figure 7.4a). This mode of information

central route to persuasion a person's careful and thoughtful consideration of the arguments presented in support of a position

processing is identical to the processes assumed by the cognitive response model. However, sometimes recipients may not be motivated (e.g., the issue is trivial) or able (e.g., they have no time or lack the knowledge) to engage in an extensive process of message evaluation. Under these conditions attitudes will be formed according to the *peripheral route to persuasion* (see Figure 7.4b). This type of persuasion refers to any attitude change mechanism that does not involve systematic processing. The peripheral route thus encompasses cognitive processes such as the use of heuristic decision rules (e.g., 'experts can be trusted'), affective processes such as classical conditioning and mere exposure, and use of information about the attitudes held by relevant others (see Chapter 11 on Social influence).

peripheral route to persuasion subsumes those persuasion processes that are not based on issue-relevant thinking (e.g., classical conditioning, heuristic processing)

The peripheral process which has been most extensively examined in studies of dual-process theories of persuasion has been *heuristic processing* (Figure 7.4b), which focuses on the simple decision rules which people use to judge the validity of messages. For example, people may have learned from previous

heuristic processing assessing the validity of a communication through reliance on heuristics, i.e., simple rules like 'statistics don't lie', 'experts can be trusted', 'consensus implies correctness', rather than through evaluation of arguments

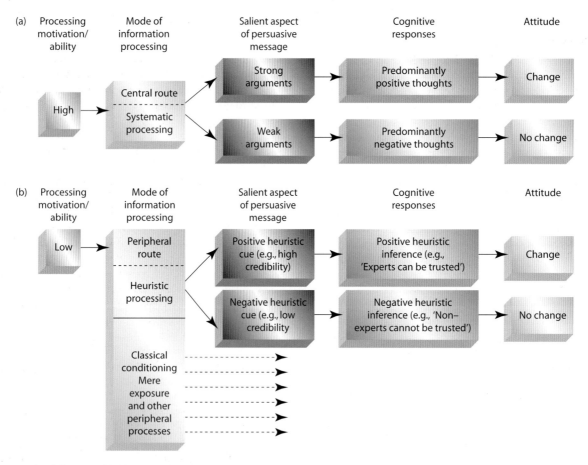

Figure 7.4 *The elaboration likelihood model: (a) central route to persuasion; (b) peripheral route to persuasion.*

experience that statements by experts tend to be more accurate than statements by non-experts. They may therefore apply the rule 'Experts can be trusted' in response to indications that the communicator is an expert (Eagly & Chaiken, 1993). Or they may have learned to trust people they like and, on finding a communicator likeable, they will apply the 'liking–agreement' heuristic, such as 'People agree with people they like' or 'People I like usually have correct opinions' (Eagly & Chaiken, 1993).

Assessing elaboration.   Petty, Cacioppo and their colleagues developed two strategies which allowed an assessment of the extent to which recipients of a message engage in message processing. One method, which was mentioned earlier, is the thought-listing technique. This technique gives some indication of the number of supportive or unsupportive thoughts stimulated by a message. If attitude change is due to central processing, then (1) recipients of a message should have generated several positive thoughts about the arguments contained in the message and (2) the relative favourability or unfavourability of these thoughts to the advocated position should be correlated with the extent of attitude change. More specifically, a favourability index based on thought-listing (e.g., ratio of favourable thoughts to total number of relevant thoughts) should act as a mediator of attitude change under central processing, but not under peripheral processing.

An even more powerful tool to assess the degree to which message recipients engage in systematic processing is the systematic variation of argument quality. With this technique, recipients are exposed to communications which consist of either strong or weak arguments. (The categorization of arguments as strong or weak is decided beforehand on the basis of a pilot study.) Exposure to strong arguments should stimulate predominantly favourable thoughts about the message in recipients who engage in central route processing. As a result, there should also be significant attitude change. On the other hand, if arguments are weak, central route processing should produce predominantly unfavourable thoughts about the message, and therefore very little attitude change. The less recipients are motivated and able to engage in central route (i.e., systematic) processing of a message, the weaker should be the effect of a manipulation of argument quality on cognitive responses and attitude change. The combined use of both thought-listing (as one of the dependent measures) and manipulation of argument quality (as one of the independent variables) therefore provides a valid tool for diagnosing the extent to which individuals engage in central processing of the content of a message.

Processing ability, elaboration and attitude change.   Variation in processing ability should affect information processing mainly when individuals are motivated to process a message. Thus studies of variables which influence processing ability have typically used issues which were highly relevant to the students who were the recipients of these communications (e.g., tuition fee increase, change in exam system). Among the most important variables influencing a person's ability to systematically process persuasive arguments are distraction and message repetition. Since we have already considered research on distraction earlier, we will focus here on message repetition. In contrast to distraction, which reduces processing ability, (moderate) argument repetition should provide recipients with more opportunity for cognitively

elaborating a communication. Thus, repetition should enhance attitude change for messages consisting of strong arguments and reduce attitude change for weak messages. Cacioppo and Petty (1990) tested this hypothesis by exposing respondents either one or three times to a message that contained either strong or weak persuasive arguments. Consistent with their predictions, increasing exposure to the same message led to higher agreement with high-quality messages, but led to decreased agreement with low-quality messages. However, the positive impact of repetition on high-quality messages will only occur if recipients are motivated to think about the communication (Claypool, Mackie, Garcia-Marques, McIntosh & Udall, 2004). Furthermore, when messages are repeated too often, boredom sets in, which can result in rejection of even high-quality arguments in high-relevance messages (Cacioppo & Petty, 1979).

Processing motivation, elaboration and attitude change.   The most influential determinant of a person's motivation to think about the argument contained in a message is the perceived *personal relevance* of the communication. Only if the issue is important to them personally should recipients of a communication be motivated to critically evaluate the arguments contained in a message. With low involvement, when the issue of the communication is of little relevance, recipients are likely to rely on peripheral cues to assess the validity of the position advocated by the communication.

Petty, Cacioppo and Goldman (1981) tested these predictions experimentally. They exposed college students to an attitude-discrepant communication advocating major changes to the examination system. This communication, on a topic about which students are very knowledgeable, contained either strong or weak arguments and was attributed either to a source with high expertise (the Carnegie Commission on Higher Education) or to one with low expertise (a class at a local high school). The researchers manipulated personal relevance by informing students either that these changes were going to be instituted the following year and would thus affect them, or that they would take effect only in ten years' time. Petty and colleagues (1981) predicted that when students believed that the changes would affect their own fate (high personal relevance), they should be motivated to scrutinize the arguments and to engage in issue-relevant thinking. For these highly involved students, argument quality would be a major factor in persuasion. Students who believed that these changes would only be instituted long after they had left the university (low personal relevance) would not be motivated to think a great deal about the communication. Instead, they would use heuristic rules such as 'Experts can be trusted' to assess the validity of the advocated position. The results strongly supported these predictions (Figure 7.5).

The extent to which individuals scrutinize message arguments is affected not only by situational factors but also by individual differences in their motivation to think about persuasive communications (see Individual Differences 7.1, p. 142). For example, people who frequently engage in and enjoy effortful cognitive activity (high *need for cognition*) should be more likely to form

need for cognition an individual difference variable which differentiates people according to the extent to which they enjoy thinking about arguments contained in a communication. When exposed to a persuasive message, individuals high in need for cognition are assumed to engage in more content-relevant thinking than individuals who are low on this dimension

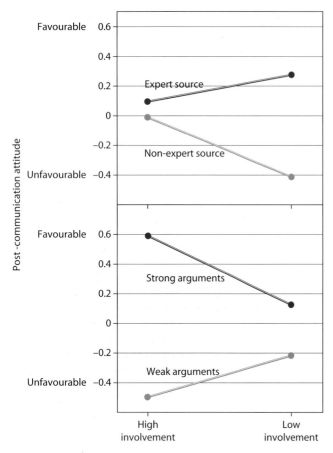

Figure 7.5 *Top panel: interactive effect of involvement and source expertise on post-communication attitudes. Bottom panel: interactive effect of involvement and argument quality on post-communication attitudes (Petty, Cacioppo & Goldman, 1981).*

attitudes on the basis of the arguments contained in a communication than are people who are low in need for cognition. Cacioppo and Petty (1982) constructed a scale to measure need for cognition (see Individual Differences 7.1). Since need for cognition reflects a cognitive motivation rather than an intellectual ability, it correlates only moderately with verbal intelligence ($r = .24$; Cacioppo, Petty, Feinstein & Jarvis, 1996). Consistent with expectations, argument quality affected attitude change mainly for individuals with high rather than low need for cognition. A study by Haugtvedt and Petty (1992) further demonstrated that attitude change in respondents with a high need for cognition was more persistent and more resistant against counterargumentation than in individuals with low need for cognition.

Multiple roles by which variables can influence persuasion. By contrasting peripheral cues with content information and by arguing that peripheral processing is determined by peripheral cues and systematic processing by the content of the message, we have given a somewhat oversimplified presentation of the elaboration likelihood model. One of the unique features of this model, but also a feature which complicates predictions, is the assumption that persuasion variables can influence persuasion in multiple ways, depending on the elaboration likelihood. Specifically the model states that at a low level of elaboration, a peripheral variable (e.g., communicator credibility, mood) will influence persuasion

The need for cognition

This scale (short version) assesses need for cognition, the tendency of individuals to engage in and enjoy effortful cognitive endeavours (Cacioppo et al., 1996). When exposed to a persuasive message, people high in need for cognition are assumed to engage in more content-relevant thinking (i.e., systematic processing) than individuals low in need for cognition.

Instructions: Indicate to what extent each statement is characteristic of you, using the following response alternatives:

1 = extremely uncharacteristic of me (not at all like me)
2 = somewhat uncharacteristic of me
3 = neither uncharacteristic nor characteristic of me
4 = somewhat characteristic of me
5 = extremely characteristic of me

1. I would prefer complex to simple problems.
2. I like to have the responsibility of handling a situation that requires a lot of thinking.
3. Thinking is not my idea of fun.
4. I would rather do something that requires little thought than something that is sure to challenge my thinking ability.
5. I try to anticipate and avoid situations where there is a likely chance I will have to think in depth about something.
6. I find satisfaction in deliberating hard and for long hours.
7. I only think as hard as I have to.
8. I prefer to think about small, daily projects to long-term ones.
9. I like tasks that require little thought once I've learned them.
10. The idea of relying on thought to make my way to the top appeals to me.
11. I really enjoy a task that involves coming up with new solutions to problems.
12. Learning new ways to think doesn't excite me very much.
13. I prefer my life to be filled with puzzles that I must solve.
14. The notion of thinking abstractly is appealing to me.
15. I would prefer a task that is intellectual, difficult and important to one that is somewhat important but does not require much thought.
16. I feel relief rather than satisfaction after completing a task that required a lot of mental effort.
17. It's enough for me that something gets the job done; I don't care how or why it works.
18. I usually end up deliberating about issues even when they do not affect me personally.

Scoring: First, reverse your scores on items 3, 4, 5, 7, 8, 9, 12, 16 and 17. On any of these items, if you gave a 1 to the question, change it into a 5. If you gave a 2, change it into a 4; if you gave a 4, change it into a 2; and if you gave a 5, change it into a 1. If you gave a 3, leave it as a 3. Scores are added, and the higher your score, the higher your need for cognition.

through heuristic processing or other non-thoughtful means. When elaboration is at a medium level, the same variable might influence persuasion by influencing the extent of the elaboration. And finally, when elaboration is high, a peripheral variable may have no impact at all, may bias processing or even act as an argument.

We will use the message recipient's *mood* as an example of how a factor can influence persuasion in different ways depending on the level of elaboration likelihood (Petty & Wegener, 1999). Under conditions of *low elaboration* mood might be linked to attitude objects via classical conditioning. There is evidence that conditioning of attitudes appears to work best when prior knowledge of the stimulus is low (Cacioppo, Marshall-Goodell, Tassinary & Petty, 1992). Another way mood can influence attitudes under conditions of low elaboration is by acting as a heuristic cue. According to the 'feelings-as-information' hypothesis (e.g., Bless, Bohner, Schwarz & Strack, 1990), people might use the 'how do I feel about it heuristic' to infer their attitude from their present mood. In line with this assumption, Schwarz and Clore (1983) found that people interviewed about their life satisfaction on a sunny day reported more satisfaction than people interviewed on cloudy days. The 'feelings-as-information' hypothesis further suggests that this type of misattribution should be eliminated when individuals are given reason to discount their mood state as information about the issue to be evaluated. In support of this assumption, the impact of weather conditions on life satisfaction disappeared when the interviewers (during the phone interview) casually asked about the local weather conditions. Presumably, this made people attribute their mood to the weather. Clore, Schwarz and Conway (1994) argued that the 'how do I feel about it heuristic' is most likely to be used when the evaluation task is affective in nature, when there are time constraints and when there is not much other information available.

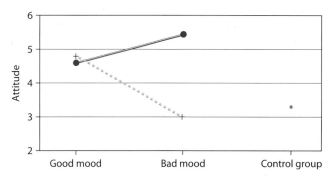

Figure 7.6 *Attitude change as function of mood and message quality (●——● strong message quality; +----+ weak message quality) (adapted from Bless et al., 1990, Experiment 1).*

Under moderate elaboration, mood can influence the recipient's motivation to elaborate on the content of a message. When in a good mood, individuals seem to be more likely to engage in simplified heuristic processing, whereas in a bad mood they may engage in more effortful systematic processing strategies. There is a great deal of support for this assumption (for a review, see Bless, 2001). For example, Bless et al. induced good or bad mood in participants in a laboratory experiment by having them dwell on either a positive or a negative life event (Bless et al., 1990). When the participants were subsequently exposed to an attitude-discrepant communication (arguing for an increase in student service fees), consisting of either high-quality or low-quality arguments, argument quality affected attitude change only for participants who were in a bad mood (Figure 7.6).

There are a number of different explanations for this effect. According to the 'feelings-as-information' hypothesis, individuals use their feelings as information about the state of their environment. Thus, happy moods inform people that their environment is safe, thereby reducing their motivation to scrutinize information in the environment (Bless et al., 1990). An alternative interpretation in terms of mood maintenance has been suggested by Wegener, Petty and Smith (1995). Wegener et al. argued that since the messages used in these studies have been either counterattitudinal or on depressing topics (e.g., fee increases, acid rain), individuals who were happy might have avoided processing these messages in order not to spoil their current pleasant state. Wegener et al. (1995) provided some evidence that with messages which could be expected to be uplifting, sad and happy individuals engaged in equally high levels of elaboration. With a message which could clearly be expected to be depressing, the pattern observed by Bless et al. (1990) was replicated.

At very high levels of elaboration, when people are already processing message arguments systematically, mood can influence information processing by affecting the material that is brought to mind when the merits of an attitude object are being considered (Petty & Wegener, 1999). There is a great deal of evidence that positive moods activate positive material in memory, whereas negative moods activate negative material (e.g., Bower, 1981). Thus, when individuals engage in effortful processing and elaboration of message arguments, positive moods might encourage positive interpretation of the information more than do negative moods. This bias in information processing is most likely when the information is relatively ambiguous.

Plate 7.2 *How does the weather affect your life satisfaction?*

The consequences of elaboration. The elaboration likelihood model predicts that persuasion induced by systematic processing (i.e., central route) is more persistent than persuasion induced by peripheral or heuristic processing. High levels of issue-relevant cognitive activity are likely to require frequent accessing of the attitude and the related knowledge structure. This activity should therefore increase the number of linkages between structural elements, making the attitude schema more internally consistent, enduring and also more resistant to counterarguments. Since examination of persistence requires a second, delayed point of attitude measurement, only a few studies have addressed this issue. These studies support the conclusion that attitude changes which are accompanied by high levels of issue-relevant cognitive activity are more persistent than changes that are accompanied by little issue-relevant thought (e.g., Haugvedt & Petty, 1992; Petty & Cacioppo, 1986a). However, as Eagly and Chaiken (1993) pointed out, heuristic processing could also result in enduring attitude change if the cue became associated with the attitude and remained salient over time (for example, I might persistently recall that my drinking two glasses of wine a day was recommended by my trusted physician). Nonetheless, such an attitude would be vulnerable to counterpropaganda, because it lacks elaborate cognitive support. Beyond the fact that my physician recommended it, I would have no rationale for supporting the habit.

The heuristic-systematic model: How does it differ from the ELM?

As we said earlier (see p. 139), the ELM and the HSM are similar both with regard to their core assumptions about determinants of persuasion and in their predictions about the impact these variables will have on persuasion. And yet, there are some differences between the two theories in the processes which they assume to mediate these effects. In our discussion of these differences, we will focus on four issues: (1) the unidimensionality of the processing continuum; (2) the interplay of processing modes;

(3) the sufficiency principle; and (4) the multiple motive assumption of the HSM.

The unidimensionality of the processing continuum. Like the ELM, the HSM assumes two modes of processing, namely, an effortful systematic mode that is identical to central route processing of the ELM and an effortless heuristic mode. Since heuristic processing is also one of the low-effort processes subsumed under the broad category of peripheral route processes by the ELM, we have already discussed it in the section on the ELM. However, in contrast to the ELM, where heuristic processing is only one of a variety of central route processes, it is the *only* low-effort process assumed by the HSM. Thus, according to the HSM, information processing ranges from heuristic processing at the low-effort end of the continuum to systematic processing at the high-effort end.

The interplay of processing modes. Like the ELM, the HSM assumes that individuals need to have high processing motivation and ability to engage in systematic processing. When people are unmotivated or unable to scrutinize the arguments contained in a persuasive message, they base their decision whether to accept or reject the position advocated in the persuasive communication on heuristic cues only. In contrast, when they are motivated to scrutinize message arguments and able to do so, they base their decision on their evaluation of these arguments, but not exclusively so. The HSM does not assume that individuals necessarily disregard the informational value of heuristic cues once they have begun to engage in systematic processing. Thus, at high levels of motivation and ability, *both* processing modes are likely to affect persuasion. The HSM makes several theoretical assumptions specifying the conditions of such interplay of processing modes (Bohner, Moskowitz & Chaiken, 1995).

According to the *additivity hypothesis* both heuristic cues and content information exert independent main effects on persuasion. This is most likely to happen when heuristic and systematic

RESEARCH CLOSE-UP 7.1

How heuristic processing can bias systematic processing

Chaiken, S. & Maheswaran, D. (1994). Heuristic processing can bias systematic processing: Effects of source credibility, argument ambiguity, and task importance on attitude judgment. *Journal of Personality and Social Psychology, 66,* 450–473.

....

Introduction

Dual-process theories regard systematic processing as more effortful and capacity limited than heuristic processing. They therefore assume that heuristic processing predominates when processing ability and motivation are low, whereas systematic processing becomes the dominant mode when processing ability and motivation are high. The heuristic-systematic model does not assume a trade-off between these processing

modes. Instead, it assumes that both processing modes affect persuasion at the high-effort end of the processing continuum, whereas only heuristic processing dominates at the low-effort end. Since systematic processing usually provides much more information than heuristic processing, the effect of heuristic processing on persuasion will often be obscured (*attenuation hypothesis*). However, there are conditions under which this will not be the case. For example, when the persuasion information is ambiguous and thus amenable to differential interpretations, the expectancies established by the individual's processing of heuristic cues can bias the interpretation of the message content (*bias hypothesis*). The present experiment manipulated task importance, source credibility and message ambiguity to test this hypothesis. With an ambiguous message and high task importance, source credibility was expected to positively bias systematic processing when credibility was high and to negatively bias systematic processing when credibility was low.

Method

Participants
Three hundred and sixty-seven students participated in this study.

Design and procedure
Participants were told that they would read and give their opinions about a new telephone answering machine, the 'XT-100'. They then read a 4-page booklet that conveyed the source credibility, message type information and task importance. A questionnaire that assessed participants' attitudes and other dependent measures followed.

Independent variables
Source credibility. The information was attributed either to the sales staff of a supermarket chain (low credibility) or to a respected consumer report magazine (high credibility).

Message type. The product description compared the XT-100 with two competing brands on six product attributes, and asserted that the XT-100 was superior to those brands. The recommendation was based either on strong arguments (superior on important attributes), weak arguments (superior on unimportant attributes) or, in the ambiguous condition, on some arguments in favour and some against the XT-100.

Task importance. Participants were told either that they were part of a small selected group being canvassed by the producers of XT-100 to decide whether the machine should be sold in their area (high task importance) or that they were part of a very large group to be canvassed and that the machine would only be sold outside the state in which the respondent lived (low task importance).

Dependent variables
Attitudes. Participants rated the extent to which they would consider buying the XT-100, their favourability towards it and the extent to which they regarded it a good product.

Cognitive responses. Subjects were given 3 minutes to list their thoughts about the product or product description. These thoughts were then categorized by two independent raters according to whether they related to the source or to the product attributes and whether they expressed positive, negative or neutral evaluations of source or product.

Manipulation checks. Participants were asked to indicate their level of motivation to read the product description, their perception of the credibility of the source and the extent to which the product description contained many (few) positive or negative features.

Results

Results supported predictions. Under low task importance, attitudes were mainly determined by source credibility (Figure 7.7, top panel). Under high task importance and unambiguously strong or weak messages, attitudes were mainly determined by argument quality, an effect mediated by systematic processing.

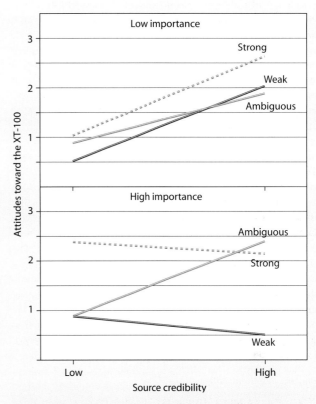

Figure 7.7 *Attitudes towards the XT-100 as a function of task importance (low vs. high), source credibility (low vs. high) and message type (strong vs. ambiguous vs. weak). Theoretical and actual range of attitude scores was −4 to 4, where higher numbers imply more positive attitudes.*

However, respondents under high task importance who had received an ambiguous message showed a strong source credibility effect, despite high levels of systematic processing (Figure 7.7, bottom panel). Under these conditions, the impact of source credibility on attitudes was mediated by both heuristic processing *and* biased systematic processing. Source credibility exerted a direct effect through heuristic processing and an indirect effect by positively biasing systematic processing when credibility was high and negatively biasing systematic processing when credibility was low.

Discussion

Results under low task importance as well as under high task importance with an unambiguously strong or weak message replicated previous research. Evidence for the bias hypothesis comes from respondents in the high task importance condition, who were exposed to an ambiguous message. Although these motivated participants displayed evidence for systematic processing, their attitudes were mainly affected by source credibility. Analysis of their cognitive responses revealed that source credibility exerted an indirect effect by positively biasing systematic processing when credibility was high and negatively biasing systematic processing when credibility was low.

processing lead to the same conclusion, for example, if an expert communicator also presents strong arguments. However, the greater the number of strong arguments presented by the expert communicator, the greater the probability that the independent effect of the heuristic cue will be submerged under this wealth of content information. As a result, the effect of the heuristic cue on persuasion may no longer be detectable (*attenuation hypothesis*). Most interesting is the *bias hypothesis* of the HSM, which predicts an interaction between the two processing modes. Such biasing is most likely to occur when the persuasive information is ambiguous and thus amenable to differential interpretations. Recipients might then give more weight to arguments which are consistent with the recommendation made by a source which is credible than by a source which is not credible. A study by Chaiken and Maheswaran (1994; Research close-up 7.1) provides support for the bias hypothesis.

The sufficiency principle: a theory of processing motivation.   The HSM and the ELM agree in their assumptions about the factors which determine processing motivation, but the HSM makes more explicit assumptions about processes which mediate the impact of these determinants on processing motivation. According to the model's **sufficiency principle**, recipients of a message try to achieve sufficient confidence in their judgement before accepting an attitudinal position (Eagly & Chaiken, 1993). What a person will consider sufficient is determined by two factors, a *sufficiency threshold* reflecting the desired level of confidence a person would like to have and the person's *actual confidence*. As long as the individual's actual confidence is below the desired level, the person will continue to process information. The desired level of confidence is likely to be higher for issues of great personal relevance than for trivial issues. Large discrepancies between actual and desired levels of confidence are therefore most likely to develop for issues which are personally relevant to recipients. Since systematic processing usually provides more information than heuristic processing, large gaps between desired and actual confidence are likely to motivate systematic rather than heuristic processing, but only if individuals expect that systematic processing will enable them to reduce this gap (Bohner, Rank, Reinhard, Einwiller & Erb, 1998). Whether recipients will actually succeed in their attempts to process a message systematically will depend on the availability of relevant resources (i.e., processing time, message-relevant knowledge).

Multiple motives.   So far we have described the information processing underlying attitude change as a relatively objective and unbiased activity. The ELM, as well as the original version of the HSM, postulates a single motive: people are motivated to hold correct attitudes. This accuracy motivation determines the processing goal, namely to assess the validity of persuasive messages.

Chaiken and her colleagues (1989; Bohner et al., 1995) have extended the HSM and incorporated two further motives or goals for heuristic and systematic processing. Whereas accuracy motivation encourages objective and unbiased information processing, the other two motives are assumed to bias the processing of

> **sufficiency principle** the heuristic-systematic model assumes that people strive for sufficient confidence in the validity of their attitudinal judgements. When people's actual confidence is below their desired level of confidence or sufficiency threshold, they will process additional information in order to close this gap

persuasive information, that is, to induce individuals to hold particular preferred attitude positions. One class of motives likely to bias information processing has been labelled *defence motivation*. The processing goal of defence-motivated individuals is to confirm the validity of preferred attitude positions and to disconfirm the validity of positions which are not preferred (Eagly & Chaiken, 1993). A number of conditions can motivate individuals to defend their present attitudinal position, such as vested interest, attitudinal commitment or a need for consistency. Defence-motivated processing can be either heuristic or systematic. The defence-motivated message recipient is assumed to use the same heuristics as somebody who is accuracy-motivated, but to use them selectively so as to support preferred attitude positions. Defence-motivated systematic processing is similarly selective. Attitude-relevant information that supports favoured positions or opposes non-favoured ones should receive more attention and be more positively interpreted than information that supports positions which are not favoured by the recipient (e.g., Das, de Wit & Stroebe, 2003; De Hoog, Stroebe & de Wit, 2005).

A second class of motives likely to bias information processing has been termed *impression motivation*. This motive refers to the desire to express attitudes that are socially acceptable. It is assumed to be aroused in influence settings, in which the identities of significant audiences are salient or when people must communicate their attitudes to others who may have the power to reward or punish them. The processing goal of impression-motivated recipients is to assess the social acceptability of alternative positions in order to accept attitudinal positions which will please or appease potential evaluators. Like accuracy- and defence-motivated processing, impression-motivated processing can be both heuristic and systematic. Impression-motivated heuristic processing is assumed to involve the use of simple rules to guide one's selection of socially acceptable attitude positions (for example, 'moderate positions minimize disagreement'). In impression-motivated systematic processing the same goal is reached through scrutinizing the available information in terms of its acceptability to the social influence context (e.g., Chen, Shechter & Chaiken, 1996).

The incorporation of impression motivation links the HSM to theories of social influence such as the model of Deutsch and Gerard (1955) discussed in Chapter 11, this volume. This model postulates that group members may accept opinions from other members either because they believe them to be valid (informational social influence) or because they think that acceptance of these beliefs will raise their status within the group (normative social influence). Informational social influence should predominate in settings which arouse accuracy motivation, whereas normative social influence should occur under conditions which arouse impression motivation.

Advertising as applied persuasion

Is subliminal advertising possible?
How can we apply dual-process theories of persuasion to advertising?

In the course of this chapter, we have already related some of the findings of persuasion studies to advertising. However, those of

Plate 7.3 *Advertising helped propel Absolut Vodka from an inconsequential brand to become America's leading premium vodka.*

you who think of advertising as a powerful force that creates consumer needs and shapes the competition in markets today might have been slightly disappointed by our discussion of persuasion techniques. After all, it is hard to imagine that the processes we discussed here can have powerful effects like creating the image of the Marlboro Man or helping to propel Absolut Vodka in the United States from an inconsequential brand with fewer than 100,000 bottles sold in 1980 to become America's leading premium vodka brand with a sales volume of 40 million litres in 2006. You might suspect that other factors have been at work (e.g., marketing, pricing strategy) or that there is some secret ingredient, a 'silver bullet' persuasion strategy which we have not discussed so far.

Subliminal advertising One candidate for such a weapon, albeit not a very secret one, is *subliminal advertising*. The term subliminal refers to the presentation of a message so briefly (or faintly) that it is below the threshold of awareness. Subliminal advertising was made notorious in 1957 through publicity surrounding James Vicary, a private market researcher, who claimed to have increased sales of Coca-Cola by 18.1 per cent and popcorn sales by 57.7 per cent in a movie theatre by secretly and subliminally flashing the message 'Drink Coca-Cola' or 'Eat popcorn'. People became so upset by the idea that they could be manipulated without their

awareness that subliminal advertising has subsequently been banned in Australia, Britain and the United States (Pratkanis & Aronson, 2001). However, while people do not want to be manipulated against their will, they quite like the idea of their willpower being buttressed by subliminal suggestion. American consumers appear to spend more than $50 million annually on audiotapes that contain subliminal messages to help them to improve their self-esteem, their memory and their study *habits* or to help them to lose weight and to stop smoking. (Pratkanis & Aronson, 2001).

> **habits** learned sequences of behaviour that have become automatic responses to specific cues and are functional in obtaining certain goals

Nobody has ever been able to replicate the findings reported by James Vicary. The study has never been published and is now believed to have been a publicity hoax (Pratkanis & Aronson, 2001). Similarly, studies of the effectiveness of self-help tapes have found no evidence of any effects. Greenwald, Spangenberg, Pratkanis and Eskenazi (1991) conducted a study in which they measured participants' self-esteem and memory and then presented them with tapes that, according to the manufacturers, contained subliminal messages that should either improve self-esteem ('I have high self-worth and high self-esteem') or memory ('My ability to remember and to recall is increasing daily'). Crosscutting the manipulation of the subliminal content of the tapes, half the respondents were led to believe that they listened to the memory tape, the other half that they listened to the self-esteem tape. Respondents took the tapes home and listened to them daily for five weeks. When their self-esteem and their memory were reassessed on their return to the laboratory, no improvements could be detected. It is interesting, though, that those participants who thought that they had received the memory tape (regardless of whether they really had been given the memory tape or had been given the self-esteem tape) believed that their memory had improved. Similarly, respondents who believed that they had received the self-esteem tape reported substantial improvements in their self-esteem. Thus, whereas the actual content of the tapes had no effect whatsoever, the *assumed* content resulted in a 'placebo effect'. Participants believed that their memory (or their self-esteem) had improved, even though, objectively, there had been no improvements at all. Obviously, such beliefs guarantee satisfied customers and the continued sales of self-help tapes.

That these subliminal messages were ineffective is hardly surprising (see Chapter 4 on Social cognition). First, subliminal verbal primes have to consist of one or perhaps two (very short) words to be effective and not of whole sentences. Second, successful priming does nothing more than increase the accessibility of the primed concept and of thoughts related to that concept. Thus, even if it were possible to prime subliminally sentences like 'My ability to remember is increasing daily' or 'I have high self-worth', they would be unlikely to improve our memory or our self-esteem. Third, effects of subliminal priming can only be demonstrated under very controlled conditions. For example, the lighting has to be right, viewers must focus on the exact spot where the prime will be displayed and there must be nothing to distract them. One could never be sure that these conditions would be met in a movie theatre or with people watching TV at home.

Coca-Cola is a relatively short brand name and thus meets the first condition for a subliminal prime. Thus, if clever advertising technicians developed a technique that enabled them to successfully prime movie or TV audiences, could Coca-Cola sales be improved through subliminal priming? This would depend on a number of conditions. First, it would depend on the thoughts members of the audience associate with Coca-Cola. If they find it too sweet a drink, priming will not change their opinion. On the other hand, if they associate it with great taste and great thirst-quenching qualities, then priming might make them want to have a Coke, but only if they are thirsty at that particular moment.

When we tried to put this hypothesis to a test, we found in a pre-test that our Dutch students attributed the greatest thirst-quenching qualities to Lipton Ice (an ice tea). We therefore decided to use Lipton Ice in our studies (Karremans, Stroebe & Claus, 2006). We conducted two experiments, in which we primed half of our participants subliminally with Lipton Ice, the other half with a neutral control word containing the same letters. The primes were presented 25 times, but each time for only 23 milliseconds, so that our participants were unaware of the priming procedure. Whereas in our first experiment we used self-ratings of thirstiness to divide participants into thirsty and non-thirsty groups, we decided to manipulate thirstiness in the second study. Participants had to suck a salty sweet (*dropje*), supposedly to see whether they could identify with their tongue the letters that were impressed on one side of the sweet. (This sweet, which is popular in the Netherlands, is known to produce thirst.) Both experiments resulted in significant prime by thirstiness interactions on choice. When offered a choice between a brand of mineral water or Lipton Ice, participants who had been primed with Lipton Ice were significantly more likely to choose it over the mineral water, *but only if they were thirsty* (Figure 7.8). They also expressed greater intentions to choose Lipton Ice in a hypothetical situation (if they were now sitting on a terrace and ordering a drink).

These findings suggest that subliminal advertising could be feasible. Exposing individuals subliminally to the brand name of a drink can increase the probability that they choose that drink, but

only under certain conditions. First, the drink has to be considered thirst-quenching and second, people have to be thirsty. But third, they also have to be in a situation in which they are able to make that choice. A known limitation of the priming procedure is that effects wear off very quickly. Thus, even thirsty, movie audiences would want their Lipton Ice immediately after they had been primed and not three days afterwards. Thus, subliminally priming movie audiences with the concept 'Lipton Ice' just before the break might induce those who are thirsty to buy a Lipton Ice during the break. However, it would not motivate them to stock up with it the next time they are at the supermarket.

But all is not lost for advertisers. There are conditions under which subliminal priming of brand names might have long-term effects. One possibility is that thirsty, Lipton Ice-loving TV audiences who, after a subliminal prime, would like to drink Lipton Ice but have none at home might decide to put it on their shopping list. A second possibility is that TV or movie audiences who are subliminally primed with the concept 'thirst' and immediately afterwards exposed to a soft drink ad emphasizing the thirst-quenching qualities of this drink might be more persuaded by this ad than they would have been otherwise. Support for this assumption comes from an experiment conducted by Strahan and colleagues (2002). They exposed respondents immediately after they had been subliminally primed with either 'thirst' or with a neutral prime to two drink advertisements, one for a thirst-quenching drink called 'Super-Quencher' and one for an electrolyte-restoring sports drink called 'PowerPro'. Respondents who had been primed with 'thirst' were more persuaded by the ad for 'Super-Quencher' (but not by the ad for 'PowerPro') than individuals who had been presented with the neutral prime.

A third possibility would be to use methods of subliminal exposure in a procedure of classical conditioning. There is evidence that classical conditioning can affect attitudes towards brand names. For example, one study on the long-term effects of conditioned attitudes towards a brand name associated positively evaluated images with a fictitious brand of mouthwash (Grossman & Till, 1998). Even three weeks after exposure, conditioning effects could still be observed. There is also evidence that classical conditioning of attitudes can work when the evaluative stimuli are presented subliminally (e.g., DeHouwer, Baeyens & Eelen, 1994; Krosnick et al., 1992). Thus, one could pair a brand name with evaluative stimuli (e.g., pictures of positive events), which are presented subliminally. The main shortcoming of this procedure would be that as a form of initial, affect-based attitude acquisition, classical conditioning may not be effective with brands of high familiarity.

A dual-process analysis of advertising Social psychological research on message processing and persuasion has focused mainly on the processing of verbal information. In contrast, advertising uses pictures, fonts, colours, music and sound effects to draw attention, evoke associations and convey meaning. All of these non-verbal modalities may affect evaluative judgements directly or through their impact on message processing. Despite these differences, the insights into persuasion processes we gained from social psychological research can be very helpful in understanding advertising.

Advertisements can adopt a variety of appeals. The three most common are arguments, emotions and endorsements (Tellis, 2004). The effectiveness of each of these strategies will depend

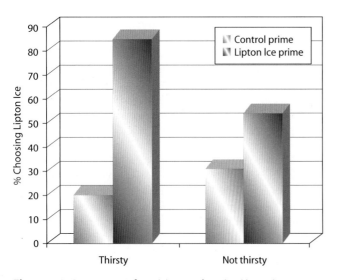

Figure 7.8 *Percentage of participants choosing Lipton Ice as a function of thirst and prime (Karremans et al., 2006, Study 2).*

Plate 7.4 *In this advertisement endorsement by an expert is used as an advertising strategy.*

mainly on two factors, namely the *type of product* being advertised and the *involvement of the audience*. Products can be classified as either feeling or thinking products (Tellis, 2004). Feeling products such as wine, paintings or soft drinks are evaluated primarily by personal preference. Examples of preference attributes are taste, flavour, style and design. In contrast, thinking products, such as washing machines, computers and most cars, are purchased because of reason attributes such as performance, reliability, quality or fit (Tellis, 2004). Obviously, some products combine aspects of both types (e.g., sports cars).

Since the attitudes towards feeling products will be mainly based on affect and will have very little cognitive content, emotional appeals are preferable for feeling products. It would be difficult to make an argument-based appeal for a particular brand of cola, given that different brands are not all that different and that purchasing decisions for soft drinks are rarely based on objective qualities. Soft drink ads therefore play on people's emotions, trying to associate these products with feelings of youth, energy and sexual attractiveness.

In contrast, the advertising strategies for thinking products usually rely on arguments praising such attributes as the performance characteristics, reliability and quality of the service. As we have discussed earlier, the problem with using argumentative appeals is that even strong arguments are only effective with audiences that are motivated and able to process the information. This may be less of a problem with ads for dishwashers or hair dryers. Although

they are not objects of great interest to most people, advertisements for these household appliances are mainly directed at those who want to buy such an appliance and would therefore be motivated to think about the arguments in an advertisement.

But what strategy should one use to advertise products such as toothpaste, washing powder or mouthwash, which neither arouse a great deal of emotion nor are considered of sufficient importance by most people to devote a great deal of effort to processing arguments? One possibility is to use endorsements by celebrities or experts. We have all seen the actor who, dressed like a dentist (i.e., expert), praises the qualities of a particular toothpaste. Another possibility is to use emotional appeals to increase the perceived importance of a product. One could try to induce guilt feelings in parents who neglect their children's welfare by not making them brush their teeth with toothpaste X.

Alternatively, one could use fear appeals (Das et al., 2003; De Hoog et al., 2005). This approach was taken by Gerald Lambert, who in 1922 hired an ad agency to improve the sluggish sales of Listerine, at the time a product used as an antiseptic in surgery and to fight throat infections (Pratkanis & Aronson, 2001). Seeking a wider market, Lambert decided to promote it as a mouthwash. The problem was that nobody in those days really used a mouthwash. Furthermore, accusing people of having 'bad breath' would not have been a popular message. Thus, the ads for Listerine used the obscure medical term 'halitosis' instead of bad breath. The slogans of this famous campaign played on people's fear of being rejected by their social environment. 'Even your best friend won't tell you. Listerine is good for halitosis.' Or, 'Often a bridesmaid . . . never a bride.' The campaign was extremely effective, turning Listerine into a household name.

But such brilliant campaigns are the exception rather than the rule, as studies of advertising effectiveness indicate (Tellis, 2004). So how can advertising contribute to such dramatic sales increases as in the example of Absolut Vodka mentioned earlier? The answer is simple: through the accumulation of small effects over a long period of time. It took 19 years and an immense advertising budget to achieve this result.

SUMMARY

This first part of the chapter has reviewed the theoretical developments that have substantially increased our understanding of the cognitive processes which mediate the impact of persuasion. Whereas McGuire's information processing model illuminated some of the processes involved in the interplay between message reception and acceptance, the cognitive response model provided powerful insights into the processes underlying the acceptance of a message. Both theories, however, still focused exclusively on systematic processing of message content. The dual-processing theories of persuasion (i.e., ELM and HSM) integrated theories of systematic processing with theories based on more peripheral processes and, furthermore, made predictions about the factors that determine whether individuals engage in systematic or peripheral processing.

INCENTIVE-INDUCED ATTITUDE CHANGE

Does the use of incentives (e.g., taxation, legal sanctions) constitute an effective strategy of behaviour change? Can incentives also be used to change attitudes?

Powerful institutions often influence behaviour directly through incentives or legal sanctions rather than relying on the uncertain effects of persuasion. For example, when Swedish drivers could not be persuaded to use their seatbelts, the government introduced a law that made seatbelt use compulsory for front-seat passengers in private cars. The introduction of this law increased the frequency of seatbelt use from 30 per cent to 85 per cent within a few months (Fhanér & Hane, 1979). Similarly, in New York, where seatbelt use ranged from 10 to 20 per cent prior to the introduction of a seatbelt law in 1984, it increased to 45–70 per cent after the law entered into force in early 1985. The introduction of these laws also resulted in substantial reductions in the deaths of vehicle occupants (Robertson, 1986).

Plate 7.5 *The introduction of compulsory seatbelt laws has increased seatbelt use and reduced deaths of vehicle occupants.*

Governments can also use taxation to reduce the occurrence of undesirable behaviour patterns. Thus, there is ample evidence that the demand for alcoholic drinks and cigarettes, like the demand for most commodities, responds to changes in price and income (see Stroebe, 2001). A review of available research from several countries concluded that, everything else remaining equal, a rise in alcohol prices generally led to a drop in the consumption of alcohol, whereas an increase in the income of consumers generally led to a rise in alcohol consumption. There is similar evidence for smoking (Stroebe, 2001).

Thus, there is ample evidence that use of incentives is an effective strategy of behaviour change. It is also likely that incentive-induced behaviour change results in a change in attitudes towards the behaviour. According to the value-expectancy models discussed in the previous chapter, one's attitude towards a given behaviour reflects the perceived consequences of engaging in that behaviour. Therefore, changes in the price of, for example, alcoholic drinks should influence one's attitude towards buying alcoholic drinks. It should have no effect, however, on one's attitude towards drinking them. Consequently, although a marked increase in the price of alcoholic drinks is likely to induce people to buy fewer of them, they might drink at their old level of consumption when not constrained by price (e.g., at a party where drinks are freely available). Furthermore, should alcohol prices come down again, people's attitude towards buying alcoholic drinks would again become more positive.

With regard to the effectiveness of legal sanctions, governments have the added problem that, to be effective, these sanctions may require continuous monitoring. It would therefore be desirable if the behaviour change induced by legal sanctions resulted in a change in attitudes. In the following sections, we will discuss conditions under which incentive-induced behaviour change might lead to attitude change.

Counterattitudinal behaviour and attitude change

One condition for attitude change following *counterattitudinal behaviour* could be that individuals find performing that behaviour much less

> **counterattitudinal behaviour** behaviour (usually induced by monetary incentives or threats) which is inconsistent with the actor's attitude or beliefs

aversive than they had anticipated. For example, seatbelt users in the 1980s, who reluctantly used their belts because of the sanctions threatened by the law, may have found them much less restrictive than they anticipated. Thus, they may have realized that their negative attitude towards seatbelt use was unjustified. This attitude change is likely to have been accompanied by a process of habit formation. Over time, putting on their seatbelts may have become habitual for most people. Thus, what was originally a conscious action, requiring cognitive resources and performed purely to avoid being sanctioned, may have turned into effortless and automatic behaviour. There is evidence that behaviour becomes habitual if it is performed frequently and in contexts which are likely to be stable (Ouellette & Wood, 1998). We would further

argue that behaviour is unlikely to become habitual if it is effortful and associated with negative consequences. Seatbelt use fulfils
all of these conditions, at least for regular car users. However, all
is not lost, if performing the behaviour is really as unpleasant as
they anticipated, because *dissonance theory* would still lead us to
expect that people will change their attitudes towards greater
consistency with their behaviour, at least under certain well-
specified conditions.

Dissonance theory According to *dissonance theory*, individuals
who are induced to behave in a way which is discrepant with
their attitude will experience
dissonance (Festinger, 1957).
Dissonance is an aversive state,
which motivates individuals
to reduce it. This motivation
will be stronger, the greater
the dissonance. One way to
reduce dissonance is to change
one's attitude towards the
behaviour.

dissonance theory a consistency theory
which assumes that dissonance is an
aversive state, which motivates individuals
to reduce it. Strategies of dissonance
reduction include belief, attitude and
behaviour change as well as the search
for consonant or the avoidance of
dissonant information

To explain this prediction, we will have to describe dissonance
theory in more detail. Whenever an individual chooses between
alternative courses of action, there have to be reasons that justify
the chosen action (consonant cognitions) otherwise the person
would not have made that particular choice. However, there are
usually also reasons which would have argued for choosing the
rejected alternative (dissonant cognitions). The more reasons there
are that would have justified choosing the rejected alternative, and
the more important these reasons are, the greater will be the dissonance the person experiences and the greater the pressure to
reduce it. For example, if Susan buys a car and decides for a Mini
over a Golf, the good looks of the Mini and the sporty feel of the
car would be consonant cognitions. However, the Golf would
probably have cost less, had a larger luggage compartment and a
more comfortable ride. These qualities of the Golf, which she gave
up by choosing the Mini, will contribute to her dissonance (i.e.,
dissonant cognitions). Since, once made, choices are difficult to reverse, the most likely means for her to reduce dissonance is to persuade herself that the Mini is even more fun and the Golf more
bourgeois than she always thought. There is empirical evidence
that people's evaluations of two objects are more discrepant some
time after a choice between them than before the choice took place
(e.g., Brehm, 1956).

If drivers use seatbelts to avoid paying a fine, their behaviour is
not completely voluntary. And yet, since they could have decided
to risk the fine, it is still a free decision. It is in this situation where
dissonance theory makes its most counterintuitive prediction.
Since the threatened sanctions are consonant cognitions for those
who comply with the law, dissonance would be greater the less
severe these sanctions. If death was the penalty for not using one's
seatbelt, few seatbelt users would feel dissonance. On the other
hand, if the penalty was $1, people who comply would probably
feel considerable dissonance. After all, a fine of $1 is not a very
substantial justification to engage in behaviour that one did not
really want to engage in. Thus, if an individual behaves counter-
attitudinally to avoid a penalty or gain some benefit, dissonance

(a)

(b)

Plates 7.6a and b *After buying one of these two cars, how are
you likely to view the other?*

will be greater if the penalty or the benefits are small rather
than large.

Festinger and Carlsmith (1959) tested these predictions in
their classic experiment. Participants had to perform two dull
motor tasks for an hour and were then asked, under some pretext,
whether they would be willing to tell the next participant that
the experimental task was really interesting. They were offered
either $20 or $1 for telling this lie. According to dissonance theory,
participants who had been offered $20 should have less problem
in justifying their behaviour than individuals who received only
$1: after all, $20 was then (and still is) a large sum of money.
Participants in the $20 condition should therefore experience less
dissonance and less need to reduce it than those who had only
been offered $1 for telling a lie (Figure 7.9). In line with these pre-
dictions, Festinger and Carlsmith found that, when asked afterwards to indicate how enjoyable they had found the two motor
tasks, participants in the $1 condition rated it more enjoyable than
did individuals who had been paid $20 or than individuals in the

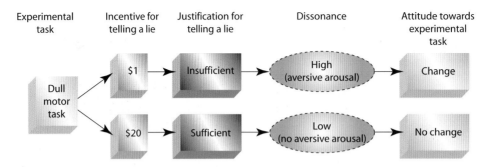

Figure 7.9 *Dissonance interpretation of the Festinger & Carlsmith (1959) experiment.*

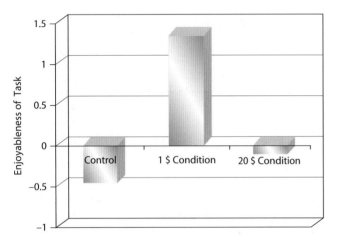

Figure 7.10 *Ratings of task enjoyableness by condition (adapted from Festinger & Carlsmith, 1959).*

control group who had merely rated the motor task without having been asked to tell a lie (Figure 7.10).

Festinger and Carlsmith intuitively built two features into their experimental situation which, though not specified by the original version of the theory, turned out to be essential for dissonance arousal. First, since the experimenter's request was not ostensibly part of the experiment, participants were free to refuse the request and thus experienced high freedom of choice. However, since most people are absolute suckers when it comes to refusing requests made in face-to-face situations (see Chapter 11, this volume), Festinger and Carlsmith did not have to worry that many participants would refuse, even in the $1 condition. Second, since the target of the lie (actually a confederate of the experimenters) had indicated that she had originally not intended to participate in the experiment because of an exam, the participants' behaviour led to aversive consequences. Both freedom of choice (Linder, Cooper & Jones, 1967) and negative consequences (Cooper & Worchel, 1970) are necessary for counterattitudinal behaviour to arouse dissonance.

Self-perception theory Dissonance theory provoked some controversy in its heyday. The major challenge to the dissonance interpretation came from *self-perception theory* (Bem, 1965, 1972). This theory assumes that people often do not know their own attitudes and, when asked about them, are in the same position as an outside observer (see Chapters 5 and 6, this volume). As we have learned in the discussion of attribution theory (see Chapter 3), people usually infer attitudes of others from relevant instances of past behaviour. Thus, when asked to state their attitude towards the motor task, participants in the Festinger and Carlsmith experiment would have remembered that they told another participant that the task was interesting. They would have used this knowledge as information about their own attitude towards the task, unless there were reasons to *discount* their own behaviour as a source of information. Being paid a large sum of money to behave in a certain way is a good reason to discount one's behaviour as a source of information about one's attitude. Thus, in the latter case, they would probably evaluate the experimental task merely on the basis of how they remembered it. Self-perception theory can thus account for the Festinger and Carlsmith findings without referring to aversive states and clashing cognitions (see Figure 7.11).

It is now generally accepted that the two theories should be regarded as complementary formulations with each theory being applicable to its own specialized domain. According to Fazio, Zanna and Cooper (1977), self-perception theory accurately characterizes attitude change in the context of less discrepant behaviour where the individual argues for a position close to his or her own initial attitude. Fazio and colleagues term such behaviour attitude-congruent and define it as any position that is still acceptable to an individual, even though it may not be in accordance with his or her actual attitude. For example, people who believe that all atomic power stations should be closed down immediately would probably also find acceptable the position that no new atomic power stations should be built and the existing ones should be phased out within 10 years. However, these opponents of atomic power stations would find completely unacceptable the argument that we need new atomic power stations to ensure future energy needs. Since it can be assumed that individuals are motivated to put considerably more cognitive effort into justifying their action if it is counterattitudinal rather than attitude-congruent, this integration is consistent with expectations from dual-process theories: low-involvement individuals (those still behaving in an attitude-congruent manner, hence exerting little effort in justification) should rely predominantly on peripheral processes (i.e., they will take their own behaviour as a source of information). In an extension of this argument, Stroebe and Diehl (1988) further demonstrated that self-perception theory can also account

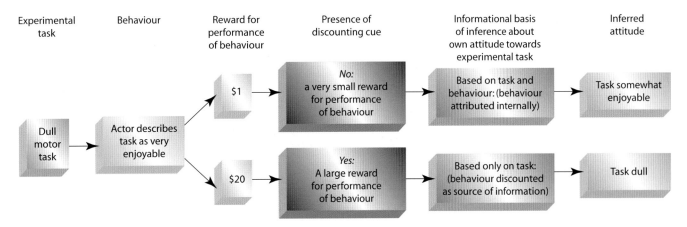

Figure 7.11 *Interpretation of the Festinger & Carlsmith (1959) experiment in terms of self-perception.*

for attitude change following highly attitude-discrepant behaviour, provided it is performed under conditions unlikely to arouse dissonance (e.g., when individuals were given no choice to refuse performing the behaviour, or when the behaviour was not associated with negative consequences).

Dissonance, self-perception and the use of incentives

Will people who smoke less or drink less because of taxation-induced price increases also change their attitudes towards smoking or drinking? Individuals who smoke less because cigarette prices have increased, or drink less because alcohol prices have gone up, may experience some dissonance. After all, their decision to reduce their consumption of cigarettes or alcohol will be the result of a decision about how to allocate their income. They would have been able to consume at the old level if they had decided to reduce *other* expenses (on food, vacations, etc.). Like all freely chosen decisions, such a decision is likely to result in dissonance and one of the ways to reduce dissonance would be to persuade oneself that one was better off by smoking and drinking less.

It is more doubtful whether dissonance or self-perception processes play an important role in mediating attitude change in the context of behaviour change induced by legal sanctions. According to dissonance theory, counterattitudinal behaviour will only result in attitude change if the incentive offers an insufficient justification for the behaviour change. A similar prerequisite according to self-perception theory is that individuals do not attribute their behaviour change to the incentive. Since legal sanctions only work if individuals are aware of the sanction and if these sanctions are *sufficiently severe* to persuade individuals to abstain from the prohibited behaviour, it is unlikely that individuals who comply will experience a great deal of dissonance or attribute their behaviour to internal causes. Support for the assumption that this type of behaviour change is rarely accompanied by attitude change comes from studies of the use of motorcycle helmets in American states which changed their helmet laws. For example, when Texas and Arkansas changed their law requiring all motorcyclists to wear helmets in 1997 to one requiring this only for riders under the age of 21, helmet use decreased from 97 per cent to 66 per cent in Texas and from 97 per cent to 51 per cent in Arkansas (Waller,

2002). This suggests that helmet use also failed to become habitual, probably because wearing a helmet is effortful and cumbersome.

Some paradoxical effects of incentives and sanctions

Unfortunately, some evidence suggests that legal sanctions or positive incentives can have paradoxical effects on attitudes, with sanctions making the behaviour seem more attractive and positive incentives decreasing the attractiveness of the behaviour they stimulate. There seems to be some truth in the old saying that forbidden fruits are the sweetest, at least for those fruits which had originally been freely available. According to **reactance theory** (Brehm, 1966), the elimination of behavioural freedom should result in reactance, a motivational state directed towards the re-establishment of this behavioural freedom. Obviously, the most direct form of the threatened or lost freedom would be to exercise it. Reactance will therefore frequently result in an intensified form of the behaviour that has been sanctioned. However, regardless of whether or not one violates the sanctions, reactance will increase the motivation to engage in the sanctioned behaviour and thus make it appear more desirable. According to this perspective, introducing a law which forbids smoking could not only induce smokers to smoke whenever they think they can get away with it, it could also make smoking for them an even more desirable activity.

There are also reasons to expect that the introduction of positive incentives to motivate individuals to engage in a particular behaviour could have negative consequences on their attitudes (e.g., Deci, Koestner & Ryan, 1999; Lepper & Greene, 1978). Paradoxically, this is most likely to happen when individuals already engaged in the behaviour before the introduction of the law because they enjoy the behaviour. Imagine that health

> **reactance theory** reactance is an aversive state caused by restriction of an individual's freedom of choice over important behavioural outcomes. Reactance is assumed to motivate the individual to re-establish the restricted freedom

insurance companies became persuaded by evidence that physical exercise extends life expectancy, reduces illness risk and saves health costs. They therefore decided to offer financial rewards (i.e., reduced premiums) for individuals who jogged regularly. This might induce many people to jog who would not have done so otherwise. But at the same time, it might also undermine the motivation of people who enjoy jogging and are already jogging regularly. At least, this is the prediction one would derive from research on the effects of external (e.g., monetary) rewards on *intrinsic motivation* and perform-ance. Intrinsically motivated behaviours are performed out of interest and because they are enjoyed. This research has demonstrated that both enjoyment and performance of an intrinsically enjoyable task can decrease once people have been given some reward for performing that task (e.g., Deci et al., 1999; Lepper & Greene, 1978).

> **intrinsic motivation** behaviour is said to be intrinsically motivated if people perform it because they enjoy it. This enjoyment is sufficient to produce the behaviour and no external reward is required. In fact, external rewards (e.g., financial contributions) are likely to reduce intrinsic motivation

Lepper, Greene and Nisbett (1973) conducted one of the early investigations of this hypothesis. They introduced an attractive drawing activity during the free-play time of nursery school chil-dren. After they had observed the baseline interest of children dur-ing free play, children who showed an initial interest in the activity were chosen as participants and asked to perform the activity under one of three conditions: In the *expected reward* condition, children were promised a reward for their performance (and later, given it); in the *unexpected reward* condition, children were unex-pectedly given a reward afterwards; in the *no reward* condition, children were neither promised nor given a reward. Two weeks later the material was again provided in the classroom and inter-est in the activity was unobtrusively observed. As predicted by the researchers, participants who expected a reward showed a signific-ant decrease in interest in the activity from the baseline to post-experimental observation, whereas participants in the *no reward* or *unexpected reward* conditions showed no significant change in overall interest. Lepper and colleagues (1973) interpreted these findings in terms of Bem's self-perception theory as an *over-justification effect*. They argued that when people are rewarded for engaging in what is already an enjoyable activity, they are likely to attribute their behaviour to the reward (i.e., dis-counting cue), and thus discount their interest in the activity as a cause of their behaviour. As a consequence, they will enjoy the behaviour less and, once the rewards are discontinued, they will be less likely to perform it.

> **over-justification effect** providing external rewards for performance of a task, which individuals previously performed because they found it enjoyable, reduces individuals' liking for, and enjoyment of, the task

In the meantime, the findings reported by Lepper and his col-leagues (1973) have been replicated in numerous studies. Based on a meta-analysis of over a hundred studies conducted with particip-ants ranging from preschool children to college students, Deci and colleagues (1999) concluded that tangible (but not verbal) rewards have a significant negative effect on intrinsic motivation for inter-esting tasks. Thus, although an offer of reduced insurance pre-miums to people who jog regularly might persuade people who never jogged to take it up, it would also spoil the enjoyment regu-lar joggers may have had in engaging in this activity.

Further limitations of the effectiveness of incentive-induced change

Since people are interested in attitude change rarely as an 'end in itself' but as a means to changing behaviour, influencing behaviour through monetary incentives or legal sanctions would seem to be the most effective of the strategies discussed in this chapter. As we have seen, there is ample evidence to support this notion. Seatbelt laws succeeded not only in increasing seatbelt use substantially, they also resulted in a change in attitudes towards seatbelt use, at least among those who complied (Fhanér & Hane, 1979). In view of the apparent effectiveness of incentive-induced behaviour change, one wonders why people still bother with persuasion.

There are actually a number of considerations to be taken into account. The most obvious is lack of power. Only governments have the power to enact laws and even they are constrained in the use of this power. For example, although the behavioural factors which are detrimental to people's health (e.g., smoking, overuse of alcohol) are well known, governments rely on persuasion as well as legal action to change behaviour.

An additional constraint on strategies of influence based on the use of monetary incentives or legal sanctions is that these strategies can only be used for behaviour that can be monitored. Thus, while efficient for publicly identifiable behaviour such as seatbelt use or speeding, positive or negative incentives are difficult to apply if the behaviour that one wishes to influence is difficult to monitor objectively. For example, in the area of race relations, governments can eliminate some of the objective and observable instances of discrimination (e.g., by introducing quotas for employment of members of racial minorities), but they cannot force people to be nice to members of outgroups, to invite them to their homes or let their children marry one of them. This is one of the reasons why the American Supreme Court mandated the end of segregated schooling. Since they could not outlaw prejudice, they attempted to reduce it by increasing interracial contact.

Finally, the effectiveness of legal sanctions is likely to depend on the acceptance of the law and on individual perception that violation of the law is associated with a high risk of sanction. For example, it is quite likely that the introduction of the law making seatbelt use compulsory would not have been effective had people not accepted that such a law was in their own best interest. In fact, without the persuasion campaigns that made it widely known that the wearing of seatbelts substantially reduced the risk of injuries in traffic accidents, it is unlikely that such a law would have been introduced. Similarly, the increases in Federal cigarette tax that occurred in the USA during the 1970s and 1980s would not have been possible without the anti-smoking campaign. The anti-smoking campaign in the USA also illustrates the fact that persua-sion and incentive-related strategies do not preclude each other and are probably most effective when used in combination. Thus, the anti-smoking campaign resulted in a non-smoking ethos that was probably responsible for the legislative successes of the non-smokers' rights movements during the 1970s and 1980s.

SUMMARY

Powerful institutions often use incentives or legal sanctions rather than persuasion to influence behaviour. There is evidence that such strategies are often effective in changing behaviour. It is less clear, however, whether these strategies also achieve a change in relevant attitudes. For incentive-induced counterattitudinal behaviour to induce dissonance, the incentive has to be small enough to offer insufficient justification for the behaviour. Similarly, self-perception theory would require that individuals do not attribute their behaviour change to the incentive. Since governmental institutions and other powerful organizations usually choose their incentives to be sufficiently powerful to persuade everybody (or nearly everybody) to change their behaviour, these incentives are not only likely to offer sufficient justification for behaviour change, but it is also likely that compliance will be attributed to these incentives. Whereas the magnitude of these incentives makes attitude change (i.e., finding the dull task enjoyable) due to dissonance or self-perception processes unlikely in the case of counterattitudinal behaviour, it increases the likelihood of attitude change (i.e., finding the previously enjoyable task less enjoyable) in the case of pro-attitudinal behaviour. This somewhat paradoxical effect is due to the fact that the presence of a discounting cue (e.g., large payment or expected reward) leads individuals to discount their counterattitudinal behaviour (i.e., describing the dull task as interesting) as well as the pro-attitudinal behaviour (performing an enjoyable drawing task) as information about their attitude.

SUMMARY AND CONCLUSIONS

- The chapter discussed two major strategies of attitude and behaviour change, namely persuasion and the use of incentives (e.g., taxation, legal sanctions).

- Persuasion involves the use of communications to change beliefs, attitudes and behaviour of others.

- Early theories of persuasion (information processing model, cognitive response theory) focused on persuasion resulting from the systematic processing of the semantic content of persuasive messages.

- More recently, dual-process theories (elaboration likelihood model, heuristic-systematic model) have accepted that people often adopt attitudes on bases other than their systematic processing of arguments. Dual-process theories integrate theories of systematic processing and persuasion processes that are based on low-effort processes (e.g., classical conditioning, self-perception, heuristic processing) and they specify the conditions under which people engage in each of these processes.

- According to dual-process theories, individuals will engage in systematic processing of message arguments only if they are motivated and able to do so.

- Processing motivation is determined by situational factors such as personal relevance of the attitude issue and by individual difference variables such as need for cognition.

- Processing ability is determined by factors such as time, absence of distraction or message repetition. Whenever individuals are unmotivated or unable to engage in systematic processing of message content, they base their decision of whether to accept or reject a persuasive communication on low-effort processing.

- Applying dual-process theories to advertising, we argued that the effectiveness of the most common appeals used in advertising (arguments, emotions, endorsements) depends on the type of product being advertised (i.e., thinking products or feeling products) and the involvement of the audience.

- Rather than relying on the uncertain effects of persuasion, powerful institutions often influence behaviour through incentives. Thus, governments may use taxation or legal sanctions to make certain behaviours like smoking, drinking alcohol or the non-use of seatbelts more costly to individuals.

- Such strategies have been effective in promoting the targeted behaviour, but less successful in also inducing attitude change.

- Since private acceptance of these government strategies is likely to aid compliance, we argued that the use of incentives *and* of persuasive appeals should be considered as complementary rather than competing strategies.

Suggestions for further reading

Bohner, G. & Wänke, M. (2002). *Attitudes and attitude change*. Hove: Psychology Press. A well-written, state-of-the-art introduction. It provides students with a comprehensive and accessible overview of theories and empirical findings in the area of attitude change.

Chen, S. & Chaiken, S. (1999). The heuristic-systematic model in its broader context. In S. Chaiken & Y. Trope (Eds.), *Dual-process theories in social psychology* (pp. 73–96). New York: Guilford Press. This chapter presents the most recent version of the heuristic-systematic model and reviews research conducted to test the theory.

Eagly, A.H. & Chaiken, S. (1993). *The psychology of attitudes*. Fort Worth, TX: Harcourt, Brace, Jovanovich. For many years the definitive text on attitudes and attitude change, the book is becoming a bit dated. And yet, it is still the most comprehensive book on the development of the field up to 1990.

Petty, R.E. & Wegener, D.T. (1999). The elaboration likelihood model: Current status and controversies. In S. Chaiken & Y. Trope (Eds.). *Dual-process theories in social psychology* (pp. 41–72). New York: Guilford Press. This chapter presents the most recent version of the elaboration likelihood model and reviews research conducted to test the theory.

8 | Aggression

Barbara Krahé

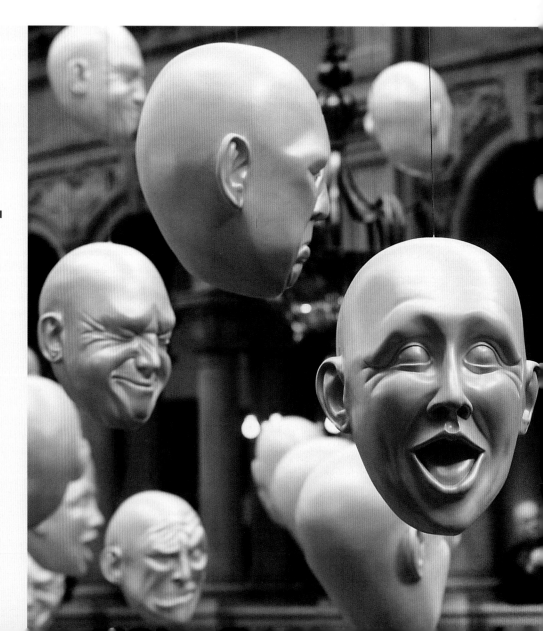

CHAPTER OUTLINE

....

This chapter presents an introduction to social psychological theory and research on aggression. After a brief discussion of how to define and measure aggression, we review the main theories of aggressive behaviour. This is followed by an analysis of individual differences in aggression and the role of situational variables, such as alcohol and high temperature, in eliciting aggressive behaviour. Special attention is devoted to the impact of violent media content on viewers' aggressive tendencies. In the second part of the chapter, different forms of aggression in society are examined, such as family violence, sexual aggression, and both school and workplace bullying. The chapter concludes with a review of strategies designed to reduce and prevent aggression.

Introduction

....

Three-year-old Karolina had a short and sad life. She was found dying in a hospital toilet in 2004, dumped there by her mother after months of torture and abuse from the mother's new partner. The list of his atrocities brought to light during the court case included tying her to a chair for hours on end, smashing a telephone over her head, and stubbing out a burning cigarette on her arm and then putting muscle warming cream on the burns to increase the pain (*Der Tagesspiegel* [German newspaper], 13 April 2005).

In April 2002, Germany was shocked by an unprecedented school shooting in which 17 people, including the assailant, were killed. It was soon established that the 19-year-old killer, a former pupil at the school who had been expelled some weeks prior to the attack, had not only been fascinated by firearms but had also spent much of his time playing violent electronic games (BBC News, Friday, 26 April 2002).

These two examples highlight the upsetting but undeniable fact that aggression as a destructive form of social behaviour is prevalent in human interactions on a large scale. Aggression permeates close relationships (e.g., child abuse and intimate partner violence), workplace interactions (e.g., bullying), intergroup relationships (e.g., gang violence and racially motivated aggression) and contacts between large-scale ethnic or political groups (e.g., international warfare). Therefore, social psychologists' concern with understanding the processes that trigger, intensify or suppress aggressive behaviour is by no means a purely scientific one. Instead, it is motivated by the aim to create a knowledge base from which we can develop interventions to reduce and prevent aggression.

The review of social psychological aggression research offered in this chapter is guided by five key questions:

1 How do social psychologists define aggressive behaviour and what are their main methods for studying it?

2   What are the major theories that explain why people engage in aggressive behaviour?

3   What are the crucial variables, both in the person and in the situation, that make aggressive behaviour more likely?

4   What do we know about the scale, causes and consequences of aggression as a social problem in different domains of life?

5   What can be done to prevent or reduce aggression?

DEFINITION AND MEASUREMENT OF AGGRESSIVE BEHAVIOUR

How do social psychologists define aggressive behaviour and what methodological tools are available to study it?
What are the main theories put forward to explain why people show aggressive behaviour?

> **aggression** any form of behaviour directed towards the goal of harming or injuring another living being who is motivated to avoid such treatment

In a widely accepted definition, Baron and Richardson (1994, p. 7) characterized *aggression* as 'any form of behavior directed toward the goal of harming or injuring another living being who is motivated to avoid such treatment'. This conceptualization has several important implications.

(1) Aggressive behaviour is defined by its underlying motivation (to harm or injure another living being), *not* by its consequences (whether or not harm or injury actually occurs). This means that a behaviour is regarded as aggressive if it was guided by the intention to harm, even if no damage was done to the target. A shot fired from a gun may miss its target, but if the shot was intended to hit the target, it is nonetheless an instance of aggression. On the other hand, your dentist may cause you pain, but it is incidental or accidental, and not intended, hence it is not aggression.

(2) A necessary feature of the intention to harm is the actor's understanding that the behaviour in question has the potential to cause harm or injury to the target. If one person's actions lead to harm or injury to another but the actor could not have expected or been aware that the behaviour could lead to those adverse effects, they do not represent instances of aggression. They could be due simply to accidental, careless or incompetent behaviour, but not aggression.

(3) Defining aggression as behaviour that the target would want to avoid means that harmful actions performed at the target's request, such as sado-masochistic sexual practices, do not represent instances of aggression.

This definition covers diverse subcategories of aggressive behaviour, such as physical and verbal aggression, spontaneous and reactive aggression, individual and group aggression. The term *violence* is more narrow in meaning and restricted to behaviours carried out with intention to harm that involve the use or threat of *physical force*, such as hitting someone over the head. Thus, not all instances of aggression are violence (e.g., shouting at someone would be aggressive, but not violent), but all acts of violence qualify as aggression.

An important conceptual distinction refers to the difference between *instrumental* and *hostile* (also called angry or affective) aggression. The two types of aggression differ with respect to the underlying motivation of the actor. People carry out acts of **instrumental aggression** for the purpose of achieving a particular goal, such as taking a hostage in order to secure a ransom. Here, the behaviour is driven by the ultimate goal the actor wants to achieve (obtaining a large sum of money), and aggression is selected as one of several possible means towards reaching that end. In contrast, **hostile aggression** is motivated by the actor's desire to express negative feelings, such as anger.

> **instrumental aggression** aggressive behaviour performed to reach a particular goal, as a means to an end
>
> **hostile aggression** aggressive behaviour motivated by the desire to express anger and hostile feelings

The *measurement of aggressive behaviour* creates particular problems for researchers due to its potentially harmful nature. It would be unethical to set up experimental situations in which research participants are given the chance to inflict genuine harm on another person or to expose them to treatments expected to increase the likelihood of subsequent aggression. The major strategies for measuring aggressive behaviour can be organized under two broad headings: *observation*, i.e., data collected by the researcher, and *recording*, i.e., data obtained from other sources, such as research participants or independent observers.

Observation of aggressive behaviour

The most common method for studying aggressive behaviour by observation is the *laboratory experiment* in which aggressive behaviour is observed as a function of experimental conditions created by the researcher. Experimental studies of aggression need to resort to paradigms in which participants can show behaviour *intended* to harm another person without actually allowing any harm to be inflicted on the target. Several experimental paradigms have been developed to address this challenge (see Krahé, 2001, for a comprehensive discussion). They create situations in which participants are given the opportunity to deliver aversive stimuli to another person, in the form of electric shocks (Taylor, 1967), loud noise (Bartholow & Anderson, 2002), cold water (Vasquez, Denson, Pedersen, Stenstrom & Miller, 2005) or unpleasantly hot spicy sauce (Lieberman, Solomon, Greenberg & McGregor, 1999).

Using the extent to which research participants deliver aversive stimuli to another person as a measure of aggression, the effects of various independent variables, such as frustration, alcohol consumption or exposure to media violence, can be studied on aggression as the dependent variable.

Despite their artificial nature, these experimental procedures for measuring aggressive behaviour do have construct validity, i.e., correspondence amongst one another and with other indicators, such as aggressive behaviour observed in natural settings (Anderson & Bushman, 1997). Because they allow researchers to observe variations in aggressive behaviour as a result of their experimental manipulations, such as creating a high vs. low level of frustration, experimental procedures facilitate the analysis of hypotheses about why, when and on what scale aggressive behaviour is shown.

Obtaining reports of aggressive behaviour

An important source of information about the occurrence of aggression in natural contexts is provided by *behavioural self-reports* in which individuals describe their own aggressive tendencies. Standardized measures have been developed to assess self-reported aggression, both at a general level (e.g., Buss & Warren's 2000 '*Aggression Questionnaire*') and with respect to particular domains, such as sexual aggression (Koss & Oros's 1982 'Sexual Experiences Survey').

Aggression Questionnaire self-report instrument to measure stable individual differences in trait aggressiveness

The problem with this strategy is that aggression is a socially undesirable behaviour and people may be unwilling to disclose their aggressive behaviour in an effort to provide socially desirable answers.

Peer/other nominations, i.e., reports by informed others, such as parents, teachers or classmates, about the aggressive behaviour of a target person, are less susceptible to the problem of social desirability. For example, Lefkowitz, Eron, Walder and Huesmann (1977) showed that peer-rated aggression was linked to the level of violence in 8-year-old boys' favourite and most frequently watched TV programmes (see the section on media violence later in the chapter). Thus those boys rated more aggressive by their peers tended to watch more violent TV. *Peer nominations* can be used to validate self-reports or to identify differences between actors and observers in the perception of aggressive behaviour.

peer nominations method for measuring (aggressive) behaviour by asking other people (e.g., classmates) to rate the aggressiveness of an individual

A final source of data on aggressive behaviour is provided by *archival records*, most notably crime statistics, such as the Uniform Crime Reports in the US or the Criminal Statistics in England and Wales. These data sources are not compiled for research purposes and therefore researchers have no influence on what is recorded in the data base. However, crime statistics are informative about the incidence of particular forms of aggression, such as intimate partner violence, child sexual abuse or homicide. They can also be used for hypothesis testing, for example about the link between high temperature and violent crime (e.g., Anderson, Anderson, Dorr, DeNeve & Flanagan, 2000; see below).

SUMMARY

Aggression is defined in social psychology as behaviour carried out with the *intention* to harm another person. The range of methods available for studying aggression is limited by the essentially harmful nature of this behaviour. For ethical reasons, researchers cannot create situations in which harm is inflicted on another person. The main methods for studying aggressive behaviour include observation under natural conditions, laboratory experiments providing an opportunity for behavioural analogues of real-life aggression (such as administering aversive noise) and the collection of reports of aggressive behaviour in the form of self-reports, reports from peers, parents or teachers, or statistical data on violent crime.

THEORIES OF AGGRESSION

How can we explain why individuals show aggressive behaviour? What are the processes that lead from an aggression-eliciting stimulus to an aggressive response?

Developing theories to explain why people engage in aggressive behaviour has been a prime objective for researchers from different disciplines, not least because understanding the factors that promote aggressive behaviour is a first step towards prevention. Table 8.1 provides a summary of the major theoretical models discussed in this section.

Biological approaches

Biological explanations of aggression refer to evolutionary and genetic principles as well as the role of hormones to explain why individuals differ in their tendency to engage in aggressive behaviour.

(1) The *ethological perspective*, represented most prominently by Konrad Lorenz (1974), looks at aggressive behaviour of animals and humans as driven by an internal energy which is released by aggression-related stimuli. In his famous *steam-boiler model*, Lorenz assumed

steam-boiler model part of Konrad Lorenz's theory of aggression, assuming that aggressive energy is produced continuously within the organism and will burst out spontaneously unless released by an external stimulus

Table 8.1 *Major theories of aggression*

	Aggression conceptualized as . . .	Data base	Empirical evidence
Biological approaches			
Ethology	. . . internal energy released by external cues; steam-boiler model	Animal studies	No support as a model for human aggression, but still popular in lay discourse
Behaviour genetics	. . . transmitted as part of genetic make-up	Twin and adoption studies	Support for the predictive value of genetic similarity
Hormonal explanations	. . . influenced by male sex hormones and cholesterol	Developmental studies	Inconclusive evidence
Psychological approaches			
Frustration-aggression hypothesis	. . . as a likely response to frustration, likelihood enhanced by aggressive cues	Experimental studies	Supported by empirical evidence
Cognitive neo-associationist model and excitation transfer	. . . as a result of affect elicited by aversive stimulation that is interpreted as anger	Experimental studies	Supported by empirical evidence
Learning theory	. . . as a result of reinforcement, either direct or indirect (observed)	Experimental + observational studies	Supported by empirical evidence
Social cognitive approaches	. . . as a result of social information processing, enactment of learned scripts	Experimental + longitudinal studies	Supported by empirical evidence

Plate 8.1 *Our genes partly determine how aggressive we are, but so too does the social environment.*

that aggressive energy is produced continuously within the organism until it is released by an external cue, such as the appearance of a rival in the contest for a mating partner. If the amount of energy rises beyond a certain level without being released by an external stimulus, it will overflow, leading to spontaneous aggression.

Psychologists have challenged Lorenz's application of his findings from animal studies to human aggression. An important criticism is directed at the assumption that once the internal reservoir of aggressive energy has been used up by an aggressive act, it is impossible to trigger another aggressive response for as long as it takes the organism to rebuild a sufficient energy level. There is ample evidence that humans can perform several aggressive behaviours in quick succession and that one aggressive act often serves to precipitate rather than suppress further aggressive acts.

(2) Researchers in the field of *behaviour genetics* examine the extent to which individual differences in aggressive behaviour can be linked to differences in genetic make-up (Plomin, Nitz & Rowe, 1990). Specifically, behaviour geneticists have sought to demonstrate that genetically related individuals are more similar in terms of their aggressive tendencies than individuals who are not genetically related. A meta-analysis of twin and adoption studies by Miles and Carey (1997) concluded that shared genetic make-up accounts to a significant extent for similarities in self-ratings as well as parents' ratings of aggressiveness, explaining up to 50 per cent of the variance. However, an important qualification comes from studies that used behavioural observation as a measure of aggression. In these studies, the impact of shared environment was substantially greater than that of genetic similarity. A subsequent meta-analysis by Rhee and Waldman (2002) also found substantial effects of genetic similarity, but the effects of environmental influences were found to be even stronger. Thus, the evidence from a broad range of studies suggests that aggressive behaviour is affected both by genetic dispositions and by socialization experiences in the course of individual development. An individual's genetic make-up may dispose him or her towards becoming an aggressive

person, but environmental factors play a crucial role in determining whether that disposition will be reinforced or counteracted.

(3) Another line of biological research on aggression is concerned with the role of *hormones* in relation to aggressive behaviour. The dramatic increase in the male sex hormone testosterone in boys during puberty has been linked to an increase in the prevalence of aggressive behaviour in this developmental period, but meta-analyses found only moderate positive correlations between testosterone and aggression among adolescent boys (Book, Starzyk & Quinsey, 2001). Cortisol has been examined as another hormonal correlate of aggression, and results were also mixed: while some studies showed that low levels of cortisol were related to aggressive behaviour and conduct problems, other studies found high cortisol levels to be predictive of aggression (cf. Ramirez, 2003, for a review). Altogether, there is as yet no conclusive evidence that hormones such as testosterone and cortisol play a causal role in the emergence of aggressive behaviour patterns.

Psychological approaches

Early psychological models also assumed aggression to be an innate response tendency. Freud's (1920) view of aggression as an instinct in the service of the pleasure principle inspired the *frustration-aggression hypothesis*, which regards aggression as driven by a desire to overcome frustration. Subsequent psychological approaches widened the frustration–aggression link into a more general model of negative affect and highlighted the role of cognitive factors, learning experiences and decision-making processes in predicting aggressive responses.

> **frustration-aggression hypothesis** assumes that frustration, i.e., blockage of a goal-directed activity, increases the likelihood of aggressive behaviour

PIONEER

Neal E. Miller (1909–2002) was the architect of the frustration-aggression hypothesis that laid the groundwork for subsequent socio-cognitive and neo-associationist models of aggression. He stressed that aggression is not inevitable but a likely response to frustration, and drew attention to the need to specify conditions under which frustration is likely to lead to aggression. Berkowitz's model of aggressive cues and subsequent cognitive neoassociationist view built upon his ideas. His views on displaced aggression were recently revitalized and elaborated by Norman Miller and colleagues in their 'triggered displaced aggression model' (Miller, Pedersen, Earleywine & Pollock, 2003).

The frustration-aggression hypothesis One of the earliest empirically tested theories about the origins of aggressive behaviour is the frustration-aggression hypothesis (Dollard, Doob, Miller, Mowrer & Sears, 1939; Miller, 1941). It states that 'frustration produces instigations to a number of different types of response, one of which is an instigation of some form of aggression' (Miller, 1941, p. 338). In this view, aggression is not the only but a possible response to frustration. Whether or not frustration will result in an aggressive response depends on the influence of additional variables in the individual or the environment. Fear of punishment for overt aggression or unavailability of the frustrator are factors that inhibit aggression. However, frustration that cannot be expressed in the form of aggressive retaliation against the original source is often '*displaced*', i.e., directed at an innocent target person who is more easily accessible or less threatening. In a meta-analysis including 49 studies, Marcus-Newhall, Pedersen, Carlson and Miller (2000) found consistent evidence that frustrated individuals show displacement of aggression from the source of the frustration onto a less powerful or more accessible target.

> **displaced aggression** tendency to respond to frustration with an aggressive response directed not at the original source of the frustration but at an unrelated, more easily accessible target

If aggression is one of several potential consequences of frustration, it is important to identify the conditions under which individuals are likely to show aggressive behaviour when frustrated. One variable shown to enhance the probability of an aggressive response to a frustration is the presence of *aggressive cues*. Aggressive cues are aspects of the situation that draw the actor's attention to the possibility of an aggressive response, such as seeing pictures of people fighting or being presented with the names of famous boxing champions. In a much-cited study, Berkowitz and LePage (1967) demonstrated that participants who had previously been frustrated by receiving negative feedback administered more electric shocks (as a measure of aggression) in the presence of weapons, i.e., aggressive cues, than in the presence of a badminton racket, i.e., a neutral object. Although subsequent studies have not always replicated the effect – some failing to find a *weapons effect* and others finding an effect in non-frustrated participants as well – overall support for the role of aggression-related cues in facilitating aggressive behaviour is impressive. From their meta-analysis of 57 studies, Carlson, Marcus-Newhall and Miller (1990, p. 632) concluded that 'aggression-related cues present in experimental settings act to increase aggressive responding'. They also found an effect, albeit weaker, of aggressive cues on participants in a neutral mood state. The finding that the impact of aggressive cues is not limited to situations where the person is already in an angry mood suggests that aggressive cues have a wide-ranging potential to activate ('prime') cognitive schemata related to aggression and thus increase the salience of aggressive response options.

> **aggressive cues** situational cues with an aggressive meaning that increase the accessibility of aggressive cognitions
>
> **weapons effect** finding that individuals who were previously frustrated showed more aggressive behaviour in the presence of weapons than in the presence of neutral objects

Plate 8.2 *Do guns make us more likely to behave aggressively?*

Cognitive neo-associationism and excitation transfer

In his *cognitive neo-associationist model*, Berkowitz (1993) extended the frustration-aggression hypothesis into a more general con-

cognitive neo-associationist model
explains aggressive behaviour as the result of negative affect that is subjected to cognitive processing and activates a network of aggression-related thoughts and feelings

ceptualization of the link between negative affect and aggressive behaviour. He argued that frustration is just one type of stimulus that elicits negative affective arousal, and that other aversive stimuli, such as pain or loud noise, may trigger aggressive responses in the same way. He proposed that aversive (unpleasant) stimuli give rise to unspecific negative feelings that evoke two immediate reactions, fight and flight. In a swift and automatic appraisal process that occurs with little or no conscious awareness, the fight impulse is associated with aggression-related thoughts, memories and behavioural responses, whereas flight is associated with escape-related responses. These responses serve to channel quickly the initially undifferentiated negative affect into the more specific emotional states of (rudimentary) anger or (rudimentary) fear. In a subsequent, more elaborate and controlled appraisal process, the person *interprets* these basic or rudimentary feelings. They are considered in relation to the situational input and the person arrives at a more specific and consolidated emotional state, i.e., anger or fear. This cognitive processing also involves the evaluation of potential outcomes, memories of similar experiences and social norms associated with the expression of different emotions. Figure 8.1 illustrates this process.

For example, when a child is hit by a stone thrown by a classmate, he will immediately experience pain associated with negative affect, probably a combination of anger, inducing the urge to fight, and fear, inducing the urge to run away. Depending on the context and the child's past experience, either the anger or the fear response is likely to dominate and guide his further analysis of the situation. Before deciding how to respond, the child will engage in a more careful appraisal process, including an assessment of his classmate's motives. If he concludes that his classmate threw the stone on purpose, the immediate feeling of anger will be

PIONEER

Leonard Berkowitz (b. 1926) is a key figure in aggression research. He has promoted both theoretical development and empirical evidence with respect to the role of negative affect and cognitive appraisal in aggressive behaviour. His study on the 'weapons effect' (Berkowitz & LePage, 1967) became a classic in social psychology. In this study, it was shown that people who were previously frustrated were more likely to show aggressive behaviour if aggressive cues, such as guns, were present in the situation. Subsequently, he developed his ideas into the cognitive neo-associationist model of aggressive behaviour. He also studied the other side of human nature, helping behavior. His book *Aggression: Its Causes, Consequences, and Control*, published in 1993, provides a comprehensive and authoritative review of aggression research.

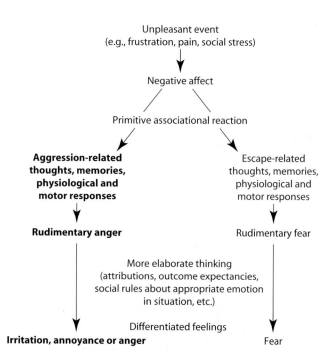

Figure 8.1 *The cognitive neo-associationist model of aggression (adapted from Berkowitz, 1993, p. 57).*

consolidated, and retaliation will be considered as an appropriate response. Because all the components of the emotional experience are associated with each other, activating one component is assumed to trigger other components relative to the strength of their association, hence the term 'associationism'. The weapons effect described earlier can be explained in the context of this model as a result of aggression-related associations elicited by the presentation of a weapon which then activate other, connected, aggressive thoughts, feelings and behaviours.

The cognitive appraisal of physiological arousal is also at the core of another influential theory of aggression, the theory of *excitation transfer* proposed by Zillmann (1978). Zillmann argued that the effects of frustration as a trigger for aggressive behaviour can be increased by physiological arousal from a neutral or non-aggression-related source. If individuals are angered and then experience unspecific arousal from a neutral source, such as physical exercise, the anger-related arousal will be magnified by the subsequent non-aggressive arousal, provided the individual is no longer aware of the source of the unspecific arousal. The neutral arousal (excitation) is transferred onto the anger-related arousal and falsely attributed as anger, intensifying the strength of the subsequent aggressive response. For example, a football player may be incensed when he sees a member of the other team foul one of his team members. He sprints the length of the pitch to confront the opposing player. As he reaches him his original anger-related arousal, based on the foul, is magnified by the exercise-induced arousal, from sprinting 70 metres. His arousal is then so great that, instead of merely protesting, he punches the opponent.

> **excitation transfer** transfer of neutral physiological arousal onto arousal resulting from frustration, thus augmenting negative affect and enhancing the strength of an aggressive response

Plate 8.3 *To what extent are footballers' levels of violence determined by their exercise-induced arousal?*

In combination, the cognitive neo-associationist model and the excitation transfer model highlight the role of negative affect as a powerful stimulant of aggression. It activates a network of affective and cognitive responses that enhance the salience of aggressive responses and thus increase the likelihood that aggressive intentions will be formed and implemented in behaviour.

Learning and aggression Studies within the behaviour-genetic approach described above suggest that an individual's genetic make-up plays a role in his or her disposition towards aggressive behaviour. However, there is no doubt that learning experiences in the course of the socialization process are as, if not more, important in affecting the development of aggressive behaviour patterns (Bandura, 1983). Learning is defined as behaviour change through experience, and two mechanisms in particular affect the acquisition of aggressive behaviour: *direct reinforcement* and *modelling* (vicarious reinforcement). Direct reinforcement involves the experience of being rewarded for aggressive behaviour, either by achieving a desired goal through the aggressive act or by winning social approval for showing aggressive behaviour. Children who are praised by their parents for 'standing up for themselves' after being provoked or who succeed in getting hold of a desired toy by grabbing it from another child learn that aggressive behaviour pays off, and they are encouraged by the positive effects of their behaviour to perform similar aggressive acts in the future. Modelling refers to learning by imitation. Watching others being rewarded for their aggressive behaviour also increases the likelihood of aggressive behaviour among the observers.

> **modelling** learning by imitation, observing a model being rewarded or punished for his/her behaviour

In a classic study, Bandura, Ross and Ross (1963) pioneered the Bobo Doll paradigm in which children are exposed to adult models behaving either in an aggressive or in a non-aggressive way towards a large, inflatable clown figure called Bobo. When the children were subsequently given the opportunity to play with the doll, those who had watched the aggressive model showed more aggressive behaviour towards the doll than those who had watched the non-aggressive model, particularly when the model had been reinforced for showing aggressive behaviour. The social learning perspective is a major theoretical approach for understanding the effects of media violence on aggressive behaviour, which can be regarded as a paradigmatic case of observational learning (see the section on violent media content below).

Social cognitive models The theoretical approaches discussed so far have stressed the role of affect and cognition as antecedents of aggressive behaviour and highlighted the importance of learning experiences in understanding aggressive behaviour. Socio-cognitive models of aggression refer to these lines of thinking and elaborate them by focusing on the role of cognitive representations in the prediction of aggressive behaviour. In his social cognitive approach, Huesmann (1998) proposed that social behaviour in general, and aggressive behaviour in particular, is shaped by abstract representations of appropriate behaviours in different situational contexts. These abstract representations are

aggressive scripts cognitive representation of when and how to show aggressive behaviour

called *aggressive scripts*, i.e., guidelines for deciding in favour of or against showing aggressive behaviour in specific situations. For example, if children have repeatedly responded (or seen others responding) to provocations by showing physical aggression, they will develop a generalized cognitive representation in which provocation and physical aggression are closely linked. When encountering a provocation they are likely to activate their scripted knowledge, which then prompts them to enact the behaviour specified by the script. The script also contains normative beliefs that tell the person when it is appropriate to show aggressive behaviour and which of various variants of the script to enact. These normative beliefs may specify that it is acceptable to respond with physical aggression when angered or provoked by a peer, but not when angered by an adult, and the likelihood of showing an aggressive response towards a peer or an adult will vary accordingly (Huesmann & Guerra, 1997).

Each of the psychological explanations of aggression highlights particular aspects of the processes that give rise to aggressive behaviour. Rather than competing against each other, they are best seen as pieces of a jigsaw that – when put together – create a clearer picture of the phenomenon called aggression. The *general aggression model* by Anderson and colleagues (Lindsay & Anderson, 2000) combines the different pieces of knowledge into a comprehensive framework, as shown in Figure 8.2.

general aggression model integrative framework explaining how personal and situational input variables lead to aggressive behaviour via cognitive appraisal and negative affective arousal

The model provides a structure that helps us to understand the complex processes through which particular input variables, such as violent media stimuli or biographical experiences of abuse, can lead to aggressive behaviour as the critical outcome variable.

SUMMARY

This section has presented the most prominent theories of the causes and mechanisms of aggressive behaviour. Biological theories focus on the role of genetic and hormonal factors accounting for differences in aggressive behaviour. In contrast, psychological theories refer to affective and cognitive reactions to aggression-eliciting stimuli and the way in which they pave the way for aggressive responses. These models show that negative affect – caused by a range of adverse stimuli such as frustration, pain or noise – is an important trigger of selective information processing that enhances the probability of aggressive behaviour. This information processing draws on aggressive scripts, i.e. abstract representations of how and when aggressive behaviour should be enacted. Another well-supported theoretical position is that aggression is a form of learned behaviour, implemented in the individual's behavioural repertoire through direct reinforcement as well as observational learning. The general aggression model integrates the diverse psychological theories of aggression into a common framework.

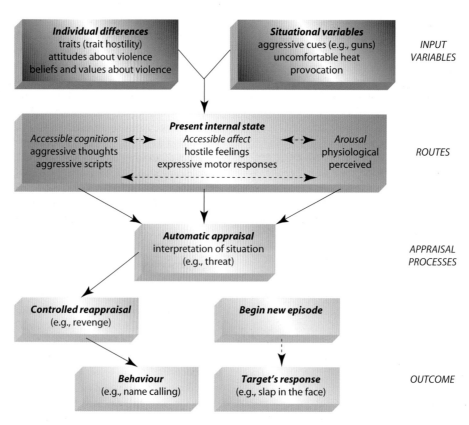

Figure 8.2 *The general aggression model (GAM) (based on Lindsay & Anderson, 2000, and Anderson et al., 2000).*

PERSONAL AND SITUATIONAL VARIABLES AFFECTING AGGRESSIVE BEHAVIOUR

Do people differ in their propensity to engage in aggressive behaviour, and what are variables associated with such individual differences?
What are critical factors in the situation or the social environment that make aggressive behaviour more likely?

In this section, we will take a closer look at some of the factors associated with differences between persons and between situations in the likelihood of aggression. In terms of the general aggression model, these are the input variables that are crucial in eliciting cognitive, affective and physiological responses that may or may not lead to an aggressive response. The guiding questions for this section are the following: how can we distinguish between more or less aggressive individuals and groups of individuals, and what situational influences of a transient or persistent nature precipitate aggressive behaviour?

Individual differences in aggressive behaviour

Researchers have suggested several variables as predictors of individual differences in aggressive behaviour. In the present section, we will focus on three of them that have received intense research attention: trait aggressiveness, hostile attributional style and gender (cf. Krahé, 2001, Ch. 3, for a coverage of additional person variables related to aggression).

trait aggressiveness denotes stable differences between individuals in the likelihood and intensity of aggressive behaviour

Trait aggressiveness The concept of *trait aggressiveness* describes dispositional, i.e., temporally and cross-situationally stable, differences between individuals with respect to the likelihood of showing aggressive behaviour. Whereas some individuals are easy to anger and quickly get 'hot under the collar', others are generally less inclined to respond with aggression. Longitudinal studies following the same research participants over many years from childhood into adulthood have shown that the tendency to engage in aggressive behaviour is remarkably stable over time. Drawing on findings from 16 studies exploring the temporal stability of men's aggressive behaviour, Olweus (1979) found a stability coefficient of $r = .76$ over a one-year period, of $r = .69$ over five years and still of $r = .60$ over a period of 10 years. These figures are matched only by the stability of intelligence scores over time and indicate that aggression in later stages of development may be predicted on the basis of earlier aggression scores. Interestingly, the stability was

highest among those individuals who had very high scores and very low scores of aggression at the beginning of the measurement period, whereas individuals with moderate aggression scores at the beginning were comparatively less stable over time.

Trait aggressiveness is conceptualized as a multidimensional construct comprising four different components: physical aggression, verbal aggression, anger and hostility. It is typically assessed by self-report questionnaires in which participants indicate the likelihood of showing different forms of physical aggression, verbal aggression, anger and hostility. The most widely used instrument is the Aggression Questionnaire (Buss & Warren, 2000; see above), but there are also instruments specially designed for adolescents (e.g., Orpinas & Frankowski, 2001).

Hostile attribution bias

Another variable linked to stable differences in the tendency to show aggressive behaviour is the *hostile attribution bias*. This construct

hostile attribution bias tendency to attribute hostile intentions to a person who has caused damage when it is unclear whether the damage was caused accidentally or on purpose

refers to the tendency to interpret ambiguous behaviour by another person as an expression of the actor's hostile intent. For example, in deciding whether or not another person causes harm accidentally or on purpose, individuals with a hostile attributional style prefer an attribution to hostile intent rather than seeing the actor's behaviour as unintentional or caused by carelessness. The hostile attribution bias is typically measured by presenting short films or written scenarios in which one actor causes harm to another person, but the stimulus material is unclear as to whether the harm was caused by accident or on purpose (e.g., Dodge, 1980). For example, children are shown a video in which two boys build a tower of bricks. One boy then knocks down the tower, and the film is ambiguous as to whether he did so intentionally. The participants are asked to indicate if they think the child knocked down the tower by mistake or on purpose. Respondents who consistently prefer explanations that attribute the damage to the actor's intent are seen as having a hostile attribution bias.

Studies with adults demonstrate that individuals with a hostile attributional style are more likely to show aggressive behaviour and that differences in trait aggressiveness are predictive of the hostile attribution bias (Dill, Anderson, Anderson & Deuser, 1997). In a longitudinal study by Burks, Laird, Dodge, Pettit and Bates (1999), children who showed hostile attributional tendencies were also more likely to develop aggressive behaviour patterns. From this perspective, individual differences in aggression may be the result of schematic, habitual ways of information processing which highlight the hostile nature of social interactions and thereby lower the threshold for aggressive responses.

To explain the development of the hostile attribution bias, several studies point to the role of exposure to violent media content. Correlational studies found a relationship between attraction to media violence and hostile attribution bias (Krahé & Möller, 2004). Other studies investigated whether hostile attributional styles are transmitted from mothers to their children. MacBrayer, Milich and Hundley (2003) found that mothers of aggressive children perceived more hostile intent and were more likely to report an intention to respond aggressively than mothers of non-aggressive children. However, mothers' and children's hostile attributions

Plate 8.4 *Mothers' and children's levels of aggression are significantly correlated only for girls.*

Plate 8.5 *Are women really less aggressive than men?*

and aggressive behavioural intentions were found to be significantly correlated only for the girls, not for the boys. The authors explain this sex-specific effect with reference to the principle of learning by modelling, which states that similar models (here: models of the same sex) are more likely to be imitated than dissimilar models. Unfortunately, no studies have yet examined the correspondence between fathers' and sons' hostile attribution biases to substantiate this explanation.

Gender differences A final variable associated with individual differences in aggression is gender, with the underlying hypothesis that men are more aggressive than women. Support for this hypothesis comes from the analysis of crime statistics across a range of countries, which show that men are overrepresented as perpetrators of violent crime at a ratio of about 8 to 1 (Archer & Lloyd, 2002). Meta-analyses of the psychological literature also found significant sex differences in aggression, with men showing more physical and verbal aggression than do women

(Archer, 2004; Eagly & Steffen, 1986). However, despite being significant, the size of the effects is moderate at best, and smaller for verbal than for physical aggression. Cross-cultural analyses suggest that this is a general pattern across different societies (Archer & McDaniel, 1995). The picture changes somewhat when relational aggression is included as a form of aggressive behaviour. Relational aggression is defined as harming others through purposeful manipulation and damage of their peer relationships (e.g., passing lies about someone to her friend, so that their relationship is harmed), and several authors have suggested that women may be as, if not more, involved than men in this type of aggression (e.g., Österman et al., 1998). Therefore, the 'myth of the non-aggressive woman' should be critically examined in the context of a broader range of behavioural types and contextual conditions of aggression (White & Kowalski, 1994).

Situational influences on aggressive behaviour

Just as it is clear that not all individuals respond with aggression in a given situation, it is clear that not all situations elicit aggressive responses to the same extent. In this section, we examine evidence concerning the role of three situational input variables that affect the occurrence of aggressive behaviour: alcohol consumption, high temperatures and exposure to violent media content.

Alcohol From the evidence available to date, it seems safe to conclude that even moderate amounts of alcohol lead to increased aggressive behaviour. Alcohol plays an important role in the perpetration of violent crime, such as homicide (Parker & Auerhahn, 1999), domestic violence, including the physical and sexual abuse of children, sexual aggression and wife battering (Wiehe, 1998), and many forms of group violence, such as sports violence, rioting and vandalism (Russell, 2004). Experimental studies show that alcohol has a causal effect on aggressive behaviour. These studies compare the aggressive responses of individuals who were given alcohol to those of individuals in a control condition who did not receive alcohol. Two meta-analyses examined evidence from a wide range of studies comparing alcohol vs. control groups and found that alcohol was a significant predictor of aggressive behaviour (Bushman & Cooper, 1990; Ito, Miller & Pollock, 1996). It is important to note, however, that general measures of the strength of the alcohol–aggression link mask the fact that the effects of alcohol may be strong for some people, but weak for others. For example, a recent study by Giancola (2003) showed that alcohol dramatically increased the administration of (supposedly) painful electric shocks to an opponent for individuals low in dispositional empathy (the ease with which people can adopt the perspective of another person), but failed to affect the behaviour of participants high in dispositional empathy (see Chapter 9, this volume, for more detail on empathy).

In terms of explaining the effects of alcohol on aggression, the *attentional hypothesis* suggests that alcohol has an indirect effect on aggression by reducing the attentional capacity of the individual, preventing a comprehensive appraisal of situational cues (Laplace, Chermack & Taylor, 1994). As a result, only the most salient cues

Plate 8.6 *Even moderate amounts of alcohol lead to increased aggressive behaviour.*

present in a situation receive attention, and if these cues suggest aggressive rather than non-aggressive responses, aggressive behaviour is likely to be shown. This view is supported by evidence on the impact of aggression-related cues discussed earlier.

High temperature Another situational input variable affecting aggressive behaviour is high temperature (Anderson et al., 2000). The *heat hypothesis* predicts that aggression should increase as temperature goes up (see Everyday Social Psychology 8.1). Two paradigms were developed to test this hypothesis under natural conditions. The first paradigm is the *geographic regions approach* comparing violent crime rates in hotter vs. cooler regions, finding support for a link between hotter climates and higher violence rates in archival data.

> **heat hypothesis** hypothesis that aggression increases with higher temperatures
>
> **geographic regions approach** method for testing the heat hypothesis by comparing violence rates in cooler and hotter climates
>
> **time periods approach** method for testing the heat hypothesis by comparing violence rates during cooler and hotter periods

However, the regions included in the comparison, typically the north vs. the south of the United States, differed in aspects other than temperature, such as unemployment rates or normative beliefs condoning violence, that could be relevant to aggression. This potential alternative explanation is ruled out by the second paradigm, the *time periods approach*, which compares changes in violent crime rates within the same region as a function of fluctuations in

EVERYDAY SOCIAL PSYCHOLOGY 8.1

The heat hypothesis and effects of global warming

The heat hypothesis states that high temperature increases the likelihood of violent behaviour. The implications of studies supporting the heat hypothesis are worrying in the face of global warming. If increases in temperature are systematically related to increases in violent crime, then the continuous rise in global temperature presents a risk factor for the rise of violent crime. Based on archival data on the link between temperature and violent crime in the United States over 48 years from 1950 to 1997, Anderson et al. (2000) estimated the magnitude of this danger, as shown in Figure 8.3.

Their analysis predicts that an increase in temperature by 2 degrees Fahrenheit increases the murder and assault rate by 9 cases per 100,000 people. For a US population of 270 million, this increase translates into 24,000 additional murder/assault cases per year. For readers more familiar with Celsius than Fahrenheit, with an increase in average temperature of just 1°C, the murder and assault rate is projected to go up by 24,000 cases in the US. As Anderson et al. (2000) point out, it is important to bear in mind that temperature is only one of many factors affecting violent crime rates. However, it remains significant

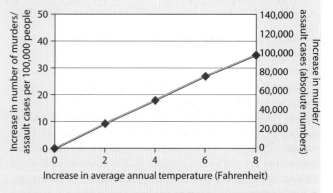

Figure 8.3 *Estimates of global warming effect on murders and assaults per year in the United States with a population of 270 million (based on Anderson et al., 2000, p. 124).*

when other contributory factors are controlled for. Research on the heat hypothesis alerts both policy makers and the general public to the fact that the dangers of global warming are not restricted to our natural environment but also pose a threat to the social functioning of human communities.

temperature, e.g., between winter and summer months or between hotter and cooler summers. This approach also provided evidence that violent crime rates were higher in the summer months than during the winter period.

Laboratory studies in which ambient temperature can be manipulated, with other factors being held constant, provide a third approach to the study of heat and aggression. Unfortunately, lab studies on the effect of high temperatures have produced divergent results. While some studies supported the conclusions from naturalistic analyses of the temperature–aggression link, other studies found a decrease in aggression when temperatures rose beyond a certain level. On the basis of a meta-analysis of 11 studies, Anderson et al. (2000) concluded that so far the results of laboratory studies on the heat hypothesis have remained inconsistent.

The effect of high temperature on aggression found under natural conditions can be explained with reference to the general aggression model. Heat gives rise to feelings of discomfort, which are proposed as input variables that trigger negative affective arousal; these, in turn, affect the cognitive processing of social stimuli and thereby enhance the likelihood of aggressive behaviour. Interestingly, no corresponding effect has been found for uncomfortably cold temperatures in natural settings. The explanation offered by Anderson et al. (2000) is that people are generally better equipped to protect themselves against the cold than they are to escape the heat, enabling them to reduce coldness-related discomfort more easily than heat-related discomfort.

Violent media content Evidence concerning the potentially harmful effect of exposure to *media violence* comes from three sources: (1) experimental studies exposing participants to either a violent or a non-violent media depiction and exploring the effects of this manipulation on subsequent aggressive thoughts, feelings and behaviours (e.g., Kirsh, 1998); (2) correlational studies collecting self-reports of violent media usage and relating them to measures of aggression (e.g., Gentile, Lynch, Linder & Walsh, 2004); and (3) longitudinal studies following the covariation of violent media consumption and aggression in the course of individual development (e.g., Huesmann & Miller, 1994; see Research close-up 8.1). Even though violent media content is discussed here in the context of situational input variables for aggressive behaviour, it is important to note that researchers and the general public are not concerned primarily with the effects of a single or short-term presentation but with the cumulative effects of repeated exposure over time

The present state of knowledge derived from each of these approaches is assessed in a recent authoritative review by Anderson et al. (2003) that culminates in the conclusion: 'Research on violent television and films, electronic games, and music reveals unequivocal evidence that media violence increases the likelihood of aggressive and violent behavior in both immediate and long-term contexts' (p. 81). Integrating the findings from almost 300 individual studies, Anderson and Bushman (2002) reported significant effect sizes (correlations weighted by sample size) for the link

> **media violence–aggression link**
> hypothesis that exposure to violent media content makes media users more aggressive

between exposure to media violence and aggression. The effect sizes vary between .17 and .23 across different methodologies (cross-sectional vs. longitudinal studies, laboratory vs. field experiments). These effect sizes are small in magnitude by conventional standards. This means that while some of the variability in aggressive behaviour can be accounted for by differences in exposure to violent media content, a much larger proportion of the variance is attributable to other factors. However, even small effect sizes can be important when extrapolated to large numbers of media users (Sparks & Sparks, 2002). Beyond demonstrating *that* media violence has a causal effect on aggressive behaviour, it is important to understand *how* this effect is produced. Several interlocking mechanisms have been identified that link violent media content as input variable and aggressive behaviour as outcome variable (see Krahé, 2001, Ch. 5 for a comprehensive discussion):

1 Watching media depictions of aggressive interactions increases the *accessibility of aggressive thoughts and feelings*. Asking participants to list their thoughts following exposure to a violent or non-violent videotape, Bushman and Geen (1990) found that more aggressive thoughts were generated by participants who had watched the violent videotape.

2 Exposure to aggression may *instigate social learning processes* which result in the acquisition of new behaviours. Much of the aggression portrayed in the media is rewarded or at least goes unpunished. Moreover, it is often shown by attractive characters with whom viewers identify. As social learning theory suggests, learning through modelling is particularly likely under these circumstances (Bandura, 1983).

3 Long-term exposure to media violence leads to *habituation*, which in turn reduces the sensitivity towards the victims' suffering.

> **habituation** process whereby the ability of a stimulus to elicit arousal becomes weaker with each consecutive presentation

Habituation describes the process whereby the ability of a stimulus to elicit arousal becomes weaker with each consecutive presentation. The person gets used to it, and the stimulus loses its impact. The decline in physiological arousal in the course of prolonged exposure to violence is well documented (e.g., Averill, Malstrom, Koriat & Lazarus, 1972).

4 Exposure to violent media content also has an indirect effect on aggressive behaviour through promoting the development of a hostile attribution bias. A recent study by Krahé and Möller (2004) showed that the frequency with which adolescents played violent electronic games predicted the extent to which they attributed hostile intentions to an actor causing harm to another person in ambiguous circumstances. As shown earlier, the hostile attribution, in turn, increases the likelihood of aggressive behaviour.

The long-term impact of TV violence on aggression

Lefkowitz, M.M., Eron, L.D., Walder, L.O. & Huesmann, L.R. (1977). *Growing up to be violent*. New York: Pergamon. Summary of the 'New York State Studies' on the long-term effects of TV violence based on Huesmann and Miller (1994).

Introduction

This study explored the long-term effects of exposure to television violence on aggression. Correlational evidence showing that viewing TV violence and behaving aggressively are linked if both constructs are measured at the same time are open to two competing explanations of the cause–effect relationship: (1) that viewing TV violence makes viewers more aggressive or (2) that more aggressive individuals are more strongly attracted by violent TV programmes. By using a longitudinal design in which the same participants were studied three times over a period of 22 years, the authors were able to examine which of the two hypotheses is more likely to be correct: if the link from viewing TV violence at the beginning of the study (time 1) to aggressive behaviour 10 years on (time 2) is stronger than the link from aggression at time 1 to the viewing of violent TV programmes at time 2, this speaks in favour of the first hypothesis, i.e., that TV violence is a causal factor in the development of aggressive behaviour patterns.

Method

The study started in 1960 with a sample of 875 children that comprised the entire population of third graders in a community in Columbia County, New York. Ten years later, 427 of the original participants, who were then 18, were re-interviewed. Another 12 years later, in 1982, data were collected from 409 of the original participants who by then had reached the age of 30. At the first assessment, measures of aggressive behaviour were obtained for each child on the basis of peer nominations. Exposure to TV violence was assessed by asking the mothers to name their child's most-watched TV programmes, which were then rated by experts for level of violent content. Aggressive behaviour and exposure to TV violence were measured again at the subsequent two data points, and additional data about criminal offences were collected at the last data point.

Results

First, concurrent correlations between exposure to TV violence and aggression were computed for each data point. At time 1, there was a significant correlation for boys, but not for girls; at time 2, there was no relationship for either sex. More important, however, are the correlations across the two data points. Cross-lagged panel analyses were conducted in which the correlations

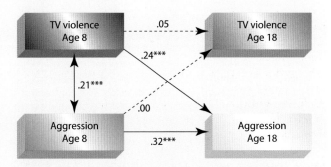

Figure 8.4 *Longitudinal link between exposure to media violence and aggression in a sample of boys (based on Huesmann & Miller, 1994, p. 169)*. Note. *The broken lines indicate non-significant links.*

between time 1 aggression and time 2 exposure to violent TV programmes were compared against time 1 TV violence exposure and time 2 aggression. No evidence was found for a longitudinal link between TV violence and aggression in girls. However, for boys, exposure to TV violence at time 1 was significantly correlated with aggression at time 2, whereas aggression at time 1 was unrelated to TV violence exposure at time 2. The path model that presents the relationships for the sample of 184 boys for whom complete data were available from both time 1 and time 2 is shown in Figure 8.4.

For the 162 male participants still in the sample at time 3, 22 years after the start of the study, a significant path (.18**) was found from exposure to TV violence at age 8 and conviction for violent crime at the age of 30.

Discussion

The study provides an impressive longitudinal data base from which causal relationships between media violence and aggression can be inferred. For boys, there was clear evidence that early exposure to TV violence predicted aggressive behaviour over a period as long as 22 years. The magnitude of the link was not dramatic, which is unsurprising given the host of other factors that affected participants in the course of that period, but it suggests that the potential long-term effects of exposure to TV violence in childhood give cause for concern. Subsequent studies, including cross-national comparisons, confirmed this finding (Huesmann & Eron, 1986). For girls, the evidence remains inconclusive. A subsequent longitudinal study by Huesmann, Moise-Titus, Podolski and Eron (2003) found parallel links among men and women between exposure to TV violence in childhood and aggression in adulthood, but studies into the impact of violent computer games also showed stronger effects for male than for female players (e.g., Bartholow & Anderson, 2002).

SUMMARY

The research reviewed in this section shows that aggressive behaviour varies both as a function of person variables and as a function of situational context. Stable individual differences in the propensity to act aggressively (trait aggressiveness) and to interpret others' actions as an expression of hostile intent (hostile attribution bias) predict differences in the ease with which aggressive responses are triggered in a particular situation. Research has also identified consistent gender differences, with men showing more physical aggression than do women. Some studies suggest that for relational aggression, such as social exclusion, the gender difference may be reversed, but more research is needed to consolidate this finding. Among the situational variables affecting the likelihood of aggressive behaviour, alcohol consumption, high temperature and exposure to media violence were shown with high consistency to lower the threshold for aggressive behaviour. In the case of media violence, longitudinal studies demonstrate that negative effects can be found over extended periods of time.

AGGRESSION AS A SOCIAL PROBLEM

Are there gender differences in the perpetration of intimate partner violence and sexual aggression?

What is bullying and what do we know about the characteristics of bullies and victims?

The theoretical and empirical contributions discussed so far identified critical input variables as well as mediating processes that explain the occurrence of aggressive behaviour. In this section, we will look at specific forms of aggressive behaviour between individuals and between groups and discuss how the theories and findings examined so far can contribute to a better understanding of these social problems.

Intimate partner violence

Intimate partner violence is defined as the perpetration or threat of an act of physical violence by one partner on the other in the context of a dating/marital relationship. It is a serious problem across the world, even though the prevalence rates vary enormously not only between but also within countries (see reviews of the international evidence by Krahé, Bieneck & Möller, 2005; Krug, Dahlberg, Mercy,

> **intimate partner violence** perpetration or threat of an act of physical violence within the context of a dating/marital relationship

Plate 8.7 *Intimate partner violence is a serious problem across the world. Research looks at whether men and women are involved as perpetrators to the same or a different degree.*

Zwi & Lozano, 2002). Mirrlees-Black (1999) found that 23 per cent of women and 15 per cent of men in the UK reported that they had experienced violence from an intimate partner at some point in their lives. In a Dutch study by Römkens (1997), 21 per cent of women and 7 per cent of men reported having experienced assault by an intimate partner at least once in their lives.

One of the most contentious issues in this field of research refers to the question of whether men and women perpetrate intimate partner violence to the same or a different degree. Two main data sources are available to address the scale of intimate partner violence and the question of men's and women's involvement as perpetrators: (1) official crime statistics and crime victimization surveys of representative samples, and (2) research collecting self-reports of perpetration of, or victimization by, relationship aggression, using the *Conflict Tactics Scales* (Straus, 1979; revised version: CTS 2, Straus,

> **Conflict Tactics Scales** instrument for measuring intimate partner violence by collecting self-reports of perpetration and/or victimization

Hamby, Boney-McCoy & Sugarman, 1996). Official crime victimization figures show that a much greater proportion of women than men are victims of partner violence and that the rate of injuries from partner violence is higher for female than for male victims (e.g., Rennison & Welchans, 2000). Studies using the Conflict Tactics Scales, however, portray a different picture. In this measure, participants are presented with a list of minor (e.g., 'I pushed or shoved my partner') and severe (e.g., 'I slammed my partner against a wall') acts of physical aggression and asked to indicate whether and how many times they have shown the behaviour in question towards an intimate partner. A large body of evidence has shown that on the CTS women feature as much or even more in the perpetration of physical aggression towards a partner than men do. In a meta-analysis of 82 studies, Archer (2000) found no evidence of the overrepresentation of men in the perpetration of physical aggression. Instead, he concluded that women were slightly more likely than men to show physical aggression towards a partner.

Critics have argued that the picture of gender symmetry portrayed by studies using the CTS is largely due to the fact that this instrument records acts of violence without considering their context. It is now widely acknowledged by researchers that progress in the understanding of the dynamics of intimate partner violence will have to pay greater attention to the specific forms and contexts in which assaults on intimate partners take place (Frieze, 2000).

Sexual aggression

Sexual aggression includes a range of forced sexual activities, such as sexual intercourse, oral sex, kissing and petting, using a range of coercive strategies, such as threat or use of physical force, exploitation of the victim's inability to resist or verbal pressure. It also includes unwanted sexual attention in the form of sexual harassment, stalking and obscene phone calls (Belknap, Fisher & Cullen, 1999; Frieze & Davis, 2002). Official crime statistics show that sexual aggression is a large-scale problem. In Germany, 8,766 cases of rape and sexual assault were reported to the police in 2003, which corresponds to a rate of 10.6 per 100,000 citizens (Polizeiliche Kriminalstatistik 2003). UK crime statistics revealed that 9,743 rapes were reported to the police in 2001, corresponding to a victimization rate of 18.7 per 100,000 members of the population (Regan & Kelly, 2003). The majority of sexual assaults are committed by a perpetrator known to the victim, either as an acquaintance or as an intimate partner. Despite the persistence of the 'real rape stereotype' picturing rape as a violent surprise attack in a dark alleyway, sexual assaults by strangers are the exception rather than the rule. Complementing crime statistics that only reflect cases reported to the police, large-scale studies have been conducted to record sexual victimization of women by men. A summary of this data base is presented in Table 8.2.

In contrast to intimate partner violence, it is undisputed that sexual violence is gender asymmetrical, with the vast majority of

sexual aggression forcing another person into sexual activities through a range of coercive strategies, such as threat or use of physical force, exploitation of the victim's inability to resist or verbal pressure

Table 8.2 *Prevalence of men's sexual aggression against women (based on Spitzberg, 1999)*

Form of sexual victimization/ aggression	Women's victimization reports (%)	Men's perpetration reports (%)	Number of studies
Rape[a]	12.9	4.7	63
Attempted rape	18.3	10.8	35
Sexual assault[b]	22.0	8.9	40
Sexual contact[c]	24.0	13.4	28
Sexual coercion[d]	24.9	24.0	39

[a] Completed sexual intercourse through threat or use of force.
[b] Penetration of the body through threat or use of force.
[c] Sexual acts without penetration of the body through continued arguments, authority, force or threat of force.
[d] Sexual intercourse through verbal pressure or abuse of position of authority.

sexual assaults committed by male perpetrators against female victims. However, it should be noted that sexual violence is also a problem in same-sex relationships (e.g., Krahé, Schütze, Fritsche & Waizenhöfer, 2000) and that women do show sexual aggression against men (Anderson & Struckman-Johnson, 1998; Krahé, Waizenhöfer & Möller, 2003).

The consequences of a sexual assault on the victim are severe. A substantial number of rape victims develop the clinical symptomatology of **post-traumatic stress disorder** (PTSD). Victims re-experience the assault in dreams, images and intrusive memories, they try to avoid cues reminding them of the assault, and experience a general emotional numbness (Foa & Rothbaum, 1998). Contrary to a widely held public belief, assaults by partners and acquaintances are equally traumatizing for the victim as stranger assaults (Culbertson & Dehle, 2001).

post-traumatic stress disorder characteristic patterns of symptoms observed in survivors of traumatic experiences such as rape

Victims of sexual aggression not only have to come to terms with the emotional trauma of the assault itself. They also have to cope with the reactions of others who learn about their fate. There is a widespread tendency to blame the victim of a sexual assault, unparalleled in judgements of victims of other criminal offences. A large body of evidence has shown that certain victim characteristics, such as low social status, higher number of sexual partners, pre-rape behaviour that is at odds with female role expectations, are linked to higher attributions of responsibility to the victim, and often correspondingly lower responsibility attributed to the attacker (Krahé, 1991). The tendency to hold victims responsible for being sexually assaulted is seen as a major factor in the low conviction rates for rape that have plagued the legal systems of many western countries (Temkin & Krahé, 2007).

Bullying in school and the workplace

The last 25 years have seen a growing concern about aggressive behaviour in school and work settings (Olweus, 1994; Randall, 1997). Referred to by different terms, such as **bullying**, mobbing or workplace aggression, this phenomenon denotes aggressive behaviour directed at victims who cannot easily defend themselves (Smith, Ananiadou & Cowie, 2003). Bullying typically carries on over extended periods of time and involves a power differential between bully and victim based on physical strength or superior status that undermines the victims' ability to defend themselves or retaliate. Forms of bullying include physical, verbal and relational aggression, i.e., behaviour directed at damaging the victim's peer relationships. The typical victim is an anxious, socially withdrawn child or adolescent, isolated from his or her peer group and likely to be physically weaker than most peers. In contrast, bullies are typically strong, dominant and assertive, showing aggressive behaviour not just towards their victims but also towards parents, teachers and other adults (cf. Griffin & Gross, 2004, for a comprehensive review). Boys feature more prominently than girls as victims as well as perpetrators of bullying (Olweus, 1994). They are also more likely to use physical aggression than are girls, who rely more on verbal and relational forms of aggression, as shown in a cross-national comparison involving 21 countries (Smith et al., 1999).

> **bullying** denotes aggressive behaviour directed at victims who cannot easily defend themselves, typically in schools and at the workplace

Workplace bullying has only recently become the object of systematic research, and empirical evidence is still limited. Like school bullying, the core of the construct refers to behaviours intended to make another person feel miserable at work over longer periods of time, with the target persons being unable to defend themselves due to an imbalance of power between perpetrator and victim. According to Hoel, Rayner and Cooper (1999), both the prevalence and the nature of experienced bullying in the workplace are similar for men and women. However, women appear to be more negatively affected by bullying than men. A large-scale study by Smith, Singer, Hoel and Cooper (2003) explored potential links between individuals' experience of bullying at school and at the workplace. A sample of more than 5,000 adults employed by a wide range of companies in the United Kingdom completed a measure of experience of workplace bullying and provided retrospective reports of bullying victimization while at school. Thirty-three per cent of participants identified themselves as victims of school bullying, and 25 per cent reported that they had experienced workplace bullying in the last five years. A significant association was found between school and workplace bullying: respondents victimized at school were more likely to have been bullied at work in the last five years than respondents who had not been bullied at school. It is important to note, however, that the relationship was inferred on the basis of retrospective reports of school bullying that may have been inaccurately recalled or distorted in the light of subsequent experiences of bullying in the workplace.

SUMMARY

Intimate partner violence, sexual aggression and bullying are widespread forms of aggression in everyday life. They can lead to lasting negative effects on the victims' psychological functioning and well-being. In research on intimate partner violence, the issue of whether men or women feature more prominently as perpetrators is controversial, but there is consistent evidence that women are more likely to be injured by an intimate partner than are men. Sexual aggression is perpetrated mostly by men against women. Bullying in school and the workplace is characterized by a power differential between perpetrator and victim. Some studies suggest that experiences of being bullied in school make victims vulnerable to subsequent workplace bullying.

Plate 8.8 *Bullying, either in schools or in the workplace, denotes aggressive behaviour directed at victims who cannot easily defend themselves.*

PSYCHOLOGICAL PREVENTION AND INTERVENTION: WHAT CAN BE DONE ABOUT AGGRESSION?

Is there evidence to support the popular catharsis hypothesis, i.e., the notion that releasing aggressive tension through symbolic action reduces the likelihood of aggressive behaviour?

What are viable strategies to reduce individuals' tendencies to show aggressive behaviour?

It has become clear that aggression poses a serious threat to the health and well-being of individuals and the functioning of societies. Psychologists not only have to deal with the task of investigating how, when and why aggressive behaviour is shown, they are also under the obligation to think about ways of counteracting and preventing its occurrence.

Aggressive behaviour is ultimately performed by individual actors. Therefore, an important aim of intervention efforts is to reduce the probability that a person will show aggressive behaviour. Three main mechanisms have been explored by which aggressive behaviour may be prevented: catharsis, punishment and anger management.

Catharsis

According to a popular belief, releasing aggressive tension in symbolic ways, such as through sarcastic humour or acting aggressively in the virtual reality of a videogame, is a successful strategy for reducing aggression. This idea is referred to as the *catharsis* hypothesis after the idea of Greek tragedy that watching tragic conflict unfold and be resolved on stage leads to a purification or 'cleansing' of the emotions (pity and fear) and brings about spiritual renewal or release from tension in the spectators. However, empirical evidence shows that the symbolic engagement in aggressive thoughts or actions is not just ineffective but even counterproductive for reducing aggression. Several studies indicate that the imaginary performance of aggressive behaviour, such as in pretend play or watching media violence, is more likely to enhance aggression than to reduce it (Bushman, 2002; Bushman, Baumeister & Stack, 1999). These findings are explained with reference to the role of aggressive cues in enhancing the likelihood of aggressive behaviour: symbolic acts of aggression can be regarded as aggressive cues that prime hostile thoughts and feelings and thereby pave the way for aggressive behaviour. Thus, the idea of catharsis is a popular myth that can be refuted on the basis of empirical evidence.

catharsis release of aggressive tension through symbolic engagement in aggressive behaviour

Punishment

Explanations of aggression as a result of learning processes suggest that we should look at punishment as an effective mechanism to suppress the performance of aggressive behaviour. However, there is general consensus that punishment can only be expected to work if several conditions are met (e.g., Berkowitz, 1993): (1) anticipated punishment must be sufficiently adverse; (2) it must have a high probability of being imposed; (3) punishment can only exert a deterrent effect if the individual's negative arousal is not too strong to prevent him or her from calculating the costs of an aggressive response in advance in a rational manner; (4) punishment will only be effective if acceptable or attractive behavioural alternatives are available to the actor in the situation; and (5) punishment must follow immediately upon the transgression so that it is perceived as contingent upon the aggressive behaviour.

Table 8.3 *Key elements of anger management training (based on Beck & Fernandez, 1998, p. 64)*

Phase 1	• Identification of situational triggers which precipitate the onset of the anger response.
	• Rehearsal of self-statements intended to reframe the situation and facilitate healthy responses (e.g., 'I can handle this. It isn't important enough to blow up over this').
Phase 2	• Acquisition of relaxation skills.
	• Coupling cognitive self-statements with relaxation after exposure to anger triggers, with clients attempting to mentally and physically soothe themselves.
Phase 3	• Rehearsal phase.
	• Exposure to trigger utilizing imagery or role play.
	• Practising cognitive and relaxation techniques until the mental and physical responses can be achieved automatically and on cue.

Apart from the fact that the co-occurrence of these factors is relatively rare, critics have argued that punitive responses may in themselves instigate aggression by functioning as aggressive cues and may reinforce beliefs about the normative acceptability of aggressive behaviour. Punishment may also convey the message that the use of aggression is a viable strategy of conflict resolution. If it is to produce desirable consequences, punishment needs to be embedded into a more general approach towards instrumental learning in which the primary aim is to reward desirable rather than penalize undesirable behaviour (Coie & Dodge, 1998).

Anger management

As we have seen, anger and negative affective arousal play a key role in many expressions of aggressive behaviour. Therefore, training people to control their anger should be effective in reducing hostile aggression. The focus of anger management approaches is on (1) teaching aggressive individuals to understand the processes that lead to anger and (2) promoting anger control by helping them to identify internal cues and external conditions that trigger aggressive outbursts. The central tasks of *anger management training*, as summarized by Beck and Fernandez (1998), are presented in Table 8.3.

anger management training approach for preventing aggression by teaching aggressive individuals to control their anger and inhibit aggressive impulses

A meta-analysis of school-based interventions using anger management approaches to reduce aggressive behaviour obtained an overall weighted effect size of $d = .64$. This indicates that aggressive behaviour goes down substantially after anger management training compared to a control group (Robinson, Smith, Miller & Brownell, 1999). Thus, it seems that this strategy works well to reduce aggression among school populations. However, anger management methods can only be expected to work with individuals who understand that their aggressive behaviour results from a failure to control their aggressive impulses and who are motivated to change their inadequate handling of these impulses. Studies including individuals with a history of violence or known to be at high risk for violent action, such as people convicted of violent crime, have found little evidence of the success of anger management approaches in promoting affect regulation and reducing violent behaviour (e.g., Watt & Howells, 1999). Therefore, one is left to conclude that the target groups who are most in need of learning effective anger control are most difficult to reach, or that anger management techniques are largely ineffective with violent offenders.

SUMMARY

Compared to the wealth of research into the causes and precipitating factors of aggressive behaviour, evidence on how to reduce it is limited. Contrary to popular wisdom, catharsis, i.e., acting out aggressive impulses in a symbolic or innocuous way, is counterproductive in reducing aggression. It leads to an increase rather than a decrease in aggressive responses. Punishment is an effective control strategy provided it is imposed swiftly after a transgression. Anger management approaches are designed to teach aggressive individuals to control their aggressive impulses, but they are effective only if the person is willing to cooperate.

SUMMARY AND CONCLUSIONS

- Aggressive behaviour is defined as behaviour carried out with the intention of harming another person. It can be a means to an end (instrumental aggression) or an expression of negative affect (affective or hostile aggression).

- Methods for studying aggressive behaviour include laboratory experiments, reports of aggressive behaviour from actors and observers, and the analysis of archival records.

- Theoretical approaches aimed at explaining aggressive behaviour include both biological and psychological lines of thinking and research. They share the assumption that the likelihood of aggressive behaviour depends on the operation of facilitating or inhibiting factors located within both the person and the environment.

- Individual differences in aggression show considerable stability from childhood to early adulthood. Dispositional aggressiveness and the hostile attribution bias have been linked to individual differences in aggression. Research on

gender differences in aggression has found that men are more physically aggressive than women, even though the difference is only moderate in size.

- Alcohol consumption and high temperatures have been identified as situational variables that exert a significant influence on the manifestation of aggressive behaviour. Studies examining the effect of violent media content have provided overall support for the proposed aggression-enhancing effect of media violence, including violent electronic games.

- Intimate partner violence is a widespread problem across the world. Studies using context-free frequency counts of aggressive acts show that men and women are equally likely to show aggressive behaviour against a partner. In contrast, crime statistics and studies taking context and consequences of aggressive acts into account show that men dominate as perpetrators and women as victims of intimate partner violence.

- Sexual violence is committed mostly by men against women, even though a few studies have documented same-sex sexual aggression and women's sexual aggression towards men. In the majority of cases, the assailant is someone previously known to the victim. The consequences of sexual victimization are severe, including negative reactions from others.

- School and workplace bullying are forms of aggressive behaviour characterized by an imbalance of power between aggressor and victim and often take place over extended periods of time.

- Imposing punishment and promoting anger management skills are strategies directed at the individual aggressor to prevent or reduce aggression.

Suggestions for further reading

Anderson, C.A. & Bushman, B.J. (1997). External validity of 'trivial' experiments: The case of laboratory aggression. *Review of General Psychology, 1,* 19–41. Provides a thought-provoking analysis of the way in which different measurement strategies in aggression research complement and cross-validate each other.

Anderson, C.A., Berkowitz, L., Donnerstein, E., Huesmann, L.R., Johnson, J.D., Linz, D., Malamuth, N.M. & Wartella, E. (2003). The influence of media violence on youth. *Psychological Science in the Public Interest, 4,* 81–110. Provides a comprehensive and critical review of the evidence on the influence of media violence on aggression, particularly among young media users.

Archer, J. (2000). Sex differences in aggression between heterosexual partners: A meta-analytic review. *Psychological*

Bulletin, 126, 651–680; Johnson, M.P. & Ferraro, K.J. (2000). Research on domestic violence in the 1990s: Making distinctions. *Journal of Marriage and the Family, 62,* 948–963. These two papers illustrate the intricacies of resolving the issue of gender differences in intimate partner violence.

Geen, R.G. (2001). *Human aggression* (2nd edn). Buckingham: Open University Press; Krahé, B. (2001). *The social psychology of aggression.* Hove: Psychology Press. Two textbooks that provide extensive and up-to-date coverage of theories, methods and main findings of social psychological research on aggressive behaviour.

9 Prosocial Behaviour

Hans W. Bierhoff

CHAPTER OUTLINE

Prosocial behaviour may range from small favours to great deeds. It may take merely a moment, or it may be a long-term endeavour. It may be done without much conscious thought or weighing up the pros and cons. It may be under the control of situational forces or may express the personality of the donor. The findings of studies on prosocial behaviour seem to be ambiguous: on the one hand, people are committed to helping victims of disasters; on the other, there are many examples of people not helping a victim in urgent need. The factors which ultimately determine the choice of the onlooker – to be either an unresponsive bystander or a 'Good Samaritan' – are topics dealt with by the social psychology of prosocial behaviour. This chapter looks first at situations when onlookers of emergencies intervene, and when they fail to do so. Next, it reviews explanations of prosocial behaviour from different theoretical perspectives. These range from the most general explanation in terms of principles of evolution to more specific explanations, including moods, personality characteristics and true altruism. This chapter also considers the importance of the relationships between people, social norms and values. Finally, we discuss why being helped is not always appreciated by the help-recipient.

Introduction

The Indian Ocean tsunami which dominated the news in late December of 2004 evoked an unprecedented outpouring of sympathy and a willingness to help all over the world. For example, charities across Europe launched appeals to help the victims and raised an unprecedented amount of money to ease their suffering. In a TV interview an expert from Oxfam explained this great helpfulness by the heartbreaking emotions that were triggered by the catastrophe and the fact that, although the disaster happened far away, it affected many European tourists.

Plate 9.1 *The Indian Ocean tsunami of late December 2004 evoked an unprecedented willingness to help all over the world.*

At the same time, reports of indifferent reactions to helpless victims are quite common. The most famous example is that of Kitty Genovese, who was killed by a psychopath in New York City in 1964. Because the appalling circumstances in which she was murdered attracted huge public attention, the terrible event was reconstructed in detail by a *New York Times* journalist (Rosenthal, 1964). It was late at night when Kitty was on her way home and parked her car at a railway station close to her apartment. On the way from the car park to her apartment she was attacked by a man who stabbed her. Unable to run away, she was attacked twice more before her assailant finally killed her. Many neighbours witnessed the incident. Interviews with 38 witnesses showed that they were not really indifferent, although they didn't help the victim. On the contrary, they followed what was going on with great attention. The entire assault lasted 35 minutes, definitely long enough either to call the police or to intervene directly. A witness finally called the police who arrived quickly at the scene of the crime, but they were too late. The murderer was arrested soon afterwards. During questioning he indicated that he was aware of possible onlookers of the crime but that he was convinced they wouldn't intervene.

This true story is only one example of numerous incidents in which urgently needed help was not given. Although the murder of Kitty Genovese took place more than 40 years ago, not much has changed in the meantime: passive onlookers are still a problem today. Thus, we are confronted with contrasting behaviours. On the one hand, people are very willing to support victims of the tsunami disaster; on the other hand, we can provide a long list of examples of people not helping a victim in dire need. The psychology of prosocial behaviour deals with the factors which ultimately determine the choice of the onlooker – to be an unresponsive bystander or to take action.

HELPING, PROSOCIAL BEHAVIOUR AND ALTRUISM

What is prosocial behaviour?
What role does the situation play in determining prosocial behaviour?

Today's altruist may be tomorrow's passive bystander; it all depends on the social situation. This is the message of Latané and Darley (1969, 1970) who were the first to investigate systematically the causes of bystander passivity. You may be the great hero after saving a child from drowning when you are the only witness. Next week, however, you may be the apathetic bystander among many others who does nothing to help a woman being harassed by a man.

Prosocial behaviour may have costs as well as benefits. Put yourself in the shoes of one of the witnesses who observed the attacks on Kitty Genovese described in the introduction. What are the potential costs that *you* would have to consider in deciding whether to help or not? Witnesses may worry about getting into danger and sustaining injury, about being embarrassed if they misperceive the situation or cannot offer effective help. They may also be concerned about the possibility of being overtaxed by the demands of the situation, or about possible material losses like damage to their belongings or missing an appointment. In contrast, the benefits helpers might gain include easing their conscience, feeling good after helping, increasing their self-esteem, earning social approval or even fame. Empirical research has indicated that rewards increase the likelihood of helping, whereas incurred costs decrease it (Piliavin, Dovidio, Gaertner & Clark, 1981).

PIONEER

Bibb Latané (b. 1937) received his PhD from the University of Minnesota in 1963. His research on the unresponsive bystander began in response to the public outcry and debate following the murder of Kitty Genovese. Together with John Darley he worked out the first decision-making model of the intervention process and coined the term 'diffusion of responsibility' as an explanation of the reduced willingness to help among groups of onlookers of emergencies. Latané also developed further the idea of the social impact of the number of persons on people's feelings and behaviour in his social impact theory.

The relevance of rewards became quite clear in some newspaper headlines after the tsunami disaster. On 1 January 2005, the *Daily Express* headline read: 'Thank you Britain for saving our lives', while the *Guardian* headline of 31 December 2004 proudly proclaimed: 'UK leads aid drive as the horror goes on'. As we will show, our definition of prosocial behaviour includes cases where people are rewarded for helping. In contrast, the term altruism is reserved for prosocial behaviour which is primarily motivated by unselfish compassion.

Definitions and examples

The terms helping, prosocial behaviour and altruism are frequently used interchangeably. To clarify the discussion, it is useful to attach

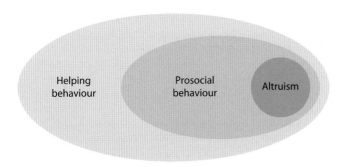

Figure 9.1 *Relationship between the concepts of helping, prosocial behaviour and altruism.*

somewhat different meanings to each of the three terms. 'Helping' is the broadest term, whereas the meaning of 'altruism' is much more narrow (cf. Schwartz & Howard, 1981, p. 190). The overlap among the three terms is illustrated in Figure 9.1.

helping refers to actions intended to improve the situation of the help-recipient

prosocial behaviour refers to helping that is not motivated by professional obligations and that is not based on an organization (except charities)

Helping refers to actions intended to improve the situation of the help-recipient. The definition of *prosocial behaviour* is narrower because 'helping' is not considered as 'prosocial behaviour' if the act is motivated by professional obligations, or if help-givers or help-recipients are organizations. However, there is one exception to the last constraint: charities are organizations whose goal is to promote the well-being of people in need (e.g., the elderly). To support a charity means that the helper uses an agent to increase the efficiency of the help that she intends to give. For example, if you wanted to help victims of the tsunami you might rely on charities like Oxfam or the Red Cross in order to get basic medical supplies to the affected parts of Asia.

altruism refers to prosocial behaviour that has the ultimate goal of benefiting another person

Finally, the term *altruism* has an additional constraint, namely that the ultimate goal of the helper is to benefit another person. The ultimate goal of prosocial behaviour might well be to receive social approval or to reduce one's own distress when witnessing an emergency involving another person. However, the term altruism is reserved for cases where the helper tries to improve the welfare of another person *as an end in itself*. In practice, prosocial behaviour is often based on a mixture of more selfish (egoistic) and more selfless (altruistic) motivations (Batson, Duncan, Ackerman, Buckley & Birch, 1981).

An example of helping that would not be considered prosocial behaviour is a cabin-crew member who helped a passenger with her luggage, because this behaviour was performed in the line of duty. An example of prosocial behaviour is someone helping a neighbour to fill out an insurance form. Since this person helped without any professional obligation to do so, the behaviour would be considered prosocial, even if the helper expected her neighbour to reciprocate with a comparable favour in the future. Finally, a

Plate 9.2 *Helping refers to actions intended to improve the situation of the recipient, e.g. an elderly person.*

classic example of altruism is found in the parable of the Good Samaritan. As recorded in the New Testament, Jesus told the story of a man who was travelling from Jerusalem to Jericho. On the road he was attacked and seriously injured by thieves. Several other people who came that way did not stop to help. Finally, a Samaritan saw the helpless victim and was immediately moved by compassion: he 'went to him, and bound up his wounds, pouring in oil and wine, and set him on his own beast, and brought him to an inn, and took care of him' (Luke 10:34, King James version). In this quotation from the Bible, the motivational force behind the altruistic behaviour of the Samaritan is called 'compassion'. We will return to the role of compassion later when we discuss Batson's (1991) theory of altruistic behaviour. The people who helped save Jews during the Nazi terror in Europe provide further examples of true altruists. Steven Spielberg's film *Schindler's List* recounts the true story of the dramatic rescue of more than 1,000 Jews from Nazi Germany by German industrialist Oskar Schindler. He took great personal risks and invested both time and money to find ways to help Jews escape from the Nazis. He was a hero, and an altruist.

Plate 9.3 *Oskar Schindler (shown here in the film) took great personal risks and invested both time and money to help Jews escape from the Nazis.*

Plate 9.4 *Bob Geldof's organization of emergency aid for the starving people of Africa is a public example of prosocial behaviour.*

Whereas many acts of prosocial behaviour take place in private, other acts of prosocial behaviour take place in public. Consider, for example, emergency aid for the starving people of Africa, organized by Bob Geldof in 1985 (Live Aid), in 2004 (Band

Aid 20) and again in 2005 as Band 8. There are, in fact, numerous examples of generosity which show that prosocial responses need not be without personal gain. For example, pop stars like Dido and Robbie Williams might profit indirectly from sacrificing their time and money for people in need, because their prosocial behaviour could promote their records. In addition, many people will admire their unselfishness.

In general, prosocial behaviour may result either from the ultimate goal of benefiting oneself (i.e., egoistically motivated behaviour) or from the ultimate goal of benefiting another person (i.e., altruistically motivated behaviour). In this chapter, the main focus is on the middle-level term prosocial behaviour, which includes egoistically and altruistically motivated helping behaviour. We use the term altruistic behaviour only to emphasize the fact that a particular behaviour serves the ultimate goal of benefiting another person.

SUMMARY

We have noted that helping others can have costs as well as benefits. We have also seen that it is important to distinguish the general class of helping behaviour (which can include behaviour performed due to professional obligations) from more specific prosocial behaviour, and from altruism, which is motivated by compassion. In the following sections we consider the psychology of the unresponsive bystander and theories of prosocial behaviour. Besides evolutionary explanations, psychological theories refer to individualistic approaches including moods and emotion, prosocial personality and compassion. In addition, interpersonal explanations contrast exchange and communal relationships. Cultural explanations refer to social norms of fairness and humanitarian values. Finally, from the perspective of the help-recipient, we consider the issue of whether aid is experienced as supporting or threatening.

WHY DON'T PEOPLE HELP?

Why does the presence of **more** *onlookers lead to* **less** *helping in emergencies?*

The question 'Why don't people help?' arises whenever we are confronted with incidents such as the murder of Kitty Genovese, who could have been saved if only one witness had intervened during the first half hour of the attack. Laypeople and experts alike explained the neighbours' failure to intervene as due to their 'apathy'. As we shall see, this explanation of what happened is false. Ingenious experiments that were stimulated by the incident show that in many cases the power of the situation is much stronger than that of personal characteristics of those involved.

When more is less

Numerous studies indicate that the willingness to intervene in emergencies is higher when a bystander is alone than when he or she is in the company of other bystanders (Latané & Nida, 1981). In one of the first experiments to show this effect, Darley and Latané (1968) systematically varied the number of bystanders (see Research close-up 9.1, below, and 14.1, p. 305). The results illustrate the *number effect*: the likelihood of intervention is reduced by the sheer number of bystanders.

> **number effect** refers to the reduced likelihood of intervention in groups of bystanders: the larger the number of bystanders, the less likely any one bystander will be to intervene and help

In a second experiment (Latané & Rodin, 1969) students heard that a woman working in an adjacent office had fallen over and was moaning in pain. This incident lasted 130 seconds. In one condition the student was alone. In the second condition another student (a confederate of the experimenter) was also present, but

RESEARCH CLOSE-UP 9.1

The impact of bystanders on helping in an emergency

Darley, J.M. & Latané, B. (1968). Bystander intervention in emergencies: Diffusion of responsibility. *Journal of Personality and Social Psychology, 8*, 377–383.

....

Introduction

If several people are witnesses of an emergency involving another person, each of the witnesses is aware of the fact that others could intervene. This awareness is the basis of diffusion of responsibility: each of the witnesses believes that full responsibility is not focused on him or her but is shared with the other witnesses. As a consequence, individual helpfulness will be reduced. Thus, we can derive the hypothesis that witnesses of an emergency who are aware of other witnesses but do not see or hear them will help less the more witnesses are present. This occurs because, as the number of witnesses increases, the process of diffusion of responsibility is likely to intensify.

Method

Participants
Seventy-two students (59 female, 13 male) participated in the experiment.

Design and procedure
The experimenter explained that the aim of the study was to find out what kind of personal problems college students had in an urban environment. A discussion via an intercom was planned in order to guarantee the anonymity of the participants. Each participant sat alone in a cubicle. There were more such rooms located along a long corridor.

Three conditions were compared: two-person, three-person and six-person groups. In the two-person group only the participant and the future victim were apparently present. In the three-person group participants believed that one additional

discussant was present. In the six-person group, the presence of four additional persons was simulated. In all conditions the participant was actually the only person present, while the presence of the other participants was simulated by pre-recorded contributions to the discussion. The plan was that in the first discussion round each participant would talk in turn. In the next round each participant would comment on what the others had talked about. The length of each contribution was limited because the microphone was on for about 2 minutes. As a consequence, only one participant could be heard over the intercom at any given time.

The first discussant, who was the future victim, talked about the difficulty of adjusting to life in New York City. He also mentioned that he was prone to seizures. When he talked again at the beginning of the second round he started choking and his speech became increasingly incoherent and louder. After 70 seconds it was evident that the person had collapsed. The intercom connection with the victim broke down after 125 seconds. The experimenter recorded the time from the beginning of the fit until the participant left the cubicle to intervene. If no participant attempted to intervene, the experimenter waited 6 minutes before terminating the experiment. Afterwards the participants filled out a questionnaire on their thoughts and feelings during the emergency and several personality scales including social desirability and social responsibility. They were fully debriefed, and given support to handle any emotions which might have been aroused in the experimental setting.

Results

All students who tried to help the person having the seizure reacted within the first 3 minutes. At any given time after the beginning of the epileptic fit the intervention rate of participants in the two-person groups was highest, followed by the intervention rate of participants in the three-person groups. Level of helpfulness was lowest in the six-person group. The strong effect of the conditions on helpfulness is revealed by the percentage of participants who intervened before the intercom

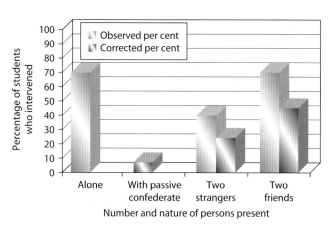

Figure 9.2 *Helping as a function of number of people present (from Darley & Latané, 1968).*

connection with the victim was cut off (see Figure 9.2). Eighty-five per cent of participants who assumed they were the only witness of the breakdown intervened. Compare this with the 62 per cent intervention rate of participants who thought that one additional student was aware of the emergency and the 31 per cent intervention rate of participants who assumed that they were among five potential helpers.

Discussion

The results confirm the hypothesis that there would be less help in larger groups of onlookers. As expected, the awareness that four others could intervene on behalf of the victim in the six-person group (which included both the participant and the victim) reduced helpfulness much more than the awareness that one or two onlookers of the emergency could offer help.

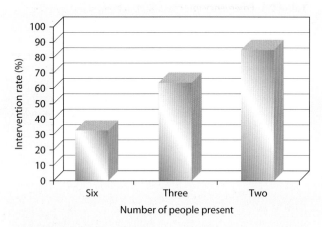

PIONEER

John M. Darley (b. 1938) earned his PhD from Harvard University and has spent most of his academic career at Princeton University. Among his first publications were studies on fear, social comparison and affiliation. Together with Bibb Latané (see p. 178), he developed the psychology of the unresponsive bystander. Their article on 'Bystander intervention in emergencies: Diffusion of responsibility' has become one of the most highly cited articles in social psychology. He has also contributed to applied social psychology and public policy by his studies on energy conservation and on the legal system.

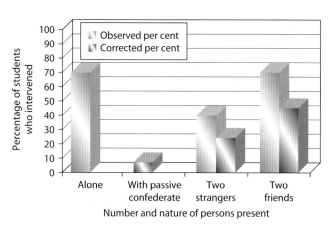

Figure 9.3 *Effect of a second bystander (confederate, stranger or friend) on emergency intervention (from Latané & Rodin, 1969).*

The theory of the unresponsive bystander: Threefold inhibitions

Several processes in combination may contribute to the social inhibition of prosocial behaviour. The theory of the unresponsive bystander highlights three inhibition processes:

was instructed to be passive. In the third condition two strangers were present at the time of the accident, and in the fourth condition two friends were present. Although two people could have intervened in the third and fourth condition, in only 40 per cent of dyads of strangers and 70 per cent of dyads of friends did at least one student intervene. The *individual* likelihood of intervention was calculated according to a special formula as 22.5 per cent for strangers and 45.2 per cent for friends.[1] These corrected intervention rates are lower than in the alone-condition, but higher than in the passive-confederate condition (see Figure 9.3). Additional analyses indicated that friends intervened faster than strangers within the 130 seconds of the emergency.

1 ***Diffusion of responsibility***: A single bystander feels that the responsibility for intervening is focused on him or her. With other bystanders present, each bystander perceives less responsibility, because it is diffused across all others present; this reduces the motivation to act prosocially on behalf of the victim.

> **diffusion of responsibility** cognitive appraisal which divides responsibility among several onlookers or bystanders. As a consequence, each individual member in the group feels less responsible than when alone. When there are several bystanders present in an emergency, the responsibility of any one of the bystanders is reduced

2 *Implicit modelling of 'nothing has happened'*: Emergencies take place rarely and, if they do occur, are quite unique in character: bystanders are not sure how to respond. Because bystanders hesitate and try to figure out what should be done, they become – unintentionally – models of passivity for one another. This modelling process defines the appropriate response in the situation: do nothing. Thus, a social definition of the situation emerges which reduces the bystander's tendency to act; passivity is then established as the social norm.

> **implicit modelling of 'nothing has happened'** because bystanders in emergencies are overwhelmed by the sudden and unexpected event, they initially hesitate to provide help. When they see that other bystanders are doing the same, they each reach the false conclusion that the other bystanders interpret the event as harmless. This is sometimes called 'pluralistic ignorance'

3 *Fear of embarrassment*: A third factor which presumably reduces the willingness to help is embarrassment. The presence of other bystanders elicits feelings of uneasiness because the others would be observers of a potential intervention. The resulting social anxiety inhibits intervention especially in situations in which bystanders are in doubt about whether they will be able to intervene successfully, because they believe they lack the ability to act in an appropriate manner. An alternative term is 'evaluation apprehension'. Potential helpers may also fear embarrassment at misconstruing a situation as an emergency when it is not. Rushing in to break up a fight leaves you feeling foolish if it turns out that two people were just kidding around.

> **fear of embarrassment** the stressful experience of a person whose behaviour in a situation is observed by bystanders. Especially when the situation is unfamiliar, social anxiety is elicited which reduces the tendency to help victims of emergencies. Related terms are 'audience inhibition' and 'evaluation apprehension'

Latané and Darley (1976) investigated these processes in an experiment which measured prosocial behaviour across five conditions. At one extreme, no inhibitory factors were present: the participant was alone while seeing on a monitor a person receiving an electric shock and then falling on the floor. At the other extreme, social inhibition was strongly manipulated. The participants assumed that a second witness was present during the incident, making it likely that diffusion of responsibility would occur (cf. Darley & Latané, 1968). In addition, two communication channels were switched on. The participant could also see the other witness, who responded passively to the emergency and thus provided a model of inaction. The participant also had two monitors in front of him, one showing the victim and one showing the other witness. This presumably increased the participant's social anxiety because he knew his responses were being observed. Thus the participant was under the combined influence of all three factors: diffusion of responsibility, implicit modelling of 'nothing has happened' and fear of embarrassment. Under these conditions helping should be minimal. The experimental hypothesis was straightforward: helping would decrease the more processes of

Table 9.1 *Emergency intervention as a function of number of inhibitory influences on the bystander (from Latané & Darley, 1976)*

Condition	Number of inhibitory processes	Level of helping
1: Alone	0	high
2: Mere awareness of other witness	1	intermediate
3 and 4: Mere awareness plus one communication channel switched on	2	low
5: Mere awareness plus two communication channels switched on	3	very low

Statistical comparisons indicated that level of helping was significantly different between rows.

social inhibition were 'switched on'. The results confirmed this prediction (see Table 9.1).

Social inhibition of prosocial behaviour in the general public clearly constitutes a social problem. Thus, it is important to learn how it might be avoided. Might it help to inform the public about the findings of studies on this topic in order to influence such negative behavioural tendencies? One experiment studied whether information on the unresponsive bystander would be effective in reducing the indifference typically shown by onlookers of emergencies. The theory of the unresponsive bystander was explained to students during a 50-minute lecture. The lecturer used research examples to illustrate each of the three inhibition processes. Later, in an apparently unrelated study, students who were accompanied by a passive confederate were confronted with the helpless victim of a bicycle accident. Compared with a control group of students who did not hear the lecture but who encountered the victim of the bicycle accident, the experimental group offered more help (Beaman, Barnes, Klentz & McQuirk, 1978). Mere knowledge of the social processes that contribute to the unresponsive bystander led students to respond in a more responsible way. Therefore, informing the public, making them aware of the problem of the unresponsive bystander, may reduce the negative impact of this problem on our society.

Another measure that can be taken against unresponsive bystanders is to increase their competence in providing help, because competence reduces fear of embarrassment. For example, people who have just completed a first-aid course will presumably stop when they encounter a person in need of help. If onlookers believe that they are competent and able to perform well, the presence of other onlookers may even serve as an incentive for them to intervene (Schwartz & Gottlieb, 1976). High competence shifts the balance of costs and rewards by adding rewards for intervention and eliminating costs. Confirming these arguments, many studies show that people who feel competent provide more help than people who feel less competent (Bierhoff, 2002a).

'Sorry, I'm in a hurry!'

The theory of the unresponsive bystander does not exhaust the range of inhibiting conditions that may be present in real life. As we have noted, intervening on behalf of a helpless victim is dependent on the level of cost that the helper incurs. Ironically, this proposition was confirmed in an experiment whose participants were students in a theological seminary (Darley & Batson, 1973; see also Research close-up 2.2, p. 26). Some of the students were told that in the second part of the study they would talk about professional problems, and others were expected to talk about the parable of the Good Samaritan. They were instructed to go to another building where they were expected by an assistant. As they left, the experimenter indicated that they would be either late ('Oh, you're late: they were expecting you a few minutes ago'), on time ('The assistant is ready for you, so please go right over') or early ('If you would like to wait over there, it shouldn't be long').

On their way, students encountered an apparent victim slumped on the floor. It was not clear what had happened to him. Figure 9.4 illustrates the percentage of these theology students who offered help. The instruction to the students had a slight effect on prosocial behaviour – those who were instructed to think about the parable tended to help more. But the time-pressure manipulation exerted a much stronger influence than the content of the message. In general, participants were less helpful when they were in a hurry.

Time pressure can exert a profound dampening effect on prosocial responses (see also Batson et al., 1978; Macrae & Johnston, 1998, Experiment 2). In our interpretation of the Kitty Genovese incident we mentioned several factors that might increase the costs of intervention. Time pressure is another factor that inhibits prosocial behaviour by increasing its costs or disadvantages.

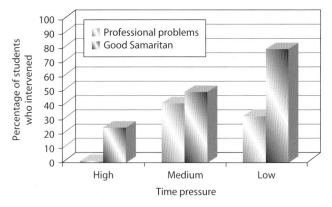

Figure 9.4 *Effect of message and time pressure on prosocial responses in an emergency situation (based on Darley & Batson, 1973; Greenwald, 1975).*

SUMMARY

Part of the answer to the question 'Why don't people help?' is that other people are around. Responsibility is diffused across all bystanders who observe an emergency. This leads people to be passive and to model this inaction to others. The presence of others also reduces helping because it increases embarrassment. Finally, people may fail to help because they lack competence, or they may simply be under time pressure.

WHY DO PEOPLE HELP ONE ANOTHER?

Are people more likely to help close family members than unrelated others?
Do people help more when in a good mood?
What are the main characteristics of the prosocial personality?
Why do people sometimes need a 'cover story' before they donate money?
Which social norms foster and hinder prosocial behaviour?

In this section we deal with the main theories of prosocial behaviour. These can be easily classified into two categories according to their level of analysis, namely evolutionary theories and psychological theories. Psychological theories can be further differentiated into individualistic, interpersonal and cultural approaches. As we shall see, these theories complement one another and together offer a comprehensive theoretical explanation of prosocial behaviour.

The evolutionary approach

Scientists from the fields of social and biological science have recognized that prosocial behaviour has strong biological roots, meaning that it is not an exception but a rule in social life (Penner, Dovidio, Piliavin & Schroeder, 2005). Evolutionary psychology is a branch of psychology which focuses on the adaptive value of preferences, feelings, attitudes and behaviour. It is based on Charles Darwin's original ideas about natural and sexual selection which were developed further through new insights of biologists like William Hamilton, Robert Trivers and others. The fact that evolutionary psychology refers to genetic determinants of behaviour does not mean that environmental influences are ignored or considered less important, because learning processes moderate any evolutionary adaptation. What an individual does in a specific environment is not pre-programmed by genes but is the result of a complex interplay of the shared human genetic make-up, individual traits, social learning and perception of the immediate social circumstances (Buss, 2004).

Kin selection and reciprocal altruism

The evolutionary approach to prosocial behaviour is based on inborn or genetic tendencies. This raises the interesting question of how the process of natural selection could favour a gene that increases the tendency of an individual to help others. Prosocial behaviour can be understood as the result of natural selection if it increases rather than decreases an individual's (or his or her relatives') chance of reproducing. The theory of *kin selection* assumes that 'kindness-to-kin genes' (Miller, 2001) have evolved. Another issue is that prosocial behaviour is part of a giving-and-receiving cycle, called *reciprocal altruism*, which may promote the survival of the individual, thus contributing to his or her reproductive success.

> **kin selection** theory developed by William Hamilton that natural selection favours those individuals who support their relatives. To provide help to relatives enhances inclusive fitness

> **reciprocal altruism** theory that people will support another person if they expect that he or she will respond prosocially. The repayment of the favour in the future is anticipated. Prosocial behaviour is embedded in a cycle of give and take

> **inclusive fitness** the sum of an individual's own reproductive success in passing on genes through the procreation of offspring (= direct fitness) and the effect of his of her support on the reproductive success of his or her relatives, weighted by their genetic relatedness coefficient (= indirect fitness)

We consider kin selection first. The reproductive success of an individual (that is, his or her *inclusive fitness*) is dependent on the distribution of his or her genes in the next generation. Inclusive fitness is the sum of two components. The first is an individual's own reproductive success – direct fitness. The second is the proportion of the reproductive success of relatives that is elicited by the helping behaviour of the individual – indirect fitness (Hamilton, 1964). For example, the genetic relatedness between siblings is .50. Therefore, one's own genes can be favoured by increasing the survival chances of brothers or sisters. In terms of reproductive success, two children of a brother count the same as one's own child.

Empirical evidence supports the theory. For example, people indicate that they are willing to help a brother (genetic relatedness .50) more than a nephew (.25), who in turn may expect more help than a cousin (.125). An acquaintance (.00) is least likely to receive help (Burnstein, Crandall & Kitayama, 1994). These results are more pronounced for scenarios which describe life-threatening situations than for everyday scenarios (when help is useful but not a life-or-death matter). Because life-threatening emergencies are directly threatening to the survival of the help-recipient, they constitute the more crucial test of the theory of kin selection.

What about friends? Why do they help each other? In this case the theory of reciprocal altruism developed by Trivers (1971) applies: this explains prosocial behaviour on the basis of reciprocity among non-relatives. The principle of reciprocal altruism is illustrated by the following example: it makes sense for Tania to lend fellow student Stephanie her lecture notes, if she expects to be helped by Stephanie when she herself misses a lecture.

Whereas evolutionary psychologists have described reciprocal altruism as part of the shared genetic make-up, social scientists have identified reciprocity as a universal cultural norm. Gouldner (1960) proposed that the *norm of reciprocity* includes two prescriptions: (1) people should help those who have helped them and (2) they should not injure those who have helped them. He assumed that the norm of reciprocity is a universal element of all human cultures. In support of this idea, cross-cultural evidence on giving and receiving help indicates that reciprocity is found in all cultures (Johnson et al., 1989). The frequency of giving and receiving aid is also highly correlated in all cultures studied.

> **norm of reciprocity** the norm that we should do to others as they do to us. Reciprocity calls for positive responses to favourable treatment but negative responses to unfavourable treatment. Prosocial reciprocity occurs when people help in return for having been helped

Prosocial reciprocity is threatened by cheating. Cheaters may exploit any prosocial tendencies which are based on the assumption that the helped person will repay the favour in the future. To avoid becoming the victim of cheats, we therefore tend to limit reciprocal altruism (and in the same vein, the norm of reciprocity) to certain circumstances and preconditions. These include a high level of trust between the parties involved (Yamagishi, 1986), but also stability of group membership, longevity of the group and a high degree of recognizability among group members (Buss, 2004).

The individualistic approach

Like the evolutionary approach, the individualistic approach explains altruism in terms of individual tendencies to be helpful. These tendencies are not, however, necessarily assumed to be genetically determined (although they can be), but rather are acquired by social learning (for reviews see Bierhoff, 2005; Kochanska & Thompson, 1997). There are basically two types of individualistic theories of prosocial behaviour: one explains it in terms of feeling states, whereas the other assumes that prosocial behaviour is determined by enduring personality characteristics. Individualistic approaches examine how you feel and who you are in order to predict your likelihood of behaving in a prosocial manner.

Moods and emotions

People's feelings fluctuate during their daily activities. They feel delighted after passing an exam, but disappointed when rejected by a friend. The intensity of feelings varies from more subtle 'background' moods to stronger emotions which may interrupt day-to-day activities. Both moods and emotions are described as varying from positive to negative affect. For example, love is a positive emotion, whereas guilt is a negative emotion.

Current mood may colour someone's willingness to respond prosocially to the needs of others. Empirical studies show that helping is fostered by a *positive mood*. For example, children who are in a happy mood share more with others than children in a neutral mood (Rosenhan, Underwood & Moore, 1974). The positive relationship between good mood and helping was confirmed in a meta-analysis by Carlson, Charlin and Miller (1988), based on 61 positive mood vs. neutral mood comparisons. In the examined studies (including student and non-student samples), positive mood was induced by a variety of methods, including success on

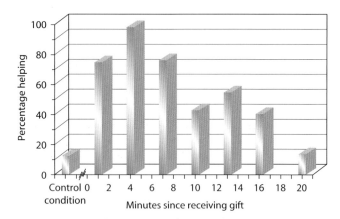

Figure 9.5 *Percentage of helpful participants depending on time elapsed between mood induction and request for help (based on Isen et al., 1976).*

a task, finding a small amount of money, thinking about a happy experience and receiving a free gift. The mean amount of time that elapsed between the positive mood induction and the request for help was about 4 minutes. This meta-analysis yielded a significant coefficient of $d = .54$, generally considered to indicate a medium-size effect which is relevant in daily life.

The effects of good mood on helping are, however, relatively short-lived, as shown in a field experiment in the USA. Participants in the study received a packet of stationery as a gift at home (Isen, Clark & Schwartz, 1976). Shortly afterwards they received a telephone call that was obviously a wrong number. Participants were asked to help the caller by making a phone call. The telephone rang 1, 4, 7, 10, 13, 16 or 20 minutes after the first contact. As illustrated in Figure 9.5, the request was highly successful if it was made 1, 4 or 7 minutes after the presentation of the gift (on average, 83 per cent of the participants made the phone call). With a time delay of 10, 13 or 16 minutes, the response rate decreased to about 50 per cent. Finally, 20 minutes later only 12 per cent of the participants made the phone call – a response rate that comes close to the results in the control condition, where no gift was received.

These results can be explained in terms of the affect-as-information model developed by Schwarz (1990). The model assumes that people follow a 'How do I feel about it?' heuristic in the sense that they use current mood as a piece of information that is integrated into their overall judgement. For example, if a person is asked to evaluate another person, he or she might simply refer to his or her feelings about the other person and then make the judgement.

From this perspective, feelings carry an informational value which may substitute for careful analytic reasoning. Specifically, positive feelings may inform the person that the current environment is a safe place (Schwarz, 1990). The affect-as-information model simply implies that actors take their mood as an index of the safety of the given situation. Since prosocial responses are suppressed by danger signals (Cacioppo & Gardner, 1993), we can infer from being in a good mood that the situation is not dangerous; this inference may encourage prosocial behaviour.

Forgas (2000) points out that positive and negative moods do not exert equal influences. The effects of a positive mood seem to be stronger and more consistent than the effects of negative moods. From an evolutionary perspective, it might be argued that *bad mood* signals problems and possibly danger (Schwarz, 1990). Thus when a person is in a state of high self-focus, bad mood undermines altruistic intentions by increasing the perceived cost of intervention (cf. Underwood, Froming & Moore, 1977).

A cursory look at the literature on negative feeling states and prosocial behaviour shows that the results are contradictory. For example, the induction of guilt feelings by a transgression (e.g. cheating on a test) increases prosocial behaviour (Freedman, Wallington & Bless, 1967), whereas participants who are induced to feel sad hesitate to help other people (Thompson, Cowan & Rosenhan, 1980). In their meta-analysis, Carlson and Miller (1987; see also Miller & Carlson, 1990) found that the effects of negative mood on helping were variable. In some studies, negative mood enhanced the level of prosocial behaviour, whereas in others the opposite effect occurred. The results are clearer, however, when effects of sadness and guilt are separated (Carlson & Miller, 1987). Sadness is associated with a low willingness to help others, while *interpersonal guilt* is associated with a high level of prosocial behaviour.

One possible explanation of the influence of guilt on helping is that participants try to compensate for their negative feelings by doing good deeds. This *negative-state-relief hypothesis* (Cialdini, Kenrick & Baumann, 1982) assumes that negative affect is accompanied by a drive to reduce unpleasant feeling states, and that prosocial behaviour is one of several techniques which the individual might employ to attain this end. But the negative-state-relief hypothesis does not explain why guilt leads to very high willingness to help, while sadness does not.

Why does interpersonal guilt exert such a strong influence on prosocial behaviour? Prosocial behaviour following a transgression can be understood as reparation. It is possible that this special meaning of prosocial behaviour in the context of a transgression explains the very high level of helpfulness of persons who feel guilty. In general, guilt feelings contribute to the maintenance of personal relationships (Baumeister, 1998; Estrada-Hollenbeck & Heatherton, 1998). Guilt is primarily aroused after hurting a relationship partner (e.g., friend, colleague). It functions like a warning signal, indicating that the person must compensate his or her partner (e.g., repair damage that they have caused) in order to restore the relationship. Guilt feelings motivate actions (e.g., reparation, apologies, compensation) which help to restore the threatened relationship and strengthen social bonds (Baumeister & Leary, 1995). Guilt is a complex emotion and there are several types of guilt, but interpersonal, situation-specific guilt is a *prosocial emotion* that functions positively to restore personal relationships (Baumeister, Stillwell & Heatherton, 1994).

> **interpersonal guilt** negative feelings about oneself which result from the knowledge that one is responsible for the distress of others or for damage done to them
>
> **negative-state-relief hypothesis** idea that prosocial behaviour is a mood-management technique. During socialization people have learned that prosocial behaviour is self-reinforcing. When they feel bad they employ prosocial behaviour to improve their feeling state

The prosocial personality Studies of the influence of *prosocial personality* focus on personality attributes associated with increased levels of prosocial behaviour. More specifically, empathy, social responsibility, internal locus of control, just-world belief and esteem enhancement have been identified as the key personality factors which explain individual differences in response to other people in need. We consider each in turn.

> **prosocial personality** the set of personality attributes (e.g., empathy, social responsibility) that contribute to willingness to help others. An alternative term is 'altruistic personality'

It seems that personality influences on prosocial behaviour are more influential when situational pressures to help are weak and when the costs of helping are high. When situational pressures are strong, they dominate personality influences; when costs are low, prosocial behaviour is performed as a routine action under the control of situational demands (Eisenberg & Shell, 1986). Evidence concerning the prosocial personality has been obtained in laboratory studies, quasi-experimental studies and field studies.

The overall pattern of relationships between prosocial personality and prosocial behaviour is quite robust (Penner et al., 2005). For example, in a laboratory study of emergency intervention, the correlation between social responsibility and prosocial behaviour was $r = .34$ (Staub, 1974). Social responsibility includes moral fulfilment of the expectations of others and adherence to social prescriptions (Bierhoff, 2002b). Social responsibility and prosocial behaviour correlated .38 in the study by Bierhoff, Klein and Kramp (1991); in their study, the highest single correlation between helpfulness and personality disposition was for *empathy* ($r = .48$). Empathy is the most obvious prosocial trait. It is a tendency to experience an emotional response that is congruent with the emotional state of another person. Empathy is based on taking the perspective of the other person (see Individual Differences 9.1).

> **empathy** tendency to experience an emotional response that is congruent with the emotional state of another person. It results from adopting the perspective of the other and compassionately understanding his or her emotions

Research has found a third aspect of the prosocial personality, namely, that those who help express stronger agreement with statements of the internal locus of control scale (Rotter, 1966; see Individual Differences 9.1) than non-helpers (Bierhoff et al., 1991; Oliner & Oliner, 1988). The fourth and final personality variable involved in prosocial behaviour is belief in a just world, defined as the generalized expectancy that people get what they deserve and deserve what they get (Lerner, 1980; see Individual Differences 9.1). *Just-world belief* correlates positively with helping when it is possible to solve the problem completely (e.g., giving £5 to a person who is hungry and wants to buy a hot meal). In contrast, when it is not possible to solve the problem completely (e.g., you hear of someone who needs to raise half a million pounds for experimental medical treatment), strong belief in a just world is a negative predictor of

> **just-world belief** generalized expectancy that people get what they deserve. Undeserved suffering of others threatens belief in a just world and motivates attempts to restore it. These include reducing the victims' suffering by helping or derogating the victims, depending on whether help can effectively be given or not

INDIVIDUAL DIFFERENCES 9.1

Do you have a 'prosocial personality'?

The prosocial personality encompasses empathy, social responsibility, internal locus of control and just-world belief. To administer the tests, use a 6-point scale with the endpoints 1 (strongly disagree) and 6 (strongly agree).

Empathy is measured by items like:

1 I am often quite touched by things that I see happen.
2 I sometimes try to understand my friends better by imagining how things look from their perspective.
3 I would describe myself as a pretty soft-hearted person.

These empathy items refer to compassion and perspective taking (Davis, 1994). They express a concern with the welfare of others, whose fate is emotionally moving. In several studies helpers consistently expressed higher empathy than did non-helpers (Bierhoff et al., 1991; Davis, 1994; Eisenberg & Fabes, 1991; Penner, Fritzsche, Craiger & Freifeld, 1995).

Social responsibility is measured by the Social Responsibility Scale (Berkowitz & Daniels, 1964), which includes items like:

1 I would never let a friend down when he expects something of me.
2 In school my behaviour has gotten me into trouble. (Negative)
3 When given a task I stick to it even if things I like to do better come along.

Interviews with rescuers of Jews in Nazi Europe revealed that the rescuers were characterized by a higher degree of social responsibility compared to a control group of people who did not help Jews (Oliner & Oliner, 1988). This result was replicated in a study of first-aiders who intervened on behalf of traffic accident victims (Bierhoff et al., 1991).

Internal locus of control is measured by statements like:

1 Trusting in fate has never turned out as well for me as making a decision to take a definite course of action.
2 What happens to me is my own doing.
3 There really is no such thing as 'luck'.

People who agree with such statements believe that their world is predictable and controllable by their own actions. These convictions may contribute to their willingness to provide help to victims. Empirically, social responsibility and internal locus of control correlate positively. Both social responsibility and internal locus of control presuppose that people see a clear link between their own behaviour and its effects.

Just-world belief is measured by the following items (Dalbert, 1999):

1 I think basically the world is a just place.
2 I believe that, by and large, people get what they deserve.
3 I am confident that justice always prevails over injustice.

Its influence on prosocial behaviour depends on what problem faces the victim (Miller, 1977b).

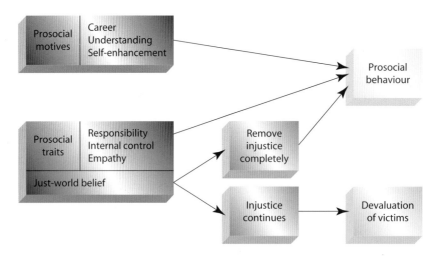

Figure 9.6 *Model of prosocial personality.*
(based on Batson, 1991)

helping (Miller, 1977b). Instead, people tend to restore their belief in a just world by devaluing the victim (Hafer, 2000). For example, in the Kitty Genovese case, derogation of the victim might have focused on blaming her for walking alone at night.

Whereas much research is devoted to spontaneous prosocial behaviour, less is known about voluntary work and regular, longer-term commitment in general. *Volunteerism* refers to unpaid work in an organizational context. It represents 'voluntary, sustained, and on-going helpfulness' (Clary et al., 1998, p. 1517) and is usually dependent on planning and individual capabilities. Figure 9.6 illustrates the combined influence of prosocial traits and motives on helpfulness.

volunteerism regular commitment to prosocial behaviour in an organizational context

The enduring motivation underlying volunteer work is measured by the Volunteer Functions Inventory (VFI; Clary et al., 1998). It is based on the functional approach to attitudes which was originally developed by Katz and Stotland (1959; see Chapter 6, this volume). In this approach it is assumed that actions serve certain functions (e.g., to acquire knowledge, to express one's values). The VFI measures six orthogonal dimensions which tap the following functions:

1 Understanding ('I can explore my own personal strengths').
2 Protective ('By volunteering I feel less lonely').
3 Values ('I feel it is important to help others').
4 Career ('I can make new contacts that might help my business or career').
5 Social ('My friends volunteer').
6 Enhancement ('Volunteering makes me feel important').

Omoto and Snyder (1995) examined the question of why people get involved in long-term helping. In a large survey of AIDS volunteers they found that some people were more motivated by altruistic reasons, whereas others were more motivated by ego-

Plate 9.5 *Altruistic motives have been found to be the best predictors of length of service in AIDS organizations.*

istic ones. Besides the motivation to volunteer, these researchers also assessed prosocial personality. They found that egoistic motives (career, understanding and self-enhancement) – but not altruistic ones – were positively related to length of service in an AIDS organization for at least one year. Thus, the 'better' motives are not always the ones that determine who will stay the course. In another study on long-term helping by AIDS volunteers, however, Penner and Finkelstein (1998) found that altruistic motives were the best predictors of length of service in AIDS organizations. This relationship was stronger in males than females. Because 90 per cent of the males in this study were gay, it was probably easier for them to identify and empathize with the primary beneficiaries of their care. This result shows that altruistic concerns can be salient and more predictive of helping under certain conditions.

The study of volunteers in charities illustrates the influence of enduring motives on satisfaction and regular commitment. These results have important practical implications. They suggest that

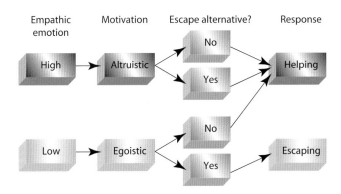

Figure 9.7 *Empathy–altruism hypothesis (based on Batson, 1991).*

volunteers may be motivated by various concerns and that either altruistic or egoistic motives, or indeed both, may play a prominent role in maintaining commitment in the long run.

Empathy-based altruism: Does true altruism exist?

Surely most of us would agree that altruistically motivated helping is somehow more worthy than egoistically motivated helping. The distinction between both types of motivation rests upon the question of whether the ultimate goal of the prosocial behaviour is to increase the helper's own welfare or to increase the welfare of another person (Batson, 1991).

Several lines of research converge in their findings that motivation to help is either egoistic or altruistic. The first evidence comes from the World Values Survey, which assessed kinds of motivation for doing unpaid voluntary work in 33 countries with a total of 13,584 respondents. A factor analysis of responses indicated the existence of four predominantly egoistic motivations and five predominantly altruistic motivations (van de Vliert, Huang & Levine, 2004). The four egoistic motivations were: 'time on my hands, wanted something worthwhile to do', 'purely for personal satisfaction', 'for social reasons, to meet people' and 'to gain new skills and useful experience'. The five altruistic motivations were: 'a sense of solidarity with the poor and disadvantaged', 'compassion for those in need', 'identifying with people who are suffering', 'religious beliefs' and 'to help give disadvantaged people hope and dignity'. Further analyses indicated that the distinction between egoistic and altruistic motivations was an almost universal finding in the cross-national comparisons.

Carefully designed experiments have tried to decide conclusively when prosocial behaviour is motivated altruistically or egoistically. The basic idea is to confront people with a victim and offer them the opportunity to leave a distressing situation. If people are egoistically motivated, they might prefer the 'escape' alternative because it allows them to reduce any negative arousal elicited by the presence of the victim. In contrast, people who are altruistically motivated are not as likely to leave the situation since their desire to alleviate the suffering of the victim would still exist after having left. Because the altruistic motivation is equated with empathy, this assumption has become known as the empathy–altruism hypothesis (Figure 9.7).

Batson and colleagues (1981) tested the empathy–altruism hypothesis in a classic experiment (see Research close-up 9.2). The results confirmed the hypothesis that altruistically motivated people will help even when it is possible to leave the situation, but egoistically motivated people only help when leaving the situation is made difficult. The pattern of results is typical of the findings of several experiments conducted by Batson and co-workers (summarized by Batson, Fultz & Schoenrade, 1987).

Further research on the empathy–altruism hypothesis is based on the distinction between two feeling states which might be aroused by perceiving a person in need (Batson, 1991). On the one hand, feelings of personal distress may arise in the observer. Personal distress is defined as a self-oriented vicarious emotion, which is described by adjectives such as 'alarmed', 'grieved', 'upset' and 'disturbed'. This unpleasant feeling state can be reduced by helping. It is also possible to reduce personal distress by leaving the situation, because the escape reduces the impact of the victim's suffering on the non-helper. The other feeling state that may follow from perceiving the other person's need is termed empathic concern. It is described by adjectives such as 'sympathetic', 'moved', 'compassionate', 'warm' and 'soft-hearted'. Studies that have *measured* empathy in this way have found results consistent with the experimental studies that *manipulated* empathy. Toi and Batson (1982) found that participants who were high on self-reported relative empathy (empathic concern minus personal distress) were willing to help a person in need even if they had an escape option. In contrast, participants who expressed more personal distress than empathic concern were quite helpful when no escape option was available, but their willingness to help decreased substantially if an escape route was available (see also Bierhoff & Rohmann, 2004).

How could the empathy–altruism hypothesis be explained from an egoistic perspective? One possibility is the negative-state-relief hypothesis, which would argue that compassionate people feel sad when they watch others suffering. The altruistic response of compassionate people would be motivated by the goal of relieving their own sadness (rather than helping the victim for her own sake). This interpretation is, however, not very convincing because empirical studies have shown that mood management related to sadness is not the decisive factor that motivates compassionate people to act (Batson et al., 1989). An alternative interpretation is based on the perception of 'oneness', which is defined as a 'sense of shared, merged, or interconnected personal identities' (Cialdini, Brown, Lewis, Luce & Neuberg, 1997, p. 483). This interpretation implies that people help similar others (see Research close-up 9.2, p. 190) due to their own self-interest (see the section on the evolutionary approach, above). People derive cues for genetic commonality from kinship, similarity and closeness, cues which are identical to the conditions mentioned by Batson (1991) as factors that elicit true altruism.

Cialdini et al. manipulated closeness by designing scenarios in which the person who needed help was a near-stranger, acquaintance, good friend or close family member of the potential helper. Participants indicated the amount of help they would offer by choosing one of seven alternatives (from no help at all to a very substantial amount of helping). They also rated the extent of 'oneness' they felt with the needy person. In one study the situation portrayed a person who was evicted from her apartment, while the second study concerned two children whose parents had died

RESEARCH CLOSE-UP 9.2

The empathy–altruism hypothesis

Batson, C.D., Duncan, B.D., Ackerman, P., Buckley, T. & Birch, K. (1981). Is empathic emotion a source of altruistic motivation? *Journal of Personality and Social Psychology, 40*, 290–302.

Introduction

To derive the hypothesis of the study, a distinction is first drawn between egoistically and altruistically motivated helping. Egoistic helping serves the ultimate goal of benefiting the helper; altruistically motivated helping serves the ultimate goal of benefiting the help-recipient. Next, the assumption is made that people who are motivated either way will not differ in their helpfulness as long as it is difficult to leave the situation, although the assumed motivation for helping is different. People who are egoistically motivated are assumed to be low in empathy: they help in order to reduce their personal distress. People who are altruistically motivated are assumed to be high in empathy: they help because of their compassion for the victim. In addition, they may anticipate feeling guilty if they don't help.

These different motivations were predicted to lead to sharp differences of responses in a situation in which it is easy for the onlooker to leave without helping. Here, altruistically motivated people will help as much as in the first situation because leaving without helping would still leave them with feelings of compassion and guilt. In contrast, egoistically motivated people are likely to leave the situation without helping, because that is all that is needed to reduce the unpleasant feeling of personal distress.

Method

Participants
Forty-four female students took part in the experiment. In each of the four conditions of the experiment the data from 11 participants were analysed.

Design and procedure
In the experimental scenario observers watched 'Elaine', a confederate of the experimenter, as she seemingly took part in a learning experiment. The observers were told that Elaine would receive random electric shocks as part of the experiment, which was supposedly designed to study learning under stressful conditions. When, after the second trial, it became obvious that Elaine was having great difficulty in continuing the experiment, the experimenter asked the observer whether she was willing

to take over Elaine's role. In one condition it had been made clear in the instructions that the observer could leave the laboratory immediately if she wished (easy-escape condition). In the other condition, the participants believed that they had to stay and observe eight further trials with Elaine suffering if they were not willing to help her (difficult-escape condition). The observer's altruistic motivation (high empathy) was induced by informing her that Elaine expressed similar values and interests, whereas an egoistic motivation (low empathy) was induced by telling the participants that Elaine was dissimilar to her with respect to values and interests.

Results

The results are summarized in Figure 9.8. Level of helping was lower towards a dissimilar Elaine in the easy-escape condition than in all other conditions ($p < .05$ for all comparisons).

Discussion

The results confirm the empathy–altruism hypothesis and provide evidence that true altruism exists. Participants led to believe that Elaine was similar to them (i.e., they were led to empathize with her) helped at the same level whether escape was easy or difficult. However, those participants led to believe that Elaine was dissimilar to them (i.e., they did not empathize with her) helped mainly if it was difficult for them to leave the experiment.

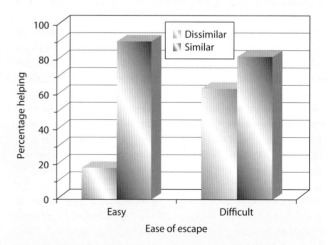

Figure 9.8 *Percentage of participants who helped Elaine depending on similarity and ease or difficulty of escape (from Batson et al., 1981).*

PIONEER

C. Daniel Batson (b. 1943) has spent most of his academic career at the University of Kansas after earning his PhD from Princeton University in 1972. He is widely known for the development of the empathy–altruism hypothesis, which is based on the assumption that people are driven by two motivational systems: an ego-istic one and an altruistic one. He developed an experimental paradigm which represents a huge step towards disentangling these two motivational systems. Batson is also widely cited for his work on religious experience.

in an accident. Results indicated that relationship closeness intensified feelings of empathy and feelings of oneness, which both correlated significantly with prosocial behaviour ($r = .45$ and $r = .76$, respectively, in Cialdini et al., 1997, Study 1). In the final step of the analysis, which took into account the combined effects of feelings of empathy and feelings of oneness on prosocial behaviour, feelings of oneness had greater weight than empathy for the prediction of prosocial behaviour.

These results, however, contradict the empathy–altruism hypothesis only on the surface. It is difficult to conceptualize empathy as a feeling state that does not involve a feeling of oneness. High empathy naturally co-varies with strong feelings of oneness. Therefore, to partial out feelings of oneness from empathy is equivalent to neutralizing empathy as a predictor of prosocial behaviour.

A different line of research has distinguished between personal distress and situational empathy in the study of children's prosocial behaviour. Eisenberg and colleagues (1993) showed that empathy (or sympathy) – and not distress – is positively related to prosocial behaviour in children. This evidence is more in line with the empathy–altruism hypothesis than with the negative-state-relief hypothesis. Eisenberg et al. used a 'baby cry helping task'. While the child (i.e., the participant) was sitting in a room with the experimenter, the sound of a crying baby could be heard through a speaker in the room. The experimenter explained that the baby was in another room and tried to calm the baby by talking to him or her via a microphone. In addition, the child was encouraged to do the same. Finally, in order to offer an 'escape' option, the child learned that it was possible to switch the speaker on or off. Then the experimenter left the room, and the baby crying episode was repeated while the children's facial and behavioural responses were videotaped. Raters assessed the extent of situational distress from the child's facial reactions. They also rated the child's tone of voice for expression of comfort and irritation, and the researchers timed how long the child talked to the baby. Results indicated that facial distress was negatively correlated with time spent talking to the baby, whereas no significant relationship was found with tone of

voice. This study again rules out personal distress as a cause of helping, because *more* facial distress was associated with talking to the baby for *less* time.

The interpersonal approach

The type of relationship (from superficial to more intimate) influences whether help is provided or not, and the contrast between exchange and communal relationships appears crucial.

Exchange vs. communal relationships Interpersonal relations may be close or superficial. In close relationships (such as between friends), but not in superficial ones, people emphasize solidarity, interpersonal harmony and cohesiveness (see Chapter 10, this volume). In addition, in close relationships rewards for successful performance of a task are distributed according to the equality norm, whereas in superficial relationships rewards are distributed according to the contributions of each person to the task (on the basis of the equity norm; cf. Bierhoff, Buck & Klein, 1986).

Clark and Mills (1993; see also Clark & Grote, 2003) have contrasted exchange and communal relationships. Examples of *exchange relationships* are those between strangers or acquaintances, whereas *communal relationships* refer to relationships between friends, family members or romantic partners. In exchange relationships people strive for maximal rewards, whereas in communal relationships people are concerned with the other's welfare. Therefore, it is plausible to assume that in exchange relationships people are motivated by egoistic motives, whereas in communal relationships they are motivated by the desire to alleviate the suffering of the victim.

In accordance with this description, empirical studies show that people in exchange relationships respond positively to repayments for given benefits and keep careful track of individual inputs into joint tasks (Clark, 1984). For communal relationships a different pattern of results emerges. In a study by Clark, Mills and Powell (1986), students were led to believe that another student might need their help. Students who were in a communal relationship with the other student paid more attention to the other's need when no opportunity to repay was expected (in comparison with students who were in an exchange relationship). In contrast, when they expected that the other person would have an opportunity to reciprocate in kind in a later part of the experiment, the participants kept track of the needs of the other person with equal care in exchange and in communal relationships. This pattern of results suggests that people in communal relationships are more helpful than people in exchange relationships if no mutual give-and-take is expected (see also Clark, Ouellette, Powell & Milberg, 1987).

We mentioned that people in exchange relationships strive for positive consequences. They firmly believe that they must decide according to their self-interest and that doing otherwise would be foolish (Miller, 1999). This widely shared assumption of the appropriateness of economic thinking in exchange relationships is likely to restrict prosocial behaviour unless people can (be made to) believe that prosocial behaviour is actually in their own best interests. We call this 'trick' an exchange fiction.

The exchange fiction To organize one's life in terms of economic exchange would seem to be highly rational and to fit with the widely shared view that self-interest rules the world. Indeed, accounts of behaviour in terms of self-interest and rational choice are the dominant lay theories that people use in explaining their actions (Miller, 1999). Lay people tend to believe that it would be a waste of time not to pursue one's self-interest; they also fear ridicule if they fail to act in their own interest.

This emphasis on rational choice has negative implications for donations to charities. Recall the example of the high level of donations after the tsunami disaster in South Asia. Such donations are not fully compatible with the image of a self-interested person that many lay people have of themselves. Holmes, Miller and Lerner (2002) assumed that such people need a 'cover story' in order to donate money to charities. They need to explain their generosity as behaviour which actually serves their own self-interest. Although they may want to do what their compassion with the victims tells them to do, they hesitate because they prefer to give a reason for their monetary transactions (even gifts to charity) which is based on their self-interest.

> **exchange fiction** people need a cover story in order to donate money to charities. To fulfil this need, people are offered something in exchange for their donation which – although it is low in value – creates the impression that a generous contribution is also a rational exchange

Holmes et al. (2002) assumed that the *exchange fiction* would be especially compelling if people were confronted with charity collections which serve high-need victims, for example a collection to establish 'a training and remedial program for handicapped and emotionally disturbed children' (p. 146). They confirmed the effectiveness of the exchange fiction in high-need situations. Passers-by were approached by a representative of a charitable organization in a field experiment. Simply asking for a donation of at least $1 (standard solicitation) resulted in an average donation of 41 cents per person. In contrast, when the exchange framing was induced by offering a candle, on average $1.85 was donated. The passer-by was told that the candle was available for a bargain price of $3 which was said to be $1 lower than the normal store price. This information presumably induced a cognitive reframing of the request (i.e., shifting it from a 'charity' context into an 'exchange' context; cf. Cialdini & Goldstein, 2004).

One might argue that people in the bargain-price condition were still acting rationally because they bought the candle. But the results in the low-need condition tell a different story. In this condition, people were told that the money was needed to buy equipment for the local softball team. Here people gave on average about 30 cents in response to both appeals (see Figure 9.9). Therefore, the offer of the candle per se did not generally increase contributions. Only when the money was for children in high need, which presumably elicited compassion, did the offer of the candle have a positive effect on generosity. The exchange fiction seems to be a reliable technique for increasing people's willingness to donate money to charities that seek to help the especially needy.

Culture and society

People are rule followers (Messick, 2000). Social rules which are applied in specific social settings are internalized as the result of social learning. Once acquired, they are incorporated in a self-reinforcement system (Bandura, 1997). Social behaviour is influenced by factors that are inherent in cultural settings. There are cultural norms, values and rituals that are shared by the whole community; there are reciprocal expectations among the holders of social roles; and there are rights and obligations based on tradition and general ethical principles, such as the Declaration of Human Rights, which mould the attitudes of people in society (Doise, 2002).

Social institutions can promote prosocial values by means of interventions that encourage children to cooperate with one another by teaching them social skills such as perspective taking, fair play and concern for others (Battistich, Schnaps, Watson, Solomon & Lewis, 1997).

Social responsibility One of the most important 'do's' that children learn is described by the *norm of social responsibility*, which prescribes that individuals should help other people who are

> **norm of social responsibility** prescribes that people should help others who are dependent on them. It is contrasted with the norm of self-sufficiency, which implies that people should take care of themselves first

dependent on their help. Berkowitz (1978) assumed that prosocial behaviour is a direct function of how responsible people feel in a social situation. Earlier research had indicated that people worked harder on behalf of their partner the more dependent the partner was. Researchers assumed that perceived dependency elicited the norm of social responsibility, which in turn motivated prosocial responses. But prosocial activities require sacrifices, which can be avoided by passing the responsibility to others; and as we have seen, the presence of other people diffuses responsibility (see Berkowitz, 1978).

Normative beliefs are learned during the socialization process. In an attempt to integrate cultural rules with individual feelings,

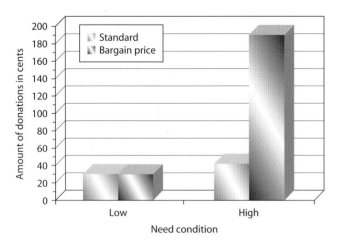

Figure 9.9 *Donations as a function of solicitation form and level of need (from Holmes et al., 2002, Exp. 2).*

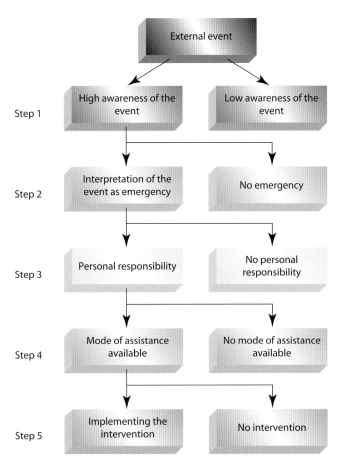

Figure 9.10 *Model of the intervention process (based on Latané & Darley, 1970).*

personal norm feeling of obligation to perform a specific action in accordance with personal values and normative beliefs

Schwartz (1977) coined the term *personal norm*. Because individuals differ with respect to their social learning of cultural values and rules, each person is characterized by a unique cognitive set of personal values and normative beliefs.

How are prosocial actions instigated? Latané and Darley (1970) proposed a five-step process model of prosocial behaviour (Figure 9.10). The first step of the process occurs when the person becomes *aware* that something is happening. The next step includes *interpretation* of the event as an emergency and recognition of the other's need. The third step centres on the generation of a sense of *personal responsibility*. In the fourth step the person may *generate available modes of assistance*. The final step of the model refers to *implementing the intervention* (i.e., acting or not) depending on the result of the decision process.

Now let us consider an example in which people were asked to read schoolbooks aloud to blind children (Schwartz, 1977). Becoming aware of the plight of blind children and recognizing their unfulfilled needs represent the first and second steps of the model (although in this case it need not necessarily be seen as an

'emergency'). In step 3 people may accept personal responsibility for improving the situation of blind children. In step 4 people ask whether effective actions to deal with the problem are available (such as reading to blind children). If the answer is positive, a decision to read to the blind children (step 5) is likely.

Personal responsibility is based on social values. Schwartz (1994) defines values as beliefs that pertain to desirable end states, transcend specific situations, guide selection or evaluation of behaviour, people and events, and are ordered by relative importance. On the basis of data from 44 countries, Schwartz identified 10 types of social values (e.g., achievement, conformity, security). Two values are immediately relevant for prosocial behaviour: benevolence and universalism. Whereas benevolence (i.e., concern for the welfare of close others) gives prosocial behaviour in personal relationships a value basis, universalism (i.e., concern for the welfare of all people and for nature) includes social justice and prosocial commitments on a worldwide scale. The tsunami disaster is a case in point: people all over the world donated money presumably because their value system told them it was the right thing to do.

Fairness norms Individuals follow normative expectations about the level of rewards that they themselves deserve and the costs that are fair and reasonable for them. In addition, people subscribe to the belief in a just world (Hafer & Bègue, 2005; Lerner, 1980). As a result, fairness norms are applied to one's own and to others' benefits and deprivations. If we receive outcomes that fall short of our standard of personal fairness, this arouses an egoistic motivation. A genuinely altruistic motivation comes into play once our own egoistic aspirations, which are related to the perceived fairness of our own position in the social system (Miller, 1977a), are met. Obviously, it is hard to act altruistically if this jeopardizes one's own fair treatment. In contrast, people who perceive their own outcomes as fair seem to be very sensitive with respect to the perceived unfair treatment of others (cf., Hoffman, 2000).

SUMMARY

In this central part of the chapter we have answered the question: 'Why do people help one another?' The answer provided integrates evolutionary and psychological theories. The evolutionary approach explains why people are more likely to help those who are genetically closer to themselves, but also to help friends, who are not genetically related. The psychological approach shows that mood and personality affect prosocial behaviour, and that some forms of helping are motivated altruistically (and not egoistically). People are also more likely to help in communal than in exchange relationships, when they believe they are acting in their own interests, and when guided by norms of social responsibility and fairness.

CONSEQUENCES OF RECEIVING HELP

How do the perspectives of helpers and of help-recipients differ from each other?

What are the possible negative consequences of being helped?

It is important to understand the differing perspectives of help-givers and help-recipients. Being helped is not always appreciated, because it sometimes has negative connotations. Receiving help can define the help-recipient as somebody who *needs* help, and it can make them indebted to the helper. To be defined as a help-recipient is particularly irritating when the help-recipient does not feel in need of help. An old man who is helped across the road, for example, may feel annoyed because he felt perfectly capable of crossing the road himself. Even if the help-recipient is in need of help, he may resent the implications of the offered help. Because receiving help establishes a debt to the helper, the freedom of choice of the help-recipient is restricted, and this is likely to arouse reactance (i.e., a desire to restore one's freedom; cf. Brehm & Brehm, 1981, and Chapter 7, this volume). In general, these negative aspects of help are assumed to become less important the greater is the need for help.

Donors and recipients have different perspectives in the giving–receiving relationship (Dunkel-Schetter, Blasband, Feinstein & Bennett, 1992). The donor profits from the fact that giving help is regarded as a desirable and fair thing to do. Although costs (time, money and effort, for example) are incurred, the positive consequences of giving help may outweigh the negative consequences. On the other hand, the recipient wants to prevent the other person from thinking that he is unable to manage on his own. Because of the negative implications of weakness and inferiority associated with receiving support, help-recipients are vulnerable to receiving aid. For example, black people who received unsolicited and unnecessary help from a white peer expressed lower self-esteem than blacks who received no imposed help (Schneider, Major, Luthanen & Crocker, 1996).

SUMMARY

Receiving and being seen to receive help is not always a positive experience. Help-givers need to be sensitive to the perspective of the help-recipient, to give help only when it is needed and without it constituting a threat to the help-recipient's self-esteem.

SUMMARY AND CONCLUSIONS

- Helping behaviour (which can include behaviour performed due to professional obligations) can be distinguished from more specific prosocial behaviour, and from altruism, which is motivated by compassion.

- Prosocial behaviour has costs as well as benefits, so sometimes does not occur, even when it is desperately needed.

- Prosocial behaviour is less likely to occur when other people are around because responsibility is diffused across bystanders, who then model passive behaviour to each other. The presence of others also reduces helping because it increases embarrassment. People may also fail to help because they lack competence, or are under time pressure.

- The theories developed to explain prosocial behaviour complement each other and may be applied simultaneously to reach a full understanding of the determinants of a specific episode of help or passivity.

- The evolutionary approach helps to explain why people are more likely to help those who are genetically closer to themselves, but also friends, who are not genetically related.

- The psychological approach shows that people are more likely to help when in a positive mood, but also when they feel guilt and when they have attributes of the prosocial personality (especially a sense of social responsibility, empathy and internal locus of control).

- Longer-term helping (e.g., volunteering) is a function of both egoistic and altruistic motivations.

- There is support for the empathy–altruism hypothesis in cases where prosocial behaviour is performed even when the helper could easily have avoided doing so; in this case the underlying motivation appears likely to be true altruism.

- People are also more likely to help in communal than in exchange relationships, when they believe they are serving their own interests, and when guided by norms of social responsibility and fairness.

- Receiving help is not unequivocally positive. It can imply weakness and need. It is therefore important that help-givers adopt the perspective of the help-recipient, give help sensitively and only when it is needed, and are careful not to threaten the help-recipient's self-esteem.

Note

1   The formula for calculating the corrected individual likelihood of intervention is $P_I = 1 - \sqrt[N]{1 - P_G}$, where P_G is the likelihood that at least one person intervenes in the group, and N is the number of group members. On the other hand, it is possible to calculate the corrected group likelihood of intervention on the basis of the individual intervention rate by the formula $P_G = 1 - (1 - P_I)^N$.

Suggestions for further reading

Batson, C.D. (1991). *The altruism question: Toward a social-psychological answer*. Hillsdale, NJ: Lawrence Erlbaum. On the basis of a historical overview of the altruism question, the empathy–altruism hypothesis is developed and research presented in its support.

Bierhoff, H.W. (2002). *Prosocial behaviour*. New York: Psychology Press. Summarizes research from developmental and social psychology. In addition, areas of applications are discussed in some detail (e.g., first aid, voluntary work engagement in organizations and unpaid volunteer work).

Clarke, D. (2003). *Pro-social and anti-social behaviour*. Hove: Routledge. Presents a short and informative overview and contrasts prosocial behaviour with aggression.

Miller, G. (2001). *The mating mind: How sexual choice shaped the evolution of human nature*. London: Vintage. A fresh approach to evolutionary psychology emphasizing the mechanism of sexual selection.

Piliavin, J.A. & Callero, P. (1991). *Giving blood: The development of an altruistic identity*. Baltimore: Johns Hopkins University Press. An example of applied research on prosocial behaviour.

Schroeder, D.A., Penner, L.A., Dovidio, J.F. & Piliavin, J.A. (1995). *The psychology of helping and altruism*. New York: McGraw-Hill. The most comprehensive monograph on prosocial behaviour currently available.

Spacapan, S. & Oskamp, S. (Eds.) (1992). *Helping and being helped: Naturalistic studies*. Newbury Park, CA: Sage. A collection of contributions examining prosocial behaviour in everyday life.

10

Affiliation, Attraction and Close Relationships

Abraham P. Buunk and Pieternel Dijkstra

CHAPTER OUTLINE

....

Humans are a very social breed. They seek each other's company in a variety of situations, they make friendships with other people, and they seem to find their ultimate happiness and despair in their intimate relationships. But what is it that drives us to interact socially with others? What determines the fact that we often quite rapidly find ourselves liking some people more than others? Such issues are dealt with in the present chapter. We begin with a discussion of affiliation, followed by a section on attraction and friendships, focusing on the factors that make individuals like other people and become friends with them. Next, we deal with the nature of romantic attraction and, finally, we deal with the development and dissolution of close relationships.

Introduction

....

Carl is in general a happy man. He enjoys having fun and spending time with his friends. Recently, he fell in love with Carin, a beautiful woman whom he had known for some time; however, Carin does not reciprocate his feelings. Since then, Carl has felt quite unhappy and at times lonely. Although he needs company because of his unhappiness, even being with his friends hardly improves his mood. Carin likes Carl, but just does not have romantic feelings for him. She feels that Carl lacks ambition, and is not the type of man she is looking for. Her closest girlfriend, with whom she discusses everything, agrees that Carl is not right for her.

Why does Carl feel so lonely? Why does being with his friends not improve his mood? And why does Carin find ambition such an important attribute in a mate? The social psychology of personal relationships helps us to answer all these questions, and explains why our close relationships with others can be such sources of personal happiness and fulfilment, but also of great sadness, even despair. This chapter will provide you with the tools to answer these questions, beginning with a consideration of why people need others in the first place.

AFFILIATION: THE NEED FOR SOCIAL CONTACT

When do we like to be in the company of others?
Does social support for other people help to reduce stress?
What are the health consequences of a lack of affiliation?

Situations fostering affiliation: When do people affiliate?

Humans have a general need to affiliate with others, and they spend a considerable part of their life in the company of other people. By *affiliation* we mean the tendency to seek out the company of others, even if we do not feel particularly close to them. According to the homeostatic model (O'Connor & Rosenblood, 1996), affiliation can be seen as a drive, in that people look for an optimal range of social contact. This model states that, when individuals experience too much solitude, they seek out social contact until their affiliative drive is satiated; and when they experience excess social contact, they seek out solitude to restore the optimum level of affiliation. It is generally assumed that the human desire for affiliation stems in large part from our evolutionary past, when joining others in the face of threat, such as predators and aggressors, enhanced our chances of survival. It has indeed been found that individuals are particularly likely to affiliate under conditions of stress, in which survival issues may become salient (e.g., Baumeister & Leary, 1995; Buunk & Schaufeli, 1993). Why would individuals affiliate when confronted with a stressful situation? Two theoretical answers to this question are particularly relevant, one stemming from social comparison theory and the other from attachment theory.

> **affiliation** the tendency to seek out the company of others, irrespective of the feelings towards such others

Social comparison According to *social comparison theory*, particularly in novel and stressful situations, individuals tend to seek out others to compare themselves with, to learn more about their own feelings and to obtain information about the most effective way of behaving. They may not know how to feel and respond: 'Am I too worried?', 'Should I be really concerned', 'Am I the only one who is so upset?' Affiliation with others facing the same situation gives individuals the opportunity to compare their responses with those of others, and thus to assess the appropriateness of their feelings (Festinger, 1954). In line with this theory, Schachter (1959) found that research participants under threat of receiving an electric shock preferred to be in the company of someone else who was also waiting to take part in the

> **social comparison theory** assumes that individuals seek out others to compare themselves with, to assess the appropriateness of their feelings and to obtain information about the most effective way of behaving

same experiment, rather than someone who was in a quite different situation, such as waiting for a professor. As Schachter concluded: 'Misery doesn't love just any kind of company, it loves only miserable company' (p. 24).

Knowledge about social comparison and affiliation has proven very useful in the area of psychology and health. Gump and Kulik (1997) found that participants who were faced with the prospect of undergoing experimentally induced pain spent more time looking at how other individuals responded who were to undergo the same threat than at individuals who were to participate in a very different experiment – their responses would not be relevant to compare with one's own responses. Social comparison with others may also provide individuals with valuable information, for example about how to deal with their own situation. As a result of this motive, individuals faced with a threat may prefer contact with someone knowledgeable, who may provide information about the potential threat. In their study Stanton, Danoff-Burg, Cameron, Snider and Kirk (1999) assigned breast cancer patients randomly to listen to an audiotaped interview in which another breast cancer patient's psychological adjustment and disease prognosis were manipulated to reflect good, poor or unspecified psychological and physical health status. Participants demonstrated a greater desire for information and emotional support from the patient with good rather than poor health status, but not more than from the patient with unspecified health status. Thus they did not profit from the opportunity to learn more about the patient with poor health status, which might in fact have been useful in putting their own situation into perspective and, indeed, making them feel comparatively better off.

Anxiety reduction A host of evidence indicates that individuals in threatening and stressful circumstances do often turn to sympathetic others who may offer them reassurance, comfort

Plate 10.1 *Social comparison with others may provide individuals with valuable information, for example about how to deal with their own illness.*

PIONEER

John Bowlby (1907–1990) started his intellectual career at the University of Cambridge where he studied developmental psychology and, later, child psychiatry and psychoanalysis. Upon returning from army service in 1945, Bowlby became head of the Children's Department at the Tavistock Clinic in London. Studying maladapted children, Bowlby felt that psychoanalysis was putting far too much emphasis on the child's fantasy world and far too little on actual events. As a result, Bowlby developed attachment theory, which states that a child's actual experiences within the family have far-reaching effects on his or her personality development. According to Bowlby, starting during the first months in their relationships with both parents, children build up so-called 'working models' of how attachment figures are likely to behave, and for the rest of their lives children's expectations are based on these models.

attachment theory proposes that the development of secure infant–caregiver attachment in childhood is the basis for the ability to maintain stable and intimate relationships in adulthood

and emotional support (e.g., Stroebe & Stroebe, 1996; Wills, 1991). The most important theory here is **attachment theory**, developed by John Bowlby (1969). This theory has both evolutionary and psychoanalytic underpinnings. With regard to evolution, in herds of social animals, stragglers on the open plains ran a greater risk of being attacked by predators, leading to a genetic propensity to respond to fear with a tendency to seek out the company of others. In psychoanalytic terms, attachment theory developed initially with a focus on new-borns and their relationships with caregivers. According to attachment theory, new-borns are equipped with a so-called attachment system, i.e., a set of built-in behaviours, such as crying and smiling, that helps keep the parent nearby, resulting in higher chances of survival and an increased level of protection. Attachment theory argues that affiliation is an innate tendency that is also apparent in other primates such as rhesus monkeys and chimpanzees, as well as in infants who, in response to danger signals, seek close contact with their mothers (Reis & Patrick, 1996; Shaver & Klinnert, 1982).

Numerous studies have demonstrated the tendency to seek out the company of reliable and dependable others in stressful situations. For instance, Kulik, Mahler and Moore (2003) found in a study of coronary-bypass patients that those who were assigned to a roommate who was post-operative rather than pre-operative were less anxious, were more mobile post-operatively and had shorter post-operative stays. Patients who had no roommate tended to have the slowest recoveries. The presence of others may, however, enhance anxiety and distress when the other person

present is nervous rather than calm. In such cases *emotional contagion* may occur: individuals unconsciously mimic others' facial expressions and feelings (e.g., Gump & Kulik, 1997, Study 2).

emotional contagion the unconscious mimicking of the facial expressions and feelings of another person

Social support and stress reduction

Whereas seeking out the company of others is an active strategy for reducing anxiety, having a supportive network of friends or relatives is something that is reliably associated with stress reduction. *Social support* refers to the feeling of being supported by others, and is usually divided into four components (House, 1981), i.e., *emotional* support (feeling cared for, loved and appreciated); *appraisal* support (feedback and social comparison on how to evaluate things); *informational* support (such as information about how to handle situations); and *instrumental* support (receiving concrete aid and help). The first three of these components correspond to the two functions of affiliation under stress that were mentioned above. In addition, social support often takes place 'invisibly', without individuals noticing that others are supporting them. A person may, for instance, not explicitly notice that his or her partner had done chores around the house, but nevertheless feel happy as a result that things at home seem to be going so well (Bolger, Zuckerman & Kessler, 2000). Numerous studies have found that social support is beneficial in terms of stress reduction, an effect that occurs with respect to such divergent stressors as the transition to parenthood, financial strain, health problems, work stress and even pain (e.g., Brown, Sheffield, Leary & Robinson, 2003; Karlin, Brondolo & Schwartz, 2003; see Stroebe & Stroebe, 1996, for a review).

social support the feeling of being supported by others, usually divided into four components: emotional support, appraisal support, informational support and instrumental support

Social support researchers have been particularly interested in the so-called **buffer effects of social support**, i.e., those instances where people who perceive that they are supported are less affected by stressful events than those who feel unsupported, because support counteracts or 'buffers' the negative consequences of stress for health and well-being. If the beneficial effects of social support are really due to the fact that it reduces stress, then these effects should be stronger for individuals in stressful situations than for individuals who are not in stressful situations. To study the stress-buffering effect of social support, a research study needs at least two levels of stress and two levels of social support. Then the buffering effect (an interaction between stress and social support) can be separated from main effects of either social support or stress on their own.

buffer effect of social support the effect that those who perceive themselves to be supported are less affected by stressful events and conditions than those who feel unsupported

For example, Winnubst, Marcelissen and Kleber (1982) found that individuals who felt more supported by their co-workers were less depressed when confronted with uncertainty about the future of their work. Another example of the buffering role of social support comes from a study by Cohen and Hoberman (1983). This

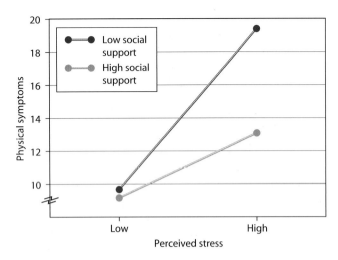

Figure 10.1 *The relationship between perceived stress and physical symptomatology for individuals low and high in social support (based on Cohen & Hoberman, 1983).*

study showed that individuals who felt that their life was very stressful had many more physical symptoms such as headaches, insomnia and weight loss if they also perceived themselves to have a low level of support from others (see Figure 10.1). Buffer effects may make individuals relatively immune to stress even when they simply *perceive* that there are others available who may be willing to help (Cohen & Wills, 1985). For instance, Sarason and Sarason (1986) found that participants who were informed they *could* turn to the experimenter if they had any questions or needed help for another reason (but actually never did) were better able to perform on a stressful task than were participants who did not have this opportunity, supposedly because this opportunity reduced feelings of stress. This effect, however, was found only for participants who scored low on the social support questionnaire, a measure of the number of others one can turn to for help, and the degree of satisfaction with this help.

Lack of affiliation, loneliness and health

One of the most direct and obvious signs of a lack of affiliation and social support is **loneliness**. Loneliness is a complex affective response stemming from a felt deficit in the number and nature of one's social relationships. According to Weiss (1975), there are two distinct forms of loneliness: *emotional loneliness*, which results from the absence of an intimate partner, and *social loneliness*, which is due to the absence of supportive friends and ties to a social network. In general, the absence of an intimate partner cannot be compensated for by supportive friends, or vice versa. Stroebe, Stroebe,

loneliness a complex affective response stemming from felt deficits in the number and nature of one's social relationships

Abakoumkin and Schut (1996) found, for instance, that widowed individuals experienced more emotional loneliness, but not more social loneliness, than married people. This study also reported that both widowed and married individuals with little social support experienced more social loneliness, but not more emotional loneliness, than individuals who had extensive social support available in their social network (see Jones & Hebb, 2003, for a review).

Why can't the loss of a marriage partner be compensated for by supportive friends? Attachment theory provides an explanation. Although attachment begins as a set of innate signals that call the adult to the baby's side, as time passes children form an enduring affectional bond with their caregivers. But the need for felt security is ageless: adult humans will also function optimally if they have a trusted figure on whom they can rely. Therefore, the attachment system will be functional throughout the human life span, with pair-bonds being the adult form of attachment in childhood. If adults lose the attachment bond with a partner, they will respond similarly to a child that is separated from her parents: they will experience great distress and, initially, a strong impulse to re-establish contact, followed by a period of depressed mood and, eventually, emotional detachment.

A lack of affiliation not only leads to loneliness, it may also have serious health consequences. In a pioneering study, Berkman and Syme (1979) examined which individuals from a sample first questioned in 1965 had died nine years later. Those who had passed away appeared to have been socially isolated: they were more often unmarried, had fewer good and frequent contacts with friends and families, and were less often members of church and other organizations. Whereas for men being married was more important for survival, for women having intense relationships with friends and family played a key role. These differences in mortality were attributed to effects of affiliation as such, rather than the fact that those less socially connected lived more unhealthily, or that those with a disability were less well able to establish and maintain social ties. Since this pioneering study, over a dozen different *epidemiological studies* have shown mortality effects of a lack of social integration, particularly for men (e.g., Rutledge, Matthews, Lui, Stone & Cauley, 2003).

epidemiological studies research studies dealing with the incidence, distribution and possible control of diseases and other factors relating to health and illness

SUMMARY

Humans generally need to affiliate with others, especially under conditions of stress. We compare ourselves with others to reduce anxiety and to gain information and emotional support. Social support from others buffers the impact of high stress, staves off loneliness and promotes better health and longevity.

ATTRACTION AND THE DEVELOPMENT OF FRIENDSHIPS

....

How does the physical environment affect interpersonal attraction and the development of friendships?

Do people tend to like others who have the same attitudes as they do?

Why is physical attractiveness so important?

What are the main characteristics of friendship?

In many situations individuals affiliate without consciously choosing the company of specific others (Berscheid, 1985). For example, individuals may join a sports club without feeling particularly attracted to the members of that club, or move to a new neighbourhood without knowing who their neighbours will be. Interestingly, however, there is ample evidence that affiliation may foster friendship. This occurs partly because of physical *propinquity*, or simply being close to others. In addition, factors such as similarity of attitudes and physical attractiveness play a role in the development of friendships.

> **propinquity** physical closeness to others, for example living in the same neighbourhood or sitting next to others in the classroom

The physical environment

Individuals tend to like those they are with – many studies have shown that simply being in the physical presence of another individual will enhance the probability of becoming friends with that person. The pioneering study on this issue was done over 50 years ago by Festinger, Schachter and Back (1950) in Westgate

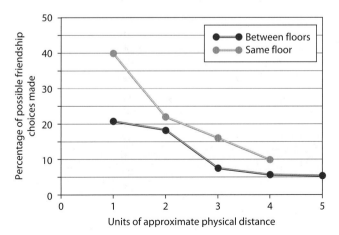

Figure 10.2 *Propinquity and friendship choice (based on Festinger et al., 1950).*

West, a housing complex for student couples consisting of 17 buildings, each with 10 apartments on two floors. Couples were assigned to them on the basis of a waiting list. After a number of months, more than 10 times as many friendships appeared to have developed with others within the same building than with others in different buildings. But even within the same building, physical propinquity, or proximity, was a powerful influence (see Figure 10.2). More friendships had developed with others on the same floor than with others on different floors, and the more doors away another couple lived on the same floor, the less often a friendship had developed with the other couple. Similar findings have been obtained in many other studies. For example, a study in a police academy found that cadets particularly became friends with those whose last names began with the same letter or with a nearby letter in the alphabet. This effect occurred because classroom seats were assigned in alphabetical order of cadets' surnames (Segal, 1974).

There may be several reasons why propinquity leads to *attraction*, as many other studies have shown. There are simply fewer barriers to developing a friendship with someone close by. Even climbing a stairway to see someone on a different floor is more trouble than just seeing the people next door. By regularly being in the company of another person, we also obtain more information about them, and have the opportunity to discover mutual interests and common attitudes. Propinquity may also lead to attraction through the so-called *mere exposure effect* (Bornstein & D'Agostino, 1992; see also Chapter 6, this volume). This was shown in a study by Saegert, Swap and Zajonc (1973), who manipulated frequency of exposure unobtrusively by having each participant spend a different number of trials of about 40 seconds with each of five other participants. The more often a participant had met another participant in the experiment, the more that person was liked.

> **attraction** positive feelings towards another individual, including a tendency to seek out the presence of the other

The role of environmental propinquity in fostering attraction may depend on various other factors. Perhaps the most important effect of propinquity is in increasing the likelihood of contact. This was shown in the Westgate West housing complex by the finding that, when asked whom they knew, apartment dwellers consistently chose next-door neighbours. If they lived on the upper floor they did not know anyone downstairs except the two families by the stairs (particularly the ones by the mailbox). The effects of propinquity are also especially pronounced when the participants are quite similar. For instance, in the Festinger et al. (1950) study, all participants were either war veterans or students. Propinquity may also *decrease* attraction by making the unpleasant characteristics of others more noticeable. As a consequence, it is often not only the most-liked others who live close by, but also the most-*dis*liked others (Ebbesen, Kjos & Konecni, 1976).

Compared to the early 1950s, when Festinger conducted his research, nowadays physical proximity seems of less importance, at least in the initial stages of affiliation and attraction. With the creation and expansion of the Internet, modern means such as dating sites, chat rooms and email have become available to large groups of individuals, making it much easier to affiliate and become friends, even lovers, with individuals at a great geographical distance. In addition to overcoming geographical distance, the Internet can help individuals overcome other barriers to relationship initiation, such as inhibitions about one's appearance, shyness and traditional sex roles (Scharlott & Christ, 1995). Although, eventually, individuals may want to meet each other in person and geographical distance then does become salient, by that time the emotional attachment may have grown so strong that individuals perceive the geographical distance as less of an obstacle to continuing their relationship compared with individuals in relationships that are initiated and maintained face to face (Ben-Ze'ev, 2004). However, the lack of physical propinquity does seem to take its toll in another way: in general (romantic) relationships that are initiated and maintained through the Internet are less committed, less serious and contain more misrepresentations than face-to-face relationships (Cornwell & Lundgren, 2001).

Despite all this evidence concerning the importance of proximity, we should emphasize that physical distance is not the only factor that determines the probability of meeting. Social factors (e.g., school, university, sports clubs) also influence the likelihood of meeting and, in addition, they have the effect of resulting in similarity on many factors. Homogamy (marriage between people from similar social or educational backgrounds) is not totally due to a preference for similar others, but to the fact that we mainly meet similar others (at least in situations that facilitate the development of romantic relationships).

The similarity of attitudes

Similarity is, in general, a potent factor fostering attraction and friendships. This is consistent with Festinger's (1954) social comparison theory, which states that we mostly compare ourselves with *similar* others. Friends have been found to be more similar to one another than non-friends in, for instance, age, marital status, race and intelligence (Hays, 1988). Attitude similarity, in particular, appears to lead to attraction. Just a century ago, in 1905, the Dutch psychologist Heymans and his colleague Wiersma found that people were more often married to others who had similar attitudes with respect to, for example, caring about good eating and drinking, politics and religion (Schuster & Elderton, 1906). However, this and other studies of similarity between married couples are open to various causal interpretations. Thus Newcomb (1961) undertook a classic study which measured attitudes *before* people met each other. In his study in a student housing complex, Newcomb found that students were most attracted to others with similar attitudes on a range of topics.

However Newcomb's evidence, like that of other studies on attitudinal similarity, was still only correlational. Therefore Byrne (1971) developed his now well-known *attraction paradigm*, in which participants fill out an attitude questionnaire such as the one presented in Figure 10.3. A few weeks later they are given an attitude questionnaire which they assume has been filled out by another person. In fact, it has been completed by the experimenter so as to express attitudes of varying degrees of similarity or dissimilarity to the participant. Experiments using this paradigm have consistently shown that attraction is a direct linear function of the

Classical Music (check one)
- I dislike classical music very much.
- I dislike classical music.
- I dislike classical music to a slight degree.
- I enjoy classical music to a slight degree.
- I enjoy classical music.
- I enjoy classical music very much.

Sports (check one)
- I enjoy sports very much.
- I enjoy sports.
- I enjoy sports to a slight degree.
- I dislike sports to a slight degree.
- I dislike sports.
- I dislike sports very much.

Welfare Legislation (check one)
- I am very much opposed to increased welfare legislation.
- I am opposed to increased welfare legislation.
- I am mildly opposed to increased welfare legislation.
- I am mildly in favour of increased welfare legislation.
- I am in favour of increased welfare legislation.
- I am very much in favour of increased welfare legislation.

War (check one)
- I feel strongly that war is sometimes necessary to solve world problems.
- I feel that war is sometimes necessary to solve world problems.
- I feel that perhaps war is sometimes necessary to solve world problems.
- I feel that perhaps war is never necessary to solve world problems.
- I feel that war is never necessary to solve world problems.
- I feel strongly that war is never necessary to solve world problems.

Strict Discipline (check one)
- I am very much against strict discipline of children.
- I am against strict discipline of children.
- I am mildly against strict discipline of children.
- I am mildly in favour of strict disciplining of children.
- I am in favour of strict disciplining of children.
- I am very much in favour of strict disciplining of children.

Divorce (check one)
- I am very much opposed to divorce.
- I am opposed to divorce.
- I am mildly opposed to divorce.
- I am mildly in favour of divorce.
- I am in favour of divorce.
- I am very much in favour of divorce.

Figure 10.3 *Attitude similarity questionnaire (based on Byrne, 1971).*

proportion of similar attitudes (i.e., the number of similar attitudes divided by the total number of similar and dissimilar attitudes). This so-called law of attraction has also been found to occur when the individual meets the other in person (e.g., Griffit & Veitch, 1974).

Why is attitude similarity so important? The major explanation given by Byrne (1971) is based on classical conditioning. Byrne showed that hearing someone express similar attitudes evokes positive affect, and that hearing someone express dissimilar attitudes evokes negative affect. Next, Byrne showed that such affective responses can be conditioned to other persons. A person whose picture was present when participants were simultaneously listening to the expression of similar attitudes was liked more than when the same picture was presented while participants listened to someone expressing dissimilar attitudes. Of course, one could argue that this could be the result of thinking that the person in the picture was the one expressing the attitudes. However, in a subsequent study, Byrne showed that conditioning also occurred when the statements could not be attributed to the person in the picture, because he or she was of the opposite sex to the person expressing the attitudes.

Although the link between attitude similarity and attraction is a very robust one, there are a number of qualifications to this general pattern. First, attitude similarity affects attraction particularly for attitudes that are *important* for an individual (Byrne, London & Griffitt, 1968). Second, individuals tend to assume that others have attitudes similar to their own, and when no information is provided about another person, they may feel as attracted to him or her as when they learn the other has similar attitudes. That is, individuals may feel more put off by dissimilar others than attracted to similar others (Rosenbaum, 1986; Singh & Ho, 2000). Third, it may be that learning that someone prefers the same free-time activities, rather than attitude similarity, is important for friendship (Werner & Parmelee, 1979), casting some doubt upon Byrne's (1971) assumption that attitude similarity leads to attraction because it is intrinsically rewarding. Finally, complementarity is more important than similarity when it comes to interpersonal styles, such as dominance and submissiveness. For example, Dryer and Horowitz (1997) found that dominant individuals were most satisfied interacting with individuals who were instructed to play a submissive role, whereas submissive individuals were more satisfied interacting with individuals who were instructed to play a dominant role.

Physical attractiveness

Like similarity, physical attractiveness is a key determinant of attraction. Although physical attractiveness is more important for romantic relationships, it also influences the development of friendships. That is, individuals tend to like physically attractive individuals. Physical attractiveness has its effect via a positive stereotype, often called the 'what is beautiful is good' stereotype: when someone is beautiful, we automatically attribute many other positive characteristics to them (Feingold, 1992). Although attractive people are viewed as more snobbish, less modest and less faithful (e.g., Singh, 2004), they are especially perceived as more sexually exciting and more socially skilled than unattractive people, but also as more sociable, more assertive and in better mental health.

These stereotypes are not completely unfounded. Although the personality and behavioural characteristics of attractive people are, overall, not very different from those of unattractive people, attractive people have been found to be less lonely, less socially anxious, more socially skilled and more popular with the opposite sex (Feingold, 1992). Probably, from the beginning of their life, attractive people receive more positive attention and will, through a so-called *self-fulfilling prophecy* (see Chapter 3, this volume),

Plate 10.2 *Attractive people have been found to be less lonely, less socially anxious, more socially skilled and more popular with the opposite sex.*

become more self-confident in their social life. This process was shown in a study by Snyder, Tanke and Berscheid (1977). These investigators led male participants to believe that they were conducting a 'getting acquainted' telephone conversation with an attractive versus an unattractive woman. Remarkably, the women who were *believed* to be attractive (though they were not actually more attractive) became, as a consequence of the more positive behaviours of the males towards them, more friendly and sociable, whereas the women assumed to be physically unattractive became cool and aloof during the conversation.

It must be noted, however, that the physical attractiveness stereotype is not as strong or general as suggested by the phrase 'what is beautiful is good' (Eagly, Ashmore & Longo, 1992). Compared to unattractive targets, attractive targets are especially perceived as more socially competent and, to a lesser extent, better adjusted and intellectually competent. However, attractive targets are generally not perceived as higher in integrity and concern for others. In addition, the physical attractiveness stereotype has less effect when individuating information is presented, for example, information about the personality and background of a target person (Eagly et al., 1992).

Friendship as a relationship

Even when environmental factors are conducive, and even when a high degree of attitude similarity exists, a friendship between two people may still not develop. The beginning of a friendship is characterized by *mutuality* of attraction, and this may give rise to the *voluntary interdependence* that is typical of friendships (Hays, 1988). That is, individuals involved in such relationships are motivated to invest in their relationship, to coordinate their behaviours and to take the interests of the other into account. In friendships throughout the life cycle, and in all social groups, such interdependence implies *reciprocity* in terms of helping, respecting and supporting each other (Hartup & Stevens, 1997; see also Chapter 9, this volume).

A useful theoretical model for analysing relationships, including friendship, is *social exchange theory*. This general approach views relationships in terms of rewards and costs to those involved. It emphasizes that individuals expect certain levels of 'outcomes' on the basis of what they put into a relationship. A related perspective is *equity theory*, according to which those who have the feeling of giving more to their friends than they receive – the 'deprived' – as well as those who feel they receive more than they give – the 'advantaged' – will be less happy in their friendships than those who perceive a reciprocal, i.e., fair or equitable, exchange (Walster, Walster & Berscheid, 1978).

It is easy to see why 'deprived' individuals are unhappy in their relationships: they are being 'cheated' and may feel angry and resentful. But why should 'advantaged' individuals also experience discomfort? Because they are doing *too* well, and may feel guilty as a consequence. Thus although, of course, it is better to be

reciprocity the basic rule in interpersonal relationships that one can expect to obtain assets such as status, attractiveness, support and love to the degree that one provides such assets oneself

social exchange theory views social relations in terms of rewards and costs to those involved; argues that social relations take the form of social exchange processes

equity theory assumes that satisfaction is a function of the ratio of outcomes to inputs of the person as compared with those of a reference other, and that individuals will try to restore equity when they find themselves in an inequitable situation

(a)

(b)

Plates 10.3a and b *Women disclose more intimate things in their relationships with friends than men do, while men look for friends with similar interests.*

'advantaged' than 'deprived', both being 'advantaged' and being 'deprived' undermine satisfaction with the relationship. Indeed, Buunk and Prins (1998) found that those who felt advantaged, as well as those who felt deprived, with respect to the giving and receiving of support in their relationship with their best friend felt more lonely than those who felt this relationship was reciprocal. The importance of reciprocity for friendships is also apparent from the most important rules in friendship: volunteering help in time of need, respecting the friend's privacy, keeping confidences, trusting and confiding in each other, standing up for the other in his or her absence and not criticizing each other in public (Argyle & Henderson, 1985). According to evolutionary theorists, the sensitivity to reciprocity in friendships and other relationships is the result of the evolution of the human species in which maintaining mutually supportive relationships was crucial for survival (Buunk & Schaufeli, 1999; see also Chapter 9, this volume).

Gender and friendship

In general, women want others as friends to whom they can talk about intimate issues such as feelings and problems. Women also disclose more intimate things in their relationships with friends than men do. In contrast, men look for friends with similar interests, emphasize more the joint undertaking of activities and do not give a high priority to discussing feelings (Fehr, 2004; Sherrod, 1989). When men and women interact with same-sex friends, men are also more dominant, whereas women are more agreeable (Suh, Moskowitz, Fournier & Zuroff, 2004).

Why are friendships between men less intimate than those between and with women? The main reason seems to be that women are simply more likely than men to engage in the kinds of behaviours that produce *intimacy*. Research shows that this difference is not due to the fact that men have a different conception of intimacy or are less socially skilled than women. For instance, in their study, Reis, Senchak and Solomon (1985) found that both men and women agreed that interactions involving personal self-disclosure (e.g., discussing a relationship break-up) are indicative of intimacy. However, when interacting with a same-sex friend, men chose not to engage in intimate self-disclosure. Thus, it seems that, although men and women agree on the path to intimacy, men simply *choose* not to follow it. The question then remains why men are less motivated than women to engage in intimate self-disclosure with same-sex friends. Evolutionary theorists argue that evolution has favoured a male preference for so-called instrumental friendships, i.e., relationships that revolve around common activities rather than shared emotions, because men had to collaborate in hunting and fighting. In contrast, women had to establish and maintain a network of nurturing relationships aimed at taking care of and raising children (De Waal, 1983).

> **intimacy** a state in interpersonal relationships that is characterized by sharing of feelings, and that is based upon caring, understanding and validation

SUMMARY

Many factors conspire to determine whether friendships develop, including physical proximity, similarity of attitudes and interests, and physical attractiveness. Friendship is a special form of relationship, guided by expectancies and rules. Women tend to be more intimate in their friendships and to disclose more than men.

ROMANTIC ATTRACTION

What characterizes and stimulates romantic attraction?
Which attachment styles can be distinguished and how does each style influence individuals' romantic relationships?
Is physical attractiveness equally important to men and women, heterosexuals and homosexuals?

Romantic love

Falling in love or feeling sexually attracted to someone is experienced quite differently from liking someone and developing a friendship with him or her. To differentiate between different types of love, Sternberg and Barnes (1988) proposed the so-called triangular theory of love, which holds that three different ingredients combine to form different types of love. The first component of love is *intimacy* and refers to close, connected and bonded feelings in loving relationships. The second component is *passion*, characterized by physical arousal and emotional and/or sexual longing. The final ingredient of love is *commitment*, that is, the decision to remain with each other and work to maintain the relationship. Each component can vary in intensity, from low to high, and when combined, eight types of love occur (see Figure 10.4): (1) non-love (intimacy, commitment and passion are all absent, such as the relationship between client and shopkeeper); (2) liking (intimacy is high but passion and commitment are low); (3) infatuation (passion is high but intimacy and commitment are low, for instance, individuals feel sexually attracted to someone they barely know); (4) empty love (commitment is high but passion and intimacy are low); (5) romantic love (intimacy and passion are high but commitment is low, such as in summer love affairs); (6) companionate love (intimacy and commitment are high but passion is low, such as in lifelong friendships); (7) fatuous love (passion and commitment are high, while intimacy is low, such as in whirlwind courtships); and (8) consummate or 'complete' love (commitment, passion and intimacy are all high).

According to the triangular theory of love, passion (or sexual attraction) is one of the defining characteristics that distinguishes romantic love from platonic love or liking. Indeed, romantic relationships are, especially in the beginning, often characterized

Plate 10.4 *According to the triangular theory of love, passion (or sexual attraction) is one of the defining characteristics that distinguishes romantic love from platonic love or liking.*

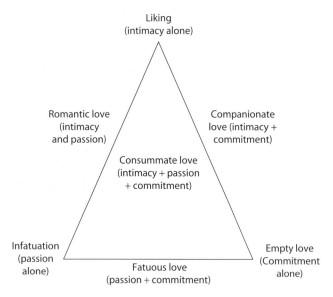

Figure 10.4 *The types of love as different combinations of the three components (Sternberg & Barnes, 1988).*

PIONEERS

Ellen S. Berscheid (b. 1936; PhD 1965, University of Minnesota; currently Regents Professor, University of Minnesota) and **Elaine Hatfield** (b. 1937; PhD Stanford University, 1963; currently Professor, University of Hawaii) have together made numerous major contributions to the study of close interpersonal relationships. Hatfield was awarded the Society of Experimental Social Psychology's Distinguished Scientist Award in 1993. Their key publications include four co-authored volumes: E. Berscheid & E. Hatfield, *Interpersonal attraction* (New York: Addison-Wesley, 1969); E. Hatfield, G. W. Walster & E. Berscheid, *Equity: Theory and research* (Boston: Allyn & Bacon, 1978); E. Hatfield & G. W. Walster, *A new look at love* (Lanham, MD: University Press of America, 1978); and E. Berscheid & E. Hatfield, *Interpersonal attraction*, 2nd edn (Reading, MA: Addison-Wesley, 1978). Berscheid also co-authored the chapter (with H. Reis) 'Attraction and close relationships' in D.T. Gilbert, S.T. Fiske & G. Lindzey (Eds.), *The handbook of social psychology*, 4th edn (Boston: McGraw-Hill, 1998), pp. 193–281.

by *passionate love* (Hatfield, 1988). Berscheid and Walster (1974) proposed that passionate love requires two components. The first is a state of physiological arousal, due to either positive emotions such as sexual gratification and excitement, or negative emotions such as frustration, fear and rejection. The second component of passionate love consists of labelling this arousal as 'passion', or 'being in love'.

passionate love a state of intense longing for union with another individual, usually characterized by intrusive thinking and preoccupation with the partner, idealization of the other and the desire to know the other as well as the desire to be known by the other

What factors enhance the feeling of love or passion? Surprisingly, not only positive but also negative emotions may fuel passion (Aron, Norman, Aron, McKenna & Heyman, 2000; see also Research close-up 10.1). For example, White, Fishbein and Rutstein (1981, Experiment 2) showed that not only seeing a comedy but also watching a film depicting killing and mutilation enhanced romantic attraction to a woman seen subsequently on a videotape. Similarly, a study by Dutton and Aron (1974) found that men who had been frightened, by giving them the prospect of receiving an electric shock, found a woman with whom they were supposed to participate in a learning experiment much sexier and more attractive than did men who had learned they were just going to receive a barely perceptible tingle of a shock. To explain the finding that fear and adrenaline can fuel sexual attraction and feelings of passion, researchers proposed that a process of *misattribution of arousal* may be involved (Dutton & Aron, 1974; White et al., 1981; see also Chapter 3, pp. 54–55). That is, when

RESEARCH CLOSE-UP 10.1

Novel activities as a way to increase relationship quality

Aron, A., Norman, C.C., Aron, E.N., McKenna, C. & Heyman, R. (2000). Couples' shared participation in novel and arousing activities and experienced relationship quality. *Journal of Personality and Social Psychology, 78,* 273–283.

Introduction

This experiment examines the effect of shared participation in novel and arousing activities on relationship quality. In the early years of a relationship initial exhilaration is due to the novelty and arousal of forming the relationship. With the inevitable decline of this novelty and arousal, relationship satisfaction usually declines too. Aron et al. hypothesize that shared participation in novel activities will increase relationship quality and suggest several mechanisms that may account for this effect. Shared participation in novel activities may, for instance, enhance relationship quality through a process of misattribution of arousal or because it reinforces a sense of interdependence and closeness.

Method

Participants
Sixty-three married couples from New York participated in the experiment.

Design and procedure
The design was a 3 (condition: novel-arousing vs. mundane vs. no activity) × 2 (measurement phase: pre-test vs. post-test) 'mixed' design, with repeated measures on the second factor. First, in separate rooms, both partners filled in a questionnaire about the quality of their relationship (pre-test index of relationship quality). Next, couples were randomly assigned to one of three experimental conditions: a novel-arousing condition, a mundane task condition and a no-activity condition. In the

novel-arousing condition, partners were invited into a large room, where they were bound to their partner on one side by means of straps at the wrist and ankle. Participants were instructed to travel back and forth throughout the room, remaining on their hands and knees, and to carry a pillow with them without using hands, arms or teeth (this could only be done by holding it between their heads or bodies). They were given four trials to complete the task in under 1 minute. The mundane task was designed to be as similar as possible but less novel and arousing. Partner 1 had to roll a ball to the centre of the room while on hands and knees. Partner 2 then crawled to the centre of the room and retrieved the ball from partner 1. Couples in the mundane task condition were ordered to carry out the task slowly. After the experiment both partners, in separate rooms, again filled in a questionnaire about their relationship containing different questions to those in the pre-test questionnaire (post-test index of relationship quality). While couples in the other conditions participated in the experimental activity, participants in the no-activity condition stayed in their separate rooms filling in some additional questionnaires.

Results

Consistent with the hypothesis, couples in the novel-arousing condition showed more change in relationship quality (between pre- and post-test) than couples in the mundane task condition and couples in the no-activity condition. The latter two showed a similar change.

Discussion

This experiment is the first to address issues of boredom and excitement in close relationships. It is also significant from an applied perspective. It shows that shared participation in novel activities provides an easily managed route for improving relationship quality. A limitation of this experiment is that it demonstrates an effect without identifying the specific mechanisms that are involved.

interpreting their feelings, individuals may attribute their arousal to the wrong source: other influences that are exciting are overlooked and individuals attribute their arousal to the presence of an attractive person. The process of misattribution, for instance, supposedly led the male participants in the Dutton and Aron study to believe that they were sexually attracted to the female participant rather than feeling apprehensive because of the prospect of receiving an electric shock.

According to Foster, Witcher, Campbell and Green (1998), the intensifying effect of arousal on attraction is not so much due to the misattribution of arousal, but rather reflects an automatic process that occurs immediately, without awareness of the person

involved. According to evolutionary theorists romantic attraction consists of such an automatic and intense emotional experience because, although affiliation and friendship may also have fostered survival, sexual attraction is crucial to the survival of the human species (Kenrick & Trost, 1989).

Individual differences in romantic love

Attachment style Intimate relationships are also affected by individual experiences and histories. According to attachment theory, introduced earlier, children unconsciously develop a specific attachment style (that is, a global orientation towards relationships and love) in response to the way they are treated by their caregivers. Individuals whose caregivers were responsive to their needs when they were in distress will most likely develop a secure attachment style. They will view others as trustworthy, dependable and helpful. In contrast, individuals whose caregivers showed a lack of responsiveness, rejection or physical and emotional abuse are more likely to develop one of two insecure attachment styles. They may adopt either an 'avoidant' style, characterized by distance from others and a cynical view of others as untrustworthy and undependable, or an 'anxious-ambivalent' style, characterized by a strong desire to be close to others, combined with a fear that others will not respond to this desire (Gallo, Smith & Ruiz, 2003; Hazan & Shaver, 1987; Mikelson, Kessler & Shaver, 1997; Reis & Patrick, 1996, see Figure 10.5). Because attachment styles are thought to be relatively stable over time, it is assumed that in adult life individuals' attachment style will influence their relationship with their partner in a manner comparable to the way that in childhood attachment styles influence the relationship between children and their parents. Research has shown that, with regard to many aspects of individuals' love lives, attachment styles exert a powerful influence. For instance, research has found that, compared to individuals with insecure attachment styles, those with a secure attachment are less jealous (e.g., Buunk, 1997), seek support more easily (Simpson, Rholes & Nelligan, 1992), are less afraid of being abandoned (Davis, Shaver & Vernon, 2003), tend to trust their partners more (Mikulincer, 1998), have more satisfying and stable relationships (Simpson, 1990) and report higher levels of the three components of love, that is, commitment, intimacy and passion.

Bartholomew and Horowitz (1991) have argued that the avoidant attachment style is, in fact, more complex than originally assumed and have suggested two types of avoidant attachment. First, individuals may want intimate relationships with others but avoid them because they are afraid of being hurt (fearful attachment style). Second, individuals may avoid intimacy because they genuinely prefer freedom and independence to closeness with others (dismissing attachment style). Bartholomew and Horowitz

Question: Which of the following best describes your feelings?

Secure: I find it relatively easy to get close to others and am comfortable depending on them and having them depend on me. I don't often worry about being abandoned or about someone getting too close to me.

Avoidant: I am somewhat uncomfortable being close to others; I find it difficult to trust them completely, difficult to allow myself to depend on them. I am nervous when anyone gets too close, and often love partners want to be more intimate than I feel comfortable being.

Anxious/Ambivalent: I find that others are reluctant to get as close as I would like. I often worry that my partner doesn't really love me or won't want to stay with me. I want to merge completely with another person, and this desire sometimes scares people away.

Figure 10.5 *Measure of attachment styles used by Hazan and Shaver (1987).*

	Views of self	
	Positive	Negative
Views of others — Positive	secure	preoccupied
Negative	dismissing	fearful

Figure 10.6 *Four-category model of adult attachment (Bartholomew & Horowitz, 1991).*

(1991) therefore proposed a four-category model in which, in addition to the secure attachment style, three insecure attachment styles are distinguished, that is, a preoccupied attachment style (similar to the anxious-ambivalent attachment style in the three-category model), a dismissing attachment style and a fearful attachment style. These four styles can be arranged along two dimensions, namely global evaluations of self (1) and global evaluations of others (2) (see Figure 10.6).

It is important to note that classification systems such as attachment styles and the types of love proposed by Sternberg and Barnes should not be strictly considered as distinct categories. The more sophisticated way to think about attachment and love is to see individuals' orientations towards relationships being shaped around certain themes, such as intimacy, commitment and passion (triangular love theory) and evaluations of self and others (attachment theory).

Partner selection criteria Despite the differences between romantic and platonic love, to some extent the chances of developing a romantic relationship with someone else are determined by the same factors that are important for the development of friendship. Propinquity makes the beginning of romantic attraction more likely, and similarity is also important for love relationships. For example, individuals feel romantically most attracted to others with the same attachment style (Klohnen & Luo, 2003) and similar attitudes (Byrne, Ervin & Lambert, 1970). Physical attractiveness is also a strong determinant of romantic attraction (e.g., Walster, Aronson, Abrahams & Rottmann, 1966).

Gender differences in preferences for physical attractiveness and status Although both men and women value physical attractiveness in a potential partner, physical attractiveness is in general a more important determinant of romantic attraction for males than it is for females. Buss (1989) found in a study conducted in 37 cultures that, although both genders rated physical attractiveness as important in most cultures, men found it more important than women did. In a study among individuals of 20, 30, 40, 50 and 60 years of age, Buunk, Dijkstra, Fetchenhauer and Kenrick (2002) found that in all age groups men preferred partners who were higher in physical attractiveness than themselves. The higher value placed by males upon physical attractiveness is in line with *evolutionary theory* (Buss, 1994). According to this perspective, males have been selected to prefer women who are likely

evolutionary theory explains human behaviour, including differences in partner preferences according to gender, from their reproductive value, i.e., their value in producing offspring in our evolutionary past

Plate 10.5 *Males in different cultures are attracted by women who have an 'hourglass figure'.*

Plate 10.6 *Personal advertisements in newspapers are one way to find a partner.*

to produce healthy babies and who are likely to raise such children successfully. Therefore, men would have become particularly sensitive to signs of youth, health and reproductive value. Signs of youth are indeed important cues for female attractiveness in all cultures (Cunningham, Roberts, Barbee, Druen & Wu, 1995). Several studies, for instance, have found that males in different cultures are attracted by women who have a waist-to-hip ratio (WHR) of 0.7 (that is, an 'hourglass figure'). Medical research has found these women to be not only relatively more healthy but also more fertile, i.e., to have a higher conception rate than women with higher WHRs (Singh, 1993).

According to the evolutionary perspective, females had a better chance of their offspring surviving when they selected males who could provide them with the necessary resources, and women would thus have become particularly sensitive to signs of status and dominance. In his study in 37 cultures, Buss (1989) found that women valued a partner's social status and wealth more than men did. In addition, women also placed a relatively high value on a partner's social dominance, i.e., a partner's level of self-confidence, initiative, assertiveness, extraversion, ascendance and authoritativeness (Sadalla, Kenrick & Vershure, 1987). These characteristics will, in general, provide a dominant man a higher status and more resources than a non-dominant man. In addition, Buunk et al. (2002) found that in all age groups that they studied (from 20 to 60 years of age) women preferred partners who were higher in income, education, self-confidence, intelligence, dominance and social position than they were themselves. In part this can be explained on the basis of economic considerations on the part of women. Since traditionally the social status of women derived from that of the husband, they had to look for status and

were therefore less free to select a mate on the basis of physical attractiveness. However, women also value physical features in men that are related to a man's social status, such as height (Buss, 1994), and physical features that are indicative of a man's level of dominance, such as strength, muscularity, athleticism, prominent jaws (e.g., Cunningham, Barbee & Pike, 1990) and a V-shaped upperbody (Dijkstra & Buunk, 2001; see also Research close-up 10.2). These latter features signal high levels of testosterone, a hormone which is responsible for muscle development as well as for dominant behaviour (Dabbs & Dabbs, 2000).

Studies examining personal advertisements have shown that homosexual men and women have very similar mate preferences to heterosexuals of the same sex. However, compared to heterosexual men, homosexual men place an even stronger emphasis on physical and sexual characteristics of potential mates (e.g., Gonzales & Meyers, 1993; Hatala & Prehodka, 1996).

Although individuals may desire partners who are physically highly attractive, they are most likely to end up with partners that have about the same degree of physical attractiveness as they have themselves (e.g., Yela & Sangrador, 2001). In general, individuals are more likely to approach those who offer acceptance than rejection. As a consequence, in order to reduce the risk of rejection, most individuals will adapt their standards for a partner to their own level of physical attractiveness (Stroebe, Insko, Thompson & Layton, 1971; Walster et al., 1966). They select as partners not those who are most attractive but those who are about as attractive as themselves and are relatively likely to respond positively to their approach. This is referred to as the *matching principle*. Matching is, however, a broad process. Although individuals tend to pair off with individuals of similar levels of physical attractiveness, sometimes notable mismatches in physical attractiveness may occur – as when, for instance, Anna Nicole Smith, a 26-year-old Play Mate, married J. Howard Marshall II, an 89-year-old billionaire (see Plate 10.7). In line with equity theory (Walster et al., 1978), however, differences in physical attractiveness such as these will be compensated for by other assets, such as money or status, as was the case in the Smith–Marshall match.

RESEARCH CLOSE-UP 10.2

Gender differences in sexual jealousy

Dijkstra, P. & Buunk, A.P. (1998). Jealousy as a function of rival characteristics: An evolutionary perspective. *Personality and Social Psychology Bulletin, 24*, 1158–1166.

Introduction

Jealousy is generated by a threat to, or the actual loss of, a valued relationship with another person, due to an actual or imagined rival for one's partner's attention. This experiment examines the extent to which men and women differ in the type of rival that evokes jealousy. In general, especially rivals with a high mate value, i.e., who are considered attractive by the opposite sex, will pose a threat to the relationship and will, consequently, evoke feelings of jealousy. According to evolutionary psychology, men and women, however, differ in the characteristics they value in a partner. Whereas men value a partner's physical attractiveness more than women do, women value a partner's social dominance – i.e., his level of self-confidence, assertiveness, extraversion, ascendance and authoritativeness – more than men do. As jealousy is evoked by characteristics of the rival that are important to the other sex, it was expected that jealousy in men would be evoked by a rival's social dominance whereas jealousy in women would be evoked by a rival's physical attractiveness.

Method

Participants

Seventy-five male and 77 female students were recruited as participants.

Design and procedure

The experimental design manipulated two factors, between subjects. The overall design was 2 (participant sex: male/female)

× 2 (physical attractiveness of the rival: low/high) × 2 (social dominance of the rival: low/high). Participants were randomly assigned to one of the experimental conditions. Participants were presented with a scenario in which the participant's partner was flirting with an individual of the opposite sex. Participants then received one of four profiles of an opposite-sex rival for their partner's attention, consisting of a photograph (low or high in attractiveness) and a personality description (low or high in social dominance). Participants rated how suspicious, betrayed, worried, distrustful, jealous, rejected, hurt, anxious, angry, threatened, sad and upset they would feel if this situation occurred to them in real life.

Results

Before analysing the main data, the researchers verified that they had successfully manipulated both a rival's social dominance and physical attractiveness. Analyses on the main dependent variable – jealousy – showed that the hypothesis was supported.

Discussion

This study contributes to the literature by illuminating sex differences in the impact of rival characteristics consistent with predictions from evolutionary psychology. A limitation of the study (for that matter, of most studies on jealousy) is that the method assesses 'projected' responses ('how would you feel if...') in contrast to 'real' responses. However, alternative methods hardly provide better solutions. Attempts to create jealousy in existing relationships would be unethical, whereas observations of naturally occurring incidents of jealousy would lack adequate experimental control.

Plate 10.7 *Mismatches in physical attractiveness may occur – as when Anna Nicole Smith, a 26-year-old Play Mate, married J. Howard Marshall II, an 89-year-old billionaire.*

SUMMARY

Psychologists have distinguished several different kinds of love and identified individual differences in romantic love, based on attachment styles. Physical attractiveness is an important factor in love for women and, especially, men, and for heterosexuals and, especially, homosexuals. But physical attractiveness is not all-important and can be offset by assets such as wealth or status.

CLOSE RELATIONSHIPS: SATISFACTION AND DISSOLUTION

....

What makes a close relationship happy and satisfying?
What is commitment, and how does it come about?
What consequences do break-up and divorce have for mental and physical well-being?

Satisfaction in relationships

Once individuals have established a mutual attraction, they may begin to develop a voluntary interdependent relationship by increasing their mutual involvement. Some relationships will become happy, satisfying and stable, while others will be characterized by conflicts and problems and are likely to end sooner or later. In general, a high degree of intimacy is characteristic for happy couples. According to Reis and Patrick (1996), interactions are experienced as intimate when three conditions are met:

1. *Caring*: we feel that our partner loves us and cares about us.

2. *Understanding*: we feel that our partner has an accurate view of how we see ourself, and that our partner knows our important needs, beliefs, feelings and life circumstances (Swann, de la Ronde & Hixon, 1994). Evidence also suggests, however, that marital satisfaction is particularly high for those whose partner does not perceive them as *accurately* as possible, but in a *more positive way* than they see themselves (Murray, Holmes & Griffin, 1996).

3. *Validation*: we feel that our partner communicates his or her acceptance, acknowledgement and support for our point of view (Fincham, Paleari & Regalia, 2002). In contrast, couples are less happy the more they show conflict avoidance, soothing (ignoring and covering up differences) and destructive communication, such as criticizing and complaining (see Noller & Fitzpatrick, 1990; Schaap, Buunk & Kerkstra, 1988).

Individuals with insecure attachment styles, in particular, have problems with developing intimacy: they are less likely to engage in cooperative problem solving, less effective in providing the partner with comfort and emotional support (Reis & Patrick, 1996) and more reactive to recent negative spouse behaviour (Feeney, 2002). When their partner says, for instance, something crude or inconsiderate, those with an insecure attachment style respond more often with destructive responses, either by actively harming the relationship (e.g., yelling at the partner) or by passively harming the relationship (e.g., refusing to discuss relationship problems). In contrast, those with a secure attachment style are more likely to respond by actively attempting to resolve the problem by,

for example, discussing the situation and suggesting solutions to problems (Gaines & Henderson, 2002; Gaines et al., 1997).

A typical feature of individuals with unhappy close relationships is that they tend to make *distress-maintaining* attributions that attribute a partner's negative actions to internal, stable and global causes. These attributions regard a partner's negative actions as deliberate, routine and indicative of the partner's behaviour in other situations. Unhappy partners also tend to attribute a partner's positive behaviour to external, unstable and specific causes, regarding it as unintended, accidental and specific to the situation. Happy people tend to make opposite, i.e., *relationship-enhancing*, attributions in which positive actions by the partner are judged to be intentional, habitual and indicative of the partner's behaviour in other situations, and negative behaviours are seen as accidental, unusual and limited. Thus, in contrast to unhappy people who blame their partner for their mistakes and flaws, happy people excuse their partner's negative behaviour with external, unstable and specific attributions. As a consequence, individuals satisfied with their relationship tend to give their partners more credit for resolving conflict, tend to blame themselves more for inconveniencing the other and tend to forgive their partners more easily for their mistakes (e.g., Fincham et al., 2002; McNulty, Karney & McNulty, 2004; Thompson & Kelley, 1981). Research has shown that a maladaptive attributional pattern predicts a decline in marital satisfaction (Fincham & Bradbury, 1991).

Happy couples also tend to interpret *social comparisons* with other couples in such a way that they feel better about their own relationship, whereas unhappy couples mainly look more at the negative implications of such comparisons. Unhappily married people often feel envious when they see others having a better marriage, and feel worried that the same might happen to them when they encounter couples with more serious marital problems than they have (Buunk, Collins, Taylor, VanYperen & Dakoff, 1990). In contrast, partners in happy couples tend to perceive their own partner and their own relationship in a very positive light compared to other partners and relationships (Buunk & Van den Eijnden, 1997), feel that they have much more control over potential difficulties than people in the typical relationship, and are more optimistic about the future of their relationship (Murray & Holmes, 1997). Perceptions of the partner and relationship have been found to predict whether the relationship persists or ends (Rusbult, Lange, Wildschut, Yovetich & Verette, 2000).

A final aspect that distinguishes happy from unhappy couples is the degree of *equity*. As noted above, equity theory assumes that individuals in close relationships expect a reciprocal and fair exchange. In evaluating this exchange, individuals may consider a variety of inputs to and outcomes from the relationship, including love, support, financial contributions and household tasks (VanYperen & Buunk, 1991). As is the case in friendships, as mentioned previously, numerous studies have shown that in romantic relationships too distress occurs among the 'advantaged', who feel guilty because they receive more from the relationship than they believe they deserve. But distress is felt especially by the 'deprived', who feel sad, frustrated, angry and hurt because they receive less than they believe they deserve. As shown in Figure 10.7, a study by Buunk and VanYperen (1991) found that those who perceived equity in their relationship were most satisfied, followed by those

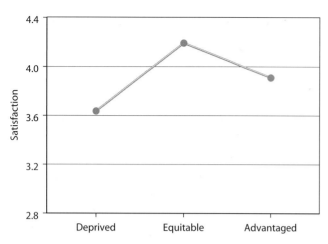

Figure 10.7 *Equity and satisfaction in intimate relationships (based on Buunk & VanYperen, 1991).*

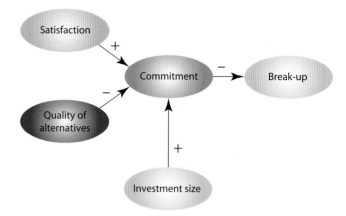

Figure 10.8 *The investment model.*

who felt advantaged; those who felt deprived experienced the lowest level of satisfaction (see also Gleason, Iida, Bolger & Shrout, 2003; Sprecher, 2001). Inequity can have serious consequences for the relationship. For instance, women (but not men) in inequitable relationships are more likely to desire and to engage in extramarital relationships than are women in equitable relationships (Prins, Buunk & VanYperen, 1992).

Commitment in relationships

It would seem self-evident that people who are satisfied with their relationship will also stick with their partners, and that unhappy couples will eventually end their relationship. Nevertheless, social scientists have long observed that happy relationships are not necessarily stable relationships, and that stable relationships are not necessarily happy relationships (Rusbult & Buunk, 1993). Rusbult (1983) proposed the ***investment model*** to explain what makes people motivated to maintain their relationships, i.e., what factors enhance ***commitment*** to these relationships (see Figure 10.8). According to Rusbult, commitment refers to the individual's tendency both to maintain a relationship and to feel psychologically attached to it. Such commitment is based upon three factors, the first two of which are: (1) a high level of *satisfaction*, i.e., an individual loves her partner and has positive feelings about the relationship, and (2) a low perceived *quality of alternatives*, i.e., the best imagined alternative relationship to the present relationship, the appeal of living alone, what is simultaneously available in addition to the present relationship (such as an interesting job or good friends) and the actual presence of an alternative partner (Buunk, 1987). When developing a relationship, individuals will gradually close themselves off,

> **investment model** theory that assumes that commitment to a relationship is based upon high satisfaction, low quality of alternatives and a high level of investments
>
> **commitment** the individual's tendency both to maintain a relationship and to feel psychologically attached to it

behaviourally and cognitively, from attractive alternatives, for instance by derogating attractive individuals of the opposite sex (Johnson & Rusbult, 1989).

Many relationships suffer unhappy periods, even including extreme aggression (see Chapter 8, this volume). But even when the alternatives are quite attractive, that does not necessarily mean they fall apart. Therefore, the investment model proposes a third variable: (3) *investment size*. This refers to the variety of ways in which individuals become linked to their partner, by putting time and energy into their relationship, by making sacrifices, by developing mutual friends, by developing shared memories and by engaging in activities, hobbies and possessions that are integrated in the relationship. High investments increase commitment, regardless of the quality of alternatives and the level of satisfaction, by increasing the costs of leaving the relationship. According to Aron and his colleagues, during the course of a relationship the selves of both partners begin to overlap and become interconnected. Benefiting the other is seen as benefiting oneself and, through identification, one begins to feel as if one shares the traits and abilities of the other (Aron, Aron & Smollan, 1992; Aron, Aron, Tudor & Nelson, 1991).

A substantial number of studies have shown that all three factors – satisfaction, alternatives and investments – are necessary to predict commitment and the likelihood of breaking up a relationship, and this applies to both heterosexual and homosexual relationships (Rusbult & Buunk, 1993). Moreover, commitment has been found to affect a wide variety of behaviours. In general, highly committed individuals are more willing to make sacrifices for their relationship: they are more likely to give up other activities in their life, such as career, religion or friends, in order to maintain their relationship (Van Lange et al., 1997). They are also more likely to forgive their partners for their betrayal and mistakes (Finkel, Rusbult, Kumashiro & Hannon, 2002). Rusbult and Martz (1995), for instance, found that battered women who sought refuge at a shelter were more likely to return to their partner after departure from the shelter when they had a high commitment to their partner prior to entering the shelter. In addition, less-committed individuals are more inclined to engage in extradyadic sex (e.g., Drigotas, Safstrom & Gentilia, 1999) and are also more likely to have unprotected sex outside the relationship without taking precautions to protect their steady partner against the possible health risks of this behaviour (Buunk & Bakker, 1997).

The consequences of break-ups

The break-up of a relationship, especially when marriage ends in a divorce, may have serious consequences, both financial and, of more interest here, psychological. Research has confirmed that the mental and physical health of divorced people is worse than that of married individuals, and even worse than that of people who have been widowed or those who never married. One of the reasons for this is that obtaining a divorce may in some cases be a consequence, instead of a cause, of mental problems (Cochrane, 1988; Stroebe & Stroebe, 1986). Nevertheless, ending a marriage through divorce is in itself a painful process. As attachment theory suggests, spouses usually develop – even in the face of the most serious hostility and fights – an emotional attachment that cannot easily be dissolved even if they want to. Indeed, many people who have divorced or separated remain emotionally attached to their ex-partner, as is shown by, for instance, spending a lot of time thinking about the former relationship, wondering what the ex-partner is doing or doubting that the divorce has really happened (Ganong & Coleman, 1994; Kitson, 1982). As suggested by attachment theory, individuals with different attachment styles respond differently to relationship break-ups. In a survey of 5,000 Internet users, Davis et al. (2003) found that preoccupied attachment was associated with more extreme emotional distress, exaggerated attempts to re-establish the relationship, angry and vengeful behaviour and dysfunctional coping strategies such as drug and alcohol use. Avoidant attachment was associated with more avoidant coping strategies, such as the suppression of emotions, whereas secure attachment was related to social coping strategies, i.e., using friends and family as 'safe havens'.

In addition to having to relinquish their attachment to a former spouse, divorced people are often confronted with the transition from being married to being single. Living alone, after having lived with a partner for a long time, usually requires considerable adjustment. It is often difficult to maintain earlier, couple-based friendships and, consequently, new relationships have to be initiated and built. Moreover, adapting to a different, lower social status can be a painful process, especially because there is still some stigma attached to being divorced. In addition, divorcees usually receive less support than widowed people, because friends may side with the former spouse. Furthermore, divorcees often have to deal with feelings of failure and rejection. Also, after the dissolution of marriage or cohabitation, former partners' economic standing often declines, leaving a substantial proportion of them, especially women, in poverty (e.g., Avellar & Smock, 2005). However, adjustment to divorce is easier for some individuals than for others. For example, individuals who took the initiative to divorce, who are embedded in social networks and who have found a new satisfying, intimate relationship are relatively better off. In addition, certain personality characteristics, including high self-esteem, independence, tolerance for change and egalitarian sex-role attitudes, facilitate coping with divorce (Price-Bonham, Wright & Pittman, 1983), as does attributing the break-up to

relationship problems rather than to oneself or one's ex-partners (Tashiro & Frazier, 2003).

SUMMARY

Happy and satisfied close relationships are characterized by high intimacy, based on caring, understanding and validation. Partners in such relationships tend to make relationship-enhancing attributions, positive social comparisons with other couples, and to perceive their relationship as equitable. People maintain their relationships because of their commitment to the relationship, based on satisfaction, low perceived quality of alternatives and high investment. The break-up of relationships is associated with serious psychological consequences which, however, can be surmounted by social support and new, satisfying relationships.

 ## SUMMARY AND CONCLUSIONS

- The need to affiliate with others is a basic human drive that is particularly enhanced in stressful situations.

- Social comparison and anxiety reduction are two major motives underlying affiliation under stress.

- Those with deficiencies in their social relationships experience relatively more loneliness and health problems.

- The physical proximity of others, as well as similarity in attitudes, promotes the development of relationships such as friendships and love relationships.

- Reciprocity, interdependence and, particularly for women, intimacy are characteristic for all personal relationships.

- More than friendships, love relationships are fostered by feelings of passion and physical attractiveness, with men paying more attention to signs of youth and health, and women more to signs of status.

- Satisfying love relationships are characterized by constructive communication, positive interpretations of the partner's behaviour, equity and favourable perceptions of one's own relationship in comparison with that of others.

- Commitment develops on the basis of a high satisfaction, combined with increasing investments in the relationship, and with decreasing attention to alternative options.

- Due to the strong attachment that usually develops in intimate relationships, break-ups and divorces are painful processes.

- Various coping strategies and personality attributes may help divorced individuals adjust to the new situation.

Suggestions for further reading

Brehm, S.S., Miller, R.S., Perlman, D. & Campbell, S.M. (2002). *Intimate relationships*. Boston: McGraw-Hill. An accessible introduction to the field of close relationships.

Buss, D.M. (1994). *The evolution of desire: Strategies of human mating*. New York: Basic Books. An interesting, well-written book on the socio-evolutionary approach to romantic attraction and close relationships.

Fletcher, G. (2002). *The new science of intimate relationships*. Malden, MA: Blackwell. A thorough and up-to-date review of the theories about and processes in intimate relationships.

Harvey, J. & Wenzel, A. (Eds.) (2001). *Close romantic relationships: Maintenance and enhancement*. Mahwah, NJ: Lawrence Erlbaum. A reader with a variety of perspectives on how individuals maintain close relationships.

Hinde, R.A. (1997). *Relationships: A dialectical perspective*. Hove: Psychology Press. A very thorough, broad and in-depth review of all aspects of close relationships.

Lerner, M.J. & Mikula, G. (Eds.) (1994). *Entitlement and the affectional bond: Justice in close relationships*. New York: Plenum Press. A useful reader on equity, social exchange and justice in dating, marital and family relationships.

Noller, P. & Fitzpatrick, M.A. (Eds.) (1988). *Perspectives on marital interaction*. Clevedon/Philadelphia: Multilingual Matters. A well-composed reader of chapters dealing particularly with marital communication.

Sarason, B.R., Sarason, I.G. & Pierce, G.R. (Eds.) (1990). *Social support: An interactional view*. New York: Wiley. An excellent volume on all aspects of and approaches to social support.

Sternberg, R.J. & Barnes, M.L. (Eds.) (1988). *The psychology of love*. New Haven, CT: Yale University Press. Chapters review various approaches to love.

11 Social Influence

Miles Hewstone and Robin Martin

KEY CONCEPTS

autokinetic effect
compliance
consistency
conversion
deindividuation
door-in-the-face technique
evaluation apprehension
foot-in-the-door technique
group polarization
groupthink
informational influence
lowballing technique
majority influence
   (conformity)
minority influence
   (innovation)
norms
normative influence
obedience to authority
referent informational
   influence
self-categorization theory
social comparison
social facilitation
social influence
whistleblowing

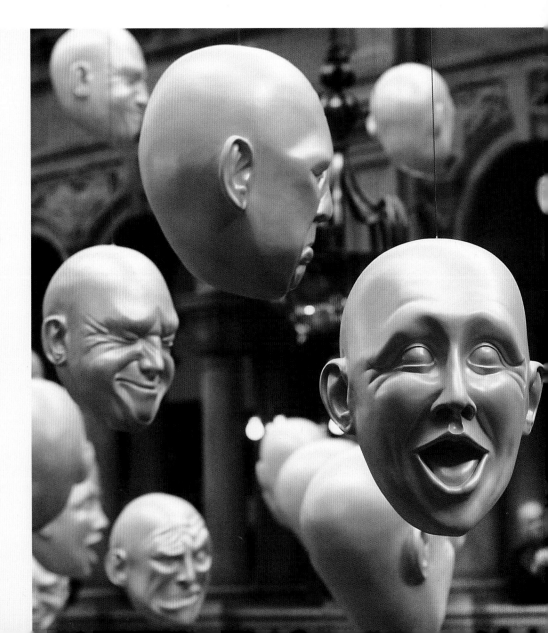

CHAPTER OUTLINE

....

This chapter considers two main types of social influence, both of which can be understood in terms of fundamental motives. First, we discuss 'incidental' social influence, where people are influenced by the presence or implied presence of others, although there has been no explicit attempt to influence them. We consider the impact of the mere presence of other people on task performance, and the impact of social norms. In the second part of the chapter, we ask why people succumb to social influence, highlighting types of social influence and motives underlying influence on the part of the target of influence. In the third part of the chapter, we turn to 'deliberate' social influence. We introduce theory and research on compliance, the influence of numerical majorities and minorities, group decision-making and obedience. Throughout we will see that social influence is an ambivalent concept. On the one hand, it is the glue of society: it makes things work, and society would be utterly chaotic without it. But on the other hand it can be a dark force, underlying some of the most extreme, even immoral, forms of human social behaviour.

Introduction

....

On a typical day most of us will be exposed to a large variety of social influences. You might be on your way to a lecture when you see three of your friends turning left, away from the psychology department, towards the café. Although no one has tried to persuade you, you are influenced to fol-low them and drink coffee instead of justifying your student loan. Why? As you later sit sipping your cappuccino, the topic turns to the use of animals in experimentation, and you find yourself out of line with your three friends, who all try to convince you that such studies are unnecessary and unethical. You try to counter their objections, doing your best to offer 'strong' persuasive counter-arguments. Then you head back to the university and run into the lecturer whom you failed to meet yesterday as agreed. She tells you to come and see her that afternoon; meekly, you obey.

As we noted when introducing the field of social psychology (see Chapter 1, this volume), one of the pioneers of the field, Gordon Allport, actually defined social psychology as 'the attempt to understand and explain how the thoughts, feelings, and behaviors of individuals are influenced by the actual, imagined, or implied presence of other human beings' (1954a, p. 5). So at one level, the study of *social influence* is as broad and diverse as the study of social psychology itself.

> **social influence** change of attitudes, beliefs, opinions, values and behaviour as a result of being exposed to other individuals' attitudes, beliefs, opinions, values and behaviour

This chapter focuses on both 'incidental' and 'deliberate' influence. We begin by looking at how the presence or implied presence of others can affect behaviour in the form of task performance, although there has been no explicit attempt at influence. We then review the impact of social norms on social behaviour, where it is more the implied presence rather than the actual presence of others that is influential. We show how norms are transmitted, and how they can influence a wide variety of human social behaviour, including our perceptions of physical phenomena and our behaviour towards other people.

Linking the two broad categories of influence, in the second part of the chapter we ask why social influence occurs. We consider group functions that social influence serves, and the key distinction between normative and informational types of social influence. Finally, we integrate different approaches by highlighting four major motives for social influence: 'effective action', 'building and maintaining relationships', 'managing the self-concept' and 'understanding'.

In the third part of the chapter we turn to deliberate influence, what might be considered the core of social influence. We introduce theory and research on compliance, the influence of numerical majorities and minorities, group decision-making and obedience. There are, obviously, close links between these instances of deliberate social influence and the area of persuasive communication and attitude change, described earlier (see Chapter 7, this volume). We will highlight these links, in particular, when

discussing majority and minority influence, where we will draw parallels with the elaboration likelihood model of persuasion (Petty & Cacioppo, 1986a; Petty & Wegener, 1999). Social influence is also involved in leadership (see Chapter 13, this volume) and in health promotion (see Chapter 15, this volume). This chapter constitutes the interface between the individualistic analysis of social influence processes and the chapters on group processes.

One important difference between the phenomena of this chapter and those of Chapter 7 is that social influence is more general than attitude change. Social influence involves change not only of attitudes but also of beliefs, opinions, values and behaviour, as a result of being exposed to other individuals' attitudes, beliefs, opinions, values and behaviour.

INCIDENTAL SOCIAL INFLUENCE

....

What effect does the presence of other people have on task performance?
What are social norms, and how are they formed and transmitted?

Social facilitation and social inhibition

The most obvious example of incidental influence is that the presence of one or more other people, even though they are not *trying* in any way to influence us, has an impact on our behaviour. We have already referred to Triplett's (1898) classic observation that cyclists rode faster when racing together than when racing alone (see Chapter 1, this volume). This is now understood to be the first demonstration of the phenomenon of *social facilitation* (F. Allport, 1924), whereby the presence of others leads to improved performance. However, neither the phenomenon nor its explanation has turned out to be straightforward. Following the initial demonstration, researchers conducted numerous studies using a variety of tasks, yielding mixed results. Some studies showed performance improvement as a result of the presence of others, while other studies showed performance impairment. Three main explanations have been proposed, but it is now widely accepted that no single explanation accounts for all the findings and a multifaceted approach is needed.

social facilitation/social inhibition an improvement in the performance of well-learned/easy tasks and a worsening of performance of poorly learned/difficult tasks due to the presence of members of the same species

Mere presence and drive theory Zajonc (1965) highlighted the importance of the task people performed in the presence of others. He suggested that mere presence of others leads to

improved performance on well-learned or easy tasks (social facilitation), but to impaired performance on tasks which are not (yet) well learned and which may therefore be perceived as difficult or complex (social inhibition). The mere presence of others facilitates responses that take precedence in an individual's behavioural repertoire (so-called dominant responses, such as pedalling when on a bicycle, which have a higher likelihood of elicitation than other responses). But mere presence inhibits novel and complicated responses that the individual has never or only infrequently performed before (so-called non-dominant responses). People will, then, perform better when others are present than when they are working alone *if* the facilitation of well-learned responses and the inhibition of novel responses are appropriate for successful task completion. Thus, performing well-learned physical motor skills or simple tasks should result in higher performance in the presence of others than when working alone. In contrast, in complex reasoning or problem-solving tasks, requiring concentration and complex cognitive activity, the presence of others interferes with successful task completion (see Figure 11.1).

Why does the mere presence of others enhance the emission of dominant responses? Zajonc (1980) used Hull-Spence drive theory (see Spence, 1956) to argue that the physical presence of others of the same species leads to an innate increase in arousal, i.e., a readiness to respond to whatever unexpected action the others might undertake. This results in an increased emission of dominant responses at the expense of non-dominant responses. In order to emphasize that the effect was based on simple drive rather than on high-level information processing, Zajonc even demonstrated social facilitation with cockroaches rather than undergraduates! (See Zajonc, Heingartner & Herman, 1969.)

Evaluation apprehension Cottrell (1968, 1972) challenged Zajonc's explanation, by suggesting that increased arousal constitutes a learned response to the presence of others rather than an innate response. According to Cottrell, task performers have learned to associate the presence of other people with performance *evaluation*, which, in turn, is linked to the anticipation of positive or negative outcomes. The presence of others will only elicit arousal and

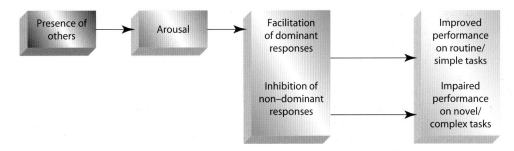

Figure 11.1 *Social facilitation/inhibition on simple versus difficult tasks (according to Zajonc, 1965, 1980).*

the accompanying facilitation of dominant responses (and inhibition of non-dominant responses) *if* task performers anticipate being evaluated by these others.

> **evaluation apprehension** concern about being appraised by others causes arousal leading to social facilitation, because people have learned to be apprehensive about being evaluated by others

Of course, we would have difficulty in applying Cottrell's concept of *evaluation apprehension* to cockroaches, ants and chickens, which have also shown social facilitation/inhibition (SFI) effects, or to tasks that involve little threat of evaluation, such as putting on or removing items of clothing, on which researchers have also demonstrated social facilitation effects (Markus, 1978). Yet, there is some experimental support for Cottrell's explanation. Research has shown that SFI effects are often eliminated when the salience of evaluation apprehension is decreased, by allowing task performers to give their responses privately rather than publicly, or by having non-evaluative audiences (Henchy & Glass, 1968; Sasfy & Okun, 1974). Further evidence comes from research showing that it is not task difficulty *per se* but the subjective expectation that one will perform well (or poorly) and that one will receive positive (or negative) outcomes that improves (or interferes with) task performance (Sanna, 1992; Sanna & Shotland, 1990). Robinson-Staveley and Cooper (1990) provided a clever demonstration of the role of expectation, in a study where participants performed a computer task alone or in the presence of another person. When participants held positive expectations about success on the task, the accuracy of their performance improved in the presence of another person, but when they held negative expectations, the reverse occurred (see Figure 11.2).

Attention conflict   Sanders and his colleagues (Sanders, 1981; Sanders, Baron & Moore, 1978) proposed that the presence of others may produce a response conflict between attending to the task itself, on the one hand, and attending to these other people, on the other hand. Others' presence may be distracting because of noises or gestures, anticipated reactions of approval or disapproval, and people's tendency to make social comparisons (see below). Since some of the attention needed to meet the task demands will be directed at the other people, one may expect a general impairment of task performance on all kinds of tasks, either well learned or not well learned. This distraction interferes with the attention given to the task and creates an internal response conflict that can only be overcome with greater effort. The attention conflict enhances

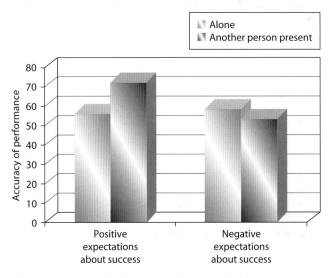

Figure 11.2 *Social facilitation as a function of task expectations and the presence of others (data from Robinson-Staveley & Cooper, 1990).*

arousal, resulting in the pattern of results noted above – facilitation of dominant responses and inhibition of non-dominant responses.

Integration   There is now general acceptance that we need to adopt a multifaceted approach to explain why the presence of others on individual task performance moves from benign to harmful as the perceived complexity of the task increases (Guerin, 1993). The presence of others may interfere with our ability to learn tasks, since learning implies that the most likely (dominant) responses are not yet the correct ones. However, once the required responses have become well learned and routine, the presence of others may improve performance. Given that most tasks in everyday life involve routine as well as non-routine activities, how important are social facilitation effects? A comprehensive meta-analysis by Bond and Titus (1983) concluded that the mere presence of others accounts for only a very small proportion of the variance in individual productivity (for other significant influences on group productivity, see Chapter 12, this volume). Nonetheless, we have seen that the presence of others can be a significant, albeit unintended, influence on task performance. As we will now see, that influence is much more significant when those others constitute a source of information about which norms should guide our behaviour in social situations.

The impact of social norms

The most fundamental concept in the study of social influence is that of social *norms*. Social norms are rules and standards that are understood by members of a group; they constitute belief systems about how (not) to behave, thus they guide behaviour but without the force of laws, and they reflect group members' shared expectations about typical or desirable activities (Cialdini & Trost, 1998; Levine & Moreland, 1998; Prislin & Wood, 2005). Norms have a number of key functions. First, they help to reduce uncertainty about how to behave appropriately (see van den Bos & Lind, 2002). For example, we know how to behave in some situations (e.g., a mosque) because we have seen how people behave in similar situations (e.g., a church). Second, norms help to coordinate individual behaviour. For example, punctuality reduces coordination losses for other group members – a meeting cannot start until all members are present, so it is important to be punctual so that others do not waste their time. Third, norms help with the distribution of outcomes. If three people are co-writing a chapter, norms help to decide the order in which the names should appear. Norms typically constrain us all, to some degree (e.g., even when you are in a hurry, you have to join the back of the queue to buy a ticket), but we each also benefit from the structure and order they provide (e.g., in the UK, at least, people waiting for some service typically form an orderly queue, and you are likely to be served when it is your turn, without having to protest).

> **norms** belief systems about how (not) to behave, which guide behaviour but without the force of laws, and which reflect group members' shared expectations about typical or desirable activities

Norms also include an evaluative component. Merely complying with a norm (e.g., waiting in line) will rarely earn you praise (or even comment). But violating a norm often generates negative responses (see Milgram, Liberty, Toledo & Wackenhut's, 1986,

Plate 11.1 *Norms constrain everyone to some degree (e.g., even when you are in a hurry, you have to join the back of the queue to buy a ticket).*

research on responses to queue-violators). Indeed, Forsyth (1995) points out that a norm often becomes salient only after it has been violated; and people who fail to comply with situationally relevant norms without an acceptable explanation are generally subjected to negative evaluation, ranging from pressure to change, through hostility, to punishment (see Schachter's, 1951, classic study on the pressure that is exerted on deviates, discussed in more detail in Chapter 12, this volume).

There are two types of norms: *descriptive* norms inform us about how others will act in similar situations (e.g., most English people throw off layers of clothing as soon as the sun comes out in summer), whereas *injunctive* norms specify what behaviour *should* be performed (e.g., when visiting a place of religious worship one should keep quiet and be respectful) (see Cialdini, Kallgren & Reno, 1991). Both kinds of norms emerge out of interaction with others, especially members of the same formal or informal group or social network. The norms may or may not be stated explicitly, and any sanctions for deviating from them come not from the legal system but from social networks. Norms appear in several other chapters of this book (e.g., subjective norms are central to the theory of reasoned action, which links attitudes to behaviour: see Chapter 6, this volume; norms of reciprocity and social responsibility affect helping: see Chapter 9, this volume; and norms are central to understanding group processes: see Chapter 12, this volume). Our social lives are made more complex by the fact that in many social situations multiple norms may apply, and some may even be incompatible; in such circumstances we are more likely to turn to other people as sources of information concerning how we should behave.

Norm formation and transmission Since some norms may appear to be arbitrary or random (e.g., rituals to which new group members are subjected), researchers have naturally questioned how norms are formed and transmitted. The three main modes of transmission appear to be (1) through deliberate instruction, demonstrations, rituals and so on; (2) more passively, via non-verbal behaviours and implicit activation of normative standards; and (3) by inferring the norm from the behaviour of others around us. As Cialdini and Trost (1998) point out, whatever their origin norms must be communicated to have any effect on behaviour. How is that done? Surprisingly, the social psychological literature on norm transmission is still very small, and one set of studies still towers above all others – Muzafer Sherif's (1935, 1936) classic research on the *autokinetic effect*. This phenomenon has long been known to astronomers, who find that when fixating on a bright stationary star in a dark

> **autokinetic effect** perceptual illusion whereby, in the absence of reference points, a stationary light appears to move

skylight, the star appears to move. Indeed, you may already have experienced yourself that, in the absence of reference points, a stationary light appears to move rather erratically in all directions.

Sherif (1935, 1936) placed participants alone or in groups of two or three in a completely darkened room. He presented participants with a single and small stationary light at a distance of about 5 metres. Sherif asked his participants to give an oral estimate of the extent of movement of the light, obviously without informing them of the autokinetic effect. Half of the participants made their

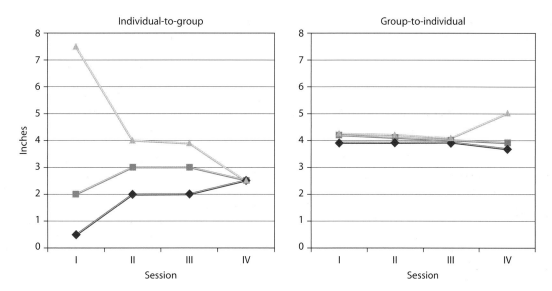

Figure 11.3 *Median judgements of movement under alone (I) or group (II, III, IV) conditions (left), and under group (I, II, III) or alone (IV) conditions (right) in Sherif's (1935) study on norm formation. In each case, judgements by three participants are shown.*

first 100 judgements alone. On three subsequent days they went through three more sets of trials, but this time in groups of two or three. For the other half of the participants the procedure was reversed. They underwent the three group sessions first and ended with a session alone.

Participants who first made their judgements alone developed a standard estimate (a *personal* norm) around which their judgements fluctuated. This personal norm was stable, but it varied highly between individuals (by as much as 7 inches [17.78 cm]). In the group phases of the experiment, which brought together people with different personal norms, participants' judgements converged towards a more or less common position – a *group norm* – within the first group session. Within groups, participants gave essentially the same estimates of movement, even though the range of movement varied by group on average 1 to 5 inches (2.54 to 12.70 cm). With the reverse procedure this group norm developed in the first session and it persisted in the later session alone. Figure 11.3 illustrates both kinds of findings. The funnel effect in the left-hand panel reveals the convergence in the (median) judgements of three participants who first judged alone (I) and later in each other's presence (II, III, IV). The right-hand panel shows the judgements of a group of three participants who went through the procedure in the reverse order. Here the convergence is already present in the first group session and the slight evidence of funnelling out in the alone-last session is much weaker than in the corresponding alone-first condition.

This famous experiment shows that, where confronted with an unstructured and ambiguous stimulus, people nevertheless develop a stable internal frame of reference against which to judge the stimulus. However, as soon as they are confronted with the different judgements of others, they quickly abandon this frame of reference so as to adjust it to that of others. Thus the apparent truth about the environment, whether social or physical, can emerge as people exchange their independent views.

There are two obvious motives for participants' responses – relating to others and understanding. Sherif himself proposed that this norm formation reflected a rational, accuracy-motivated assessment of the situation (Hood & Sherif, 1962). He concluded that, under unstable conditions, where participants were confused about how to respond, they assumed that 'the group must be right' (Sherif, 1936, p. 111). Interestingly, the joint frame of reference formed in the presence of others endured when the source of influence was no longer present, over considerable time, and it transferred to new settings – including when participants joined a new group, and when they were re-tested individually, even up to a year after their initial exposure to others' estimates (Hood & Sherif, 1962; Rohrer, Baron, Hoffman & Swander, 1954).

In subsequent studies Sherif (1935, 1936) placed a single individual who made extreme judgements in each of several groups. This one person influenced the remaining group members, whereby a more extreme norm guided their judgements. Then, once this arbitrary standard was established, Sherif removed the extreme individual from the group, replacing him with a new member. Intriguingly, the remaining group members retained as their norm the higher estimate, and the new group member gradually adapted to the higher standard. Research has even shown that old members can be gradually removed from the group and replaced with new members (naïve participants), and the old norm continues to impact on estimates for a long time until, in fact, the group members have been changed five times (see Jacobs & Campbell, 1961, in Research close-up 11.1). But there is a finite limit to arbitrary norms, and they tend to decay more rapidly across generations the more contrived they are (MacNeil & Sherif, 1976).

What kind of social influence does Sherif's study demonstrate? It is incidental rather than deliberate influence because there were no explicit attempts to influence others. Sherif's work is important precisely because it shows how, at least for an ambiguous

RESEARCH CLOSE-UP 11.1

Norm transmission in a small group

Jacobs, K.C. & Campbell, D.T. (1961). The perpetuation of an arbitrary tradition through several generations of a laboratory microculture. *Journal of Abnormal and Social Psychology*, 62, 649–658.

....

Introduction

We select this study for two main reasons. First, because, although published in 1961, it remains a brilliant demonstration, and thus should encourage you not to focus only on the most recently published findings as if they were necessarily 'better' or more interesting, which is not the case. Second, because the full design and write-up are very complex, and you would be unlikely to read the original paper yourself. Indeed, we have simplified the presentation here.

The study builds on Sherif's (1936) use of the autokinetic effect to study the *formation* of norms in order to explore the *transmission* of norms across generations of group members. If you gradually change the group members, will the original norm remain? How long will it take to die out? Jacobs and Campbell studied these questions by using experimental confederates, instructed to give extreme estimates of the amount that the light moved. Once they had inculcated an extreme cultural norm, they were then removed from the group, one by one, across generations, and were replaced by naïve participants.

Method

Participants

One hundred and seventy-five students (no gender given), unaware of the autokinetic phenomenon, took part in the study.

Design and procedure

The complete experiment consisted of six conditions, but we present only five to simplify, while highlighting the main findings. Participants were seated in a row, 8 feet (2.44 m) from a box designed to emit the small pinpoint of light, in a darkened room. Their task was to estimate the distance the light moved, from the time it appeared until it was turned off. They wore blindfolds when admitted to the room, and whenever old participants left and new ones arrived, so that they would not know which, and how many, group members had changed. In group trials, the 'oldest' member of the group was removed at the end of each block of 30 trials, and a new member was added.

The five conditions include one control condition and four experimental conditions. The conditions varied in terms of the size of the group and, most importantly, the number of confederates (from 0 to 3) who accompanied the participant. This variation was used to manipulate the strength of the norm inculcated and transmitted, these confederates being the vehicles

for the transmission of the group's culture. The confederates who were present in the starting condition were removed one at a time, after each round of 30 judgements. The participant always sat to the left of any confederates, who always gave their judgements before he did; they were instructed to give estimates between 15 and 16 inches (38.1 to 40.6 cm).

The five conditions are listed below, each designated by a letter and two numbers. The letters C or X designate *Control* or e*X*perimental conditions, respectively. The first number indicates the size of the group, while the second number indicates the number of confederates present.

1 C-1-0; each participant judged the movement of the light alone for four periods (called 'generations' for the group conditions) of 30 judgements.

2 X-2-1; the initial generation consisted of a solitary naïve participant and one confederate; 9 generations.

3 X-3-2; the initial generation consisted of a solitary naïve participant and two confederates; 10 generations.

4 X-4-3; the initial generation consisted of a solitary naïve participant and three confederates; 11 generations.

5 X-3-1; two naïve participants were paired with one confederate; 9 generations.

Results

The key research question was whether or not the naïve participants, once 'indoctrinated' by the confederates, would themselves pass on the arbitrary norm at all, once the original indoctrinators had left the group.

To answer this question, Jacobs and Campbell examined the judgements of the first generation of respondents to judge without any confederates present. The estimated movement of the light was quite substantial as long as the confederate was not outnumbered (see Figure 11.4). Thus when there were only two members of the group, one of whom was a confederate (condition (2) X-2-1), and when either two-thirds or three-quarters of the original group members were confederates (conditions (3) X-3-2 and (4) X-4-3), estimates were significantly greater than the mean in the control condition (condition (1) C-1-0). However, when the confederate was just one of three group members (condition (5) X-3-1), the average estimate after he had left the group was not significantly different from the control group.

Further analyses pooled conditions 2, 3 and 4 and then compared them with condition 1 to investigate the responses of experimental participants introduced at each of several generations after the final confederate had left the group. Estimates declined, as expected, over generations (see Figure 11.5). But the first four generations all showed significantly greater estimates of the light's movement than in the control condition. By the fifth generation the effect was marginal, and by the sixth

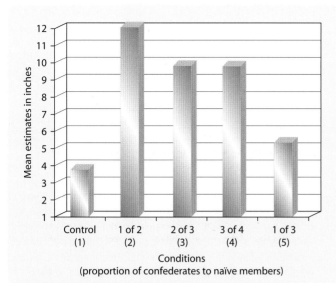

Figure 11.4 *Mean estimates of autokinetic effect as a function of proportion of confederates to naïve group members (data from Jacobs & Campbell, 1961).*

generation the difference from the control condition was no longer evident. Thus the arbitrary social norm was transmitted over four generations.

Discussion

This study was highly successful in its aim of showing cultural transmission of norms that survived total replacement of the original group members responsible for the norm. However, it also placed limits on the perpetuation of an arbitrary norm.

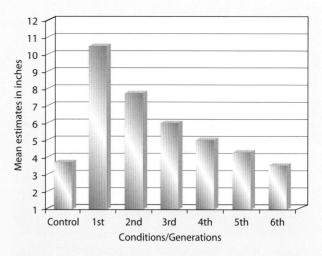

Figure 11.5 *Mean estimates of autokinetic effect as a function of number of 'generations' since last confederate left the group (data from Jacobs & Campbell, 1961).*

Without other sources of support, such norms eventually die out (and in this case quite quickly, after four generations). The study is an ingenious experimental analogue of many real-life situations in which the make-up of group members, or members of the 'culture', changes gradually over time, often every year. At your university, for example, the most senior students graduate and leave each year, but are replaced the following year by a new cohort of the most junior students; yet somehow norms and traditions endure. The same process can be seen in any large institution or organization, or in sports teams.

stimulus, norms can be adopted implicitly, how they develop through reciprocal influence and how they become internalized.

Influence via social norms in more social settings

Sherif's autokinetic studies demonstrated the emergence of arbitrary social norms in response to ambiguous stimuli presented in a stark experimental context. But social norms have the power to influence our behaviour in many more realistic situations outside the laboratory. Often we are guided by norms without even being aware of the fact, as Cialdini and his colleagues demonstrated in a series of clever field experiments to determine the effects of descriptive norms on behaviour (Cialdini, Reno & Kallgren, 1990). Cialdini and colleagues manipulated the descriptive norm for littering behaviour by controlling the amount of litter in a variety of settings (e.g., a parking garage); the setting was either clean (anti-littering norm) or littered (pro-littering norm). The researchers also helpfully provided a leaflet for the participant to discard (e.g., they placed a reminder to drive carefully under the windscreen wipers of the car parked in the garage). In general, the studies showed that people were more likely to drop litter into a littered environment than into a clean environment. Somehow, the presence of litter on the ground seems to send the message that it is normative to litter in this space, while the clean environment sends

the message that it is normative to take your litter home with you. This tendency was especially strong when the researchers directed the participants' attention to the descriptive norm in the setting. For example, when a confederate dropped litter in an already dirty setting, this focused attention on the littered environment and people were most likely themselves to litter. When the confederate dropped litter into a clean environment, however, this highlighted the lack of litter; people then littered *less* than they did when there was a clean environment with no confederate who littered.

In an even more compelling demonstration of the power of social norms, Crandall (1988) studied the norm-transmission process associated with *bulimia* (a cycle of binge-eating followed by self-induced vomiting or other forms of purging, aimed at keeping one's weight low). He showed that the reward of social popularity was sufficiently powerful to elicit seriously health-threatening behaviour. Crandall capitalized on the fact that bulimia is prevalent in certain groups where it is seen as an accepted means of weight control (the groups include dance troupes, cheerleading squads and – the groups he studied – sororities, female-only student societies found on American campuses). Crandall studied two sororities and found that those who had not initially binged began this practice and, during their first year living in the sorority house, binge eating increased generally among members. In an echo of

(a)

(b)

Plates 11.2a and b *The power of social norms: people are more likely to drop litter into a littered environment than into a clean one.*

Sherif's studies, the amount that these 'sorority sisters' binged also moved towards the average of their friendship network over time. There were, however, also differences between the two sororities studied. In one case, binge eating was positively correlated with popularity – the most popular and well-connected 'sisters' binged more. In the other sorority, the most popular members binged a moderate amount, at the rate established by the group's norms. These studies provide a fairly dramatic example of social influence, via norms, in pursuit of the goal of building and maintaining social relationships.

Perhaps the most dramatic social psychological study of norms is the renowned Stanford Prison Experiment (Haney, Banks & Zimbardo, 1973; see www.prisonexp.org/links.htm). These researchers demonstrated that normal people could be brought to behave in extremely anti-social ways, in part at least by assigning them to specific roles and allowing them to develop norms in line with these roles. These researchers randomly assigned 24 'normal, average, and healthy' (Zimbardo, Maslach & Haney, 2000, p. 199) students to play the roles of mock prisoners or mock guards in a simulated prison established in the basement of the psychology department at Stanford University, California. The study was intended to last two weeks but had to be halted after six days, due to the 'sadistic' (Zimbardo et al., 2000, p. 202) punishment by the 'guards' of the 'prisoners', whose psychological suffering was deemed unacceptably great. This study was recently replicated for a BBC television programme, yielding different results (Reicher & Haslam, 2006) and fierce controversy (Zimbardo, 2006), and appears also to have been quite strongly influenced by demand characteristics (see Chapter 2, this volume).

The extreme forms of behaviour observed by Zimbardo and his colleagues – stripping prisoners naked, depriving them of food, humiliating them and subjecting them to solitary confinement – were partly a result of the **deindividuation** of both guards and prisoners (who each wore role-consistent clothing), depriving them of their sense of individual identity and responsibility. But the power of the contrived situation also encouraged the development of new norms of behaviour, disinhibiting traditionally disapproved ways of treating others, even though there had been no explicit influence from the experimenters to encourage these forms of behaviour. If this all sounds too contrived to be true, or at least to have any consequences beyond the boundaries of this study, consider the treatment by some personnel of the United States Army of their Iraqi prisoners in Abu Ghraib prison in 2003 (see Hersh, 2004). Norms within that real prison sanctioned terrorizing the prisoners with dogs, making them simulate sex acts with each other, and degrading them in various other ways that violated the Geneva Convention on the treatment of prisoners of war.

deindividuation a state in which individuals are deprived of their sense of individual identity and are more likely to behave in an extreme manner, often anti-socially and violating norms

Plate 11.3 *Extreme forms of behaviour, such as the mistreatment of Iraqi prisoners in Abu Ghraib by US soldiers, result from deindividuation and the development of new behavioural norms that disinhibit traditionally disapproved ways of treating others.*

SUMMARY

We have presented social facilitation and norms as examples of incidental influence. The mere presence of others can improve or worsen performance, depending on task complexity. Norms guide our social behaviour in most settings, helping to reduce uncertainty about how to behave appropriately, but typically have a limited domain of application. Norms can be transmitted in various ways, and often have 'carry-over' effects, across time and settings. Often social influence takes the form of our being influenced by the norm that we infer from other people's behaviour.

WHY DOES SOCIAL INFLUENCE OCCUR?

What functions of group membership are served by group pressures towards uniformity?
What is meant by normative and informational social influence?

Having illustrated some forms of social influence (incidental influence) and before introducing alternative forms (deliberate influence), this is a good place to ask *why* people are influenced by others. As we have indicated, some forms of influence are low-level, rather trivial effects (e.g., social facilitation), which appear to lack motivation. Other forms of influence are much more interesting, because they illustrate some of the fundamental goals that guide human social behaviour and their underlying motives.

One of the earliest theoretical analyses of this question was that of Festinger (1950). Focusing on task-oriented groups with face-to-face communication, he argued that norm formation as well as norm following were outcomes of pressures towards uniformity. Uniformity itself serves two functions of group membership, *social*

reality testing and *group locomotion*. When we follow established social norms, we are confident that our behaviour is appropriate, correct and socially desirable – we have subjective validity (Turner, 1991). Although we can test the subjective validity of some beliefs against physical reality ('Is this water hot? I will put a thermometer in it to check'), other beliefs can only be tested against social reality. Agreement with other members of the relevant group (be it immediate task group or wider reference group), by comparing our views with theirs (Festinger, 1954), provides us with subjective validity for our beliefs (see also Chapters 5, 10 and 12, this volume, on social comparison theory).

Social comparison is most likely to occur in situations that are novel, ambiguous or objectively unclear (Sherif, 1936; Tesser, Campbell & Mickler, 1983), and when people are unsure, they are most likely to look to, and be guided by, the beliefs and behaviours of *similar* others. Thus social reality testing is the consensual validation of beliefs through social comparison. This is seen as necessary for the group to reach its desired goals, what Festinger (1950) called group locomotion. Coordination of goals and activities among group members is necessary for the group to move, as a group, effectively and efficiently in the direction it wants or needs to go. Consider conformity, going along with the group (which we introduced in Chapter 1, this volume, and will return to in more detail below). Even though it tends to have negative connotations in western, individual societies (Markus & Kitayama, 1994), conformity can help us to achieve group goals quickly and easily (Cialdini & Trost, 1998). Think for a few seconds how chaotic society would be in the complete absence of conformity.

> **social comparison** the act of comparing one's own attitudes, abilities or emotions with those of others in order to evaluate one's standing on the abilities, or the correctness of the attitudes and emotions

Festinger suggested that opinion discrepancies within groups elicit pressures towards uniformity, which produces communication between members of the group. Uniformity is achieved by group members convincing others to move towards their position, by themselves shifting towards the position held by others, or by redefining the group by rejecting those members who disagree (see Levine, 1989; Turner, 1991).

Deutsch and Gerard (1955) proposed a simple but highly significant analysis of motives for social influence. They argued that people agree with others for *normative* or *informational* reasons. *Normative influence* presumes a need for social approval or harmony with others, and occurs when people conform to the positive expectations of others – they avoid behaving in ways that will lead to social punishment or disapproval. The main goal, then, is to build and maintain satisfactory relationships with others, and accuracy becomes correspondingly less important (Prislin & Wood, 2005). *Informational influence* presumes a need to reduce uncertainty and involves accepting the information obtained from others as evidence about reality. The main goal, in this case, is to make accurate and valid judgements.

> **normative influence** influence based on conforming to the positive expectations of others – people avoid behaving in ways that will lead to social punishment or disapproval

> **informational influence** influence based on accepting the information obtained from others as evidence about reality

Notwithstanding the impact Deutsch and Gerard's framework has had on the whole social influence literature, Prislin and Wood

(2005) have criticized the interpretation of it, which emphasizes only whether people are (public settings) or are not (private settings) under *surveillance*. According to a simplistic application of the normative–informational distinction, social influence based on normative influence is temporary, evidenced in public settings but not maintained in private settings, in which judgements do not have social consequences, whereas informational influence yields enduring change in judgements and holds in both public and private settings. In contrast to this view, Prislin and Wood emphasize that normative motives can have informational consequences that hold up later in time, and in private settings.

One way to integrate these different approaches to understanding *why* social influence occurs is to highlight four major motives (Cialdini & Trost, 1998; see also Prislin & Wood, 2005): 'effective action', 'building and maintaining relationships', 'managing the self-concept' and 'understanding'. This approach emphasizes the goals of the *target* of influence rather than the influencing agent. Thus, for example, a participant in Sherif's autokinetic studies could have shifted his or her estimate of how much the point of light appeared to move, in the direction of the group norm, in order to facilitate the group's working effectively, to gain approval and acceptance from others in the group, to avoid a self-conception as someone who is different or deviant, and to believe that he or she now sees things more accurately.

We will return to these goals throughout the remainder of this chapter. We emphasize, here, that individuals will process the information available in social situations so as to meet whatever goal is salient. Thus, depending on whether the focus is on action, relationships, the self-concept or understanding, the target of social influence will focus information processing on its implications for behavioural effectiveness, social relations, the desired view of the self or the validity of the available information. Each of these goals can also be addressed in various ways (see Lundgren & Prislin, 1998; Prislin & Wood, 2005). When the implications are important, people can address the relevant goal(s) through careful thought and systematic analysis, yielding change that endures across time and settings. Or, when the goals are less compelling and people have less need to be confident in their judgements, they can meet them through less systematic, more heuristic strategies (see Chapter 7, this volume, on dual-route models of attitude change).

SUMMARY

When we look at why social influence occurs, we see some of the fundamental motives that direct human social behaviour. Pressures towards uniformity and agreement among group members help us to validate social beliefs and guide the group towards its goals. We can also agree with others because we wish to be liked (or to avoid being disliked), or because we accept information from others as evidence about how things 'really are'. Ultimately, we are influenced by others so that we behave effectively, build and maintain relationships with others, manage our own self-concept and understand the social world more effectively.

DELIBERATE SOCIAL INFLUENCE

What are the main techniques of compliance, and how and when do they work?

Under what circumstances do numerical majorities and minorities exert influence?

How can different theories be integrated to explain group polarization?

What are the main situational determinants of obedience to authority?

Compliance

Compliance refers to a particular kind of response whereby the target of influence acquiesces to a request from the source of influence (Cialdini & Trost, 1998). The request may be explicit or implicit, but the target recognizes that

> **compliance** a particular kind of response whereby the target of influence acquiesces to a request from the source of influence. The term is also used more generally to refer to change in public behaviour to match a norm, without corresponding change on a private level

he or she is being pressured to respond in a desired way. We emphasize that even though these forms of influence may appear relatively mild – all are based on *requests* – they are also all quite manipulative, and you are likely to encounter them in your interactions with skilled professional salespeople – so beware! But they can also be used for positive ends, as in eliciting donations to charity. (As you will see below, the term *compliance* is also used more generally in the research on conformity to refer to change in public behaviour to match a norm, but without corresponding change on a private level.) We consider below the three main techniques of compliance.

The door-in-the-face technique In the *door-in-the-face technique* (also known as a 'reciprocal concessions' procedure), the requester begins with an extreme request that is almost always refused (e.g., 'Can you lend me £20?'). The requester then retreats to a more moderate request, in fact the one that the requester had in mind all along (e.g., 'Can you lend me £5?'). By acting in this way, the

> **door-in-the-face technique** compliance technique in which the requester begins with an extreme request that is almost always refused, then retreats to a more moderate request, which he or she had in mind all along (also known as a 'reciprocal concessions' procedure)

requester hopes that the concession from an extreme to a moderate request will encourage the target of the request to make a similar, reciprocal, concession and move from initial refusal of the larger request to acceptance of the smaller one (e.g., Cialdini et al., 1975).

As Cialdini and Trost (1998) point out, this technique is widely used in fundraising. For example, after refusing a larger request for a donation, people are much more likely than before to give any contribution (Reingen, 1978). It has also been used to solicit blood donors (Cialdini & Ascani, 1976). Researchers first asked people to take part in a long-term donor programme. When that request was declined, the requester asked for a one-time donation. Again, compliance with the small request was significantly greater after refusal of the large request (50%) than in a control condition, in which people were asked only to perform the smaller favour (32%). You can even use this technique on your lecturers . . . Harari, Mohr and Hosey (1980) found that if students asked faculty members to spend 15 to 20 minutes talking to them about an issue of interest, some 59 per cent of the faculty agreed. But as many as 78 per cent acquiesced if they had first been asked for a much bigger favour (giving 2 hours a week of help to the student for the rest of the semester), which they had of course refused.

The success of this technique relies on two explanations. First, when the salesperson makes a concession, it is normative for the consumer to *reciprocate*, which he does by accepting the concession. The tactic is much less effective if the time between the two requests is perceived as too long (Cann, Sherman & Elkes, 1975), if the two requests are made by two different people (Snyder & Cunningham, 1975) and if the first request is excessive (Schwarzwald, Raz & Zvibel, 1979). Second, when the target (e.g., the consumer, faced with a salesperson) makes a concession, he has re-established *equity* with the salesperson. The motives underlying compliance of this sort include our desire to build and maintain social relationships, but also our wish to view ourselves as, for example, generous (Brown & Smart, 1991) or consistent (Cialdini, Trost & Newsom, 1995).

The foot-in-the-door technique

The *foot-in-the-door technique* adopts the reverse strategy, with the requester first asking for a small favour that is almost certain to be granted, and then following this up with a request for a larger, related favour (Freedman & Fraser, 1966). For example, a car salesperson may ask a potential buyer to test drive a car. Compliance to the critical request (buying the car) will be enhanced if the customer can first be made to comply with the initial, smaller request. The requester uses initial compliance as a means of committing the target to behave in a way that is consistent with it, and there is plentiful evidence that people are suckers for this approach (see Beaman, Cole, Preston, Klentz & Stenblay, 1983, for a review). It can also be used for charitable donations: respondents who had agreed to accept and wear a small lapel pin promoting a local charity were also more likely to give money to that charity when approached at a later point in time (Pliner, Hart, Kohl & Saari, 1974).

The success of this technique relies on the general idea of consistency (Cialdini et al., 1995; Cialdini & Trost, 1998). Thus the person who agreed to wear the lapel pin will wish to behave consistently when contacted later. This is closely linked to an explanation in terms of self-perception theory (see Chapters 6 and 7, this volume). For example, the car-buying customer may infer from her behaviour that she is the kind of person who drives that sort of car.

> **foot-in-the-door technique** compliance technique in which the requester first asks for a small favour that is almost certain to be granted, then follows this up with a request for a larger, related favour

Lowballing

In the *lowballing technique*, which Cialdini and Trost (1998, p. 178) refer to as one of the 'more unsavoury' techniques, compliance to an initial attempt is followed by a more costly and less beneficial version of the same request (Cialdini, Cacioppo, Bassett & Miller, 1978). For example, a car dealer may induce the customer to decide on a particular model of car by offering a low price for it, or an attractive trade-in deal on the customer's old vehicle. Then, after the decision has been made, the dealer goes back on the deal, giving some reason why the car is no longer available at the originally agreed price. Really unscrupulous dealers may even strengthen the customer's commitment by allowing him to arrange financing, or even take the car home overnight (Joule, 1987).

> **lowballing technique** compliance to an initial attempt is followed by a more costly and less beneficial version of the same request

This technique seems to rely on the target, even though he or she has been duped, feeling an unfulfilled obligation to the requester. The target is also already psychologically committed to the purchase, and so proceeds anyway. The technique is primarily effective when used by a single requester (Burger & Petty, 1981), and when the target freely made the initial commitment (Cialdini et al., 1978; see Chapter 7, this volume, on cognitive dissonance theory).

Integration

These techniques of compliance rely on general principles such as equity, reciprocity and self-consistency. One other general principle guiding compliance concerns perceived rewards and costs. People are not quite the suckers that these phenomena may imply, and in general they are likely to comply with a request for help if the costs are low but not if costs are high (Cialdini & Goldstein, 2004). Under low costs they may display relative 'mindlessness' (Langer, Blank & Chanowitz, 1978), for example not listening carefully to the exact words of a requester who asks to jump ahead of them in the queue for the Xerox machine, with the lame excuse that they 'have to make some copies'. However, when the requester asks to copy a larger number of pages (implying costs for the target, who will have to hang around and wait), then the requester's words are listened to carefully and compliance only follows a convincing justification (e.g., 'I have to visit my sick mother in hospital').

The influence of numerical majorities and minorities

Whereas compliance strategies involve interpersonal influence, social influence is also a key phenomenon in small groups. The first studies to examine the conditions under which an individual yields or conforms to a numerical majority were conducted by Solomon Asch (e.g., Asch, 1951, 1956; see Levine, 1999, and Leyens & Corneille, 1999, for commentaries on the impact of Asch's research). The 'Asch experiments' have become a classic in the literature and we have already described the basic paradigm (see Chapter 1, this volume). In this section we will, first, review the main findings from the Asch paradigm, and then consider when and why people conform. Next, we introduce

PIONEER

Solomon E. Asch (1907–1996) was born in Warsaw, Poland. He received his BS from the College of the City of New York in 1928, and his MA and PhD from Columbia University in 1930 and 1932, respectively. He taught at Brooklyn College, the New School for Social Research and Swarthmore College, and held visiting posts at Harvard and MIT. He was Distinguished Professor of Psychology and Director of the Institute for Cognitive Studies at Rutgers University from 1966 to 1972, when he joined the University of Pennsylvania. He is best known for his famous experiments on conformity (or 'group forces in the modification and distortion of judgements'). These studies deliberately opposed physical and social reality and showed that most people succumb to the pressure to conform to majority opinion, even when stimuli are unambiguous. Asch also contributed classic research on impression formation (see Chapter 3, this volume), and he influenced many subsequent social psychologists (Stanley Milgram was greatly influenced by, and worked for, Asch). He wrote a distinctive and authoritative textbook on *Social Psychology*, first published in 1952 and reprinted as recently as 1987.

Source: www.upenn.edu/almanac/v42/n23/asch.html

minority influence (innovation) situation in which either an individual or a group in a numerical minority can influence the majority

majority influence (conformity) social influence resulting from exposure to the opinions of a majority, or the majority of one's group

minority influence and *innovation*, the situation in which either an individual or a group in a numerical minority can influence the majority. Finally, we review the major theoretical approaches to explain both *majority influence* and minority influence.

Majority influence: The Asch paradigm and beyond

Asch (1956) began his famous work expecting to show that people were *not* as suggestible as was generally believed at that time. He also believed that the norm-following behaviour shown in Sherif's (1936) studies could be attributed to the ambiguous nature of the autokinetic stimulus. He contended that when unambiguous stimuli were used, and where there was a clearly correct answer, people would remain independent of the group's inaccurate judgements. As you will see, the results turned out rather differently.

Asch used a task in which participants were shown two cards. On one card were three lines of different lengths with each line having a number. The second card contained just one line (the standard line) that was of the same length as one of the three lines on the first card (the task is discussed and illustrated in Chapter 1, see p. 7). The participant's task was simply to state publicly which of the three lines was the same length as the standard line. This task was repeated 18 times, and on each trial different cards were shown

using different lengths of lines. In a control condition in which participants performed alone with no group influence, over 99 per cent of the responses were correct, showing that the task was simple and unambiguous.

What Asch did next was very interesting. He had participants perform the task publicly, answering aloud, in groups of six to nine. He arranged that all the participants (all male), except one, would be confederates of the experimenter – i.e., they were instructed by the experimenter to give a set pattern of answers, some of which were clearly incorrect. In some studies the confederates all gave the wrong answer to the task. In addition, the seating arrangement was such that the naïve participant always gave his answers last but one. In other words, the naïve participant heard several people give the wrong answer before he was required to give his own response. Asch's research question was: how would the naïve participant respond when faced with a consistent majority giving an (obviously) incorrect response? In fact, Asch found that the naïve participants gave the same incorrect response as the majority on 36.8 per cent of occasions.

It might be easy to brush aside these findings and assert that participants were just publicly agreeing with the majority. In one variation of the study (Asch, 1956) a situation was arranged so that the naïve participant believed he had arrived too late and so could write down his responses while the other group members (the confederates) still gave their responses aloud. The rate of conforming to the majority fell to 12.5 per cent, but this is still much higher than when no confederates were present (0.7 per cent).

Subsequent studies on conformity tended to move away from Asch's paradigm, which was costly and time-consuming, because each naïve participant had to be tested alongside a group of confederates. Instead, using the Crutchfield (1955) paradigm, there are no confederates and the numerical majority is implied through feedback about other people's responses. Each participant sits in a separate cubicle (with no visual or verbal contact) and they all respond to the task via response switches. In addition, the response of each other group member is displayed on each participant's console. Each participant believes that he is receiving the responses of the group members but, in fact, he is not; and the response pattern can be programmed by the experimenter to show either agreement or disagreement with the participants. More recently still, most studies of conformity have abandoned the group context completely and participants receive feedback concerning other people's responses in summary form (e.g., being told that 82 per cent of the population hold a particular attitude). Comparison between different paradigms shows reliable differences, with conformity rates being highest in face-to-face situations (e.g., Levy, 1960). This is not surprising as literally facing the majority increases normative pressures to conform.

When do people conform?
Asch's first studies were followed by many variants. Among the most important factors found to influence the level of conformity are group size, unanimity and social support, and culture.

In terms of the numerical size of the majority, conformity increased quite dramatically as the number of majority members (faced with a minority of one) increased from one to three, but the influence of additional members was minimal (Asch, 1951; see

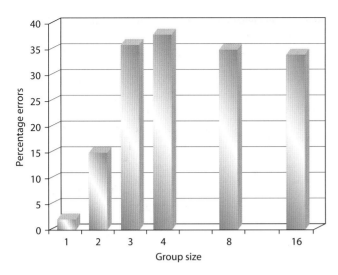

Figure 11.6 *Percentage of errors as a function of majority size (based on Asch, 1951).*

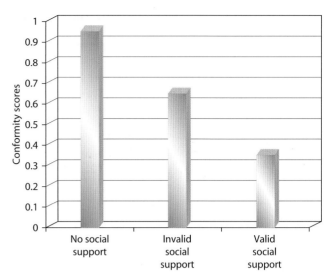

Figure 11.7 *Conformity in the absence and in the presence of types of social support (based on Allen & Levine, 1971).*

Figure 11.6). However, results are rather inconsistent (see Gerard, Wilhelmy & Connolley, 1968; Reis, Earing, Kent & Nezlek, 1976). A crucial factor for the levelling off of conformity after the third participant seems to be that the members of the majority must be seen to be independent, and not simply 'sheep' (Wilder, 1977); once that is the case, there is a linear increase in conformity as group size increases (Gerard et al., 1968).

In one study Asch arranged for one of the confederates, who responded before the naïve participant, to give the correct answer. The level of conformity by the naïve participant dropped dramatically, but was this due to the correct respondent breaking the majority's unanimity, or his giving the naïve participant 'social support' for the correct answer? Another of Asch's studies was designed to answer this question and showed that breaking the majority's unanimity was most important. When he had one of the confederates deviate from the majority, but by giving a different incorrect answer, this broke unanimity but did not give the naïve participant a supporter. The results showed that the rates of conformity by the naïve participant reduced to nearly the same level as when there had been a social supporter. Genuine social support does, however, have a value over and above breaking unanimity when social influence concerns attitudes and opinions rather than unambiguous stimuli (see Allen, 1975, for a review). The true value of the social supporter is in providing a valid and independent assessment of reality (see Allen, 1975). Using the Asch task, Allen and Levine (1971) varied whether the participant had social support, and what type of support. In one of their two support conditions the social support was 'invalid', because the supporter was wearing spectacles with thick lenses. Although giving correct answers, this supporter could not possibly be perceived as a valid source of information on a visual discrimination task. The results, shown in Figure 11.7, indicate that, although invalid support was better than none, valid social support was clearly most effective.

Finally, Bond and Smith (1996) conducted a meta-analysis on the Asch conformity paradigm and found greater acceptance of others' judgements in collectivistic cultures (which tend to subordinate individual goals to group goals) than in individualistic cultures (which tend to place an emphasis on individual goals and achievement; see Chapter 5, this volume). Indeed, the impact of culture was much greater than any other moderator of group influence, including the size of the majority.

Why do people conform? In post-experimental interviews conducted by Asch (see Asch, 1952/1987), participants gave a number of reasons why they yielded to the majority. Some thought the majority was wrong but went along with it simply to feel they belonged to the group and to avoid being ostracized. Others thought that the majority must be right as they were the only person to see the task differently, i.e., 'several pairs of eyes' are more likely to be correct than the one pair of the naïve participant.

These different reasons given for yielding to the majority map closely onto theoretical accounts of conformity. The most popular explanation for conformity is based upon the dependency perspective on small group behaviour, which we described earlier in this chapter. Group members are cognitively and socially dependent on each other (Festinger, 1950) because opinion uniformity helps them to validate their opinions (social reality) and to move the group towards its goals (group locomotion).

Explanations for the Asch studies also relied on Deutsch and Gerard's (1955) distinction between normative and informational social influence, introduced earlier. If conformity is related to the desire to be liked (normative influence) and the desire to be right (informational influence), then factors that affect these desires should increase the likelihood of conformity. In terms of normative social influence, conformity should be greater when people believe they are part of a group than when they do not. Making the group salient will increase people's desire to be part of the group and therefore increase conformity. This was shown in the study by Deutsch and Gerard (1955) that used the Asch lines. They found that conformity increased when participants were told they were part of a group, and that the best-performing groups in the study would win a prize, compared to a condition where no such information was given. On the other hand, conformity decreased when participants' responses were anonymous (via the Crutchfield paradigm discussed earlier). In terms of informational influence, factors that increase the credibility of the majority as a valid source of reality (e.g., status and expertise) lead to more conformity (Kiesler & Kiesler, 1969). Also, factors that weaken the credibility of the majority as a valid source of information (e.g., breaking the majority consensus as shown above) reduce conformity.

More generally, we can understand conformity by considering three main goals that it can serve (Cialdini & Trost, 1998). A shift towards a group consensus can allow the individual: (1) to believe that he or she now sees things more accurately; (2) to gain the approval and acceptance of positively viewed others; and (3) to avoid a self-concept as different, deviant or as refusing to compromise for the good of the group.

Minority influence and innovation Research on conformity focused on the ability of the majority to influence the individual, and therefore neglected the possibility that the individual (or minority) could influence the majority. According to the dependency account, which was the dominant early explanation of conformity, minorities lack the resources to make majority members dependent on them. Minorities, by definition, lack power, status and numerical size and therefore do not have the means to enforce normative or informational influence.

Yet, history is replete with examples of individuals and minorities who, through their actions, have had a tremendous impact upon the majority in society. It was this observation in the late 1960s by the French social psychologist Serge Moscovici that led to a theoretical reshaping of the area. Moscovici argued that if social influence only relied upon conformity to the majority, then it would be difficult to see how groups change, new ideas develop and innovation might occur. Moscovici argued that minorities are distinctive – they stand out from the crowd – and from this distinctiveness they can create conflict within the majority by challenging the dominant majority view, and in so doing offer a new and different perspective. Since people wish to avoid conflict, they will often dismiss the minority position by attributing its deviancy to some underlying, undesirable psychological dimension (Papastamou, 1986). For example, the minority might be seen as 'crazy', 'biased' or 'provocative' in an attempt to explain its deviant view. Indeed, if one considers many 'successful' minorities (such as Galileo, Freud and Copernicus, or, more recently, Bob Geldof), they often suffered ridicule and rejection by the majority before their views became accepted.

In order to overcome people's inclination to reject the deviant minority, the minority must adopt a particular style of behaviour that communicates to the majority that the minority is sure of, and committed to, its position. Moscovici termed this the minority's behavioural style, and he emphasized above all *consistency*, the need for the minority to respond with the same response to the same stimulus, across trials. Moscovici, Lage and Naffrechoux (1969) demonstrated these ideas experimentally. They presented groups

consistency a behavioural style indicating that the same position is maintained across time; seen as central to minority influence

Serge Moscovici (b. 1925) was born in Romania to Jewish parents. Following systematic discrimination, including exclusion from high school, he was a victim of the 1941 Bucharest pogrom and was interned in a Nazi forced labour camp. He made his way secretly to France, where he studied psychology at the Sorbonne. His professional career has been spent at the Ecole des Hautes Etudes en Sciences Sociales, Paris, with visiting appointments in Princeton, and at the New School for Social Research, New York. He became director of the Laboratoire Européen de Psychologie Sociale (European Laboratory of Social Psychology) at the Maison des sciences de l'homme, Paris. His ground-breaking contributions to the study of minority influence, which opposed the dominant American focus on majority influence, themselves illustrate the impact that a consistent, outspoken minority can have, without which there would be neither innovation nor social change. He has also written on the history of science and promoted the study of social representations, originating with his classic analysis of how ideas about psychoanalysis infused and influenced French society.

Source: www.answers.com/topic/serge-moscovici

of six female participants with a series of slides that were unambiguously blue and differed only in their light intensity. In a control condition, participants not exposed to influence named the colour of the slide as 'blue' on 99.75 per cent of trials. However, in one condition the group contained two confederates (a numerical minority) who were instructed to call the blue slides 'green' on every trial. When this occurred the naïve participants also called the slide green on 8.45 per cent of occasions, and this was significantly higher than in the control condition (0.25 per cent) that had no confederates. The importance of the minority responding consistently was shown in a third condition of the experiment, where the confederates were inconsistent (they responded randomly green to only some of the slides, and blue to others). When the minority was inconsistent, the percentage of green responses from the naïve participants fell to 1.25 per cent, which was not different from the control condition (see Figure 11.8). It is clear that for a minority to be successful it must respond consistently (see also Nemeth, Swedlund & Kanki, 1974).

Mugny (1975, 1982) made a further distinction between 'behavioural style' and 'negotiating style'. Because the minority lacks power and the means to exact dependency, the minority has to negotiate its influence with the majority. Mugny (1975) identified two negotiating styles – a rigid style, where the minority refuses to compromise on any issue, and a flexible style, where the minority is prepared to adapt to the majority position and accept certain compromises. Through numerous studies, Mugny

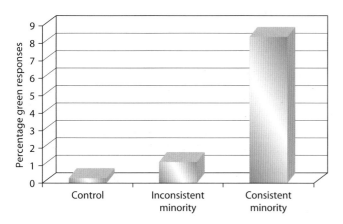

Figure 11.8 *Percentage of green responses given by majority participants in the experiment by Moscovici et al. (1969).*

has shown that a minority that uses a flexible style is more likely to influence the majority than one that uses a rigid style (at least on a public level).

Theoretical approaches to majority and minority influence There are currently two broad explanations for majority–minority influence phenomena, each of which subsumes several theories (Levine & Moreland, 1998). We term these the 'conflict' and 'social categorization' approaches.

Moscovici (1976, 1980) argued that conflict was the critical factor underlying influence. According to him, all forms of influence, whether from a majority or a minority, result in conflict and individuals are motivated to reduce that conflict. However, Moscovici argues that people employ different processes, with different outcomes, depending on whether the source of the conflict is a majority or a minority. He proposed a contrast between two types of process, *comparison* and *validation*, which has some similarities to Deutsch and Gerard's (1955) distinction between normative and informational influence. Moscovici argued that majorities induce a comparison process, in which the target of influence focuses on the discrepancy between his or her position and that advocated by the majority. The minority targets, because they wish to gain the majority's acceptance, show compliance (public influence) towards the majority position, but not **conversion** (private influence). In contrast, minorities induce a validation process, in which majority members focus on the content of the minority's position or message.

> **conversion** a change in private response after exposure to influence by others; internalized change; a change in the way one structures an aspect of reality

An important addition to Moscovici's earlier theorizing is the idea that, while minority influence may not lead to public agreement, for fear of being categorized as a minority member (Mugny, 1982), the close examination of the validity of the minority's arguments may bring about attitude conversion on an indirect, latent or private level.

The most provocative claim was made by Moscovici and Personnaz (1980). Using the blue–green slide paradigm, they claimed that if a minority consistently responded that a blue slide was 'green', then even though they could not bring that participant to accept that direct influence, they would exert influence on an indirect level. In this case the indirect level was the chromatic complementary after-image of the slide. The after-image is what one sees when one views a white screen after viewing a coloured slide: the after-image of blue is yellow-orange, and of green it is red-purple. Of course, the experimenters did not tell participants that different colours were linked to different after-images, and it is assumed that participants were ignorant of this too.

Moscovici and Personnaz did indeed find that when minority-influenced participants reported what colour after-image they saw on a white screen, they tended to see the after-image of a blue slide as more yellow-orange than did majority-influenced participants, consistent with the idea that they had begun to see the slide as the minority saw it, as 'green'. However, this claim is implausible, given what we know about the physiology of after-images. There have also been failures to replicate, and the study has been criticized on methodological grounds (see Martin & Hewstone, 2001a, for a discussion).

A much less contentious way of measuring indirect influence is to measure influence on a target attitude and on an indirectly related attitude. For example, Pérez and Mugny (1987) exposed participants to a counterattitudinal pro-abortion message that was attributed to either a majority or minority source. The researchers then measured participants' attitudes towards both the target issue, abortion, and an indirectly related issue, birth control. Although the issue of birth control had not been mentioned in the source's message, it is related to it at a superordinate level (i.e., someone who is pro-abortion would also tend to be pro-birth control). While the minority had little impact on the direct abortion issue, it had a large impact on the birth control issue – participants had become more favourable to birth control. This was not found when the source was a majority. This result shows that the impact of the minority was low on direct attitudes (presumably because participants did not want to identify publicly with the minority), but the minority had a 'hidden impact' (Maass & Clark, 1984) on a related indirect attitude (see also Alvaro & Crano, 1997).

Moscovici's theory has received partial support from an extensive meta-analysis by Wood and colleagues (1994). Overall, they reported that majorities had greater influence than minorities on both public measures and direct measures responded to in private. Minorities were, however, equally or more influential than majorities on indirect measures responded to in private.

An important recent development in this area has been the increased use of theory and methodology derived from the persuasion literature (see Chapter 7, this volume) to understand majority and minority influence. Specifically, researchers have drawn a parallel between Moscovici's concepts of comparison and validation and the distinction between non-systematic and systematic processing made in models of persuasion (the elaboration likelihood model and the heuristic-systematic model) (see Maass & Clark, 1983; Martin & Hewstone, 2001b). Thus studies have manipulated source status (majority vs. minority) and argument quality (strong vs. weak arguments). This design allows the researcher to investigate which source is associated with systematic processing; if processing is systematic, there should be greater persuasion by the strong than the weak message, as well as more message-congruent thoughts, and these thoughts should mediate attitude change. There is, however, disagreement amongst researchers concerning which source condition (majority or minority) should elicit the most cognitive scrutiny of the message, with some advocating superior message processing associated with a minority (e.g., Moscovici, 1980), others advocating this for the majority (e.g., Mackie, 1987), and still others proposing that both a majority and minority can lead to message processing under different circumstances (e.g., Baker & Petty, 1994).

Although results are quite mixed (e.g., Baker & Petty, 1994; Martin & Hewstone, 2003; Martin, Hewstone & Martin, 2007), there is now considerable evidence that both majorities and minorities can lead to systematic processing, and hence influence, but this depends on the elaboration level present when targets are exposed to the message (see also Crano & Chen, 1998; De Dreu & De Vries, 1993). For example, Martin et al. (2007) showed that when either motivational or cognitive factors encouraged low

message elaboration, there was heuristic acceptance of the majority position without detailed message processing (i.e., no difference between the impact of strong and weak arguments). When the level of message elaboration was intermediate, there was message processing only for the minority source (for the minority source, strong arguments had more impact than weak arguments). And when message elaboration was high, there was message processing for both source conditions.

However, although both majority and minority sources can, in principle and in practice, instigate systematic message processing, there is growing evidence that minorities lead to 'stronger' attitudes than do majorities (as defined by Krosnick, Boninger, Chuang, Berent & Carnot, 1993; see Chapter 6, this volume). Specifically, minority-instigated attitudes are more resistant to counterpersuasion (Martin, Hewstone & Martin, 2003; see Research close-up 11.2), and are more predictive of behaviour, than are majority-instigated attitudes (Martin, Martin, Smith & Hewstone, 2007).

RESEARCH CLOSE-UP 11.2

Resisting persuasion: The value of minority influence

Martin, R., Hewstone, M. & Martin, P.Y. (2003). Resistance to persuasive messages as a function of majority and minority source status. *Journal of Experimental Social Psychology, 39,* 585–593.

....

Introduction

As the main text of the chapter explains, Moscovici's (1980) conversion theory predicts that minority influence leads to greater message processing than does majority influence. This paper reports three studies that take a different, and novel, approach to examining this hypothesis. We describe one study here. In this study the participants were exposed to two messages that argued different positions in relation to the same topic. The messages were delayed in time, and participants completed attitude measures after each message. The first message (initial message) argued a counterattitudinal position while the second argued the opposite pro-attitudinal position (countermessage).

If attitudes following the initial message had been formed from processing the message in detail, then these attitudes should resist the second countermessage. Active processing of the arguments in the initial message (i.e., thinking of issues in agreement with the message) should provide individuals with arguments to resist the attack from the second countermessage. If, however, the attitudes formed following the first message were *not* based upon detailed message processing, then these attitudes should be influenced by (or yield to) the second message.

The authors predicted that if minority influence leads to greater message processing, as proposed by Moscovici (1980), then attitudes formed following exposure to a minority should

be more resistant to a second countermessage than are attitudes formed following majority influence.

Method

Participants and design
The participants were 69 students (25 males and 44 females) who were randomly assigned to one of two conditions (majority vs. minority support of initial message).

Stimulus materials
The topic of the message was the legalization of voluntary euthanasia (i.e., the right to end life if suffering from a terminal illness). Pre-testing had shown that the participants were moderately in favour of voluntary euthanasia. Two messages were employed which used strong and persuasive arguments that were either against (initial message) or in favour of (countermessage) voluntary euthanasia.

Procedure
Participants were tested in groups of between two and five. The study had five stages. First, participants rated their attitude towards voluntary euthanasia on a 9-point scale from 1, *Totally disagree* to 9, *Totally agree* (pre-test). Second, they were informed that a recent survey at their university showed that either 82 per cent (majority) or 18 per cent (minority) of students were against legalizing voluntary euthanasia. They then read several arguments that summarized the majority or minority position against voluntary euthanasia (initial message) (note: the researchers presented the same arguments in each condition, only the majority/minority label changed). Third, participants' attitudes towards voluntary euthanasia were measured

again on the same 9-point scale employed in the first booklet (post-test I: initial message). Fourth, participants were then shown arguments that conveyed the opposite perspective to the initial message, i.e., in favour of voluntary euthanasia (countermessage). Fifth, participants rated their attitude towards voluntary euthanasia for a third time on the 9-point scale (post-test II: countermessage).

Results

Scores on the one-item scale were reverse coded so that high scores indicated greater influence to the initial message while low scores indicated greater influence to the countermessage. As can be seen from Figure 11.9, the participants were influenced by both the majority and minority, as there was a significant change in attitudes between pre-test and post-test I:

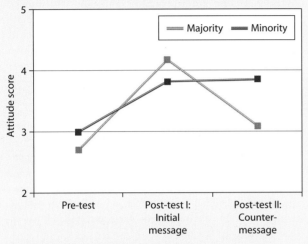

Figure 11.9 *Mean attitudes as a function of majority vs. minority source and pre-test, post-test I (initial message) and post-test II (countermessage) (data from Martin et al., 2003). Note: greater agreement with the source is reflected by high scores on the initial message and low scores on the countermessage. The difference between initial message and countermessage reflects the degree of resistance – the smaller the difference, the greater the resistance.*

initial message in the direction of the source of influence. The amount of change in the majority and minority conditions was the same. At this stage, it appears that the majority and minority led to the same amount of influence, but the results for the countermessage show this was derived from different processes.

The prediction was that attitudes following majority influence would result from compliance, without thinking about the message arguments in detail, and, therefore, these attitudes should yield to a countermessage. This is what happened as the scores following the countermessage (post-test II) were significantly lower than scores following the initial message (post-test I). In fact, attitudes following the countermessage reduced to nearly the same level as the pre-test attitude; this suggests that the attitude change to the initial message was only superficial, as attitudes returned to their pre-test level when exposed to the countermessage.

By contrast, the prediction was that attitudes following minority influence would be due to detailed evaluation of the minority's arguments, and this should enable participants to resist the countermessage. Again, this is what happened. There was no difference in attitude scores between the initial message (post-test I) and the countermessage (post-test II), showing participants had not changed their attitude (i.e., had resisted) when exposed to the second message.

Discussion

This is the first investigation of resistance to persuasion in the context of majority and minority influence and it offers a new demonstration, consistent with conversion theory, of greater message processing induced by a minority, compared with a majority, source. However, the authors acknowledge that majorities can, and often do, encourage systematic message processing, although in situations that encourage message elaboration. This was shown in another study where participants were told, before they read the majority message, that they would later be asked to recall the arguments contained in it (this procedure should encourage message processing). With these instructions, attitudes following majority influence also resisted the countermessage (Martin, Hewstone & Martin, 2007).

There is stronger support for the conflict explanation of majority–minority influence from Nemeth's (1986, 1995) research (see De Vries, De Dreu, Gordijn & Schuurman, 1996, for a theoretical integration of Moscovici's and Nemeth's approaches). According to Nemeth, majority vs. minority status does not affect the *amount* of thinking about the message but the *type* of thinking and the focus of thoughts. She has consistently found that majorities produce a narrow focus on the message they present, whereas minorities produce a broader focus on new information and attitudinal positions. Her explanation for this effect is that learning that the majority has a different position to oneself creates stress, particularly if the majority is physically present, and stress is known to narrow the focus of attention. Specifically, exposure to majority dissent leads to message-relevant, convergent thinking, which

yields uncreative solutions to problems. In contrast, exposure to minority dissent leads to issue-relevant, divergent thinking, producing creative problem-solving solutions (e.g., Maass & Volpato, 1994; Mucchi-Faina, Maass & Volpato, 1991; Nemeth & Kwan, 1985). Consistent with this view, exposure to majority dissent is more helpful than exposure to minority dissent when a task requires convergent thinking, while minority dissent is more effective on tasks requiring divergent thinking (Nemeth, Mosier & Chiles, 1992). The value of dissent within groups will also be seen later, in the section on group decision-making. There we see that an overemphasis on harmony and consensus, and a failure to encourage and attend to diverse viewpoints, can lead to disastrous decision-making.

Whereas the dependence and conflict approaches focus on intragroup processes, the social categorization account focuses on intergroup *and* intragroup processes (Mugny, 1982; Mugny & Pérez, 1991; Turner, Hogg, Oakes, Reicher & Wetherell, 1987). Mugny and Pérez argue that minority influence occurs if identification with the source is compatible with a positive social identity (essentially, the extent to which one feels positive about membership of a group; see Chapter 14, this volume). According to this view, minorities categorized as outgroups have little direct influence, but can have indirect influence if they induce a validation process. Minorities categorized as ingroups can produce direct influence because the target of influence identifies with the source of influence.

The impact of group identification on social influence also lies at the heart of the ***self-categorization theory*** analysis of majority and minority influence (see Turner, 1991). According to self-categorization theory (for a fuller account see Chapters 5 and 14, this volume), individuals identify with a particular group and conform to a prototypical group position. This form of social influence is termed ***referent informational influence***. The prototypical position maximizes both similarities between ingroup members and differences between ingroup and outgroup (Hogg, Turner & Davidson, 1990; Mackie, 1986). Self-categorization theory predicts that social influence will occur only if three conditions are met: (1) the target perceives that the source disagrees with his or her position; (2) the source and target are perceived as members of the same group; and (3) the source's position is prototypical of the group norm (i.e., it is most typical of the ingroup, and least typical of the outgroup; van Knippenberg, Lossie & Wilke, 1994). People have a need to hold attitudes consistent with their social identities, and according to self-categorization theory people adopt ingroup positions to reduce subjective uncertainty about their responses. Disagreement with others categorized as similar to the self, however, conveys subjective uncertainty and motivates people to resolve the discrepancy by means of mutual social influence.

David and Turner (1996, 1999) provided some evidence for self-categorization theory. They found majority compliance and minority conversion only when the source of influence was categorized as similar to the target of influence; when the source was characterized as being dissimilar to the target of influence, there was no direct or indirect influence. However, research on majority–minority influence conducted within the self-categorization theory framework has failed to show that self-categorization (or perceived similarity between target and source) is the mediating process (for an exception see Gordijn, Postmes & de Vries, 2001).

Research by Crano and colleagues has also demonstrated the beneficial effects of being an ingroup minority (e.g., Alvaro & Crano, 1997; Crano & Alvaro, 1998; Crano & Chen, 1998). One interesting idea proposed by Crano is that ingroup minorities can exert influence because, as members of the same group, their

self-categorization theory theory explaining how the process of categorizing oneself as a group member forms social identity and brings about various forms of both group (e.g., group polarization, majority–minority influence) and intergroup (e.g., intergroup discrimination) behaviours

referent informational influence individuals identify with a particular group and conform to a prototypical group position

counterattitudinal positions are listened to and evaluated in a lenient, open-minded way, promoting changes on indirect measures (the minority is still considered too dissimilar to produce acceptance on direct measures). However, it would be a mistake to argue that only ingroup minorities exert influence (for a review of the impact of outgroup minorities, see Pérez & Mugny, 1998). Furthermore, social change has often come from extreme individuals who are unlikely to be seen as ingroup members. This is true historically, when considering social movements, and in more modern times, when one looks at minorities as sources of new fashions or musical trends.

The upshot of these theoretical analyses is that there is clear support for Moscovici's (1980) addition of minority influence to this area. However, there is mixed support for his theory, as there is for self-categorization theory's prediction that only ingroup minorities will have an impact. There is evidence that majorities and minorities can instigate detailed processing of their messages, under specific circumstances, and that both ingroup and outgroup minorities can exert influence; typically, however, the influence of ingroup minorities will be greater, and it will be shown primarily on indirect private measures of influence and on measures of divergent thinking.

Group polarization

Imagine that you get together with a group of friends and discuss your favourite lectures. If you reach a group decision on, say, your evaluation of the social psychology course, is it likely to be the average of your individual views? In fact, although this was originally thought to be how groups made decisions, research has shown that, far from an 'averaging' process, group discussion is associated with a 'polarizing' process. ***Group polarization*** refers to the tendency to make decisions that are more extreme than the average of group members' initial positions, in the direction already favoured by the group. Individual members' private opinions then converge on this polarized decision. Although many of the relevant studies demonstrate *attitude* polarization, we emphasize that, consistent with our description of the field of social influence in general, the same phenomenon has been demonstrated for many kinds of judgements and decision, including stereotypes, interpersonal impressions and jury decisions (see Lamm & Myers, 1978, and Everyday Social Psychology 11.1, p. 235).

group polarization tendency to make decisions that are more extreme than the average of group members' initial positions, in the direction already favoured by the group

The phenomenon of group polarization was clearly demonstrated by Moscovici and Zavalloni (1969). They had small groups of French high school students first write down in private their attitudes towards two topics, one on which they were initially somewhat positive (their attitude to the then president, Charles de Gaulle) and one on which they were initially somewhat negative (their attitude towards North Americans). Then they had to reach consensus, as a group, on each item. Finally, they made another private attitude rating. As a result of the discussion, participants became more extreme in the same direction as their initial

Juries

Although we have focused on experimental studies of social influence in this chapter, there is no shortage of examples of these phenomena in the real world, nor of applications of the relevant theory and research. One prime example is the work of juries, a group of 12 laypeople who, primarily in countries with English common-law traditions, decide on culpability in criminal trials or liability in civil trials. These groups make important, sometimes literally life-and-death, decisions. But they are often quite homogeneous – famously described by British judge Lord Devlin as 'middle-aged, middle-minded and middle class' – and illustrate several of the phenomena discussed in this chapter.

Social psychologists have studied juries for many years, typically using an experimental trial-simulation methodology (because, for legal reasons, researchers are not permitted direct access to jurors' deliberations). While this may appear to be a fundamental weakness of the relevant research, because the laboratory analogue cannot exactly reproduce the pressures and responsibilities of a real jury, Kerr (1995) notes that laboratory and jury groups are similar in that they are both ad hoc collections of people who, initially, do not know each other.

Although some key aspects of how juries operate involve individual decision-making tendencies and biases (involving the *juror* rather than the *jury*; see Hastie, 1993), social psychologists have focused on jury deliberation processes (e.g., Hastie, Penrod & Pennington, 1983; Stasser, Kerr & Bray, 1982). Many of the phenomena considered in this chapter (and the two subsequent chapters on groups) can be seen at work in juries. Here we will highlight some of those relating to social influence, focusing on group polarization, majority influence and minority influence.

Juries clearly show group polarization. A classic legal source noted that verdicts handed down are more extreme than the individual jury members' initial judgements, but always in the same direction as the initial judgements (Kalven & Zeisel, 1966). Moreover, bias found in individual jurors' judgements (e.g., attention paid to pre-trial publicity) tends to be accentuated by deliberating juries (Stasser et al., 1982). Myers and Kaplan (1976) studied this issue experimentally, by forming mock juries that had to determine the guilt of defendants. Via a manipulation of the strength of the evidence, some groups already initially favoured conviction, while other groups initially favoured acquittal. Discussions within each of these kinds of groups led to a polarization of these initial tendencies (see also Hastie et al., 1983).

Juries also illustrate majority influence, because initial, pre-deliberation majorities nearly always prevail in the criminal courts (Kalven & Zeisel, 1966). Moreover, social psychologists studying juries emphasize that jury deliberation involves more than simple persuasion (i.e., informational influence), and, in fact, there is a strong normative component (Kerr, 1995).

Smith and Tindale (in press) demonstrate that once it achieves a two-thirds majority, the majority view tends to determine the outcome of the jury decision process (Davis, 1980; Tindale & Davis, 1983). They note, however, that, overall, jurors

who support acquittal tend to be more influential than those who support conviction (Davis, Kerr, Stasser, Meek & Holt, 1977; Kerr & MacCoun, 1985; Tindale, Davis, Vollrath, Nagao & Hinsz, 1990), most likely because the not guilty verdict is in keeping with social norms. Therefore, even if seven members of a 12-person jury favour guilty at the beginning of their deliberation, the final verdict is more likely than not to be defined by the five-person minority favouring not guilty; thus minority influence is at work too.

The 'reasonable doubt' criterion used in law requires that jurors vote for conviction only in the event that they cannot generate any reasonable doubts concerning the defendant's guilt. Therefore, arguing in favour of acquittal is often much easier than is arguing in favour of conviction, because only one reasonable doubt needs to be generated in order to validate the acquittal position. Consistent with this notion, Kerr and MacCoun (1985) found that minority factions favouring acquittal were not influential when the reasonable doubt criterion was replaced by a 'preponderance of the evidence' criterion. Under this latter criterion, neither verdict is inherently easier to validate, and, therefore, majority factions tend to prevail.

Banned, as you are, from ever actually observing a jury, you could at least take a well-justified break from your studies of social influence to watch the classic film *Twelve Angry Men* (directed by Sidney Lumet, 1957). This film illustrates the strong normative component within juries, as the majority attempts to coerce opposed and undecided jurors. But most famously it demonstrates minority influence, as the main protagonist (played by Henry Fonda) succeeds in overturning an 11-to-1 jury favouring a guilty judgement (see www.filmsite.org/twelve.html). Or you could read Grove's (1998) interesting account of what it is like to serve on a jury, *The Juryman's Tale*.

Plate 11.4 *Henry Fonda wins over a previously unanimous majority of other jurors in the film* Twelve Angry Men.

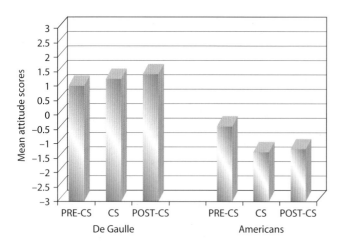

Figure 11.10 *Group polarization: attitudes towards de Gaulle and towards Americans in pre-consensus, consensus and post-consensus conditions (data from Moscovici & Zavalloni, 1969).*

attitudes. As Figure 11.10 shows, attitudes towards de Gaulle became more positive, and attitudes towards Americans became more negative, after the discussion.

There are three main explanations for this effect – persuasive arguments, social comparison and self-categorization – which we will first review, and then try to integrate.

Persuasive arguments As the discussion in a group unfolds, individuals typically learn something from each other; the discussion allows for an exchange of knowledge, opinions and, above all, *arguments*, as group members try to convince one another (Burnstein & Vinokur, 1977). Vinokur and Burnstein (1974) highlighted three kinds of information that circulate among members of a group, information that: (1) expresses a view pro or contra the issue; (2) contains some novelty (which is intrinsically persuasive); and (3) has cogency (the ability to persuade). During the exchange of arguments, each individual is likely to learn novel reasons for holding the consensual view, whereby attitudes become more extreme (indeed, arguments consistent with the dominant tendency are rated more persuasive than those that contradict it; Burnstein, Vinokur & Trope, 1973). Discussion also provides an opportunity for individuals both to repeat their own views and to hear those views repeated by others; repetition contributes to the shift towards more extreme judgements (Brauer & Judd, 1996; Brauer, Judd & Gliner, 1995).

Three lines of evidence support the persuasive arguments approach, also called the informational approach because it argues that polarization is based on informational social influence (Deutsch & Gerard, 1955). First, polarization is correlated with the ratio of pro vs. con arguments available to group members; second, polarization can be produced by manipulating this ratio; and third, polarization increases with the novelty and validity of the arguments that group members hear (Kaplan & Miller, 1977). Thus, this explanation is essentially parallel to that offered by cognitive theories of persuasion (see Chapter 7, this volume): a group member's attitude is a function of the number and persuasiveness of pro and con arguments recalled from memory when he or she formulates this position (Eagly & Chaiken, 1993).

Social comparison An alternative account of group polarization is based on social comparison theory (Festinger, 1954). It is also known as the normative explanation for polarization, because it contends that polarization is due to normative influence (Deutsch & Gerard, 1955). According to this view, group members tend to compare themselves with others, and have a need to view themselves positively and gain approval from others (Goethals & Zanna, 1979; Myers & Lamm, 1976). Moreover, they wish to be different from other group members, but in a socially desirable direction; so, after learning others' positions, they shift to an even more extreme position themselves (Myers, 1978).

The main line of support for this explanation is that group polarization can be brought about, quite simply, by learning of other group members' attitudinal *positions*. Participants who received information about the distribution of other group members' positions before they made their own decisions took more extreme positions than those unaware of other group members' positions (Myers, Bach & Schreiber, 1974). They did so, moreover, without ever hearing others' arguments (Burnstein & Vinokur, 1973), and only when they were informed about the distribution of opinions held by all other members of the group, not simply when they were informed of the group average (Myers & Kaplan, 1976).

Self-categorization A more recent normative account of group polarization acknowledges the importance of both persuasive arguments *and* members' positions, but emphasizes that group membership is essential to group polarization (Turner, 1991). Polarization arises from tendencies to accentuate similarities within members of one's own group, but to differentiate from members of outgroups. Consistent with this view, polarization is enhanced by reference to an outside group (Doise, 1969), which emphasizes the ingroup–outgroup division. Indeed, even in the absence of actual discussion between members of the same group, group members' attitudes shift towards a perceived ingroup norm that best defines the group in contrast to the relevant outgroup (Hogg et al., 1990).

Whereas the earlier accounts define the group norm as the *average* position of all the group's members, and view polarization as movement beyond that norm, the self-categorization account argues that the group norm can be more extreme than the average position, and polarization can reflect movement *towards* that norm. According to self-categorization theory (which we introduced earlier, in the section on theoretical approaches to majority and minority influence), individuals identify with a particular group and conform to a prototypical group position, one that defines views held in their group. Prototypes are individual representations of group norms and are formed by making comparisons, both within the group and between the group, which maximize the perceived difference between the two groups (see earlier section on minority influence). Thus, group members perceive the group's position to be more extreme than it actually is, based on the average of the group members' responses. This referent informational influence helps to define the ingroup as different from the outgroup (Hogg et al., 1990; Mackie, 1986).

There are four main lines of empirical support for the self-categorization account of group polarization. First, polarization produced by listening to a group discussion or learning others' positions depends on participants believing that they are members of the *same* group (i.e., ingroup members), and not a competing group (i.e., outgroup members) (Mackie & Cooper, 1984; Turner et al., 1987; Turner, Wetherell & Hogg, 1989). Second, listeners perceive the *content* of the discussion to be more polarized when they think the discussants are ingroup members than when they do not (Mackie, 1986). Third, polarization is mediated by group members' perceptions of the ingroup's position (Turner et al., 1989). Fourth, intergroup attitudinal polarization is more extreme (ingroup and outgroup positions are further apart) when group membership is more salient, or members identify more strongly with their group (e.g., Mackie, 1986; Mackie & Cooper, 1984; Turner et al., 1989).

Integration   It has long been acknowledged that informational and normative approaches appear to work together to produce group polarization (Kaplan & Miller, 1987). Isenberg's (1986) meta-analysis, which predates the self-categorization account, reported significant effect sizes for effects produced by both the normative account and, especially, persuasive arguments theory. Which kind of influence is more important depends on the context. Kaplan (1987) concluded that normative influence was more likely with judgemental issues, a group goal of harmony, person-oriented group members and public responses, whereas informational influence was more likely with intellectual issues, a group goal of making a correct decision, task-oriented group members and private responses. The self-categorization account can integrate the other two approaches because it contends that *arguments* from other ingroup members will be more persuasive than those of outgroup members, and that learning the *positions* of ingroup members will be more persuasive than learning about the positions of outgroup members.

Groupthink

Part of the explanation for research activity on group polarization is the potentially serious implications of polarization for decision-making in natural settings (Eagly & Chaiken, 1993). Such decisions

Plate 11.5 *Group polarization can have potentially serious implications for decision-making in natural settings such as cabinet meetings.*

are typically made by groups composed of like-minded participants (e.g., councils, committees, juries, the cabinets of ruling governments), and the processes involved may lead the groups to make decisions that are incorrect, unwise or, in the worst case, disastrous. This is most evident in the case of *groupthink*, a syndrome of poor group decision-making in which members of a cohesive ingroup

> **groupthink** a syndrome of poor group decision-making in which members of a cohesive ingroup strive for unanimity at the expense of a realistic appraisal of alternative courses of action

strive for unanimity at the expense of a realistic appraisal of alternative courses of action (Janis, 1982; see Figure 11.11 and Chapter 2, this volume). Groupthink does not necessarily arise from group polarization, but it is an extreme form of problems associated with the failure to exchange information (or, at least, different views) among group members (Levine & Moreland, 1998). In essence, groupthink constitutes an extreme form of normative influence, where the norm to reach and maintain consensus and harmony within the group completely eliminates any informational influence that could show how disastrous the group's intended decision is likely to be.

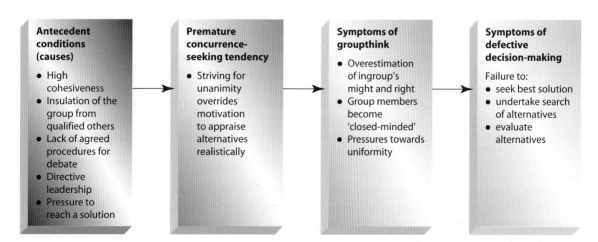

Antecedent conditions (causes)	Premature concurrence-seeking tendency	Symptoms of groupthink	Symptoms of defective decision-making
• High cohesiveness • Insulation of the group from qualified others • Lack of agreed procedures for debate • Directive leadership • Pressure to reach a solution	• Striving for unanimity overrides motivation to appraise alternatives realistically	• Overestimation of ingroup's might and right • Group members become 'closed-minded' • Pressures towards uniformity	Failure to: • seek best solution • undertake search of alternatives • evaluate alternatives

Figure 11.11 *Schematic analysis of groupthink model (after Janis, 1982).*

The concept of groupthink (which alludes to Big Brother's attempt to control the way people think, in George Orwell's 1949 novel *Nineteen eighty-four*) has received a great deal of popular attention because it claims to explain a series of US foreign policy fiascos, including the calamitous Bay of Pigs invasion of Cuba (1961) and the escalation of the Vietnam War (1964–1967). Janis applied work on group decisions to elite political settings by carrying out a series of case studies, in which he researched government records, political diaries and politicians' accounts of these turbulent periods (see also Raven, 1974; t'Hart, 1990). According to Janis, the main causes of groupthink include high cohesiveness, insulation of the group from external critics, opinionated leadership, lack of agreed procedures for debate and pressure to reach a solution. Specifically, Janis (1982) claimed that high cohesiveness in interaction with a stressful situation leads to groupthink; this outcome will be more likely the more structural weaknesses are present in the group (e.g., insulation, directive leadership and lack of agreed decision-making procedures).

In turn, some of the main characteristics of groupthink decision-makers are that they are more prone to: jump to premature conclusions, dismiss contradictory information, bolster preferred options, suppress dissent within the group and display excessive optimism about the outcomes (Tetlock, 1998). Such decision-making is, moreover, not restricted to foreign policy issues. Esser and Lindoerfer (1989) argued that the ill-fated decision to launch the *Challenger* space shuttle in 1986 (in which seven astronauts died as the shuttle exploded 59 seconds after ignition) had many of the hallmarks of groupthink (see also Starbuck & Farjoun, 2005).

Popular as the notion of groupthink is, its empirical basis is rather weak. Analysis of case studies, often based on content analysis of archival records (see Chapter 2, p. 23), does show increased rigidity and more simplistic thinking among decision-makers involved in groupthink decisions compared to more favourable outcomes (Tetlock, 1979). Herek, Janis and Huth (1987) also reported a negative association between the number of symptoms of groupthink and the quality of the decision. But there is little evidence that cohesiveness alone, or in combination with other supposed antecedents, contributes to defective decision-making. As Tetlock (1998) also points out, one can quite easily find successful political decisions in cases with evidence of groupthink (e.g., Churchill suppressed dissent in cabinet meeting in 1940–1941, when some group members advocated a negotiated peace with Hitler), but also instances where vigilant decision-making failed to prevent disastrous outcomes (e.g., President Jimmy Carter's failed mission to rescue hostages from Iran in 1980, despite his encouragement of open debate).

Laboratory studies are even less supportive, perhaps because it is difficult, if not impossible, to create in the laboratory true analogues of highly cohesive, insulated groups, working under high pressure to make decisions with massive political consequences (Esser, 1998; Mullen, Anthony, Salas & Driskell, 1994). Manipulations of groupthink have generally not produced poor-quality discussions and decisions (Flowers, 1977; Leana, 1985), and groupthink has been found in groups with either high or low cohesiveness (see Aldag & Fuller, 1993; Turner, Pratkanis, Probasco & Love, 1992).

There are also fundamental weaknesses of the groupthink model. It does not allow precise predictions, it is difficult to operationalize the concept (must all the characteristics of groupthink be present to define it as such?) and it is often only applied after the fact. Thus Aldag and Fuller (1993) proposed a more general, but also more complex, group problem-solving model (see also t'Hart, Stern & Sundelius, 1995). It includes many of the features discussed by Janis, but also includes others. For example, it allows for cohesiveness to play a role, but it is seen as just one aspect of *group structure* (see Chapter 12, this volume) which, along with *decision characteristics* and *decision-making context*, determine *emergent group characteristics* (e.g., perceptions that the ingroup is moral and unanimous in its opinions). These characteristics, in turn, affect *decision process characteristics* (e.g., how carefully objectives are surveyed and whether alternatives are generated), leading ultimately to *outcomes*. We present a simplified version of this model in Figure 11.12.

Obedience to authority

As we have seen in this chapter, social influence emanates from many sources, often group members of equal status to the target of influence. Research on *obedience to authority*, which began with Stanley

obedience to authority complying with orders from a person of higher social status within a defined hierarchy or chain of command

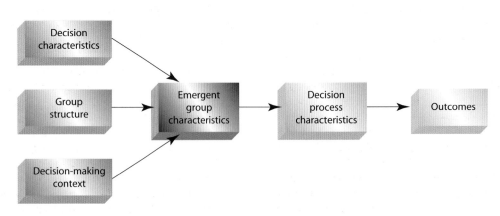

Figure 11.12 *Simplified general problem-solving model (after Aldag & Fuller, 1993).*

Stanley Milgram (1933–1984) earned his Bachelor's degree at Queens College, New York, in 1954, but it was in political science and he never took a psychology course as an undergraduate. He completed his PhD at Harvard University, and taught at Yale University and the New School for Social Research, New York. Although best known for his research on obedience, Milgram also studied conformity, life in cities, and did pioneering work on non-reactive measures. His research across many diverse fields is characterized by its phenomenological approach, the salience of moral issues and the importance he attached to situational determinants of social behaviour.  Milgram has recently received the honour of a full-length biography, entitled *The Man Who Shocked the World: The Life and Legacy of Stanley Milgram* (Blass, 2004, Basic Books).

Source: www.stanleymilgram.com/

Plate 11.6 *Milgram's research into obedience was originally intended to help us to understand how the Nazi Holocaust could have taken place.*

Milgram's (1963) famous research, addresses a different form of influence, namely, obedience to a source who is not an equal but an authority figure. Obedience here is defined as complying with orders from a person of higher social status within a defined hierarchy or chain of command (Miller, 1995). It is often an example of the functioning of legitimate power, whereby an internalized framework of norms, values, customs and procedures specifies that such influence is appropriate (Turner, 1991; e.g., we are told to 'do as your parents/teachers/senior officers tell you'). The motives underlying obedience are diverse, including respect for the expertise of authority and fear of the consequences of disobedience. Below we shall: (1) outline Milgram's paradigm and initial results; (2) review some of the findings on the situational determinants of obedience; (3) evaluate the theoretical analysis of obedience; (4) consider ethical issues; and (5) introduce the phenomenon of disobedience.

Milgram's obedience paradigm The classic research was conducted by Milgram (1963, 1974), who intended that his experimental research should help us to understand better how the Nazi Holocaust (and all the individual acts of obedience involved in that systematic annihilation) could have taken place. Milgram was, specifically, fascinated with the trial in Jerusalem of the arch-architect of the 'Final Solution', Adolf Eichmann, as reported by the philosopher Hannah Arendt (1965) in her book *Eichmann in Jerusalem: A Report on the Banality of Evil*. If such evil were 'banal', or unexceptional, then would most people show destructive obedience? Prior to his research Milgram doubted it, and indeed his first study was intended to be the 'baseline', a situation in which few people would obey. Later research was then to manipulate key variables and investigate their impact on rates of obedience (see Milgram, 1963, 1974; see also Blass, 1999, 2000; Miller, Collins & Brief, 1995).

We have already referred to some details of this notorious research to lay out principles of research methodology (see Chapter 2, this volume). Now we go into more detail, highlighting crucial aspects of the research and referring to some of the 18 studies reported by Milgram in his 1974 book. For his first study Milgram recruited 40 male participants via newspaper advertisements (no mention was made of obedience). At the laboratory, the investigator explained that a teacher–learner scenario would be used, and participants were led to believe that roles had been determined by chance. The 'victim' was, in fact, an experimental confederate. The experimenter explained that, by means of a simulated shock generator, the participant (as 'teacher') was to deliver increasingly more intense electric shocks to the 'learner' each time he made a mistake on the learning task (participants were informed that the shocks were extremely painful, but that they would cause no permanent damage; Milgram, 1963). In fact, no shocks were delivered, but the impact of the experimental scenario was so high that all participants believed that they were shocking the learner.

The learner was strapped into a chair and electrodes were fixed to his wrists. The teacher was taken to a different room, where he was instructed to punish the learner's first mistake with a shock of 15 volts, increasing in intensity by 15 volts with every new mistake. A shock generator in front of him showed the teacher 30 buttons, and clear verbal labels, ranging from 15 volts, through 60 volts ('slight shock'), to 120 volts ('moderate shock') and finally to 450 volts ('danger: severe shock, XXX'). In a clever touch, Milgram ensured that all participants experienced the reality of a relatively low-intensity electric shock (45 volts) so that they could not later claim that they had not believed they were really shocking the victim.

Milgram, a dramatist as much as an experimenter (see Blass, 1992), carefully *scripted* the whole scenario, down to the detail of having the experimenter wear a *grey* lab coat (indicating that he was a mere technician) rather than, as is frequently *mis*reported, a white coat (which might have signified that he was a higher-status physician or scientist). The victim's responses were a predetermined series, rising in intensity with the level of shock: 'Ugh' (75, 90, 105 volts); 'Hey, this really hurts' (120 volts); 'Experimenter, get me out of here! I won't be in the experiment any more! I refuse to go on' (150 volts); screams of agony (270 volts); screams and refusal to answer (300, 315 volts); and an intense and prolonged agonized scream (330 volts). Likewise the experimenter used a graded set of commands ('prods') to keep the teacher going: 'Please continue'; 'The experiment requires that you continue'; 'It is absolutely essential that you continue'; and 'You have no other choice, you *must* go on'. In this way Milgram ensured that his experimental scenario had a very high impact on participants without sacrificing control over the situation.

The results of this baseline study were staggering. Far from the minimal level of obedience expected, no participant stopped before administering a 300 volt shock. Across the sample, maximal obedience was shown by 26 of 40 respondents: 65 per cent. By comparison, in a later study, when participants were free to choose any shock level, only 2 out of 40 participants exceeded the 150 volt level, and 28 never went beyond 75 volts.

Situational determinants of obedience
The main thrust of Milgram's subsequent studies was to explore variation in the rate of obedience across different social situations. In various conditions, for example, Milgram manipulated the proximity of the victim, the authority of the experimenter and the behaviour of peers.

Four conditions varied the physical (and emotional) proximity of the victim. In one condition he pounded heavily on the wall separating his room from the teacher's; in another the participant heard his crying and shouting (as described earlier). In two other conditions the teacher and the victim were actually in the same room; in one condition, the teacher not only heard but also saw the victim; in the other condition, the teacher had to hold the victim's hand down on a shock plate. The obedience rates corresponding to these four conditions of increasing proximity are shown in Figure 11.13. Maximal obedience fell from 65 per cent of the participants to 30 per cent.

Milgram also varied the authority of the experimenter and how much control he exerted. This was hugely influential. When the experimenter was absent from the participant's room and gave his

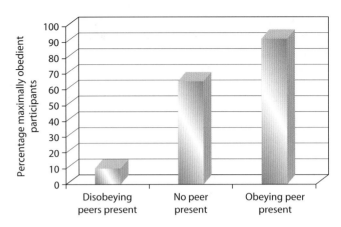

Figure 11.14 *Obedience as a function of peer behaviour (data from Milgram, 1974).*

orders over the telephone, maximal obedience dropped to 21 per cent (a number of participants said over the phone that they were giving higher shocks than they in fact did!). In another variation, the experimenter had to leave the room before instructing the participant to increase shock levels. He handed over his authority to a second participant who was present, and who would only have to record the learner's reaction times. This second participant then came up with the idea of increasing the shock level with every error and, throughout the learning session, he insisted that the teacher applied his rules. Only 20 per cent of the participants obeyed the equal-status authority to the end. In addition, when a participant refused to obey and the 'authority' decided that he would administer the shocks himself, a number of participants physically attacked the 'torturer' or tried to unplug the shock generator. Participants did not, however, show such heroism when the authority was the high-status scientist.

Two experimental variations investigated the role of peer pressure. In the first there were three co-teachers, the participant and two confederates. The first confederate presented the task, the second recorded the learner's responses and the participant administered the shocks. The first confederate refused to continue at 150 volts, and was joined by the second confederate at 210 volts. Their refusal had a dramatic effect on the participants, only 10 per cent were maximally obedient compared with 65 per cent when no peer was present (see Figure 11.14). In contrast, if the teacher, who administered the learning task, was accompanied by a co-teacher, who gave the shocks (obedient peer), 92 per cent of the participants participated in the experiment to the end.

Why do people obey?
It is not convincing to argue that the participants (a majority of whom obeyed to high levels across most studies) were sadists. In one study by Milgram participants *chose* their own level of shock, and they opted for very low-level shocks. Surely sadists would have seized their opportunity here? Participants also appeared to be distressed by the experience, often appearing tense, displaying nervous laughter, sweating profusely and even begging the experimenter to stop. This tends to rule out both the possibility that participants were sadists and the claim that

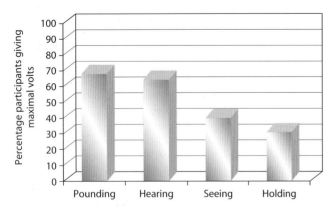

Figure 11.13 *Obedience as a function of physical proximity (data from Milgram, 1974).*

they did not believe Milgram's cover story. Milgram's own theoretical analysis of obedience included four factors, which have received varying levels of support.

First, and rather descriptively, Milgram argued for the importance of socio-cultural factors. We grow up in a society where we learn (indeed, we are taught) to obey authorities, beginning with parents and school teachers, and ending with police officers. Moreover, we expect those authority figures to be legitimate and trustworthy. Second, and more persuasively, Milgram pointed to 'binding factors', the subtle creation of psychological barriers to disobedience. He used the notion of 'entrapment' to refer to the experimenter's gradual increase in punishment levels ordered (cf. the 'foot-in-the-door' technique for obtaining compliance, discussed earlier), rather than beginning with an outrageous demand which most participants would probably have refused. This subtle progression towards destructive obedience may be crucial in helping us to understand how ordinary individuals can ultimately commit acts of evil (see Browning, 1992; Darley, 1992; Kelman & Hamilton, 1989; Miller, 1986).

Third, Milgram argued that the subordinate in a hierarchical system does not accept personal responsibility for his or her actions, but allocates this responsibility to someone higher up in the organization. He referred to this as an 'agentic shift', where the obedient participants switch off their own conscience and see themselves as *agents* for carrying out a more senior person's wishes. This, of course, is a convenient, self-serving account used by many perpetrators of evil, such as the former Iraqi torturer's statement that 'I was following orders. Saddam is responsible' (reported in the *Observer*, 14 May 2006). Empirical support for this notion is, however, weak (see Nissani, 1990; Waller, 2002). Mantell and Panzarella (1976) reported no relationship between participants' degree of obedience and their assignment of responsibility. In post-experimental interviews, Milgram asked participants to divide up responsibility between the experimenter, themselves and the victim. He reported that both obedient and defiant participants attributed almost equal responsibility to the experimenter, which contradicts the claim that obedient participants somehow pass responsibility up the 'chain of command'. However, defiant participants saw themselves as more responsible (and the learner-victim as less responsible) than did the obedient participants (see Milgram, 1974, Appendix II).

Fourth, and finally, Milgram's whole research programme placed huge emphasis on the power of the situation, something that is fundamental to the study of social psychology (see Chapter 1, this volume). His findings suggest that destructive obedience is well within the behavioural repertoire of most people (Miller, 1986). Personality is not irrelevant (individuals who hold authoritarian beliefs are more likely to obey authorities; Elms & Milgram, 1966; Kelman & Hamilton, 1989), but it pales into insignificance when compared with the power of the situation. To acknowledge this fact, however, is not to exonerate the perpetrators of evil deeds and adopt a morally condoning attitude towards them (Miller, Gordon & Buddie, 1999). Harm-doing, which may well have been instigated by situational factors initially, demands self-regulation processes that definitely involve the actor-person himself (see Bandura, 1999).

Ethical issues Milgram's research has become the most famous of all experiments in social psychology (it spawned TV programmes, a play and even a song by Peter Gabriel, *We Do What We're Told*). It speaks to the darkest side of human nature, and has been used in attempts to understand better phenomena such as genocide (Staub, 1989) and war crimes (Bourke, 1999). But it also became infamous, generating controversy centred on ethical issues (see Baumrind, 1964; Miller, 1986; see also Chapter 2, this volume). Milgram was severely criticized for inducing suffering in his participants. Using a procedure that would be impossible to replicate today given ethical guidelines for research, he induced stress and anxiety in his participants and, among those who did obey, guilt about how they had behaved. No contemporary study could inform participants that, although blatantly untrue, 'it is absolutely essential that you continue' or 'you have no other choice, you *must* go on'. Indeed, the furore caused by this research is credited with generating regulations that control the use of human participants in psychological research. More generally, some of the questions you may care to consider are: Could the participants' psychological suffering be dealt with in normal debriefing? How would participants react on learning that they were – apparently – capable of heinous acts in response to orders? Should the experiment ever have been carried out? Is the research sufficiently important to justify such deception of, and stress experienced by, participants? To what extent was the criticism triggered by the results rather than by the research itself?

Disobedience Another valuable perspective on Milgram's research is whether the results are, in fact, so surprising. Later critics suggested that the experimenter may have played a more active role in instigating obedience than is evident from Milgram's (1965) early report (perhaps inducing obedience through demand characteristics), and that the evidence of *dis*obedience is itself remarkable (35 per cent of the participants defied the experiment at some point). Early resistance seems crucial (only 17 per cent of those showing early signs of protest delivered shocks of more than 150 volts), a finding that is consistent with Rochat and Modigliani's (1995) historical study of French citizens who, during World War II, refused to persecute war refugees in the village of Le Chambon.

Whistleblowing is a specific form of disobedience, occurring when people report corruption or unethical practice within an organization. Such behaviour is, however,

> **whistleblowing** a specific form of disobedience in which an 'insider' (e.g., an employee) reports corruption or unethical practice within an organization

relatively rare, not least because a significant proportion of whistleblowers are subjected to harassment from senior members of the organization or ostracism from peers (Glazer & Glazer, 1989; MacNamara, 1991; Miceli & Near, 1992). Whistleblowers are, in effect, critics of the ingroup, who are generally damned for their temerity (see Hornsey, 2005), and there is evidence from the medical domain suggesting that willingness to blow the whistle declines with time in training (Goldie, Schwartz, McConnachie & Morrison, 2003). Apparently, medical students learn to keep quiet by seeing the retaliation meted out to whistleblowers (Bolsin, 2003). Yet such courageous action is necessary, whether to stop medical malpractice (as in the case of the junior doctor who blew the whistle on a senior surgeon responsible for abnormally high mortality rates in paediatric heart surgery at a hospital in Bristol, UK, during the 1990s) or mistreatment of prisoners of war (as in the case of the Navy dog handler who refused to be drawn into the abuse of Iraqi prisoners in Abu Ghraib prison; see Greenberg & Dratel, 2005).

Research on obedience in perspective Whatever your view of Milgram's experiments (ethically acceptable or not; due to demand characteristics or not), every social psychologist should read and have an opinion about Milgram's research on obedience (see Blass, 1992). Subsequent studies, in different countries and with various paradigms, have demonstrated the generality of the effect he first demonstrated (e.g., Mantell, 1971; Meeus & Raaijmakers, 1986, 1995; Shanab & Yahya, 1978) and highlighted the importance of obedience in a range of settings, including medical (Hofling, Brotzman, Dairymple, Graves & Pierce, 1966; Rank & Jacobson, 1977) and organizational contexts (cf. the financial scandal in the USA, involving Enron and Arthur Andersen; Lee Toffler & Reingold, 2003; Swartz & Watkins, 2003), and not just military ones. Milgram specifically sought to extend Asch's conformity experiment to 'something more consequential than judging lengths of lines' (Blass, 1992, p. 286). In this he was hugely successful: destructive obedience is more widespread than most of us would ever have imagined. This research can, however, provide only part of the explanation for the excesses of the Third Reich, which Milgram set out to understand. The Nazi Holocaust included many acts that were not simply acts of obedience to authority (see Browning, 1992; Goldhagen, 1996; Johnson & Reuband, 2005; Newman & Erber, 2002).

SUMMARY

The study of deliberate social influence introduces some of the most celebrated experiments ever carried out by social psychologists. We began by considering three main techniques of compliance, based on requests – the door-in-the-face, the foot-in-the-door and lowballing. Next, we reviewed the literature on majority vs. minority social influence, showing how the field has moved from a narrow focus on majority influence only to an understanding that both majorities and minorities can be influential, and in various ways. We then reported on the tendency of groups to polarize individual members' views and linked this to some of the extreme consequences of social influence in groups, as seen in groupthink. Finally, we reviewed research on obedience to authority, including Milgram's classic research and its ethical consequences, and the phenomenon of whistleblowing.

SUMMARY AND CONCLUSIONS

- This chapter discussed two main types of social influence, 'incidental' and 'deliberate', and how they can be understood in terms of fundamental motives.

- Social influence refers to change of attitudes, beliefs, opinions, values and behaviour as a result of being exposed to other individuals' attitudes, beliefs, opinions, values and behaviour. It forms the interface between individualistic and group approaches to social psychology.

- Incidental social influence refers to situations in which people are influenced, although there has been no explicit attempt to influence them.

- People are influenced by the presence or implied presence of others, which tends to improve performance on simple / well-learned tasks but worsen performance on complex / novel tasks.

- Social norms are the most fundamental concept in the study of social influence. They can be descriptive or injunctive, we can infer them from other people's behaviour, and they can be easily established and transmitted.

- Social influence is driven by some of the fundamental motives directing human social behaviour. Ultimately, we are influenced by others so that we behave proficiently, build and maintain relationships with others, manage our own self-concept, and understand the social world more effectively.

- Deliberate social influence includes compliance with requests, the influence of numerical majorities and minorities, group decision-making and obedience to authority.

- There is evidence for each of the three main techniques of compliance – door-in-the-face, foot-in-the-door and lowballing – which rely greatly on general principles such as equity, reciprocity and self-consistency.

- Both numerical majorities and minorities can exert influence, and the major explanations concern conflict and social categorization. Majorities tend to have greater influence on public and direct measures, but minorities can be more effective on indirect, private measures.

- Groups tend to polarize decisions, due to normative, informational and referent influence. So-called groupthink is an extreme form of poor decision-making, but this model has fundamental weaknesses.

- Obedience to immoral authority is primarily driven by situational factors, but we still lack a clear explanation of why it occurs. Research on this topic poses important ethical questions, and more recent work on whistleblowing underlines the moral importance of disobedience.

- Social influence is an ambivalent concept. The very existence of a society depends on it, but it can be a force for good (e.g., donations to charity) as well as for bad (e.g., tyranny of the majority), and even evil (e.g., obedience to authority leading to immoral behaviour).

Suggestions for further reading

Asch, S.E. (1956). Studies of independence and conformity: A minority of one against a unanimous majority. *Psychological Monographs*, 70(9), Whole no. 416. This text presents Asch's own account of his famous conformity experiments. The best way to learn about these studies is to read them first hand.

Baron, R.S. & Kerr, N. (2003). *Group process, group decision, group action* (2nd edn). Buckingham: Open University Press. Extends the material presented in this chapter on social facilitation, majority and minority influence and group decision-making.

Cialdini, R.B. & Trost, M.R. (1998). Social influence: Social norms, conformity, and compliance. In D.T. Gilbert, S.T.

Fiske & G. Lindzey (Eds.), *The handbook of social psychology* (4th edn, Vol. 2, pp. 151–192). New York: McGraw-Hill. Authoritative source, especially good on norms and compliance strategies.

Janis, I.L. (1972). *Victims of groupthink*. Boston: Houghton Mifflin. Janis's original presentation of groupthink, illustrated with case materials showing disastrous decision-making in the area of foreign policy.

Martin, R. & Hewstone, M. (2003). Social influence. In M. Hogg & J. Cooper (Eds.), *Sage handbook of social psychology* (pp. 347–366). London: Sage.

Milgram, S. (1974). *Obedience to authority*. New York: Harper & Row. Compelling and readable overview of Milgram's own programme of 18 experiments, and the furore they unleashed.

Miller, A.G., Collins, B.E. & Brief, D.E. (Eds.) (1995). Perspectives on obedience to authority: The legacy of the Milgram experiments. *Journal of Social Issues*, 51, 1–212. A journal special issue on reactions to Milgram's obedience research and subsequent theory and research on obedient and defiant behaviour.

Turner, J.C. (1991). *Social influence*. Buckingham: Open University Press. A scholarly overview of the whole field, with a sophisticated theoretical analysis from the perspective of self-categorization theory.

12

The Psychology of Groups: Basic Principles

Bernard A. Nijstad and Daan van Knippenberg

CHAPTER OUTLINE

....

Groups are pervasive in social life. In this chapter, we discuss why people form and join groups, and what types of groups can be distinguished. We further discuss three levels of analysis. At the individual level, we discuss the (changing) relations between the group and its members. At the group level, we discuss group development, group structure (status and roles) and group norms. At the intergroup level, we discuss how the (intergroup) context shapes the behaviour of group members and the structure of groups.

Introduction

....

Imagine you're spending a weekend in Amsterdam. You enter a subway station, which is quite crowded. From the way people are dressed – many are wearing red and white Ajax shirts – you infer that they must be Ajax fans going to support their football team. These fans show remarkable behaviour: they sing and shout in ways they would not normally behave in public. Yet, most of them are adults (and not all are drunk), and they only show this behaviour when there is an Ajax match. The most striking aspect of their behaviour is that the fans behave so similarly. However,

Plate 12.1 *These fans share membership of a social group: they are all Ajax football supporters.*

many of them do not even know each other, and their behaviour is quite out of the ordinary: normally, people would not sing and shout in a subway.

The only reason these fans behave so similarly is that they share membership of a social group: they are all Ajax fans. In this chapter, we argue that in order to understand their behaviour and behaviour in other groups, we need to consider three *levels of analysis*: the individual level, the group level and the wider context in which groups are situated. At the individual level, all Ajax fans in the subway are individually aware of their group membership (being an Ajax fan) and of the fact that the other people in the subway are Ajax fans as well. At the group level, the fact that their behaviour is so similar indicates that it cannot be caused by idiosyncratic tendencies of individual Ajax fans, such as their individual personalities. Rather, there is something 'groupy' going on which guides

their behaviour. At the broader level, one could argue that these fans only show this behaviour because of the context: there is going to be a football match in which Ajax will play against another team. Indeed, if there had been no such match, the fans would behave quite differently.

In this chapter, we use this three-level framework to discuss some basic characteristics of groups and some basic processes in groups. We first examine the issues of what a group is, why people form or join groups, and what types of groups can be distinguished. We then move on to the individual level and discuss how individuals join groups and how their group membership develops over time. We then consider the group level, as we discuss group development and group structure. Finally, we discuss the (intergroup) context in which groups exist and how this context affects processes that occur in groups.

THE PHENOMENOLOGY OF GROUPS

....

What is a group?
Why do people form, join and distinguish groups?
What kinds of groups can be distinguished, and what are their characteristics?
What is group entitativity, and what contributes to perceptions of entitativity?

Defining groups

Groups are everywhere: we see groups of friends in a bar, groups of colleagues in an organization, groups of fans in a stadium. But what exactly do we mean by the word 'group?' Many authors have suggested different ingredients towards a definition of groups. Lewin (1948) suggested that common fate is critical: people are a group to the extent that they experience similar outcomes. Sherif and Sherif (1969) proposed that some form of social structure (status or role differentiation, e.g., a leadership role) is essential, because otherwise the 'group' would just be a loose collection of individuals. Bales (1950) stressed the importance of face-to-face interaction. We suggest a broader definition of groups: following Tajfel (1981), we argue that *a group exists when two or more individuals define themselves as members of a group.*

A few things should be noted. First, many different groups would fit this definition, including religious groups (Christians), national groups (the British), organizational groups (the psychology department) and friendship groups (a student society). Second, it is subjective and does not include any 'objective' characteristics of groups, such as common fate or face-to-face interaction. Rather, it emphasizes common identity: sharing the view with others that you belong to the same group. Third, it is important to recognize

that one can only talk about groups to the extent that there are people who do not belong to the group, although they belong to other groups.

Why groups?

Why do humans form, join and distinguish groups? Several theoretical perspectives can be applied to answer that question. We will discuss three: a sociobiological, a cognitive and a utilitarian perspective (also see Baron & Kerr, 2003). These three perspectives are complementary rather than mutually exclusive.

Following Darwin's evolution theory, the *sociobiological perspective* (e.g., Bowlby, 1958) emphasizes the adaptive value of forming groups. Forming groups enables humans (and other social animals) to deal more effectively with enemies or predators, and allows cooperation in such areas as raising children, farming or hunting. Especially earlier in our evolutionary history, when food was often scarce and enemies and predators were dangerous, forming groups had a significant advantage. A predisposition to form groups increased the chances of survival of the individual and, through the evolutionary principle of natural selection, this predisposition was selected and passed on to later generations. This human predisposition to form and maintain stable, strong and positive relationships with others is called the ***need to belong*** (Baumeister & Leary, 1995). Baumeister and

> **need to belong** the fundamental and innate human motivation to form positive, strong and stable bonds with others

Leary argued that this human need is innate and universal. Indeed, evidence indicates that the tendency to form groups is found across all cultures and situations, suggesting that this tendency is evolutionarily 'built in'.

According to the *cognitive perspective*, groups help us to understand our world. *Social comparison theory* (Festinger, 1954; see Chapters 5 and 10, this volume) argues that people want to hold accurate views of the world. They can do this by validating their beliefs either against 'physical reality' (e.g., 'Will this glass crack if I hit it with a hammer?') or against 'social reality' (e.g., 'I like this new music; I wonder what my friends think about it?'). People turn to others especially for beliefs for which there is no physical reality (e.g., preferences). Building on these ideas, *social identity theory* (e.g., Tajfel & Turner, 1986; see Chapter 5, this volume) and *self-categorization theory* (Turner, Hogg, Oakes, Reicher & Wetherell, 1987; see Chapters 5 and 11, this volume) argue that people define themselves and others partly in terms of group membership. The theory argues that seeing oneself and others as members of groups helps to reduce uncertainty and make sense of our world (e.g., Hogg & Abrams, 1993). Being a member of a group often provides guidelines for the way we should behave and think. If you think about the Ajax football fans we started this chapter with, their behaviour is clearly guided by their group membership and the behaviours thought to be appropriate for that group (see our later discussion of group norms). Further, seeing other people as members of certain groups helps to interpret their behaviour: knowing that the people in the subway are Ajax fans makes it much easier to understand what is going on.

A *utilitarian perspective* argues that people derive benefits from groups. *Social exchange theory* (e.g., Thibaut & Kelley, 1959; see Chapter 10, this volume) argues that social relations (including those within groups) help to fulfil the individual's needs and often take the form of exchange processes. These exchanges might involve material goods (e.g., borrowing a tool, selling your car) or interpersonal helping (helping a friend move house), but also psychological 'goods' such as love, friendship or approval. Enduring exchange relations between two or more people are more effectively organized when people form a (more or less stable) group. Thus, groups exist because they facilitate mutually beneficial social exchange.

Social exchange theory argues that social relations involve costs as well as benefits, and as long as the benefits exceed the costs the relation will yield a 'profit'. There is much evidence that people are unhappy about relations if they feel that they invest more in them (e.g., time) than they get back (e.g., approval) (e.g., Le & Agnew, 2003; see also Chapter 10). Furthermore, satisfaction with an exchange relationship depends on the degree to which alternative relationships exist that yield more profit. Thus, people join groups because they derive benefits from their group membership. People may leave groups (if possible) when they are unhappy about the benefits relative to the costs of group membership, or when alternative groups exist that have a better cost–benefit ratio (also see Rusbult & Farrell, 1983). In general, people will leave groups when better alternatives are available, including the option of being alone.

Types of groups and group entitativity

As we noted earlier, our definition of groups is relatively broad and many types of groups may be included. However, there are different types of groups with different characteristics. Further, some groups seem more 'groupy' than other groups, a phenomenon often referred to as the **entitativity** of groups: the degree to which a collection of persons is perceived as being bonded together in a coherent unit (Campbell, 1958).

> **entitativity** the degree to which a collection of persons is perceived as being bonded together in a coherent unit

So, what different types of groups can we distinguish? Lickel et al. (2000) wondered whether people spontaneously distinguish between different types of groups. They provided their participants (American and Polish students) with a sample of 40 different groups, such as 'members of a family', 'blacks', 'members of a jury' and 'people in line at a bank'. Participants had to rate these different groups on eight dimensions: importance of group members to each other, common goals and common outcomes for group members, degree of interaction among members, size, duration, permeability (how easy it is to join or leave the group) and similarity among group members. The groups were also rated on the degree to which the group really was a group (group entitativity). After they had done the ratings, participants were asked to sort the 40 groups into different categories using their own individual criteria, including as many or as few categories as they wanted.

Lickel et al. (2000) found that some of their 40 groups were consistently sorted into one common category, whereas other groups were consistently sorted into other categories. Further, groups that were sorted into the same category were also rated similarly on the eight dimensions. Lickel et al. identified four types of groups: intimacy groups, task groups, social categories and loose associations. In Table 12.1 we give a summary of their findings and some examples of the different types of groups. As can be seen in the table, the types of groups differed along the different dimensions. For example, intimacy groups (e.g., a family) were seen as

PIONEER

John Walter Thibaut (1917–1986) was born in Marion, Ohio. He studied philosophy at the University of North Carolina. During World War II, he came into contact with psychology when he was assigned to the Aviation Psychology Program. In 1946, he moved to the Massachusetts Institute of Technology to study with Kurt Lewin. After Lewin's death in 1947, Thibaut moved to the University of Michigan where he received his PhD. His subsequent career took him to Boston University, Harvard University and back to the University of North Carolina. Thibaut is best known for his 1959 book (co-authored with Harold Kelley) *The Social Psychology of Groups*. In that book, Thibaut and Kelley laid out the foundations of social exchange theory, arguing that social relations take the form of social exchange processes.

Plate 12.2 *Intimacy groups, e.g. a family, are seen as high in entitativity.*

et al. (2000) also considered which of their eight group characteristics best predicted group entitativity. They found that the single most important predictor was interaction among group members: higher levels of interaction were associated with higher entitativity. The other characteristics also contributed to entitativity: importance, common goals and outcomes, group member similarity and duration showed a positive relation (the higher the importance, common goals, etc., the higher the perceived entitativity), whereas group size and permeability showed a weak negative relation (larger groups and highly permeable groups were rated lower in entitativity). Note that some of the possible components of a definition of groups that we described earlier (common fate, face-to-face interaction) were positively associated with perceived group entitativity: they indeed make groups more 'groupy'.

important, with high levels of interaction, common goals and outcomes, a high degree of similarity, fairly small, of long duration and low permeability. Social categories (e.g., women), in contrast, were rated low on importance of members to each other, with low levels of interaction, common goals and outcomes, and member similarity, and were rated to be large, of long duration and low in permeability.

With regard to group entitativity, intimacy groups and task groups were seen as high in entitativity, loose associations as low, and social categories occupied an intermediate position. Lickel

SUMMARY

Forming, joining and distinguishing groups has a number of advantages: groups help us to make sense of our world and to coordinate more effectively mutually beneficial social exchange. The tendency to form groups probably is evolutionarily built in, as groups are found everywhere. However, not every type of group is equally important or 'groupy': especially intimacy groups and task groups are seen to be important and high in entitativity, while social categories and loose associations are less so.

Table 12.1 *Characteristics of different types of groups (based on Lickel et al., 2000)*

Characteristic	Type of group (examples)			
	Intimacy group (family members, friends, romantic partners)	*Task group (jury members, cast of a play, sports team)*	*Social category (women, blacks, Americans)*	*Loose association (people at a bus stop, at the cinema, living in same area)*
Entitativity	High	High	Moderate	Low
Interaction	High	Moderate/High	Low	Low
Importance	High	Moderate/High	Low	Low
Common goals	High	Moderate/High	Low	Low
Common outcomes	High	Moderate/High	Low	Low
Similarity	High	Moderate	Low	Low
Duration	Long	Moderate	Long	Short
Permeability	Low	Moderate	Low	High
Size	Small	Small	Large	Moderate

INDIVIDUALS IN GROUPS: THE INDIVIDUAL LEVEL OF ANALYSIS

What stages of group socialization can be distinguished?
What are role transitions and what determines their occurrence?
How does dissonance theory explain severity of initiation?

In this section we consider the individual within the group: that is, we focus on the individual level of analysis. In particular, we discuss Moreland and Levine's (1982) model of *group socialization*, which is depicted in Figure 12.1. The model is applicable to groups that exist for comparatively long periods of time and have direct interaction between members, but that experience changes in membership. Examples would include a sports team, a team within an organization or a student society (i.e., many intimacy groups and task groups).

Moreland and Levine's model distinguishes five stages of group membership: investigation, socialization, maintenance, resocialization and remembrance. According to the model, moving from one stage to the next involves a *role transition*. Thus, moving from prospective member (the stage of investigation) to new member (the stage of socialization) involves the role transition of entry. Further role transitions are acceptance (from new member to full member), divergence (from full member to marginal member) and exit (from marginal member to ex-member). As can be seen in Figure 12.1, the five different stages differ in the degree of *commitment* of the individual to the group, in other words, the degree to which a group member identifies with the group and its goals and wishes to maintain group membership. Commitment increases gradually as people become full members, after which it decreases towards the point that individuals wish to leave the group.

Role transitions occur as a result of evaluation processes in which the group and the individual evaluate one another's 'rewardingness', or the extent to which the group is rewarding for the member and the member is valued by the group. When the group is rewarding for members, they will try to enter the group or maintain group membership (i.e., feel commitment). Similarly, when a group values a (prospective) member, the group will encourage the person to become or stay a member of the group (i.e., the group is committed to the member). This is related to our earlier discussion of social exchange processes and the benefits people

> **group socialization** the efforts of the group to assimilate new members to existing group norms and practices

> **role transition** a change in the relation between a group member and a group

> **commitment** the degree to which a group member identifies with the group and its goals and wishes to maintain group membership

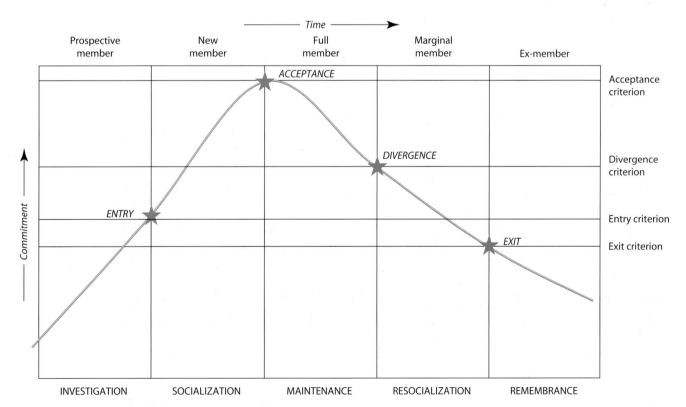

Figure 12.1 *The Moreland and Levine (1982) model of group socialization.*

can derive from them (e.g., to gain social approval or receive help or material goods). Indeed, according to Moreland and Levine (1982), commitment is a function of the past, present and expected future rewardingness of the group as compared to the rewardingness of alternative groups. In the remainder of this section, we consider the five stages shown in Figure 12.1.

Joining a group and group socialization: Becoming a full member

Investigation   In the stage of investigation, groups look for people who might make a contribution to the attainment of group goals. Task groups will often search for people who have the required skills and abilities, whereas intimacy groups will tend to emphasize compatibility (e.g., similarity) with the existing membership. Prospective members, on the other hand, will look for groups that may potentially fulfil their needs. For example, when you have just moved to a new city to start college, you will probably try to identify certain groups that may help to fulfil your social needs. Thus, you may join a student society, hoping to find people with whom you can start a new, positive and stable relation (i.e., fulfil your need to belong).

Entry and initiation   When the level of mutual commitment between group and prospective member reaches an entry criterion, a role transition will occur: *entry*. Entry is often marked by some ritual or ceremony that makes it clear that the relation between the group and the (prospective) member has changed. In an organization, this may take the form of a welcome speech, and in social groups it may be a party. At other times the entry or *initiation* ritual can be quite unpleasant and painful for the prospective member.

> **initiation**   the role transition of entry into a group, often accompanied by some ritual

Lodewijkx and Syroit (1997) studied initiation into a Dutch sorority (a student society for female students). The novices first stay in a campsite for a week. Everyone wears a shapeless, sack-like uniform, they are not called by their real names and they have to undergo physical hardship (hard work and lack of sleep and food). After a week they return to the city and participate in 'evening gatherings' for a further one and a half weeks. During these gatherings, which are regarded as threatening by the novices, they are often bullied and embarrassed. Then, finally, the inauguration ceremony takes place, after which they have a meal with the senior members – the so-called 'integration party' – and the initiation is ended.

As these severe initiations take place in many different groups (e.g., the military, some sports teams, student societies), the question arises as to why groups perform these harsh rituals. Aronson and Mills (1959) suggested a classic argument. They maintained that severe initiations increase the liking for and commitment to the group. Their argument is based upon *cognitive dissonance theory* (Festinger, 1957; see Chapter 7, this volume). Suppose a prospective member has undergone harsh treatment but it later appears that the group is not as attractive as initially believed. This would lead to cognitive dissonance: members can no longer maintain that they had good reasons to undergo the harsh treatment when they admit that the group is not so attractive after all. Thus, the member will deny that the group is unattractive and will maintain a high level of commitment to the group.

Aronson and Mills (1959) performed an experiment to test this reasoning. They offered female students the opportunity to join a discussion group about sexuality. However, some of the prospective members first had to undergo the embarrassing experience of reading aloud sexually explicit passages, while other prospective members did not have to do this. Next, the participants listened to an actual group discussion that was recorded on tape. This discussion was in fact quite boring and was about the secondary sexual behaviour of lower animals. Participants were next asked to rate the attractiveness of the group. In line with the dissonance explanation, the women who had to read the embarrassing passages rated the group more attractive than those who did not.

Lodewijkx and Syroit (1997), however, did not find a positive relation between severity of initiation and group liking. They conducted a field study among the prospective members of the sorority mentioned above and found, in fact, that severe initiations *decreased* the liking for the group. Thus, prospective members of the sorority who rated the initiation as more severe liked the group less. The reason was that severe initiations led to loneliness and frustration, and this in turn reduced the liking for the group. What Lodewijkx and Syriot did find was that, during the initiation, positive relations developed among prospective members and these increased liking for the group.

Thus, severe initiations do not always increase liking for the group, as they may lead to loneliness and frustration. In the Aronson and Mills study, in which the initiation was very brief, this probably did not happen. Severe initiations may also have other functions: they deter potential members who are not eager enough to join the group, and prospective members can show their interest in the group by undergoing these harsh treatments (Moreland & Levine, 1982).

Socialization   After entry, the stage of socialization begins. In this stage, new members learn the *norms* of the group: the (unwritten) rules that prescribe the attitudes and behaviours that are (or are not) appropriate in the context of the group. In addition, new members may acquire the necessary knowledge and skills to function effectively as a group member (i.e., learn their *role* in the group: the set of behaviours associated with a certain position in the group).

> **role**   the behaviours expected of a person with a specific position in the group

Thus, the group tries to assimilate the member to fit the expectations of the group. However, socialization is a two-way street, and the new member may also try to influence the group in such a way that the member's needs are best met. For example, a new member may try to change the group's norms or customs (e.g., 'I think that we should meet more often'). Research close-up 12.1 describes a study of newcomer influence.

During socialization, the commitment of the member towards the group and the commitment of the group towards the member

RESEARCH CLOSE-UP 12.1

Conditions under which newcomers can influence a group

Choi, H.S. & Levine, J.M. (2004). Minority influence in work teams: The impact of newcomers. *Journal of Experimental Social Psychology, 40*, 273–280.

Introduction

Choi and Levine studied the impact of newcomers on groups. In particular, they were interested in the degree to which the other group members would accept a newcomer's suggestion to change the way in which the group works. Choi and Levine argued that this would be dependent on task success: when the group had been successful before the newcomer's arrival, they would be unmotivated to change their strategy, whereas they would more likely consider it after failure. Second, they argued that when the group had chosen their own way of working, they would be less likely to give it up because they would feel more committed to it. On the other hand, groups that had been assigned a specific way of working would more easily accept the newcomer's suggestion.

Method

Participants
Participants were 141 male undergraduates who took part in 47 three-person groups.

Design and procedure
Participants performed a task twice. After the first task trial, one of the group members was replaced by a newcomer, who suggested changing the way of working. The experimental design was a 2 (group performance: failure/success) × 2 (group choice: no choice/choice) factorial. Group performance was manipulated by giving false feedback after the first task trial. Group choice was manipulated by having the groups choose their own way of working before the first trial or not giving them that choice.

The task the groups had to perform was an air-surveillance task. The three group members were seated at different computers. One of them was randomly appointed commander, the other two specialists. The two specialists had to monitor eight characteristics of planes flying through a simulated airspace, such as airspeed, direction and weapons. They had to pass the information on to the commander, who had to use a formula to integrate the information and assign a threat value to each plane. Based on the accuracy of that value, the group could earn points.

After task training, the first independent variable was introduced. Groups were given a description of two strategies of how to divide the workload between the two specialists – one according to the importance and one based on the difficulty of

monitoring plane characteristics. Some groups could choose their preferred strategy, while others were given no choice. Then the first trial, lasting 15 minutes, was performed. The groups received either positive or negative feedback about how well they had done in that first trial (the performance manipulation). One of the specialists was then replaced by a newcomer, who in fact was a confederate of the experimenter. To get acquainted, the two real participants were allowed to have an electronic chat with the newcomer. During this chat, the newcomer proposed using the other strategy (i.e., the one the group had not used in the first trial). A second 15 minute trial followed, in which the groups made an assessment whether to stay with their old strategy or adopt the newcomer's suggestion to change.

Results

Results are shown in Figure 12.2. As predicted, both group choice and group performance affected the adoption of the newcomer's suggestion. After failure and when the initial strategy had been assigned, groups were more likely to change strategies than after success or when they had chosen their initial strategy themselves.

Discussion

Choi and Levine conclude that newcomers are not merely passive recipients of influence. Under some conditions, such as failure on the group task, newcomers can have a substantial influence on the practices of the group. As such, newcomers can bring about changes and introduce innovations to the group.

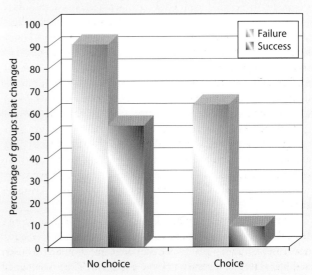

Figure 12.2 *Effects of performance feedback and group choice on acceptance of newcomer suggestions (after Choi & Levine, 2004).*

will generally increase (except when the new member or the group is dissatisfied). At a certain point in time (when the acceptance criterion is reached), the member will no longer be treated as somebody who needs special attention, the socialization stage is ended and the new member is accepted as a full member. The new members may gain access to information that was previously hidden, join certain informal cliques, and their behaviour is monitored less strictly. As with entry, there may be some ritual to mark the transition of acceptance as a full member. A well-known example is the bar mitzvah ceremony for Jewish boys at the age of 13, after which the boy is accepted as a full member of Jewish society instead of being considered a child.

Being accepted as a full member is easier in some groups than in others. In part, it depends on the ***staffing level*** of the group: the degree to which the actual number of group members is similar to the ideal number of group members. Groups can be overstaffed (have too many members) as well as understaffed (have too few members). One might expect that understaffed groups will be less demanding of new members (it is easier to become a full member) than overstaffed groups.

> **staffing level** the degree to which the actual number of group members is similar to the ideal number of group members

Cini, Moreland and Levine (1993) conducted a study among 93 student groups, including fine arts clubs, social groups and political groups. They held interviews with the president of each group in which they gathered information about the staffing level of the groups and about recruitment and socialization practices. It appeared that both understaffing and overstaffing caused problems. Understaffing led to a loss of resources (e.g., too few members contributing membership fees), poorer group performance and fatigue among group members. Overstaffing led to apathy and boredom, alienation (i.e., group members felt 'lost in the crowd'), and confusion and disorganization. The solution to understaffing, not surprisingly, was to recruit new members. Consequently, the groups that were understaffed were more open: they were less selective (it was easier to become a new member), and also less demanding for new members (it was easier to become a full member). For example, new members were evaluated and expected to perform special duties less often in understaffed as compared to overstaffed groups. Solutions to overstaffing, in contrast, were to restrict membership, but also to punish deviance from group norms more harshly, in the hope that deviant members would leave the group.

Being in a group: Maintenance and role negotiation

After acceptance, the stage of maintenance begins. This stage is characterized by high levels of commitment, and for both the member and the group the relation is seen as rewarding (see Figure 12.1). The major way in which groups and members try to increase the rewardingness of their relationship is through role negotiation. Thus, the member tries to occupy the role within the group that best satisfies his or her need, whereas the group tries to appoint roles to members in such a way that the group's goals can be best achieved. One of the more important roles within the group is that of group leader (see Chapter 13, this volume). However, there are often other roles that need to be fulfilled within groups, such as those of 'recruiter' (who identifies and evaluates prospective members) and 'trainer' (who has a role during socialization of new members). According to the model, the relation between the group and the member will be rewarding and commitment will remain high to the degree that role negotiations are successful. Being in a group is more extensively examined in the next section, where we discuss norms, roles and status.

Leaving a group: Divergence and exit

Divergence After a time, group members may lose interest in the group, for example because they are dissatisfied with their role in the group or because they have identified other groups that are more rewarding. On the other hand, the commitment of the group to its members may decline when members fail to live up to group expectations. For example, members may not perform well in their role or may violate important group norms. This will lead the group to relabel these members as marginal members or deviates. The group might, for instance, no longer give marginal members full information, or other group members may exclude marginal members from informal cliques (e.g., they are no longer asked to come along for a drink after work). Often, considerable pressure is exerted on deviates to realign or even to leave the group (especially if the group is overstaffed).

Schachter (1951) experimentally demonstrated the pressure that is exerted on deviates. He had groups discuss a delinquency case. In each of the experimental groups there were confederates playing different roles: the 'mode' who accommodated to the group's average judgement, the 'slider' who initially took an extreme position but then moved towards the group norm, and the 'deviate' who also took an extreme position but maintained it throughout the discussion. Initially, the group discussion was primarily aimed at the two deviating members (the slider and the deviate) in each group, trying to change their minds. When it became apparent that the deviates would not change, the groups eventually excluded them, refusing to talk to them and ignoring their contributions (see Figure 12.3).

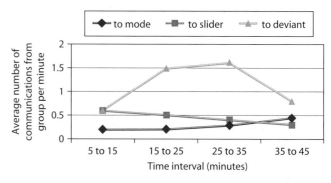

Figure 12.3 *Communications directed towards the mode, slider and deviant over time (based on Schachter, 1951).*

Resocialization and exit Divergence might be followed by a period of resocialization. In this period, the group might try to persuade marginal members not to leave, or they might try to accommodate to the wishes of marginal members (e.g., give them a different role). Similarly, group members may try to convince the group not to expel them, and might try to assimilate to the group's expectations again. This might result in re-entry to the group when successful. However, when resocialization fails, group members may reach an exit criterion and leave the group. As with other role transitions, this may involve some ritual, such as a goodbye speech or a party. Alternatively, the group may expel the member, which can be quite a painful experience. For example, an employee might be fired or a church member might be excommunicated.

Research has shown that social exclusion from groups has enormous negative effects on excluded members. Consider the following situation. You are invited to come to the psychology lab to participate in an experiment and are asked to wait in a waiting room until the experiment starts. In that room two other participants are also waiting (they are, in fact, confederates of the experimenter). One of them has brought a tennis ball and playfully throws it to the other participant. That participant joins in and throws the ball to you. For a while, the three of you play this ball-tossing game. After some time, however, the other participants no longer throw the ball to you, but only to each other, and this goes on for several minutes. How would you feel?

Williams (2001) reports extensive evidence concerning the power of social exclusion. Using the ball-tossing game (and other situations), he found that social exclusion produces severe negative moods and anger, and leads to lower ratings on belongingness and self-esteem. Further, Eisenberger, Lieberman and Williams (2003) found that exclusion quite literally is a form of 'social pain'. These researchers had participants play a computerized version of the ball-tossing game while lying in an fMRI (functional magnetic resonance imaging) brain scanner. Using the fMRI scanner, the researchers could identify which brain areas were active during social exclusion. Participants were led to believe that, by pushing a button, they could throw a (virtual) ball to another participant, who could then throw the ball back to them or to a third participant. In fact, there was only one real participant, and the computer was programmed in such a way that this participant received the ball nine times, after which the ball was no longer thrown to him or her. While being excluded from the game, an fMRI brain scan was made. Eisenberger et al. (2003) found that social exclusion activates an area in the brain (the anterior cingulate cortex) that is normally activated when a person is in physical pain. Furthermore, the level of activation of that brain area was correlated with participants' reports of distress.

Remembrance The last stage of the Moreland and Levine model is remembrance (see again Figure 12.1). In this stage, the ex-member and the group retrospectively evaluate each other. Thus, remaining group members will evaluate the ex-member's contributions to the group and will maintain some degree of commitment to the ex-member if these contributions are seen as positive. Similarly, ex-members look back on their time with the group with either fond or bitter memories. In extreme cases, ex-members may even try to destroy their former group in an act of revenge. Workplace shootings (e.g., in Kansas City, USA, in 2004), in which employees who had been dismissed shot their boss or former colleagues, are extreme examples. Fortunately, these incidents are rare.

SUMMARY

Individuals move through different phases of group membership (prospective member, new member, full member, marginal member and ex-member). These stages of group membership differ in the degree of commitment of the group and the member to each other. Moving from one stage to the next involves a role transition, and role transitions can both be extreme (e.g., severe initiation rituals) and have a large impact on members (e.g., after exit).

GROUP DEVELOPMENT AND STRUCTURE: THE GROUP LEVEL OF ANALYSIS

What are the five stages of group development?
What is interaction process analysis, and how is it helpful when studying group development and group structure?
What are the functions of group norms?
How do status and role differences come about?

In the previous section we discussed the (changing) relation of the group member with the group. In this section we explore the group level of analysis. First, we discuss how groups themselves can also change over time. Second, groups have certain characteristics, such as norms to govern their behaviour and a group structure, in which certain members have more **status** than others or in which different members occupy different roles in the group. These issues are examined below. It should be noted that this section is mainly relevant for groups with direct (usually face-to-face) interaction.

> **status** evaluation of a role by the group in which a role is contained or defined

Group development

Some groups are formed for a special reason and end after a certain time. Examples include therapy groups, project teams and the group of students in a psychology seminar. These groups will generally develop: the interaction patterns among group members

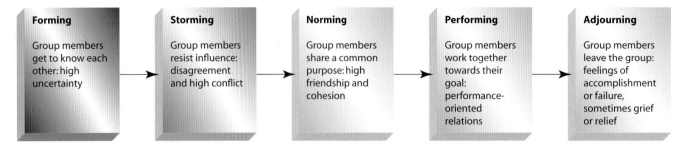

Forming	**Storming**	**Norming**	**Performing**	**Adjourning**
Group members get to know each other: high uncertainty	Group members resist influence: disagreement and high conflict	Group members share a common purpose: high friendship and cohesion	Group members work together towards their goal: performance-oriented relations	Group members leave the group: feelings of accomplishment or failure, sometimes grief or relief

Figure 12.4 *The five stages of group development (after Tuckman & Jensen, 1977).*

change over time. Further, there may be similarities in the way different groups develop. The basic idea is that every group faces certain challenges and has certain goals, and these challenges and goals change over time. This, in turn, has consequences for the way group members interact with each other, as well as for group performance and the rewardingness of the group to its members.

Tuckman (1965) and Tuckman and Jensen (1977) introduced a classic five-stage model of group development: forming, storming, norming, performing and adjourning (see Figure 12.4). In the first stage, when the group is *forming*, group members feel insecure because they do not know each other and do not know what is expected of them. As a consequence, interactions are usually polite and inhibited. In this first stage, people get to know each other and develop a shared identity as members of the same group. This might happen at the beginning of a psychology seminar: students still feel insecure, engage in polite conversation, and the atmosphere is quite subdued. Once people have got to know each other, they enter the second stage (*storming*). The challenge in the second stage is to develop a group structure. Here issues of leadership and influence are at stake, and as group members may compete about different roles in the group, there may be conflicts and disagreements. Most groups will overcome this, and when a group structure and group roles have been established, they can move

on to the third stage. In the third stage, *norming*, group members develop close ties. In this stage, the group members come to agree upon the group's goals and develop norms that govern group interaction. Once this has been achieved, the group enters the *performing* stage. Because group structure and group norms have been established, the group's efforts can be directed towards achieving the group's task. Although it is probably still necessary to engage in behaviours to maintain a positive atmosphere in the group, most activities will be task-related. The final stage of group development is *adjourning*. When the task has been accomplished or is abandoned, the group will end. This might be associated either with feelings of accomplishment or with feelings of disappointment (dependent, of course, on task success).

According to the Tuckman and Jensen (1977) model, the different stages of group life should be characterized by different interaction patterns within the group. But how can we establish whether this really is true? To answer that question, it is necessary to code group interactions into certain categories and see whether certain types of behaviour are more frequent in the early or the later stages of group life. Probably the best-known coding system of group interaction is Bales's (1950) *interaction process analysis* (IPA; see also Bales & Slater, 1955, and Chapter 2, this volume). IPA makes the basic and important distinction between *task behaviours* (all behaviours directed at task completion) and *socio-emotional behaviours* (all behaviours directed at interpersonal relations within the group). In the socio-emotional domain it further distinguishes between positive and negative behaviours. According to Bales, task-related behaviour is necessary for task completion but can lead to conflicts when people disagree. In order not to disturb the functioning of the group, socio-emotional behaviour is necessary to restore group harmony. The coding system of IPA is shown in Figure 12.5. As can be seen in the figure, the scheme distinguishes between 12 different categories, divided into socio-emotional behaviours that are positive, task-related behaviours (which are emotionally neutral) and negative socio-emotional behaviours.

Now, according to the Tuckman and Jensen (1977) stage model, these 12 categories of behaviour should occur to differing degrees in the different stages of group life. The forming stage

task behaviour behaviours during group interactions that are directed at task completion

socio-emotional behaviour behaviours during group interactions that are directed at interpersonal relations

Plate 12.3 *Some groups are formed for a special reason and also end after some time, e.g., a group of students in a psychology seminar.*

Socio-emotional behaviour, positive	1. Shows solidarity, raises other's status, gives help, reward.
	2. Shows tension release, jokes, laughs, shows satisfaction.
	3. Agrees, shows passive acceptance, understands, concurs, complies.
Task behaviour, neutral	4. Gives suggestions, directions, implying autonomy for other.
	5. Gives opinion, evaluates, analyses, expresses feelings and wishes.
	6. Gives orientation, information, repeats, clarifies, confirms.
	7. Asks for orientation, information, repetition, confirmation.
	8. Asks for opinion, evaluation, analysis, expression of feeling.
	9. Asks for suggestion, direction, possible ways of action.
Socio-emotional behaviour, negative	10. Disagrees, shows passive rejection, formality, withholds help.
	11. Shows tension, asks for help, withdraws out of the field.
	12. Shows antagonism, deflates other's status, defends or asserts self.

Figure 12.5 *The coding scheme of interaction process analysis (after Bales, 1950).*

PIONEER

Robert F. Bales (1916–2004), a pioneer in the development of systematic methods of group observation and measurement of interaction processes, received his BA and MS degrees in Sociology from the University of Oregon. He entered graduate study in sociology at Harvard in 1940 (with Talcott Parsons as his dissertation advisor), received his PhD in sociology in 1945, and was appointed Professor of Social Relations in 1957, retiring in 1986. During the 1944–45 academic year, Bales spent a formative year as Research Associate at the Section on Alcohol Studies at Yale University. His research on the interactions in therapeutic group settings for alcohol addicts formed the basis for his first and classic book, *Interaction process analysis: A method for the study of small groups*, published in 1950. Bales hoped that by studying the interaction of many such groups, he would discover recurring patterns that might help to understand and to predict the functioning of problem-solving groups. His interaction process analysis proved an extremely useful tool for studying group interaction, group member roles and group development. This research reflected his conception of social psychology as the scientific study of social interaction with the group and its activity, rather than the individuals, as the primary unit of analysis. With this research program he sought to integrate the psychological and sociological sources of social psychology.

should be characterized by much positive socio-emotional behaviour, whereas in the storming stage more negative socio-emotional behaviour should occur. In the norming stage, there should be both positive socio-emotional behaviour and task-related behaviour, and the performing stage should be dominated by task-related behaviour. Is this what really happens? At a general level, the answer seems to be yes. For example, Wheelan, Davidson and Tilin (2003) found time together to be related to socio-emotional behaviours (the longer the group was together, the *fewer* of these behaviours) as well as to task-related behaviours (the longer the group was together, the *more* of these behaviours).

On the other hand, stage models such as Tuckman and Jensen's can easily be criticized as an oversimplification of reality. Some groups, for example, may never have a storming stage, whereas other groups are in conflict continuously. Further, groups may sometimes return to a previous stage instead of progressing to the next (as the model would assume). Finally, it will often be impossible to establish which stage the group is in, and the assumption that the different stages are qualitatively different from each other is difficult to maintain. Rather, different activities occur in each stage, although they may vary in intensity. Most researchers would therefore argue that there are no abrupt changes in the way group members interact with each other, but rather that these changes occur gradually and that one can see this as a gradual development of groups over time.

On being similar: Norms, shared cognition and cohesion

Group norms Group norms are (unwritten) rules shared by the members of a group, which prescribe the attitudes, behaviour and beliefs that are, and are not, appropriate in the context of the group (see Everyday Social Psychology 12.1). Because norms are prescriptive, they serve as guides for attitudes and behaviour and in that way perform an important regulatory function. Group members tend to conform to group norms (i.e., think and act in accordance with group norms), either because group norms are internalized, that is, become part of the individual's belief and value system (Turner, 1991), or because group norms are enforced by the (anticipated) reaction of other group members to normative and anti-normative behaviour (Deutsch & Gerard, 1955). Because of this adherence to group norms, groups function more smoothly than without norms. For instance, if everybody adheres to group norms, other group members' behaviour becomes more predictable and therefore can be anticipated. In that sense, group norms help regulate group interaction. Group norms are also an important source of information about social reality. Often, people rely on what many people see as valid and true as an accurate reflection of (social) reality. Another important function of norms is that conformity to group norms illustrates one's commitment to the group – it shows that one is 'a good group member' (cf. Hollander, 1958).

This is not to say, however, that all group members always conform to group norms. Individual group members may show deviant behaviour. If they do, however, they are likely to run into the negative responses of their fellow group members, even to the extent that they may be excluded from the group (Schachter, 1951). Because social exclusion is a highly unpleasant experience (Williams, 2001; see above), such pressures to conform to group

EVERYDAY SOCIAL PSYCHOLOGY 12.1

Jonestown

On 18 November 1978, more than 900 men, women and children died in a mass suicide/murder in Jonestown, a jungle encampment in Guyana, South America. Most of them drank, or were forced to drink, a fruit punch that had been laced with cyanide and tranquillizers. Parents first gave it to their children, then they drank it themselves. How could this have happened? Why did a whole group of people resort to this desperate measure?

The people of Jonestown were members of a religious cult, called the People's Temple. The cult was founded in the USA by James Warren Jones and had moved to the jungle encampment in Guyana in the mid-1970s. There, the members of the cult had to work hard on the fields and lived in isolation from the outside world. Immediately before the tragedy, US Congressman Ryan had visited Jonestown with some journalists, investigating accusations that people were being held there against their will. Eighteen people indeed wanted to leave with Ryan. However, cult members attacked them at the airstrip as they were leaving, killing the congressman, three journalists and one defector, and wounding 12 others. Back in Jonestown, Jones proclaimed that the end had come, and that in this extreme situation 'revolutionary suicide' was their only option. The members of the People's Temple obeyed, committing mass suicide and killing those who were unable or unwilling to kill themselves (including children and the elderly).

To begin to understand why they chose death, one must firstly realize that the members of the People's Temple were socialized to accept the norms of the cult. One of the more important norms was loyalty to the group, a norm that was quite strictly enforced. Second, the members of the People's Temple lived in isolation from the outside world and had no contacts with relatives or others outside Jonestown. One implication of their isolation was that an end to Jonestown would imply a loss of all their current social ties. It also implied that they were only in contact with like-minded people. As this chapter shows, one function of groups is to provide us with knowledge of our social and physical world. In isolation, people may even begin to believe bizarre things, such as the concept of 'revolutionary suicide'. The members of the cult, for example, believed that an end to Jonestown would mean not only an end to the promised land they had believed in, but also torture and imprisonment by the US government. When faced with the grim prospect of losing all social ties, all hopes, everything they believed in, and torture and imprisonment, they saw no reason to live.

Although the Jonestown case is clearly extreme, and fortunately very rare, it does illustrate the power of the social group (and of an autocratic leader). It is one of social psychology's goals to understand these tragedies and hopefully prevent them in the future.

Plate 12.4 *Members of the People's Temple at Jonestown, Guyana, committed mass suicide in 1978. They were socialized to accept the cult's norms, especially group loyalty.*

norms tend to be quite effective in many situations. Thus, groups may enforce and maintain their group norms.

As already noted in the discussion of group development, groups develop group norms relatively early in their existence (Tuckman, 1965). This is not to say that group norms do not change. Norms may change over time. This change may occur because the environment of the group changes. It may also occur because the membership of the group changes. New members tend to be socialized into the group and its norms (Moreland & Levine, 1982), but they may also introduce changes to the group. Indeed, as research on minority influence shows (see Chapter 11, this volume), if the conditions are right, a deviant minority may convert a whole group towards a different way of thinking. Group norms should therefore be seen, on the one hand, as enforcing their own maintenance and, on the other hand, as subject to change over time and situations. Group norms are thus both an influence on group process and an outcome of group process.

Socially shared cognition and affect

An aspect of groups that is receiving more attention in recent years is shared cognition (Thompson, Levine & Messick, 1999; Tindale & Kameda, 2000). Over time, groups may develop a shared understanding of different aspects of group life, such as the tasks the group performs, the role of each member in the group, and each member's particular knowledge, skills and abilities. For each individual group member, such understanding is important, but when it is shared within the group it has the added advantage of setting the stage for smooth coordination, communication and cooperation, because all group members have a similar understanding of what they are supposed to do and who does what. Socially shared cognitions, when accurately reflecting the demands faced by the group, may therefore improve group functioning and performance (Mohammed & Dumville, 2001).

> **transactive memory** a system of knowledge available to group members with shared awareness of each other's expertise, strengths and weaknesses

A nice illustration of the influence of shared cognition is found in work on **transactive memory**. Transactive memory refers to shared knowledge about how knowledge is distributed in the group. Rather than having all the information themselves, group members know who knows what and whom to ask for information about specific things (Wegner, 1986). Transactive memory makes it possible for groups to operate efficiently and adequately because it helps locate information and 'the right person for the job'.

Liang, Moreland and Argote (1995) experimentally studied groups that had to assemble a radio. Before they assembled the radio as a group, participants received training to prepare them for the task. The critical manipulation was whether individuals received this training as a group or individually (after which they performed the task in newly formed groups). As predicted, groups that were trained together performed better than those who were trained alone. This effect could be explained because groups that were trained together had more accurate knowledge about who was good at which part of the task: they had thus formed a better transactive memory system (see also Chapter 13, this volume).

Groups may share not only cognition but also emotions (George, 1990). Research in group emotions is still in its infancy, but there is emerging evidence that groups may come to share emotions, and that these shared emotions affect group functioning. Barsade (2002), for instance, found that affect introduced by a confederate in an experiment spread within the whole group and affected group members' ratings of group functioning. In a similar vein, Sy, Coté and Saavedra (2005) showed that the affect displayed by a confederate leader of a group transferred to the members of the group and affected group performance: groups performed better when the leader displayed positive affect than when the leader displayed negative affect.

Group cohesion

Group *cohesion* (or 'cohesiveness') is the force that binds members to the group and induces them to stay with the group (Festinger, 1950). Group cohesion is assumed to be important to group functioning, because it helps keep the group together and motivates group members to exert themselves on behalf of the group. Evidence for this proposition is mixed, however, and research suggests that it is useful to distinguish between types of cohesion. **Task cohesion** refers to the shared commitment to the group's tasks, while *interpersonal cohesion* refers to the attraction to the group. As a meta-analysis by Mullen and Copper (1994) shows, only task cohesion is (positively) related to group performance. Further, cohesion may not always improve performance, as can be seen in Research close-up 12.2.

> **cohesion** the force that binds members to the group
>
> **task cohesion** cohesion based on attraction of group members to the group task
>
> **interpersonal cohesion** cohesion based on liking of the group and its members

On being different: Status and roles

Whereas norms make group members' behaviour more alike, there are also clear differences between group members in the way they behave and the position they have in the group. Take, for instance, a football team. Clearly, different players have different roles defined by their position in the field (goalkeeper, defender, forward). Besides these formal roles, there will also be informal roles. For example, a more experienced team member (even though not formally the team captain) may have more influence on the other players than a newcomer, and another team member may always take the initiative to reconcile people after an argument.

Earlier, we discussed Bales's (1950) interaction process analysis (IPA). It appears that IPA is a useful tool for looking at status and roles inside a group: it is possible to keep track of the 12 different types of behaviour (see Figure 12.5) for each group member, to see whether there are differences among group members. Research using IPA (or other coding systems) to code behaviour in freely interacting groups has revealed a number of important insights (see McGrath, 1984, for a summary of findings), two of which we will discuss now.

RESEARCH CLOSE-UP 12.2

Group cohesiveness leads to better performance when the group accepts performance goals

Podsakoff, P.M., MacKenzie, S.B. & Ahearne, M. (1997). Moderating effects of goal acceptance on the relation between group cohesiveness and productivity. *Journal of Applied Psychology, 82*, 974–983.

Introduction

Podsakoff and colleagues argued that higher cohesion does not always lead to better performance. They argued that the relationship between cohesiveness and performance should be contingent on the group's acceptance of performance goals. If the group accepts the performance goals of the organization, cohesiveness should be positively related to group performance. If, however, the group does not accept performance goals, then cohesiveness is expected to be unrelated (or even negatively related) to performance.

Method

Participants
The study participants were 218 members of 40 work crews at a paper mill in the USA. Crews consisted of 5.25 members on average, most participants were male (96 per cent), and their average age was 39 years old.

Measures and procedure
Two measures were obtained through a questionnaire distributed among the crew members: group cohesiveness and acceptance of the performance goals of the company. Thus, all group members individually rated their perception of group cohesiveness and their acceptance of performance goals. Performance of each crew was obtained from company records. It consisted of the amount of paper produced as a percentage of total machine capacity.

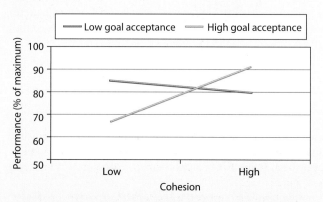

Figure 12.6 *The relation between cohesion and performance for crews high and low in goal acceptance (after Podsakoff et al., 1997).*

Results

Figure 12.6 shows the results. As predicted, group cohesion and group goal acceptance interacted in predicting task performance. When groups were relatively accepting of performance goals, the relationship between group cohesion and group performance was positive. However, when groups were not accepting of performance goals, the relationship between group cohesion and performance tended to be negative.

Discussion

This study illustrates that group cohesion does not necessarily motivate performance. Rather, it motivates group members to exert themselves for causes that are seen as important to the group (see van Knippenberg & Ellemers, 2003). When group members do not accept the company's performance goals, higher cohesion will generally not improve performance.

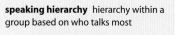

speaking hierarchy hierarchy within a group based on who talks most

First, some group members talk more than others, and the discrepancy increases with the size of the group. Thus, groups develop a *speaking hierarchy* (Bales, 1953) in which members higher in that hierarchy talk more than those lower in the hierarchy (see Figure 12.7). Further, people who talk more are usually seen as more influential. Later research has shown that group members do not distribute their participation evenly throughout the discussion, but rather that contributions are concentrated in periods of high activity (Dabbs & Ruback, 1987). Thus, if a person has recently spoken, he or she is more likely to speak again. Often this takes the form of a dyadic exchange, in which two group members alternate speaking turns. When this happens, we say that the group is in a *floor* position (i.e., two group members

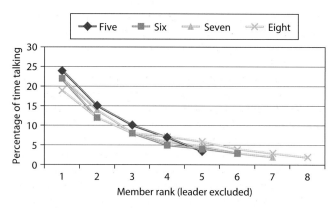

Figure 12.7 *Speaking hierarchy for groups of five, six, seven and eight members (taken from Stephan & Mischler, 1952).*

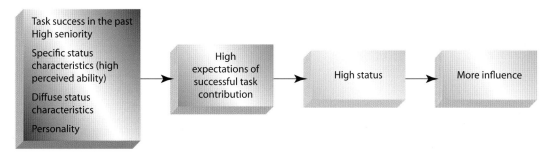

Figure 12.8 *Expectation states theory (Berger et al., 1980).*

'hold the floor'; Parker, 1988). Parker found that four-person groups were in a floor position no less than 61 per cent of their time, much more than would be expected if all group members contributed equally.

Second, research using IPA has found that some people are consistently more task-oriented (i.e., they engage mostly in task-related behaviours, categories 4–9 in Figure 12.5), whereas others are more relationship-oriented (i.e., they engage more in socio-emotional behaviours) (Slater, 1955). The former person has been labelled the task specialist, and the latter the socio-emotional specialist: clearly a case of (informal) role differentiation. It further appeared that these two group members interacted with each other quite frequently, and much more than would be expected according to chance (i.e., they were often in a floor position). Finally, the task specialist was seen as most influential, but he or she was liked less than the socio-emotional specialist.

Who talks most in the group and who takes which role is dependent on personality and individual abilities. For example, an extroverted person will probably talk more than an introverted person. However, this is not the whole story. There are other factors that determine who is more and who is less influential.

The most comprehensive theory about status in groups is ***expectation states theory*** (Berger, Rosenholtz & Zelditch, 1980). It deals with the issue of how status structures emerge in groups, and how they are shaped by the outside status of group members (see Ridgeway, 2001, for an overview of the theory and the evidence for it). A simplified graphical depiction of the theory is presented in Figure 12.8.

expectation states theory argues that status differences within a group result from different expectations that group members have about each other

Expectation states theory is applicable to groups in which members strive for a common goal or perform a common task. It assumes that several inequalities within a group, such as inequalities in participation and influence, are highly correlated because they are all derived from *performance expectations*. That is, because of certain characteristics of group members, other group members form expectations about the usefulness of each group member's contributions. These expectations then serve as a self-fulfilling prophecy: the greater the expectations, the more likely a person is to speak up, offer suggestions and be evaluated positively by the others. The lower the expectations, the less likely it is that these things happen. The important question, then, is: what determines these performance expectations?

The theory assumes that performance expectations are influenced by so-called *status characteristics*. The theory distinguishes between *diffuse* status characteristics (not necessarily related to the group task), including, for example, gender, age and race, and *specific* status characteristics, such as skills and abilities (i.e., characteristics that are necessary for the group task, previous task success). These characteristics carry certain cultural expectations about competencies. For example, women are generally seen as less competent than men (especially on tasks that are more 'masculine'; e.g., Pugh & Wahrman, 1983), and more senior people may be seen as more competent (up to a certain age) than younger people (Freese & Cohen, 1973). Similarly, higher expectations are formed for people who are more experienced, have a higher status in society more generally, or have a relevant area of expertise. Obviously, these expectations may sometimes be false (i.e., a woman may in fact be more competent than a man), but they nevertheless affect people's status in the group and the amount of influence they have. The reason is that expectations need to be explicitly falsified before they lose their influence, and as long as they are not, they continue to have their effect in a self-fulfilling way. There is extensive evidence supporting the theory. For example, Driskell and Mullen (1990) found that characteristics of group members affected their status and power through the expectations of other group members (for more evidence, see Ridgeway, 2001).

SUMMARY

Groups develop over time, in the sense that their interaction patterns change. Further, some processes cause group members to become more similar to each other, both in terms of their behaviour (as prescribed by group norms) and in terms of their cognitions and emotions. Finally, differences between group members may also emerge, for which expectation states theory offers a theoretical account. We now turn to the last level of analysis: the contextual or intergroup level.

GROUPS IN THEIR ENVIRONMENT: THE INTERGROUP LEVEL OF ANALYSIS

In what ways does the (intergroup) context affect intragroup behaviour?

How does behaviour in groups change when group membership is made salient?

Going back to our opening example of the football fans, it is clear that these people do not always behave in this way. They are also supporters of their team when the team is not playing, but it is the context of the match that draws them together and that brings out their behaviour in the subway station. Playing against another team renders these supporters' affiliation with their favourite team salient and evokes the quite uniform behaviour that clearly identifies them as a group.

What holds for these supporters holds for all groups. Groups do not live in isolation. Other groups are part of the environment in which groups function. Understanding the psychology of groups therefore requires studying the influence of the *intergroup context* on the thoughts, feelings and behaviour of group members. Part of this involves the study of intergroup relations – the way group members think, feel and act towards members of other groups (see Chapter 14, this volume). The intergroup context may, however, also affect intragroup processes, and that is an issue we deal with here.

The intergroup context and the salience of group membership

The fact that individuals are members of a certain group does not mean that this group membership is always at the forefront of their minds. Self-categorization as a group member needs to be cognitively activated, or rendered *salient*, for the group membership to exert its influence on people's self-definition (see Chapter 5, this volume). Group membership then influences group members' attitudes and behaviour via this self-definition (i.e., social identity; see Turner et al., 1987; see also Chapters 11 and 14, this volume). An important influence of the intergroup context is that of rendering group membership salient. Exposure to other groups in a sense 'reminds' us of our own group memberships. Especially in the context of an intergroup confrontation of some kind, this may work to render group membership a salient influence on group members' thoughts, feelings and behaviour. Such confrontations may involve explicit competition, as in sports or in the political arena, or competition for scarce goods (e.g., customers, funding), but may also involve more implicit forms of competition, such as competition for social status (e.g., which is the most important department within an organization? which street gang has the toughest reputation?).

These processes are well illustrated in a study by James and Greenberg (1989). They conducted two experiments in which they had students from their university work on a task solving anagrams. The task objective was to solve as many anagrams as possible and participants' performance on the task (i.e., the number of anagrams solved) was the main variable of interest. James and Greenberg argued that students would be more motivated, and therefore perform better, when their university membership was made salient in the context of a comparison between students from their university and students from another university.

James and Greenberg experimentally manipulated the extent to which students' affiliation to their university was salient. In their first experiment, they manipulated group membership salience by letting participants work in a room that was painted either white (low salience condition) or red and blue (the colours of the university: high salience condition). All participants were led to believe that the experiment was part of a larger study comparing the performance of students from their university with that of students from a 'rival' university. As expected, participants in the high group membership salience condition solved more anagrams than did participants in the low group membership salience condition.

In their second experiment, James and Greenberg aimed to show that this effect would only be found in the presence of intergroup comparison and not in the absence of this intergroup comparison. In order to demonstrate this, they manipulated not only group membership salience but also the presence or absence of the comparison with the other university. Intergroup comparison was manipulated by telling half of the participants that their performance would be compared with that of the rival university, whereas the other half did not receive this instruction. This time, salience was manipulated by giving participants a practice anagram that solved either as *wildcats*, which referred to their university mascot (high salience condition), or as *beavers*, which had no relevance for university membership (low salience condition). Results indicated that group salience had no effect when the intergroup comparison was absent, but that group salience led to higher (and the highest) performance when intergroup comparison was present (see Figure 12.9).

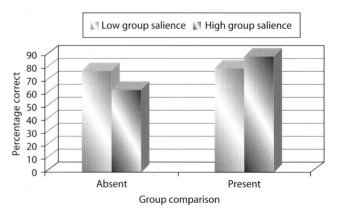

Figure 12.9 *Percentage of anagrams solved correctly as a function of ingroup salience and comparison condition (after James & Greenberg, 1989).*

What this study shows is that group membership needs to be salient to affect behaviour, but that the context in which it is rendered salient affects whether and how group membership salience translates into behaviour (for more on this issue, see Haslam, 2001; van Knippenberg, 2000). In the intergroup context created by James and Greenberg, performing well could help establish that one's own group was superior to the comparison group. Because salient group memberships reflect on how we see ourselves, the relative standing of our group vis-à-vis other groups (i.e., are we 'better'?) reflects on how good or bad we can feel about ourselves. Obviously, then, we prefer our groups to compare favourably to other groups, and are willing to contribute actively to our group achieving such a favourable comparison (Tajfel & Turner, 1986). In the situation created by James and Greenberg, this led individuals for whom group membership was made salient in the context of intergroup comparison to work harder.

An important influence of the intergroup context on group members is, thus, that it may render group membership salient, and may inform the translation of this salient self-categorization into attitudes and behaviour. The intergroup context may also affect group members' perceptions of their own group, and by doing so may affect attitudes and behaviour that are contingent on these perceptions. This is an issue that is addressed next.

The intergroup context, group perceptions and social influence

Part of what defines a group is the distinction between who is 'in' and who is 'out'. Groups exist by virtue of their members, but also by the fact that there are some people who are *not* members of the group and may indeed be members of *other* groups. Accordingly, people's perceptions of their membership groups are affected by the comparison between their own group and other groups, and group members' perceptions of their group are also contingent on what differentiates their group from other groups (Turner et al., 1987). Put differently, we ascribe characteristics to ourselves and to our groups on the basis of our perception that we possess these characteristics to a greater degree than others. For example, we will only come to the conclusion that the members of our group are intelligent if we perceive our group to be more intelligent than certain other groups. Indeed, such social comparison processes evaluating ourselves permeate social life (see Chapter 14 for further detail on intergroup social comparison). The important point for our present discussion is that if the intergroup context changes, comparison groups may change and as a consequence our perceptions of our group may change.

Take, for instance, the case of political parties. Members of a party that is the most conservative party within a country's political spectrum will probably think of their party as conservative. However, when a new party emerges that is perceived to be more conservative, the attribute conservative may become less suited to distinguish the party from other parties, and party members' perceptions of their party may change to emphasize other characteristics of their party. Or consider, for example, the discussion about Turkey's prospective membership of the European Union.

In contrast to the other countries of the European Union, the largest religious denomination in Turkey is Islam rather than Christianity. This fact seems to have highlighted the shared roots in Christianity of the current EU countries in the perception of many parties partaking in the discussion – an attribute that until now never really seemed at the forefront of perception within the European Union.

Changes in the intergroup context may occur because old groups disappear from the scene (e.g., a competitor goes bankrupt) or new groups emerge, or because an existing group becomes more relevant as a comparison group (as in the example of Turkey and the European Union) or less relevant as a comparison group (e.g., because a competing firm focuses more on other markets than one's own firm). Such changes may affect which attributes of the group are salient (i.e., what differentiates the group from relevant other groups), but they may also alter our perception of a given attribute of the group. Take the example of a group of psychology students who think of themselves as intelligent. Within the larger context of society, this probably makes a lot of sense. Imagine, however, that this group finds itself in a context where comparison with a group of the proverbial rocket scientists becomes relevant. Intelligence may not be seen as the most relevant dimension of comparison, but if it were, the attribute intelligent would likely be ascribed not to one's own group but to the other group.

SUMMARY

In sum, the intergroup context may both affect the salience of group membership and inform group members' behaviour within this context (cf. the intergroup comparison in the James & Greenberg 1989 study), and influence perceptions of group norms that may feed into attitudes and behaviour.

 ## SUMMARY AND CONCLUSIONS

Let us return to the example we began with: the Ajax fans in the subway. The individual Ajax fan is probably looking for an entertaining and enjoyable game of football. However, there is more than that. As you will probably agree, 'real' football fans identify very much with their teams: they are proud of the team when the team wins, and feel sad and depressed when the team loses. Being an Ajax fan is thus part of an individual's identity, and self-esteem is derived from the team's success. When an individual Ajax fan now enters the subway, he or she will know what to expect: watching a game of football implies singing and shouting. Because most of the other people in the subway are Ajax fans, and because they have similar expectations, the behaviour becomes normative: it is seen as appropriate. However, the only reason why this behaviour is seen as appropriate (or at least acceptable) is because of the context: Ajax is about to play another team, and this both makes group membership salient and affects the perception of group norms. Thus, the behaviour in the subway is caused by individual expectations (individual level), which are shared among the fans and constitute behavioural norms (group level), and arise in a context that makes group membership salient (context level).

- A group exists when two or more people define themselves as members of a group.

- The reasons why people form, join and distinguish groups are sociobiological (evolutionarily built in), cognitive (understanding our world) and utilitarian (gaining benefits).

- Different types of groups, such as task groups, intimacy groups, social categories and loose associations, differ on a number of important dimensions such as group entitativity, importance and shared objectives.

- Group members move through the different stages of group membership (prospective member, new member, full member, marginal member and ex-member) separated from each other by role transitions, and these different stages are characterized by different levels of commitment.

- The role transition of entry can be marked by a harsh transition ritual. A classic explanation for these rituals is given by dissonance theory, which argues that such rituals increase commitment to the group.

- An important determinant of group openness is staffing level: it is easier to become a full member of an understaffed as compared to an overstaffed group.

- Social exclusion from groups can lead to quite severe anger and depression.

- Groups develop over time, because the challenges they face and the goals they have change. Tuckman's classic theory distinguishes five stages: forming, storming, norming, performing and adjourning.

- Interaction process analysis is a useful coding scheme for group interactions and makes a basic distinction between socio-emotional and task behaviours.

- Groups develop shared cognitions, such as transactive memory systems (i.e., knowing who knows what) and shared emotions.

- Cohesion can be based on attractiveness of the group (interpersonal cohesion) or on attractiveness of the group task (task cohesion). In general, cohesion motivates group members to exert effort for causes that are important to the group.

- Groups develop status and role differences. Expectation states theory explains the emergence of a status structure in a group. It argues that certain status characteristics lead to performance expectations that subsequently lead to differences in status and influence.

- The presence of other groups can make group membership salient. As a consequence, group members will be more strongly influenced by their group membership.

Suggestions for further reading

Haslam, S.A. (2001). *Psychology in organisations: The social identity approach*. London: Sage. A detailed review of the influence of group norms and intergroup context on attitudes and behaviour in groups.

Lickel, B., Hamilton, D.L. & Sherman, S.J. (2001). Elements of a lay theory of groups: Types of groups, relational styles, and the perception of group entitativity. *Personality and Social Psychology Review*, 5, 129–140. An in-depth discussion of types of groups and 'lay theories' about them (i.e., how lay people look at groups).

Moreland, R.L. & Levine, J.M. (1982). Socialization in small groups: Temporal changes in individual–group relations. In L. Berkowitz (Ed.), *Advances in experimental social psychology* (Vol. 15, pp. 137–192). New York: Academic Press. An extensive discussion of group socialization.

Ridgeway, C.L. (2001). Social status and group structure. In M.A. Hogg & S. Tindale (Eds.), *Blackwell handbook of social psychology: Group processes* (pp. 352–375). Oxford: Blackwell. A good summary of the research on expectation states theory.

Wheelan, S.A. (1994). *Group process: A developmental perspective*. Boston: Allyn & Bacon. A discussion of group development that examines different stages of group life.

13

Group Performance and Leadership

Stefan Schulz-Hardt and Felix C. Brodbeck

CHAPTER OUTLINE

In this chapter we examine the question of how social interdependence and social interaction affect group performance. More specifically, we provide answers to the following questions: How can we identify group-level influences on performance? What are the major pitfalls and opportunities for performance when people work together in a group? What can we do to systematically optimize group performance? Why is leadership so critical for group performance, and how can it contribute to the optimization of group performance? We answer these questions by outlining the basic underlying principles, applying them to specific group tasks, with examples, and selectively illustrating them with empirical research.

Introduction

We all often work in groups. Some of these groups are informal, as, for example, a group of students preparing for an exam. Other groups are more or less formal, for example, a work team on the production line, a personnel selection committee or a sports team. Thus, work in groups is an essential part of our society. Whereas in some cases groups are indispensable to perform a specific task (e.g., you can only play volleyball in a team), in many other cases groups are used because we expect them to raise performance on a specific task. For example, personnel selection might also be carried out by a single person, but we often believe that a group of people will make better selection decisions. To see whether such assumptions are correct, we have to find out what determines group performance and how group performance compares with performance in an individual setting.

The comparison of group vs. individual performance is a fundamental question in social psychology and actually triggered some of the earliest experiments in the field (e.g., Ringelmann, 1913; Triplett, 1898; see Chapter 1, this volume). As it has turned out, the relation between group and individual performance strongly depends on the type of task. For example, we would all expect that the more heads involved in solving a problem, the greater the chances of the problem being solved. However, most of us would not claim that a climbing team will climb a mountain faster the more people are involved.

In addition, simply comparing individual performance with group performance is often misleading. Imagine the following situation. You investigate weight pulling and find that individuals pull an average weight of 100 kg, whereas four-person groups pull an average weight of 105 kg. Here, group performance is superior to individual performance. Will this finding make you praise the benefits of group work? We suspect the answer is 'no'; instead, this result might make you wonder what has happened in these groups that led to their performance being only slightly above that of individuals. Thus, what is needed to determine whether group performance raises or lowers individual performance is an appropriate standard against which to compare this performance. As we

(a)

(b)

(c)

Plates 13.1a, b and c *Different kinds of groups: a work team on the production line, a sports team and a personnel selection committee.*

will see, the appropriate baseline is again strongly dependent on the type of task. For example, you might expect the four-person group to pull four times the weight of an individual, but you wouldn't expect them to climb a mountain four times faster or four times slower than one person.

With that in mind, we introduce the core concepts of actual group performance, potential group performance and different task types in the next section. In particular, we outline how potential group performance is defined for different types of tasks and how this potential changes with group size. In the third section, we deal with the psychological processes that determine how groups perform against the standard of their potential performance. In particular, we describe several *process losses* that make groups perform below their potential, and also outline several *process gains* that make them surpass their potential. As we further show, the relative prevalence of process losses vs. process gains in groups depends on how group performance is *managed*, that is, how groups are designed and how their process is being controlled. In the fourth section, we will describe three basic principles of group performance management, namely *group composition*, *group synchronization* and *group learning*, which facilitate process gains rather than process losses.

The extent to which these principles are realized depends on many factors. We highlight one factor – leadership – that is particularly important in this context. Therefore, in the fifth section we give a brief introduction to leadership concepts and leadership research, and in the sixth section we outline how leadership affects group performance via the principles of *group performance management*. In the final section we summarize the core messages of this chapter.

SOME CORE CONCEPTS: ACTUAL GROUP PERFORMANCE, GROUP POTENTIAL AND TASK TYPE

What performance potential do groups have for different types of task?

How does group size affect performance potential?

Actual and potential group performance

As outlined, a meaningful evaluation of group performance requires a baseline against which one can judge that performance. Naturally, group performance depends on individual performance: the better the group members are, the better – on average – group performance will be, and this also implies that what makes individual members better will – again on average – also make the group better. This individual component of group performance, however, is not what social psychologists are interested in. Instead, they are interested in the group component of group performance, that is, the question of how this performance is affected by group members' awareness that common outcomes also depend on what other group members do (social interdependence) and on their interaction with these other group members (social interaction).

To determine this group-specific component, we have to know what performance would have occurred if the same members had worked independently of each other (i.e., not as a group). This latter performance will be labelled *potential group performance* or (more simply) **group potential**. The potential is contrasted with how the group actually performs, which is called *actual group performance*.

> **potential group performance (group potential)** the performance that would have occurred if the members of a group had worked independently of each other and not as a group; a common benchmark to evaluate actual group performance

This group potential is determined in two steps. The first is to measure how the same group members or similar persons perform individually. The second is to combine these individual contributions into a (hypothetical) group product. As we will see, this second step depends strongly on the type of task under investigation.

Basic types of group tasks and their implications for group potential

Dimensions of group tasks   In his seminal classification of *group task types*, Steiner (1972) distinguished three dimensions. The first refers to whether the task is *unitary* or *divisible*: divisible tasks allow for the assignment of different subtasks to different members, whereas for unitary tasks all members have to perform the same task. The second dimension consists of whether the ultimate focus of task fulfilment is quantity (*maximization tasks*) or quality (*optimization tasks*). Finally, the third dimension classifies tasks by how group performance is related to the performance of each individual member. Here, Steiner made an important distinction between *additive*, *disjunctive* and *conjunctive* tasks.[1] We describe each of these tasks in some detail and show how group potential is defined for them (see the overview in Table 13.1). To further illustrate how group potential

> **group task type**   distinguishes group tasks depending on whether the task is divisible between group members, whether the quality or quantity of the output is relevant, and how individual contributions are related to the group's performance

Table 13.1 *Important types of unitary group tasks and their implications for group potential*

Task type	Examples	Group potential
Additive	Pulling a rope; brainstorming; shovelling snow	Sum of members' individual performance
Disjunctive	Problem solving; decision-making; mathematical calculations	Best member's individual performance
Conjunctive	Mountain climbing; precision work; keeping something confidential	Weakest member's individual performance

PIONEER

Ivan D. Steiner (1917–2001) graduated from Central Michigan University before receiving a master's degree and a doctorate from the University of Michigan. He was a PhD student of Ted Newcomb, and later on he also taught social psychology at the University of Illinois. He spent the last 10 years of his academic career at the University of Massachusetts (Amherst). Steiner contributed greatly to the research on group performance and became famous for his classification of group tasks. Depending on how the individual's effort contributes to the overall performance of the group, he distinguished between additive, conjunctive and disjunctive tasks, each of which are affected differently by process losses and process gains.

works for each task type, we also explain how group potential changes with group size.

Additive tasks Additive tasks are those in which the performance of a group is simply the sum of their members' individual performances. Additive tasks are usually maximization tasks. Weight pulling is an example: the weight pulled by the whole group should be the sum of the weights that the individual members pull in this situation. Another example is *brainstorming*: if a group has the task of generating as many ideas as possible about a particular topic, group performance is the sum of the different ideas generated by the individual members.

> **brainstorming** a group technique aimed at enhancing creativity in groups by means of the uninhibited generation of as many ideas as possible concerning a specified topic

Hence, potential group performance is defined by the sum of member performances measured in an individual situation. As a consequence, group potential is higher than the best group member's individual potential and – for groups consisting of members with identical individual performance – it increases linearly with group size. This means that if you double the number of members in a group, you get twice the group potential as before.

Disjunctive tasks In a disjunctive task, a group has to choose one of several judgements or proposals. A good example is problem solving, where a group has to decide on one particular solution to a problem. Here, actual group performance depends solely on the quality of the one particular proposal which is chosen by the group. Due to this restriction, disjunctive tasks are usually optimization tasks, where quality matters. Potential group performance in disjunctive tasks is determined by the best member's individual performance. As group size increases, group potential also increases, but the increase in potential gained if another member is added to the group becomes smaller the larger the size of the group. If, for example, the individual chances of solving a problem are 50 per cent, a relatively large increase in potential is obtained if there are three instead of two members. In contrast, if you already have 20 members, adding another person changes very little.

> **eureka effect** describes the situation when the correct solution to a problem, once it is found, is immediately recognized as being correct by group members

Disjunctive tasks are often differentiated into tasks with or without a so-called *eureka effect*, which means that the correct solution, once found, is immediately recognized as being correct. A eureka effect increases the chances that a group will realize its potential: if the best member in the group is able to solve the problem, but the group fails to realize the correctness of his or her solution (no eureka effect), the group might choose a different, suboptimal option.

Conjunctive tasks Whereas in disjunctive tasks one successful member can be enough to solve the problem, a conjunctive task requires all group members to be successful for the group to

Plate 13.2 *This group is only as fast as its slowest member.*

complete the task. An example is climbing a mountain as part of a roped team. Suppose that in order to reach the peak the climbers have to pass a difficult overhang. The climbing team will only reach the peak if all members are successful in passing the overhang. Or, if we use the speed of a climbing team as a continuous measure of performance, we can say that the group is only as fast as its slowest member. The group potential for conjunctive tasks is given by the individual performance of the group's weakest member. As a consequence, group potential *decreases* with increasing group size, because the larger the group gets, the more likely it is to have a very weak member in the group.

Hence, it can be ineffective to have large groups for conjunctive tasks. This problem is lessened if the conjunctive task is divisible and specific subtasks can be matched to group members' abilities. For example, the climbing party might decide that for difficult passages it would be useful to have the better members going ahead, fixing ropes and then helping the weaker members over these passages. In this case, potential group performance is higher than the individual performance of the weakest member.

SUMMARY

To determine group-specific influences on the performance of groups, we have to establish what performance would have occurred in the absence of group processes. This is given by the group potential. Determining the group potential depends on the type of group task. For example, in additive tasks (e.g., brainstorming), the potential is given by the sum of the members' performances in an individual situation. The group potential in a disjunctive task (e.g., problem solving) is determined by the quality of the best proposal individually generated by a group member. In a conjunctive task (e.g., mountain climbing), the group potential is given by the weakest member's individual performance.

PROCESS LOSSES VS. PROCESS GAINS IN GROUP PERFORMANCE

What processes influence whether actual group performance remains below or surpasses potential group performance? How does the occurrence of these processes depend on task type?

Types of process losses and process gains

Group potential and actual group performance often diverge. This divergence is due to *process losses* and *process gains*, both of which occur due to social interdependence and social interaction in groups. This is expressed in the following formula by Hackman and Morris (1975):

Actual group performance = Group potential – process losses + process gains

Thus, when actual group performance is below group potential, process losses must have occurred. If, in contrast, actual group performance exceeds group potential, process gains must have been present.

Different types of process losses and process gains can occur. For a group to perform, its members have to make individual contributions, and these contributions have to be coordinated. As a result, group processes can affect performance by influencing either the coordination of individual contributions or the individual contributions themselves. With regard to individual contributions, they depend on how much the person *can* contribute and how much the person is *motivated* to contribute. Hence, group processes can influence both group members' ability and motivation to contribute to the group product. In sum, we have three levels of process losses and gains, namely *coordination*, *motivation* and *individual capability*.

Coordination losses By definition, coordination in groups can only lead to process losses, not to process gains. This is due to the fact that, as outlined, group potential is measured on the basis of an *optimal* combination of individual contributions.[2] Consequently, *coordination losses* are said to occur if a group fails to optimally coordinate its members' individual contributions. For example, in his classic investigations of group performance in physical tasks, Ringelmann (1913) found that the average individual weight that people pull when performing such a task in a group decreases as the size of the group increases, the

> **coordination losses** describe the diminished performance of a group if it fails to optimally coordinate its members' individual contributions

PIONEER

Max Ringelmann (1861–1931) was professor of agricultural engineering at the French National Institute of Agronomy and director of the Machine Testing Station. His main field of research lay in determining the efficiency of work in agricultural applications. In what may be considered one of the first experiments in social psychology, he discovered a decrease in individual performance that occurs when the individual works in a group rather than alone. He also found that each group member's individual contribution to group performance decreases as group size increases. These findings are referred to as the Ringelmann effect.

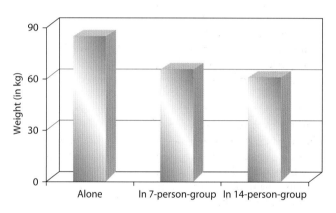

Figure 13.1 *Average individual weight pulled dependent on the number of persons pulling together (Ringelmann, 1913).*

so-called *Ringelmann effect*. An illustration of one of his findings is given in Figure 13.1. Later investigations showed that this process loss is due to both insufficient coordination

> **Ringelmann effect** describes the finding that in physical tasks such as weight pulling, the average performance of individual group members decreases with increasing group size

(members fail to exert their maximal effort at the same moment) and decreased motivation (individuals work less hard when they are part of a group) (Ingham, Levinger, Graves & Peckham, 1974). An experiment that disentangles coordination losses and motivation losses is described in Research close-up 13.1.

Another well-known coordination loss occurs in brainstorming. Osborn (1957) proposed that brainstorming in a group would lead to the generation of far more and better ideas than would be obtained if the same persons generated ideas individually. Experiments testing this assumption contain at least two conditions: in one condition, the participants come together in a group and conduct a brainstorming session. For example, the task could be to generate as many ideas as possible concerning ways to

Why groups under-perform: separating coordination and motivation losses

Latané, B., Williams, K. & Harkins, S. (1979, Experiment 2). Many hands make light the work: The causes and consequences of social loafing. *Journal of Personality and Social Psychology, 37*, 822–832.

....

Introduction

The aim of this study was to replicate Ringelmann's findings of process losses in collective work using a different task, and to demonstrate to what extent the process losses are due to insufficient coordination vs. motivation losses in groups. Latané and his colleagues therefore conducted two experiments with a cheering and hand clapping task (see below). In the first experiment, they successfully replicated the Ringelmann effect by showing that the more people there were in a group, the less noise was produced per person. To distinguish between motivation and coordination, in Experiment 2, which we examine more closely below, Latané et al. used an elegant strategy, namely the introduction of 'pseudo-groups'. In a pseudo-group, participants are led to believe they are working in a group while actually working alone. Since no coordination losses are possible in this situation, all process losses found in pseudo-groups would have to be due to motivation losses (because individual capability losses are hardly possible with this type of task).

Method

Participants
Thirty-six male students participated in the experiment, with 6 participants per experimental session.

Design and procedure
The experimental design was a within-subjects design with five conditions. Each participant completed several trials (1) alone, (2) in actual two-person groups, (3) in actual six-person groups, (4) in two-person pseudo-groups and (5) in six-person pseudo-groups. The participants' task was to shout as loudly as possible when the experimenter gave a signal. They were blindfolded and wore headsets on which constant noise was played. This manipulation ensured that during the pseudo-group trials participants believed they were shouting with one or five other persons respectively, when in fact they were shouting alone.

Results

The data were analysed with two separate analyses of variance (ANOVAs), one comparing the individual trials with the actual two-person group and six-person group trials, the other doing the same for the pseudo-groups. Both analyses showed that the average noise produced per person decreased with the increasing number of persons. People shouted less loudly in the two-person groups than when alone, and they shouted less loudly in six-person groups than in two-person groups. This was true for actual groups as well as for pseudo-groups. However, the decrement in individual performance was about twice as high in the

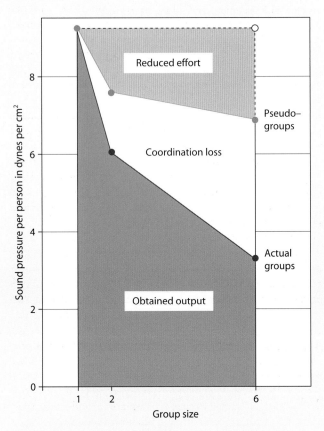

Figure 13.2 *Intensity of sound produced per person when cheering alone vs. in actual or pseudo-groups of two or six persons (Latané et al., 1979, p. 827).*

actual groups compared with the pseudo-groups (no statistical comparisons between these conditions were made). This relationship is illustrated in Figure 13.2. The decrements in sound intensity between shouting alone and shouting in a pseudo-group can be traced back to reduced effort, since no differences in coordination requirements exist between these conditions. In contrast, the differences between pseudo-groups and actual groups can be attributed to coordination losses such as, for example, group members not reaching their maximum sound intensity synchronously.

Discussion

The results demonstrate that, in accordance with the authors' hypotheses, coordination losses are not the only source of process losses when people perform a task collectively instead of individually or co-actively. Instead, reduced effort also contributes to this effect. Although one might object that no direct measures of motivation and coordination losses existed, it has to be conceded that the arrangement of the experimental setting and conditions hardly leaves room for alternative explanations of the observed performance decrements (e.g., cognitive interference among members is implausible). In sum, the study successfully demonstrates two reasons why groups may fail to realize their full potential.

nominal group a number of individuals who perform a task individually and work independently of each other. Nominal groups are used to determine the potential performance of groups

protect the environment. The other condition determines the group potential. This is done in **nominal groups**. Nominal groups contain the same number of persons as the real groups do; however, each person is seated in a different room and asked to generate and write down ideas individually about the topic. The experimenter collects their lists and puts them together. Ideas that are mentioned by more than one member (redundant ideas) enter the list only once, because in a group the same idea would also be generated and counted only once.

In all of these experiments, brainstorming groups hardly ever reached the number of ideas generated by nominal groups; in most cases they were significantly below this group potential (for an overview see Mullen, Johnson & Salas, 1991). This disadvantage is not compensated by increased quality of ideas: on average, interactive brainstorming groups do not generate better (i.e., more creative or more practicable) ideas than nominal groups. As Diehl and Stroebe (1987) have shown in a series of experiments, the most important reason for this suboptimal performance in interactive brainstorming groups is a coordination loss called **production blocking**: when people generate ideas in an interacting group, at any given time only one person can articulate her idea. During this time all other members are 'blocked' and are unable to express their own ideas.

production blocking a process loss typical of brainstorming tasks in face-to-face groups. Since in a group only one person can speak at a time, the other group members cannot express their own ideas at the same time

Coordination losses also occur in disjunctive or conjunctive tasks. For example, groups often fail to choose the best among their members' proposals, even if one member actually proposes the optimal solution. In a study by Torrance (1954), three-person groups were given several tasks, one of which was a problem-solving task with a definite answer. The participants were members of the US Airforce; each group consisted of a pilot, a navigator and a gunner. In a military aircrew, pilots have the highest status, whereas gunners are lowest in status. Torrance's results showed that if the pilot had found the correct solution prior to discussion, the group failed to choose this option in less than one out of ten cases. In contrast, when the gunner had found the correct solution, more than one-third of the groups failed to adopt this solution. Hence, the group's choice of one of their members' proposals was influenced by member status. Similarly, groups often prefer an incorrect solution proposed by the majority over a correct solution proposed by a minority (Smith, Tindale & Steiner, 1998; see also Chapter 11, this volume). In both of these examples the individual contributions would have allowed the groups to succeed, but successful coordination (choosing the right proposal) often did not occur.

Motivation losses and gains If actual group performance differs from group potential, this difference can be due to the fact that the group members' individual contributions become better or worse in a group setting compared to an individual situation. One reason for this is that working in a group can lower or increase

people's motivation to contribute to task performance (**motivation losses and gains**). We first turn to motivation losses, three of which have so far been identified in group performance research:

- *Social loafing* (Latané et al., 1979): Social loafing occurs if group members reduce their effort due to the fact that their individual contribution to the group product is not identifiable.

- *Free-riding* (Kerr & Bruun, 1983): In the case of free-riding, group members reduce their effort because their individual contribution seems to have little impact on group performance.

- *Sucker effect* (Kerr, 1983): The sucker effect occurs if group members perceive or anticipate that other group members lower their effort. To avoid being exploited (being the 'sucker'), they reduce their effort themselves.

motivation losses and gains decreases or increases in group members' motivation to contribute to group task performance

social loafing a motivation loss in groups that occurs when group members reduce their effort due to the fact that individual contributions to group performance are not identifiable

free-riding a reduction in group members' task-related effort because their individual contribution seems to have little impact on group performance

sucker effect a motivation loss in groups that occurs when group members perceive or anticipate that other group members will lower their effort. To avoid being exploited, they reduce their effort themselves

Both the extent and type of motivation loss that occurs depend on task type. Additive tasks allow for all of the above-mentioned losses. For example, some members of the weight-pulling group could pull less hard because they believe that it is almost impossible to determine how hard each member has tried to pull (social loafing) or because they feel that – given the large number of group members – it will hardly make a difference how hard they pull (free-riding). At the same time, other group members might be aware of such tendencies and, thus, reduce their effort to avoid being the 'sucker'. These losses are typically stronger the larger the group size (Latané et al., 1979). Why is this the case? The larger the group, the more difficult it is to identify individual contributions, which gives rise to more social loafing and more suspicion that others will exploit one's performance. At the same time, the relative impact of each member's individual contribution becomes smaller with increasing group size.

In disjunctive and conjunctive tasks, social loafing is less of a problem because individual contributions in these tasks are normally visible: when a group solves a problem, it is more or less evident who came up with which proposal; and when a climbing team scales a mountain, it is evident who slows down the group. However, both free-riding and sucker effects can be a problem, especially if the group contains weaker and stronger members and the members are aware of these differences. In a disjunctive task, this awareness particularly pushes weak members towards free-riding, since they know that even if they invest a lot of effort, it is fairly unlikely that their contribution (e.g., their proposal) will be good enough to be chosen by the group. In contrast, stronger members know that they are expected to take responsibility for good performance and, thus, are particularly prone to feel they are the 'sucker'. In conjunctive tasks, the opposite happens: here the stronger members are aware that their effort is not very important for group performance, because even if they invest less effort they should be able to perform at the level of the weaker members. Hence they tend to free-ride, which may cause problems if, by investing more effort, they could help the weaker members to perform better (Kerr & Bruun, 1983). If conjunctive tasks are divisible, such problems can be avoided by matching subtasks to members' abilities. However, since this means that stronger members get more to do than weaker members, this can also induce sucker effects among the stronger members, especially if their acceptance of the division of labour is low.

While most social psychological research on group performance has focused on motivation losses, more recent studies have established three motivation gains in groups:

> **social competition** a motivation gain in groups that occurs if the group members want to outperform each other during group tasks in which the individual contributions are identifiable
>
> **social compensation** a motivation gain in groups that occurs if stronger group members increase their effort in order to compensate for weaker members' suboptimal performance
>
> **Köhler effect** a motivation gain in groups which involves weaker group members' working harder than they would do individually in order to avoid being responsible for a weak group performance

- *Social competition* (Stroebe, Diehl & Abakoumkin, 1996): If individual contributions are identifiable, group members can be more motivated during group performance compared to individual performance because they want to outperform other members. Social competition is particularly likely if group members have relatively equal abilities.

- *Social compensation* (Williams & Karau, 1991): Social compensation occurs if stronger members work harder in a group than they would do individually in order to compensate for a weaker member's suboptimal performance.

- *Köhler effect* (Köhler, 1926; Witte, 1989): The Köhler effect was discovered in the 1920s but remained largely unrecognized until Witte rediscovered it in 1989. A Köhler effect is said to occur if weaker members work harder than they would do individually in order to avoid being responsible for a weak group performance.

The occurrence of motivation gains also depends on the type of task. Social competition can operate within all task types as long as individual contributions are identifiable and comparable. As we have already pointed out, this is the case for most disjunctive and conjunctive tasks, but it is often not so in additive tasks. Hence, social competition is more likely to occur in disjunctive or conjunctive tasks than in additive tasks. In contrast, social compensation is mainly restricted to additive tasks because only in additive tasks can stronger group members really compensate for another member's weak performance. Finally, the Köhler effect is mainly restricted to conjunctive tasks, since only in conjunctive tasks can weaker members anticipate that an inferior group performance will be attributed to them by other group members (Hertel, Kerr

& Messé, 2000). The effect is strongest if there are moderate discrepancies between group members' individual capabilities and they are aware of these differences (Messé, Hertel, Kerr, Lount & Park, 2002): if individual capabilities are almost equal, it is less clear who is to blame for an inferior performance. If, however, the discrepancies are very large, the weaker members hardly have any hope of being able to match the stronger members' performance.

In sum, within the same task type both motivation gains and motivation losses can occur. Thus, one of the challenges for group performance research is to find variables that determine whether gains or losses dominate. One key variable that has been found so far is the *importance of group goals*. Social compensation is particularly likely to occur if the common group goal is highly valued by members, otherwise motivation losses are more likely. This is well demonstrated in a series of experiments by Williams and Karau (1991). Participants performed an idea-generation task and were told that they were working with a partner (supposedly in another room) who, in fact, did not exist. The researchers manipulated whether participants expected their partner to show strong or weak performance and whether the performance goal (generating as many ideas as possible) was relevant to them or not. In addition, for half of the participants, the task was labelled a collective task (i.e., the number of collectively generated ideas would be counted), while for the other half the task was co-active (although performed with the other person, the number of individually generated ideas would be counted). The results are shown in Figure 13.3. When participants expected to work with a *strongly performing* partner, there was no need to compensate. In fact, those working on the collective task even engaged in a bit of social loafing: their performance was always below their potential (i.e., less than in the co-active situation) regardless of task relevance.

In contrast, if participants worked with a *weakly performing* partner, there was a need to compensate, but only when the task was both *relevant* (i.e., the outcome was important to them) and

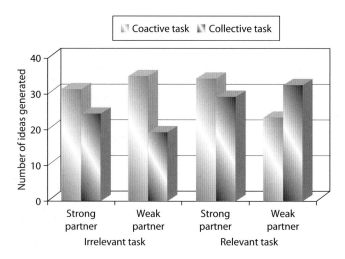

Figure 13.3 *Social loafing and social compensation as a function of task relevance and partner ability (Williams & Karau, 1991, Experiment 3).*

collective (i.e., joint productivity would be evaluated). In this condition, performance in the collective task was actually higher than in the co-active task: they performed beyond their potential. If, however, the group goal was irrelevant, there was a motivation loss instead of a motivation gain. Regardless of their co-worker's ability, participants produced fewer ideas in collective conditions than in co-active conditions. Similar effects can be expected for disjunctive and conjunctive tasks. For example, a Köhler effect should only occur if the group goal is important and, thus, the weaker members do not want to feel responsible for inferior performance.

Losses and gains in individual capability

If group members contribute more or less than they would do in an individual setting, this can be due to the motivation losses and gains described above. However, the same effects can be due to the fact that the group setting influences their *ability* to make such contributions. Social interaction in a group may help members to make better contributions than they might have made individually, for example by other group members' providing intellectual stimulation or demonstrating effective strategies. However, social interaction may also have a detrimental effect on their individual capability, for example by restricting their attention or offering role models of ineffective strategies. Surprisingly, such *individual capability gains and losses* due to social interaction have so far been almost neglected in group performance research. As a consequence, compared to coordination and motivation losses or gains, there is a need for more research in this area.

> **individual capability gains and losses** improvements or impairments in individual group members' ability to successfully perform a task due to social interaction with the group

Individual capability losses and capability gains, however, can be clearly illustrated in brainstorming tasks (e.g., Nijstad, Stroebe & Lodewijkx, 2002). If, for example, the task is to generate as many ideas as possible for promoting environmental protection, then hearing an idea from another group member about reducing traffic can make you focus on ideas for diminishing fuel consumption, whereas in the individual situation you might also have thought about sustainable development and other issues. Hence, if you fail to come up with ideas about sustainable development in the group situation, this is not due to the fact that you're not trying hard enough (motivation loss); rather, due to social influence, you simply aren't capable of producing these ideas at that moment. This

> **cognitive restriction** a capability loss in group tasks that involve idea generation, which occurs when an idea mentioned by another group member makes people focus on the particular category this idea belongs to, at the expense of generating ideas from other categories

socially determined capability loss can be termed *cognitive restriction*. On the other hand, it is also possible that you would never have thought about reducing fuel consumption, and it was only after another group member came up with the idea of reducing traffic that you generated new ideas on this issue. Again, the reason for the difference between your contribution in an individual setting and in the group is not motivational: you don't try harder in the group setting, but stimulation from other group members makes you more capable of producing diverse ideas.

Plate 13.3 *Computer-mediated communication allows group members to brainstorm electronically.*

Thus, the corresponding socially determined capability gain can be termed *cognitive stimulation*.

Since both cognitive restriction and cognitive stimulation effects can occur, brainstorming in groups can lead either to more uniformity (Ziegler, Diehl & Zijlstra, 2000) or to greater variety (Paulus & Yang, 2000) in idea generation. However, to demonstrate individual capability gains (stimulation), many of the well-known process losses in brainstorming – particularly production blocking – have to be eliminated first, otherwise they are so strong that individual capability gains are totally submerged. Such process losses can be eliminated, for example, by using computer-mediated communication (Dennis & Valacich, 1993): instead of brainstorming in face-to-face interaction, group members are linked together via a chat system. Since each member is free to type in ideas at the same time as other members, production blocking cannot occur and, hence, there are better conditions for cognitive stimulation.

> **cognitive stimulation** a capability gain in group tasks that involve idea generation, which occurs when an idea mentioned by another group member stimulates a cognitive category one would otherwise not have thought of

For an overview of the different process losses and process gains discussed in this chapter, see Table 13.2.

Table 13.2 *Overview of process losses and process gains in group performance that have been documented in research so far*

Level of process	Process losses	Process gains
Coordination	Ringelmann effect Production blocking	–
Motivation	Social loafing Free-riding Sucker effect	Social compensation Social competition Köhler effect
Individual capability	Cognitive restriction	Cognitive stimulation

SUMMARY

If group performance is below group potential, process losses have occurred. If, instead, group performance exceeds group potential, then process gains have taken place. Process losses and gains are possible at three different theoretical levels: motivation, individual capability and coordination. Three types of motivation loss (social loafing, free-riding and the sucker effect) and three types of motivation gain (social competition, social compensation and the Köhler effect) have been shown so far. Far less frequently, research has demonstrated that individual capabilities can be restricted (capability loss) as well as stimulated (capability gain) in a group. Studies have focused almost exclusively on coordination losses so far, due to the fact that group potential is usually defined in terms of the optimal combination of group members' individual efforts.

GROUP PERFORMANCE MANAGEMENT

Why do process losses seem to be more frequent than process gains? How can group performance be optimized?

Three basic principles of group performance management

Over the last century, social psychological research on group performance has provided impressive evidence for process losses but far less evidence for process gains. This might suggest that negative aspects dominate when people work together in a group. In our view this conclusion is unjustified. Social psychological experiments on group performance predominantly use randomly composed ad hoc groups, with no further means or techniques of support accompanying the group process. Furthermore, experiments are usually restricted to one or, in some cases, two task trials. While these restrictions are useful for certain types of research questions (and often also have pragmatic reasons), they systematically disfavour groups in the evaluation of group performance. If you're comparing a car with a unicycle on speed or safety criteria, you would hardly use a car that had four randomly composed wheels with no means to synchronize them. In addition, you would hardly restrict your comparison to the first 10 metres. Unfortunately, this is analogous to what usually happens in group performance research.

Gaining insight into factors that disfavour groups is not only interesting for research purposes (e.g., to develop new research programs on group performance), it also provides a key to solving the problem of how to optimize group performance. If group performance is underestimated because no systematic *group composition* and support of group functioning take place, and because the time frame is too limited, then systematically optimizing these aspects should provide a promising way to optimize group performance. Accordingly, Schulz-Hardt, Hertel and Brodbeck (in press) term the sum of activities aimed at improving the group-specific component of group performance (i.e., maximizing process gains and minimizing process losses) *group performance management* and propose three basic underlying principles:

1 Groups should be composed according to the requirements of task structure.
2 Group processes during performance should be specifically synchronized.
3 Groups should be given the opportunity to perform multiple similar tasks to allow for group learning to occur.

In the following sections, we briefly explain each of the three principles and give examples of how they can be applied to specific group tasks.

Group composition Group performance depends on the kind of people who are brought together in a group. This is true in a trivial sense, in that the more capable group members are of performing the task, the better the group will perform (in general). It is, however, also true in a non-trivial sense, in that certain compositions make it more likely than others that a group will fully realize or even surpass its potential, thereby realizing process gains.

To illustrate this principle, we take a look at an important task in group decision-making research, the *hidden profile* task. Consider the following situation. A personnel selection committee consisting of group members X, Y and Z has to decide which of the three candidates, A, B and C, should be chosen for a sales management position. The information about the candidates (advantages and disadvantages) and the way it is distributed among the committee is illustrated in Table 13.3.

If the full information (the 'whole group' column in Table 13.3) is considered, candidate A is the best choice, with three advantages and two disadvantages, compared to candidates B and C (two advantages, three disadvantages). However, as becomes apparent from the first three columns, none of the committee members individually possesses this full information set. The advantages of candidates B and C as well as the disadvantages of candidate A are held by all group members prior to discussion; they are termed *shared information*. In contrast, each disadvantage of candidates B

> **group composition** specifies how certain characteristics are distributed within a group
>
> **group performance management** the sum of activities aimed at maximizing (or improving) the group-specific component of group performance

> **hidden profile** a group decision situation in which task-relevant information is distributed among group members in such a way that no individual group member can detect the best solution based on his or her own information. Only by sharing information within the group can the optimal solution to the task become evident

Table 13.3 *Information distribution in a hidden profile task*

	Group member X	Group member Y	Group member Z	Whole group (X + Y + Z)
Candidate A	Good analytical expertise (+)	Stays calm under pressure (+)	Works well with the team (+)	Good analytic expertise (+) Stays calm under pressure (+) Works well with the team (+)
	Lacks humour (–) **Not very creative (–)**	**Lacks humour (–)** **Not very creative (–)**	**Lacks humour (–)** **Not very creative (–)**	**Lacks humour (–)** **Not very creative (–)**
Candidate B	**Good communication skills (+)** **Known to be very reliable (+)** Tends to be short-tempered (–)	**Good communication skills (+)** **Known to be very reliable (+)** Often resentful in conflicts (–)	**Good communication skills (+)** **Known to be very reliable (+)** Refuses to do overtime (–)	**Good communication skills (+)** **Known to be very reliable (+)** Tends to be short-tempered (–) Often resentful in conflicts (–) Refuses to do overtime (–)
Candidate C	**Knows the market inside out (+)** **Works well with the team (+)** Inattentive in meetings (–)	**Knows the market inside out (+)** **Works well with the team (+)** Delays uncomfortable tasks (–)	**Knows the market inside out (+)** **Works well with the team (+)** Said to be arrogant (–)	**Knows the market inside out (+)** **Works well with the team (+)** Inattentive in meetings (–) Delays uncomfortable tasks (–) Said to be arrogant (–)
Implied choice	Either B or C	Either B or C	Either B or C	A

+ candidate's advantages; – candidate's disadvantages; shared information is indicated in bold.

and C as well as each advantage of candidate A is held by only one group member; these items are termed *unshared information*. Due to this distribution, prior to discussion none of the group members can detect that A is the best choice – it is 'hidden' from the group members, which is why this situation is called a hidden profile. This task is particularly important for group decision-making research, because it constitutes the prototype of situations where groups can make better decisions than individual members can. If, in contrast, the committee in our example had representative individual information that already implied candidate A to be the best choice (in which case it is called a *manifest profile*), making the decision in a group could hardly yield any surplus in decision quality.

Unfortunately, research has shown that most groups fail to solve hidden profiles (Stasser & Birchmeier, 2003). As Brodbeck, Kerschreiter, Mojzisch and Schulz-Hardt (2007) and Mojzisch and Schulz-Hardt (2006) have outlined, this failure is caused by three different processes, summarized in Figure 13.4. (To date, there is no solid evidence to indicate whether these processes

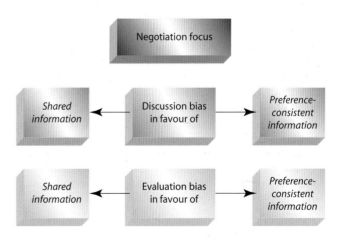

Figure 13.4 *Explanations for the failure of groups to discover hidden profiles (adapted from Brodbeck et al., 2007, and Mojzisch & Schulz-Hardt, 2006).*

constitute coordination losses, motivation losses or individual capability losses, so we do not categorize them as such.)

(1) *Negotiation focus*: Groups tend to negotiate the decision on the basis of their members' pre-discussion preferences rather than openly exchanging the relevant information (Gigone & Hastie, 1993). Because no member can individually detect the best alternative in a hidden profile prior to discussion, pre-discussion preferences are usually in favour of suboptimal alternatives (in our example, candidates B or C). Thus, one of the suboptimal alternatives is chosen by the group.

(2) *Discussion bias*: Even if the relevant information is exchanged in the group, this discussion is typically biased. Groups spend more time discussing shared than unshared information (Larson, Foster-Fishman & Keys, 1994), because shared information can be introduced by more members than unshared information. Furthermore, group members predominantly introduce or repeat information that is consistent with their initial preferences (Dennis, 1996; Schulz-Hardt, Brodbeck, Mojzisch, Kerschreiter & Frey, 2006), which can be due to a perceived 'advocacy role' (Stasser & Titus, 1985), that is, group members believe that their primary task in a discussion is to explain why they prefer a particular alternative. However, most of the critical information for solving the hidden profile is both unshared and inconsistent with the members' initial preferences (in our example, the advantages of candidate A and the disadvantages of candidates B and C). As a consequence, the group does not exchange enough of this critical information to detect the best alternative.

(3) *Evaluation bias*: The evaluation of information in the group is also biased in favour of shared and preference-consistent information: group members judge shared information to be more credible and valid than unshared information, because each member individually 'owns' the shared information (Chernyshenko, Miner, Baumann & Sniezek, 2003) – so one can be relatively sure that this information is correct – and shared information can also be socially validated by other group members (Wittenbaum, Hubbell & Zuckerman, 1999). Furthermore, they judge information that is consistent with their preferences to be more credible and important than information that is inconsistent with their preferences (Greitemeyer & Schulz-Hardt, 2003), because preference-consistent information is accepted at face value, whereas preference-inconsistent information is critically tested. As a consequence, even if all information is exchanged in the group, group members often undervalue the critical information and, thus, fail to detect the best alternative.

As recent studies have demonstrated, these processes and, thus, the chances of groups' solving hidden profiles depend substantially on a particular aspect of group composition, namely, consent vs. dissent in group members' individual pre-discussion preferences (see Brodbeck, Kerschreiter, Mojzisch, Frey & Schulz-Hardt, 2002; Schulz-Hardt, Brodbeck et al., 2006). Imagine you had two three-person groups in our personnel selection case. In one group, all three group members prefer candidate B (consent group). In another group, two members prefer B, whereas one member prefers candidate C (dissent group). With regard to group potential, neither group differs – in both groups, no member individually prefers the correct choice (candidate A). However, the dissent group should be less likely than the consent group to reach a premature consensus via negotiation. Furthermore, due to minority influence, there should be less bias in gathering information (Schulz-Hardt, Frey, Lüthgens & Moscovici, 2000) and its evaluation (Nemeth, 1986) in the dissent group (see also Chapter 11, this volume). To test these ideas experimentally, Schulz-Hardt, Brodbeck et al. (2006) first gave participants individual information about a hidden profile case. Groups with pre-discussion consent or dissent were then formed, based on the participants' individual preferences. Dissent groups were more likely to solve the hidden profile than were consent groups, even if none of the dissenting opinions was correct (i.e., in favour of the best candidate). This facilitative effect of pre-discussion dissent was mediated by a more intensive information exchange (less negotiation focus) and by less discussion bias.

Whereas composing groups with pre-discussion dissent is facilitative for performance in decision-making tasks, other tasks require other methods of group composition. For example, in a conjunctive task such as mountain climbing, it should be facilitative to have groups with moderate discrepancies among members' abilities, because this increases the likelihood of motivation gains among the weaker members (Messé et al., 2002) – and the weakest member determines group performance in a conjunctive task. So, if you had four climbers and had to split them into two two-person teams, teams of mixed ability should give better performance than teams of similar ability, in terms of facilitating process gains. Generally, whenever there is freedom to compose groups for particular tasks, the type of task should first be classified and then a group composition chosen that counteracts process losses and facilitates process gains for this task type.

Group synchronization Working together in a group requires generating or modifying individual contributions (e.g., physical effort, thoughts and ideas) collaboratively and integrating these different individual contributions in a way that is functional for high performance. For many tasks, we do not 'naturally' know how to do this or might even hold misleading preconceptions. For instance, for many people making a group decision means that everybody offers his or her preferred solution and states the arguments in its favour; finally the group chooses the solution with the most convincing arguments. As we have seen above, a group will hardly ever solve a hidden profile in this way.

Hence, just as four wheels need a differential in the axis to enable the vehicle to drive around corners, groups need synchronization to perform well. By **group synchronization** we mean the sum of activities aimed at optimizing the collaborative generation, modification and integration of individual contributions in a group. Means promoting group synchronization can vary from very simple tools (e.g., feedback about members' individual contributions) to rather complex procedures (e.g., group decision-making techniques).

> **group synchronization** the sum of activities aimed at optimizing the collaborative generation, modification and integration of individual contributions in a group

As in the case of group composition, optimal synchronization depends on the type of task at hand. However, some means of group synchronization can be applied across a wide range of group tasks. One of these is the *continuous visibility of individual contributions*. In a physical task such as pulling a weight, this can simply mean providing group members with feedback about their own as well as other group members' individual performance. In a cognitive task such as brainstorming or making a group decision based on distributed information, this can take the form of documenting group members' ideas and informational input on a documentation board or, as often used for these and other purposes, on an information board during computer-mediated group communication. In all cases, such permanent visibility of individual contributions counteracts motivation losses like social loafing or sucker effects and facilitates motivation gains due to social competition or Köhler effects (DeShon, Kozlowski, Schmidt, Milner, & Wiechmann, 2004; Hoeksema-van Orden, Gaillard & Buunk, 1998). It also facilitates coordination within the group, for instance by making it easier to identify the best proposal in a disjunctive task (Henry, Strickland, Yorges & Ladd, 1996) or by helping group members to match their own contributions to the contributions of other group members. Finally, in cognitive tasks, continuous visibility promotes individual capability gains by facilitating cognitive stimulation (Brodbeck, Mojzisch, Kerschreiter & Schulz-Hardt, 2006).

In contrast, some methods of group synchronization are unique for specific tasks such as group decision-making. As already outlined, our 'normal' preconceptions about how to make a decision in a group run counter to the way in which high-quality group decisions are actually made. Therefore, it can be useful to 'guide' group discussion on a decision problem by means of specific techniques. Some of these techniques are rather simple, such as dividing the decision process into an information collection phase and an information evaluation/decision-making phase. Even such simple guidance for the discussion process facilitates the solution of

hidden profiles (Brodbeck et al., 2006). Other techniques are more complex. For example, dialectical techniques divide a decision-making group into two subgroups that are given different roles. Based on these roles, they act out a controversial debate independent of the members' real opinions. This facilitates stimulation by including arguments or information that hardly anyone in the group would have mentioned if group members had, as they usually do, acted on their own preferences. Indeed, such dialectical techniques raise the quality of group decisions (see Katzenstein, 1996).

Group learning   The use of groups for a particular task is an investment, and the return on this investment often takes time to be realized. At the beginning, groups have considerably high costs, for example coordination losses due to the fact that group members are not used to working together on this particular task, or the effort of synchronizing the group adequately. If the group gains experience with the task over time, these costs should decrease and the chance of process gains should increase. Of course, individuals also increase their own performance if they repeatedly perform similar tasks. However, repeatedly performing similar tasks *in a group* allows for further learning processes (*group learning*) that cannot occur if people perform individually.

> **group learning** a generic term for several learning processes that can only occur if several people co-actively or cooperatively work on the same task

That the group collaborative context can stimulate learning processes which result in improved performance on the part of both individual members *and* the whole group has been demonstrated by Brodbeck and Greitemeyer (2000a, b; see Research close-up 13.2). They identified four different learning processes within group collaborative settings.

RESEARCH CLOSE-UP 13.2

Different components of group learning

Brodbeck, F.C. & Greitemeyer, T. (2000a). A dynamic model of group performance: Considering the group members' capacity to learn. *Group Processes and Intergroup Relations*, 3, 159–182.

Brodbeck, F.C. & Greitemeyer, T. (2000b). Effects of individual versus mixed individual and group experience in rule induction on group member learning and group performance. *Journal of Experimental Social Psychology*, 36, 621–648.

Introduction

In two experimental studies Brodbeck and Greitemeyer investigated the effects of individual experience vs. mixed individual and group experience on individual and group learning

(performance increments) in rule induction tasks. Rule induction is the search for descriptive, predictive and explanatory generalizations, rules or principles. Individuals or members of a group observe patterns and regularities in a particular domain and propose hypotheses to account for them. They then evaluate the hypotheses by observation and experiment and revise them accordingly. The experimental design allowed for the measurement of change in individual and group performance over consecutive task trials and various related variables, such as the exchange of hypotheses, error detection and error correction, the use of strategies for testing hypotheses, and so on. The level of task difficulty was manipulated across the two experiments in order to account for potential ceiling effects (i.e., maximum performance levels have been reached and thus no improvement in performance is possible).

Method

Participants

One hundred and thirty-two students (44 three-person groups) took part in the first experiment and 174 students (58 three-person groups) in the second experiment.

Design and procedure

Random series of eight and ten rule induction tasks were performed by sets of three participants randomly assigned to either *individual training* (performing all tasks in a nominal group) or to *mixed training* (alternating nominal and collaborative group task performance). Individual and group performance measures were taken across all tasks. For each task, a rule had to be induced that partitioned a deck of 52 playing cards with four suits (clubs = C, diamonds = D, hearts = H, spades = S) of 13 cards (ace = 1, two = 2, . . . , jack = 11, queen = 12, king = 13) into examples and non-examples of the rule. The instructions indicated that the rule could be based on suit, number, colour (red = r, black = b) or any combination of numerical and logical operations on these attributes (e.g., odd = o, even = e). The rule sequence length consisted of either three or four cards. First, the experimenter demonstrated a correct instance of the rule. Participants could then conduct a series of up to 10 'experiments', by presenting one card per experiment that they assumed constituted a correct continuation of the card(s) already on the table. For each card presented, they received feedback as to whether the card played was 'correct' (in line with the rule to be discovered) or 'wrong' (not in line with the rule to be discovered). Before presenting each card, participants formulated a hypothesis by writing down the rule that they thought plausible at the stage of their experimental sequence. There were four types of rules: (1) combination of suits (e.g., S-S-H-C), (2) combination of colours (e.g., r-r-b), (3) combination of odd and even numbers (e.g., e-o-e) and (4) combination of colour and odd vs. even numbers (e.g., ro-bo-re). The most difficult rule was S-S-H-C (32 per cent solution rate) and the easiest rule was r-r-b-b (71 per cent solution rate).

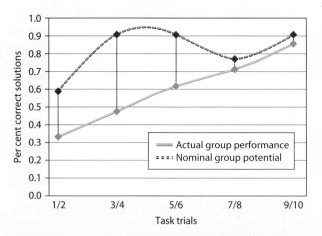

Figure 13.5 *Development of potential and actual group performance over consecutive task trials (Brodbeck & Greitemeyer, 2000a, Experiment 1: **Simple** rule induction tasks).*

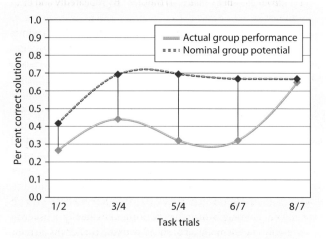

Figure 13.6 *Development of potential and actual group performance over consecutive task trials (Brodbeck & Greitemeyer, 2000a, Experiment 2: **Difficult** rule induction tasks).*

Results

As predicted, in both experiments nominal group performance improved as a function of improved individual resources for performing the task individually and (with some time lag) collective group performance improved as a function of collaboratively working in groups, thereby reducing or even eliminating process losses completely (see Figures 13.5 and 13.6, the last two task trials). In Experiment 1 a *ceiling effect* could have caused group performance to catch up with respective levels of individual performance in later trials. Thus, in the second experiment, more difficult tasks were used; there was no evidence of a ceiling effect due to nominal group performance reaching 100 per cent solution rates (see Figure 13.6).

Brodbeck and Greitemeyer (2000b) analysed in more detail the participants' formation of hypotheses about rules, their error-checking strategies and their success in finding correct rules. For example, in individual post-tests it was found that mixed training participants performed error checking more promptly and as a result generated fewer non-plausible hypotheses than did individual training participants. In the group post-test, mixed training groups were superior in collective error checking and more effective in collective truth detection than were individual training groups.

Discussion

The results demonstrated that group learning is a function of various sources of learning: (1) improvements in individual resources for performing the task individually (individual-to-individual (I–I) transfer); (2) improvements in individual resources as a consequence of prior collaboration (group-to-individual (G–I) transfer); and (3) individual learning to collaborate more smoothly and more effectively during collective task performance (group-to-individual-in-group (G–IG) transfer). Furthermore, the research demonstrated that process loss can be reduced or even eliminated when participants performed several task trials (n = 5) in a group collaborative context. The different learning processes identified by these experiments are further described and illustrated with examples in the main body of the chapter.

(1) *Individual-to-individual (I–I) transfer.* By repeatedly and individually performing similar tasks, individual learning takes place, that is, a relatively permanent change in individual behaviour or cognition, which usually results in performance increments. A performing group can profit from ***individual-to-individual (I–I) transfer*** because the group potential increases when the individual group members improve their abilities and skills in a way that affects their individual performance. For example, the level of potential performance of a party of climbers depends on the climbers' training, which they perform individually in order to be physically and mentally up to speed with the challenges on their next mountain tour.

> **individual-to-individual (I–I) transfer**
> denotes individual learning processes whereby a group member's ability to perform a task on his or her own improves as a result of repeated individual task performance

(2) *Group-to-individual (G–I) transfer.* When individual resources for performing a task *individually* improve as a function of social interaction between group members during repeated collective task performance, this is termed '***group-to-individual (G–I) transfer***' (cf. Laughlin & Sweeney, 1977). G–I transfer comes about when, for example, the effectiveness of a task performance strategy becomes evident (demonstrable to others) in the group collaborative context. The strategy can be adopted by other group members who are not using it already, and thus can be profitably transferred to later individual task performance contexts. Imagine our party of climbers again. Sometimes the climbers perform parts of their training together so that they can exchange ideas about strategies to better 'read the wall', that is, to identify grips and holes and potential slips. In doing so, they increase their repertoire of technical skills individually, which comes in handy when they are up the mountain as a team.

> **group-to-individual (G–I) transfer**
> denotes a group learning process whereby a group member's ability to perform a task *on his or her own* changes as a result of social interaction between group members during repeated collective task performance

(3) *Group-to-individual-in-group (G–IG) transfer.* If the individuals' resources for performing a task *collectively* improve as a function of prior collaborative task performance, then ***group-to-individual-in-group (G–IG) transfer*** takes place. With this type of transfer group-specific skills are learned that can be used in subsequent group performance situations. In the mountain climbing team this could, for example, mean that the members learn to support each other in finding the best possible grips and avoiding potential slips via communication, or to proactively correct each other's technical faults in climbing difficult overhangs. These individual skills for collaborative mountain climbing are transferable to a large extent to climbing as part of other teams as well.

> **group-to-individual-in-group (G–IG) transfer** denotes a group learning process whereby a group member's ability to perform a task *within groups* changes as a result of social interaction between group members during repeated collective task performance

(4) *Group-level learning or group-to-group (G–G) transfer.* ***Group-level learning (G–G transfer)*** is a relatively permanent change of collective behaviour resulting in performance increments for a particular group. Although the term group-level learning suggests that the group as a whole learns, this does not imply that there is a 'group mind' or something similar that would be capable of such learning. Instead, and in accordance with the previous terminology, group learning might also be called group-to-individual-in-same-group (G–IsG) transfer. By repeatedly performing similar tasks in the *same* group, group members learn how to optimally match subtasks to their specific capabilities and how to coordinate with particular other group members.

> **group-level learning (G–G transfer)**
> denotes a group learning process whereby a *particular* whole group's capability to perform a group task changes as a result of social interaction between its group members during repeated collective task performance

Only one group-level learning phenomenon in accordance with this criterion has been demonstrated so far: transactive memory in groups (Moreland, Argote & Krishnan, 1996; Wegner, 1987; see also Chapter 12, this volume). Transactive memory refers to a system of knowledge possessed by particular group members with shared awareness of each other's expertise, strengths and weaknesses ('knowing who knows what'). In the mountain climbing example, such group-to-group transfer would occur if the members had specialized in specific subtasks such as fixing ropes, helping weaker members during difficult passages or finding passages in unknown terrain, and if each member were aware of this specialization.

Due to these four group-learning processes, group performance should benefit more from repeated trials than individual performance does. In addition, over time it should become more likely that groups (1) increase their potential, (2) use their potential more optimally (reduce process losses), (3) perform at the level of their potential (no process loss, or process losses and process gains balance out) or (4) surpass their potential (process gains are larger than process losses). Direct empirical evidence for (1), (2) and (3) has been provided by Brodbeck and Greitemeyer (2000a, b). Solid replicable experimental evidence for (4) is not yet available.

The experiments on the dynamic model of group performance described in Research close-up 13.2 capture individual capability gains and reduction of coordination losses as a consequence of learning in groups. It is, however, plausible that the reduction of motivation losses and the development of motivation gains can also be 'learned' in groups. If the same group repeatedly performs similar tasks, group members become more familiar with each other and develop interpersonal trust. Interpersonal trust facilitates the pursuit of collective instead of individual goals (Dirks, 1999). As a consequence, group members should be less prone to social loafing or sucker effects, and should be more likely to show social compensation. Indirect evidence for this comes from a study by Erez and Somech (1996) showing that hardly any social loafing occurs in groups whose members have known each other for at least six months.

SUMMARY

In sum, our consideration of group performance and group learning has shown that effective group performance management requires an analysis of the task structure, followed by careful group composition and choice of adequate synchronization measures, both with regard to task structure. Furthermore, group learning should be facilitated by using the same group for a range of structurally similar tasks. As we have illustrated, these three basic principles affect all three categories of process losses and process gains by optimizing group coordination as well as stimulating individual motivation and capabilities during collective work. Figure 13.7 summarizes these effects.

So far we have investigated basic aspects of group performance, namely task types, group process gains and losses, and principles for the management of group performance, without referring to the structure of natural groups at work (i.e., work groups within their social settings, e.g., in organizations). We therefore turn next to a fundamental process for structuring group activity: leadership.

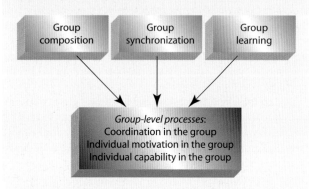

Figure 13.7 *The three basic elements of group performance management as affecting all three levels of performance-related group processes.*

LEADERSHIP

What makes leadership effective?
What are the major approaches to the study of leadership?

Leadership is about *influencing others*. This admittedly very short and broad definition is the only common denominator of the many definitions that exist in the leadership literature (e.g., Bass, 1990; Yukl, 2005). We define leadership in accordance with researchers from Project GLOBE, an international research program of some 170 scholars from more than 60 different countries, who study leadership across cultures (Chhokar, Brodbeck & House, 2007; House, Hanges, Javidan, Dorfman & Gupta, 2004). GLOBE researchers have developed a definition of leadership which specifies

what is meant by 'influencing' others within organizational settings: *leadership (in organizations)* means *influencing, motivating, or enabling others to contribute towards the effectiveness of work units and organizations.*

The central questions that have received and continue to receive attention in leadership research are: How can we identify effective leaders? What makes leaders effective? How do leaders influence others? How are leaders perceived by others? How do leaders emerge and develop? Therefore, most leadership research focuses on at least one of the following criteria of *leadership effectiveness*: (1) the impact of leadership on the accomplishment of group and organizational objectives (e.g., high-quality decisions, solutions to problems); (2) the extent of influence on followers that can be exerted via leadership (e.g., change in behaviour, attitudes, values, motivation, well-being); (3) the perception of a person as a leader in the 'eye of the beholder'; and (4) the emergence of a person as a leader and how quickly leaders are promoted to higher ranks in an organization. Here we focus on a specific question: How can leadership help to improve group performance? This question relates mainly to the first two classes of criteria of leadership effectiveness.

In this section we describe approaches to the study of leadership which cover major developments in the history of leadership research. For reasons of space, only a small selection of theories and research can be described. For broader coverage see Pierce and Newstrom (2003), and for comprehensive reviews see Bass (1990) and Yukl (2005). Thereafter, we develop a group performance perspective on leadership that integrates the research on group functioning described in the first part of this chapter with findings from leadership research.

> **leadership (in organizations)** influencing, motivating or enabling others to contribute towards the effectiveness of work units and organizations
>
> **leadership effectiveness** the impact of leadership on the accomplishment of group and organizational objectives, on the behaviour, perceptions, attitudes, values, motivation or well-being of followers and peers, and on the accomplishments of those who lead

Approaches to the study of leadership

The systematic study of leadership has been dominated by *leader-oriented approaches*, many of which were developed in the first half of the twentieth century. They focus on personality characteristics and behaviours of leaders in order to distinguish leaders from non-leaders and to identify effective leaders in organizations. From about the 1960s, *contingency approaches* were developed which incorporate relevant situational factors (e.g., characteristics of the organization, the task or the followers) for predicting the success of certain leader characteristics and leadership behaviours. The latest developments in leadership research emphasize the nature and dynamics of leader–follower relationships (e.g., *transformational-transactional leadership*) as well as *shared leadership* within work groups. For effective leadership in groups there is something to learn from all approaches described here.

Leader-oriented approaches The view of the leader as a 'hero' or a 'great person' has dominated leadership research for a long time, and thus the study of leadership has mainly been the study of *leaders*, that is, their characteristics, skills and behaviours, on the one hand, and their effects on followers, groups and organizations, on the other.

Leader traits. Since the pioneering systematic studies of leadership in the first half of the last century, a major proportion of research have focused on stable *leader traits* (e.g., personality, intelligence, motivational dispositions), on the basis of which leader emergence and leadership effectiveness may be predicted – following the idea that 'a leader is born, not made'. Today, relatively small but consistent correlations between effective or emergent leaders and the so-called 'Big Five' personality characteristics are reported (Judge, Bono, Ilies & Gerhard, 2002): for example, with Extraversion ($r = .31$), Openness to Experience ($r = .24$), Conscientiousness ($r = .28$) and Neuroticism ($r = -.24$) (the correlation with the fifth personality dimension, Agreeableness, is lower, $r = .08$).

leader traits relatively stable person characteristics (e.g., personality, intelligence, motivational dispositions) which are thought to predict leader emergence and leadership effectiveness

Intelligence was also found to relate positively to leader effectiveness ($r = .27$; Judge, Colbert & Ilies, 2004).

Only a few empirical studies have rigorously tested the assumption that personality traits have a causal impact on leader effectiveness or the emergence of an individual as a leader in an organization. The commonly used cross-sectional designs, by which measures of leader personality and performance are taken at about the same point in time, cannot test directional causal assumptions. With such correlational designs, the possibility remains that the commonly implied causal relationship (i.e., that personality has an influence on leadership success) may work the other way around. Individuals who find themselves in leadership positions more often than others, by being pushed into them by chance or because of their technical expertise (at school, in higher education, at work), may learn and develop the sets of skills, attitudes and behaviours necessary to succeed – or just to maintain their leadership position. By trying to satisfy respective role expectations and social norms typically applied to leaders, individuals are likely to develop or exhibit those personal characteristics that match expectations.

(a)

(b)

(c)

Plates 13.4a, b and c *What stable traits are characteristic of leaders?*

A general critique of leader-trait approaches is that they don't explain in sufficient detail how the link between person characteristics and leadership success is established: what are the variables that *mediate* this relationship?

Leadership behaviour. The search for variables that can predict leadership success better than personality traits shifted the focus of interest towards what leaders actually do – **leadership behaviour**. During the late 1940s, two research programs began to work in this area independently of each other. They have shaped our understanding of leadership behaviour up to the present day. One was established at Ohio State University (e.g., Hemphill, Stogdill), the other at the University of Michigan (e.g., Likert, Katz). The two programs identified a large number of leader behaviours and grouped these into quite similar categorization schemes.

leadership behaviour observable acts that are meant to influence, motivate or enable others to contribute towards the effectiveness of a work unit or organization

The *Ohio group* sought to classify relevant aspects of leadership behaviours by assembling about 1,800 leader behaviour descriptions, which were subsequently reduced to about 150 items. A preliminary questionnaire was administered to thousands of employees in civic and military organizations, who indicated the extent to which their supervisors displayed these behaviours. The final questionnaire, called the Leader Behaviour Description Questionnaire (LBDQ), is a hallmark in the history of leadership research. By using factor-analytic methods to analyse patterns of relationships among all the LBDQ items, two independent dimensions emerged: *initiating structure* (i.e., task-oriented behaviours) and *consideration* (i.e., people-oriented behaviours).

Judge, Piccolo and Ilies (2004) conducted a meta-analysis of 200 studies, with 300 samples. They found that both consideration ($r = .49$) and initiating structure ($r = .29$) have moderately strong relations with leadership outcomes. Consideration was more strongly related to leader effectiveness ($r = .39$), followers' motivation ($r = .40$), satisfaction with leaders ($r = .68$) and job satisfaction ($r = .40$) than was initiating structure ($r = .28$, $r = .26$, $r = .27$, $r = .19$ respectively), and both were equally strongly ($r = .23$) related to group/organizational performance (see Judge, Piccolo & Ilies, 2004, p. 40, Table 3). The literature published prior to this meta-analysis indicated that initiating structure is more susceptible to situational differences than is consideration; for example, in some situations task orientation is positively associated with satisfaction, in others it even has negative effects (cf. Pierce & Newstrom, 2003). This may explain why in the meta-analysis reported above, where correlations were sampled across a whole range of different situations, correlations were weaker for initiating structure than for consideration.

The *Michigan group* characterized the four dimensions of leadership behaviour they identified – interaction facilitation, work facilitation, goal emphasis and individual support – as the 'basic structure of what one may term "leadership"' (Bowers & Seashore, 1966, p. 247). Their understanding of 'leadership' provides the foundation for a leadership perspective which differs considerably from leader-oriented approaches. While the Ohio group's research clearly focused on the individual (formal) leader, the Michigan group stated that effective work groups require the presence of each of the four classes of behaviours they identified, but *anyone* in a group can provide them successfully. These behaviours need not all be shown by one and the same (formal) leader as long as they are present in the work group to a sufficient extent. Because this view is of particular interest to our chapter's focus on group performance, we elaborate on it later in this section.

Cross-sectional designs are also commonly used for the empirical study of leadership behaviour. As was noted above, such designs do not allow us to make causal inferences about the direction of relationship between leadership behaviour and leadership success. Again, the true causal pathways may go in the opposite direction. For example, leaders may show more consideration behaviour because followers are already motivated and high-performing (Greene, 1975). Another threat to the correct interpretation of results from cross-sectional studies is the so called 'third variable problem'. For example, mutual sympathy between leader and followers, due to a match in personal values or sociocultural backgrounds, may have a similar positive impact on both leader behaviour and follower behaviour. Equally, mutual trust can lead to more consideration on the leader's part and to higher performance on the follower's part. Thus, an apparent correlation between consideration on the part of leaders and high performance on the part of followers can be caused by a third variable (mutual sympathy or mutual trust) that makes leader behaviour and follower performance *appear to be directly* linked with each other, when in fact they are not.

Problems with correctly interpreting results from cross-sectional studies are aggravated when relying on followers' self-report measures for leader behaviours (as occurs, for example, in the LBDQ) in conjunction with followers' perceptions of leadership effectiveness (e.g., their motivation, satisfaction with the leader or job satisfaction). In the worst case all these variables are assessed by asking the same followers (*common source effect*) and by using the same questionnaire as measurement instrument (*common method effect*). Under these circumstances, the strengths of relationships between leader behaviour and leader effectiveness are likely to be overestimated.

Contingency approaches Leader-oriented approaches which focus solely on leaders' traits and behaviours have a tendency to look for simple answers to complex problems. They can account for only a limited proportion of the variance in leadership effectiveness, because the effects of leader traits and behaviours are likely to average out across different situations that may require different types of leaders or different leader behaviours. *Contingency approaches* emphasize the role of situational factors and how these moderate the relationship between leadership traits or behaviours and leadership effectiveness, such as task characteristics (e.g., task structure, task complexity), followers' characteristics (e.g., their level of motivation, competencies, maturity) or characteristics of the social context (e.g., quality of social relationships, group cohesion, group size).

contingency approaches emphasize the role of situational factors in the study of leadership (e.g., characteristics of the task, the followers or the social context) and how these moderate the relationship between leader traits or leadership behaviours and leadership effectiveness

Many contingency theories have been proposed, each of which stresses the importance of a particular array of situational factors and different leadership characteristics (for reviews, see Bass, 1990; Yukl, 2005). One message contained in all contingency approaches is that leaders must be able to recognize, adapt to or change different situational circumstances, otherwise they may lose their influence on followers. To date, there is no unified theory from which we can derive the most critical situational factors that moderate relationships between leader characteristics and behaviours, on the one hand, and leadership effectiveness, on the other. We therefore describe here only one of the more widely cited contingency theories, *path-goal theory*, which has been presented by House and his colleagues (House, 1971, 1996; House & Mitchell, 1974).

Path-goal theory. Leaders are considered effective when their behaviour impacts on the subordinates' motivation, satisfaction and ability to perform effectively. A major concern of path-goal theory is how a leader influences the followers' perceptions of their work goals, their personal goals and the paths to goal attainment. To maximize their impact in these aspects, leaders need to master a range of leadership behaviours and use them flexibly depending on certain situational contingencies. Five classes of leadership behaviours are distinguished in newer versions of path-goal theory (House, 1996). *Clarifying behaviour* (e.g., about rewards and punishments, performance goals and means to achieve them) reduces role ambiguity and increases follower beliefs that effort in a certain direction will result in good performance, and that performance will be rewarded. *Work facilitation behaviour* (e.g., planning, scheduling, coordinating, guiding, coaching, counselling and giving feedback) eliminates roadblocks and bottlenecks, provides resources, stimulates self-development and helps to delegate authority to subordinates. *Participative behaviour* (e.g., consulting with subordinates, incorporating subordinate opinions in decision-making) increases followers' self-confidence and the personal value of job-related effort. *Supportive behaviour* (e.g., creating a friendly and psychologically supportive environment, displaying concern for subordinates' welfare) increases the followers' involvement with the work group and both organizational and goal commitment. *Achievement-oriented behaviour* (e.g., setting high goals and seeking improvement, emphasizing excellence, showing confidence in subordinates, stressing pride in work) increases subordinate confidence and the personal value of goal-directed effort.

The extent to which the described leadership behaviours are successful depends on two classes of contingency factors. (1) *Personal characteristics of the followers* (e.g., internal vs. external locus of control, self-efficacy beliefs, knowledge, skills and abilities) influence the degree to which followers see the leadership behaviour as a source of satisfaction or as instrumental to future satisfaction. (2) *Characteristics of the environment* (e.g., task structure, formal authority system of the organization, primary work group) are not within the direct control of followers but are important to satisfy their needs or their ability to perform well. For example, followers with an internal locus of control, high self-efficacy beliefs or high competence in their job respond more positively to participative leadership behaviour than do followers with external locus of control (who need more work facilitation behaviour), low self-efficacy (who need more supportive behaviour) or low job competence (who need more clarifying behaviour). Examples of leadership behaviour contingencies with characteristics of the primary work group are described in detail in the section below on group leadership.

Despite inconclusive research results and some conceptual deficiencies (e.g., House, 1996; Wofford & Liska, 1993), path-goal theory is still in use because it provides a valuable conceptual framework for identifying situational factors relevant to leadership effectiveness. The theory's underlying idea, that certain leadership behaviours are helpful and successful under certain circumstances, has been adopted in several newer leadership theories (cf. Pierce & Newstrom, 2003). Another idea that path-goal theory has infused into leadership research and practice is that the followers and their characteristics matter in the leadership process. Not only is their performance-related behaviour important, so too are their perceptions, cognitions and beliefs about work-related issues.

Transactional, transformational and charismatic leadership

In the past 25 years a substantial amount of research evidence has been accumulated about what leaders and followers offer one another. *Transactional leaders* focus on the proper exchange of resources. They give followers something they want in exchange for something the leader wants (cf. Burns, 1978; Conger & Kanungo, 1998). *Transformational and charismatic leaders*, in contrast, develop an appealing vision and focus on the alignment of the group or organizational goals with the followers' needs and aspirations in order to influence them to make sacrifices and put the needs of the organization above their own interests. *Laissez-faire leaders* offer very little to followers ('non-leadership'). They avoid making decisions, hesitate in taking action and are often absent when needed.

> **transactional leaders** leaders who focus on the proper exchange of resources: they give followers something in exchange for something the leaders want
>
> **transformational/charismatic leaders** leaders who focus on aligning the group or organizational goals with the followers' needs and aspirations by developing an appealing vision. The goal is to influence followers to make sacrifices and put the needs of the organization above their self-interest
>
> **laissez-faire leaders** leaders who engage in 'non-leadership', e.g., they avoid making decisions, hesitate in taking action and are often absent when needed

Bass (1985) has refined the concept of transformational leadership into four subdimensions (known as the 4 Is of transformational leadership, because all dimensions begin with the letter 'I').

1 *Idealized influence*: Leaders behave in admirable ways (e.g., display conviction, display role-modelling behaviours consistent with the vision, appeal on an emotional level) so that followers tend to identify with them.

2 *Inspirational motivation*: Leaders articulate a vision (e.g., provide meaning for the work task, set high standards, communicate optimism about the achievability of the vision) which is appealing and inspiring to followers.

3 *Intellectual stimulation*: Leaders stimulate and encourage creativity in their followers (e.g., challenge assumptions, take risks, ask followers to put into practice their own ideas).

4 *Individualized consideration*: Leaders attend to each
   follower individually (e.g., act as a mentor or coach, listen
   to their concerns and needs).

The concepts of transformational leadership and *charismatic leadership* (Conger & Kanungo, 1987, 1998) have much in common (Judge & Piccolo, 2004). Charismatic leaders can be described as self-confident, enthusiastic leaders able to win followers' respect and support for their vision. They also show role-modelling behaviours consistent with the vision, take personal risks and express strong confidence in their followers. On the part of the followers, charismatic leadership results in, for example, *internalization* (i.e., followers adopt the leader's ideals and goals and become inspired to attain them because they are inherently satisfying) and *social identification* (i.e., followers create a connection in their minds between their self-concepts and the shared values and identities of their group or organization). For ease of description, our use of the term transformational leadership includes charismatic leadership, although we acknowledge that the different theories underlying each concept do make a clear distinction between them (e.g., Conger & Kanungo, 1998).

Transactional leadership consists of three dimensions underlying leaders' behaviour:

1 *Contingent reward*: Leaders set up constructive transactions
   or exchanges with followers (e.g., clarify expectations,
   establish rewards for meeting expectations).

2 *Active management by exception*: Leaders monitor follower
   behaviour, anticipate problems and take corrective action
   before serious difficulties occur.

3 *Passive management by exception*: Leaders wait until the
   followers' behaviour has created problems before taking
   action (cf. Avolio, 1999). Laissez-faire leadership
   represents the absence of leadership and thus can be
   differentiated from passive management by exception,
   where at least some leadership influence is exerted,
   although often after the damage is done.

The research on theories of transformational, transactional and laissez-faire leadership combines and complements the leadership-oriented and contingency approaches described above in four ways. First, it proposes that leadership is a process that is partially determined by leader traits, trainable behaviours and skills. Second, it identifies situational factors under which the different types of leadership vary in effectiveness. Third, it proposes a bidirectional influence between leader characteristics, on the one hand, and attributions of followers and how they react to the leader's characteristics, on the other. Fourth, it proposes that followers' responses to leadership are moderated and mediated by their needs, self-concepts, interpretations of goals and events, motivations and emotions.

Transformational and transactional theories of leadership have been tested with a whole variety of methods, including longitudinal studies, field studies and laboratory experiments. In a meta-analysis of 87 studies (total N > 38,000), Judge and Piccolo (2004) determined the contribution of transformational, transactional and laissez-faire leadership to the prediction of organizational criteria relevant to leadership effectiveness (follower job satisfaction, satisfaction with leader, motivation, leader job performance,

effectiveness and group/organization performance). Overall, by combining the different effectiveness criteria, this analysis revealed that three leadership dimensions were positively related to outcome variables: transformational leadership ($r = .44$), transactional–contingent reward leadership ($r = .39$) and transactional–active management by exception ($r = .15$). In contrast, two of the leadership dimensions were negatively related to leadership outcomes: transactional–passive management by exception ($r = -.15$) and laissez-faire leadership ($r = -.37$). The authors conclude that contingent reward (transactional) leadership and transformational leadership predict outcome variables to a similar extent. This is troublesome considering that transformational–transactional leadership theory predicts that contingent reward will be reasonably effective, but not as effective as any of the transformational leadership dimensions (Bass & Avolio, 1994, p. 6). The superiority of one theory relative to the other seems to depend on the context. For example, Judge and Piccolo (2004) note that contingent reward leadership works best in business settings. Perhaps it is the resource-dependent nature of this kind of setting that is crucial, that is, business leaders are more able to reward followers tangibly (e.g., via financial incentives) in exchange for their efforts than are leaders in the other domains studied (universities/colleges, military settings, public sector). In situations in which leaders have access to fewer or no resources, contingent reward leadership may be less effective because it is more difficult for leaders to meet their side of the bargain. Thus, transformational leadership may be more robust in these settings than is contingent reward leadership.

Another observation from Judge and Piccolo's (2004) meta-analysis is that transformational and contingent reward leadership predicted leadership outcomes about equally strongly under weak research designs (leadership and outcomes were measured at the same time and with the same source). In contrast, under strong research designs (longitudinal designs and designs in which the leadership and the criterion were measured with different sources of data), transformational leadership predicted leadership outcomes more strongly than did contingent reward leadership.

SUMMARY

In this section we have reviewed various approaches to the study of leadership: leader-oriented approaches, which focus on traits; contingency approaches, which emphasize both situational factors and traits; and approaches to transactional, transformational and charismatic leadership, which combine and complement the trait and contingency approaches, conceptualizing leadership as 'a quality attributed to people as a result of their interrelations with others' (Smith, 1995, p. 358). This implies that leadership is inherent neither solely in people nor solely in the situational context. Instead, both categories of variables can be seen as conditions that facilitate or inhibit the expression of effective leadership processes. This view is in accord with Kurt Lewin's famous formula, $b = f(P, E)$, which identifies human behaviour (b) as a function of person characteristics (P) *and* characteristics of the environment (E). Note that both leaders and followers are to be seen in Lewin's formula as person (P) and as part of the environment (E) within which they interact with each other. This is part of the reason why leadership is a complex social phenomenon and the scientific study of it is a very complex task.

Most of the approaches to the study of leadership focus on the leader as a person and less on 'leadership' as a process. For an exception, the leadership perspective taken by the Michigan group explicitly suggests that *anyone* in a work group can provide leadership functions. The more of the necessary leadership behaviours are effectively provided by group members, the less a (formal) leader needs to infuse them into the work group (and the less harmful are passive or laissez-faire leaders). We believe that it is in an organization's interest for their leaders to develop employees and whole work groups such that the group members facilitate each other's performance by also engaging in effective leadership behaviour. This comes very close to modern concepts of shared or team leadership, which are discussed in the next section.

LEADERSHIP IN GROUPS

Why is leadership critical for group performance?
How can leadership help to improve group performance?

The first researchers to turn their attention to how leadership can affect groups as a whole were Kurt Lewin and his co-workers, Lippitt and White. In a series of experiments they observed in detail how different leadership behaviours of adult leaders affected the 'social climates' of after-school clubs of 10-year-old boys (e.g., Lewin, Lippitt & White, 1939; White & Lippitt, 1976). They implemented three different *leadership styles* (i.e., a repeatedly shown pattern of leadership behaviour evident across a variety of situations): *autocratic leadership* (directive, non-participative, domineering behaviours), *democratic leadership* (participative, communicative, egalitarian) and *laissez-faire leadership* ('hands-off' leadership, with few attempts made to influence others at all). Not surprisingly, democratic leaders were liked more than autocratic or laissez-faire leaders. They created a group-minded, friendly and task-oriented atmosphere. In contrast, autocratic leadership resulted in more frequent hostile behaviours, but also in 'apathetic' patterns of behaviour with no instances of smiling or joking. Although the quantity of work done in autocracy was somewhat greater than in democracy, there were indications that work motivation was greater in democracy. There was more 'work-minded' conversation in democratically led groups and members continued to work hard, even when the group leader was temporarily absent. In contrast, members of autocratically led groups often stopped working when the leader left the room. Finally, there was some informal evidence that the work produced

> **leadership style** a pattern of leadership behaviour which is repeatedly shown and evident across a variety of situations

in democratically led groups showed higher levels of originality than under either of the other types of leadership. Note that laissez-faire was not the same as democracy: there was less work done, the work was poorer and less satisfaction with the laissez-faire leader was expressed. These findings show that leadership has an impact on how groups function as a whole, that there are more or less effective ways to manage groups, and that absence of leadership (laissez-faire) can seriously disrupt group activity.

Because we focus on characteristics of group functioning and how these can be facilitated by leadership, we define **group leadership** as influencing, motivating or enabling (oneself and) others to contribute towards the effectiveness and viability of work groups. This definition is also meant to comprise *leaderless groups* (e.g., self-managed work groups), which may be led by agents external to the group as well as by *shared or team leadership*. The latter two concepts have recently been introduced into the leadership literature.

> **group leadership** influencing, motivating or enabling (oneself and) others to contribute towards the effectiveness and viability of work groups
>
> **leaderless groups** groups that have no appointed leader (e.g., self-managed work groups) but which may be led by agents external to the group or by shared or team leadership
>
> **shared or team leadership** responsibility for leadership functions, the exercise of leadership behaviour and perceptions about leadership roles are shared among group members

Bradford and Cohen (1984) argued that the predominant conception of a 'heroic leader' undermines the principally positive effects of shared responsibility for leadership functions and empowerment of followers on leadership effectiveness. In contrast, *shared leadership* (e.g., Pearce & Sims, 2000) and *team leadership* (e.g., Sivasubramaniam, Murry, Avolio & Jung, 2002) denote group-level leadership concepts that go beyond the commonly held concept of a single leader, in that the responsibility for leadership functions, the exercise of leadership behaviour and the perceptions of leadership roles are shared among group members. These concepts complement the view of a singular leader who is more informed and confident than others with the view that leadership is a mutual influence process (e.g., Smith, 1995).

Based on the propositions about group functioning and performance described in the first part of this chapter, we argue that effective group leadership needs to ensure that the functions critical to (1) group and task design, (2) group synchronization and (3) group learning are taken care of. Note that there are further tasks that should be addressed by leadership in groups (Zaccaro, Rittman & Marks, 2001) which are not reviewed here. To our knowledge, these have, however, not yet been explicitly linked to social psychological theorizing and research about group performance and group decision-making.

Group and task design

According to the first principle of group performance management, group leadership requires that groups are composed in accordance with the requirements of the task structure (group design). At the same time, group leaders should attempt to (re)structure tasks in accordance with group composition (task design).

Wageman's (2001) study of self-managed teams demonstrated that effective group leadership is indeed a group and task design activity. The author measured the extent to which group leaders made sure that their work group was a 'real team', with clear membership, stable over time, and group members working in close physical proximity to each other. Furthermore, she measured whether leaders infused a clear direction, with few, memorable objectives that focused on the ends to be achieved rather than on the details of the means for achieving them. This study also measured to what extent leaders enabled an effective team structure, with adequate group size, sufficient skill variety (not too much heterogeneity so that coordination problems remained manageable), high task interdependence, challenging task goals, challenging performance targets, and clearly articulated strategies and norms for planning and decision-making. Finally, it measured the degree to which organizational context factors (e.g., quality of reward and feedback systems, adequacy of training offered and availability of resources needed) supported effective group functioning. Wageman (2001) used a sample of 34 self-managed teams to test the extent to which the desired leadership activities were linked with objective group performance criteria, obtained from company records. The more leaders engaged in the above-described task/group design activities, the higher was group performance and the more self-management was practised within groups.

A similar point highlighting the importance of a proactive team design in relation to team task objectives and leadership was made by Erez, Lepine and Elms (2002). These authors investigated learning groups of students whose purpose it was to share information and views freely for group discussion and group task performance. They found that teams that rotated leadership among their members had higher levels of voice (participation), cooperation and performance relative to teams that relied on leader emergence (usually the most dominant group member emerges as a leader in such groups). This is an example of how the way in which leadership comes about and is practised directly influences the manner in which the group members' resources are used.

Group synchronization

Group leadership implies the monitoring and management of ongoing group processes, for example the exchange of information, views and opinions and the social dynamics involved. The contribution of leadership to group synchronization has been most extensively demonstrated for information management during group decision-making. Via information management, effective leadership keeps the group focused on the problem at hand, facilitates communication, stimulates decision-relevant contributions and keeps them alive during discussion (e.g., Larson & Christensen, 1993; Maier, 1967). In a study on medical diagnostic teams, Larson, Christensen, Abbott and Franz (1996) investigated how designated leaders (the most experienced medical doctor per group) manage the processing of distributed information during group decision-making. They observed that

Plate 13.5 *How does the designated leader in a group such as this manage the processing of distributed information during group decision-making?*

leaders repeated unshared information (i.e., information held by only one group member) at a steadily increasing rate over time and raised more questions concerning concrete factual information than other group members did. In a follow-up study, again in the domain of medical decision-making, Larson, Christensen, Franz and Abbott (1998) replicated the above results and found positive correlations between information management behaviour and group decision quality. This is an example of how information management behaviours can counteract 'asymmetries' in the discussion and evaluation of information that were identified as a weakness of group decision-making (see Figure 13.4).

Larson, Foster-Fishman and Franz (1998) also explored the effects of leadership style on group decision-making. They trained individuals to display either directive or participative leadership behaviours. Directive leadership groups outperformed participative leadership groups only when their leaders possessed sufficient information favouring the best decision alternative. In contrast, when directive leaders possessed information that favoured a sub-optimal choice (as did the information held by other group members), group decision quality deteriorated considerably. This was not the case in groups with a participative leader who managed the group in a way that encouraged more (shared *and* unshared) information to surface. In contrast, directive leaders tend to 'sell' their opinion by emphasizing their own unshared information that is consistent with their decision preference. Likewise, Cruz, Henningsen and Smith (1999) concluded from their hidden profile study that the quality of the group's choice depends on the quality of a directive leader's preferred decision alternative. Overall, these findings are in line with Vroom and Jago's (1988) notion that autocratic forms of decision-making are feasible only when leaders possess sufficient information to make a high-quality decision. Considering that in situations of a hidden profile most or all group members (including the leader) are likely to hold information that does not imply the best possible decision alternative, a directive leadership style seems less functional for high-quality decision-making than does a participative leadership style. However, Larson, Foster-Fishman and Franz's (1998) study also demonstrates that a participative leadership style does not guarantee high-quality decision-making under all conditions of distributed knowledge. When the leader indeed knows best, directive leadership results in better group decisions than participative leadership does. Thus, wise leaders should know when they know best and when not and adjust their leadership style accordingly.

Group development and learning

Group leadership implies supporting group learning and development. For example, effective group leadership seeks to further the development of transactive memory systems by fostering a team learning orientation (Bunderson & Sutcliffe, 2003). This can be established by promoting mutual collaboration among group members and developing a decentralized communication structure instead of using directive leadership, which is associated with a communication structure that centres around the leader. In a decentralized transactive memory system, a large proportion of group members hold significant parts of the group knowledge. If knowledge is distributed, not centralized, a transactive memory system is less subject to disruption when, for instance, a centrally positioned leader is overloaded with work, cannot communicate with adequate frequency and thus is not able to transmit the group's knowledge adequately.

Interdependent work in groups entails uncertainty about others' motivation, competency and behaviours: will they do the work they said they would do? Will they perform to the standards set? Will they deliver their part in time? Especially in geographically dispersed groups, the continuous communication essential for sharing group knowledge and information about individual activities related to the task is difficult to maintain. This leaves members of geographically dispersed groups to cope with particularly high levels of uncertainty. Delays in remote communication make feedback about others' activities difficult to obtain. Delayed or inaccurate feedback requires several iterations for clarification. In face-to-face groups, feedback about others' activities is more immediate and can be obtained more easily, for example by observing who attends meetings or who participates in hallway communications. In contrast, members in distributed groups (called *virtual groups* because they mainly communicate electronically) may go for long periods without feedback about each other's activities.

team awareness understanding of the ongoing activities of others which provides a context for one's own activity

Team awareness is the group members' understanding of the ongoing activities of others which provides a context for their own activity. It reduces the effort needed to coordinate tasks and resources by providing a context to interpret communications and others' actions more adequately (Weisband, 2002). Leadership can foster the development of team awareness, for example by taking actions to monitor the progress of others and to include everyone by sharing the respective information. This helps to better cope with individual group members' work overload. Weisband (2002) studied leadership influence on team awareness with geographically dispersed student project teams working on a four-week project (writing a consensus policy document) via email and a web-based conferencing system. The more the above-described leadership actions were *shared* (i.e., several group members engaged in the leadership activities), the more team awareness individual group members developed (i.e., they were better informed about others' activities) and the better was overall project performance. Developing team awareness among group members takes effort and time. It is an investment that becomes profitable after longer or repeated group task performance and under certain conditions, for example in distributed or virtual work teams.

In general, leadership for group learning not only means providing the training resources for each group member to learn to perform the job better individually (I–I transfer), it also involves developing a collaborative learning orientation where group members can discuss and improve each others' task performance strategies and behaviours (G–I transfer). Furthermore, the development of transactive memory systems and team awareness benefits from encouraging group members to reflect and constantly improve the ways they collaborate and interact with each other (G–IG transfer), and to learn about other group members' areas of expertise, strengths and weaknesses (G–G transfer). The more this knowledge and awareness are developed and leadership functions are shared within the group, the more likely it is that group members can support each other, fill gaps for each other, correct and manage each other's errors and anticipate and cope with capacity shortages on the part of particular group members before problems arise. All this improves group performance over time.

SUMMARY

In sum, group leadership means careful composition of work groups, proactive design of task structures and active synchronization of group decision-making processes and task execution in groups. Apart from an active coaching of individual group members (e.g., via transformational leadership), leadership functions in groups also comprise the systematic development of effective transactive memory systems and team awareness among group members (which may take some time). As the Michigan group has already shown, all these leadership functions do not necessarily need to be performed by just one (formal) leader. Especially when high task interdependence and geographically distributed virtual teamwork is involved, the shared performance of leadership functions seems to work best.

SUMMARY AND CONCLUSIONS

In this chapter we have reviewed basic group processes and leadership that influence group performance. With regard to the specific questions outlined in the introduction, the following conclusions can be derived from this review.

- *How can we identify group-level effects on performance?* Group performance is, first and foremost, influenced by individual performance. Group members' individual performances (or abilities) constitute the basis for the definition of potential group performance. Potential group performance differs based on task type (e.g., additive, disjunctive and conjunctive tasks) because individual contributions are differently related to group performance for these different task types.

- *What are the major pitfalls and opportunities when people work together in a group?* Actual group performance diverges from potential group performance due to process losses and process gains. Process losses are coordination losses, motivation losses and individual capability losses; process gains are motivation gains and individual capability gains. These processes constitute the group-level influences on group performance.

- *What can we do to systematically optimize group performance?* Process losses can be reduced and process gains can be facilitated if three basic principles of group leadership are applied: composing groups in accordance with task requirements, synchronizing group members' efforts during collective performance and allowing for group learning across multiple task trials.

- *What makes leadership effective?* Leadership effectiveness depends on many factors: leader traits, leadership behaviour, situational factors (e.g., task, followers, social context) and whether leader–follower relationships are transformational, transactional or non-existent (laissez-faire leadership). Note that focusing solely on the leader as the focal point of leadership limits our understanding of the complex nature of leadership, which is a mutual influence process that can also be shared among group members.

- *Why is leadership so critical for group performance, and how can it contribute to the optimization of group performance?* Leadership, be it in the form of an individual leader or shared leadership, is about influencing others for the benefit of individual, group and organizational goals. Group leadership helps (or hinders) groups to optimize their performance.

- *How can leadership help to improve group performance?* Derived from the basic principles of group leadership, we identified three categories of situational contingencies that are important: composition (e.g., align group and task structure), synchronization (e.g., manage information and activity for reducing process loss and increasing process gain) and group learning (e.g., foster individual and group development by supporting all learning processes within groups).

As we mentioned at the beginning of this chapter, research on group performance was one of the very first topics that social psychology investigated. Some of the most intriguing current directions in this field include the systematic detection of process gains, the analysis of collective information processing in groups and the optimization of group performance via basic principles of group and shared leadership. We are confident that group performance and leadership will remain central topics of social psychology at the interface between basic research, applied research and the application of social psychological findings in organizations.

Notes

1 Steiner also included a fourth task type, the 'discretionary' task, but since this has not been a focus of empirical work we will not discuss it here.

2 It is debatable whether this approach leads to an overestimation of group potential and, thus, disfavours groups in the evaluation of their actual performance. Some authors actually discuss the possibility of coordination gains on the basis of different conceptions of group potential; however, this lies outside the scope of this introductory chapter.

Suggestions for further reading

Baron, R.S. & Kerr, N. (2003). *Group process, group decision, group action* (2nd edn). Buckingham: Open University Press. One of the best and most comprehensive introductions to the diverse facets of performance and performance-related processes in groups.

Pierce, J.L. & Newstrom, J.W. (2003). *Leaders and the leadership process: Readings, self-assessments and applications*. Boston: McGraw-Hill Irwin. In addition to concise descriptions of leadership theory and practice, this textbook contains many excerpts of classic theoretical and research-oriented papers, as well as self-assessments, practical applications and useful further readings in the domain of leadership.

Steiner, I.D. (1972). *Group processes and productivity*. New York: Academic Press. Steiner's book remains *the* classic and pioneering analysis of group performance on various tasks. Although more than 30 years old, many insights from this book are still highly relevant, and some of them still await their realization in group performance research.

Turner, M.E. (2001). *Groups at work: Theory and research*. Mahwah, NJ: Lawrence Erlbaum. This book's social psychological and organizational perspectives on the fundamental topics of group performance research are a useful tool for students and researchers who are interested in the organizational application of group performance research, and for practitioners who want to learn more about the theoretical basis of groups and group performance.

Witte, E.H. & Davis, J.H. (Eds.) (1996). *Understanding group behavior* (Vols. 1 and 2). Mahwah, NJ: Lawrence Erlbaum. These two volumes contain a series of insightful papers from well-known group researchers. They are particularly valuable to readers who would like to broaden the scope from 'pure' group performance research to many other facets of intragroup and intergroup behaviour that are nevertheless relevant for group performance.

Yukl, G. (2005). *Leadership in organizations* (6th edn). Upper Saddle River, NJ: Prentice-Hall. This classic book contains a comprehensive review of leadership theories and research. New editions appear regularly.

14 Prejudice and Intergroup Relations

Thomas Kessler and Amélie Mummendey

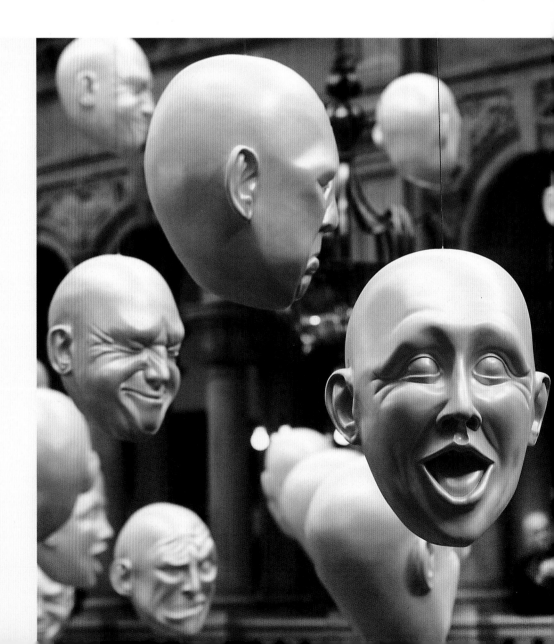

CHAPTER OUTLINE

....

This chapter introduces prejudice and social discrimination together with explanations of their causes. After a brief discussion of prejudice at the level of the individual, the chapter focuses mainly on prejudice and social discrimination as intergroup phenomena. We present classic and contemporary intergroup explanations of intergroup conflict such as realistic conflict theory and social identity theory. Furthermore, we introduce basic psychological processes such as social categorization, identification with a social group, group evaluation and group-based emotions, and consider the intergroup motivations regulating intergroup behaviour. The remainder of the chapter presents various approaches explaining when and how prejudice and intergroup conflict can be reduced.

Introduction

....

As in most parts of the modern world, social and economic change in Europe is currently characterized by an internationalization of all domains of life. Consequently, countries are forced to deal with a permanent and increasing flow of migration of people with different cultural, religious or ethnic backgrounds. We find ourselves confronted with people who appear to be different from us. Obviously, societal changes such as migration are not the only way in which different others are introduced into our social contexts. We are already used to differentiating between people on the basis of gender, sexual orientation or nationality.

These 'others' enter into various areas of our lives. We have to deal with those who are different from us. We form impressions and judgements about what sort of people they are, and we experience feelings and emotions towards them:

> 'Catholics are bigots; Protestants are uptight.' 'Women are born to support and maintain the family, they're not cut out for top management positions.' 'Men are not really competent to rear children.' 'Homosexuals should not be parents and cannot raise children in an appropriate way.' 'East Germans are always complaining; they are incompetent.' 'West Germans are arrogant and cold.' 'Muslims are conservative and sexist; they threaten the fundamental values of modern Europe.'

What information do we gain from this list of impressions and judgements?

Firstly, in all examples, the content of judgement is connected with negative feelings. Secondly, our behaviour towards these groups of people tends to be in line with our judgements and emotions. Given the above statements, female applicants are unlikely to be shortlisted for senior managerial positions. Turkish families are also unlikely to be openly welcomed into new neighbourhoods. Thirdly, our judgements, emotions and behaviours obviously apply to both social groups as a whole and to individual members of the particular group. We approach these 'others' in a generalized way and neglect interindividual differences.

An integration of the individual aspects listed above leads us to a more comprehensive picture, and ultimately to the concepts of prejudice and discrimination. Although both prejudice and discrimination can, in principle, occur in positive forms, the literature on intergroup relations (and hence this chapter) focuses on their negative forms. *Prejudice* can be defined as an antipathy, or a derogatory social attitude, towards particular social groups or their members, combined with the feeling and expression of negative affect. *Social discrimination* refers to the explicit display of negative or disadvantaging behaviour towards particular social groups or their members (Allport, 1954b; Brown, 1995; Hewstone, Rubin & Willis, 2002).

prejudice a derogatory attitude or antipathy towards particular social groups or their members

social discrimination negative, disadvantaging or derogatory behaviour towards a social group or its members

The selection of social groups appearing in the statements above consists of groups who are often made a target of prejudice. Groups defined in terms of religious beliefs, gender, sexual orientation and ethnicity prove to be chronic victims of prejudice. This may be due to the fact that these groups are all formed on the basis of categories which are meaningful for defining the self and for differentiating between the self and others in many social contexts.

Prejudice is often expressed in various forms of discrimination against the target group or any of its members. Discrimination can take the form of underprivilege, disadvantage, social exclusion, maltreatment or even physical extermination (in its most extreme forms, 'ethnic cleansing' and genocide). In everyday life, these forms of overt and blatantly negative treatment are, however, less frequent than more subtle forms such as tokenism or reverse discrimination.

Tokenism involves conceding a minor favour to a minority in order to justify negative discrimination on a broader scale. For example, employers hiring a woman or a black person on the basis of their gender or race, and not their individual competence, can use this 'token minority' to demonstrate that they do not discriminate against minorities, and that there is no need for more fundamental changes in equal opportunity policy (see Pettigrew & Martin, 1987).

tokenism conceding a minor favour to a social minority in order to justify negative discrimination on a broader scale

Sometimes, prejudiced individuals act *against* their prejudice and show *reverse discrimination*: they systematically evaluate or treat members of a target group *more favourably* than non-members (e.g., Dutton & Lake, 1973). For those individuals engaging in reverse discrimination, such subtle forms of discrimination offer protection against public accusations of bias in a society where prejudice may be deemed unacceptable. For the targets of reverse discrimination, however, it is not only extremely blatant forms of discrimination but also the more subtle forms that pose a problem. They may experience detrimental effects to their self-esteem and self-worth and internalize negative evaluations and low expectations of their own competence, because they attribute positive feedback and success to their category membership rather than to their personal merits.

reverse discrimination systematically more positive evaluation or treatment of members of a target outgroup than members of one's own group, which can have negative effects on the self-esteem of members of the outgroup

Plate 14.1 *Hiring a woman can be a way for an employer to use a 'token minority' to demonstrate that he does not discriminate.*

SUMMARY

Prejudice consists of a derogatory attitude towards social groups or their members. Social discrimination is the behavioural manifestation of prejudice ranging from explicit negative treatment of others based on their group membership to tokenism and reverse discrimination.

EXPLANATIONS OF PREJUDICE AND DISCRIMINATION

Do personality factors contribute to prejudice and intergroup conflict?
How does the relationship between ingroup and outgroup influence attitudes and behaviours of group members?
What are the minimal conditions for intergroup conflict to develop?
How do group members manage their social identity?

The destructive consequences of extremely negative forms of prejudice and discrimination such as devaluation, hostile aggression, dehumanization and even genocide lead us to ask why people are prejudiced and how social discrimination can be explained. Whilst prejudice and discrimination are widespread phenomena, not all individuals express prejudiced views in the same way and to the same degree. The question of interest is therefore how the pervasiveness and ubiquity of prejudice can be explained.

The prejudiced personality

During the final victory against the German Third Reich in 1945, the Allied troops uncovered crimes committed against millions of men, women and children whom the Nazi Germans had identified as belonging to certain groups and who, according to the Nazi ideology, were a threat to the purity of the German or Aryan race. These were principally but not exclusively Jews. Gypsies such as the Sintis and Romanies, homosexuals, communists, and physically and mentally handicapped people also belonged to those groups identified as 'inferior'. The dimensions of these crimes in terms of numbers of victims and perpetrators involved, administrative and organizational sophistication, cruelty and brutality clearly exceed anything ever experienced or imagined thus far in history. It might, then, be thought that the extent of these atrocities was so great that those individuals who were willing and able to commit them must be considered to have been people with dysfunctional personalities. In their famous book *The Authoritarian Personality*, published in 1950, Adorno, Frenkel-Brunswik, Levinson and Sanford took exactly this approach to explaining the Nazi Holocaust, and presented the first personality-based approach to prejudice. The *authoritarian personality* is conceived as a syndrome made up of a number of basic personality dimensions. These dimensions determine the degree to which individuals would be generally prone to prejudice and susceptible to fascist ideologies prevalent in a given society within a certain era.

authoritarian personality a particular type of personality, overly submissive to authority figures, which is thought to be especially prone to prejudice

The primary personality dimension is authoritarianism. Authoritarianism relates to an overly subservient attitude towards authority figures as well as an authoritarian attitude towards lower-status minorities. Such personality characteristics are presumed to originate from a particular style of socialization in families, with authoritarian repressive parents using extremely harsh punishments to discipline their children into strict conformity with conventional norms.

As a result the children are subject to conflicting tendencies of admiration and aggression towards their parents. The children do not, however, dare to act upon their hostile impulses towards the parental authorities. Instead, the children's negative feelings and aggressive tendencies are displaced and directed at 'scapegoats'; these are groups which deviate from prevalent societal conventions, for example social minorities, against whom derogation and even aggression are socially sanctioned.

Based on these theoretical assumptions, Adorno and colleagues developed a personality inventory to assess the various dimensions of the authoritarian personality. These dimensions included: attitudes towards minorities (e.g., anti-Semitism); admiration for authorities; political and economic conservatism; and a cognitive style of thinking, whereby the world is simply divided into good and bad. The central scale within this inventory is the well known Fascism scale (F-scale) measuring the potential for fascism and distinguishing those individuals who are susceptible to fascist propaganda from those with democratic and tolerant attitudes. Since the Nazis adhered to an extreme right-wing conservative ideology, the authors of the authoritarian personality restricted their personality inventory to right-wing political attitudes (for a more recent interpretation of authoritarianism, see Altemeyer, 1998).

The concept of the authoritarian personality was originally very influential, but later provoked severe methodological as well as conceptual criticism. The neglect of the influence of current social situations, prevailing norms and socio-cultural conditions on the degree of prejudice was at the centre of the conceptual critique. In a most important series of studies carried out in South Africa and in the southern and northern United States, Pettigrew (1958) showed, that – as expected – the level of racial prejudice against black people was lower in the northern states than in both the southern states and South Africa. With respect to their authoritarian personality, however, the three samples did not differ. Pettigrew's data showed that personality had less of an impact on whether white individuals expressed anti-black prejudice than did conformity to the contemporary social norms of the segregated and non-segregated societies.

As mentioned above, the authoritarian personality approach as an explanation of the causes of prejudice had been instigated by the extreme crimes of Nazi Germany. A more recent approach that includes an individual difference explanation of prejudice and its causes is social dominance theory (Sidanius & Pratto, 1999). Although this is a wide-ranging theory, including a focus on ideological and societal factors, it also highlights the importance of *social dominance orientation* (SDO), an individual difference measure of individuals' acceptance of general cultural ideologies concerning equality or inequality in societies (Pratto, 1999; Sidanius & Pratto, 1999; see Individual differences 14.1). Facing widespread status and power differences between social groups in our societies, some individuals accept or even favour a clear stratification of dominant and subordinate groups

social dominance orientation degree of individual acceptance of and desire for group-based social hierarchy and the domination of 'inferior' groups by 'superior' groups as being just and consistent with a natural order. Individuals who score highly on SDO have a strong desire to promote intergroup hierarchies and for their ingroups to dominate their outgroups; they also reject policies aimed at establishing equality. Those with low SDO scores, in contrast, argue that inequality is unjust and support views and political programs against inequality between social groups. At the centre of the more general construct of SDO are various *legitimizing myths*, defined as consensually held values, attitudes, beliefs, stereotypes or cultural ideologies that provide moral and intellectual justification for group-based oppression and inequality. They serve to justify the oppression of some groups by others, hence status differences between powerful and less powerful groups in a society are made acceptable. Ultimately, social dominance theory offers an evolutionary-psychological explanation for the organization of human societies as group-based hierarchies.

The SDO-scale includes statements that support or reject such legitimizing myths (see Individual Differences 14.1). Interindividual differences in agreement or disagreement with these myths are measured, whereby agreement is assumed to represent a desire for group-based dominance and an opposition to equality. Several studies have shown that SDO relates to non-egalitarian political and social attitudes, including sexism, racism and nationalism (Pratto, Sidanius, Stallworth & Malle, 1994; Sidanius & Pratto, 1999; Sidanius, Pratto & Bobo, 1996). However, there is less evidence that people with high SDO engage in specific instances of intergroup bias in order to achieve or maintain ingroup dominance (Sidanius et al., 1996). Even if we accept the idea of a dysfunctional personality syndrome or individual orientation as explaining the causes of prejudice and discrimination, the pervasiveness and ubiquity of prejudice towards particular groups such as the Jews in Nazi Germany or blacks in South Africa and the United States remain unexplained. It is hard to believe that millions of citizens all share a certain dysfunctional personality structure or a specific individual orientation. Even if this were the case, how can we explain that specific groups are selected as targets within one country and one historical period but not in another? Pettigrew's evidence has already demonstrated that the content of a societal norm and consensus about how to behave leads ordinary people, irrespective of their individual differences, to adopt and express prejudice to a higher or lower degree.

INDIVIDUAL DIFFERENCES 14.1

The Social Dominance Orientation (SDO) Scale (Pratto et al., 1994; Sidanius & Pratto, 1999)

Social dominance theory (Sidanius & Pratto, 1999) proposes that society contains ideologies that either promote or attenuate intergroup hierarchies. Individual differences in the extent to which these competing ideologies are accepted are represented by social dominance orientation (SDO). This scale, developed by Sidanius and Pratto (1999), measures the extent to which individuals have a strong desire to promote intergroup hierarchies and for their ingroups to dominate their outgroups.

Instructions for completion: Below is a series of statements with which you may either agree or disagree. For each statement, please indicate the degree of your agreement/disagreement by **circling** the appropriate number from '1' to '7'.

	Strongly Disagree/Disapprove				Strongly Agree/Favour		
1. Some groups of people are just more worthy than others.	1	2	3	4	5	6	7
2. In getting what your group wants, it is sometimes necessary to use force against other groups.	1	2	3	4	5	6	7
3. It's OK if some groups have more of a chance in life than others.	1	2	3	4	5	6	7
4. To get ahead in life, it is sometimes necessary to step on other groups.	1	2	3	4	5	6	7
5. If certain groups of people stayed in their place, we would have fewer problems.	1	2	3	4	5	6	7
6. It's probably a good thing that certain groups are at the top and other groups are at the bottom.	1	2	3	4	5	6	7
7. Inferior groups should stay in their place.	1	2	3	4	5	6	7
8. Sometimes other groups must be kept in their place.	1	2	3	4	5	6	7
9. It would be good if all groups could be equal.	1	2	3	4	5	6	7
10. Group equality should be our ideal.	1	2	3	4	5	6	7
11. All groups should be given an equal chance in life.	1	2	3	4	5	6	7
12. We should do what we can to equalize conditions for different groups.	1	2	3	4	5	6	7
13. We should increase social equality.	1	2	3	4	5	6	7
14. We would have fewer problems if we treated different groups more equally.	1	2	3	4	5	6	7
15. We should strive to make incomes more equal.	1	2	3	4	5	6	7
16. No one group should dominate in society.	1	2	3	4	5	6	7

Instructions for scoring: Items 9–16 (which should *not* be presented in a block, as they are shown here) should be reverse coded.

A further limitation of the personality approach must also be mentioned: prejudice is a socially pervasive phenomenon. However, whilst individuals broadly share cognitions, emotions and behavioural dispositions towards target groups, not everybody, and not even every prejudiced individual, carries the entire range of prejudices known to exist. Moreover, the groups which we ourselves belong to define, in turn, which groups appear to be 'the other'. Depending on how we view the characteristics of our own group, we perceive and evaluate in what respect 'others' are seen as different. Thus, to return to the stereotypes we introduced earlier, although it is almost never true that *all* members of one group hold the same stereotype about an outgroup, the stereotypes held are always views of an outgroup from a specific perspective. Thus East Germans are often judged incompetent from a West German perspective, Catholics may be judged to be bigots from a Protestant perspective, and homosexuals might be judged inadequate parents from a heterosexual perspective.

In order to overcome the limitations of personality approaches and increase our understanding of prejudice as a social phenomenon, we must therefore consider the intergroup context within which the prejudice is embedded. This entails examining not only the target group but also the complementary group expressing the prejudice and carrying out the acts of social discrimination.

Realistic conflict theory

According to individual difference explanations of the causes of prejudice, positive and negative attitudes towards other groups are based on characteristics of the individual personality. These attitudes determine whether relations between one's own group and other groups are positive or negative. The social pervasiveness of prejudice and discrimination is explained by the coming together of large numbers of authoritarian or SDO personalities. They, in turn, will disseminate prejudice, and the result will be a relationship

PIONEER

Muzafer Sherif (1906–1978) made ground-breaking contributions to the psychology of attitudes, the study of group norms and intergroup relations. Born in Izmir, Turkey, he completed a higher degree at Harvard and spent most of his life as professor at the University of Oklahoma, USA. His work on the development of group norms using the autokinetic phenomenon (see Chapter 11, this volume) showed that other group members provide us with a frame of reference, especially, but not only, when stimuli are ambiguous. His Robbers Cave study of intergroup relations demonstrated the powerful impact of group goals on intergroup relations, and showed that group conflict was easier to induce than to reduce. This research contributed to the development of realistic conflict theory.

to members of outgroups that is characterized by conflict. The difficulty with this theory is that it does not seem likely that, just by chance, a selection of equally prejudiced personalities will appear in a certain context at a certain time. Sherif (1966) proposed a radically different view. Instead of beginning with individual attitudes, which then lead to acceptance or rejection of others, he postulated that the reverse sequence explains the origins of prejudice and discrimination. He suggested that it is the particular relationship between social groups which influences the attitudes and behaviour of its members.

This basic assumption led Sherif to develop his realistic conflict theory (RCT) (Campbell, 1965; Sherif, 1966). Imagine that a group of social psychology students and a group of neuropsychology students have succeeded in reaching the final of a competition for the most innovative and socially relevant research project in the field of psychology. The award is highly prestigious and carries a considerable amount of prize money; your group definitely wants to win. So, however, does the other group. Only one group can win and the other must lose. You compete with the other group; to reach the goal of winning, both your group and the other group are *negatively dependent* on one another. In contrast, imagine that the award is advertised for the most innovative and socially relevant interdisciplinary research project. Now both groups from different disciplines have a common goal; neither you nor the other group could win the prize on its own. Both groups can only achieve their goal by mutual cooperation. They share a superordinate goal and both groups are therefore positively dependent on one another.

Under the condition of *negative interdependence* between own and other group, the other group is a barrier to achieving the own group's goals. Accordingly, members will devalue, dislike and reject the other group. In contrast, *positive interdependence* means that the other group is necessary and therefore highly func-

> **positive and negative interdependence** interdependence denotes that one can only achieve one's own goals dependent on how others behave. If the ingroup's goals can only be achieved when the outgroup achieves its goal, then both are positively interdependent. If ingroup goals can only be achieved at the expense of the outgroup's goals, both are negatively interdependent

tional for the achievement of the ingroup's goal. Positive interdependence leads to more positive evaluations and greater acceptance of the other group. The type of intergroup interdependence reflects the structural conditions in which the groups can achieve their goals, such as obtaining valued goods or necessary resources.

According to RCT, it is these structural intergroup conditions, for example the type of interdependence relationship between groups, that determine the attitudes and behaviour of group members. Examples of specific attitudes and behaviours include: identification with ingroup, solidarity within groups (van Vugt & Hart, 2004) and the respective evaluation of ingroup and outgroup (Blake & Mouton, 1986; Campbell, 1965).

In several famous field studies based at summer camps for boys in the USA, Sherif and colleagues examined the basic assumptions of RCT concerning the influence of functional relationships between groups on intergroup attitudes and behaviour (Sherif, Harvey, White, Hood & Sherif, 1961; Sherif & Sherif, 1953; Sherif, White & Harvey, 1955). They aimed to test the hypotheses that

ethnocentrism rating ingroup attributes and characteristics above those of the outgroup; literally, a view of things in which other groups are rated against the standard of the ingroup

whilst competition for scarce resources (negative interdependence) fosters intergroup conflicts and *ethnocentrism*, common superordinate goals (positive interdependence) reduce conflict and enhance positive intergroup attitudes. In order to test their hypotheses rigorously, Sherif and colleagues ruled out all other explanations for expected effects, including personality differences, prior personal ties and pronounced differences in socio-economic background and physical appearance, and concentrated solely on functional intergroup relationships. They carefully selected their participants: recruiting white middle-class American boys who were approximately 12 years old, psychologically well adjusted, and who did not know each other prior to the camp. In addition, to control for interpersonal attraction, the first summer camp studies included an initial phase in which the boys could form friendships. These friendships were split up in a later phase when the boys were divided into two groups.

Let us take a closer look at the most famous study, conducted at Robbers Cave, Oklahoma. This study consisted of three different phases. In the first phase of *group formation*, the boys were divided into two groups matched for boys' size and skills. The two groups were unaware of the presence of the other group: they lived in separate areas and engaged separately in activities such as cooking, constructing areas for swimming and transporting canoes over rough terrain. During the days, which were filled with these kinds of segregated activities, each group developed its own norms and symbols (e.g., they created group names such as the 'Eagles' and the 'Rattlers'). Each group developed a status hierarchy, with some boys moving to higher positions of respect and power and others landing at the bottom of the heap. The boy who came up with the best ideas and proved most efficient at coordinating the group's endeavours became group leader. After a while, both groups became aware of the presence of the other group in the same summer camp. Both groups then increasingly began to make references to the other group, and suggested that contests such as sports matches be arranged, so that the two groups could compete and establish which was the best group.

In the second phase of *intergroup competition*, the experimenters arranged a series of such direct competitive encounters, all designed to establish negative interdependence between the groups: they participated in sports contests and other competitive activities such as tug of war. Members of the winning group received highly attractive rewards, for example a penknife; members of the losing group received nothing. Not surprisingly, these contests produced fierce competition. The boys became more and more attached to their own group, and cohesiveness and solidarity within groups increased. At the same time, the boys became increasingly hostile and aggressive towards the respective outgroup, which rapidly generalized beyond competition situations. For instance, the boys began to call outgroup members 'stinkers', 'cheats' or 'sneaks'; they produced threatening posters, planned raids and collected secret hoards of green apples as ammunition. After only a few days, the intergroup conflict escalated so dramatically that the experimenters were forced to hastily end this phase.

In the third phase of *intergroup cooperation*, the experimenters established positive interdependence between both groups by

introducing *superordinate goals*, goals which were desired by both groups, but which could only be achieved by them acting together, and not by

superordinate goals goals which are desired by two or more groups, but which can only be achieved by both groups acting together, not by either group on its own

either group on its own. After a breakdown of the water supply, the two groups had to cooperate in finding a solution to restore water to the camp. In another case, the boys learned that a truck that was supposed to bring their lunch was stuck in the mud. In order to receive their lunch, the boys from both groups had to join forces to pull the truck out of the mud. Interestingly, they now cooperatively used the same rope which they had previously used competitively in a tug-of-war. These joint efforts to achieve superordinate goals did not immediately reduce the hostility between the groups. However, a series of activities, all designed to achieve a superordinate goal, gradually led to a reduction in intergroup conflict and the development of increasing intergroup acceptance accompanied by more friendly attitudes towards one another.

It is worth mentioning several points in connection with Sherif's experiment. (1) The experimenters observed some signs of negative intergroup attitudes even before the groups were drawn into competition with one another. Sherif and colleagues did not rate this observation as important. (2) Ingroup solidarity, ingroup identification and negative outgroup attitudes increased with intergroup competition. (3) Individual factors were ruled out as explanatory factors for intergroup conflict because the members of both groups were normal in terms of their personality and psychological make-up at pre-test. Moreover, both groups, the proud winners and the frustrated losers, developed hostile intergroup attitudes and opposition. Hence, frustration at losing the contest cannot be the major explanatory variable (see Chapter 8, this volume). (4) It took several joint and positive interdependent activities to reduce intergroup hostility.

Realistic conflict theory (Campbell, 1965; Sherif, 1966) identifies social groups and their goal relations as the basis for cooperation and conflict. Accordingly, it is the type of intergroup relationship which explains intergroup attitudes and behaviours. For Sherif, intergroup cooperation and conflict are rational, with each group striving to maximize its share of real resources.

Mere categorization

RCT proposes that realistic conflict between groups is the necessary condition for prejudice and discrimination between group members. However, later research within the theoretical framework of RCT, but also evidence from Sherif's own studies, raised some doubts about this assumption. As mentioned above, the boys asked for competitive games as soon as they had become aware of the outgroup and before negative interdependence had been established. Furthermore, competitive *intergroup behaviour* has been shown to emerge between

intergroup behaviour behaviour of individuals acting as members of a particular social group towards members of another group

groups that are not interdependent groups (Rabbie & Horowitz, 1969), between groups in explicitly non-competitive relations (Ferguson & Kelley, 1964; Rabbie & Wilkins, 1971) and even between groups in explicitly positive interdependent relations (Rabbie & de Brey, 1971). Realistic conflict and negative interdependence are clearly significant but not necessary conditions for competitive intergroup behaviour to occur. What, then, are the necessary conditions for the occurrence of prejudice and discrimination?

Tajfel and colleagues (Tajfel, Billig, Bundy & Flament, 1971; see also Rabbie & Horowitz, 1969) attempted to address this question: they proceeded systematically, beginning with a situation in which two groups were present and all additional determinants that could contribute to intergroup conflict were removed. They established the **minimal group paradigm**, designed to represent a baseline condition for intergroup behaviour. The idea was that by successively adding further factors to this baseline, information could be gained about which factors were necessary to produce **ingroup favouritism** and

> **minimal group paradigm** a set of experimental procedures designed to create groups on essentially arbitrary criteria (with no interaction within or between them, and with no knowledge of who else belongs to each group) whose members show intergroup discrimination
>
> **ingroup favouritism** the tendency to treat the ingroup or members of the ingroup more favourably than the outgroup or its members

intergroup discrimination. The typical characteristics of a minimal group situation were (1) meaningless or even arbitrary categorization into ingroup and outgroup; (2) complete anonymity of individual group membership; (3) no face-to-face interaction between members within and between groups; (4) no personal benefit of behavioural decisions concerning ingroup and outgroup members; and (5) explicit importance of the decisions for the recipients.

Based on these characteristics of the minimal group paradigm, the researchers allocated participants into two groups according to an arbitrary criterion. For instance, in one experiment, Tajfel and colleagues allegedly divided the participants according to their preference for paintings by the two artists Paul Klee or Vassilij Kandinsky. The participants in these minimal group paradigms were, however, randomly assigned to the groups. Other ingroup and outgroup members were denoted only by a code number indicating their group membership. Participants worked on their experimental task in individually separated cubicles. They were instructed to distribute money (or another resource of some importance, such as 'points') to ingroup and outgroup members but explicitly never to themselves.

In order to measure intergroup behaviour, the researchers studied the extent to which participants used one or more of several strategies for distributing the money between ingroup and outgroup members. Participants could adopt a *fairness* strategy and distribute equal amounts of money between ingroup and outgroup; or they could *maximize ingroup profit* by allocating the most money to ingroup members; or they could *maximize joint profit* by choosing the highest possible amount of money, irrespective of whether it went to ingroup or outgroup; finally, they could *maximize the difference* between ingroup and outgroup.

Given that the baseline was such a meaningless distinction between the ingroup and outgroup, it was not surprising that participants tended to be fair and distributed the money fairly equally between members of their ingroup and outgroup. But they also used the other strategies. Beyond the tendency towards fairness, participants also significantly favoured the ingroup over the outgroup. The most challenging result from a rational or instru-

PIONEER

Henri Tajfel (1919–1982) was born in Wloclawek, Poland. He escaped from the Nazis to join the French army, but was later captured. He owed his life to having been captured whilst wearing his uniform as a French soldier – it meant that he was treated as a (French) prisoner of war rather than being sent to the death camps as a Polish Jew. It was this experience which revealed to him the impact of social categorization. He moved to the United Kingdom and studied at Birkbeck College, University of London, subsequently teaching at Oxford University and then becoming Professor of Social Psychology at Bristol University. It was in a laboratory at Bristol that he and his collaborators carried out the first minimal group experiments, demonstrating that mere categorization could induce intergroup discrimination. These studies stimulated the development of social identity theory, the most significant influence from European social psychology on the discipline of social psychology as a whole.

mental perspective was that participants were prepared to sacrifice absolute gains for their ingroup (and for both groups together) in order to maximize the difference between their ingroup and the outgroup *in favour of the ingroup*. Numerous studies have replicated these results: it appears to be a robust finding that mere categorization is sufficient for the emergence of competitive intergroup behaviour (Brewer, 1979; Brown & Brewer, 1998; Tajfel, 1978).

Social identity theory

The minimal group paradigm and its findings pose two challenges. Firstly, why do people begin to show competitive intergroup behaviour in such a trivial intergroup situation where there is neither meaningful categorization nor conflict or competition between ingroup and outgroup? Secondly, why do individuals favour their ingroup by maximizing not only the outcome for their ingroup but also the difference between ingroup and outgroup? Tajfel and Turner (1986) developed social identity theory (SIT) to explain the findings of the minimal group paradigm and, more generally, to address the central phenomena of intergroup relations, by means of studies both within and beyond the laboratory. The theory builds upon four interrelated concepts: social categorization, social comparison, social identity and positive distinctiveness.

Social categorization divides the social context into own group, which the individual belongs to, and outgroup, which the individual does not belong to, on the basis of particular features

> **social categorization** the process of organizing information about the social world (especially concerning social groups), emphasizing similarities within categories and differences between categories.

such as gender, religion or ethnic background. Categorization enables individuals to gain information concerning their position in the world; they get to know both who they are and who they are not. As members of certain social categories, individuals do not perceive themselves or others as unique individuals, but rather in terms of their category membership. The more important and meaningful the category membership, the more it constitutes the basis for individuals' social identity, a key part of their self-concept.

Individuals generally strive for a positive self-concept. Accordingly, they strive for a positive social identity (the view of oneself derived from one's group membership; see Chapter 5, p. 104). Social comparisons between own and other groups on valued dimensions provide the information which individuals require for the formation of a positive or negative social identity. For example, many of you reading this chapter may have a positive social identity as a psychology student when compared with social work students, but not so positive when compared with medical students (based, in each case, on social status, prestige and salaries of the respective graduates in each field). If, however, social competence and not prestige is the dimension of comparison, then the comparison outcome involving psychology students and social work students, and its effect on social identity, would possibly be reversed.

The need for a positive social identity is satisfied when a social comparison outcome is clearly in favour of the ingroup and the ingroup is positively distinct from comparison outgroups. From the perspective of SIT, intergroup behaviour serves the need to establish, maintain and defend positive ingroup distinctiveness. In the minimal group paradigm, distribution of money between ingroup and outgroup is the only form of intergroup behaviour available for serving positive ingroup distinctiveness: by maximizing the difference between groups in favour of the ingroup, the **positive distinctiveness** of the ingroup is explicitly established and underlined.

Beyond the minimal group situation, in the real social world outside the laboratory, social groups are usually not of a minimal nature and group members use more information about the social context and the characteristics of the relationship between groups than mere categorization. Imagine the following situation. In many countries primary school teachers currently enjoy lower public prestige and are paid less than secondary school teachers. Primary school teachers have a lower status than secondary school teachers and are therefore forced to face an unfavourable outcome when comparing their own group with the other group. Given their striving for positive social distinctiveness, how will members of the lower-status group deal with this status quo? The first question asked will be whether group members can imagine alternatives to the status quo: are the boundaries between the groups permeable, and is it possible to move upwards by becoming a member of the higher-status group? Or can the relationship between groups as a whole be changed, are they stable or unstable? And should the relationships be changed or not, are they legitimate or illegitimate?

positive distinctiveness motivation to show the superiority of one's ingroup compared to an outgroup on valued dimensions

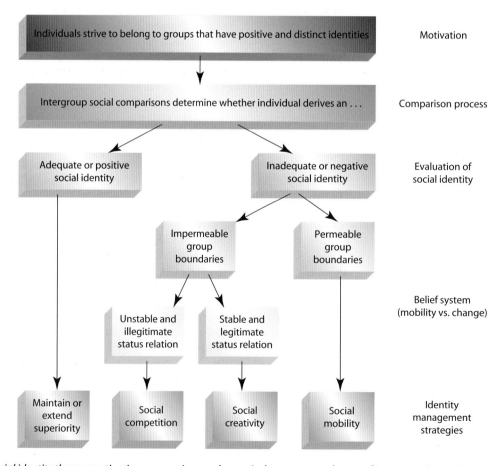

Figure 14.1 *Social identity theory: motivation, comparison and appraisal processes and types of intergroup behaviour.*

If the boundaries between own and other group are permeable, a primary school teacher might try to leave her low-status group and move into the high-status group in order to re-establish positive ingroup distinctiveness. She can return to university, try to obtain a higher qualification entitling her to the position of a secondary school teacher, and thus use *social mobility* to move into the higher-status group.

If, however, even given boundaries which seem permeable, the primary school teacher conceives the status relationship to be unstable and illegitimate, she will engage in *social competition* and will attempt to demonstrate the superiority of her group of primary school teachers in comparison to secondary school teachers. All this seems unlikely when the status relationship is perceived as stable and legitimate. In this case, our primary school teacher will be more likely to use *social creativity* to re-evaluate her group. Social creativity comprises attempts to change the nature of the comparison context such as finding other outgroups (e.g., kindergarten teachers) for which intergroup comparison leads to favourable outcomes. Moreover, she can also change the comparison dimension (e.g., 'it is not public recognition that is important, but the basic education of children'), which may also lead to a more positive evaluation of her ingroup.

The strategies of social mobility, social competition and social creativity are means of restoring a positively distinct view of the ingroup compared with outgroups. The selection of these various forms of intergroup behaviour is determined by group members' evaluation of intergroup comparisons. These evaluations are, in turn, based upon characteristics of status relationships such as stability and legitimacy as well as permeability of group boundaries (Ellemers, 1993; Mummendey, Kessler, Klink & Mielke, 1999; see Figure 14.1 for a flow chart of social identity processes).

SUMMARY

Authoritarian personality and social dominance orientation are personality-based explanations of prejudice. Realistic conflict theory posits that it is not personality but the relationship between social groups that determines the attitudes and behaviour of group members. Mere categorization into ingroup and outgroup, however, is sometimes sufficient to elicit ingroup favouritism. Social identity explains how striving for a positive social identity leads to various intergroup behaviours including prejudice.

INTERGROUP BEHAVIOUR: BASIC PROCESSES

What psychological processes guide intergroup behaviour?
How are individuals and social groups connected?
What motivates a more favourable treatment of an ingroup
  compared to an outgroup?

In analysing and explaining the causes of prejudice and discrimination as intergroup behaviour, it will be useful to take a closer look at the general nature of intergroup behaviour, including its basic concepts and processes. Imagine two people, Meltem and Karola. Both women are in their mid-twenties and study psychology in Munich. They have joined a common work group to prepare for their exams. They are also members of different political students' communities: Meltem works for the Muslim, Karola for the Catholic student community. Imagine both women, firstly, in the work group situation and, secondly, in a public political discussion about headscarves for Muslim women. In the work group, Meltem and Karola support each other in studying the various issues of their degree subject. They share their personal feelings of anxiety before an exam; they exchange their individual aspirations and their personal views about their professors. And now imagine switching to the topic of Muslim and Christian culture and religion in a European country.

Within the first context, Meltem and Karola view and interact with each other in terms of their idiosyncratic personal characteristics as unique individuals. When it comes to the topic of different religions, their opinions and statements will be strongly determined by the beliefs they share with other members of the religious communities they each belong to. This will be even more true the more meaningful it is for Meltem and Karola to be members of their groups, that is, the stronger their distinct social identities. Each will act together with other members of their respective groups regardless of their personal differences. More generally speaking, intergroup behaviour takes place whenever persons individually or collectively interact in terms of their group identification (Sherif, 1966).

Individuals derive their identity from their membership in a particular ingroup relative to an outgroup. They act as group members and like other members of the category they belong to when in a given social situation a particular social categorization becomes meaningful. This may even be the case when a person is alone and perhaps thinking about whether to sign a petition in favour of her own group or against other groups; it may also occur within dyadic interactions (e.g., when Meltem and Karola discuss issues concerning their respective religions); or it may arise in social situations with larger numbers of individuals belonging to different groups.

Individuals demonstrate intergroup behaviour whenever they *categorize* themselves and others into ingroup and outgroups and when they *identify* themselves with their own group. The basic processes of *categorization* and *identification* influence the way in which individuals perceive and evaluate both themselves and others. Furthermore, these processes have an important impact on motivational processes and behaviour. Based on evidence from current research, Figure 14.2 summarizes which basic processes are important and how they relate to one another in regulating intergroup behaviour.

In the following parts of this chapter, we will describe the processes that are relevant for the regulation of intergroup behaviour in more detail.

Social categorization

Social categorization and knowledge One of the basic abilities we possess is to categorize objects, events or people into

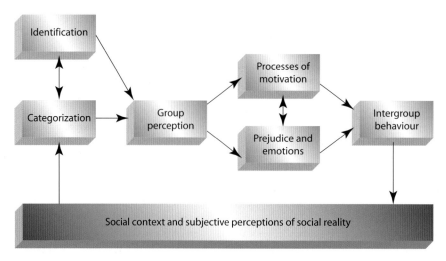

Figure 14.2 *Flow chart of basic psychological processes regulating intergroup behaviour.*

similar clusters and differentiate between dissimilar clusters. For instance, we categorize apples or oranges as fruits and differentiate them from vegetables. The central function of categorization is to gain knowledge about things identified as elements of a particular category (Millikan, 1998). Having, for example, categorized a person as being Catholic or Muslim, we can then relate everything we have learned about Catholics or Muslims to the person belonging to this category. Categorization structures our social and non-social environment and gives meaning to things because it relates category-based knowledge to actual perception (Smith & Medin, 1981; see Chapter 4, this volume). Categories involve inductive and deductive processes. Induction involves going from the particular to the general. For instance, if we meet a person from Norway and discover that he eats a lot of fish, drinks a lot of spirits and wears a warm woollen sweater, we may, on the basis of this individual, draw conclusions about Norwegians in general. Deduction involves going from the general to the particular. Thus we may use our category-based knowledge to infer the characteristics of any Norwegian we meet in the future.

Assimilation and contrast Categorization not only organizes our knowledge but also affects the way we perceive and remember information about objects or people. Taylor, Fiske, Etcoff and Ruderman (1978) designed the 'who said what?' paradigm to study this effect. Participants hear or read statements from several target persons allegedly involved in a discussion about a particular topic. Participants additionally receive information regarding the group membership of each target person (e.g., half the people are black and the other half white; or four are female and two are male). In a second phase, participants read through the statements in a scrambled order, this time without group membership information. Their task is to identify *who said what* in the previous phase.

There are three kinds of possible response in this paradigm. First, participants can correctly assign a particular statement to a particular individual (but they rarely do, because the task seems to be quite difficult). Second, they can make a 'within-category error', assigning the statement to a member of the correct category but to the wrong individual within the category. Third, they

can make a 'between-category error', assigning the statement to someone from the wrong category (e.g., it was said by a black person but the participant erred in attributing it to a white person). Participants tend to make many more within-category than between-category errors, which indicates that they organize their knowledge categorically (e.g., van Knippenberg, van Twuyver & Pepels, 1994). Generally, when individuals are categorized, this leads to both an underestimation of differences within categories (*assimilation*) and an overestimation of differences between categories (*contrast*; Corneille, Klein, Lambert & Judd, 2002; Krueger & Clement, 1994; Tajfel & Wilkes, 1963).

Salience of social categories The 'who said what?' paradigm demonstrates the effects of categorization on perception and person memory. We must next address the question: when does a particular categorization become salient? Consider, for instance, several long queues of people waiting at an airport. You could categorize the people in the queues simply according to the type of queue, i.e., those who are travelling first, business or economy class. You could also use profession (business people or workers), origin (foreigners or locals), age (younger or older) and so on. Obviously, objects or persons can be categorized in many different ways. The question arises: which factors determine which category you will use, which one will become salient in a particular situation? *Category salience* refers to the activation and attraction of attention that leads a particular category to stand out compared to other categories. According to an influential early approach (Bruner, 1957), category salience depends both on the perceivers' readiness to use a particular category and on the fit of a particular category in the current social context (Oakes, 1987; Oakes, Haslam & Turner, 1994).

Perceiver's readiness, also referred to as the *accessibility* of categories to the perceiver, pertains to the perceiver's goals and motivation within a specific situation, or more generally across many situations. The use of a category is more likely if a perceiver uses

> **category salience** the activation of a particular social category within a particular context. It depends on normative and comparative fit as well as a readiness to apply this category

it habitually (Bruner, 1957; Higgins, 1996; see also Chapter 4, this volume). For example, individuals who are used to structuring their world according to gender tend also in a particular situation to use gender as a basis for categorization (Stangor, Lynch, Dunn & Glass, 1992). A particular category will also be used if it matches the current goals and motives of the perceiver. Imagine yourself in a big department store trying to get some advice about where to find a certain product: you will categorize people as being either employees or customers in order to approach the right person in pursuit of your goal.

It is not, however, only the perceiver's readiness or category accessibility that determines whether a category is likely to be used; there are also conditions of the situational context which contribute to category salience. These are the conditions of *category fit*. According to Campbell (1958), people use factors such as similarity, proximity and common fate to group entities such as persons in their social environment. Several studies by Gaertner and colleagues (e.g., Gaertner, Mann, Murrell & Dovidio, 1989) illustrate clever manipulations of these factors.

They first divided participants experimentally into two groups by giving them either red or blue labels. In a second step, they induced three different group conditions by varying the way in which individuals were seated ('two groups', 'one group' and 'individuals'). In the 'two groups' condition, members wore the original labels of their respective groups (similarity), they sat together with their group at the opposite side of the table from the other group (proximity), and each group expected to win a prize for the best solution in an experimental task (common fate within groups). In the 'one group' condition, participants received a new common label; they were seated alternately around one table and were told that there was a single prize for the best common solution. Finally, in the 'individual condition', each participant sat at a separate table, had to create a new individual name, and expected to win a prize for the best individual solution.

The factors of similarity, proximity and common fate determine the *comparative fit* of a category. Comparative fit depicts how well a given category fits to the perceived entities within the current social context. Comparative fit is based on the meta-contrast principle. This principle looks at how much categories differentiate between observed stimuli, thereby minimizing the differences within a category (assimilation) and maximizing the differences between the categories (contrast). The notion of comparative fit can easily be applied to the 'who said what?' paradigm (Taylor et al., 1978). Assume a group discussion in which all male participants defend one position (e.g., pro-affirmative action policies for women) whereas all females defend the opposite position (e.g., anti-affirmative action policies for women). In such a case, the gender category would differentiate perfectly between opposing positions in the discussion (Klauer & Wegener, 1998; van Knippenberg & van Knippenberg, 1994).

In addition to comparative fit, *normative fit* refers to the background knowledge of the perceiver that specifies which similarities and differences are relevant in a current context. Let us go back to the discussion concerning gender equality. In our example given above, if men happened to be contra and women happened to be pro affirmative action policies, this would fit our expectations and we would be even more likely to use gender in order to categorize

the members of the discussion parties. Hence, a higher normative fit enhances the salience of categories.

Self-categories Try to answer the question 'who am I?' Several answers will come into your mind: 'I'm Karola Schmidt, I'm from Germany and I'm a psychology student.' In categorizing people, we don't refer only to others but very often also include ourselves. Self-categories are part of our self-concept: they tell us who we are and where our position is relative to various categories (see Chapter 5, this volume). Self-categories constitute our personal and social identity. Categories are organized in a hierarchical structure (Turner, Hogg, Oakes, Reicher & Wetherell, 1987). We can categorize ourselves as 'I, Karola,' that is, as a unique individual distinct from all others, or on a more inclusive level as 'We, West Germans,' that is, as a member of a social category who is similar to other ingroup members and at the same time distinct from individuals belonging to a salient outgroup such as East Germans. This categorization into ingroup and outgroup could be dissolved by moving up to a superordinate level and to a more comprehensive category, 'We (are all) Germans', as one common ingroup that may, however, then be contrasted to a new outgroup, e.g., Belgians (see Figure 14.3).

Identification and its components

Just as categories and categorization give meaning to a particular situation, self-categories give meaning to the self, whereby not all categories are equally relevant for self-identity. The concept of identification denotes the relationship of the self to a particular social category. Generally, if individuals do identify with a particular social category, they will be affected by issues related to this category. If I am from Germany and this is significant to me and I care about German customs, language or traditions, then I will be concerned about events or actions affecting Germans as a whole, such as derogatory statements aimed at German people.

Identification with a social category leads individuals to perceive and evaluate events with respect to their implications for this particular social category. They also tend to be motivated to act according to the goals and values that they associate with the category. The notion of identity is closely related to identification. *Identity* comprises the content of a social category such as knowledge about that particular category. *Identification* denotes the relation of self to the social category which is, globally, the strength of this particular identity. Initially, Tajfel (1978, p. 63) conceived identification as a multi-component construct including the particular knowledge of group membership and the value and the emotional significance attached to this group membership. More recent research has suggested that we should explore identification in more detail as a multi-component construct (e.g., Ashmore, Deaux & McLaughlin-Volpe, 2003; Ellemers, Kortekaas & Ouwerkerk, 1999).

Ashmore et al. (2003) have provided a comprehensive review of the various components of identification which have been mentioned in the literature, including, amongst others, categorization, evaluation, importance and attachment (see Table 14.1 for definitions and examples of measures of each of the components of

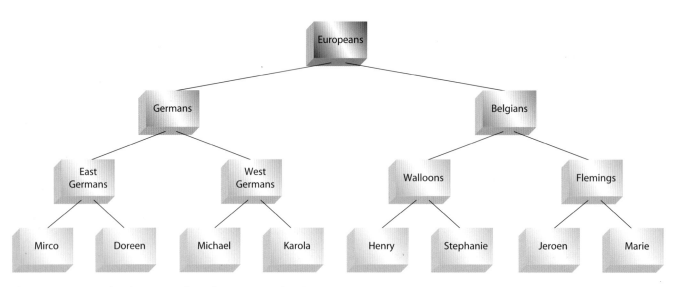

Figure 14.3 *Hierarchical structure of social categories with individuals as the least inclusive category, regional and national categorizations as moderately inclusive levels, and European categorization as the most inclusive level.*

Table 14.1 *Components of identification, definition and measurement examples (based on Ashmore et al., 2003)*

Component	Definition	Measurement example
Self-categorization	Identifying self with a social category	'I identify myself as being East German'
Evaluation	Positive or negative attitude towards the category	'I like being East German' (positive) 'I am angry about being East German' (negative)
Importance	Importance of a particular group membership for an individual's overall self-concept	'Being an East German is an important reflection of who I am'
Attachment or emotional involvement	Emotional involvement felt with a particular social group	'I have a strong sense of belonging to East Germans'
Social embeddedness	Degree to which a group membership is embedded in the person's everyday social relations	'I am often involved in issues related to East Germans'
Behavioural involvement	Degree to which an individual engages in actions on behalf of a social group	'I often engage in actions that improve the situation of East Germans'
Content and meaning	Attributes and traits associated with a social group, beliefs about one's group's experience, history and position in society	'East Germans are . . . [e.g., tolerant, active, etc.]'

identification). However, research on this topic is in its early stages and the number of components of identification which can be distinguished and the diverse effects these components have are not yet known.

The most central and basic aspect of identification is self-categorization, that is, the definition of the self in terms of a social group. For instance, without self-categorization as a member of a particular group, one cannot feel proud about the achievements of one's social group compared to those of another group. Another important component of identification is evaluation, that is, how

the group is evaluated in relation to a relevant other group on an important dimension. The ingroup can be positively or negatively evaluated depending on the comparison outcome. Importance of identity refers to whether group membership and the associated attributes are central to the self. Attachment denotes the affective involvement a person feels with a social category and the degree to which the fate of the group is perceived as their own. Finally, strong identification leads individuals to perceive those things which are good for the group as being their own preferences. When group issues come to be seen also as personal preferences and goals, this explains why group members engage in various intergroup behaviours including collective action and participation in social movements (Simon & Klandermans, 2001).

Intergroup perception

Group homogeneity Self-categorization and identification as a member of a particular group have important consequences for the way we perceive own and other groups. We have already outlined assimilation and contrast as general effects of categorization. When examining various types of intergroup relations more closely, the picture appears to be more differentiated: assimilation and contrast do not necessarily affect both groups symmetrically.

A number of studies have consistently shown that people perceive outgroups as more homogeneous than their ingroup: 'they' are all the same, but 'we' are all different (Judd & Park, 1988; Quattrone & Jones, 1980). Several explanations for this 'outgroup homogeneity effect' have been proposed. For example, if individuals are more familiar with their own group than with an outgroup or they know more ingroup than outgroup members, then this should lead to a more differentiated and complex representation of the ingroup than of an outgroup (Linville, Fischer & Salovey, 1989). Alternatively, the effect may not only be due to the more detailed knowledge about various other ingroup members, but rather to the fact that the self is always included in the ingroup: the ingroup is more important and more concrete because at least one of its members is very well known – the self. This gives the individual access to greater knowledge of the range of behaviours and expressed beliefs within the ingroup (e.g., we know that we ourselves sometimes behave differently and even express different views across different social situations).

Simon and Brown (1987) presented a series of experimental studies challenging the outgroup homogeneity effect and its explanations by demonstrating an *ingroup* homogeneity effect. A review of the evidence on the outgroup homogeneity effect clearly showed that minority groups are perceived as homogeneous on highly relevant dimensions, irrespective of whether this was an outgroup or ingroup (Brown & Smith, 1989; Kelly, 1989; Simon, 1992). An active minority preparing to engage in a social movement, for instance, perceives itself as more homogeneous than the majority, in particular on group-relevant attributes that differentiate the minority from the majority.

Recent studies have also analysed the effects of power on perceived group variability (see Guinote, 2004, for a review). Positions of power and control over important outcomes are often held by members of social majorities rather than minorities. It would make sense for less powerful minority members to perceive greater variability in a more powerful majority outgroup, because they should attend carefully to how they behave. However, powerful groups are in fact objectively more variable than powerless groups (Brauer, 2001; Guinote, Judd & Brauer, 2002). Members of high-status groups tend to seek gains from their advantaged position, thereby more easily violating group norms. In contrast, minority members tend to avoid offending others because of their disadvantaged position, thereby showing more norm-conforming behaviour (Keltner, Gruenfeld & Anderson, 2003).

Varieties of prejudice

So far we have discussed prejudice as a derogatory social attitude towards a social group. Prejudice can be conceived as a special case of the multicomponent model of attitudes (see Chapter 6, Figure 6.1, p. 115), with stereotypes as the cognitive component, prejudice as the affective component and social discrimination as the behavioural component. The affect felt towards own and other groups (Smith, 1993), be it positive, negative or mixed (Fiske, Cuddy, Glick & Xu, 2002), results from intergroup comparisons. A prejudice, being a negative judgement of a whole group, can be perceived as fair or unfair, accurate or unjustified. Importantly, like stereotypes, prejudices are socially shared evaluations showing a close relation to societal norms (Crandall, Eshleman & O'Brien, 2002).

As already noted, gender, race and age are among the most prevalent bases of stereotyping and therefore also of prejudice (Fiske, 1998; Mackie, Hamilton, Susskind & Rosselli, 1996). However, at least in today's modern western societies, it is no longer socially acceptable to express overt prejudice against minority groups. This does not automatically mean that prejudice has vanished: it is merely expressed less frequently in a direct and blatant form, and more often in subtle forms that are more compatible with modern norms (see also Chapter 6, this volume).

Several concepts of modern prejudice have been proposed (see Table 14.2), for example *aversive racism* (Gaertner & Dovidio, 1986; see Research close-up 14.1), *ambivalent racism* (Katz & Hass, 1988) and *modern racism* (Sears & Henry, 2003). These concepts all share the common assumption of an uncomfortable internal conflict associated with attitudes towards target groups. Individuals hold a prejudice against particular groups, yet at the same time they accept and want to comply with the societal norms of tolerance and egalitarianism, both of which demand positive evaluations of the target groups.

As a consequence of the change from blatant to more subtle forms of prejudice, researchers have had to change how they

Plate 14.2 *Gender, race and age are among the most prevalent bases of stereotyping and prejudice.*

Table 14.2 *Modern forms of prejudice*

Aversive racism (e.g., Gaertner & Dovidio, 1986)

Aversive racism consists of the endorsement of egalitarian values, fairness and justice for all social groups. It comprises a strong self-image of being non-prejudiced. At the same time, it is associated with negative feelings towards minority groups.

Aversive racists will not discriminate in situations in which their prejudice would be revealed, thereby threatening their non-prejudiced self-image. However, discrimination against minority groups is likely in all situations in which the normative structure is weak, the guidelines of appropriate behaviour are vague and the bases of social judgement are ambiguous.

Ambivalent racism (e.g., Katz & Hass, 1988)

Ambivalent racism involves ambivalent feelings towards minority groups, implying simultaneously strong positive and negative feelings.

Ambivalent racism leads to response amplification: positive actions and achievements of minority group members lead to extremely positive evaluations (i.e., reverse discrimination), whereas negative actions and failures lead to extremely negative evaluations.

Modern racism (Sears & Henry, 2003)

Modern racism replaces mostly old-fashioned, openly racist attitudes because open expression of negative intergroup attitudes (e.g., racial attitudes) is frowned upon socially.

Negative affect is no longer attached to race *per se* but to newly emerging racial issues such as affirmative action and welfare programs. For instance, modern racists deny the existence of social discrimination and thus claim that affirmative action is an unfair gain for minority groups.

measure prejudice. They have developed new 'implicit' measures of prejudice that tap unintentional bias of which well-intentioned individuals are largely unaware. These implicit measures include indirect self-report measures (e.g., Maass, 1999; von Hippel, Sekaquaptewa & Vargas, 1997) and response-latency measures following priming procedures (e.g., Dovidio, Kawakami, Johnson, Johnson & Howard, 1997).

For instance, Wittenbrink, Judd and Park (1997) used a semantic priming paradigm (see Chapter 4, this volume). Their results showed that the prime word 'black' led to faster response latencies for negative stereotypic attributes of African Americans than the prime word 'white'. In contrast, the prime word 'white' led to faster responses to positive stereotypic attributes of white Americans than the prime word 'black'. Wittenbrink and colleagues (1997) interpret this pattern as evidence for implicit prejudice. Moreover, additional scales assessing explicit prejudice were only moderately related to the measure of implicit prejudice. This provides some validation that the implicit measure does indeed assess prejudice, but demonstrates also that the explicit and implicit measures tap different aspects of prejudice.

More recently, researchers have turned to the developing area of social neuroscience to investigate brain activity involved in prejudice. Phelps et al. (2000, Study 1) measured activity in the amygdala (an area of the brain involved in processing fear-related information) when white participants viewed unfamiliar black and white faces. Although there was no overall difference in amygdala activation as a function of stimulus race, differences in amygdala activation to own- and other-race faces were significantly correlated with implicit racial prejudice (as measured by the Implicit Association Test (IAT); Greenwald, McGhee & Schwartz, 1998; see Chapter 6, this volume), but not with an explicit measure of racial attitudes. White participants with the most negative implicit

attitudes towards blacks showed greatest amygdala activation responses to black versus white faces. These effects disappeared, however, when participants viewed faces of famous and well-liked black and white individuals (Phelps et al., 2000, Study 2).

A different way of exploring varieties of prejudice involves conceiving prejudice as both an attitude and a group-based emotion (see Figure 14.4). Smith (1993) developed a new conception of prejudice as group-based emotions. Conceptualizing prejudice in this way has several advantages. Firstly, prejudice is more complex than the evaluation along a single dimension ranging from positive to negative. For instance, the emotions of anger and fear are both negative in valence but have different meanings. Secondly, group-based emotions are conceptualized as evaluations of in- and outgroups from a particular ingroup perspective, in other words, the particular intergroup situation is taken into account. Hence prejudice is less static and may vary, depending on the social context. Moreover, intergroup attitudes are seen to represent more permanent intergroup evaluations, whereas intergroup emotions reflect more transient evaluations.

The concept of prejudice as group-based emotion has some thought-provoking implications. Whilst the level of prejudice aimed at two different target groups might be identical when measured on a positive–negative scale, it is possible that the emotions associated with evaluations of the two different targets are completely different. In a recent study, Cottrell and Neuberg (2005) showed that whilst the level of general prejudice is roughly the same across several groups, the underlying emotions differ considerably. Moreover, patterns of intergroup evaluation on dimensions of threat consistently predict these emotions, and the emotions lead to different behavioural tendencies. For instance, Cottrell and Neuberg showed that prejudice in terms of an attitude held by white American participants towards African Americans, Asian

Race and helping: Subtle forms of aversive prejudice

Gaertner, S.L. & Dovidio, J.F. (1977). The subtlety of white racism, arousal, and helping behavior. *Journal of Personality and Social Psychology, 35*, 691–707.

Introduction

In a series of papers, Gaertner and colleagues (Gaertner, 1975; Gaertner & Bickman, 1971) examined the effects of race on helping behaviour. Experimental evidence showed that victims' race influenced the likelihood of helping behaviour. On the one hand, victims of the same race as potential helpers more readily elicited helping behaviour. For instance, white participants tended to offer help (or show a lower bystander effect) more often to white than to black victims. On the other hand, however, several studies showed no differential bystander effect or even that white participants behaved more favourably towards black than white victims.

Dutton and colleagues (e.g., Dutton & Lake, 1973) showed that whites may be more favourable towards blacks in order to avoid the self-attribution of bigotry (i.e., being prejudiced). Gaertner (1976) suggested that people who claim not to be prejudiced may nonetheless have negative feelings towards black people, leading to an aversive state in which they dissociate the negative feelings from a non-prejudiced self-image. The basic thesis examined in this research was that people with this aversive type of prejudice may avoid behaviour that reveals their prejudice. However, they are more likely to discriminate against black people (i.e., will not help) in situations in which their failure to help could be attributed to factors other than race.

Method

Participants
Seventy-five white female students participated in the study.

Design and procedure
The design of the study was a 2 (race of the victim: white vs. black) × 2 (diffusion of responsibility: alone vs. presence of others) factorial design. Participants assumed that they communicated via intercom with the target person in another room. The race of the target person was manipulated by showing a student identification card revealing either a white or a black female. In the 'alone' condition, participants knew that they were the only person interacting with the target person. In the 'presence of others' condition, participants learned that two other participants (in separate rooms) also interacted with the target person. During the experiment, participants heard sounds of falling chairs and the target person screaming, indicating an emergency. Then, within the next 3 minutes, the helping

Table 14.3 *Effects of diffusion of responsibility and race of the victim on the likelihood of helping, time taken to stand up and time taken to open the door*

	N	% help	Time taken to stand up (sec.)	Time taken to open door (sec.)
Alone				
Black victim	16	93.8	36.6	45.0
White victim	16	81.3	55.0	62.6
Presence of others				
Black victim	16	37.5	124.9	128.5
White victim	16	75.0	72.4	89.2

behaviour and how long the participant took to intervene (i.e., time taken to stand up, time taken to open the door) were recorded.

Results

The results (see Table 14.3) showed the typical bystander effect; that is, participants in the 'alone' condition helped more than those in the 'presence of others' condition for whom responsibility could be diffused across three people. Results showed no main effect of race of the victim. However, there was a significant interaction between race of the victim and diffusion of responsibility. Participants in the 'alone' condition were more likely to help a black than a white victim, and they did so more quickly. In contrast, participants in the 'presence of others' condition offered significantly less help to the black compared to the white victim and they took more time to offer this help.

Discussion

The study showed that prejudice can express itself in subtle ways. Whites offered less help to black than white victims only when diffusion of responsibility provided them with a plausible alternative explanation for their prejudice (i.e., they could still claim that the reason they did not help the black victim was that there were two other people who could also have helped). This study, together with other similar studies, gave rise to the development of the concept of aversive racism. Aversive racists endorse fair and just treatment of all groups whilst occasionally (sometimes unconsciously) harbouring negative feelings towards particular groups (e.g., blacks) and therefore avoiding intergroup interaction. These individuals also avoid unfair behaviour in intergroup situations. However, they manifest their prejudice in subtle and rationalizable ways.

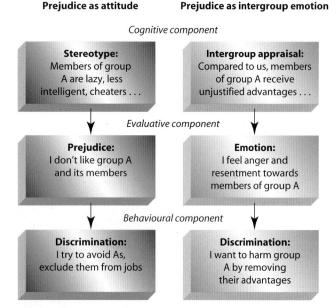

Figure 14.4 *Prejudice as attitude and prejudice as group-based emotion.*

Americans and Native Americans does not differ, whereas the emotions associated with the different racial prejudices are quite different. Native Americans elicit most pity, whereas African Americans also evoke anxiety and Asian Americans elicit, if anything at all, some envy. Thus, traditional measures of prejudice as an attitude mask the differential emotional reactions underlying prejudice. Given that emotions are connected with particular action tendencies (Frijda, 1986), different group-based emotions should also lead to distinct behavioural tendencies towards outgroup members. Mackie, Devos and Smith (2000) indeed showed that anger and anxiety, both of which are negative emotions, lead to different behavioural reactions: anger enhances approach tendencies, while anxiety is more often associated with avoidance tendencies.

Fiske et al. (2002) attempted to integrate the content of stereotypes with prejudice as specific emotions. According to their stereotype content model, there are two underlying dimensions of stereotype content, 'competence' and 'warmth'. Competence comprises attributes such as intelligent, confident, independent and competitive, whereas warmth comprises attributes such as likeable, sincere, good-natured and tolerant. Fiske and colleagues (2002) propose that stereotyped groups can be characterized and compared in terms of these two dimensions, and that stereotype content implies specific emotions. Hence, some social groups are perceived as being nice but not particularly competent (e.g., housewives), eliciting emotions such as sympathy but also pity; other groups are perceived as competent but not warm (e.g., rich people), evoking emotions such as envy and jealousy; and groups that are perceived as neither competent nor warm (e.g., welfare recipients) will awaken emotions such as contempt and anger. Finally, there remain those 'good' groups who are not only competent but also warm: interestingly, these happen to be ingroups and their close allies. They trigger emotions such as pride and admiration.

Intergroup motivation

Different motives In previous parts of this chapter we discussed prejudice as being both an important determinant and an outcome of intergroup relations. We examined the central effects of ingroup identification on prejudice as perception and emotion associated with groups to which we either belong or do not belong. We have already seen some of the consequences of conceiving ourselves to be members of a group and identifying ourselves with this group. Let us now turn to the question of the motivation of prejudice. What motivates individuals to engage in intergroup behaviour such as favouring their ingroup? One way to answer the question of *why* people are prejudiced is to propose several motives. Tajfel and Turner (1986), the pioneers of social identity theory, postulate that group members are motivated to establish, maintain and foster a positive distinctiveness for their ingroup in relation to an important outgroup (see p. 298). If intergroup comparisons do not support positive distinctiveness for the ingroup, either because of a negative comparison outcome or because others question the positive outcome, the motive for positive distinctiveness becomes active and instigates actions to change the status quo and re-establish positive distinctiveness. Intergroup behaviour is driven by the motive of positive ingroup distinctiveness and responds when this is threatened or challenged.

Hogg (2000) proposed that individuals are also motivated to reduce subjective uncertainty, and he proposed the *uncertainty reduction* hypothesis. In joining a group and defining and identifying the self in terms of group membership, individuals reduce subjective uncertainty about themselves, their attitudes, beliefs and their position in the social world. They join social groups because these provide clear normative prescriptions that structure the social environment and help to predict the actions of others. Experimental evidence shows that under high compared to low subjective uncertainty, both identification with and positive evaluation of the ingroup increase (Grieve & Hogg, 1999).

Brewer (1991) addressed the question of why individuals choose a certain level of self-categorization and proposed her theory of *optimal distinctiveness*. She assumes that individuals tend to find an optimal solution for the trade-off between two concurrent needs, namely the need to be like others (to 'belong') and the need to be distinguishable from others (to 'be distinct'). Individuals will choose self-categorizations which simultaneously enable them to be connected to some people whilst remaining different from others. For example, as a student you may feel that the identity of 'student at the university of X' is too broad and inclusive, and does not satisfy your need for exclusivity. In contrast, the identity of a 'student in professor Y's class' may be too exclusive. An optimally distinct identity may be conveyed by the identity of being a 'psychology student', which is often how you will feel, and be treated, during your time as a student.

Social identities that simultaneously meet the needs for affiliation and differentiation are termed optimally distinct; when one need is not met, these identities are termed non-optimal. Optimal identities are those that provide sufficient inclusiveness within the group and sufficient differentiation *between* ingroup and outgroups.

(a)

(b)

(c)

Plates 14.3a, b and c *Different groups in society evoke different emotions.*

Leonardelli and Brewer (2001) provided evidence for both motives in several experiments. Members of optimally distinctive groups show greater ingroup identification, greater satisfaction with their group, higher ingroup favouritism and higher self-esteem than members of less optimally distinct groups.

Other motivational theories such as terror management theory (Greenberg, Solomon & Pyszczynski, 1997) have also been used to explain ingroup favouritism. This theory is based on the general assumption that people strive for self-preservation. When people, for one reason or another, contemplate their own mortality, a feeling of existential terror is elicited ('what will happen to me when I die?'). One way to cope with this feeling is to foster one's own world view. World views buffer against terror and anxiety by giving assurance that the universe is meaningful and orderly and that immortality is attainable, be it literally (e.g., through the concept of a soul and afterlife) or symbolically (e.g., through potential accomplishments and culture). By conforming strongly to the norms and values of their cultural world view, individuals additionally become particularly valuable members of their group within a meaningful universe and thus enhance their self-esteem.

Outgroup members who do not share the adopted world view pose a challenge to both the ingroup members' world view and their self-esteem and will therefore be devalued. In a series of experiments testing terror management theory, participants in experimental conditions were asked to think about their own death (a 'mortality salience' manipulation). After a short distractor task, they then evaluated events which violated either ingroup or outgroup norms. For instance, Harmon-Jones, Greenberg, Solomon and Simon (1996) demonstrated that when mortality was salient, participants in a minimal group experiment showed stronger ingroup favouritism than when mortality was not salient (see also Castano, Yzerbyt, Paladino & Sacchi, 2002).

We have discussed various motives which have been proposed as triggers of identification, evaluation and behaviour related to own and other groups. However, research has not yet shed light on the question of *how* these motives function, or what motivational process might control intergroup behaviour. One approach to investigating underlying motivational processes was the *self-esteem hypothesis* (Hogg & Abrams, 1988). This hypothesis comprises two corollaries. Firstly, group members will enhance their self-esteem by discriminating against a relevant outgroup on important dimensions. Secondly, group members will show an enhanced tendency to discriminate against an outgroup when their self-esteem is low. In an insightful review, Rubin and Hewstone (1998) showed that the first corollary of the self-esteem hypothesis, wherein favouring the ingroup increases self-esteem, is generally well supported by several studies. However, the second corollary, wherein low self-esteem enhances ingroup-favouring behaviour, not only received less support but was also actually contradicted by several studies showing that *high* self-esteem enhances ingroup favouritism (e.g., Crocker, Thompson, McGraw & Ingerman, 1987). This failure to provide a convincing explanation of motivational processes of positive distinctiveness leads us to further direct our attention towards processes regulating intergroup behaviour.

Ingroup favouritism and outgroup derogation Let us return to the assumption of a motive for positive ingroup distinctiveness. Positive distinctiveness refers to the value difference between ingroup and outgroup. It can be established either by upgrading the ingroup above the outgroup or by downgrading the outgroup (or both). Some evidence suggests, however, that ingroup favouritism and outgroup derogation are driven by different psychological processes: ingroup favouritism is well predicted by the strength of ingroup identification, and outgroup derogation is predicted by perceived threat towards the ingroup (Struch & Schwartz, 1989). Applied to the minimal group situation, ingroup favouritism means that more positive outcomes are distributed to the ingroup, whereas outgroup derogation means that more

negative outcomes will be distributed to the outgroup. Research has shown a positive–negative asymmetry based on whether participants assign positive or negative outcomes to ingroup and outgroups. Individuals favour their ingroup over outgroups in terms of positive outcomes, but they do not generally disfavour outgroups by assigning them more negative outcomes than they do to the ingroup (Mummendey & Otten, 1998). Indeed, generally ingroup-favouring responses are more common than outgroup derogation, and 'aggravating conditions' such as negative intergroup emotions, threat or insult are required before group members demonstrate outgroup derogation (see Hewstone, Fincham & Jaspars, 1981).

The question now arises as to why people prefer to strive for positive distinctiveness through the distribution of positive rather than negative outcomes. Are positive outcomes more functional in fulfilling the need for positive distinctiveness than negative outcomes? One explanation for this asymmetry is the motivational orientation indicating how goals guide an individual's behaviour in a certain situation. These orientations may be focused either on gains and positive events or on losses and negative events. Higgins (1997) conceptualized these general goal orientations as *promotion* vs. *prevention* focus.

Based on Higgins's theory of motivational processes, Sassenberg, Kessler and Mummendey (2003) manipulated promotion focus within a gain/non-gain frame and prevention focus within a non-loss/loss frame concerning the money to be distributed between the groups. Moreover, valence of outcomes was manipulated by describing them as either an increment or a decrement in money for ingroup and outgroup. The results showed the predicted interaction between promotion/prevention and valence of outcomes. Group members with a promotion focus established positive distinctiveness only by distributing positive outcomes in favour of their ingroup. Group members with a prevention focus established positive distinctiveness only by distributing negative outcomes in favour of their ingroup (i.e., the ingroup receives less negative outcomes). Hence, group members attempt to establish positive distinctiveness only when their general motivational orientation fits the opportunities for differentiation. This could explain the positive–negative asymmetry in social discrimination if we assume that participants in previous experiments have been predominantly promotion focused. Arguably, in most psychological experiments, participants are made to expect gains (e.g., more or less money or course credits) or are even chronically promotion focused, which has been shown to be prevalent in western culture (Lee, Aaker & Gardner, 2000).

SUMMARY

The basic psychological processes guiding intergroup behaviour comprise social categorization, identification, intergroup perception and intergroup motivation. Identification connects individuals to social groups. Various motives (e.g., positive distinctiveness, uncertainty reduction) explain why group members favour their ingroup over an outgroup, but this more often takes the form of ingroup favouritism than outgroup derogation.

REDUCTION OF INTERGROUP CONFLICT

How can intergroup conflict be reduced?
What role does social categorization play in the reduction of prejudice?
What psychological processes improve attitudes towards outgroups and their members?

Prejudice, social discrimination and intergroup conflict are some of the most pressing current societal problems. How can social psychology contribute towards improving intergroup relations? More than half a century ago, Gordon Allport (1954b) proposed the highly influential *contact hypothesis*. He suggested that contact between members of different groups would improve intergroup relations and reduce prejudice provided that it occurred under certain conditions. These conditions were (1) equal status for the members of both groups in the contact situation; (2) superordinate goals (i.e., members should be positively interdependent within the contact situations); (3) no competition between the group members; and (4) support by norms and institutional authorities. According to Pettigrew (1998), these four conditions were initially conceived as being necessary for contact to reduce prejudice. It was thought that if one of these conditions was not fulfilled, then contact between members of different social groups might not only fail to reduce prejudice, it might even confirm and strengthen prejudice.

contact hypothesis the idea that contact between members of different social groups under appropriate conditions will reduce their prejudice against each other

Allport's conjectures stimulated a vast number of empirical studies concerning the effect of contact on prejudice as well as numerous policy-making programs concerned with improving ethnic relations in schools and workplaces. In a meta-analysis of more than 500 studies, Pettigrew and Tropp (2000, 2006) found that the greater the contact between groups, the lower the prejudice expressed. Only about 6 per cent of the studies showed the reverse effect of more contact being associated with increased prejudice. For the various studies included in the meta-analysis, Allport's conditions for contact were sometimes fulfilled, sometimes only to a lesser extent, and sometimes not at all. Nevertheless, across all studies there was a substantial positive effect of contact on the reduction of prejudice. Pettigrew and Tropp (2000, 2006) therefore conclude that Allport's original contact conditions are not *necessary* for positive contact effects to occur, but are *facilitating* conditions that are likely to make contact more effective. Confirming this view, studies that realized Allport's conditions showed stronger effects of contact than those that did not.

In many of the studies analysed by Pettigrew and Tropp, contact and prejudice were assessed at the same time using cross-sectional designs. It is therefore not clear whether contact reduces prejudice or whether perhaps less prejudiced individuals simply seek more contact with outgroup members whereas more prejudiced individuals avoid contact with outgroup members. Experimental studies and longitudinal studies have, however, now resolved this issue. Experimental studies (e.g., Wilder, 1986) have shown that participants who engage in positive intergroup contact show less prejudice than those in control conditions. Longitudinal studies have revealed that contact assessed at earlier points in time reduces prejudice at later points in time (e.g., Levin, van Laar & Sidanius, 2003).

A detailed analysis of those few studies which show that contact is associated with increased prejudice indicates that there may be 'negative contact conditions' that must be avoided if contact is to have a positive effect. Negative contact conditions include when contact is *not frequent enough* for acquaintanceship to develop, or when the contact situation is *threatening* or even *anxiety provoking*. Based on their analysis, Pettigrew and Tropp (2006) proposed a

---

PIONEER

Gordon Willard Allport (1897–1967) was born in Montezuma, Indiana. He received his PhD in psychology in 1922 from Harvard, following in the footsteps of his brother Floyd, who also became an important social psychologist (see Chapter 1, this volume). He completed additional studies in Berlin, Hamburg and Cambridge before returning to Harvard. His career was spent examining social issues such as prejudice and developing personality tests. Allport's most significant books are *Pattern and Growth in Personality* (1965), *The Person in Psychology* (1968) and *The Nature of Prejudice* (1954). His work on contact between social groups has inspired a huge amount of research on ways to reduce prejudice and decrease conflict in intergroup relations. In commenting on his 1954 book, he considered that it 'had done something good in the world'.

Plate 14.4 *People who engage in positive intergroup contact show less prejudice.*

reformulation of the contact hypothesis, moving away from conditions necessary for positive contact towards negative conditions that must be avoided in order that positive contact effects are not wiped out. Contact opportunities should occur frequently enough and particular attention should be given to assuring that the contact situation will not stimulate feelings of threat and anxiety in the participants. Pettigrew and Tropp placed great emphasis on the importance of developing cross-group friendships. In general, this reformulation of the contact hypothesis leads to a much more optimistic view of contact than the original formulation, since preconditions for positive effects can now be met more easily.

Three models of contact between social groups

When considering positive effects of contact on intergroup relations, we obviously want to see these effects reach beyond those group members involved in the particular situation where contact was established. We are interested in generalizing the positive effects of contact beyond the specific situation to as many other situations as possible and beyond specific group members to the outgroup as a whole.

Precisely this issue of generalization lead to the development of three different models of intergroup contact: The *decategorization* model (Brewer & Miller, 1984), the *common ingroup identity* model (Gaertner et al., 1989) and the *mutual distinctiveness* model (Brown & Hewstone, 2005; Hewstone & Brown, 1986).

Although all three models are built on the same foundation of social identity theory (Tajfel & Turner, 1986), they yield very different predictions. According to social identity theory, categorization into ingroup and outgroup with its assimilation and contrast effects (see above) often enforces ingroup favouritism and lessens outgroup acceptance. Therefore, Brewer and Miller (1984) suggested that contact situations should be created in which categorization between groups is prevented, whilst encouraging group members to perceive differences between all individuals irrespective of their group member-

decategorization reduction of the salience of ingroup–outgroup distinctions in order to establish interpersonal contact

ship. In their *decategorization* model, the contact situation is designed to provide conditions in which participants can interact more in terms of their personal identity (i.e., as individuals) than in terms of their social identity (i.e., as group members). The original categorization is designed to become less and less meaningful as well as less useful. Brewer and Miller consider Allport's original contact conditions to provide support for their model. They claim that the conditions expected to strengthen the potential of interpersonal friendships specifically function by strengthening decategorization.

Several studies support the decategorization model (e.g., Bettencourt, Brewer, Croak & Miller, 1992). In these studies, participants, having been categorized into two groups, had to interact. In an *interpersonal focus* condition, participants were instructed to form an accurate impression of their co-workers as individuals; in a *task-oriented* condition, they had to focus on the characteristics

Plate 14.5 *Cross-cutting categorizations that are of equal importance to the pre-existing categorizations (e.g. religion in Northern Ireland) are difficult to find outside the laboratory.*

of the task. The results show that an interpersonal focus leads to more individuated perceptions of outgroup members, more positive evaluation of outgroup members, and less bias between ingroup and outgroup compared to the task-focus condition (see also Ensari & Miller, 2002). Decategorized contact reduces prejudice because former outgroup members are perceived in a more differentiated manner. Another form of differentiation can be achieved by introducing cross-cutting social categories (see Crisp & Hewstone, 1999, for a review). Bias can be reduced when members belonging to ingroup and outgroup on one dimension (e.g., an Asian vs. a white person) are simultaneously made to be ingroup members on a second dimension (e.g., an Asian and a white person who both support the same political party). Because people simultaneously belong to multiple groups, there ought to be great potential to find cross-cutting categorizations that can be used to provide individuals with some form of shared group membership. However, there are limits to this approach because, outside the laboratory, it is so difficult to find cross-cutting categorizations that are of equal importance to the pre-existing categorizations (e.g., race in the United States, or religion in Northern Ireland).

Interventions based on the decategorization model provide conditions whereby individuals no longer approach others in terms of group membership, but instead recognize them as individuals. The next question to be addressed is, how might processes of decategorization be generalized beyond individuals in a particular contact situation, thus more generally reducing intergroup bias and prejudice? The answer to this question does not involve generalizing the particular attitude or evaluation represented by a particular individual who was encountered in a particular contact situation. What must be generalized is a new habit of ignoring categories and focusing on interindividual differences when evaluating and interacting with others.

This would mean that in order to reduce prejudice and increase acceptance of outgroups, individuals would have to abandon their ingroup and their social identity. Realistically, however, individuals very often cherish their specific group memberships and social identities. Gaertner, Dovidio and their colleagues therefore

common ingroup identity model of intergroup contact which replaces salient ingroup–outgroup distinctions at a subordinate level with a common ingroup identity at a superordinate level that includes former ingroup and outgroup members

looked for a way to improve intergroup relations whilst retaining explicit salience of individuals' ingroup and social identity. They proposed the *common ingroup identity* model (e.g., Gaertner et al., 1989). In contrast to decategorization, they proposed replacing existing categorizations with recategorization on a higher, superordinate level. The problematic distinction between ingroup and outgroup is thus replaced by a new common ingroup, which makes the former outgroup part of an extended new ingroup. The former outgroup now profits from ingroup favouritism and former outgroup members are correspondingly evaluated more positively.

Several studies have demonstrated that recategorization of ingroup and outgroup members and forming a common ingroup identity actually improve the evaluation of former *outgroup* members, whereas decategorization led to less favourable evaluations of former *ingroup* members (Gaertner & Dovidio, 2000; Gaertner, Dovidio, Nier, Ward & Banker, 1999). Thus conditions of contact between members of different groups which increase the salience of a common ingroup identity decrease prejudice against former outgroups.

Unfortunately, the blessing of a common identity for the former outgroup may be accompanied by perils for a new outgroup. The former intergroup categorization may simply be replaced by a new one, and prejudice and devaluation of the new outgroups may resurface (Kessler & Mummendey, 2001). For example, enlargement of the European Union may promote more positive attitudes of Germans towards Poles (both share membership of the EU), but it may worsen attitudes towards Americans as a new outgroup (at this new level of categorization). The decategorization and recategorization models predict that contact will have positive effects by reducing the salience of prior social categorizations. Although there is empirical support for both approaches, people are in many cases reluctant to give up their social identity outside the laboratory. Does this lead to the conclusion that intergroup prejudice and discrimination are therefore inevitable?

Hewstone and Brown (1986; Brown, Vivian & Hewstone, 1999) searched for a solution to this dilemma and proposed their *mutual distinctiveness* model. This model assumes that neither interpersonal (i.e., decategorization) nor intragroup (i.e., recategorization) contact has the potential to reduce negative attitudes and emotions towards a particular outgroup. Neither model is able to repair the problematic relationship between ingroup and outgroup; instead, they both avoid it, either by decategorizing or by recategorizing as a new identity. The mutual distinctiveness model, in contrast, explicitly addresses and aims to improve the problematic intergroup relationship.

Earlier studies on intergroup evaluations demonstrated that overall ingroup favouritism could be eradicated if ingroups could make intergroup comparisons on more than one dimension and

mutual distinctiveness recommendation to establish intergroup contact while keeping group memberships salient in order to foster generalization of contact experience to the whole outgroup

create positive ingroup distinctiveness on ingroup-relevant dimensions at the same time as conceding outgroup superiority on other dimensions (Mummendey & Schreiber, 1983; Mummendey & Simon, 1989). For example, university lecturers might acknowledge that they earn lower salaries than lawyers, but they could emphasize that their jobs are more interesting and satisfying.

Corresponding to this principle, Hewstone and Brown stress the importance of members of both groups developing their positive distinctiveness by recognizing the mutual superiority of groups when evaluated across various dimensions. This model was supported by evidence from several lines of empirical research. Most importantly, there is now extensive evidence that intergroup contact has a stronger effect on prejudice reduction when group members' social categories are salient than when they are not (see Brown & Hewstone, 2005, for a review). In a series of studies, Wilder (1986) led participants to interact with an individual who was allegedly an outgroup member (actually she was a confederate) who behaved in either a positive or negative manner, and who was either typical or atypical of the outgroup. As one would expect, the outgroup member was evaluated more positively when she behaved in a positive and cooperative manner. However, the evaluation of the outgroup as a whole was moderated by the perceived typicality of the outgroup member: it was only when the outgroup member was seen as typical that the positive contact experience led to a significantly more positive evaluation of the outgroup as a whole (see also González & Brown, in press; Harwood, Hewstone, Paolini & Voci, 2005; Voci & Hewstone, 2003).

A potential problem of the mutual distinctiveness model is that it could be especially difficult to achieve positive intergroup contact experiences when intergroup categorization remains salient (e.g., Islam & Hewstone, 1993). In the meantime, however, several studies have shown that positive contact experiences are, as a general rule, found even under high salience of group membership (see Brown & Hewstone, 2005, for a review).

Obviously, all three approaches (decategorization, recategorization and mutual distinctiveness) carry their respective benefits. Pettigrew (1998) proposed that the three models, each with its individual advantages, can be integrated into a more comprehensive approach by ordering them on a time scale. He suggested that contact might be much more easily initiated under conditions of decategorization, especially if the groups involved find themselves in strong conflict. Only after individuals from the two groups have experienced a certain degree of positive contact would their group memberships then be made increasingly salient, thereby leading to the generalization of positive contact experiences to the outgroup as a whole. In a final step, members of the two groups could be made not only to recognize their mutual superiority, but also to perceive ingroup and outgroup as belonging to one superordinate group with complete assimilation of prior ingroup and outgroup into one common identity. Pettigrew (1998) pointed out, however, that this sequence may terminate before all three stages have been achieved. This may be especially likely when original group memberships are not easily abandoned and recategorization is resisted. In this case, group members may prefer to maintain mutual recognition as separate groups, but also to acknowledge that they share a common group identity at a superordinate level

RESEARCH CLOSE-UP 14.2

Some of my best friends have friends who are . . . : Effects of direct and indirect contact

Paolini, S., Hewstone, M., Cairns, E. & Voci, A. (2004). Effects of direct and indirect cross-group friendships on judgments of Catholics and Protestants in Northern Ireland: The mediating role of an anxiety-reduction mechanism. *Personality and Social Psychology Bulletin, 30,* 770–786.

Introduction

Contact between members of rival social groups can reduce prejudice between them. Friendships across the group divide (so-called direct friendships) are a particularly powerful way of reducing prejudice (Pettigrew, 1998). In addition, the indirect friendship hypothesis suggests that simply knowing other ingroup members who have friendships with outgroup members can also lead to a reduction in prejudice (Wright, Aron, McLaughlin-Volpe & Ropp, 1997). A survey study tested these two hypotheses in the context of the long and continuing intergroup conflict between Catholics and Protestants in Northern Ireland, where the vast majority of school pupils attend schools with members of the same religious groups as themselves, but those who go on to university experience a desegregated social environment. The study focused on the reduction of prejudice and an increase in perceived outgroup variability as a further indicator of improvement of intergroup relations. It also assessed intergroup anxiety as a potential mediator variable between direct and indirect friendship experiences and outcome measures.

Method

A survey study measured direct and indirect friendship as predictor variables, intergroup anxiety as a mediator, and prejudice and perceived outgroup variability as criterion variables.

Participants

Three hundred and forty-one students in Northern Ireland participated in the survey. The sample involved 148 male and 190 female participants with a mean age of 23.13 years (three respondents did not report their gender). Participants identified themselves as belonging to either the Catholic ($N = 178$) or the Protestant ($N = 163$) community.

Design and procedure

Students participated voluntarily in the study. The questionnaires included the following main items: (1) direct cross-group friendships (number of close outgroup friends at home and at university); (2) indirect cross-group friendships (number of ingroup friends who had close friendships with members of the other community); (3) intergroup anxiety ('imagine you meet members of the other community that are complete strangers to you: how would you feel compared to an occasion where you meet members of your own community?'; participants rated feelings such as awkward, relaxed, defensive, etc.); (4) prejudice (a 'feeling thermometer', ranging from extremely unfavourable to extremely favourable feelings towards the outgroup); and (5) perceived outgroup variability (e.g., 'there are many different types of people in the other community').

Results

As predicted, both direct and extended contact were associated with lower levels of prejudice and with increased perceived outgroup variability. Moreover, both contact variables were also substantially and negatively correlated with intergroup anxiety, which itself was negatively associated with prejudice and positively associated with outgroup variability. Further analyses revealed that anxiety *completely* mediated the relationship between direct contact and perceived variability and between extended contact and prejudice. Anxiety *partially* mediated the link between direct contact and prejudice and between extended contact and variability.

Discussion

The results of the study demonstrate a positive association between both direct and indirect cross-group friendships and improved intergroup relations. Moreover, the research identified intergroup anxiety as a strong mediating variable between outgroup friendships and the outcome variables. Hence, intergroup contact is associated with reduced anxiety; reduced anxiety, in turn, is associated with lower prejudice and greater perceived outgroup variability. These results were replicated in a second survey reported in the same paper, based on a representative sample of the population of Northern Ireland.

Although very compelling, the authors point out that the findings should be read with some caution due to the cross-sectional design of their research, which cannot demonstrate causal relationships between variables. Thus, it may be equally plausible that higher prejudice also relates to higher intergroup anxiety and to fewer direct and indirect outgroup friendships. Research on intergroup contact in general, however, shows a stronger effect from contact to prejudice than vice versa (see Brown & Hewstone, 2005; Pettigrew & Tropp, 2006) and effects of contact have been confirmed in experimental and longitudinal studies.

(e.g., the English, Welsh and Scots who are all also British). Gaertner and Dovidio refer to this as a 'dual identity' model.

Psychological processes in prejudice reduction

In his initial presentation of the contact hypothesis, Allport (1954b) did not explicitly describe the psychological processes involved in the reduction of prejudice. How, then, does contact reduce prejudice? What psychological processes mediate the effect of the contact situation on prejudice reduction? Pettigrew (1998) proposes four main classes of psychological processes that may mediate the influence of contact on prejudice reduction: (1) increased information about the outgroup; (2) changing behaviour; (3) affective ties; and (4) reappraisal of the ingroup.

In contact situations it is possible to gather new information about the outgroup and its members, thereby changing initial stereotypes. According to Rothbart and John's (1985) cognitive analysis, modifying stereotypes is difficult because stereotype-inconsistent information only changes existing stereotypes under certain conditions. An outgroup member who strongly contradicts a particular stereotype is easily explained away as an exception (a process known as 'subtyping'; see Chapter 4, this volume). For example, a female who has all the qualities of a manager (such as assertive and confident, i.e., stereotype-disconfirming information for a woman) may be subcategorized as a 'career woman', thereby leaving the stereotype of 'women' unchanged. Stereotype-disconfirming information will most effectively change an existing stereotype if it is distributed across many exemplars who are generally seen to be typical members of the group (Hewstone, 1994; Richards & Hewstone, 2001). This is consistent with the idea that group membership must be salient during contact for existing stereotypes to be changed.

According to Pettigrew (1998), alternative psychological processes of prejudice reduction are guided by behavioural changes. When prejudiced individuals have contact with outgroups and experience this contact positively (or, at least, less negatively than expected), they will experience a feeling of 'cognitive dissonance' due to the fact that their behaviour is inconsistent with their pre-existing attitude (see Chapter 7, this volume). This dissonance may, in turn, lead to a subsequent reduction in prejudice (Aronson & Patnoe, 1997). In addition, according to self-perception theory (Bem, 1972; see Chapter 6, this volume), individuals without strong prejudices may simply observe themselves in new contact situations and thereby infer from their own friendly behaviour that they are not prejudiced.

Research has recently redirected the focus away from cognitive towards affective processes in reducing prejudice (see Brown & Hewstone, 2005), and Pettigrew and Tropp (2006) reveal that contact has markedly strong effects on affective measures. Emotions are clearly critical when it comes to intergroup contact. As a prime example, *intergroup anxiety* is a negative affective reaction that plays a central role in contact situations (Greenland & Brown, 1999; Stephan & Stephan, 1985). Initial intergroup encounters carry an especially strong potential for intergroup anxiety. Several studies have underlined the role of intergroup anxiety within contact settings, typically showing a positive relationship between anxiety and prejudice (Islam & Hewstone, 1993; Voci & Hewstone, 2003). Thus, research on contact between Catholics and Protestants in Northern Ireland (see Research close-up 14.2) has shown that quality and quantity of outgroup contact are associated with reduced intergroup anxiety, which, in turn, is associated with more positive views of the outgroup (Paolini et al., 2004). Sustained contact typically reduces intergroup anxiety. Moreover, recent research indicates that not only direct contact but also 'indirect' or 'extended' contact (knowing other ingroup members who have outgroup friends) reduces negative attitudes towards the outgroup (Liebkind & McAlister, 1999; Wright et al., 1997).

A final broad psychological process through which contact may reduce prejudice is that of ingroup reappraisal (Pettigrew, 1998). Intergroup contact leads to new insights not only concerning the outgroup but also regarding the *ingroup*. Positive contact with members of outgroups can lead to a reappraisal of the ingroup and a weakening of the conviction that the ingroup is the standard against which other groups must be compared. Pettigrew (1997) showed that outgroup friendship reduces ingroup pride and produces more generally positive attitudes towards outgroups. Moreover, the positive experiences of intergroup contact with members of one outgroup (e.g., contact between white and black people) can lead to more positive evaluations of quite different outgroups whose members one has not even encountered (e.g., immigrants).

Finally, as pointed out by Hewstone (2003), an important question remains as to why contact does not always prevent intergroup conflict. There are abundant examples of intergroup conflicts that emerge after a long period of contact between groups (e.g., Yugoslavia, Rwanda). Why did previous contact not prevent these

intergroup anxiety the feeling of uneasiness or anxiety when one imagines having contact with unknown members of an outgroup

Plate 14.6 *Why did previous contact not prevent conflict in former Yugoslavia?*

conflicts? One possible answer can be found in the previous pages of this chapter. As soon as changes in structural conditions result in negative interdependence concerning valuable resources, or as soon as a group recognizes a threat to its values posed by an out-group (which may well have remained undetected over a long period of time), then intergroup conflicts can re-emerge. Intense negative emotions towards the outgroup can quickly escalate the conflict. Intergroup anxiety reduces trust and enhances a group's or group member's need for safety. And resentment towards an outgroup leads to collective actions aimed at changing intergroup relations perceived as unjust.

SUMMARY

Contact between members of different social groups can help to reduce prejudice and intergroup conflict. Three models of intergroup contact (i.e., decategorization, recategorization and mutual distinctiveness) propose ways in which the contact situation should be structured in order to improve intergroup relations. This can occur via a number of mediating psychological processes, especially reduced intergroup anxiety.

SUMMARY AND CONCLUSIONS

- Prejudice is a negative and hostile attitude towards a social group and its members based on their group membership.

- The authoritarian personality approach and social dominance theory attempt to explain prejudice by focusing on the prejudiced individual.

- The relations between social groups determine the attitudes and behaviours of group members: negative interdependence leads to intergroup conflict, whereas positive interdependence carries the potential for harmonious relations.

- Intergroup behaviour under minimal conditions can be explained by social categorization, identification, social comparison and the need for positive distinctiveness.

- Social categorization leads to assimilation of individuals within and contrast of individuals between categories.

- Ingroup identification associates the self with a particular social group, thereby conveying psychological relevance to this social category.

- Intergroup comparisons lead to the evaluation of an ingroup relative to an outgroup on valued dimensions.

- Prejudice is the outcome of intergroup evaluation, which can be conceptualized as either an attitude or a group-based emotion.

- Intergroup contact is very effective in reducing prejudice and intergroup conflict.

- Allport's conditions for positive contact are not essential but, rather, facilitate positive contact effects. The reformulated contact hypothesis suggests that contact should be frequent enough and neither threatening nor anxiety-provoking. Under these conditions, contact tends to reduce prejudice, especially where cross-group friendships occur.

- Affective ties and the reduction of intergroup anxiety are powerful processes of prejudice reduction.

Suggestions for further reading

Brewer, M.B. (2001). *Intergroup relations* (2nd edn). Buckingham: Open University Press. Provides an overview of intergroup phenomena and their explanations.

Brown, R. (1995). *Prejudice: Its social psychology*. Oxford: Blackwell. A readable and comprehensive introduction to the topic of prejudice.

Brown, R. & Hewstone, M. (2005). An integrative theory of intergroup contact. In M. Zanna (Ed.), *Advances in experimental social psychology* (Vol. 37, pp. 355–343). San Diego, CA: Academic Press. A comprehensive overview of research on contact, with a strong focus on salient intergroup contact and mediating variables.

Dovidio, J., Glick, P. & Rudman, L.A. (Eds.) (2005). *On the nature of prejudice: Fifty years after Allport*. Oxford: Blackwell. A review of the field since Allport, organized around the themes that he originally outlined.

Gaertner, S.L. & Dovidio, J.F. (2000). *Reducing intergroup bias: The common ingroup identity model*. Philadelphia: Psychology Press. Describes new developments concerning the common ingroup identity model with respect to the reduction of modern forms of prejudice.

Mackie, D.M. & Smith, E.R. (Eds.) (2002). *From prejudice to intergroup emotions: Differentiated reactions to social groups*. New York and Hove: Psychology Press. An edited collection of various perspectives on the emerging field of intergroup emotions.

15

Social Psychology in Action

Klaus Jonas and Carmen Lebherz

CHAPTER OUTLINE

We begin by addressing how social psychology can be applied to real life, what methodological issues are involved in this endeavour, and how application can inform social psychological theories. We then describe the application of social psychology to three important topics: advertising, the workplace and health.

First, we discuss social psychological foundations of advertising. After reviewing some of the major theoretical models developed by advertising researchers, we argue that these models can be fruitfully subsumed under the more general dual-process approach to attitude change (introduced in Chapter 7, this volume). To illustrate the usefulness of the dual-process approach, we then discuss several advertising techniques in terms of dual-process theories of attitude change. Second, we apply social psychology to the workplace. We show how individuals form attitudes about their jobs, the organizations in which they work and the fairness of everyday work life. We discuss how to increase employees' job satisfaction levels, how to motivate them to be supportive towards their colleagues, and how to increase their commitment towards the organization. Finally, we turn to matters of health. We describe social psychology's important contributions to the prediction of health behaviour and to bringing about change of maladaptive behaviours, and the important role of social psychological factors in coping with stressors.

Introduction

This chapter begins with some thoughts on how we can apply the wide array of social psychological theories and research to our everyday lives, including attempts to find remedies for individual and societal problems as well as providing instruments for increasing the effectiveness of economic or political endeavours. This involves both methodological questions and the relationship between basic and applied research. We then move on to three specific areas of everyday life that have benefited greatly from social psychological research.

The first area involves advertising, i.e., attempts to influence our attitudes and behaviour regarding consumer products. Billions of Euros are invested every year with the aim of influencing consumers to buy items for daily consumption, luxury goods, technical products, services and so on (Solomon, 2004). Marketers and advertisers have long been developing influence strategies, some of which are more intuitive, while others are more scientifically based. Of course, advertising has many points of contact with social psychological theories of persuasion (see Chapter 7, this volume). One of the most effective theoretical frameworks in persuasion is the dual-process approach. Social psychologists developed dual-process models during the 1970s, long after advertisers began to practise successful advertising. We will show below, however, that most, if not all, types of advertising can be better understood by being analysed within the conceptual framework of dual-process models. Thus, we will argue that familiar advertising techniques such as comparative advertising or publicizing brand extensions are instances of processes operating under the high or low elaboration mode, respectively.

The second major part of this chapter deals with organizational behaviour. Workplace activity is inherently social in nature. Indeed, most employees spend a large proportion of their work time communicating with colleagues, evaluating their organization's fairness and forming an opinion about their team's work atmosphere and support. Every day, team members make decisions that directly affect work outcomes, e.g., whether to fill in for an overloaded colleague to ensure that the work gets done. We will look at the major work outcomes of organizational behaviour and how they are affected by employees' attitudes, job characteristics and the social processes common in the workplace. Although organizational behaviour appears to bear few similarities to advertising and consumer behaviour, we will illustrate how both areas have profited greatly from social psychological research on attitudes. Of course, much of organizational behaviour also has to do with the issues of group processes and leadership; these questions have already been dealt with in Chapter 13, this volume.

As a final example of addressing real-life problems by means of social psychological theorizing, we will address the topic of health. Health and illness are among the most pressing concerns of today's society, given the increasing costs of health services and the demographic trends according to which populations all over the world are becoming increasingly older. Social psychological theories can help us to identify the determinants of health-impairing behaviours, such as smoking or having unprotected sex, and to design interventions aimed at changing these behaviours. Apart from maladaptive behaviour, a major threat to the health and well-being of today's populations is stress. We will show how social psychological research generates predictions regarding stress-ameliorating factors such as coping styles as well as social support from one's partner, friends or colleagues. We will place special emphasis on stress at the workplace, thus linking our coverage of health to the preceding discussion of organizational behaviour, because of the large number of hours that many members of today's population spend working.

APPLYING SOCIAL PSYCHOLOGY

Social psychology and its relation to the 'real world'

Why is social psychology important to our society's most crucial issues?

Social psychology is the discipline within psychology that focuses on how social situations determine human behaviour. A major aspect of situations is the presence of fellow humans: if two or more individuals come together, a social context for individuals develops. Recall Gordon Allport's (1954a) definition from Chapter 1: 'Social psychology is the attempt to understand and explain how the thoughts, feelings, and behaviors of individuals are influenced by the actual, imagined, or implied presence of other human beings' (p. 5). As humans are a thoroughly social species, large parts of our lives take place in the company of others: we grow up in families, kindergartens and schools; we play on sports teams, attend committees and form work teams; we communicate face to face or via telephone, letters or email with family and friends, colleagues and supervisors.

Indeed, social psychology is ubiquitous in our daily lives, and this is why social psychology is readily applicable and has been widely applied to the 'real world'. For example, medical emergency teams have to make decisions of utmost importance under great time pressure, and social psychology has suggested how team members should be coordinated to prevent bad decisions (e.g., Tschan et al., 2006). Aggression is prevalent in hooligans who gather to attack opposing groups or destroy property, or in neo-Nazis who attack immigrants (see Chapter 8, this volume); social psychology helps us to understand how prejudice shapes behaviour, what instigates intergroup aggression and how to reduce such hostility (see Chapter 14). Applying social psychology to some

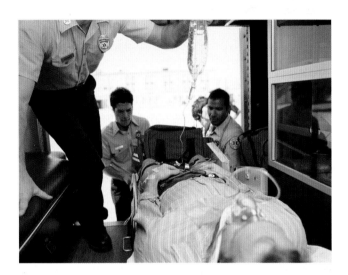

Plate 15.1 *Medical emergency teams have to make vital decisions under great time pressure.*

of our society's most pressing social problems and phenomena comes naturally. Indeed, throughout the previous chapters, we have already introduced many successful applications of social psychological knowledge.

Applied social psychology and its relation to basic research

How do basic and applied research benefit from each other?

Applied social psychology is the part of the discipline of social psychology that takes what we have learned from basic research and seeks to apply it in real life. In part, social psychology helps to solve, or at least ameliorate, social problems. To do so, applied research asks about the causes of a social problem and designs, implements and evaluates interventions accordingly. For example, alcohol consumption on student campuses is a huge problem in many countries. Especially 'binge drinkers', i.e., those who have more than four drinks in a row, are likely to experience alcohol-related problems such as missing classes, having unprotected sex or being physically injured (Wechsler et al., 2002). When traditional interventions such as awareness campaigns failed to reduce drinking rates, social psychological evidence on the influence of norms on behaviour came into play.

Recall that norms are rules that prescribe attitudes and behaviours appropriate in a group (see Chapters 11 and 12, this volume). Social psychological research has shown that group members tend to conform to group norms because norms become part of the individual's belief and value system (Turner, 1991). Furthermore, norms can be misperceived. With regard to alcohol consumption, research has shown that when students consider other students, they assume that more of them binge drink than is actually the case (Perkins & Berkowitz, 1986; see also Chapter 3, this volume). Thus, a misperception of an 'on-campus drinking norm' exists ('everybody binge drinks') that leads students to conform to the norm. If this hypothesis is correct, changing perceptions of the norm should lead to decreased drinking on campus. This is indeed what researchers and health practitioners found

(a)

(b)

Plates 15.2a and b *When students consider other students, they assume that more of them binge drink than is actually the case.*

when they first intervened and tried to change norms by way of flyers, posters and advertisements (Haines & Barker, 2003; Haines & Spear, 1996). Figure 15.1 depicts a poster that shows the actual norm as found in surveys, i.e., that most students drink alcohol rather moderately. By informing students about these facts, moderate drinking behaviour is normalized and normative pressure to drink among students decreases.

Whereas basic research develops and tests theories that explain relationships between social constructs, e.g., the influence of (misperceived) norms on behaviour, applied social psychology centres around a social problem and searches for solutions to this problem, e.g., binge drinking on campus. Only if we can identify the social causes of behaviour can we predict future behaviour and develop interventions aimed at changing that behaviour. We need sound theories in order to derive sound hypotheses about how to intervene in a real-life problem.

Thus, real-life problems profit from basic research in that theories, paradigms, concepts and basic research results guide the search for solutions. Theories and research results restrict the wide range of possible actions to a set derived from prior scientific knowledge. With regard to binge drinking, hypotheses about which intervention to choose after others had failed were not developed in a vacuum but deduced from theories of social norms, which also summarize how misconceptions of norms develop and why individuals adapt their behaviour to such norms. Can successful application also improve basic research and theory?

We can think of the relationship between basic and applied social psychology as a reciprocal process, like the one depicted in Figure 15.2. Theories (box 1) that have been developed and tested in basic research (box 2) are applied to social problems (box 3). These theories can provide important insights into the nature and causes of these problems, insights that can help to suggest solutions (box 4). Based on these theoretical ideas, interventions are

DRINKING AT NIU

MOST
NIU students (72%) drink 5 or fewer drinks when they "party"

MOST
NIU students did not cause physical harm to self (80%) or others (91%) as a consequence of drinking.

NEARLY ALL
NIU students (97%) disapprove of drunkenness which interferes with responsibilities.

*A DRINK = a bottle of beer,
            a glass of wine,
            a wine cooler,
            a shot of liqueur
            or a mixed drink

Figure 15.1 *Changing the social norm of drinking (www.socialnorms.org).*

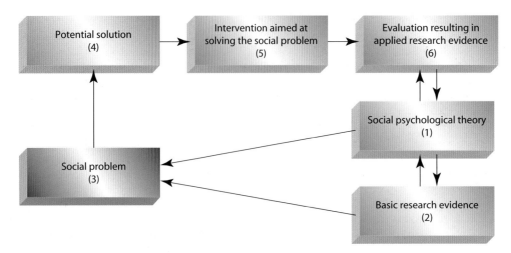

Figure 15.2 *The relation between theory and practice.*

developed with the aim of reducing or solving the social problem (box 5). The process does not end here, however. The efficacy of these interventions has to be evaluated (box 6), and the information gained from this evaluation reflects on the validity of the theory on which the intervention has been based and thus might lead to modification of that theory (box 1). Empirical confirmation in a real-life setting increases our confidence in the predictive power of that theory, whereas disconfirmation often shows us ways to improve the theory and thus promotes theoretical advancement. Improved theories will enable us to suggest better solutions for change, or optimization, when faced with future practical problems.

Sometimes applied social psychology starts from theories developed in basic research. At other times the starting point is in the real world, with a pressing social issue at hand and an observation that leads to an initial hypothesis and, later, theory building. Whatever the starting point, however, basic and applied social psychology should never be viewed and implemented separately, but in a way that promotes the advancement of both. We can thus complement Kurt Lewin's famous statement that 'there is nothing so practical as a good theory' (1951, p. 169) by adding that 'there is also nothing so good for theory as practice and application'.

Methodological differences between basic and applied social psychology

How do we adapt our methods to real-life situations?

Note that we described the experiment as the dominant research method in social psychology (see Chapter 2, this volume) because it can identify whether a manipulated (independent) variable causes a change in the measured (dependent) variable. We also pointed out that random assignment of participants to experimental conditions was the key feature of experimental research. In applied research, however, there are three major barriers to the use of random assignment which make it necessary to adapt our methods to the circumstances.

First, in some situations random assignment is impossible for ethical or practical reasons. For example, if we want to investigate school bullying (e.g., Smith & Brain, 2000), we cannot randomly assign pupils to the roles of victims and bullies. Similarly, if we want to study the impact of marital bereavement on health, we cannot assign participants randomly to bereaved or non-bereaved conditions (Stroebe, 2001). In these situations, we have to rely on quasi-experimental studies, which are in fact cross-sectional or longitudinal observational studies that compare groups that experience a given stressor (e.g., bullying or partner loss) to matched control groups that did not suffer this stress experience.

Second, there are also situations in which random assignment would be possible in principle, but difficult or impossible to implement in practice. For example, if we want to study the effects of job rotation at an assembly line, we could, in principle, implement rotation in 10 departments with an assembly line and compare the productivity and work satisfaction of workers in those departments with those of workers in 10 other departments with assembly lines, but without job rotation. The problem with this plan is that even large organizations rarely have 20 departments that use comparable assembly lines. Furthermore, even if an organization had sufficient departments for such a study, the time and effort of doing this research would be prohibitive. In practice, we would therefore end up with one or two intervention departments where we rotated jobs and one or two control departments where we did not. Since these departments would differ in many other respects, we would be conducting a quasi-experiment rather than a proper field experiment.

Third, in the real world the external context in which we conduct our study often changes, subjecting research participants to sources of influence that are beyond the control of the researcher. For example, the organization in which we do our research might implement organization-wide changes, or some people will leave departments during the study and new people will come in. In community interventions that assess the impact of health campaigns, the problem frequently arises that mass media or government sources may provide additional health information that affects both the intervention and the control communities (e.g., Luepker et al., 1994).

Thus, although applied researchers conduct experiments, some in the laboratory but mostly using field settings, they have greater difficulty than basic researchers in safeguarding the internal validity of their studies. Fortunately, they have at their disposal sophisticated statistical methods that allow them to deal with many of the threats to the internal validity of their research. Furthermore, applied research gains from being more externally and ecologically valid than laboratory studies because it is conducted in the field and under natural circumstances. Since the different strengths of basic and applied research complement each other, the reciprocal link between these two approaches is of great value for progress in social psychology.

SUMMARY

It comes naturally to social psychology to help develop solutions for some of the major problems of today's society, such as unhealthy or aggressive behaviour. Sometimes a pressing problem stimulates interventions and only later advances theory building. At other times, theories already exist and guide practitioners to new paths that will bring improvements. In either direction, basic and applied research, theory and practice, work together and complement each other. As field research does not allow for as much control over situational circumstances as laboratory research, applied researchers have to deal with different methodological issues than basic researchers. It is more difficult to establish causality in applied studies conducted in the field than it is in laboratory experiments. However, applied studies often benefit from high external validity and bring the satisfaction of helping to solve problems and implement change.

SOCIAL PSYCHOLOGY AND ADVERTISING

Models of advertising effectiveness

How does advertising influence consumers?
What are the similarities and differences between models of advertising and general theories of persuasion?

A recent video clip on MySwitzerland.com, the official homepage of the national Swiss tourism organization, contains a photo session and an interview with Michael Schumacher, famous Formula 1 driver, after he landed by helicopter on the spectacular Aletsch glacier in the Swiss Alps. The interviewer asks him to describe his

Plate 15.3 *Could a famous personality such as Michael Schumacher be used to sell a product, such as taking holidays in Switzerland?*

image of Switzerland. His answer includes associating Switzerland with terrific landscapes, freedom and security. Do you think this clip will advance tourism in Switzerland? If so, why? You have already read an introduction to the topic of attitude change and persuasion (see Chapter 7, this volume). The earlier chapter paid particular attention to dual-process models and relevant supportive evidence. In this section, we will show that dual-process models are also powerful for guiding advertising campaigns and interpreting their effects.

But before we discuss this topic, we will give a brief overview of the main theoretical approaches that have been developed specifically for advertising. As we will see, over the last decades advertising specialists have abandoned the unrealistic conception of a recipient who always attends to, and thinks deeply about, the information and arguments contained in an advertisement. Given the millions of advertisements recipients are exposed to, it is unlikely that they will be able or willing to devote attention to most of them. Thus, the development of advertising research shows parallels to the development of more general theories of attitude change, which – by adopting the dual-process framework – also conceded that recipients might often lack motivation and/or ability to process messages systematically. Of course, apart from parallels between persuasion research and advertising, advertising has some unique features that are not found in other types of persuasion, such as speeches delivered by politicians or lifestyle advice dispensed by physicians. But as we will see, even the seemingly specific features of advertising can be dealt with successfully by the dual-process framework. We will explore these issues now by considering some of the most influential models of the effects of advertising.

Hierarchy of effects models *Lavidge and Steiner's six-step model.* Lavidge and Steiner's (1961) model is one of the oldest and most influential models in advertising. It argues that successful advertising must bring about a sequence of six steps among consumers: awareness → knowledge → liking → preference → conviction → purchase. For example, to successfully influence the prospective buyer of a new camera, (1) an advertisement must create *awareness* that a certain new camera model exists (e.g., a digital camera from a certain manufacturer); (2) the advertisement must transmit some *knowledge* of what qualities the camera offers (e.g., good pixel quality); (3) building upon this knowledge, the potential buyer must develop *liking* for the product; (4) not only must she like the camera, she also has to develop a *preference* for the product over all other possibilities (e.g., other digital cameras); (5) she must couple her preference with a desire to buy and the *conviction* that it is wise to purchase; and (6) she must actually *purchase* the product.

Thus, Lavidge and Steiner (1961) assume, as does McGuire's (1968, 1985) information processing model, that the recipient of an advertisement has to go through a number of steps until he or she carries out the intended behaviour change. Lavidge and Steiner argue that each of the intervening steps is a necessary condition for subsequent steps; omitting a step will effectively prevent progress to the following steps. Thus, for example, the process may stop at the awareness step (e.g., due to lack of information), or before purchasing (e.g., due to lack of money). Many practitioners see this step model as helpful because each step offers a possible starting point for designing campaigns (e.g., increasing awareness by increasing publicity for the respective product, designing persuasive TV commercials to convince consumers of the advantages of the product). Meanwhile, however, doubts have been cast on step models by evidence that recipients can be influenced without going through all of the specified steps. For example, recipients may develop a positive attitude towards a product without comprehending the arguments contained in the message (e.g., because the advertisement shows an admired celebrity endorsing the product; cf. Greenwald, 1968; Petty & Wegener, 1998a). Furthermore, recipients may be influenced by subliminal persuasion without showing conscious attention towards the ad or the TV commercial, and without learning much about the respective product (e.g., Karremans, Stroebe & Claus, 2006; Strahan, Spencer & Zanna, 2002; see Chapter 7, this volume).

Ray's three-orders hierarchy model. In Lavidge and Steiner's (1961) and McGuire's (1985) models, learning about features of the product is seen as the basis for developing a positive attitude towards the product, which in turn is regarded as the determinant

Learning hierarchy (learn-feel-do)	Dissonance-attribution-hierarchy (do-feel-learn)	Low-involvement-hierarchy (learn-do-feel)
If recipients are involved and alternatives are clearly distinguishable	If recipients are involved, but alternatives are not clearly distinguishable	If recipients are not involved and alternatives are not clearly distinguishable
1. learning 2. attitude change 3. behaviour change	1. behaviour change 2. attitude change 3. learning	1. learning 2. behaviour change 3. attitude change

Figure 15.3 *The three-orders hierarchy model (Ray, 1973, 1982).*

of subsequent behaviour (e.g., purchase). In his ***three-orders hierarchy model***, Ray (1973; see Figure 15.3) calls this sequence of steps the 'learning hierarchy', i.e., learning about the features of the object is followed by attitude change, which is followed by behaviour. According to Ray (1973, 1982), the learning hierarchy ('learn-feel-do') accurately describes only situations in which the audience is involved (i.e., interested in the product) and when there are clear differences between alternatives (e.g., a recipient who is looking for a new car sees an advertisement that offers a 10 per cent discount for a car if it is bought before the end of the year). In this situation, recipients thoughtfully examine the information shown, make evaluations and then carry out the respective behaviour.

> **three-orders hierarchy model** a model according to which people undergo different orders of cognitive, evaluative and behavioural reaction processes in response to an advertisement, depending upon whether they are involved and whether clear alternatives between the products can be distinguished

Requiring recipients' involvement and the existence of clear differences between alternatives already sets limits on the applicability of the learning hierarchy, because people are typically exposed to many advertisements in a given day and are unlikely to devote attention to most of them. Therefore, Ray (1973) specifies two additional sequences or hierarchies of steps that can lead to advertising effectiveness and that differ from the conditions underlying the learning hierarchy. First, there are situations where even involved recipients have difficulties in discerning the advantages and disadvantages of the products offered. For example, a customer may have to choose between different banks or services without having adequate knowledge or while being under time pressure. For such situations, Ray predicts the *dissonance-attribution hierarchy* ('do-feel-learn'), i.e., behaviour constitutes the first step (e.g., time pressure may enforce a purchase even before learning has taken place). In turn, the fact that the behaviour has been carried out induces attitude change (Festinger, 1957) or triggers self-perception processes (e.g., 'I bought this product, therefore I seem to like it'; cf. Bem, 1972; Olson & Stone, 2005). In addition to dissonance reduction or self-perception processes, direct experience associated with the consumption of the product may give rise to new information about the product, its assets and disadvantages. For example, the customer may find out that there are certain 'hidden' costs of the bank account that she did not anticipate. Therefore, in the dissonance-attribution hierarchy, not only is the order of steps different from the learning hierarchy, but also the 'learning' involved is different: rather than receiving indirect knowledge about the product through an advertisement, the consumer gains *direct* knowledge, and information processing may be guided by dissonance reduction or self-perception.

The second alternative hierarchy distinguished by Ray (1973), the *low-involvement hierarchy* ('learn-do-feel'), is based on a notion developed by Krugman (1965). According to Krugman (1965), TV audiences are often passive and not really involved, mainly when they are exposed to advertising for trivial products that have little or no advantage over competing products (e.g., different brands of sweets, detergents, toothbrushes). Nevertheless, in these cases, advertisements might influence viewers by improving their recognition of the brand name or image. The next time they are in a shop, they might prefer to buy this product rather than one of its competitors due to its increased *accessibility* (see Chapter 4, this volume). The subsequent direct experience with the product may then change their attitude towards it, provided it turns out to be a good product that serves its function. In this case, the proposed sequence is learning-behaviour-attitude change, where the 'learning' is somewhat superficial and much less elaborate than envisaged in the learning hierarchy. Thus, for low-involvement products, the three-orders hierarchy model recommends that advertisers invest money in advertising with the aim of maximizing mere exposure and/or accessibility of the respective brand. This should give the brand an advantage in situations where the consumer has to choose among different brands from the same product category, for example when faced with an array of products in a supermarket aisle (Solomon, 2004).

It should be obvious that the low-involvement hierarchy parallels the notion of peripheral or heuristic processing (see Chapter 7, this volume) if the assumption is made that the improved recognition of the brand is accompanied by processes of mere exposure and/or by a heuristic such as 'I like what I know'. The learning hierarchy corresponds closely to the notion of central or systematic processing in the dual-process framework. In contrast, the dissonance-attribution hierarchy cannot be unambiguously related to either peripheral/heuristic or central/systematic processing, because it constitutes a mixture of peripheral processing (self-perception; e.g., 'I must like it since I chose it') and more elaborated processing (information gathered from direct experience with the product). To sum up, the three-orders hierarchy model anticipated key assumptions of dual-process theories, but its conceptual clarity seems lower than that of the elaboration likelihood model (ELM; Petty & Cacioppo, 1986a) and the heuristic-systematic model (HSM; Chaiken, Liberman & Eagly, 1989). The dissonance-attribution hierarchy involves both peripheral and central processes, yet since peripheral and central processes have been shown to have different antecedents and consequences (Petty & Wegener, 1998a), they should be kept theoretically separate, as is the case in the ELM and HSM.

The integrated information response model

Although Ray's (1973) concept of the dissonance-attribution hierarchy is somewhat difficult to categorize in terms of dual-processing theories, its more general idea, that the sequence of steps aimed at influencing consumers often involves the consumer's own behaviour, is well taken. Frequently, marketing practitioners supplement advertisements by providing consumers with direct experience with the product, such as a free trial of the product, a trial subscription or a test drive. Advertisers hope that this combined strategy will increase the resulting influence. Precisely this position is held in the integrated information response model (Smith & Swinyard, 1982), which takes into account information from two sources, information from the advertisement and information from direct experience with the product. Smith and Swinyard argue that low involvement among advertisement recipients is by far the most common situation because, with thousands of advertisements vying for their attention, consumers cannot be expected to examine all of them carefully. It may therefore be wise for advertisers to provide consumers with direct experience with the respective product in addition to indirect experience such as an advertisement. For example, consumers can be given a small sample of a new chocolate bar or persuaded to take out a trial subscription to a magazine. This (supplementary) strategy may be effective in cases when advertisers can be sure that the information resulting from this experience will be positive and when the adoption of this strategy is cost effective (as is the case with cheap products such as samples of sweets or with letting consumers test drive a new car).

Smith and Swinyard (1982) assume that exposure to advertising will normally generate only minimal message acceptance because recipients show a lack of interest or perceive advertising as being guided by a vested interest of the source. Therefore, recipients will discount the message, derogate the source or begin to counterargue (cf. Obermiller & Spangenberg, 1998). As a result, advertising in this case will produce only a weak positive evaluation, which is insufficient to motivate the consumer to buy the product. However, the positive evaluation of a product due to a skilfully produced advertisement should at least be strong enough to induce recipients to *test* the product. This test, on the other hand, yields direct experience, leading to stronger convictions and stronger (positive) evaluations, which may result, finally, in commitment. Smith and Swinyard (1982) ascribe the stronger effects of direct

Plate 15.4 *Providing free trials of a product is one advertising strategy to increase influence on consumer behaviour.*

experience as compared to advertising to the fact that people tend to trust their own senses more than persuasion by other parties, and that direct experience is more vivid and leads to better recall.

Basic research yields support for Smith and Swinyard's (1982) reasoning. Research on attitudes has shown that direct experience produces stronger attitudes than indirect experience, that is, a higher correlation between attitudes and behaviour, attitudes that are more persistent, more resistant and more likely to guide information processing (Fazio, Chen, McDonel & Sherman; 1982; Priester & Petty, 2003; Regan & Fazio, 1977). This is a good example of the fruitfulness of basic research in generating a theoretical explanation for (commercial) practice.

Attitude towards the advertisement and the dual mediation hypothesis Advertisements are complex messages that combine arguments with humour, music and/or attractive visuals, integrate story elements and thus try to persuade, irritate, relax or soothe (Batra & Ray, 1985). Given this variety of effects, it is not surprising that advertising researchers postulate that not only do recipients' attitudes towards the advertised product predict their purchasing intentions, so too do their **attitudes towards the advertisement** itself (e.g., Yoo & MacInnis, 2005). This is especially likely when advertisements themselves achieve a kind of cult status, be it footballer Thierry Henri promoting Renault cars, or model Claudia Schiffer dispensing with her clothes before getting into a Citroën. Indeed, as a meta-analysis by Brown and Stayman (1992) shows, the attitude towards the advertisement exerts an influence that is independent of the attitude towards the product itself. The fact that these two different attitudes have to be taken into consideration is a unique feature of the advertising domain.

> **attitude towards the advertisement** evaluation of the advertisement (rather than the product itself) that is determined by its characteristics (e.g., visual, acoustic, humorous).

Relevant research shows that the attitude towards the advertisement can assume at least three different roles (e.g., Gardner, 1985; Park & Young, 1986). (1) Affective reactions to the advertisement may influence the attitude towards the brand, as in classical conditioning or in priming when a positively evaluated stimulus in the advertisement (e.g., a beautiful woman) improves the perceivers' evaluation of the brand (see also MacKenzie, Lutz & Belch, 1986). In terms of the ELM, this would be regarded as a peripheral effect. (2) The exposure to the advertisement elicits the expectation that using the brand will result in positive consequences (e.g., a TV commercial for a food product creates the expectation of the pleasures of cooking or eating the food; cf. Gardner, 1985). In terms of the ELM, in this case, the advertisement (or parts thereof) functions as an argument for using the product. (3) The attitude towards the advertisement can facilitate or bias the processing of the message (e.g., when a celebrity is depicted in the advertisement, it attracts attention, or pleasant music facilitates its elaboration; cf. Park & Young, 1986). In terms of the ELM, such variables influence the elaboration of a message by increasing the extent of argument processing (Petty, Cacioppo, Sedikides & Strathman, 1988).

Brown and Stayman's (1992) meta-analysis also found evidence for a twofold influence of attitude towards the advertisement upon the attitude towards the brand, namely, a direct and an indirect

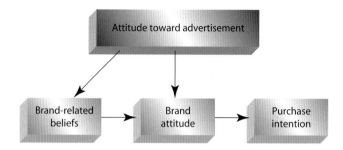

Figure 15.4 *The dual mediation model (Brown & Stayman, 1992).*

influence. The *direct* influence consisted of a significant relationship between attitude towards the advertisement and attitude towards the brand. The *indirect* influence consisted of (1) a significant relationship between attitude towards the advertisement and brand-related beliefs on the one hand, and (2) a significant relationship between brand-related beliefs and attitude towards the brand on the other. Taken together, these two influences are called the *dual mediation model* (e.g., Brown & Stayman, 1992; Coulter & Punj, 2004; MacKenzie et al., 1986; see Figure 15.4). Brown and Stayman (1992) did not analyse the psychological processes underlying the two paths of the dual mediation model, but both are consistent with the analysis above. The direct effect is presumably due to affective processes such as conditioning or to aspects of the advertisement acting as arguments for using the brand. The indirect effect is possibly due to variables that influence the extent and/or direction of processing, such as elements of the advertisement including celebrity endorsers or attention-grabbing effects that influence the extent or direction of processing.

According to the results of research on the dual mediation model, advertisers should use either (or a combination) of the following strategies: advertisements should try to transfer positive affect to the respective product (e.g., by showing beautiful landscapes), but they should also try to create positive expectations in the recipients if they use the respective product (e.g., by portraying a character who shows how easy it is to install a new piece of furniture from IKEA in one's home and/or by trying to present a well-known actor in the advertisement who increases the recipients' interest in listening to the message). Returning to our previous example involving Michael Schumacher, the designers of the video clip seem to have achieved all three aims by associating Switzerland with beautiful landscapes and portraying an attention-grabbing celebrity who argues that visiting or living in Switzerland will increase one's quality of life.

The dual-process perspective

What is a brand extension?
How might comparative advertisements increase the persuasive impact of an advertisement?

As can be seen from the above description, the dual-process approach is suitable as a framework for the different models and concepts described above. Advertising situations can be assigned to some more or less extreme point of the elaboration continuum:

direct experience (which is assumed to be an important source of information in the integrated information response model) can be regarded as increasing the elaboration likelihood and decreasing the tendency for biased processing. The concept of attitude towards the advertisement can also be integrated into the ELM: this type of attitude may be related to peripheral cues, to arguments for consuming the product, or it may influence the extent or direction of the elaboration.

As our discussion of the dual-process perspective in advertising is necessarily selective, we will conclude our discussion of the application of dual-process models here by discussing only two additional important mechanisms in advertising. One of them is located on the low end of the elaboration continuum – advertising by using *brand extensions* – while the other is associated with more elaboration – *comparative advertising*.

Advertising under conditions of low elaboration likelihood: Brand extensions

We have already addressed low elaboration mechanisms such as classical conditioning and subliminal advertising (see Chapter 7, this volume). An additional low elaboration mechanism has to do with *categorization*. To create a new image for every new product would be much too costly. Therefore, the majority of new products are launched under a well-established brand name such as Adidas, Gucci, Nestlé or Volvo (Shavitt & Wänke, 2004; Wänke, 1998). Such launches are called **brand extensions** because their aim is that consumers categorize

brand extension new product that is launched under an already established brand name

the new product in the established brand category and transfer its associated image to the new product.

One factor facilitating whether a new product is categorized as part of an existing brand is *fit*, that is, the degree of similarity of the new product to either the brand category or the brand image (Loken, 2006; Wänke, Bless & Schwarz, 1998). For example, a new compact car with typical features of a Volkswagen or a Toyota (such as design of front end, headlights, etc.) fits in the category of other cars from the respective car producer. After consumers have categorized the new product as an extension of the familiar brand, they can be expected to assimilate the image of the new brand member to the image and evaluation of the existing brand. In addition to the degree of similarity, another factor that facilitates the categorization of a new product as a brand extension is simply the *brand name* given to the extension (Wänke, 1998; Wänke et al., 1998): employing the same name for the extension, independently of physical similarity, may facilitate categorization and thus enhance the transfer of brand beliefs to the extension. An interesting example is the new smaller Volvo, the S40. The shape of the new model differs considerably from the well-established 'square' lines of the redoubtable Volvo (called by its detractors a 'tank on wheels', with its association with safety and reliability). Tellingly, Volvo marketed the new product with advertisements showing its sleek new shape, but alongside the slogan: 'Underneath it's a Volvo' (i.e., with the same motor, safety features, etc.).

Wänke et al. (1998, Experiment 1) found evidence for the assumption that the brand name facilitates the categorization of a new product as a brand extension (see Research close-up 15.1).

RESEARCH CLOSE-UP 15.1

Social psychology and marketing: Categorization and brand extensions

Wänke, M., Bless, H. & Schwarz, N. (1998). Contrast and assimilation in product line extensions: Context is not destiny. *Journal of Consumer Psychology, 7*, 299–322.

Introduction

Often, new products are launched as extensions of already established brands. Marketing departments adopt this strategy in the hope that consumers will transfer the evaluation and/or image of the core brand to the extension. As Wänke et al. argued, this transfer can be conceptualized as a categorization, namely, assigning the extension to the brand category. Such categorization decisions can be influenced by several variables, e.g., by similarity of the extension to the brand, or just by the name assigned to the extension. In two studies (only the first is presented here), the authors investigated whether names of car models that resembled the names of previous models would facilitate the transfer of brand beliefs. The researchers tested two hypotheses:

Hypothesis 1   A new model (e.g., a compact car) should be rated higher on attributes *typical* of a previous product line (e.g., a series of sports cars) when the name of the new model suggests *continuation* of the previous line rather than discontinuation.

Hypothesis 2   A new model should be rated lower on attributes *atypical* of the previous product line when the name of the new model suggests *continuation* of the previous line rather than discontinuation.

Method

Participants
Forty-nine students took part in this study.

Design and procedure
Participants first formed impressions of a fictitious brand of cars ('Winston') by reading descriptions of the company's three

recent models. The models were described as sports cars and had the names *Winston Silverhawk*, *Winston Silverpride* and *Winston Silverstar*. After reading the three descriptions, participants read the description of a compact car that was presented as small but roomy and neat looking. There were two experimental conditions. In the first (continuation) condition, the compact car was introduced as *Winston Silverray*. In the second (discontinuation) condition, the car was named *Winston Miranda*. After reading the description, participants had to evaluate the car along 10 dimensions.

According to the results of a pre-test, five of these dimensions typically apply to sports cars (advanced technology, fast, sports car, high quality, great design) and five dimensions typically do not apply to sports cars (safe, family car, roomy, comfortable, practical). According to another pre-test, the different names of the extension did not evoke significantly different evaluations on the 10 dimensions among participants who read the descriptions of the compact car (with the name assignment *Winston Silverray* vs. *Winston Miranda*) but were not exposed to descriptions of the previous models.

In a first step, scores on the five dimensions with high typicality and scores on the five dimensions with low typicality were averaged to yield two reliable indices. These two indices were then analysed in a 2 (continuation vs. discontinuation) $\times$ 2 (typicality for sports cars: low vs. high) mixed design, with continuation as a between-subjects factor and typicality as a within-subjects factor.

Results

Results revealed a significant interaction between the two factors, continuation and typicality (see Figure 15.5). Further analyses showed that participants rated the compact car slightly higher on sports car-typical attributes (and significantly lower on sports car-atypical attributes) when the name suggested continuation rather than discontinuation.

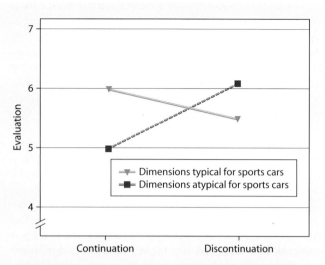

Figure 15.5 *Average evaluation of target car as a function of typical vs. atypical dimensions and continuation vs. discontinuation of product line of a sports car brand (Wänke et al., 1998). Scores reflect a compound measure of five ratings that were all assessed on a scale ranging from 1 (does not apply at all) to 9 (applies very much).*

Discussion

The significant interaction between the two factors was generally consistent with the predictions, although the effect was only significant for sports car-atypical attributes (thus confirming only hypothesis 2). In seeking to explain why the result was not significant for sports car-typical attributes, the authors referred to the particular materials used. Some of the dimensions selected as typical for sports cars were not necessarily atypical for compact cars (e.g., high quality, great design). Although this explanation is post hoc, the results of a second experiment with a different design were also consistent with the authors' categorization predictions.

Plate 15.5 *This advertisement tries to extend the safety image of the Volvo 200 series to the new S40, although the two models differ considerably in shape.*

They also argued that the transfer of brand beliefs to a new extension may be influenced not only by perceived fit with respect to features of already established brand names but also by several additional characteristics such as product display, communication strategies or packaging. These strategies may be used individually or in combination. Thus, marketing executives have a wide array of potential tools to influence consumers' perception of a new product under conditions of low elaboration.

Advertising under conditions of high elaboration likelihood: Comparative advertising *Comparative advertising* involves one brand (the *sponsor brand*) comparing itself to another brand (the *comparison brand*).

A famous example of this is the 'Pepsi Challenge' advertisement, used by Pepsi-Cola to challenge its rival, Coca-Cola. In the advertisement,

comparative advertising an advertisement that compares one brand ('sponsor brand') with a comparison brand with the aim of convincing recipients of the sponsor brand's superiority

drinkers are shown to prefer the taste of Pepsi in a blind tasting. Several studies have provided evidence that comparative advertising increases elaboration of the advertisement (e.g., Dröge, 1989; Pechmann & Esteban, 1994). Of course, from an advertiser's perspective, increased elaboration is desirable because it fosters rather strong attitudes. Thus, provided that the comparative advertisement offers strong positive arguments for the sponsor brand, we would expect the advertisement to cause strong positive attitudes that eventually lead consumers to purchase the product.

As Priester, Godek, Nayakankuppum and Park (2004) argued, however, previous research did not establish a clear explanation of the facilitative effects of comparative advertising on elaboration. Normally, comparative advertising involves a comparison brand that belongs to the leading market brands. Thus, consumers are quite familiar with such comparison brands and – assuming that the high market share of the comparison brand is due to the positive qualities of this brand – tend to perceive that the comparison brand has some desirable attitudes. But how does this lead to high elaboration of a comparative advertisement? In an attempt to provide an explanation, Priester et al. (2004) argue that often in comparative advertising, not only does familiarity vary between sponsor and comparison brand, so too does *similarity*. Arguably, an unfamiliar sponsor brand may be seen as 'new' or 'small', whereas the comparison brand may be regarded as dissimilar, e.g. 'old' or 'big', in contrast. Perceiving dissimilarity should enhance elaboration. If this reasoning is correct, comparing two high market share products should lead to less elaboration (because both are perceived as having common attributes such as 'old' and 'big') than comparing a high market share product to a low market share comparison.

To test these predictions, Priester et al. (2004) conducted an experiment with a 2 (brand similarity: high vs. low) × 2 (argument quality: strong vs. weak) design. They confronted college students with an advertisement that compared a high market share toothpaste brand (Crest) to either another high market share brand (Colgate) or to a low market share brand (Zact). The sponsor brand (i.e., Crest) and the comparison brand (Colgate or Zact, respectively) were presented together in a mock-up advertisement in a health magazine. Both toothpastes were depicted visually on one

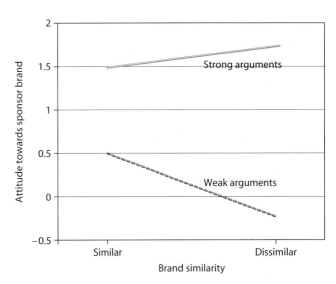

Figure 15.6 *Attitudes as a function of similarity of brands and argument quality (Priester et al., 2004, Experiment 1).*

page, with the comparison brand displayed as about a quarter of the size of the sponsor brand. The text at the top of the page read either 'Why should you choose Crest toothpaste instead of Colgate?' or 'Why should you choose Crest toothpaste instead of Zact?', respectively. Argument quality was manipulated by presenting either strong or weak arguments for Crest toothpaste. As Figure 15.6 shows, the results were consistent with the predictions of Priester et al. (2004). The impact of strong vs. weak arguments on attitudes was greater under conditions of dissimilarity (Crest vs. Zact) than similarity (Crest vs. Colgate), thus indicating greater message elaboration in this condition.

SUMMARY

Advertising has several powerful instruments at its disposal to influence consumers: providing consumers with arguments about the advertised products, working with affective techniques (classical conditioning, mere exposure), creating advertisements that increase the amount and extent of elaboration of the accompanying arguments, supplementing advertisements with direct experience in the form of product trials, and working with brand extensions or comparative advertisements. Each of these strategies represents a potentially powerful instrument provided that the influencing agents ensure the respective antecedent conditions, in terms of motivation and ability of the recipients. As our selective treatment of advertising has also shown, the diverse theoretical approaches that were designed specifically for advertising can be translated into the dual-process framework. This framework is not only empirically well supported, it is also much more powerful and integrative than the lower-order theories described above and avoids some of their ambiguities.

Plate 15.6 *The 'Pepsi Challenge' is an example of comparative advertising.*

SOCIAL PSYCHOLOGY IN THE WORKPLACE

If we asked you what was the most important type of behaviour in organizations, the first thing that might come to mind is the employees' (work) performance. Organizations need motivated and productive employees to carry out their jobs and therefore ensure that the organization remains profitable and prosperous. However, organizations are also very social places that involve interactions with colleagues, customers and supervisors, and thus a great deal of interdependence between people – even more so today than in the past because team work has evolved, over the years, as the dominant form of work organization (Ilgen & Pulakos, 1999). In team work, but also in individual work with colleagues and supervisors, maximizing one's own performance does not necessarily lead to the best possible outcome for the team or the organization as a whole; in fact, an exclusive focus on individual performance can make everybody worse off, because people may be unwilling to help each other, share information and pull together towards a common goal. Therefore, research has broadened its focus to include team-supportive performance behaviours such as being helpful or courteous to colleagues, acknowledging the fact that workplaces are social places in which individuals act interdependently.

When we are interested in the social groups that form organizations and the social processes that take place in organizations, we look at how social contexts affect the thoughts, feelings and behaviours of individuals. Recall the view of Floyd Allport (1924, p. 4) that '[t]here is no psychology of groups which is not essentially and entirely a psychology of individuals' (see Chapter 1, this volume). One important social psychological measure that you have become familiar with during the previous chapters is that of attitude. Therefore, we will make a case for the importance of the attitudes that individuals develop in organizational contexts. These attitudes mediate the impact of job characteristics and the social context on work outcomes. Figure 15.7 shows three foci of organizational behaviour research: work outcomes, job attitudes and the determinants of job attitudes. We will first turn to the right

side of Figure 15.7 and describe four categories of organizational behaviours that subsume the work outcome in organizations: task performance, contextual performance, counterproductive work behaviour and withdrawal.

Work outcome

Why do we differentiate task performance from contextual performance?
What are counterproductive work behaviours?

Task performance Most people would agree that the key outcome variable in work settings is job performance. In former times, job performance was treated as equivalent to *task performance*, i.e., how well one accomplishes the duties and tasks one is hired to do, what comprises one's current job description. For instance, car sales personnel need to sell cars, secretaries have to schedule their bosses' agendas and journalists must hand in articles for deadlines. Task performance can be measured in formal or informal performance appraisals, using supervisory or peer ratings or, in some areas such as production or service, in quantifiable, objective measures, e.g., number of units produced or number of incoming calls answered.

> **task performance** the degree of accomplishment of the duties and tasks one is hired to do

Sometimes, however, high task performers still lack what it takes in the workplace. Think, for example, of a computer nerd who develops the most complex codes with great enthusiasm but feels unable to present them to his supervisor and does not consider it necessary to instruct non-experts how to use them.

Contextual performance In our example, the computer nerd fails to maintain or enhance the context of work for his colleagues and supervisor. This aspect of performance is called *contextual performance*. One important reason for the increasing attention towards

> **contextual performance** an employee's extra-role behaviour, e.g., helping colleagues, which is not part of the job description but which promotes the effective functioning of the organization

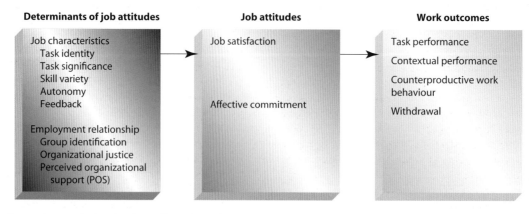

Determinants of job attitudes

Job characteristics
  Task identity
  Task significance
  Skill variety
  Autonomy
  Feedback

Employment relationship
  Group identification
  Organizational justice
  Perceived organizational
    support (POS)

Job attitudes

Job satisfaction

Affective commitment

Work outcomes

Task performance

Contextual performance

Counterproductive work
behaviour

Withdrawal

Figure 15.7 *Determinants of job attitudes and how they relate to work outcomes.*

Plate 15.7 *Employees have to fulfil individual tasks as well as work together as a team.*

correlation that they are indeed distinct performance dimensions: not all high task performers also engage in helpful or courteous behaviour, and not all employees who show strong extra-role engagement earn high scores on formal work appraisals. Contextual performance has been linked to enhanced organizational effectiveness such as increased efficiency and productivity (e.g., Podsakoff, Ahearne & MacKenzie, 1997; Walz & Niehoff, 1996). However, little is yet known about how, precisely, contextual performance affects these outcomes. Theoretically, contextual performance should lead to more efficient use of resources, enhanced coordination between employees and better-qualified employees (because teams with supportive work contexts are more attractive to applicants).

Counterproductive work behaviour *Counterproductive work behaviour* is the opposite of contextual performance and subsumes all voluntary behaviours that violate organizational norms and thus threaten the well-being of the organization. From Chapter 13, you are already familiar with many negative consequences that can be associated with teamwork, such as reduced individual performance (social loafing). Although applied research has, to date, focused on how individual behaviour harms the organization as a whole, while basic social psychological research has focused on small groups, you can easily identify social loafing as one form of counterproductive behaviour in work teams. Other forms of counterproductive behaviour include theft and sabotage, which cause financial losses, or harassment and bullying, which cause psychological problems (see Chapter 8, this volume). Questionnaires such as the 'Workplace Deviant Behaviour Scale' by Bennett and Robinson (2000) assess counterproductive work behaviour by asking employees and/or supervisors about employee behaviour directed against the organization (e.g., 'Taken property from work without permission') and behaviour directed against individuals (e.g., 'Made fun of someone at work').

> **counterproductive work behaviour**
> all voluntary behaviours that violate organizational norms and thus threaten the well-being of the organization, e.g., sabotage, theft

contextual performance is that employees not only have to fulfil their individual tasks, they also have to work together as a team and create an environmental context that promotes individual *and* team performance.

Whereas task performance is highly job specific, contextual performance behaviours such as volunteering and cooperating apply to almost all tasks. They support the environment in which task performance occurs. Supervisors attach great importance to contextual performance behaviours. Indeed, an additional reason for the broadened research perspective on performance is the empirical finding that supervisors look at both task *and* context behaviours when evaluating their employees' performance (e.g., Rotundo & Sackett, 2002) or when judging applicant behaviour in the selection interview (Mackenzie, Podsakoff & Fetter, 1991).

The original concept related to contextual performance was suggested by Organ (1988) and named *organizational citizenship behaviour* (OCB). Since its redefinition by Organ in 1997, OCB has become highly similar to contextual performance (Borman & Motowidlo, 1993), and we will use the concepts interchangeably in this chapter. Thus, contextual performance is an employee's extra-role behaviour that is not part of the job description, which may or may not be explicitly recognized by the organization's reward system but which promotes the effective functioning of the organization. Researchers have proposed several taxonomies concerning the dimensions of such extra-role behaviour. For example, Smith, Organ and Near (1983) asked managers in interviews to identify 'instances of helpful but not absolutely required . . . job behaviour' (p. 656) and to rate how characteristic each behaviour was for the employee. They performed a factor analysis on the ratings and found a specific altruism factor, i.e., helping a specific person in a specific situation, and a generalized compliance factor, i.e., impersonal behaviours such as conforming to organizational norms.

Task performance has been found to correlate at around $r = .25$ with contextual performance, and we can see from the size of the

Withdrawal Withdrawal is another outcome that organizations should be eager to avoid. It subsumes turnover (termination of an individual's employment with a given company), absenteeism and lateness, with lateness being the mildest form of withdrawal and turnover being the most extreme. What makes people drop out of an organization is one of the important questions when we consider organizational behaviour. Recruiting is costly for the organization, and it is also strenuous for the individual employee who is looking for a new job: it involves writing applications, undergoing assessments and interviews, and socializing with a new team and organization.

You are now familiar with the most crucial forms of organizational behaviour, namely task and contextual performance, counterproductive behaviour and withdrawal. Let us now move to the middle box of Figure 15.7 and look at how these behaviours are linked to employees' job attitudes. Can we predict positive and negative organizational behaviour from employees' attitudes?

Job attitudes

What kinds of organizational behaviour can we predict from employees' job attitudes?

What makes employees put in extra effort, cooperate and work together as a team?

Every day, people form, confirm and change opinions about specific aspects of their work situation. They also develop general evaluations of their job situation as a whole. We call such specific and general evaluations *job attitudes*. Just like the social attitudes you are familiar with from Chapter 6, job attitudes lie on a continuum ranging from positive to negative reactions and have cognitive, affective and behavioural components (e.g., Hulin & Judge, 2003).

> **job attitudes** an employee's evaluations of the job situation, on a continuum ranging from positive to negative reactions, subsuming cognitive, affective and behavioural components

> **job satisfaction** the most general job attitude, regarding how an employee evaluates the job as a whole

The most general measure of how employees evaluate their jobs is called overall *job satisfaction*. It is important in its own right, because people should be content with their work and workplace. In addition, job satisfaction is an important concomitant of the work outcomes we discussed above, because, as you know, attitudes are related to behaviour and, consequently, job attitudes are related to work behaviour. For example, job satisfaction has been found to correlate at around $r = .30$ with the contextual performance behaviours that promote teamwork and cooperation (Organ & Ryan, 1995). Because, as is the case for most organizational research, data from several self-report measures of different concepts are gathered at one point and correlated, we do not know whether contented employees engage more readily in contextual behaviours or whether contextual performance causes employees to be more satisfied with their job because the work context is more pleasant and supportive.

The relationship between job satisfaction and task performance has long been a hot topic in applied psychology. From the 1950s to the 1990s, most researchers agreed that there is hardly any relationship at all (Brayfield & Crockett, 1955; Iaffaldano & Muchinsky, 1985). However, the most comprehensive and methodologically sound meta-analysis on this question showed that there is a reliable correlation around $r = .30$ (Judge, Thoresen, Bono & Patton, 2001). In their influential article, Judge et al. (2001; see Suggestions for Further Reading, this chapter) also discuss all possible causal relationships but state that, just as with contextual performance, we cannot conclude to date whether satisfaction causes performance, whether performance causes satisfaction, or whether they influence each other reciprocally over time.

With regard to turnover, longitudinal studies in which predictors have been measured at an earlier point in time than turnover occurrence found that earlier dissatisfaction with one's job predicts later turnover in a reliable way (Griffeth, Hom & Gaertner, 2000; Sutton & Griffin, 2004).

A more specific job attitude is an employee's commitment to the organization and its goals, an attachment that exists between the individual and the organization. We can further specify affective,

PIONEER

Timothy A. Judge (b. 1962) graduated from the University of Iowa and the University of Illinois and received his doctorate from the University of Illinois at Urbana-Champaign in 1990. He was a professor at Cornell University and the University of Iowa and is currently at the University of Florida. He has conducted applied research on job attitudes and work outcome, leadership and individual differences, and has published some highly influential meta-analyses and reviews on job attitudes and work outcomes. His work has been influential for both research and organizations because he combines real-world data with psychological concepts and publishes in psychology as well as in management journals. He has received awards from, among others, the Society of Industrial and Organizational Psychology and the Academy of Management.

continuance and normative organizational commitment, which are influenced by different aspects of the workplace and imply different consequences for work outcomes, but which employees can experience simultaneously to some degree. Figure 15.8 depicts the proposed relationships between the forms of organizational commitment and their determinants and consequences (Meyer, Stanley, Herscovitsch & Topolnytsky, 2002). However, we will restrict our attention to affective commitment because it has received by far the most research attention to date and has been shown to be a good predictor of task and contextual performance.

Affective commitment is an employee's degree of emotional attachment to, identification with and involvement in the organization. Measures of affective commitment contain questions on employees' dedication and loyalty. Employees who show strong affective commitment in the questionnaire measures are rarely absent from work and unlikely to quit their job (e.g., Jaramillo, Mulki & Marshall, 2005; Mowday, Porter & Steers, 1982). They are more satisfied with their job (correlations are around $r = .60$) and score more highly on task performance (correlations are around $r = .30$) than employees who show weak affective commitment (Van Scotter, 2000). Both turnover and performance are caused by degree of commitment: the more committed employees feel towards the organization, the more strongly they perform and the less likely they are to look for new jobs (Cohen, 1993; Vandenberghe, Bentein & Stinglhamber, 2004). Indeed, meta-analyses of turnover behaviour have established that low affective commitment is, together with job dissatisfaction, the best available predictor of turnover (Griffeth et al., 2000; Sutton & Griffin, 2004).

> **affective commitment** specific job attitude depicting an employee's degree of emotional attachment to, identification with and involvement in the organization

As you can see, job attitudes predict organizational behaviour rather well, and this is what makes them important for organizations.

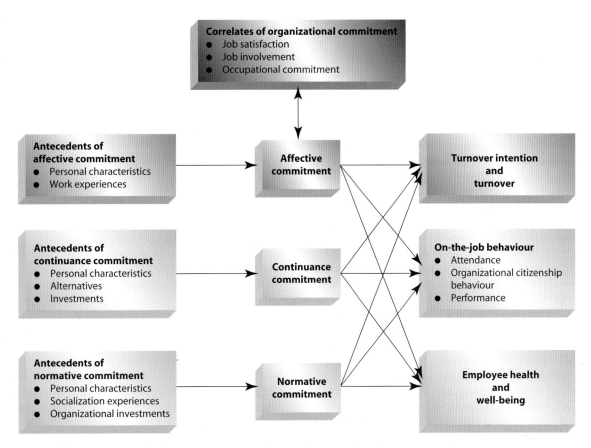

Figure 15.8 *Three-component model of organizational commitment (Meyer et al., 2002).*

Two key questions follow from these links between job attitudes and work outcome: How can organizations ensure that their employees hold positive job attitudes? What can supervisors do to foster high job satisfaction and affective commitment in their teams?

Determinants of job attitudes

How does group identification influence cooperation within work teams?

Under which circumstances do employees perceive their organization as fair and rewarding?

What can supervisors do to ensure their subordinates' commitment to the organization?

Have another look at Figure 15.7. We will now turn to the left-hand box and draw on two major aspects of work to answer this question. First, a job itself, its structure and content, determines job attitudes. Second, the daily social interactions that take place in teams and organizations are significant influences on job attitudes. We will therefore show what a motivating job should look like and describe some of the most influential processes in the employment relationship that affect job attitudes and determine organizational behaviour.

Job characteristics Job characteristics summarize the situational variables that form a job. A theory that makes concise predictions about the influence of such characteristics on job attitudes is Hackman and Oldham's (1976) job characteristics model (JCM). As you can see in Figure 15.9, the JCM states that there are five

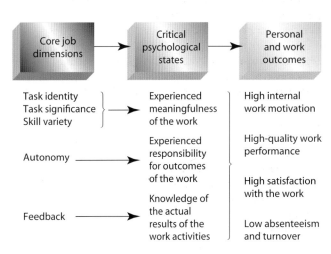

Figure 15.9 *Job characteristics model (JCM) (Hackman & Oldham, 1976).*

characteristics that make a job satisfying to employees. The first three, task identity, task significance and skill variety, are summed to form a total measure of work content. This sum is maximal if an employee's tasks are comprehensive as opposed to fragmented into small individual units (high task identity), if the tasks are important to oneself, other teams and/or people outside the organization (high task significance) and if the employee is allowed to perform several different tasks as opposed to always having to perform the same or similar ones (high skill variety). Because the three factors are summed to form a work content score, high scores on one factor can compensate for low scores on another. The other two factors of the model, autonomy and feedback, are multiplied by the work content score.

The model therefore states that autonomy and feedback are absolutely necessary characteristics of the job, and if either one is lacking (i.e., score of zero) or if the work content score is zero, job satisfaction, or the job's 'motivating potential' as Hackman and Oldham (1976) called it, is necessarily zero. For example, according to the JCM, a rather dreary job can nevertheless be satisfying if it is very important to many people, e.g., the job of an air traffic controller who observes radar points on a monitor all day, thus ensuring the safety of thousands of air passengers. This is because jobs such as air traffic control create feelings of meaningfulness and responsibility and make employees perceive their jobs as challenging and interesting (Judge, Bono & Locke, 2000).

The model also predicts that a job can never be perceived as satisfying if it totally lacks autonomy concerning how to do the job, or if it totally lacks feedback about how well the job is done, because such jobs cannot lead to such positive psychological states as meaningfulness. Thus, a mathematical function of the five characteristics determines the degree of job satisfaction an employee experiences, and organizations can estimate the motivating potential of each job.

The JCM has received a great deal of empirical support over the years. Employees state that they are satisfied and motivated if their jobs provide task identity, task significance, skill variety, autonomy and feedback. Although the job characteristics of the JCM are also correlated with task performance, the JCM is more powerful in predicting job satisfaction than in predicting task performance (Fried, 1991; Fried & Ferris, 1987; Loher, Noe, Moeller & Fitzgerald, 1985).

The employment relationship What are the most influential social processes in the workplace that affect job attitudes and determine organizational behaviour? Employees react to their work situation cognitively and emotionally. When it comes to job attitudes and satisfaction, it is the employee's perception that counts. Managers in human resources cannot debate with people about how to perceive and interpret management decisions or organizational support, but they can make an effort to understand *how* employees develop attitudes and then suggest interpretations accordingly. If supervisors know what influences their subordinates' impressions, they can design the terms of their relationship in a way that fosters positive job attitudes.

We will now look at three aspects of the employment relationship that can be traced back to social psychological theories and research and that have been successfully applied to the workplace: group identification in teams, the degree of organizational justice and the support employees receive from supervisors and the organization. All predict job attitudes and organizational behaviour quite well, and we will now have a closer look at the underlying processes.

Group identification. Take a moment to think about your own experiences with teamwork, e.g., in study groups or during team assignments. Would you agree that you are more likely to put in a lot of effort to make the assignment a success if you feel a strong sense of belonging to the team? Research has shown that it is especially contextual performance that is enhanced by team members' group identification within the team. It makes a difference to contextual performance whether you think of yourself as a single, autonomous individual who happened to be assigned to a work team based on an organization chart or whether, by contrast, you regard yourself as sharing identification with your team. As you know from social identity theory (see Chapters 5 and 14, this volume), we tend to attribute positive characteristics to members of our own ingroup (e.g., Brewer, 1996). Therefore, the more strongly you identify with your team, the more you will be likely to find your colleagues honest, cooperative and trustworthy. Recall from Chapter 13 that trust between group members facilitates the pursuit of collective instead of individual goals (Dirks, 1999). Thus, employees who strongly identify with their team tend to trust their colleagues, expect them to reciprocate effort and helping behaviour, and are therefore more willing to engage in contextual performance behaviours (Kramer, 1999; Kramer, Hanna, Su & Wei, 2001; Messick et al., 1983).

Organizational justice. Imagine that you have started your first job. You are enjoying the new challenges, you appreciate the team climate and you are very eager to make the project a success. After six months, your supervisor carries out a first performance appraisal, during which she tells you how much she likes your work and how your team colleagues enjoy working with you. She also says that now that the project is doing so well, there will be bonuses for some team members. Although she considers you one of the most productive and hard-working team members, she will distribute bonuses according to seniority, and you therefore have no chance of receiving any reward. How would you feel about this?

Organizational justice concerns how fair members of the organization perceive the resource allocation among employees to be (Greenberg, 1990). Some authors prefer the term 'fairness' over justice, but we will use the terms interchangeably in this chapter. Justice perceptions can concern how fairly a certain amount of outcome (e.g., income) is *distributed*, quantitatively and relatively between employees or between organizational groups, and is then called **distributive justice**. Perceptions of distributive justice are strong if outcomes are distributed in proportion to an individual's input. In the above example, you might have felt a sting because your supervisor considers you to be one of her best employees but gave rewards

> **distributive justice** perceptions in organizations about how fairly a certain amount of outcome (e.g., income) is distributed, both absolutely and relatively, between employees or between organizational groups

to others. Consequently, the input-to-outcome ratio in your team seems unfair. This is supported by research on how social comparison processes are affected by a team's wage dispersion, i.e., the variance of pay within the team. If team members contribute the same amount but dispersion is known to be wide, people at the low end of the pay scale are dissatisfied, reduce their effort and consider turnover (Pfeffer & Langton, 1993).

Justice perception can also concern how fair the *processes* of resource allocation are, and is then called ***procedural justice***. The conditions for procedural justice include, for example, opportunities to express one's view during decision-making, consistency of procedures across people and time, and the extent to which all parties' concerns are fairly represented. Recently, a third justice dimension besides distributive and procedural justice has been established. *Interactional justice* concerns the fairness of interpersonal treatment (Bies & Moag, 1986) and encompasses two aspects. First, it reflects how respectfully and politely an organization treats its employees (interpersonal justice), and second, it concerns how well an organization explains and informs about why procedures are as they are, or why outcomes

> **procedural justice** perceptions in organizations about how fair the processes of resource allocation are

are distributed in the way they are (informational justice). Research close-up 15.2 gives you an example of how fair interpersonal treatment can make a difference in organizations.

Procedural justice in particular has been found to predict job satisfaction and task performance (Cropanzano, Rupp, Mohler & Schminke, 2001; Tekleab, Takeuchi & Taylor, 2005); and both procedural and distributive justice are highly positively correlated with organizational commitment and trust, moderately positively correlated with contextual performance, and strongly negatively correlated with withdrawal and absenteeism. Some longitudinal studies suggest that procedural justice determines the degree of organizational commitment. For example, Kim and Mauborgne (1993) found that unit managers of large international organizations were more committed to, and more willing to comply with, strategic decisions made by their organization when they perceived the decision-making process to be fair. Specifically, they showed high commitment to strategic decisions when decision-making processes were consistent throughout the organization, when there was bilateral communication between their units and the overall organization, and when they felt fully informed about the decisions made.

Why and how does the perception of fair procedures lead to more positive reactions? Three answers have been offered to this

RESEARCH CLOSE-UP 15.2

Interpersonal and informational justice

Greenberg, J. (1994). Using socially fair treatment to promote acceptance of a work site smoking ban. *Journal of Applied Psychology, 79,* 288–297.

Introduction

The adverse effects of smoking concern not only smokers but also non-smokers who inhale secondary, or side-stream, smoke. In recent years, smoking bans have been implemented in more and more public places and organizations throughout Europe and North America. This study is a field experiment that investigates how organizations can increase acceptance among smoking employees when implementing a worksite smoking ban.

Previous research had shown that employees feel fairly treated if supervisors provide explanations of decisions (informational justice) and if supervisors treat them with respect and dignity (interpersonal justice). The author therefore hypothesized that the smoking ban would gain greater acceptance if employees received high rather than low amounts of information, and if the ban were announced in a manner demonstrating high rather than low social sensitivity. In addition, the authors

hypothesized that heavy smokers, especially, would show greater acceptance of the ban if high amounts of information were presented and high amounts of social sensitivity were shown.

Method

Participants

Participants were 732 clerical employees who worked in a large financial services organization, most of whom had no managerial responsibilities (63.25 per cent were white, 29.78 per cent black and 5.33 per cent Hispanic; 60.25 per cent were female; 28.96 per cent were smokers). With regard to smoking behaviour, the sample was representative of US national trends and highly similar to samples used in previous research.

Design and procedure

The experimental design manipulated two between-subjects factors and used level of smoking as a third, quasi-experimental factor. The overall design was 2 (social sensitivity: high/low) × 2 (information level: high/low) × 3 (smoking: no/light/heavy). Participants were randomly assigned to one of the experimental conditions by being asked to return to one of four different meeting rooms in which they had previously met for a training program.

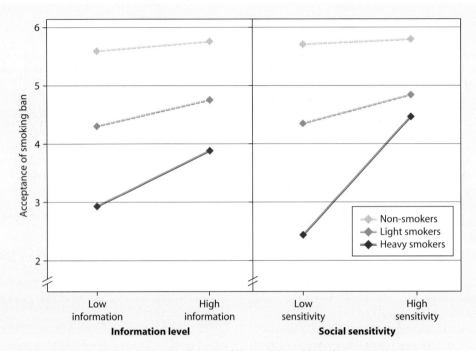

Figure 15.10 *Improving acceptance of a smoking ban by using fair procedures (Greenberg, 1994).*

Participants watched a videotape in which their company president announced the new worksite smoking ban (participants thought it was a live broadcast from corporate headquarters). In the tape, the president presented either only the most cursory information about the reason for the smoking ban (low-information condition) or a large amount of detailed information by means of charts and graphs detailing the hazards of smoking, remarks about health risks to smokers and non-smoking co-workers, and information about the costs of smoking to the company (high-information condition).

The president also expressed either little concern about whether the ban might be hard on smokers (low social sensitivity condition) or strong concern by acknowledging that smokers might find it difficult to refrain from smoking, and by explaining the health concerns that prevailed in the decision (high social sensitivity condition).

Immediately after the president's announcement, participants stated their acceptance of the ban in a questionnaire. After the experiment, participants were provided with a thorough explanation of the study. Participants in the low-information and low social sensitivity conditions watched a debriefing tape in which the president provided high amounts of information and social sensitivity. This was done to ensure that all participants, regardless of condition, could yield the expected positive reactions to the smoking ban.

Results

Manipulation checks showed that the author had successfully manipulated both the amount of information and the amount of social sensitivity. Analyses of the main dependent variable,

acceptance of the smoking ban, showed that the hypotheses were supported. As depicted in Figure 15.10, both light and heavy smokers showed higher acceptance of the ban when confronted with high as opposed to low information and high as opposed to low sensitivity. The effect was stronger for heavy than for light smokers, as the author hypothesized. Non-smokers rated the ban most favourably, but the manipulations did not further increase their acceptance (although they passed the manipulation check, i.e., they were aware of the fair procedure). Also, when the author looked at the overall sample, without differentiating between smokers and non-smokers, the effect of information and sensitivity was additive, i.e., acceptance was overall greatest in the condition with high information *and* high sensitivity.

Discussion

This study showed that organizations can buffer negative reactions of their employees to new company policies, such as a smoking ban, by providing thorough information and by announcing the policies in a manner that shows considerable awareness of the inconvenience it is likely to cause. The author states that high information provides informational justice, whereas awareness of inconvenience (social sensitivity) shows interpersonal justice. Thus, employees feel fairly treated and respond to such treatment with higher acceptance. Interestingly, it was especially the heavy smokers who significantly increased their acceptance, although light smokers also increased their acceptance, albeit less prominently. One limitation of the study is that the more informative and more socially sensitive message was also considerably longer than the control message. Length of message was thus confounded with the manipulation.

question. The original, *instrumental* explanation is that people want to have control over the processes that lead to decisions in order to make sure that the outcome is fair, and that fair procedures suggest that they have such control (Thibaut & Walker, 1978). A second explanation is that people think that procedural justice indicates how much they are appreciated by the team, supervisor or organization, and how well they are accepted in the team or organization (Tyler & Lind, 1992). According to this *relational* approach, people infer their social standing from procedural information and reciprocate this degree of belongingness by being more accepting of outcomes.

The most integrative explanation to date was offered by van den Bos and colleagues (e.g., van den Bos, Lind, Vermunt & Wilke, 1997) in their *substitutability* explanation. They attempted to integrate distributive and procedural justice by suggesting that most everyday situations provide relatively more procedural than distributive information. We will now take a closer look at this explanation.

According to Adams's (1965) equity theory, we judge our outcomes to be fair when our input-to-outcome ratio is comparable to other people's input-to-outcome ratio (see Chapters 10 and 12, this volume). It is therefore not a question of absolute outcome but outcome relative to the individual input. However, as van den Bos (2005) states, we often lack information about others' inputs or outcomes. We often do not know what our colleagues earn, and it is even harder to estimate how much they work and how well they perform. What we do have access to, however, is procedural information. According to van den Bos and Lind (2001), using procedural information as a substitute for missing distributive information is a form of uncertainty management, a heuristic to judge the fairness of outcomes when social comparison information is missing and we are uncertain of the fairness of our share of outcome. The more fair we think the procedures of selection, performance appraisal, resource allocation and so on are, the more satisfied we will be with our personal outcome of these procedures, i.e., the selection decision, our performance ratings and the resources we receive.

perceived organizational support
employees' beliefs about how much the organization values their contribution and cares about their well-being

Perceived organizational support. The concept of *perceived organizational support* (POS) summarizes the employees' beliefs that their organization values their contribution and cares about their well-being. POS strongly influences the employment relationship. It is usually measured with Likert-type scales, as in the eight-item short form of the Survey of Perceived Organizational Support (SPOS) developed by Eisenberger, Cummings, Armeli and Lynch (1997) and depicted in Table 15.1.

A meta-analysis by Rhoades and Eisenberger (2002) shows that POS correlates most strongly and positively with procedural justice perceptions. Job conditions such as pay, rewards and promotions, as well as autonomy (a job characteristic you know from Hackman and Oldham's theory of work design and job satisfaction), are related to POS. The degree of support that employees experience should be of interest to supervisors and organizations because it mediates the relationship between perceived justice and work outcome. Thus if employees perceive their organization as

Table 15.1 *SPOS 8-item short form (Eisenberger et al., 1997)*

Perceived organizational support

1	My organization really cares about my well-being.
2	My organization strongly considers my goals and values.
3	My organization shows little concern for me. (R)
4	My organization cares about my opinions.
5	My organization is willing to help me if I need a special favour.
6	Help is available from my organization when I have a problem.
7	My organization would forgive an honest mistake on my part.
8	If given the opportunity, my organization would take advantage of me. (R)

(R) denotes that items are reverse scored.

fair, they feel that their organization is supportive, and this then increases their affective commitment to the organization, makes them contribute to the work context more readily and lowers turnover intentions (Moorman, Blakely & Niehoff, 1998; Rhoades, Eisenberger & Armeli, 2001).

Both organizational justice and POS are employees' appraisals of treatment by their organization, and both are based on fairness. They differ, however, in that justice perceptions are based on specific decisions and on how these decisions are made, whereas POS assesses employees' beliefs about the commitment the organization has to them. These beliefs evolve over the course of an individual's tenure with an organization and include many decisions made during that period of time. Thus, a single unfair decision might decrease perceived justice, but not necessarily the more general perceived support.

For human resource managers, POS might be a reliable and attractive way of assessing the quality of the employment relationship, not only because it affects job attitudes, but also because it relates directly to performance. It seems that feelings of support create a feeling of obligation in employees to aid the organization. Recall from Chapters 10 and 12 what you know about social exchange theory. Relationships are based on an exchange of material and psychological goods that follows the reciprocity norm: the more you receive, the more you are inclined to give back to the donor (Gouldner, 1960). If we apply this norm to the employee–employer relationship, employees who perceive their organization as supportive feel obliged to reciprocate and increase both task and contextual efforts (Eisenberger, Armeli, Rexwinkel, Lynch & Rhoades, 2001).

SUMMARY

Organizations should be concerned about the job attitudes of their employees. Employees who are content with their job and committed to their organization are an asset to their organization: they are likely to remain with the organization, fulfil their designated tasks and work beyond job descriptions to support colleagues and further the well-being of their employer.

We have shown that organizations have available the means to foster positive job attitudes. First, organizations can design jobs in a way that demands a variety of skills in the employees, grants high degrees of autonomy and provides feedback on job fulfilment. Second, organizational structures and supervisor team leadership behaviour should be transparent and ensure just procedures. Organizations should be eager to communicate that they appreciate their employees' contributions and support their efforts.

In sum, you have seen that practitioners in the workplace can benefit from basic research and social psychological theories to better understand the social processes in the workplace. Applied researchers have fruitfully extended the well-established concept of social attitudes to job attitudes, and found it useful for predicting work outcomes.

SOCIAL PSYCHOLOGY AND HEALTH

The present section focuses on the contributions of social psychological theories and research to the study of two major sources of health and illness, namely, *patterns of health behaviour* and *psychosocial stress*. First, we will show how social psychological knowledge can be used to explain why people engage in behaviours that are damaging to their health. We will sketch how such detrimental health behaviour patterns can be changed by social psychological means. Second, we will address the topic of psychosocial stress and its impact on health. We will discuss several stress-ameliorating factors such as dispositional optimism and the availability of social support. We will place special emphasis on stress at the workplace, given the many hours that members of the population spend working.

Behaviour and health

What are the major determinants of health behaviour?
What are the main strategies of behaviour change?

The impact of behaviour on health No single set of data can better illustrate the fact that our health is influenced by the way we live than the findings from a prospective study, conducted in the United States, of the association of certain health behaviours with longevity (Breslow & Enstrom, 1980; see also Conner & Norman, 2005). In 1965, participants in this study were asked whether they engaged in the following seven health practices: sleeping seven to eight hours daily, eating breakfast almost every day, never eating between meals, currently being at or near prescribed height-adjusted weight, never smoking cigarettes, moderate use of alcohol and regular physical activity. When the researchers recontacted this sample nine and a half years later, they discovered that those who had engaged in these health practices in 1965, and usually had continued to do so over the intervening years, tended to live longer. The men who had followed all seven health practices had a death rate that was only 28 per cent of that of men who followed three or fewer of these practices. The death rate of women who followed all the practices was 43 per cent of those who followed three or fewer of them. Several other studies have confirmed the association between health behaviours and longevity (see Taylor, 2005).

Determinants of health behaviour Why do people continue to engage in health-impairing behaviours even if they know that they are damaging their health? Is there any way to influence them? This section presents two major theoretical models that provide a framework for the cognitive determinants of health behaviour (for other models of health behaviour, see Conner & Norman, 2005). Such models are eminently important because it is only after we have identified the determinants of a particular health behaviour that we will be able to change it. The two models described below were developed especially to predict health behaviour, although they have much in common with more general models of attitude–behaviour relations such as the theory of reasoned action and the theory of planned behaviour (see Chapter 6, this volume).

Protection motivation theory. According to **protection motivation theory** (PMT), which was developed by Rogers (1983; see also Norman, Boer & Seydel, 2005), exposure to a health threat, or a threat in general, evokes two cognitive processes, namely, threat appraisal and coping appraisal (cf. Lazarus & Folkman, 1984). The concept of threat appraisal refers to a cognitive process targeted at evaluating the severity of a threat and one's individual vulnerability to it. Threat appraisal also includes an assessment of the advantages of continuing the present maladaptive behaviour. For example, a sexually active individual may assess the severity of contracting AIDS when having unprotected sex together with his or her perceived probability of developing AIDS under these circumstances; these two assessments are then weighed against the rewards of practising the maladaptive behaviour, such as, in this example, the perceived pleasures of having sex without a condom.

The second process that is important to the individual according to PMT is coping appraisal. It consists of assessing the response

> **protection motivation theory** the model assumes that the motivation to protect oneself from a danger is a positive function of four beliefs: the threat is severe, one is personally vulnerable, one has the ability to perform the coping response and the coping response is effective in reducing the threat. Two further beliefs are assumed to decrease protection motivation: the rewards of the maladaptive response are great and the costs of performing the coping response are high

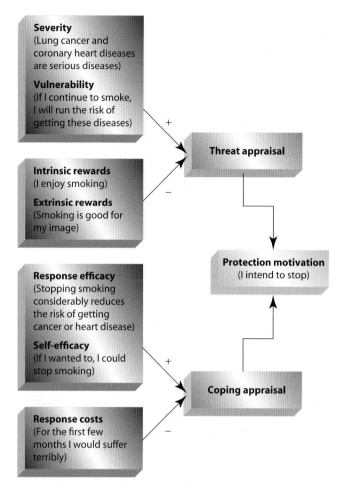

Figure 15.11 *Protection motivation theory applied to the reduction of smoking (Stroebe, 2001; based on Rogers, 1983).*

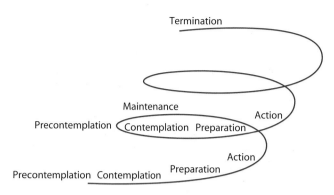

Figure 15.12 *Spiral pattern of the stages of change of the transtheoretical model (Prochaska et al., 1992).*

efficacy (effectiveness) of a given recommendation (e.g., using a condom while having sexual intercourse) and one's self-efficacy (Bandura, 1997) in carrying out the respective behaviour, that is, an individual's perception that he or she is able to carry out the pertinent behaviour (e.g., an individual may feel unsure whether she is able to enforce use of a condom for sex with her partner). In addition, the 'costs' of the adaptive response (e.g., perceived awkwardness of using a condom) are subtracted from the assessments of response efficacy and self-efficacy. 'Protection motivation' results from the two appraisal processes. Protection motivation is roughly identical to the concept of intention in the theory of planned behaviour (Ajzen, 2002; see Figure 15.11).

As described, according to Rogers (1983), the factors *within* a process combine *additively* (i.e., threat appraisal is conceived as the sum of severity plus vulnerability minus rewards, whereas coping appraisal is conceived as the sum of response efficacy and self-efficacy minus costs). However, Rogers postulates a *multiplicative* combination *between* the two appraisal processes. This assumption is plausible insofar as threat appraisal should increase protection motivation only if the individual feels able to perform a coping response and this response is effective in reducing the danger. Several studies have tested these predictions concerning the relationship

between the variables specified by protection motivation theory, but to date the relationship between PMT variables is far from being clear. Most tests of PMT only consider the main effects of its variables (Norman et al., 2005). PMT has been applied to many different health behaviours such as exercise behaviour, breast self-examination, AIDS-related behaviour and smoking (for overviews see Milne, Sheeran & Orbell, 2000; Norman et al., 2005). The main predictions of the model have received support, that is, health-related intentions (i.e., protection motivation) were significantly correlated with subsequent behaviour and all threat and coping appraisal variables were significantly correlated with intention. However, coping appraisal variables were more strongly related to intentions than were threat appraisal components. Self-efficacy emerged as the strongest predictor of intentions (Milne et al., 2000).

The transtheoretical model. One limitation of theories of health behaviour such as PMT is that they are relatively static. Implicitly or explicitly, they assume that the determinants of an individual's intention are stable. However, observations of smokers and people who are trying to lose weight tell a different story. For example, some smokers may not take the threats associated with smoking very seriously as long as there are no symptoms such as coughing or shortness of breath. In contrast, stage models of behaviour change include a longitudinal dimension and emphasize that the psychological basis of the intention to change a certain behaviour may change drastically over time (cf. Sutton, 2005). One of the most well-known stage models is the *transtheoretical model* (TTM) developed by Prochaska, DiClemente and Norcross (1992; cf. also Prochaska, Redding & Evers, 2002; see Figure 15.12). The model describes the process of achieving a particular health goal (such as giving up smoking) as a sequence of five stages that have to be passed successfully (cf. Armitage, Povey & Arden, 2003; Sutton, 2005).

In the *precontemplation* stage, individuals do not even consider changing their problematic behaviour (e.g., smoking, alcohol abuse). For example, a smoker may not deliberate much about smoking, let alone intend to quit. When individuals reach the *contemplation* stage, they do think about their problematic behaviour

> **transtheoretical model** a stage model of behaviour change developed to understand how people intentionally change their behaviour

and its possible adverse consequences. For instance, the smoker in our example may have heard about the possible serious consequences of prolonged smoking and may wonder whether he should quit. The third stage – the *preparation* stage – consists of mental preparation of a behaviour change, i.e., formulation of intentions and action plans. Thus, a smoker may formulate the intention to stop smoking after his next vacation and may plan to use nicotine gum as a substitute. The fourth stage, the *action* stage, is characterized by explicit attempts to change or abandon the problematic behaviour, although at this stage relapses are frequent (thus in Figure 15.12 the precontemplation, contemplation, preparation and action phases are repeated). Thus, a smoker may quit several times, interrupted by relapses. The fifth stage, *maintenance*, consists of maintaining the changed behaviour successfully over a relatively long period of time (often operationalized as a 6-month period without relapse).

The TTM assumes that two important psychological variables accompany the (successful) transition from stage to stage. The first is *self-efficacy* (Bandura, 2001; e.g., an individual's perception that he or she is able to stop smoking). The second variable is the so-called *decisional balance*, a concept borrowed from Janis and Mann's (1977) decision theory. Decisional balance concerns a consideration of the positive and the negative consequences (pros and cons) of a particular (negative health) behaviour such as smoking. According to the theory, the pros and cons are polarized at the precontemplation and at the maintenance stages (that is, primarily advantages of the maladaptive behaviour are seen at the precontemplation stage, but primarily disadvantages are seen at the maintenance stage). Pros and cons are more or less equally strong during the three stages in between.

The TTM has been very influential and has helped to make popular the idea that behaviour change progresses through a series of stages. However, to make it a reliable tool for interventions to induce behaviour change and match these interventions to the respective stage, more theoretical specifications are needed regarding the variables that determine the stage transitions (Sutton, 2005).

Strategies of health behaviour change
Given the fact that many people show maladaptive behaviours such as smoking, practising unprotected sex, eating a fatty diet or failing to exercise, the question arises as to how these undesirable behaviours can be changed. Public interventions designed to achieve large-scale behaviour change rely on two strategies: *health education* or *modification of the incentive structure*. Health education involves the transfer of knowledge and skill. It provides individuals or groups with knowledge about the health consequences of certain lifestyles and the skills to enable them to change their behaviour. This strategy often consists of exposing people to persuasive messages that are designed to motivate them to

health education the provision of knowledge and/or training of skills that facilitate voluntary adoption of behaviour conducive to health

modification of the incentive structure strategies of behaviour change that influence behaviour by increasing the costs of undesirable (e.g., health-impairing) behaviour and decreasing the costs of desirable (health-promoting) behaviour. Governments often use fiscal measures (e.g., tax increases on cigarettes) or legal measures (e.g., laws enforcing use of seatbelts) to influence behaviour

change their maladaptive behaviours. Thus, persuasive health messages rely heavily upon the principles of persuasion you have already learned about in Chapter 7, and they have much in common with advertising, which we dealt with in an earlier section of this chapter. Strategies that rely on modification of relevant incentives increase the costs of engaging in unhealthy behaviours or decrease the costs of healthy behaviours. Examples are the ban on smoking in restaurants or public buildings that is practised in several countries, the imposition of a fine on people who do not use seatbelts, and free inoculations for certain risk groups.

Persuasion. Persuasive attempts to change people's unhealthy behaviours have often used so-called *fear appeals* or fear-arousing communications (de Hoog, Stroebe & de Wit, 2005; Leventhal, 1970). Fear appeals are communications that depict the threats associated with a certain maladaptive behaviour such as smoking and offer a recommendation concerning how to avert the threat (e.g., quit smoking). Early accounts of fear appeals (e.g., Hovland, Janis & Kelley, 1953) placed emphasis upon the amount of fear aroused by a fear appeal as the most important factor determining its effectiveness. Indeed, strong evidence was found for a positive linear relationship between amount of fear aroused and acceptance of the recommendation (Sutton, 1982). However, later social psychological research guided by protection motivation theory (e.g., Rippetoe & Rogers, 1987; Rogers & Mewborn, 1976) helped to establish the fact that it is not the emotion of fear as such that is mainly responsible for this positive effect. Rather, the concomitant cognitive processes such as assessing one's vulnerability to the threat and the effectiveness of the recommended action are more important determinants of acceptance (Das, de Wit & Stroebe, 2003; de Hoog et al., 2005).

Due to the growing empirical support for dual-process theories of persuasion such as the ELM and the HSM, several researchers have also applied these theories to fear appeals (e.g., Gleicher & Petty, 1992; Liberman & Chaiken, 1992). According to these analyses, fear appeals can have two different effects. On the one hand, the threat to which the fear appeal refers (e.g., contracting AIDS due to unprotected sex) motivates the message recipient to process the message intensively and accurately. On the other hand, the threat of being possibly unwell or unsafe induces a defence motivation, because the individual feels threatened by the outcome and his or her inability to cope effectively. Thus, the individual will critically evaluate the message, process information selectively, try to find weaknesses in the argumentation, tend to minimize the impending threat and tend to exaggerate the effectiveness of his or her coping abilities.

The stage model of the processing of fear-arousing communications (Das et al., 2003; de Hoog et al., 2005; Stroebe, 2001) is a particularly promising theory of the effects of fear appeals, because it integrates ideas from dual-process theories of persuasion (cf. Chapter 7, this volume), previous fear appeal theories (e.g., PMT) and cognitive stress theory (Lazarus & Folkman, 1984). According to this stage model, individuals exposed to fear appeals engage in two types of appraisal: (1) the appraisal of threat and (2) the

fear appeals persuasive communications that attempt to motivate recipients to change behaviour that is deleterious to their health by inducing fear about the potential health hazards and recommending an action that will reduce or eliminate the threat

appraisal of coping strategies for reducing or averting the threat. The appraisal of threat is assumed to happen in the first stage, whereas the appraisal of the recommendation is assumed to follow in a second stage. The model assumes that the perception of a severe health risk increases deep elaboration of the fear appeal, because such a threat deserves thorough elaboration. If the individual perceives high severity and low personal vulnerability, the elaboration is assumed to be guided by accuracy motivation. If, however, high perceived severity is combined with high perceived vulnerability, defence motivation is aroused, because the individual feels threatened.

Therefore, the combination of high severity with high vulnerability should lead to deep *biased* elaboration. In other words, the appraisal of the threat in the first stage is assumed to be biased in a *negative* direction (i.e., the individual is motivated to play down the threat and search selectively for flaws in the argumentation concerning the threat). Likewise, an individual perceiving high severity and high vulnerability will be biased in a *positive* direction when evaluating the recommendation and the existing coping strategies. No arousal of defence motivation is assumed for the other two combinations of severity and vulnerability (low severity, low vulnerability: shallow processing and accuracy motivation; low severity, high vulnerability: deep processing and accuracy motivation).

On the basis of these assumptions, these investigators carried out two studies (Das et al., 2003; de Hoog et al., 2005) that involved the manipulation of vulnerability and severity of threat as well as the quality of arguments supporting a protective action recommendation. The depicted threats included the health consequences of stress and of RSI (repetitive strain injury). On the whole, the results were consistent with the model. Higher vulnerability led to higher systematic processing and stronger intention to act. There was also evidence showing that the positive influence of vulnerability on intentions was not moderated by argument quality. This latter result is suggestive of defence motivation, i.e., individuals who were highly vulnerable seemed to be positively biased; they intended to carry out the recommendation irrespective of whether they received strong or weak supporting arguments for the recommendation to attend stress management training (de Hoog et al., 2005).

Changing the incentive structure. Persuasion often turns out to be a relatively ineffective means of changing the behaviour of large numbers of the population. For example, Swedish drivers could not be *persuaded* to use their seatbelts, so the government decided to introduce a law that made seatbelt use compulsory for front-seat passengers in private cars. This law increased the frequency of seatbelt use from 30 to 85 per cent within a few months (Fhanér & Hane, 1979). A meta-analysis comparing the impact of seatbelt education programs with the effects of legal measures indicated that legal measures resulted in substantially greater behaviour change than did education (Johnston, Hendricks & Fike, 1994). Thus, clearly the incentives (or sanctions) associated with such compulsory strategies are much more powerful than the relatively weak impact of persuasive arguments (Stroebe, 2001). In addition to gaining incentives or avoiding sanctions, the incentive-based strategy of behaviour change may help to establish healthy habits. Thus, behaviours such as putting on a seatbelt or stopping at a red traffic light become habitual if they are performed frequently under

environmental conditions that are stable (Ouellette & Wood, 1998; Verplanken & Aarts, 1999). In addition, after having been induced to perform the requested behaviour, individuals may find that the behaviour is not as bad as they had anticipated. Therefore, the positive direct experience provides them with information about the behaviour and they are induced to elaborate on its consequences. This should lead to strong attitudes that predict the behaviour irrespective of sanctions or incentives (cf. Fazio et al., 1982).

If persuasion turns out to be less effective than alternatives in cases such as seatbelt use, why then bother at all with persuasion, and why not rely completely on changes in the incentive structure? For several reasons, this would be unrealistic and, in addition, undesirable. First, incentive-based attitude change does not apply to all health behaviours. For example, people would not accept a law forcing them to jog daily, and, in addition, such a law would be difficult to enforce. Second, in some cases health education tends to build up an intrinsic motivation to carry out the recommended behaviour (e.g., 'I really do feel better now that I've stopped smoking'). In contrast, the danger of incentive-based behaviour change is that people may attribute their own changed behaviour to the power of the sanctioning or reward-providing institution (e.g., 'I still don't think it is necessary to use a seatbelt, but I can't afford to pay a fine'; cf. Lepper & Greene, 1978). Thus, health education is based upon the idea that respondents who are convinced of the advantages of the respective health behaviour will carry it out even in situations (e.g., privately) in which surveillance through sanctioning institutions is absent.

Stress and health

How does stress affect health?
What factors moderate the stress–health relationship?
What types of stressors exist in the workplace?

Like smoking or eating a fatty diet, leading a stressful life can have an adverse effect on your health. There are two ways in which stress can affect health, namely through changes in health behaviour and through bodily changes (e.g., changes in the immune system). People who are stressed tend to stop eating regularly, increase their alcohol consumption or take tranquillizers and sleeping pills. For example, widows and widowers in the Tübingen Longitudinal Study of Bereavement reported increased use of tranquillizers and sleeping tablets and increased consumption of both alcoholic beverages and cigarettes after the loss of a partner (Stroebe, 2001). However, stress may also have indirect effects upon health, by reducing the body's resistance to diseases. An especially clear-cut study to confirm this mechanism was conducted by Cohen, Tyrell and Smith (1993; see also Cohen et al., 1998). They intentionally exposed healthy participants to a common cold virus, then quarantined and monitored them for the development of (latent) infection and (manifest) clinical colds. Results showed that participants with higher scores on scales of psychological stress were at greater risk of developing a cold. The stress scales that these researchers employed referred to previous negative life events, perception that current demands exceeded capabilities, and negative affect such as feeling distressed and nervous. The researchers also took numerous precautions to preclude alternative explanations of the effect (e.g., confounding with personality variables, different health practices).

The concept of stress has been made popular through Selye's (1956) research on patterns of bodily responses that occur when an organism is exposed to a stressor such as intensive heat or infection. These ideas were then adapted by psychiatrists, who began to study stressful life events as factors contributing to the development of a variety of physical and mental illnesses (e.g., Cobb & Lindemann, 1943). Basic to this work was the idea that psychosocial stress caused by *critical life events* leads to the same bodily changes as tissue damage. Critical life events represent major changes in an individual's life, which range from short term to enduring and which are potentially threatening. Examples are major illnesses, divorce or the death of a spouse (Holmes & Rahe, 1967).

critical life events events that constitute major changes in an individual's life, which range from short term to enduring and which are potentially threatening

stress the condition that arises when individuals perceive the demands of a situation as challenging or exceeding their resources and endangering their well-being

Numerous definitions of *stress* have been suggested. The common element is their emphasis on a process in which 'environmental demands tax or exceed the adaptive capacity of an organism, resulting in psychological and biological changes that may place persons at risk for disease' (Cohen, Kessler & Gordon, 1995, p. 3). Whereas the early research focused on critical life events as stressors, later research has proposed that minor life events ('daily hassles') such as 'misplacing or losing things', 'troublesome neighbours' or 'concerns about owing money' may also have a negative impact on individuals' health and well-being (DeLongis, Folkman & Lazarus, 1988; Kanner, Coyne, Schaefer & Lazarus, 1981). As research has shown, the negative impact of stress on health and well-being includes several illnesses such as coronary heart disease (e.g., Hemingway & Marmot, 1999; Siegrist, 1996), disorders of the immune system (e.g., Cohen et al., 1993; Steptoe, 2001) and musculoskeletal ailments (e.g., Hemingway, Shipley, Stansfield & Marmot, 1997). The evidence of health-impairing effects is clear-cut for critical life events and for work-related stress (see below), but more ambiguous for daily hassles.

What makes stressors stressful? One of the most influential psychological theories of stress is the transactional stress model developed by Lazarus (1966; Lazarus & Folkman, 1984; for other stress models see Edwards, Caplan & van Harrison, 2000; Karasek & Theorell, 1990). As we noted earlier, two central processes determine the extent of stress that an individual experiences in a given situation, namely, *cognitive appraisal* and *coping* (Lazarus & Folkman, 1984). Regarding appraisal, Lazarus and Folkman distinguish between three types. *Primary appraisal* designates the process by which the individual assesses a certain event according to whether it is stressful or harmless. *Secondary appraisal* refers to

cognitive appraisal the evaluative process that determines why, and to what extent, a particular situation is perceived as stressful

coping the cognitive and behavioural strategies that individuals use to manage both a stressful situation and the negative emotional reactions elicited by the event

the individual assessing his or her own coping competencies and resources with respect to the potential threat. *Reappraisal* refers to a reassessment of the situation to find out whether the threatening situation has possibly changed after the individual's attempts to cope with it.

Coping encompasses the cognitive and behavioural strategies that individuals use to manage both a stressful situation and the negative emotional reactions elicited by that event. Lazarus and Folkman (1984) distinguish two forms of coping. *Problem-focused coping* is instrumental behaviour directed at reducing or eliminating the threat. It is the type of behaviour predicted by models of health behaviour such as protection motivation theory and the transtheoretical model.

problem-focused coping instrumental behaviour aimed at reducing or eliminating the risk of harmful consequences that might result from a stressful event

emotion-focused coping coping strategies that do not focus on the stressful event but on ameliorating the distressing emotional reactions to the event

Emotion-focused coping is aimed at reducing emotional distress. In coping with their emotions, individuals may use cognitive strategies such as reappraising the situation as less threatening or engaging in wishful thinking. But they may also try to 'calm their nerves' by taking tranquillizers or drinking alcohol.

The extent to which a situation is experienced as stressful, as well as the individual's success in mastering it, will depend on his or her *coping resources*. Lazarus and Folkman (1984) distinguish resources that are primarily properties of the person and resources that are primarily environmental. *Intrapersonal resources* include

coping resources the extrapersonal (e.g., social support) and intrapersonal (e.g., optimism) resources available to the individual for coping with the demands of a critical event

physical resources such as good health and energy, psychological resources such as optimism or a positive self-concept, and competencies such as problem solving and social skills. Examples of *extrapersonal* (or environmental) *resources* are financial resources or social support, i.e., the availability of others (e.g., family, friends, colleagues) who can help the individual to cope with the stressful situation.

Moderators of the stress–health relationship There are tremendous individual differences in the extent to which stress experiences affect people's health. These differences are attributed to the fact that coping resources function as *moderators* of the stress–health relationship. In this case, moderation means that the relationship is obtained only for a low value of the resource (e.g., stress is related to ill health when the individual lacks social support), whereas a high value of the resource weakens the relationship or even makes it disappear (e.g., high social support can prevent stress leading to illness).

Strategies of coping. Several empirical instruments exist for measuring coping strategies, one of the most widely used being the 'Ways of Coping Inventory' (Folkman, Lazarus, Dunkel-Schetter, DeLongis & Gruen, 1986). This measures eight distinct coping strategies, three of which are given here for illustration: confrontive coping (e.g., 'Tried to get the person responsible to change his or her mind'), self-controlling ('I tried to keep my feelings to myself')

PIONEER

Susan Folkman (b. 1938) came late to psychology after having studied history and then for a decade concentrating fully on being a housewife and mother of four children. In the mid-1970s, after a second degree in educational psychology, she began her fruitful collaboration with Richard S. Lazarus at Berkeley, first as a PhD student, later as a research member of the faculty. In 1988, she moved to the University of California at San Francisco. She is internationally recognized for her theoretical and empirical contributions to the field of psychological stress and coping. Her 'Ways of Coping Questionnaire' pioneered empirical research into coping processes and has become a widely used instrument in the study of coping. The monograph *Stress, Appraisal, and Coping* (Lazarus & Folkman, 1984) shaped the area of stress research for decades and has become a classic. After her move to San Francisco, her work focused on stress and coping in the context of HIV diseases and other chronic illness, especially on issues to do with caregiving and bereavement. Since 2001 she has been Director of the Osher Center for Integrative Medicine at the University of California, San Francisco.

INDIVIDUAL DIFFERENCES 15.1

Life Orientation Test (LOT)

Scheier, M.F., Carver, C.S. & Bridges, M.W. (1994). Distinguishing optimism from neuroticism (and trait anxiety, self-mastery, and self-esteem): A reevaluation of the life orientation test. *Journal of Personality and Social Psychology, 67,* 1063–1178.

This scale assesses optimism, the tendency to hold positive expectations for one's future. Optimists differ from pessimists in the way they cope with challenges and in the kind of coping responses they show. Optimists persist longer in their efforts to overcome adversity and adjust more favourably to important life transitions. Although optimism as assessed by the LOT has moderate correlations with neuroticism, trait anxiety, self-mastery and self-esteem, Scheier et al. (1994) show that it is a distinct psychological trait with unique contributions to the prediction of depression and coping. The LOT version described below is an improved version of the original measure (Scheier & Carver, 1985). The complete scale also includes four filler items, not shown here.

Instructions: Respondents are requested to indicate the extent of their agreement with the following items (using the response format: 0 = *strongly disagree*, 1 = *disagree*, 2 = *neutral*, 3 = *agree* and 4 = *strongly agree*):

1. In uncertain times, I usually expect the best.
2. If something can go wrong for me, it will.
3. I'm always optimistic about my future.
4. I hardly ever expect things to go my way.
5. I rarely count on good things happening to me.
6. Overall, I expect more good things to happen to me than bad.

Scoring: Items 2, 4 and 5 are reverse scored before scoring. Items 2, 4 and 5 are then summed with responses to items 1, 3 and 6 to compute an overall optimism score (theoretical range: 0–24).

and planful problem solving ('I made a plan of action and followed it'). However, this apparent diversity of strategies can be further reduced because the various strategies can be distinguished according to two functions (Lazarus & Folkman, 1984): they are carried out to reduce the risk of harmful consequences that might result from a stressful event (problem-focused coping) or to adjust the negative emotional reactions to the event (emotion-focused coping).

In addition to the functions served by coping strategies, a second dimension of each coping strategy is approach vs. avoidance (Roth & Cohen, 1986; Stroebe, 2001). For example, somebody may confront a possible health threat by undergoing the relevant diagnostic procedures, or they may deny any possible threat. As a general conclusion, frequent reliance on avoidant coping strategies seems to have adverse effects on health (Carver et al., 1993; Epping-Jordan, Compas & Howell, 1994; Stanton & Snider, 1993).

Personality traits. Dispositional optimism is an important personality variable that has been proposed as a moderator of the stress–health relationship (for other individual difference variables see Stroebe, 2001). Scheier and Carver (1987) have argued that optimistic people see positive outcomes as more attainable compared with pessimists. This expectation should protect them from giving up in times of stress and hardship. Expecting that things will turn out positively in the long run should have a calming effect on one's well-being and should encourage one to persist in the face of obstacles. In contrast, pessimists should prematurely abandon their efforts to overcome their respective difficulties. These different expectations should function much like a self-fulfilling prophecy, leading to relatively more positive outcomes and more positive

health for optimists. An instrument for measuring optimism developed by Scheier and Carver (1985; revised by Scheier, Carver & Bridges, 1994) assesses the general expectation with which people expect that good things are likely to happen to them (see Individual Differences 15.1).

Several researchers have obtained evidence for the assumption that optimism is indeed associated with less mood disturbance and fewer negative effects of stress on health (e.g., Scheier et al., 1989; Segerstrom, Taylor, Kemeny & Fahey, 1998). An interesting study by Scheier et al. (1989) showed that optimists recovered faster from surgery (bypass patients and women who underwent surgery for breast cancer). There was also a positive relationship between optimism and post-surgical quality of life several months after surgery. Recall that part of the hypothesis regarding the construct of optimism relates to coping as a mediator: optimists are assumed to engage more in problem-focused coping in the face of stressful situations. Several longitudinal studies have provided empirical support for the important role played by active coping among optimists as compared to pessimists and the mediational impact of active coping upon health (e.g., Aspinwall & Taylor, 1992; Segerstrom et al., 1998).

Social support. In the earlier section on social psychology in the workplace, we pointed to the importance of perceived organizational support (POS) for the employment relationship. A more general concept of *social support* is also important in the analysis of stress and well-being: social support is a major resource against stress. Social support reflects the information from others that one is loved and cared for, esteemed and valued, and part of a network of communication and mutual obligation (Cobb, 1976; for typologies of social support see House, 1981; cf. also Chapter 10, this volume). A literature review by Cohen and Wills (1985) shows that social support does indeed have a moderating ('buffering') effect upon health. There is even consistent evidence that low levels of social support are associated with an increased risk of mortality (e.g., Berkman & Syme, 1979; cf. Stroebe, 2001).

Stress in the workplace

The topic of workplace stress provides a link between the topics of organizations and health, which we have so far treated separately. Since people spend a large amount of their lifetime at work, research on organizations has addressed stress due to working in organizations (e.g., Barling, Kelloway & Frone, 2005). Stressors at the workplace may be divided into *non-social* stressors such as long work hours or innovative or complex work technology (e.g., Coovert, Thompson & Craiger, 2005; Totterdell, 2005) and *social* stressors such as role conflicts (Beehr & Glazer, 2005) or severe forms of social conflict such as harassment or workplace aggression (Rospenda & Richman, 2005; Schat & Kelloway, 2005; cf. also Chapter 8, this volume). However, the distinction between social and non-social stressors is somewhat crude, since clearly some social aspects (e.g., poor leadership) may be the more distal cause of a 'non-social' stressor (e.g., inadequate introduction of a new technology), and vice versa.

Competent leadership is a major factor fostering good work outcomes and higher organizational commitment (see Chapter 13, this volume). But leadership is also important for subordinates' health and well-being. Poor leadership has been implicated as a major factor of stress at work (Kelloway, Sivanathan, Francis & Barling, 2005). For example, Wagner, Fieldman and Hussey (2003) reported that nurses experienced significant increases in systolic and diastolic blood pressure on days when they worked for supervisors they did not like compared to days on which they worked for a supervisor they liked. Indeed, the increases were of such a magnitude that long-term exposure to such stress would put the nurses at serious risk of coronary failure and increased risk of stroke. Kelloway et al. (2005) regard poor leadership as being a 'root cause' of stress in organizational settings. By root cause they mean that poor leadership cannot simply be regarded as another single stressor, such as a high workload or high work demands, because it may give rise to *several* important stressors. Thus, some of the most salient problems created by poor leaders may consist in creating work overload for their subordinates, failing to clarify subordinates' work obligations and neglecting to set specific goals, and failing to intervene in cases of harassment and aggression among subordinates (Kelloway et al., 2005).

Take goal setting as an example (Locke & Latham, 2002). Leaders influence the goals their subordinates set themselves, the pace of work, and the amount of work required. Research has shown that specific, high, but realistic goals are an important determinant of productivity (Locke & Latham, 2002). The achievement of goals, on the other hand, has a positive influence upon individuals' self-efficacy (Bandura, 2001). Thus, by failing to set goals for subordinates, by setting unrealistic or diffuse goals ('do your best'), by showing a lack of individual consideration for the strengths and weaknesses of the respective subordinate in reaching the goals, or by not giving necessary feedback, a passive or incompetent leader may create stress. He or she does so by impairing the subordinates' self-efficacy, or by creating an unrealistic gap between the leader's demands and subordinates' capabilities. These adverse effects may even spill over into subordinates' private life as they 'take home' their stress, thereby creating work–family conflicts (Bellavia & Frone, 2005).

According to Kelloway et al.'s (2005) analysis of leadership as a root cause of stress in the workplace, poor leadership has a *direct* effect upon subordinates' well-being and health. But of course, leadership is also a major factor with regard to social support (or lack of it) and therefore has a *moderating* effect in the stress–health relationship (e.g., Cummings, 1990; Karlin, Brondolo & Schwartz, 2003). For example, the supportive leader may show consideration for a worker (e.g., for his or her dual role as a worker and a parent), offer task-specific help or provide appropriate feedback. By offering these types of support, the amount of stress can be expected to be reduced. Incompetent or passive leaders may fail to provide these kinds of support and may thereby pose risks to the subordinate's health.

It is clear that poor leadership also has close connections with organizational justice, which we discussed in an earlier section. For example, a manager who assigns an unrealistically high workload to his or her subordinates or lacks careful planning will be perceived as unfair (Cropanzano, Goldman & Benson, 2005). Recent research has implicated a lack of organizational justice as a stressor and suggested that perceived lack of justice is associated with an increase in (self-reported) physical symptoms (e.g., De Boer, Bakker, Syroit & Schaufeli, 2002; Elovainio, Kivimäki & Vahtera, 2002).

SUMMARY

Health education professionals can profit a great deal from social psychological research. Research concerning the determinants of health behaviour has shown that coping appraisal, especially one's perceived self-efficacy, is a major factor in predicting intentions to carry out health-related behaviour. Attempts to change health-related behaviour can involve attempts to persuade people, via communicative appeals, or to change the incentive structure. Research on fear appeals has yielded evidence that recipients must feel vulnerable to the respective health threat to be motivated to accept the protective message. But vulnerability may also be associated with recipients' tendencies to downplay the threat. Thus, the threat must be described carefully and convincingly. Changes in the incentive structure, such as introducing rewards or imposing sanctions, may sometimes be more effective than persuasion, but persuasion can be expected to yield more long-lasting, intrinsic changes.

Health is influenced not only by unhealthy behaviour but also by stress. Stress may be engendered by a variety of stressors, such as major critical life events, daily hassles and stress in the workplace, such as stress associated with bad leadership. Bad leadership may function as a 'root cause' of stress in the workplace, because it gives rise to several stressors such as creating work overload, neglecting to set specific realistic goals and failing to give necessary feedback. Several variables moderate stress, such as personality traits and social support.

SUMMARY AND CONCLUSIONS

- Social psychological theory, basic research and applied research have a reciprocal relationship. Theories help us to understand and address real-life phenomena, while confirmation of a theory's central predictions in practice increases our confidence in the theory and enhances its generalizability.

- In this chapter we have described the application of social psychology to three main areas: advertising, the workplace and health.

- The dual-process perspective (e.g., ELM and HSM models) is a powerful framework for explaining the diverse effects of advertising and is suitable for integrating some of the older models that were designed specifically for advertising.

- Because recipients of advertisements typically lack time and motivation, they can often only be influenced by low-elaboration strategies. Among others, such strategies

encompass classical conditioning, mere exposure and categorizing a new product as an exemplar of an already established brand category (brand extension).

- A unique feature distinguishing advertising from other types of persuasion is the role of the attitude towards the advertisement. Because this specific attitude exerts direct and indirect effects upon the brand attitude, it is a main target of advertisers.

- We have stressed that job attitudes are useful in predicting work outcome. Both the most general job attitude, job satisfaction, and one of the more specific job attitudes, affective commitment, determine employees' performance and withdrawal behaviour.

- We have identified job design as one major influence on job attitudes. The job characteristics model predicts that satisfaction is stronger if the jobs require a variety of skills and tasks that are both important and comprehensive; employees will also only be satisfied with jobs that provide a certain degree of autonomy and feedback.

- The employment relationship is also central in determining job attitudes. If employees feel that the organization treats them fairly and supports their efforts, they are more satisfied with their job, more highly committed to the organization and work harder towards task achievement.

- Perceptions regarding procedural justice are influential in the workplace, as explained by the instrumental, relational and substitutability approaches.

- Vulnerability and self-efficacy are important determinants of health behaviour. These variables are given prominent attention in one of the most influential social cognitive models of health behaviour, protection motivation theory. Its further predictors are severity, intrinsic and extrinsic rewards, response efficacy and response costs.

- Modifications in the incentive structure involve attempts to increase the costs of health-impairing behaviour (e.g., by taxes on cigarettes) and decrease the costs of health-promoting behaviour (e.g., by laws enforcing use of seatbelts). Such attempts to influence health behaviour are often more effective than persuasive appeals, but run the risk that respondents will not internalize their behaviour change.

- Stress has a negative impact upon health and well-being. The impact of stress is moderated by strategies of coping and several intrapersonal (e.g., dispositional optimism) and extrapersonal (e.g., social support) resources.

- For today's workforce, a critical factor determining stress levels is the quality of leadership. Bad leadership is a root cause of stress (e.g., by creating work overload, by neglecting to set specific goals and by failing to intervene in cases of conflicts among subordinates).

Suggestions for further reading

Conner, M. & Norman, P. (Eds.) (2005). *Predicting health behaviour: Research and practice with social cognition models* (2nd edn). Maidenhead: Open University Press. A highly readable theoretical and empirical evaluation of the major social cognitive models of health behaviour, including suggestions for their further development and synthesis.

Greenberg, J. & Colquitt, J.A. (Eds.) (2005). *Handbook of organizational justice*. Mahwah, NJ: Lawrence Erlbaum. This comprehensive reader offers a state-of-the-art introduction to the field of organizational justice. Many experts in the field give their insights, e.g., into the different justice constructs, the process of judging justice and how justice relates to stress and discrimination.

Judge, T.A., Thoresen, C.J., Bono, J.E. & Patton, G.K. (2001). The job satisfaction–job performance relationship: A qualitative and quantitative review. *Psychological Bulletin, 127*, 376–407. This influential article gives an excellent review of the possible relationships between job satisfaction and job performance and summarizes the state of research.

Priester, J.R. & Petty, R.F. (2003). The influence of spokesperson trustworthiness on message elaboration, attitude strength, and advertising effectiveness. *Journal of Consumer Psychology, 13*, 408–421. An exemplary application of the ELM to the topic of advertising with a special focus on spokesperson trustworthiness.

Solomon, M.R. (2004). *Consumer behavior: Buying, having, and being*. Upper Saddle River, NJ: Pearson. An excellent introduction to all facets of consumer behaviour and advertising, including important social psychological contributions.

Stroebe, W. (2001). *Social psychology and health* (2nd edn). Buckingham: Open University Press. An important, integrative approach to health topics from a social-psychological perspective.

Taylor, S.E. (2005). *Health psychology* (6th edn). New York: McGraw-Hill. One of the best textbooks on health psychology, written by a leading researcher in the field.

Glossary

accessibility the extent to which information is easily located and retrieved.

accountability a processing goal whereby perceivers believe they will have to justify their responses to a third party and be held responsible for their impressions; this typically leads to less stereotypical impressions.

actor–observer difference general tendency for people to explain their own behaviour in more situational terms but other people's behaviour in more dispositional terms.

affective commitment specific job attitude depicting an employee's degree of emotional attachment to, identification with and involvement in the organization.

affective component of attitude the feelings or emotions associated with an attitude object.

affiliation the tendency to seek out the company of others, irrespective of the feelings towards such others.

aggression any form of behaviour directed towards the goal of harming or injuring another living being who is motivated to avoid such treatment.

Aggression Questionnaire self-report instrument to measure stable individual differences in trait aggressiveness.

aggressive cues situational cues with an aggressive meaning that increase the accessibility of aggressive cognitions.

aggressive scripts cognitive representation of when and how to show aggressive behaviour.

altruism refers to **prosocial behaviour** that has the ultimate goal of benefiting another person.

analysis of non-common effects observers infer intentions behind actions by comparing the consequences of the behavioural options that were open to the actor and identifying distinctive outcomes (*see* **correspondent inference theory**).

anger management training approach for preventing aggression by teaching aggressive individuals to control their anger and inhibit aggressive impulses.

attachment theory proposes that the development of secure infant–caregiver attachment in childhood is the basis for the ability to maintain stable and intimate relationships in adulthood.

attitude an overall evaluation of a stimulus object.

attitude–behavior relation the degree to which an attitude predicts behaviour.

attitude function the psychological need fulfilled by an attitude.

attitude towards the advertisement evaluation of the advertisement (rather than the product itself) that is determined by its characteristics (e.g., visual, acoustic, humorous).

attitudinal ambivalence an instance where an individual both likes and dislikes an attitude object.

attraction positive feelings towards another individual, including a tendency to seek out the presence of the other.

attributional bias systematic distortions in the sampling or processing of information about the causes of behaviour.

augmentation principle the assumption that causal factors need to be stronger if an inhibitory influence on an observed effect is present. The converse of the **discounting principle**.

authoritarian personality a particular type of personality, overly submissive to authority figures, which is thought to be especially prone to prejudice.

autokinetic effect perceptual illusion whereby, in the absence of reference points, a stationary light appears to move.

automatic process a process that occurs without intention, effort or awareness and does not interfere with other concurrent cognitive processes.

behavioural component of attitude past behaviours associated with an attitude object.

brainstorming a group technique aimed at enhancing creativity in groups by means of the uninhibited generation of as many ideas as possible concerning a specified topic.

brand extension new product that is launched under an already established brand name.

buffer effect of social support the effect that those who perceive themselves to be supported are less affected by stressful events and conditions than those who feel unsupported.

bullying (mobbing) denotes aggressive behaviour directed at victims who cannot easily defend themselves, typically in schools and at the workplace.

categorization the tendency to group objects (including people) into discrete groups, based upon shared characteristics common to them.

category salience the activation of a particular social category within a particular context. It depends on normative and comparative fit as well as a readiness to apply this category.

catharsis release of aggressive tension through symbolic engagement in aggressive behaviour.

causal power an intrinsic property of an object or event that enables it to exert influence on some other object or event.

causal schema a knowledge structure shaping attributions. Causal schemas may be either abstract representations of general causal principles (e.g., multiple necessary and multiple sufficient causes schemas) or domain-specific ideas about how particular causes determine particular effects.

central route to persuasion a person's careful and thoughtful consideration of the arguments presented in support of a position. *See also* **peripheral route to persuasion**; **systematic processing**.

central trait a dispositional characteristic viewed by social perceivers as integral to the organization of personality.

cognitive algebra a proposed process for averaging or summing trait information when forming impressions of other people.

cognitive appraisal the evaluative process that determines why, and to what extent, a particular situation is perceived as stressful.

cognitive component of attitude thoughts, beliefs and attributes associated with an attitude object.

cognitive neo-associationist model explains aggressive behaviour as the result of negative affect that is subjected to cognitive processing and activates a network of aggression-related thoughts and feelings.

cognitive response model assumes that attitude change is mediated by the thoughts, or 'cognitive responses', which recipients generate as they receive and reflect upon persuasive communications, and that the magnitude and direction of attitude change obtained by a persuasive communication are functions of the extent of message-relevant thinking as well as its favourability.

cognitive restriction a capability loss in group tasks that involve idea generation, which occurs when an idea mentioned by another group member makes people focus on the particular category this idea belongs to, at the expense of generating ideas from other categories.

cognitive stimulation a capability gain in group tasks that involve idea generation, which occurs when an idea mentioned by another group member stimulates a cognitive category one would otherwise not have thought of.

cohesion the force that binds members to the group. *See also* **interpersonal cohesion; task cohesion**.

commitment the individual's tendency both to maintain a relationship and to feel psychologically attached to it (Chapter 10); the degree to which a group member identifies with the group and its goals and wishes to maintain group membership (Chapter 12).

common ingroup identity model of intergroup contact which replaces salient ingroup–outgroup distinctions at a subordinate level with a common ingroup identity at a superordinate level that includes former ingroup and outgroup members.

comparative advertising an advertisement that compares one brand ('sponsor brand') with a comparison brand with the aim of convincing recipients of the sponsor brand's superiority.

compliance a particular kind of response whereby the target of influence acquiesces to a request from the source of influence. The term is also used more generally to refer to change in public behaviour to match a norm, without corresponding change on a private level.

confederate an accomplice or assistant of the experimenter who is ostensibly another participant but who in fact plays a prescribed role in the experiment.

configural model a holistic approach to impression formation, implying that social perceivers actively construct deeper meanings out of the bits of information that they receive about other people.

Conflict Tactics Scales instrument for measuring intimate partner violence by collecting self-reports of perpetration and/or victimization.

conformity *see* **majority influence**.

confounding a variable that incorporates two or more potentially separable components is a confounded variable. When an independent variable is confounded, the researcher's ability to draw unambiguous causal inferences is seriously constrained.

consensus information evidence relating to how different actors behave towards the same entity.

consistency a behavioural style indicating that the same position is maintained across time; seen as central to **minority influence**.

consistency information evidence relating to how an actor's behaviour towards an entity varies across different situations.

construct an abstract theoretical concept (such as social influence).

construct validity the validity of the assumption that independent and dependent variables adequately capture the abstract variables (constructs) they are supposed to represent.

contact hypothesis the idea that contact between members of different social groups under appropriate conditions will reduce their prejudice against each other.

contextual performance an employee's extra-role behaviour, e.g., helping colleagues, which is not part of the job description but which promotes the effective functioning of the organization.

contingency approaches emphasize the role of situational factors in the study of leadership (e.g., characteristics of the task, the followers or the social context) and how these moderate the relationship

between **leader traits** or **leadership behaviour** and **leadership effectiveness**.

continuum model of impression formation a theoretical model advanced by Fiske and Neuberg (1990) that views impression formation as a process going from category-based evaluations at one end of the continuum to individuated responses at the other. Progress along the continuum is thought to depend upon the interplay of motivational and attentional factors.

control group a group of participants who are typically not exposed to the independent variable(s) used in experimental research. Measures of the **dependent variable** derived from these participants are compared with those derived from participants who are exposed to the **independent variable** (i.e., the **experimental group**), providing a basis for inferring whether the independent variable determines scores on the dependent variable.

controlled process a process that is intentional, under the individual's volitional control, effortful and entailing conscious awareness.

convergent validity established by showing that different measures of the same **construct** (e.g., self-report, implicit, observation) are significantly associated with each other.

conversion a change in private response after exposure to influence by others; internalized change; a change in the way one structures an aspect of reality.

coordination losses describe the diminished performance of a group if it fails to optimally coordinate its members' individual contributions.

coping the cognitive and behavioural strategies that individuals use to manage both a stressful situation and the negative emotional reactions elicited by the event.

coping resources the extrapersonal (e.g., social support) and intrapersonal (e.g., optimism) resources available to the individual for coping with the demands of a critical event.

correspondence bias the proposed tendency to infer a personal disposition corresponding to observed behaviour even when the behaviour was determined by the situation.

correspondent inference theory proposes that observers infer correspondent intentions and dispositions for observed intentional behaviour under certain circumstances.

counterattitudinal behaviour behaviour (usually induced by monetary incentives or threats) which is inconsistent with the actor's attitude or beliefs.

counterproductive work behaviour all voluntary behaviours that violate organizational norms and thus threaten the well-being of the organization, e.g., sabotage, theft.

covariation theory proposes that observers work out the causes of behaviour by collecting data about comparison cases. Causality is attributed to the person, entity or situation depending on which of these factors covaries with the observed effect.

cover story a false but supposedly plausible explanation of the purpose of an experiment. The intention is to limit the operation of **demand characteristics**.

critical life events events that constitute major changes in an individual's life, which range from short term to enduring and which are potentially threatening.

debriefing the practice of explaining to participants the purpose of the experiment in which they have just participated, and answering any questions the participant may have. It is especially important to debrief participants when the experimental procedure involved deception – in which case the debriefing should also explain why the deception was considered to be necessary.

decategorization reduction of the salience of ingroup–outgroup distinctions in order to establish interpersonal contact.

deindividuation a state in which individuals are deprived of their sense of individual identity and are more likely to behave in an extreme manner, often anti-socially and violating norms.

demand characteristics cues that are perceived as telling participants how they are expected to behave or respond in a research setting, i.e., cues that 'demand' a certain sort of response.

dependent variable the **variable** that is expected to change as a function of changes in the **independent variable**. Measured changes in the dependent variable are seen as 'dependent on' manipulated changes in the independent variable.

depersonalization the shift from personal to social identity, entailing the accentuation of intragroup similarities and intergroup differences.

depressive realism the idea that depressed people's interpretations of reality are more accurate than those of non-depressed people.

diffusion of responsibility cognitive appraisal which divides responsibility among several onlookers or bystanders. As a consequence, each individual member in the group feels less responsible than when alone. When there are several bystanders present in an emergency, the responsibility of any one of the bystanders is reduced.

discounting principle the presence of a causal factor working towards an observed effect implies that other potential factors are less influential. The converse of the **augmenting principle**.

discourse analysis a family of methods for analysing talk and texts, with the goal of revealing how people make sense of their everyday worlds.

displaced aggression tendency to respond to frustration with an aggressive response directed not at the original source of the frustration but at an unrelated, more easily accessible target.

dissociation model a model that proposes that two different processes can occur independently, and that one does not inevitably follow from the other (e.g., Devine's theoretical model that proposes a dissociation between automatic and controlled processes in stereotyping).

dissonance theory a consistency theory which assumes that dissonance is an aversive state, which motivates individuals to reduce it. Strategies of dissonance reduction include belief, attitude and behaviour change as well as the search for consonant or the avoidance of dissonant information.

distinctiveness information evidence relating to how an actor responds to different entities under similar circumstances.

distraction while listening to a persuasive communication, individuals are distracted by having to perform an irrelevant activity or by experiencing sensory stimulation irrelevant to the message.

distributive justice perceptions in organizations about how fairly a certain amount of outcome (e.g., income) is distributed, both absolutely and relatively, between employees or between organizational groups.

door-in-the-face technique compliance technique in which the requester begins with an extreme request that is almost always refused, then retreats to a more moderate request, which he or she had in mind all along (also known as a 'reciprocal concessions' procedure).

dual-process theories of persuasion theories of persuasion postulating two modes of information processing, systematic and non-systematic. Modes differ in the extent to which individuals engage in content-relevant thoughts and critical evaluation of the arguments contained in a message in order to accept or reject the position advocated. The mode used is assumed to depend on processing motivation and ability. See **elaboration likelihood model**; **heuristic-systematic model**.

ego depletion a temporary reduction in the self's regulatory capacity.

elaboration refers to the extent to which a person thinks about the issue-relevant arguments contained in a message.

elaboration likelihood model (ELM) assumes that attitude change in response to persuasive communications can be mediated by two different modes of information processing (central and peripheral). Elaboration denotes the extent to which a person thinks about the issue-relevant arguments contained in a message. The probability that a recipient will critically evaluate arguments (the elaboration likelihood) is determined by both processing motivation and ability. See **dual-process theories of persuasion**.

emotion-focused coping coping strategies that do not focus on the stressful event but on ameliorating the distressing emotional reactions to the event.

emotional contagion the unconscious mimicking of the facial expressions and feelings of another person.

empathy tendency to experience an emotional response that is congruent with the emotional state of another person. It results from adopting the perspective of the other and compassionately understanding his or her emotions.

encoding the way in which we translate what we see into a digestible format to be stored in the mind.

entitativity the degree to which a collection of persons is perceived as being bonded together in a coherent unit.

epidemiological studies research studies dealing with the incidence, distribution and possible control of diseases and other factors relating to health and illness.

equity theory assumes that satisfaction is a function of the ratio of outcomes to inputs of the person as compared with those of a reference other, and that individuals will try to restore equity when they find themselves in an inequitable situation.

ethnocentrism rating ingroup attributes and characteristics above those of the outgroup; literally, a view of things in which other groups are rated against the standard of the ingroup.

eureka effect describes the situation when the correct solution to a problem, once it is found, is immediately recognized as being correct by group members.

evaluation apprehension concern about being appraised by others causes arousal leading to **social facilitation**, because people have learned to be apprehensive about being evaluated by others.

evolutionary theory explains human behaviour, including differences in partner preferences according to gender, from their reproductive value, i.e., their value in producing offspring in our evolutionary past.

exchange fiction people need a **cover story** in order to donate money to charities. To fulfil this need, people are offered something in exchange for their donation which – although it is low in value – creates the impression that a generous contribution is also a rational exchange.

excitation transfer transfer of neutral physiological arousal onto arousal resulting from frustration, thus augmenting negative affect and enhancing the strength of an aggressive response.

expectation states theory argues that status differences within a group result from different expectations that group members have about each other.

experiment a method in which the researcher deliberately introduces some change into a setting to examine the consequences of that change.

experimental group a group of participants allocated to the 'experimental' condition of the experiment, i.e., the condition in which participants are exposed to that level of the **independent variable** that is predicted to influence their thoughts, feelings or behaviour. See **control group**.

experimental scenario the 'package' within which an experiment is presented to participants. In **field experiments** it is, ideally, something that happens naturally. In laboratory experiments it is important to devise a scenario that strikes the participant as realistic and involving.

experimenter expectancy effects effects unintentionally produced by the experimenter in the course of his or her interaction with the participant. These effects result from the experimenter's knowledge of the hypothesis under test, and they increase the likelihood that the participants will behave in such a way as to confirm the hypothesis.

explicit measures of attitude attitude measures that directly ask respondents to think about and report an attitude.

external validity refers to the generalizability of research findings to settings and populations other than those involved in the research.

factorial experiment an experiment in which two or more independent variables are manipulated within the same design.

false consensus bias the assumption that other people generally share one's own personal attitudes and opinions.

fear appeals persuasive communications that attempt to motivate recipients to change behaviour that is deleterious to their health by inducing fear about the potential health hazards and recommending an action that will reduce or eliminate the threat.

fear of embarrassment the stressful experience of a person whose behaviour in a situation is observed by bystanders. Especially when the situation is unfamiliar, social anxiety is elicited which reduces the tendency to help victims of emergencies. Related terms are 'audience inhibition' and **evaluation apprehension**.

field experiment a true randomized experiment conducted in a natural setting.

foot-in-the-door technique **compliance** technique in which the requester first asks for a small favour that is almost certain to be granted, then follows this up with a request for a larger, related favour.

free-riding a reduction in group members' task-related effort because their individual contribution seems to have little impact on group performance.

frustration-aggression hypothesis assumes that frustration, i.e., blockage of a goal-directed activity, increases the likelihood of aggressive behaviour.

general aggression model integrative framework explaining how personal and situational input variables lead to aggressive behaviour via cognitive appraisal and negative affective arousal.

geographic regions approach method for testing the **heat hypothesis** by comparing violence rates in cooler and hotter climates.

goal dependent where an outcome is conditional upon a specific goal being in place (e.g., goal-dependent automatic stereotype activation).

group composition specifies how certain characteristics are distributed within a group.

group leadership influencing, motivating or enabling (oneself and) others to contribute towards the effectiveness and viability of work groups.

group learning a generic term for several learning processes that can only occur if several people co-actively or cooperatively work on the same task.

group-level learning (G–G transfer) denotes a group learning process whereby a *particular* whole group's capability to perform a group task changes as a result of social interaction between its group members during repeated collective task performance.

group performance management the sum of activities aimed at maximizing (or improving) the group-specific component of group performance.

group polarization tendency to make decisions that are more extreme than the average of group members' initial positions, in the direction already favoured by the group.

group socialization the efforts of the group to assimilate new members to existing group norms and practices.

group synchronization the sum of activities aimed at optimizing the collaborative generation, modification and integration of individual contributions in a group.

group task type distinguishes group tasks depending on whether the task is divisible between group members, whether the quality or quantity of the output is relevant, and how individual contributions are related to the group's performance.

groupthink a syndrome of poor group decision-making in which members of a cohesive ingroup strive for unanimity at the expense of a realistic appraisal of alternative courses of action.

group-to-individual (G–I) transfer denotes a group learning process whereby a group member's ability to perform a task *on his or her own* changes as a result of social interaction between group members during repeated collective task performance.

group-to-individual-in-group (G–IG) transfer denotes a group learning process whereby a group member's ability to perform a task *within groups* changes as a result of social interaction between group members during repeated collective task performance.

habits learned sequences of behaviour that have become automatic responses to specific cues and are functional in obtaining certain goals.

habituation process whereby the ability of a stimulus to elicit arousal becomes weaker with each consecutive presentation.

Hawthorne effect a term used to describe the effect of participants' awareness that they are being observed on their behaviour.

health education the provision of knowledge and/or training of skills that facilitate voluntary adoption of behaviour conducive to health.

heat hypothesis hypothesis that aggression increases with higher temperatures. *See also* **geographic regions approach; time periods approach**.

helping refers to actions intended to improve the situation of the help-recipient. *See also* **prosocial behaviour**.

heuristic a well-used, non-optimal rule of thumb used to arrive at a judgement that is effective in many but not all cases; stereotypes are often said to function as heuristics.

heuristic processing assessing the validity of a communication through reliance on heuristics, i.e., simple rules like 'statistics don't lie', 'experts can be trusted', 'consensus implies correctness', rather than through evaluation of arguments. *See* **systematic processing**.

heuristic-systematic model (HSM) assumes that attitude change in response to persuasive communications can be mediated by two different modes of information processing, heuristic and systematic processing (*see* **dual process theories of persuasion**), which can operate concurrently. When motivation and ability are high, systematic processing is likely; when they are low, individuals rely on heuristic cues to accept or reject the attitudinal position recommended.

hidden profile a group decision situation in which task-relevant information is distributed among group members in such a way that no individual group member can detect the best solution based on his or her own information. Only by sharing information within the group can the optimal solution to the task become evident.

hostile aggression aggressive behaviour motivated by the desire to express anger and hostile feelings.

hostile attribution bias tendency to attribute hostile intentions to a person who has caused damage when it is unclear whether the damage was caused accidentally or on purpose.

hypothesis a prediction derived from a theory concerning the relationship between variables.

implicit measures measures of constructs such as attitudes and stereotypes that are derived from the way respondents behave (such as how long they take to make a decision or to answer a question) rather than from the content of their answers to explicit questions about these constructs. They are a class of **unobtrusive measures**.

implicit measures of attitude attitude measures that assess attitudes without directly asking respondents for a verbal report of an attitude.

implicit modelling of 'nothing has happened' because bystanders in emergencies are overwhelmed by the sudden and unexpected event, they initially hesitate to provide help. When they see that other bystanders are doing the same, they each reach the false conclusion that the other bystanders interpret the event as harmless. This is sometimes called 'pluralistic ignorance'.

implicit personality theory an integrated set of ideas held by social perceivers about how different traits tend to be organized within a person.

inclusive fitness the sum of an individual's own reproductive success in passing on genes through the procreation of offspring (= direct fitness) and the effect of his of her support on the reproductive success of his or her relatives, weighted by their genetic relatedness coefficient (= indirect fitness).

inconsistency resolution the way in which we reconcile inconsistent information with a pre-established **schema**.

independent self self as an autonomous entity defined predominantly in terms of abstract, internal attributes like traits, abilities and attitudes.

independent variable the **variable** that an experimenter manipulates or modifies in order to examine the effect on one or more **dependent variables**.

individual capability gains and losses improvements or impairments in individual group members' ability to successfully perform a task due to social interaction with the group.

individual-to-individual (I–I) transfer denotes individual learning processes whereby a group member's ability to perform a task on his or her own improves as a result of repeated individual task performance.

individuating information information about a person's personal characteristics (not normally derived from a particular category membership).

informational influence influence based on accepting the information obtained from others as evidence about reality.

ingroup favouritism the tendency to treat the ingroup or members of the ingroup more favourably than the outgroup or its members.

initiation the role transition of entry into a group, often accompanied by some ritual.

innovation *see* **minority influence**.

instrumental aggression aggressive behaviour performed to reach a particular goal, as a means to an end.

interaction effect a term used when the combined effects of two (or more) independent variables in a **factorial experiment** yield a pattern that differs from the sum of the main effects.

interaction process analysis (IPA) a formal observational measurement system devised by Bales for coding the interactions of members of small social groups. It consists of categories and procedures for coding interaction in terms of these categories.

interdependent self self construed as socially embedded and defined predominantly in terms of relationships with others, group memberships and social roles.

intergroup anxiety the feeling of uneasiness or anxiety when one imagines having contact with unknown members of an outgroup.

intergroup behaviour behaviour of individuals acting as members of a particular social group towards members of another group.

internal validity refers to the validity of the inference that changes in the **independent variable** result in changes in the **dependent variable**.

Internet experiments experiments that are run on a server which participants access via the Internet.

interpersonal cohesion cohesion based on liking of the group and its members.

interpersonal guilt negative feelings about oneself which result from the knowledge that one is responsible for the distress of others or for damage done to them.

intimacy a state in interpersonal relationships that is characterized by sharing of feelings, and that is based upon caring, understanding and validation.

intimate partner violence perpetration or threat of an act of physical violence within the context of a dating/marital relationship.

intrinsic motivation behaviour is said to be intrinsically motivated if people perform it because they enjoy it. This enjoyment is sufficient to produce the behaviour and no external reward is required. In fact, external rewards (e.g., financial contributions) are likely to reduce intrinsic motivation.

introspection the examination of one's own thoughts, feelings, motives and reasons for behaving in a particular way. It does not guarantee valid knowledge about oneself, but involves a constructive process of putting together a coherent and acceptable narrative of one's self and identity.

investment model theory that assumes that commitment to a relationship is based upon high satisfaction, low quality of alternatives and a high level of investments.

job attitudes an employee's evaluations of the job situation, on a continuum ranging from positive to negative reactions, subsuming cognitive, affective and behavioural components.

job satisfaction the most general job attitude, regarding how an employee evaluates the job as a whole.

just-world belief generalized expectancy that people get what they deserve. Undeserved suffering of others threatens belief in a just world and motivates attempts to restore it. These include reducing the victims' suffering by helping or derogating the victims, depending on whether help can effectively be given or not.

kin selection theory developed by William Hamilton that natural selection favours those individuals who support their relatives. To provide help to relatives enhances **inclusive fitness**.

Köhler effect a motivation gain in groups which involves weaker group members' working harder than they would do individually in order to avoid being responsible for a weak group performance.

laissez-faire leaders leaders who engage in 'non-leadership', e.g., they avoid making decisions, hesitate in taking action and are often absent when needed.

leader traits relatively stable person characteristics (e.g., personality, intelligence, motivational dispositions) which are thought to predict leader emergence and **leadership effectiveness**.

leaderless groups groups that have no appointed leader (e.g., self-managed work groups) but which may be led by agents external to the group or by **shared or team leadership**.

leadership (in organizations) influencing, motivating or enabling others to contribute towards the effectiveness of work units and organizations.

leadership behaviour observable acts that are meant to influence, motivate or enable others to contribute towards the effectiveness of a work unit or organization.

leadership effectiveness the impact of leadership on the accomplishment of group and organizational objectives, on the behaviour, perceptions, attitudes, values, motivation or well-being of followers and peers, and on the accomplishments of those who lead.

leadership style a pattern of **leadership behaviour** which is repeatedly shown and evident across a variety of situations.

learned helplessness theory the proposal that depression results from learning that outcomes are not contingent on one's behaviour.

loneliness a complex affective response stemming from felt deficits in the number and nature of one's social relationships.

lowballing technique compliance to an initial attempt is followed by a more costly and less beneficial version of the same request.

main effect a term used to refer to the separate effects of each independent variable in a **factorial experiment**.

majority influence (conformity) social influence resulting from exposure to the opinions of a majority, or the majority of one's group.

manipulation check a measure of the effectiveness of the **independent variable**.

media violence–aggression link hypothesis that exposure to violent media content makes media users more aggressive.

mediating variable a variable that mediates the relation between two other variables. Assume that independent variable X and dependent variable O are related. If a third variable Z is related to both X and O, and if the X–O relation disappears when we take the role of Z into account, then Z is said to mediate the relation between X and O.

mere exposure effect increase in liking for an object as a result of being repeatedly exposed to it.

meta-analysis a set of techniques for statistically integrating the results of independent studies of a given phenomenon, with a view to establishing whether the findings exhibit a pattern of relationships that is reliable across studies.

minimal group paradigm a set of experimental procedures designed to create groups on essentially arbitrary criteria (with no interaction within or between them, and with no knowledge of who else belongs to each group) whose members show intergroup discrimination.

minority influence (innovation) situation in which either an individual or a group in a numerical minority can influence the majority.

mobbing *see* **bullying**.

MODE model a model of **attitude–behaviour relations** in which motivation and opportunity are necessary to make a deliberative consideration of available information.

modelling learning by imitation, observing a model being rewarded or punished for his/her behaviour.

modification of the incentive structure strategies of behaviour change that influence behaviour by increasing the costs of undesirable (e.g., health-impairing) behaviour and decreasing the costs of desirable (health-promoting) behaviour. Governments often use fiscal measures (e.g., tax increases on cigarettes) or legal measures (e.g., laws enforcing use of seatbelts) to influence behaviour.

motivation losses and gains decreases or increases in group members' motivation to contribute to group task performance. See **Köhler effect**; **social compensation**; **social competition**; **social loafing**; **sucker effect**.

multicomponent model of attitude a model of attitude that conceptualizes attitudes as summary evaluations that have affective, cognitive and behavioural components.

mutual distinctiveness recommendation to establish intergroup contact while keeping group memberships salient in order to foster generalization of contact experience to the whole outgroup. *See* **contact hypothesis**.

naïve scientist model a metaphor for how social information is processed that likens social perceivers to academic researchers who attempt to develop theories and explanations for the purposes of prediction and control of behaviour.

need for cognition an individual difference variable which differentiates people according to the extent to which they enjoy thinking about arguments contained in a communication. When exposed to a persuasive message, individuals high in need for cognition are assumed to engage in more content-relevant thinking than individuals who are low on this dimension.

need to belong the fundamental and innate human motivation to form positive, strong and stable bonds with others.

negative-state-relief hypothesis idea that **prosocial behaviour** is a mood-management technique. During socialization people have learned that prosocial behaviour is self-reinforcing. When they feel bad they employ prosocial behaviour to improve their feeling state.

nominal group a number of individuals who perform a task individually and work independently of each other. Nominal groups are used to determine the potential performance of groups (*see* **potential group performance**).

norm of reciprocity the norm that we should do to others as they do to us. Reciprocity calls for positive responses to favourable treatment but negative responses to unfavourable treatment. Prosocial reciprocity occurs when people help in return for having been helped. *See also* **reciprocity**.

norm of social responsibility prescribes that people should help others who are dependent on them. It is contrasted with the norm of self-sufficiency, which implies that people should take care of themselves first.

normative influence influence based on conforming to the positive expectations of others – people avoid behaving in ways that will lead to social punishment or disapproval.

norms belief systems about how (not) to behave, which guide behaviour but without the force of laws, and which reflect group members' shared expectations about typical or desirable activities.

number effect refers to the reduced likelihood of intervention in groups of bystanders: the larger the number of bystanders, the less likely any one bystander will be to intervene and help.

obedience to authority complying with orders from a person of higher social status within a defined hierarchy or chain of command.

one-dimensional perspective of attitudes a perspective that perceives positive and negative elements as stored along a single dimension.

one-shot case study a research design in which observations are made on a group after some event has occurred or some manipulation has been introduced. The problem is that there is nothing with which these observations may be compared, so one has no way of knowing whether the event or manipulation had an effect.

operationalization the way in which a theoretical **construct** is turned into a measurable **dependent variable** or a manipulable **independent variable** in a particular study.

outcome dependency a motivational objective in which participants believe they will later meet a target and work together on a jointly judged task; shown to lead to less stereotypical target impressions.

over-justification effect providing external rewards for performance of a task, which individuals previously performed because they found it enjoyable, reduces individuals' liking for, and enjoyment of, the task.

participant observation a method of observation in which the researcher studies the target group or community from within, making careful records of what he or she observes.

passionate love a state of intense longing for union with another individual, usually characterized by intrusive thinking and preoccupation with the partner, idealization of the other and the desire to know the other as well as the desire to be known by the other.

peer nominations method for measuring (aggressive) behaviour by asking other people (e.g., classmates) to rate the aggressiveness of an individual.

perceived organizational support employees' beliefs about how much the organization values their contribution and cares about their well-being.

peripheral route to persuasion subsumes those persuasion processes that are not based on issue-relevant thinking (e.g., classical conditioning, **heuristic processing**). *See also* **central route to persuasion**.

peripheral trait within impression formation, a trait whose perceived presence does not significantly change the overall interpretation of a person's personality.

personal identity self-definition as a unique individual in terms of interpersonal or intragroup differentiations ('I' or 'me' versus 'you').

personal norm feeling of obligation to perform a specific action in accordance with personal values and normative beliefs.

positive distinctiveness motivation to show the superiority of one's ingroup compared to an outgroup on valued dimensions.

positive and negative interdependence interdependence denotes that one can only achieve one's own goals dependent on how others behave. If the ingroup's goals can only be achieved when the outgroup achieves its goal, then both are positively interdependent. If ingroup goals can only be achieved at the expense of the outgroup's goals, both are negatively interdependent.

post-experimental enquiry a technique advocated by Orne for detecting the operation of **demand characteristics**. The participant is carefully interviewed after participation in an experiment, the object being to assess perceptions of the purpose of the experiment.

post-test only control group design a minimal design for a true experiment. Participants are randomly allocated to one of two groups. One group is exposed to the **independent variable**; another (the **control group**) is not. Both groups are assessed on the **dependent variable**, and comparison of the two groups on this measure indicates whether or not the independent variable had an effect.

post-traumatic stress disorder characteristic patterns of symptoms observed in survivors of traumatic experiences such as rape.

potential group performance (group potential) the performance that would have occurred if the members of a group had worked independently of each other and not as a group; a common benchmark to evaluate actual group performance.

prejudice a derogatory attitude or antipathy towards particular social groups or their members.

primacy effect the tendency for information presented earlier to be more influential in social perception and interpretation.

priming activating one stimulus (e.g., bird) facilitates the subsequent processing of another related stimulus (e.g., wing, feather).

problem-focused coping instrumental behaviour aimed at reducing or eliminating the risk of harmful consequences that might result from a stressful event.

procedural justice perceptions in organizations about how fair the processes of resource allocation are.

production blocking a process loss typical of **brainstorming** tasks in face-to-face groups. Since in a group only one person can speak at a time, the other group members cannot express their own ideas at the same time.

propinquity physical closeness to others, for example living in the same neighbourhood or sitting next to others in the classroom.

prosocial behaviour refers to **helping** that is not motivated by professional obligations and that is not based on an organization (except charities).

prosocial personality the set of personality attributes (e.g., empathy, social responsibility) that contribute to willingness to help others. An alternative term is 'altruistic personality'.

protection motivation theory the model assumes that the motivation to protect oneself from a danger is a positive function of four beliefs: the threat is severe, one is personally vulnerable, one has the ability to perform the coping response and the coping response is effective in reducing the threat. Two further beliefs are assumed to decrease protection motivation: the rewards of the maladaptive response are great and the costs of performing the coping response are high.

quasi-experiment an experiment in which participants are not randomly allocated to the different experimental conditions (typically because of factors beyond the control of the researcher).

quota sample a sample that fills certain pre-specified quotas and thereby reflects certain attributes of the population (such as age and sex) that are thought to be important to the issue being researched.

random allocation (sometimes called random assignment) the process of allocating participants to groups (or conditions) in such a way that each participant has an equal chance of being assigned to each group.

reactance theory reactance is an aversive state caused by restriction of an individual's freedom of choice over important behavioural outcomes. Reactance is assumed to motivate the individual to re-establish the restricted freedom.

reactivity a measurement procedure is reactive if it alters the nature of what is being measured (i.e., if the behaviour observed or the verbal response recorded is partly or wholly determined by the participant's awareness that some aspect of his or her behaviour is being measured).

rebound effect where suppression attempts fail; used to demonstrate how a suppressed stereotype returns to have an even greater impact upon one's judgements about a person from a stereotyped group.

reciprocal altruism theory that people will support another person if they expect that he or she will respond prosocially. The repayment of the favour in the future is anticipated. **Prosocial behaviour** is embedded in a cycle of give and take.

reciprocity the basic rule in interpersonal relationships that one can expect to obtain assets such as status, attractiveness, support and love to the degree that one provides such assets oneself. *See also* **norm of reciprocity**.

referent informational influence individuals identify with a particular group and conform to a prototypical group position.

reliability the degree to which a measure is free from measurement error; a measure is reliable if it yields the same result on more than one occasion or when used by different individuals.

retrieval the process of recovering information from memory once it has been encoded.

reverse discrimination systematically more positive evaluation or treatment of members of a target outgroup than members of one's own group, which can have negative effects on the self-esteem of members of the outgroup.

Ringelmann effect describes the finding that in physical tasks such as weight pulling, the average performance of individual group members decreases with increasing group size.

role the behaviours expected of a person with a specific position in the group.

role transition a change in the relation between a group member and a group.

salience a property of stimuli in relation to perceivers that causes them to attract attention.

sampling the process of selecting a subset of members of a population with a view to describing the population from which they are taken.

schema a cognitive structure or mental representation comprising pre-digested information about objects or people from specific categories; our expectancies about objects or groups; what defines them.

self-awareness a psychological state in which one is aware of oneself as an object, just as one is aware of other objects such as buildings or other people.

self-categorization the formation of cognitive groupings of oneself and other people as the same in contrast to some other class of people.

self-categorization theory theory explaining how the process of categorizing oneself as a group member forms social identity and brings about various forms of both group (e.g., **group polarization**, **majority influence**, **minority influence**) and intergroup (e.g., intergroup discrimination) behaviours.

self-complexity a joint function of the number of self-aspects and the degree of their relatedness. High self-complexity occurs with a large number of independent self-aspects, whereas low self-complexity occurs with a small number of highly interrelated self-aspects.

self-concept a cognitive representation of oneself that gives coherence and meaning to one's experience, including one's relations to other people. It organizes past experience and helps us to recognize and interpret relevant stimuli in the social environment.

self-consciousness people differ in the degree to which they attend to private (e.g., emotions, feelings, thoughts) or public (e.g., behaviour, speech, physical appearance) aspects of the self. This dimension is known as public vs. private self-consciousness.

self-efficacy beliefs in one's ability to carry out certain actions required to attain a specific goal (e.g., that one is capable of giving up smoking or doing well in an exam).

self-enhancement tendency to achieve or maintain a high level of **self-esteem** by way of different strategies (e.g., self-serving attributions or basking in reflected glory).

self-esteem attitude towards oneself along a positive–negative dimension.

self-evaluation evaluation of one's own behaviours, physical appearance, abilities or other personal attributes against internalized standards or social norms.

self-fulfilling prophecy when an originally false social belief leads to its own fulfilment. Social belief refers to people's expectations regarding another group of people. When a self-fulfilling prophecy occurs, the perceiver's initially false beliefs cause targets to act in ways that objectively confirm those beliefs.

self and identity from a social psychological point of view, self and identity are shorthand expressions for an ensemble of psychological experiences (thoughts, feelings, motives, etc.) that reflect and contribute to a person's understanding of his or her place in the social world.

self-knowledge knowledge about one's own characteristics, abilities, opinions, thoughts, feelings, motives, etc. **Introspection** seems to be a rather limited source of self-knowledge. Better sources are observation of one's own behaviour, careful examination of other people's perceptions of us and self–other comparisons.

self-monitoring an individual difference construct concerning differences in how people vary their behaviour across social situations.

self-perception theory a theory which assumes that individuals often do not know their own attitudes and, like outside observers, have to engage in attributional reasoning to infer their attitudes from their own behaviour.

self-regulation the process of controlling and directing one's behaviour in order to achieve desired goals. It involves goal setting, cognitive preparations for behaving in a goal-directed manner as well as the ongoing monitoring, evaluation and correction of goal-directed activities.

self-schema a cognitive generalization about the self, derived from past experience, that organizes and guides the processing of self-related information contained in the individual's social experiences.

self-serving biases motivated distortions of attributional conclusions that function to preserve or increase **self-esteem**.

sexual aggression forcing another person into sexual activities through a range of coercive strategies, such as threat or use of physical force, exploitation of the victim's inability to resist or verbal pressure.

shared or team leadership responsibility for leadership functions, the exercise of **leadership behaviour** and perceptions about leadership roles are shared among group members.

simple random sample a sample in which each member of the population has an equal chance of being selected and in which the selection of every possible combination of the desired number of members is equally likely.

social categorization the process of organizing information about the social world (especially concerning social groups), emphasizing similarities within categories and differences between categories.

social comparison the act of comparing one's own attitudes, abilities or emotions with those of others in order to evaluate one's standing on the abilities, or the correctness of the attitudes and emotions.

social comparison theory assumes that individuals seek out others to compare themselves with, to assess the appropriateness of their feelings and to obtain information about the most effective way of behaving.

social compensation a motivation gain in groups that occurs if stronger group members increase their effort in order to compensate for weaker members' suboptimal performance.

social competition a motivation gain in groups that occurs if the group members want to outperform each other during group tasks in which the individual contributions are identifiable.

social desirability refers to the fact that research participants are likely to want to be seen in a positive light and may therefore adjust their responses or behaviour in order to avoid being negatively evaluated.

social discrimination negative, disadvantaging or derogatory behaviour towards a social group or its members.

social dominance orientation degree of individual acceptance of and desire for group-based social hierarchy and the domination of 'inferior' groups by 'superior' groups.

social exchange theory views social relations in terms of rewards and costs to those involved; argues that social relations take the form of social exchange processes.

social facilitation/social inhibition an improvement in the performance of well-learned/easy tasks and a worsening of performance of poorly learned/difficult tasks due to the presence of members of the same species.

social identity that part of a person's **self-concept** which derives from the knowledge of his or her membership in a social group (or groups) together with the value and emotional significance attached to that membership.

social influence change of attitudes, beliefs, opinions, values and behaviour as a result of being exposed to other individuals' attitudes, beliefs, opinions, values and behaviour.

social loafing a motivation loss in groups that occurs when group members reduce their effort due to the fact that individual contributions to group performance are not identifiable.

social support the feeling of being supported by others, usually divided into four components: emotional support, appraisal support, informational support and instrumental support.

socially desirable responding a deliberative attempt to misrepresent responses so as to present oneself in a favourable way (*see* **social desirability**).

socio-emotional behaviour behaviours during group interactions that are directed at interpersonal relations.

speaking hierarchy hierarchy within a group based on who talks most.

staffing level the degree to which the actual number of group members is similar to the ideal number of group members.

status evaluation of a role by the group in which a role is contained or defined.

steam-boiler model part of Konrad Lorenz's theory of aggression, assuming that aggressive energy is produced continuously within the organism and will burst out spontaneously unless released by an external stimulus.

stereotype a cognitive structure that contains our knowledge, beliefs and expectancies about some human social group.

stereotype suppression the act of trying to prevent an activated stereotype from impacting upon one's judgements about a person from a stereotyped group.

stress the condition that arises when individuals perceive the demands of a situation as challenging or exceeding their resources and endangering their well-being.

sucker effect a motivation loss in groups that occurs when group members perceive or anticipate that other group members will lower their effort. To avoid being exploited, they reduce their effort themselves.

sufficiency principle the **heuristic-systematic model** assumes that people strive for sufficient confidence in the validity of their attitudinal judgements. When people's actual confidence is below their desired level of confidence or sufficiency threshold, they will process additional information in order to close this gap.

superordinate goals goals which are desired by two or more groups, but which can only be achieved by both groups acting together, not by either group on its own.

survey research a research strategy that involves interviewing (or administering a questionnaire to) a sample of respondents who are selected so as to be representative of the population from which they are drawn.

systematic processing thorough, detailed processing of information (e.g., attention to the arguments contained in a persuasive communication); this kind of processing relies on ability and effort. *See also* **central route to persuasion**; **heuristic processing**.

task behaviour behaviours during group interactions that are directed at task completion.

task cohesion cohesion based on attraction of group members to the group task.

task performance the degree of accomplishment of the duties and tasks one is hired to do.

team awareness understanding of the ongoing activities of others which provides a context for one's own activity.

theory a set of abstract concepts (i.e., **constructs**) together with propositions about how those constructs are related to one another.

theory of planned behavior an extension to the **theory of reasoned action** that includes the concept of perceived behavioural control.

theory of reasoned action a model in which behaviour is predicted by behavioural intentions, which are determined by attitudes and subjective norms.

thought-listing a measure of cognitive responses. Message recipients are asked to list all the thoughts that occurred to them while being exposed to a persuasive message. These thoughts are categorized as favourable or unfavourable to the position advocated by the message. Neutral or irrelevant thoughts are not considered.

three-orders hierarchy model a model according to which people undergo different orders of cognitive, evaluative and behavioural reaction processes in response to an advertisement, depending upon whether they are involved and whether clear alternatives between the products can be distinguished.

time periods approach method for testing the **heat hypothesis** by comparing violence rates during cooler and hotter periods.

tokenism conceding a minor favour to a social minority in order to justify negative discrimination on a broader scale.

trait aggressiveness denotes stable differences between individuals in the likelihood and intensity of aggressive behaviour.

transactional leaders leaders who focus on the proper exchange of resources: they give followers something in exchange for something the leaders want.

transactive memory a system of knowledge available to group members with shared awareness of each other's expertise, strengths and weaknesses.

transformational/charismatic leaders leaders who focus on aligning the group or organizational goals with the followers' needs and aspirations by developing an appealing vision. The goal is to influence followers to make sacrifices and put the needs of the organization above their self-interest.

transtheoretical model a stage model of behaviour change developed to understand how people intentionally change their behaviour.

triangulation the use of multiple methods and measures to research a given issue.

true randomized experiment an experiment in which participants are allocated to the different conditions of the experiment on a random basis.

two-dimensional perspective of attitudes a perspective that perceives positive and negative elements as stored along separate dimensions.

unobtrusive measures (also called non-reactive measures) measures that the participant is not aware of, and which therefore cannot influence his or her behaviour.

validity a measure is valid to the extent that it measures precisely what it is supposed to measure. *See* **construct validity**; **convergent validity**; **external validity**; **internal validity**.

variable the term used to refer to the measurable representation of a **construct**. *See also* **confounding**; **dependent variable**; **independent variable**; **mediating variable**.

volunteerism regular commitment to **prosocial behaviour** in an organizational context.

weapons effect finding that individuals who were previously frustrated showed more aggressive behaviour in the presence of weapons than in the presence of neutral objects.

whistleblowing a specific form of disobedience in which an 'insider' (e.g., an employee) reports corruption or unethical practice within an organization.

References

Aarts, H., Verplanken, B. & van Knippenberg, A. (1998). Predicting behavior from actions in the past: Repeated decision making or a matter of habit? *Journal of Applied Social Psychology, 28*, 1355–1374.

Abelson, R.P. (1995). Attitude extremity. In R.E. Petty & J.A. Krosnick (Eds.), *Attitude strength: Antecedents and consequences* (pp. 25–42). Hillsdale, NJ: Lawrence Erlbaum.

Abramson, L.Y., Seligman, M.E.P. & Teasdale, J.D. (1978). Learned helplessness in humans: Critique and reformulation. *Journal of Abnormal Psychology, 87*, 49–74.

Adams, J.S. (1965). Inequity in social exchange. In L. Berkowitz (Ed.), *Advances in experimental social psychology* (Vol. 2, pp. 267–299). San Diego, CA: Academic Press.

Adorno, T.W., Frenkel-Brunswick, E., Levinson, D.J. & Sanford, R.N. (1950). *The authoritarian personality*. New York: Harper.

Ajzen, I. (1991). The theory of planned behavior. *Organizational Behavior and Human Decision Processes, 50*, 179–211.

Ajzen, I. (2002). Perceived behavioural control, self-efficacy, locus of control, and the theory of planned behaviour. *Journal of Applied Social Psychology, 32*, 1–20.

Ajzen, I. & Fishbein, M. (1977). Attitude–behavior relations: A theoretical analysis and review of empirical research. *Psychological Bulletin, 84*, 888–918.

Ajzen, I. & Madden, T.J. (1986). Prediction of goal-directed behavior: Attitudes, intentions, and perceived behavioral control. *Journal of Experimental Social Psychology, 22*, 453–474.

Albarracin, D., Cohen, J.B. & Kumkale, G.T. (2003). When communications collide with recipients' actions: Effects of post-message behavior on intentions to follow the message recommendation. *Personality and Social Psychology Bulletin, 29*, 834–845.

Albarracin, D., Johnson, B.T., Fishbein, M. & Muellerleile, P.A. (2001). Theories of reasoned action and planned behavior as models of condom use: A meta-analysis. *Psychological Bulletin, 127*, 144–161.

Aldag, R.J. & Fuller, S.R. (1993). Beyond fiasco: A re-appraisal of the groupthink phenomenon and a new model of group decision making processes. *Psychological Bulletin, 113*, 533–552.

Allen, D.G., Weeks, K.P. & Moffitt, K.R. (2005). Turnover intentions and voluntary turnover: The moderating roles of self-monitoring, locus of control, proactive personality, and risk aversion. *Journal of Applied Psychology, 90*, 980–990.

Allen, V.L. (1965). Situational factors in conformity. In L. Berkowitz (Ed.), *Advances in experimental social psychology* (Vol. 2, pp. 133–176). New York: Academic Press.

Allen, V.L. (1975). Social support for nonconformity. In L. Berkowitz (Ed.), *Advances in experimental social psychology* (Vol. 8, pp. 1–43). New York: Academic Press.

Allen, V.L. & Levine, J.M. (1971). Social support and conformity: The role of independent assessment of reality. *Journal of Experimental Social Psychology, 7*, 48–58.

Allport, F.H. (1924). *Social psychology*. Cambridge, MA: Riverside Press.

Allport, F.H. (1933). *Institutional behaviour*. Chapel Hill: University of North Carolina Press.

Allport, F.H. (1955). *Theories of perception and the concept of structure*. New York: Wiley.

Allport, G.W. (1935). Attitudes. In C. Murchison (Ed.), *Handbook of social psychology* (pp. 798–844). Worcester, MA: Clark University Press.

Allport, G.W. (1954a). The historical background of modern social psychology. In G. Lindzey (Ed.), *Handbook of social psychology* (2nd edn, Vol. 1, pp. 3–56). Reading, MA: Addison-Wesley.

Allport, G.W. (1954b). *The nature of prejudice*. Reading, MA: Addison-Wesley.

Allport, G.W. (1955). *Becoming*. New Haven, CT: Yale University Press.

Allport, G.W. (1961). *Pattern and growth in personality*. New York: Holt, Rinehart & Winston.

Allport, G.W. (1968). Is the concept of self necessary? In C. Gordon & K.J. Gergen (Eds.), *The self in social interaction* (Vol. 1, pp. 25–32). New York: Wiley.

Altemeyer, B. (1998). The other 'authoritarian personality'. In M. Zanna (Ed.), *Advances in experimental social psychology* (Vol. 30, pp. 47–92). San Diego, CA: Academic Press.

Alvaro, E.M. & Crano, W.D. (1997). Indirect minority influence: Evidence for leniency in source evaluation and counterargumentation. *Journal of Personality and Social Psychology, 72*, 949–964.

Alwin, D.F., Cohen, R.L. & Newcomb, T.M. (1991). *Political attitudes over the life span: The Bennington women after fifty years*. Madison: University of Wisconsin Press.

American Psychological Association (1985). *Standards for educational and psychological testing*. Washington, DC: Author.

Amoroso, D.M. & Walters, R.H. (1969). Effects of anxiety and socially mediated anxiety reduction on paired-associate learning. *Journal of Personality and Social Psychology, 11*, 388–396.

Anderson, C.A. & Bushman, B.J. (1997). External validity of 'trivial' experiments: The case of laboratory aggression. *Review of General Psychology, 1*, 19–41.

Anderson, C.A. & Bushman, B.J. (2002). Media violence and the American public revisited. *American Psychologist, 57*, 448–450.

Anderson, C.A., Anderson, K.B., Dorr, N., DeNeve, K.M. & Flanagan, M. (2000). Temperature and aggression. In M.P. Zanna (Ed.), *Advances in experimental social psychology* (Vol. 32, pp. 63–133). New York: Academic Press.

Anderson, C.A., Berkowitz, L., Donnerstein, E., Huesmann, L.R., Johnson, J.D., Linz, D., Malamuth, N.M. & Wartella, E. (2003). The influence of media violence on youth. *Psychological Science in the Public Interest, 4*, 81–110.

Anderson, N.H. (1981). *Foundations of information integration theory*. New York: Academic Press.

Anderson, P.B. & Struckman-Johnson, C. (Eds.) (1998). *Sexually aggressive women*. New York: Guilford Press.

Archer, D. & McDaniel, P. (1995). Violence and gender: Differences and similarities across societies. In B.R. Ruback & N.A. Weiner (Eds.), *Interpersonal violent behaviors* (pp. 63–87). New York: Springer.

Archer, J. (2000). Sex differences in aggression between heterosexual partners: A meta-analytic review. *Psychological Bulletin, 126*, 651–680.

Archer, J. (2004). Sex difference in aggression in real-world settings: A meta-analytic review. *Review of General Psychology, 8*, 291–322.

Archer, J. & Lloyd, B.B. (2002). *Sex and gender* (3rd edn). New York: Cambridge University Press.

Archives and Records Management, Syracuse University (undated). Floyd Henry Allport. archives.syr.edu/arch/faculty/fallbio.htm.

Arendt, H. (1965). *Eichmann in Jerusalem: A report on the banality of evil*. New York: Viking Press.

Argyle, M. & Henderson, M. (1985). *The anatomy of relationships*. Harmondsworth: Penguin.

Armitage, C.J. & Conner, M. (2001). Efficacy of the theory of planned behaviour: A meta-analytic review. *British Journal of Social Psychology, 40*, 471–499.

Armitage, C.J., Povey, R. & Arden, M.A. (2003). Evidence for discontinuity patterns across the stages of change: A role for attitudinal ambivalence. *Psychology and Health, 18*, 373–386.

Aron, A., Aron, E.N. & Norman, C. (2001). Self-expansion model of motivation and cognition in close relationships and beyond. In M. Clark & G.J.O. Fletcher (Eds.), *Blackwell handbook of social psychology: Interpersonal processes*. Oxford: Blackwell.

Aron, A., Aron, E.N. & Smollan, D. (1992). Inclusion of the other in the self scale and the structure of interpersonal closeness. *Journal of Personality and Social Psychology, 63*, 596–612.

Aron, A., Aron, E.N., Tudor, M. & Nelson, G. (1991). Close relationships as including other in self. *Journal of Personality and Social Psychology, 60*, 241–253.

Aron, A., Norman, C.C., Aron, E.N., McKenna, C. & Heyman, R.E. (2000). Couples' shared participation in novel and arousing activities and experienced relationship quality. *Journal of Personality and Social Psychology, 78*, 273–284.

Aronson, E. & Mills, J. (1959). The effects of severity of initiation on liking for a group. *Journal of Abnormal and Social Psychology, 59*, 177–181.

Aronson, E. & Patnoe, D. (1997). *The jigsaw classroom*. New York: Longman.

Aronson, E., Ellsworth, P.C., Carlsmith, J.M. & Gonzales, M.H. (1990). *Methods of research in social psychology* (2nd edn). New York: McGraw-Hill.

Aronson, E., Wilson, T.D. & Brewer, M.B. (1998). Experimentation in social psychology. In D.T. Gilbert, S.T. Fiske & G. Lindzey (Eds.), *Handbook of social psychology* (4th edn., Vol. 1, pp. 99–142). New York: McGraw-Hill.

Asch, S.E. (1946). Forming impressions of personality. *Journal of Abnormal and Social Psychology, 41*, 258–290.

Asch, S.E. (1951). Effects of group pressure upon the modification and distortion of judgments. In H. Guetzkow (Ed.), *Groups, leadership, and men* (pp. 177–190). Pittsburgh, PA: Carnegie Press.

Asch, S.E. (1955). Opinions and social pressure. *Scientific American, 193*, 31–35.

Asch, S.E. (1956). Studies of independence and conformity: A minority of one against a unanimous majority. *Psychological Monographs, 70*(9), Whole no. 416.

Asch, S.E. (1987). *Social psychology*. New York: Oxford University Press. (Original work published 1952.)

Ashmore, R.D., Deaux, K. & McLaughlin-Volpe, T. (2003). An organizing framework for collective identity: Articulation and significance of multidimensionality. *Psychological Bulletin, 130*, 80–114.

Aspinwall, L.G. & Taylor, S.E. (1992). Modeling cognitive adaptation: A longitudinal investigation of the impact of individual differences and coping on college adjustment and performance. *Journal of Personality and Social Psychology, 63*, 989–1003.

Avellar, S. & Smock, P.J. (2005). The economic consequences of the dissolution of cohabiting unions. *Journal of Marriage and the Family, 67*, 315–328.

Averill, J.R., Malstrom, E.J., Koriat, A. & Lazarus, R.S. (1972). Habituation to complex emotional stimuli. *Journal of Abnormal Psychology, 80*, 20–28.

Avolio, B.J. (1999). *Full leadership development*. Thousand Oaks, CA: Sage.

Bakeman, R. (2000). Behavioral observation and coding. In H.T. Reis & C.M. Judd (Eds.), *Handbook of research methods in social and personality psychology* (pp. 138–160). New York: Cambridge University Press.

Baker, S.M. & Petty, R.E. (1994). Majority and minority influence: Source-position imbalance as a determinant of message scrutiny. *Journal of Personality and Social Psychology, 67*, 5–19.

Bales, R.F. (1950). *Interaction process analysis: A method for the study of small groups*. Chicago: University of Chicago Press.

Bales, R.F. (1953). The equilibrium problem in small groups. In T. Parsons, R.F. Bales & E.A. Shils (Eds.), *Working papers in the theory of action* (pp. 444–476). New York: Free Press.

Bales, R.F. & Slater, P.E. (1955). Role differentiation in small decision-making groups. In T. Parsons & R.F. Bales (Eds.), *Family, socialization, and interaction process* (pp. 259–306). Glencoe, IL: Free Press.

Banaji, M.R. & Hardin, C.D. (1996). Automatic stereotyping. *Psychological Science, 7*, 136–141.

Bandura, A. (1983). Psychological mechanisms of aggression. In R.G. Geen & E.I. Donnerstein (Eds.), *Aggression: Theoretical and empirical reviews* (Vol. 1, pp. 1–40). New York: Academic Press.

Bandura, A. (1997). *Self-efficacy: The exercise of control*. New York: Freeman.

Bandura, A. (1999). Moral disengagement in the perpetration of inhumanities. *Personality and Social Psychology Review, 3*, 193–209.

Bandura, A. (2001). Social cognitive theory: An agentic perspective. *Annual Review of Psychology, 52*, 1–26.

Bandura, A., Ross, D. & Ross, S.A. (1963). Imitation of film-mediated aggressive models. *Journal of Abnormal and Social Psychology, 66*, 3–11.

Barber, J.P., Abrams, M.J., Connolly-Gibbons, M.B., Crits-Christoph, P., Barrett, M.S., Rynn, M., & Siqueland, L. (2005). Explanatory style change in supportive-expressive dynamic therapy. *Journal of Clinical Psychology, 61*, 257–268.

Bargh, J.A. (1982). Attention and automaticity in the processing of self-relevant information. *Journal of Personality and Social Psychology, 43*, 425–436.

Bargh, J.A. (1994). The four horsemen of automaticity: Awareness, intention, efficiency, and control in social cognition. In R.S. Wyer, Jr. & T.K. Srull (Eds.), *Handbook of social cognition* (2nd edn, Vol. 1, pp. 1–40). Hillsdale, NJ: Erlbaum.

Bargh, J.A. (1999). The cognitive monster: Evidence against the controllability of automatic stereotype effects. In S. Chaiken & Y. Trope (Eds.), *Dual process theories in social psychology* (pp. 361–382). New York: Guilford Press.

Bargh, J.A. (2002). Losing consciousness: Automatic influences on consumer judgment, behavior, and motivation. *Journal of Consumer Research, 29*, 280–285.

Bargh, J.A. & Chartrand, T.L. (2000). The mind in the middle: A practical guide to priming and automaticity research. In H.T. Reis & C.M. Judd (Eds.), *Handbook of research methods in social and personality psychology* (pp. 253–285). New York: Cambridge University Press.

Bargh, J.A. & Pietromonaco, P. (1982). Automatic information processing and social perception: The influence of trait information presented outside of conscious awareness on impression formation. *Journal of Personality and Social Psychology, 43*, 437–449.

Bargh, J.A., Chen, M. & Burrows, L. (1996). Automaticity of social behavior: Direct effects of trait construct and stereotype activation on action. *Journal of Personality and Social Psychology, 71*, 230–244.

Barling, J., Kelloway, E.K. & Frone, M.R. (Eds.) (2005). *Handbook of work stress*. Thousand Oaks, CA: Sage.

Baron, R.A. & Richardson, D.R. (1994). *Human aggression* (2nd edn). New York: Plenum Press.

Baron, R.M. & Boudreau, L.A. (1987). An ecological perspective on integrating personality and social psychology. *Journal of Personality and Social Psychology, 53*, 1222–1228.

Baron, R.M. & Kenny, D.A. (1986). The mediator–moderator variable distinction in social psychological research: Conceptual, strategic, and statistical considerations. *Journal of Personality and Social Psychology, 50*, 869–878.

Baron, R.S. & Kerr, N.L. (2003). *Group process, group decision, group action* (2nd edn). Buckingham: Open University Press.

Barsade, S. (2002). The ripple effect: Emotional contagion and its influence on group behavior. *Administrative Science Quarterly, 47*, 644–675.

Bartholomew, K. & Horowitz, L.M. (1991). Attachment styles among young adults: A test of a four-category model. *Journal of Personality and Social Psychology, 61*, 226–244.

Bartholow, B.D. & Anderson, C.A. (2002). Effects of violent video games on aggressive behavior: Potential sex differences. *Journal of Experimental Social Psychology, 38*, 283–290.

Bartlett, F.C. (1932). *Remembering*. Cambridge: Cambridge University Press.

Bass, B.M. (1985). *Leadership and performance beyond expectations*. New York: Free Press.

Bass, B.M. (1990). *Bass and Stogdill's handbook of leadership: A survey of theory and research* (3rd edn). New York: Free Press.

Bass, B.M. & Avolio, B.J. (1994). *Improving organizational effectiveness through transformational leadership.* Thousand Oaks, CA: Sage.

Batra, R. & Ray, M.L. (1985). How advertising works at contact. In L.F. Alwitt & A.A. Mitchell (Eds.), *Psychological processes and advertising effects* (pp. 13–43). Hillsdale, NJ: Lawrence Erlbaum.

Batson, C.D. (1991). *The altruism question: Toward a social-psychological answer.* Hillsdale, NJ: Lawrence Erlbaum.

Batson, C.D., Batson, J.G., Griffith, C.A., Barrientos, S., Brandt, J.R., Sprengelmeyer, P. & Bayly, M.J. (1989). Negative-state relief and the empathy–altruism hypothesis. *Journal of Personality and Social Psychology, 56*, 922–933.

Batson, C.D., Cochran, P.J., Biederman, M.F., Blosser, J.L., Ryan, M.J. & Vogt, B. (1978). Failure to help when in a hurry: Callousness or conflict? *Personality and Social Psychology Bulletin, 4*, 97–101.

Batson, C.D., Duncan, B.D., Ackerman, P., Buckley, T. & Birch, K. (1981). Is empathic emotion a source of altruistic motivation? *Journal of Personality and Social Psychology, 50*, 212–220.

Batson, C.D., Fultz, J. & Schoenrade, P.A. (1987). Distress and empathy: Two qualitatively distinct vicarious emotions with different motivational consequences. *Journal of Personality, 55*, 21–39.

Battistich, V., Schnaps, E., Watson, M., Solomon, D. & Lewis, C. (1997). Caring school communities. *Educational Psychologist, 32*, 137–151.

Baumeister, R.F. (1986). *Identity: Cultural change and the struggle for the self.* New York: Oxford University Press.

Baumeister, R.F. (1998a). Inducing guilt. In J. Bybee (Ed.), *Guilt and children* (pp. 127–138). San Diego, CA: Academic Press.

Baumeister, R.F. (1998b). The self. In D.T. Gilbert, S.T. Fiske & G. Lindzey (Eds.), *Handbook of social psychology* (4th ed., Vol. 1, pp. 680–740). New York: McGraw-Hill.

Baumeister, R.F. (2002). Ego depletion and self-control failure: An energy model of the self's executive function. *Self and Identity, 1*, 129–136.

Baumeister, R.F. & Leary, M.R. (1995). The need to belong: Desire for interpersonal attachments as a fundamental human motivation. *Psychological Bulletin, 117*, 497–529.

Baumeister, R.F., Bratslavsky, E., Muraven, M. & Tice, D.M. (1998). Ego depletion: Is the active self a limited resource? *Journal of Personality and Social Psychology, 74*, 1252–1265.

Baumeister, R.F., Stillwell, A.M. & Heatherton, T.F. (1994). Interpersonal aspects of guilt: An interpersonal approach. *Psychological Bulletin, 115*, 243–267.

Baumrind, D. (1964). Some thoughts on the ethics of research after reading Milgram's 'Behavioral Study of Obedience'. *American Psychologist, 19*, 421–423.

Beaman, A.L., Barnes, P.J., Klentz, B. & McQuirk, B. (1978). Increasing helping rates through information dissemination: Teaching pays. *Personality and Social Psychology Bulletin, 4*, 406–411.

Beaman, A.L., Cole, C.M., Preston, M., Klentz, B. & Stenblay, N.M. (1983). Fifteen years of foot-in-the-door research: A meta-analysis. *Personality and Social Psychology Bulletin, 9*, 181–196.

Beck, R. & Fernandez, E. (1998). Cognitive-behavioral therapy in the treatment of anger: A meta-analysis. *Cognitive Therapy and Research, 22*, 63–74.

Beehr, T.A. & Glazer, S. (2005). Organizational role stress. In J. Barling, E.K. Kelloway & M.R. Frone (Eds.), *Handbook of work stress* (pp. 7–33). Thousand Oaks, CA: Sage.

Belknap, J., Fisher, B.S. & Cullen, F.T. (1999). The development of a comprehensive measure of sexual victimization of college women. *Violence against Women, 5*, 185–214.

Bell, D.W. & Esses, V.M. (2002). Ambivalence and response amplification: A motivational perspective. *Personality and Social Psychology Bulletin, 28*, 1143–1152.

Bellavia, G.M. & Frone, M.R. (2005). Work–family conflict. In J. Barling, E.K. Kelloway & M.R. Frone (Eds.), *Handbook of work stress* (pp. 113–147). Thousand Oaks, CA: Sage.

Bem, D.J. (1965). An experimental analysis of self-persuasion. *Journal of Experimental Social Psychology, 1*, 199–218.

Bem, D.J. (1972). Self-perception theory. In L. Berkowitz (Ed.), *Advances in experimental social psychology* (Vol. 6, pp. 1–62). New York: Academic Press.

Bennett, R.J. & Robinson, S.L. (2000). Development of a measure of workplace deviance. *Journal of Applied Psychology, 85*, 349–360.

Ben-Ze'ev, A. (2004). *Love online: Emotions on the Internet.* Cambridge: Cambridge University Press.

Berger, J., Rosenholtz, S.J. & Zelditch, M., Jr. (1980). Status organizing processes. In A. Inkeles, N.J. Smelser & R. Turner (Eds.), *Annual review of sociology* (pp. 479–508). Palo Alto, CA: Annual Reviews, Inc.

Berglas, S. & Jones, E.E. (1978). Drug choice as a self-handicapping strategy in response to noncontingent success. *Journal of Personality and Social Psychology, 36*, 405–417.

Berkman, L.F. & Syme, S.L. (1979). Social networks, host resistance, and mortality: A nine-year follow-up of Alameda County residents. *American Journal of Epidemiology, 109*, 186–204.

Berkowitz, L. (1978). Decreased helpfulness with increased group size through lessening the effects of the needy individual's dependency. *Journal of Personality, 46*, 299–310.

Berkowitz, L. (1993). *Aggression: Its causes, consequences, and control.* Philadelphia: Temple University Press.

Berkowitz, L. & Daniels, L.R. (1964). Affecting the salience of the social responsibility norm: Effects of past help on the response to dependency relationships. *Journal of Abnormal and Social Psychology, 68*, 275–281.

Berkowitz, L. & LePage, A. (1967). Weapons as aggression-eliciting stimuli. *Journal of Personality and Social Psychology, 7*, 202–207.

Berry, D.S. & McArthur, L.Z. (1986). Perceiving character in faces: The impact of age-related craniofacial changes on social perception. *Psychological Bulletin, 100*, 3–18.

Berscheid, E. (1985). Interpersonal attraction. In G. Lindzey & E. Aronson (Eds.), *Handbook of social psychology* (Vol. 2, pp. 413–484). New York: Random House.

Berscheid, E. & Walster, E. (1974). A little bit about love. In T. Huston (Ed.), *Foundations of interpersonal attraction* (pp. 356–382). New York: Academic Press.

Bettencourt, B.A., Brewer, M.B., Croak, M.R. & Miller, N. (1992). Cooperation and the reduction of intergroup bias: The role of reward structure and social orientation. *Journal of Experimental Social Psychology, 28*, 301–309.

Bickman, L. & Henchy, T. (Eds.) (1972). *Beyond the laboratory: Field research in social psychology.* New York: McGraw-Hill.

Bierhoff, H.W. (2002a). *Prosocial behavior.* New York: Psychology Press.

Bierhoff, H.W. (2002b). Just world, social responsibility, and helping behavior. In M. Ross & D.T. Miller (Eds.), *The justice motive in everyday life* (pp. 189–203). Cambridge: Cambridge University Press.

Bierhoff, H.W. (2005). The psychology of compassion and prosocial behaviour. In P. Gilbert (Ed.), *Compassion: Conceptualizations, research and use in psychotherapy* (pp. 148–167). Hove: Routledge.

Bierhoff, H.W. & Rohmann, E. (2004). Altruistic personality in the context of the empathy–altruism hypothesis. *European Journal of Personality, 18*, 351–365.

Bierhoff, H.W., Buck, E. & Klein, R. (1986). Social context and perceived justice. In H.W. Bierhoff, R.L. Cohen & J. Greenberg (Eds.), *Justice in social relations* (pp. 165–185). New York: Plenum Press.

Bierhoff, H.W., Klein, R. & Kramp, P. (1991). Evidence for the altruistic personality from data on accident research. *Journal of Personality, 59*, 263–280.

Bies, R.J. & Moag, J.F. (1986). Interactional justice: Communication criteria of fairness. In R.J. Lewicki, B.H. Sheppard & M.H. Bazerman (Eds.), *Research on negotiations in organizations* (Vol. 1, pp. 43–55). Greenwich, CT: JAI Press.

Binet, A. & Henri, V. (1894). De la suggestibilité naturelle chez les enfants. *Revue Philosophique, 38*, 337–347.

Birnbaum, M.H. (2000). Introduction to psychological experiments on the Internet. In M.H. Birnbaum (Ed.), *Psychological experiments on the Internet* (pp. 3–34). San Diego, CA: Academic Press.

Black, S.L. & Bevan, S. (1992). At the movies with Buss and Durkee: A natural experiment on film violence. *Aggressive Behavior, 18*, 37–45.

Blair, I.V. & Banaji, M.R. (1996). Automatic and controlled processes in stereotype priming. *Journal of Personality and Social Psychology, 70*, 1142–1163.

Blake, R.R. & Mouton, J.S. (1986). From theory to practice in interface problem solving. In S. Worchel & W.G. Austin (Eds.), *Psychology of intergroup relations* (2nd edn, pp. 67–81). Chicago: Nelson-Hall.

Blass, T. (1992). The social psychology of Stanley Milgram. In M. Zanna (Ed.), *Advances in experimental social psychology* (Vol. 25, pp. 227–329). San Diego, CA: Academic Press.

Blass, T. (1999). The Milgram paradigm after 35 years: Some things we now know about obedience to authority. *Journal of Applied Social Psychology, 29*, 955–978.

Blass, T. (Ed.) (2000). *Obedience to authority: Current perspectives on the Milgram paradigm*. Mahwah, NJ: Lawrence Erlbaum.

Blass, T. (2004). *The man who shocked the world: The life and legacy of Stanley Milgram*. New York: Basic Books.

Blau, P.M. (1964). *Exchange and power in social life*. New York: Wiley.

Blazer, D. (1982). Social support and mortality in an elderly community population. *American Journal of Epidemiology, 115*, 684–694.

Bless, H. (2001). The consequences of mood on the processing of social information. In A. Tesser & N. Schwarz (Eds.), *Blackwell handbook of social psychology: Intraindividual processes* (pp. 391–412). Oxford: Blackwell.

Bless, H., Bohner, G., Schwarz, N. & Strack, F. (1990). Mood and persuasion: A cognitive response analysis. *Personality and Social Psychology Bulletin, 16*, 331–345.

Bless, H., Fiedler, K. & Strack, F. (2004). *Social cognition: How individuals construct social reality*. New York: Psychology Press.

Bodenhausen, G.V. (1990). Stereotypes as judgmental heuristics: Evidence of Circadian variations in discrimination. *Psychological Science, 1*, 319–322.

Bohner, G. & Wänke, M. (2002). *Attitudes and attitude change*. Hove: Psychology Press.

Bohner, G., Moskowitz, G. & Chaiken, S. (1995). The interplay of heuristic and systematic processing of social information. In W. Stroebe & M. Hewstone (Eds.), *European review of social psychology* (Vol. 6, pp. 33–68). Chichester: Wiley.

Bohner, G., Rank, S., Reinhard, M.A., Einwiller, S. & Erb, H.P. (1998). Motivational determinants of systematic processing: Expectancy moderates effects of desired confidence on processing effort. *European Journal of Social Psychology, 28*, 185–206.

Bolger, N., Zuckerman, A. & Kessler, R.C. (2000). Invisible support and adjustment to stress. *Journal of Personality and Social Psychology, 79*, 953–961.

Bolsin, S.N. (2003). Whistle blowing. *Medical Education, 37*, 294–296.

Bond, C.F. & Titus, L.J. (1983). Social facilitation: A meta-analysis of 241 studies. *Psychological Bulletin, 94*, 265–292.

Bond, R. & Smith, P.B. (1996). Culture and conformity: A meta-analysis of studies using Asch's (1952b, 1956) line judgment task. *Psychological Bulletin, 119*, 111–137.

Book, A.S., Starzyk, K.B. & Quinsey, V.L. (2001). The relationship between testosterone and aggression: A meta-analysis. *Aggression and Violent Behavior, 6*, 579–599.

Borman, W.C. & Motowidlo, S.J. (1993). Expanding the criterion domain to include elements of contextual performance. In N. Schmitt & W.C. Borman (Eds.), *Personnel selection in organizations* (pp. 71–98). San Francisco: Jossey-Bass.

Bornstein, R.F. & D'Agostino, P.R. (1992). Stimulus recognition and the mere exposure effect. *Journal of Personality and Social Psychology, 63*, 545–552.

Bourke, J. (1999). *An intimate history of killing: Face-to-face killing in the twentieth century*. London: Granta.

Bower, G.H. (1981). Mood and memory. *American Psychologist, 36*, 129–148.

Bowers, D.G. & Seashore, S.E. (1966). Predicting organizational effectiveness with a four-factor theory of leadership. *Administrative Science Quarterly, 2*, 238–263.

Bowlby, J. (1958). The nature of a child's tie to his mother. *International Journal of Psycho-analysis, 39*, 350–373.

Bowlby, J. (1969). *Attachment and loss*. Vol. 1: *Attachment*. London: Hogarth Press; New York: Basic Books; Harmondsworth: Penguin.

Bradford, D.L. & Cohen, A.R. (1984). *Managing for excellence: The guide to developing high performance organizations*. New York: Wiley.

Bransford, J.D. & Johnson, M.K. (1972). Contextual prerequisites for understanding: Some investigations of comprehension and recall. *Journal of Verbal Learning and Verbal Behavior, 11*, 717–726.

Brauer, M. (2001). Intergroup perception in the social context: The effects of social status and group membership on perceived out-group homogeneity and ethnocentrism. *Journal of Experimental Social Psychology, 37*, 15–31.

Brauer, M. & Judd, C.M. (1996). Group polarization and repeated attitude expressions: A new take on an old topic. In W. Stroebe & M. Hewstone (Eds.), *European review of social psychology* (Vol. 7, pp. 173–207). Chichester: Wiley.

Brauer, M., Judd, C.M. & Gliner, M.D. (1995). The effects of repeated attitude expressions on attitude polarization during group discussions. *Journal of Personality and Social Psychology, 68*, 1014–1029.

Brayfield, A.H. & Crockett, W.H. (1955). Employee attitudes and employee performance. *Psychological Bulletin, 52*, 396–424.

Brehm, J.W. (1956). Postdecision changes in the desirability of alternatives. *Journal of Abnormal and Social Psychology, 52*, 384–389.

Brehm, J.W. (1966). *A theory of psychological reactance*. New York: Academic Press.

Brehm, S. & Brehm, J.W. (1981). *Psychological reactance: A theory of freedom and control*. New York: Academic Press.

Breslow, L. & Enstrom, J.E. (1980). Persistence of health habits and their relationship to mortality. *Preventive Medicine, 9*, 469–483.

Brewer, M.B. (1979). In-group bias in the minimal intergroup situation: A cognitive motivational analysis. *Psychological Bulletin, 86*, 307–324.

Brewer, M.B. (1988). A dual process model of impression formation. In T.K. Srull & R.S. Wyer, Jr. (Eds.), *Advances in social cognition* (Vol. 1, pp. 1–36). Hillsdale, NJ: Lawrence Erlbaum.

Brewer, M.B. (1991). The social self: On being the same and different at the same time. *Personality and Social Psychology Bulletin, 17*, 475–482.

Brewer, M.B. (1996). In-group favoritism: The subtle side of intergroup discrimination. In D.M. Messick & A. Tenbrunsel (Eds.), *Codes of conduct: Behavioral research and business ethics* (pp. 160–171). New York: Russell Sage Foundation.

Brewer, M.B. (2000). Research design and issues of validity. In H.T. Reis & C.M. Judd (Eds.), *Handbook of research methods in social and personality psychology* (pp. 3–16). New York: Cambridge University Press.

Brewer, M.B. (2001). *Intergroup relations* (2nd edn). Buckingham: Open University Press.

Brewer, M.B. & Miller, N. (1984). Beyond the contact hypothesis: Theoretical perspectives on desegregation. In N. Miller & M.B. Brewer (Eds.), *Groups in contact: The psychology of desegregation* (pp. 281–302). Orlando, FL: Academic Press.

Briñol, P. & Petty, R.E. (2003). Overt head movements and persuasion: A self-validation analysis. *Journal of Personality and Social Psychology, 84*, 1123–1139.

Brodbeck, F.C. & Greitemeyer, T. (2000a). A dynamic model of group performance: Considering the group members' capacity to learn. *Group Processes and Intergroup Relations, 3*, 159–182.

Brodbeck, F.C. & Greitemeyer, T. (2000b). Effects of individual versus mixed individual and group experience in rule induction on group member learning and group performance. *Journal of Experimental Social Psychology, 36*, 621–648.

Brodbeck, F.C., Kerschreiter, R., Mojzisch, A., Frey, D. & Schulz-Hardt, S. (2002). The dissemination of critical, unshared information in decision making groups: The effects of pre-discussion dissent. *European Journal of Social Psychology, 32*, 35–56.

Brodbeck, F.C., Kerschreiter, R., Mojzisch, A. & Schulz-Hardt, S. (2007). Improving group decision making under conditions of distributed knowledge: The Information Asymmetries Model. *Academy of Management Review, 32,* 459–479.

Brodbeck, F.C., Mojzisch, A., Kerschreiter, R. & Schulz-Hardt, S. (2006). Dual task structuring and group documentation as means to improve decision making in hidden profile situations. Unpublished manuscript, Aston University, Birmingham, UK.

Brown, C. (1990). *My left foot.* London: Minerva. (Original work published 1954.)

Brown, J.D. & Smart, S.A. (1991). The self and social conduct: Linking self-representations to prosocial behavior. *Journal of Personality and Social Psychology, 60,* 368–375.

Brown, J.L., Sheffield, D., Leary, M.R. & Robinson, M.E. (2003). Social support and experimental pain. *Psychosomatic Medicine, 65,* 276–283.

Brown, R. (1995). *Prejudice: Its social psychology.* Oxford: Blackwell.

Brown, R. & Brewer, M.B. (1998). Intergroup relations. In D.T. Gilbert, S.T. Fiske & G. Lindzey (Eds.), *The handbook of social psychology* (Vol. 2, 4th edn, pp. 554–594). New York: McGraw-Hill.

Brown, R. & Fish, D. (1983). The psychological causality implicit in language. *Cognition, 14,* 237–273.

Brown, R. & Hewstone, M. (2005). An integrative theory of intergroup contact. In M. Zanna (Ed.), *Advances in experimental social psychology* (Vol. 37, pp. 355–343). San Diego, CA: Academic Press.

Brown, R. & Smith, A. (1989). Perceptions of and by minority groups: The case of women in academia. *European Journal of Social Psychology, 19,* 61–75.

Brown, R., Vivian, J. & Hewstone, M. (1999). Changing attitudes through intergroup contact: The effects of group membership salience. *European Journal of Social Psychology, 29,* 741–764.

Brown, S.P. & Stayman, D.M. (1992). Antecedents and consequences of attitude toward the ad: A meta-analysis. *Journal of Consumer Research, 19,* 34–51.

Browning, C.R. (1992). *Ordinary men: Reserve Police Battalion 101 and the Final Solution in Poland.* New York: HarperCollins.

Bruner, J.S. (1957). On perceptual readiness. *Psychological Review, 64,* 123–152.

Bruner, J.S. (1994). The 'remembered' self. In U. Neisser & R. Fivush (Eds.), *The remembering self: Constructions and accuracy in the self-narrative* (pp. 41–54). New York: Cambridge University Press.

Bruner, J.S. & Tagiuri, R. (1954). The perception of people. In G. Lindzey (Ed.), *Handbook of social psychology* (Vol. 2, pp. 634–654). Reading, MA: Addison-Wesley.

Bunderson, J.S. & Sutcliffe, K.M. (2003). Management team learning orientation and business unit performance. *Journal of Applied Psychology, 88,* 552–560.

Burger, J.M. & Petty, R.E. (1981). The low-ball compliance technique: Task or person commitment? *Journal of Personality and Social Psychology, 40,* 492–500.

Burks, V.S., Laird, R.D., Dodge, A., Pettit, G.S. & Bates, J.E. (1999). Knowledge structures, social information processing, and children's aggressive behavior. *Social Development, 8,* 220–236.

Burns, J.M. (1978). *Leadership.* New York: Harper & Row.

Burnstein, E. & Branigan, C. (2001). Evolutionary analyses in social psychology. In N. Tesser & N. Schwarz (Eds.), *Blackwell handbook of social psychology: Intraindividual processes* (pp. 3–21). Oxford: Blackwell.

Burnstein, E. & Vinokur, A. (1973). Testing two classes of theories about group-induced shifts in individual choices. *Journal of Personality and Social Psychology, 9,* 123–137.

Burnstein, E. & Vinokur, A. (1977). Persuasive argumentation and social comparison as determinants of attitude polarization. *Journal of Experimental Social Psychology, 13,* 315–332.

Burnstein, E., Crandall, C. & Kitayama, S. (1994). Some Neo-Darwinian decision rules for altruism: Weighting cues for inclusive fitness as a function of the biological importance of the decision. *Journal of Personality and Social Psychology, 67,* 773–789.

Burnstein, E., Vinokur, A. & Trope, Y. (1973). Interpersonal comparison versus persuasive argumentation: A more direct test of alternative explanations for group-induced shifts in individual choice. *Journal of Experimental Social Psychology, 9,* 236–245.

Bushman, B.J. (2002). Does venting anger feed or extinguish the flame? Catharsis, rumination, distraction, anger, and aggressive responding. *Personality and Social Psychology Bulletin, 28,* 724–731.

Bushman, B.J. & Cooper, H.M. (1990). Effects of alcohol on human aggression: An integrative research review. *Psychological Bulletin, 107,* 341–354.

Bushman, B.J. & Geen, R.G. (1990). Role of cognitive-emotional mediators and individual differences in the effects of media violence on aggression. *Journal of Personality and Social Psychology, 58,* 156–163.

Bushman, B.J., Baumeister, R.F. & Stack, A.D. (1999). Catharsis, aggression, and persuasive influence: Self-fulfilling or self-defeating prophecies? *Journal of Personality and Social Psychology, 76,* 367–376.

Buss, A.H. & Warren, W.L. (2000). *The Aggression Questionnaire manual.* Los Angeles: Western Psychological Services.

Buss, D.M. (1988). The evolution of human intrasexual competition: Tactics of mate attraction. *Journal of Personality and Social Psychology, 54,* 616–628.

Buss, D.M. (1989). Sex differences in human mate preferences: Evolutionary hypotheses tested in 37 cultures. *Behavioral and Brain Sciences, 12,* 1–49.

Buss, D.M. (1994). *The evolution of desire: Strategies of human mating.* New York: Basic Books.

Buss, D.M. (2004). *Evolutionary psychology* (2nd edn). Boston: Pearson Education.

Buss, D.M. & Bedden, L.A. (1990). Derogation of competitors. *Journal of Social and Personal Relationships, 7,* 395–422.

Buss, D.M. & Kenrick, D.T. (1998). Evolutionary social psychology. In D.T. Gilbert, S.T. Fiske & G. Lindzey (Eds.), *The handbook of social psychology* (4th edn, Vol. 2, pp. 982–1026). New York: McGraw-Hill.

Buss, D.M. et al. (1990). International preferences in selecting mates. A study of 37 cultures. *Journal of Cross-Cultural Psychology, 21,* 5–47.

Buunk, B.P. (1987). Conditions that promote break-ups as a consequence of extradyadic involvements. *Journal of Social and Clinical Psychology, 5,* 237–250.

Buunk, B.P. (1994). Social comparison processes under stress: Towards an integration of classic and recent perspectives. In W. Stroebe & M. Hewstone (Eds.), *European review of social psychology* (Vol. 5, pp. 211–241). Chichester: Wiley.

Buunk, B.P. (1995). Comparison direction and comparison dimension among disabled individuals: Towards a refined conceptualization of social comparison under stress. *Personality and Social Psychology Bulletin, 21,* 316–330.

Buunk, B.P. (1997). Personality, birth order and attachment styles as related to various types of jealousy. *Personality and Individual Differences, 23,* 997–1006.

Buunk, B.P. & Bakker, A.B. (1997). Commitment to the relationship, extradyadic sex, and AIDS-preventive behavior. *Journal of Applied Social Psychology, 27,* 1241–1257.

Buunk, B.P. & Prins, K.S. (1998). Loneliness, exchange orientation and reciprocity in friendships. *Personal Relationships, 5,* 1–14.

Buunk, B.P. & Schaufeli, W.B. (1993). Burnout: A perspective from social comparison theory. In W.B. Schaufeli, C. Maslach & T. Marek (Eds.), *Professional burnout: Recent developments in theory and research* (pp. 53–69). Washington, DC: Taylor & Francis.

Buunk, B.P. & Schaufeli, W.B. (1999). Reciprocity in interpersonal relationships: An evolutionary perspective on its importance for health and well-being. In W. Stroebe & M. Hewstone (Eds.), *European review of social psychology* (Vol. 10, pp. 259–291). Chichester: Wiley.

Buunk, B.P. & Van den Eijnden, R.J.J.M. (1997). Perceived prevalence, perceived superiority, and relationship satisfaction: Most relationships are good, but ours is the best. *Personality and Social Psychology Bulletin, 23,* 219–228.

Buunk, B.P. & VanYperen, N.W. (1991). Referential comparisons, relational comparisons, and exchange orientation: Their relation to marital satisfaction. *Personality and Social Psychology Bulletin, 17*, 709–717.

Buunk, B.P., Collins, R., Taylor, S.E., VanYperen, N.W. & Dakoff, G. (1990). Upward and downward comparisons: Either direction has its ups and downs. *Journal of Personality and Social Psychology, 59*, 1238–1249.

Buunk, B.P., Dijkstra, P., Fetchenhauer, D. & Kenrick, D.T. (2002). Age and gender differences in mate selection criteria for various involvement levels. *Personal Relationships, 9*, 271–278.

Byrne, D. (1971). *The attraction paradigm*. New York: Academic Press.

Byrne, D., Ervin, C.R. & Lambert, J. (1970). Continuity between the experimental study of attraction and real-life computer dating. *Journal of Personality and Social Psychology, 16*, 157–165.

Byrne, D., London, O. & Griffit, W. (1968). The effect of topic importance and attitude similarity–dissimilarity on attraction in an intra-stranger design. *Psychonomic Science, 11*, 303–304.

Cacioppo, J.T. & Berntson, G.G. (Eds.) (2005). *Social neuroscience*. New York and Hove: Psychology Press.

Cacioppo, J.T. & Gardner, W.L. (1993). What underlies medical donor attitudes and behavior? *Health Psychology, 12*, 269–271.

Cacioppo, J.T. & Petty, R.E. (1979). Effects of message repetition and position on cognitive response, recall and persuasion. *Journal of Personality and Social Psychology, 37*, 97–109.

Cacioppo, J.T. & Petty, R.E. (1982). The need for cognition. *Journal of Personality and Social Psychology, 42*, 116–131.

Cacioppo, J.T. & Petty, R.E. (1990). Effects of message repetition on argument processing, recall, and persuasion. *Basic and Applied Social Psychology, 10*, 3–12.

Cacioppo, J.T., Gardner, W.L. & Berntson, G.G. (1997). Beyond bipolar conceptualizations and measures: The case of attitudes and evaluative space. *Personality and Social Psychology Review, 1*, 3–25.

Cacioppo, J.T., Marshall-Goodell, B.S., Tassinary, L.G. & Petty, R.E. (1992). Rudimentary determinants of attitudes: Classical conditioning is more effective when prior knowledge about the attitude stimulus is low than high. *Journal of Personality and Social Psychology, 37*, 2181–2199.

Cacioppo, J.T., Petty, R.E., Feinstein, J. & Jarvis, B. (1996). Individual differences in cognitive motivation: The life and times of people varying in need for cognition. *Psychological Bulletin, 119*, 197–253.

Cacioppo, J.T., Priester, J.R. & Berntson, G.G. (1993). Rudimentary determinants of attitudes: II. Arm flexion and extension have differential effects on attitudes. *Journal of Personality and Social Psychology, 65*, 5–17.

Calvert-Boyanowsky, J. & Leventhal, H. (1975). The role of information in attenuating behavioral responses to stress: A reinterpretation of the misattribution phenomenon. *Journal of Personality and Social Psychology, 32*, 214–221.

Campbell, D.T. (1950). The indirect assessment of attitudes. *Psychological Bulletin, 47*, 15–38.

Campbell, D.T. (1958). Common fate, similarity, and other indices of the status of aggregates of persons as social entities. *Behavioral Science, 3*, 14–25.

Campbell, D.T. (1965). Ethnocentric and other altruistic motives. In D. Levine (Ed.), *Nebraska symposium on motivation* (Vol. 13). Lincoln: University of Nebraska.

Campbell, D.T. & Fiske, D.W. (1959). Convergent and discriminant validation by the multitrait–multimethod matrix. *Psychological Bulletin, 56*, 81–105.

Campbell, J.D. & Fehr, B. (1990). Self-esteem and perceptions of conveyed impressions: Is negative affectivity associated with greater realism? *Journal of Personality and Social Psychology, 58*, 122–133.

Cann, A., Sherman, S.J. & Elkes, R. (1975). Effects of initial request size and timing of second request on compliance. *Journal of Personality and Social Psychology, 32*, 774–782.

Cannon, W.B. (1927). The James–Lange theory of emotions: A critical examination and an alternative theory. *American Journal of Psychology, 39*, 106–124.

Carey, M. (1978). Does civil inattention exist in pedestrian passing? *Journal of Personality and Social Psychology, 36*, 1185–1193.

Carlson, M. & Miller, N. (1987). Explanation of the relation between negative mood and helping. *Psychological Bulletin, 102*, 91–108.

Carlson, M., Charlin, V. & Miller, N. (1988). Positive mood and helping behaviour: A test of six hypotheses. *Journal of Personality and Social Psychology, 55*, 211–229.

Carlson, M., Marcus-Newhall, A. & Miller, N. (1990). Effects of situational aggression cues: A quantitative review. *Journal of Personality and Social Psychology, 58*, 622–633.

Carpenter, E.M. & Kirkpatrick, L.A. (1996). Attachment style and presence of a romantic partner as moderators of psychophysiological responses to a stressful laboratory situation. *Personal Relationships, 3*, 351–367.

Cartwright, D. (1979). Contemporary social psychology in historical perspective. *Social Psychology Quarterly, 42*, 82–93.

Carver, C.S. & Scheier, M.F. (1981). *Attention and self-regulation: A control-theory approach to human behavior*. New York: Springer.

Carver, C.S., Pozo, C., Harris, S.D., Noriega, C., et al. (1993). How coping mediates the effects of optimism on distress: A study of women with early stages breast cancer. *Journal of Personality and Social Psychology, 65*, 375–390.

Castano, E., Yzerbyt, V., Paladino, M.-P. & Sacchi, S. (2002). I belong, therefore, I exist: Ingroup identification, ingroup entitativity, and ingroup bias. *Personality and Social Psychology Bulletin, 28*, 135–143.

Chaiken, S. & Baldwin, M.W. (1981). Affective–cognitive consistency and the effect of salient behavioral information on the self-perception of attitudes. *Journal of Personality and Social Psychology, 41*, 1–12.

Chaiken, S. & Maheswaran, D. (1994). Heuristic processing can bias systematic processing: Effects of source credibility, argument ambiguity, and task importance on attitude judgment. *Journal of Personality and Social Psychology, 66*, 460–473.

Chaiken, S., Liberman, A. & Eagly, A.H. (1989). Heuristic and systematic information processing within and beyond the persuasion context. In J.S. Uleman & J.A. Bargh (Eds.), *Unintended thought* (pp. 212–252). New York: Guilford Press.

Chen, S. & Chaiken S. (1999). The heuristic-systematic model in its broader context. In S. Chaiken & Y. Trope (Eds.), *Dual-process theories in social psychology* (pp. 73–96). New York: Guilford Press.

Chen, S., Shechter, D. & Chaiken, S. (1996). Getting at the truth or getting along: Accuracy- vs. impression-motivated heuristic and systematic information processing. *Journal of Personality and Social Psychology, 71*, 262–275.

Cheng, P.W. (1997). From covariation to causation: A causal power theory. *Psychological Review, 104*, 367–405.

Cheng, P.W. & Novick, L.R. (1990). A probabilistic contrast theory of causal induction. *Journal of Personality and Social Psychology, 58*, 545–567.

Chernyshenko, O.S., Miner, A.G., Baumann, M.R. & Sniezek, J.A. (2003). The impact of information distribution, ownership, and discussion on group member judgment: The differential cue weighting model. *Organizational Behavior and Human Decision Processes, 91*, 12–25.

Chhokar, S., Brodbeck, F.C. & House, R.J. (2007). *Culture and leadership across the world: The GLOBE Book of in-depth studies of 25 societies*. Mahwah, NJ: LEA Publishers.

Choi, H.S. & Levine, J.M. (2004). Minority influence in work teams: The impact of newcomers. *Journal of Experimental Social Psychology, 40*, 273–280.

Choi, I. & Nisbett, R.E. (1998). Situational salience and cultural differences in the correspondence bias and actor–observer bias. *Personality and Social Psychology Bulletin, 24*, 49–60.

Choi, I., Nisbett, R.E. & Norenzayan, A. (1999). Causal attribution across cultures: Variation and universality. *Psychological Bulletin, 125*, 47–63.

Cialdini, R.B. & Ascani, K. (1976). Test of a concession procedure for inducing verbal, behavioral, and further compliance with a request to give blood. *Journal of Applied Psychology, 61*, 295–300.

Cialdini, R.B. & Goldstein, N.J. (2004). Social influence: Compliance and conformity. *Annual Review of Psychology, 55,* 591–622.

Cialdini, R.B. & Richardson, K.D. (1980). Two indirect tactics of image management: Basking and blasting. *Journal of Personality and Social Psychology, 39,* 406–415.

Cialdini, R.B. & Trost, M.R. (1998). Social influence: Social norms, conformity, and compliance. In D.T. Gilbert, S.T. Fiske & G. Lindzey (Eds.), *The handbook of social psychology* (4th edn, Vol. 2, pp. 151–192). New York: McGraw-Hill.

Cialdini, R.B., Brown, S.L., Lewis, B.P., Luce, C. & Neuberg, S.L. (1997). Reinterpreting the empathy–altruism relationship: When one into one equals oneness. *Journal of Personality and Social Psychology, 73,* 481–494.

Cialdini, R.B., Cacioppo, J.T., Bassett, R. & Miller, J.A. (1978). Low-ball procedure for producing compliance: Commitment then cost. *Journal of Personality and Social Psychology, 36,* 463–476.

Cialdini, R.B., Kallgren, C.A. & Reno, R.R. (1991). A focus theory of normative conduct: A theoretical refinement and reevaluation of norms in human behavior. In L. Berkowitz (Ed.), *Advances in experimental social psychology* (Vol. 21, pp. 201–234). San Diego, CA: Academic Press.

Cialdini, R.B., Kenrick, D.T. & Baumann, D.J. (1982). Effects of mood on prosocial behavior in children and adults. In N. Eisenberg (Ed.), *The development of prosocial behaviour* (pp. 339–362). New York: Academic Press.

Cialdini, R.B., Reno, R.R. & Kallgren, C.A. (1990). A focus theory of normative conduct: Recycling the concept of norms to reduce littering in public places. *Journal of Personality and Social Psychology, 58,* 1015–1026.

Cialdini, R.B., Trost, M.R. & Newsom, J.T. (1995). Preference for consistency: The development of a valid measure and the discovery of surprising behavioural implications. *Journal of Personality and Social Psychology, 69,* 318–328.

Cialdini, R.B., Vincent, J.E., Lewis, S.K., Catalan, J., Wheeler, D. & Darby, B.L. (1975). Reciprocal concessions procedure for inducing compliance: The door-in-the-face technique. *Journal of Personality and Social Psychology, 31,* 206–215.

Cini, M.A., Moreland, R.L. & Levine, J.M. (1993). Group staffing levels and responses to prospective and new members. *Journal of Personality and Social Psychology, 65,* 723–734.

Clark, M.S. (1984). Record keeping in two types of relationships. *Journal of Personality and Social Psychology, 47,* 549–557.

Clark, M.S. & Grote, N.K. (2003). Close relationships. In T. Millon & M.J. Lerner (Eds.), *Handbook of psychology: Personality and social psychology* (Vol. 5, pp. 447–461). New York: Wiley.

Clark, M.S. & Mills, J. (1993). The difference between communal and exchange relationships: What it is and is not. *Personality and Social Psychology Bulletin, 19,* 684–691.

Clark, M.S., Mills, J. & Powell, M.C. (1986). Keeping track of needs in communal and exchange relationships. *Journal of Personality and Social Psychology, 51,* 233–238.

Clark, M.S., Ouellette, R., Powell, M.C. & Milberg, S. (1987). Recipient's mood, relationship type, and helping. *Journal of Personality and Social Psychology, 53,* 94–103.

Clary, E.G., Snyder, M., Ridge, R.D., Copeland, J., Stukas, A.A., Haugen, J. & Miene, P. (1998). Understanding and assessing the motivations of volunteers: A functional approach. *Journal of Personality and Social Psychology, 74,* 1516–1530.

Claypool, H.M., Mackie, D.M., Garcia-Marques, T., McIntosh, A. & Udall, A. (2004). The effects of personal relevance and repetition on persuasive processing. *Social Cognition, 22,* 310–335.

Clore, G.L., Schwarz, N. & Conway, M. (1994). Cognitive causes and consequences of emotion. In R.S. Wyer & T.K. Srull (Eds.), *Handbook of social cognition* (2nd edn, Vol. 1, pp. 323–417). Hillsdale, NJ: Lawrence Erlbaum.

Cobb, S. (1976). Social support as a moderator of life stress. *Psychosomatic Medicine, 38,* 300–314.

Cobb, S. & Lindemann, E. (1943). Neuropsychiatric observations after the Coconut Grove fire. *Annals of Surgery, 117,* 814–824.

Coch, L. & French, J.R.P. (1948). Overcoming resistance to change. *Human Relations, 11,* 512–532.

Cochrane, R. (1988). Marriage, separation and divorce. In S. Fisher & J. Reason (Eds.), *Handbook of life stress, cognition and health* (pp. 137–160). Chichester: Wiley.

Cohen, C. (1981). Person categories and social perception: Testing some boundaries of the processing effects of prior knowledge. *Journal of Personality and Social Psychology, 40,* 441–452.

Cohen, M.H. (1993). The unknown and the unknowable: Managing sustained uncertainty. *Western Journal of Nursing Research, 15,* 77–96.

Cohen, S. & Hoberman, H.M. (1983). Positive events and social supports as buffers of life change stress. *Journal of Applied Social Psychology, 13,* 99–125.

Cohen, S. & Wills, T.A. (1985). Stress, social support, and the buffering hypothesis. *Psychological Bulletin, 98,* 310–357.

Cohen, S., Frank, E., Doyle, W.J., Skoner, D.P., Rabin, B.S. & Gwaltney, J.M. (1998). Types of stressors that increase susceptibility to the common cold in healthy adults. *Health Psychology, 17,* 214–223.

Cohen, S., Kessler, R.C. & Gordon, L.U. (1995). Strategies for measuring stress in studies of psychiatric and physical disorders. In S. Cohen, R.C. Kessler & L.U. Gordon (Eds.), *Measuring stress* (pp. 3–26). New York: Oxford University Press.

Cohen, S., Tyrell, D.A.J. & Smith, A.P. (1993). Negative life events, perceived stress, negative affect, and susceptibility to the common cold. *Journal of Personality and Social Psychology, 64,* 131–140.

Coie, J.D. & Dodge, K.A. (1998). Aggression and antisocial behavior. In W. Damon & N. Eisenberg (Eds.), *Handbook of child psychology* (5th edn, pp. 779–862). New York: Wiley.

Conger, J.A. & Kanungo, R.N. (1987). Toward a behavioral theory of charismatic leadership in organizational settings. *Academy of Management Review, 12,* 637–647.

Conger, J.A. & Kanungo, R.N. (1998). *Charismatic leadership in organizations.* Thousand Oaks, CA: Sage.

Conner, M. & Norman, P. (Eds.) (2005). *Predicting health behaviour: Research and practice with social cognition models* (2nd edn). Maidenhead: Open University Press.

Converse, P.E. (1994). Theodore Newcomb. Biographical Memoirs V. 64. The National Academies Press. Retrieved October 2005 from books.nap.edu.books/0309049784/html/320.html.

Cook, T.D. & Campbell, D.T. (1979). *Quasi-experimentation: Design and analysis issues for field settings.* Chicago, IL: Rand McNally.

Cooper, H. (1990). Meta-analysis and the integrative research review. In C. Hendrick & M.S. Clark (Eds.), *Research methods in personality and social psychology* (*Review of Personality and Social Psychology,* Vol. 11, pp. 142–163). Newbury Park, CA: Sage.

Cooper, H. & Hedges, L.V. (Eds.) (1994). *The handbook of research synthesis.* New York: Russell Sage.

Cooper, J. & Worchel, S. (1970). Role of undesirable consequences in arousing cognitive dissonance. *Journal of Personality and Social Psychology, 16,* 199–206.

Coovert, M.D., Thompson, L.F. & Craiger, J.P. (2005). Technology. In J. Barling, E.K. Kelloway & M.R. Frone (Eds.), *Handbook of work stress* (pp. 299–324). Thousand Oaks, CA: Sage.

Corneille, O., Klein, O., Lambert, S. & Judd, C.M. (2002). On the role of familiarity with units of measurement in categorical accentuation. *Psychological Science, 13,* 380–383.

Cornwell, B. & Lundgren, D.C. (2001). Love on the Internet: Involvement and misrepresentations in romantic relationships in cyberspace vs. realspace. *Computers in Human Behavior, 17,* 197–211.

Cottrell, C.A. & Neuberg, S.L. (2005). Different emotional reactions to different groups: A sociofunctional threat-based approach to 'Prejudice'. *Journal of Personality and Social Psychology, 88,* 770–789.

Cottrell, N.B. (1968). Performance in the presence of other human beings: Mere presence, audience and affiliation effects. In E.C. Simmel, R.A. Hoppe & G.A. Milton (Eds.), *Social facilitation and imitative behavior* (pp. 91–109). Boston: Allyn & Bacon.

Cottrell, N.B. (1972). Social facilitation. In C.G. McClintock (Ed.), *Experimental social psychology* (pp. 185–236). New York: Holt, Rinehart & Winston.

Coulter, K.S. & Punj, G.N. (2004). The effects of cognitive resource requirements, availability, and argument quality on brand attitudes. *Journal of Advertising, 33*, 53–64.

Crandall, C. (1988). Social contagion of binge eating. *Journal of Personality and Social Psychology, 66*, 588–598.

Crandall, C.S., Eshleman, A. & O'Brien, L. (2002). Social norms and the expression and suppression of prejudice: The struggle for internalization. *Journal of Personality and Social Psychology, 82*, 359–378.

Crano, W.D. & Alvaro, E.M. (1998). The context/comparison model of social influence: Mechanisms, structure, and linkages that underlie indirect attitude change. In W. Stroebe & M. Hewstone (Eds.), *European review of social psychology* (Vol. 8, pp. 175–202). Chichester: Wiley.

Crano, W.D. & Chen, X. (1998). The leniency contract and persistence of majority and minority influence. *Journal of Personality and Social Psychology, 74*, 1437–1450.

Crisp, R.J. & Hewstone, M. (1999). Differential evaluation of crossed category groups: Patterns, processes, and reducing intergroup bias. *Group Processes and Intergroup Relations, 2*, 307–333.

Crocker, J., Karpinski, A., Quinn, D.M. & Chase, S.K. (2003). When grades determine self-worth: Consequences of contingent self-worth for male and female engineering and psychology majors. *Journal of Personality and Social Psychology, 85*, 507–516.

Crocker, J., Thompson, L.J., McGraw, K.M. & Ingerman, C. (1987). Downward comparison, prejudice, and evaluations of others: Effects of self-esteem and threat. *Journal of Personality and Social Psychology, 52*, 907–916.

Cropanzano, R., Goldman, B.M. & Benson III, L. (2005). Organizational justice. In J. Barling, E.K. Kelloway & M.R. Frone (Eds.), *Handbook of work stress* (pp. 63–87). Thousand Oaks, CA: Sage.

Cropanzano, R., Rupp, D.E., Mohler, C.J. & Schminke, M. (2001). Three roads to organizational justice. In J. Ferris (Ed.), *Research in personnel and human resource management* (pp. 1–113). Greenwich, CT: JAI Press.

Crutchfield, R.S. (1955). Conformity and character. *American Psychologist, 10*, 191–198.

Cruz, M.G., Henningsen, D.D. & Smith, B.A. (1999). The impact of directive leadership on group information sampling, decisions and perceptions of the leader. *Communication Research, 26*, 349–369.

Csikszentmihalyi, M. & Figurski, T.J. (1982). Self-awareness and aversive experience in everyday life. *Journal of Personality, 50*, 15–28.

Culbertson, K.A. & Dehle, C. (2001). Impact of sexual assault as a function of perpetrator type. *Journal of Interpersonal Violence, 16*, 992–1007.

Cummings, R.C. (1990). Job stress and the buffering effect of supervisory support. *Group and Organizational Studies, 15*, 92–104.

Cunningham, M.R. (1986). Measuring the physical in physical attractiveness: Quasi experiments on the sociobiology of female facial beauty. *Journal of Personality and Social Psychology, 50*, 925–935.

Cunningham, M.R., Barbee, A.P. & Pike, C.L. (1990). What do women want? Facialmetric assessment of multiple motives in the perception of male physical attractiveness. *Journal of Personality and Social Psychology, 59*, 61–72.

Cunningham, M.R., Roberts, A.R., Barbee, A.P., Druen, P.B. & Wu, C. (1995). 'Their ideas of beauty are, on the whole, the same as ours': Consistency and variability in the cross-cultural perception of female physical attractiveness. *Journal of Personality and Social Psychology, 68*, 261–279.

Cunningham, W.A., Preacher, K.J. & Banaji, M.R. (2001). Implicit attitude measures: Consistency, stability, and convergent validity. *Psychological Science, 12*, 163–170.

Dabbs, J.M. & Dabbs, M.G. (2000). *Heroes, rogues and lovers: Testosterone and behavior.* New York: McGraw-Hill.

Dabbs, J.M. & Ruback, R.B. (1987). Dimensions of group process: Amount and structure of vocal interaction. In L. Berkowitz (Ed.), *Advances in experimental social psychology* (Vol. 20, pp. 123–169). San Diego, CA: Academic Press.

Dalbert, C. (1999). The world is more just for me than generally: About the personal belief in a just world scale's validity. *Social Justice Research, 12*, 79–98.

Darley, J. (1992). Social organization for the production of evil. *Psychological Inquiry, 3*, 199–218.

Darley, J.M. & Batson, C.D. (1973). From Jerusalem to Jericho: A study of situational and dispositional variables in helping behaviour. *Journal of Personality and Social Psychology, 27*, 100–108.

Darley, J.M. & Latané, B. (1968). Bystander intervention in emergencies: Diffusion of responsibility. *Journal of Personality and Social Psychology, 8*, 377–383.

Das, E., de Wit, J. & Stroebe, W. (2003). Fear appeals motivate acceptance of action recommendations: Evidence for a positive bias in the processing of persuasive messages. *Personality and Social Psychology Bulletin, 29*, 650–664.

Dashiell, J.F. (1935). Experimental studies of the influence of social situations on the behavior of individual human adults. In C. Murchison (Ed.), *Handbook of social psychology* (pp. 1097–1158). Worcester, MA: Clark University Press.

David, B. & Turner, J.C. (1996). Studies in self-categorization and minority conversion: Is being a member of the outgroup an advantage? *British Journal of Social Psychology, 35*, 179–199.

David, B. & Turner, J.C. (1999). Studies in self-categorization and minority conversion: The ingroup minority in intragroup and intergroup contexts. *British Journal of Social Psychology, 38*, 115–134.

Davidson, A.R. & Jaccard, J.J. (1979). Variables that moderate the attitude–behavior relation: Results of a longitudinal survey. *Journal of Personality and Social Psychology, 37*, 1364–1376.

Davis, D., Shaver, P.R. & Vernon, M.L. (2003). Physical, emotional and behavioral reactions to breaking up: The roles of gender, age, emotional involvement and attachment style. *Journal of Personality and Social Psychology, 29*, 871–884.

Davis, J.H. (1980). Group decision and procedural justice. In M. Fishbein (Ed.), *Progress in social psychology* (Vol. 1, pp. 157–229). Hillsdale, NJ: Lawrence Erlbaum.

Davis, J.H., Kerr, N.L., Stasser, G., Meek, D. & Holt, R. (1977). Victim consequences, sentence severity, and decision processes in mock juries. *Organizational Behavior and Human Performance, 18*, 346–365.

Davis, M.H. (1994). *Empathy: A social psychological approach.* Madison, WI: Brown & Benchmark.

De Boer, E.M., Bakker, A.B., Syroit, J.E. & Schaufeli, W.B. (2002). Unfairness at work as a predictor of absenteeism. *Journal of Organizational Behavior, 23*, 181–197.

DeCharms, R. (1968). *Personal causation: The internal-affective determinants of behavior.* New York: Academic Press.

Deci, E.L., Koestner, R. & Ryan, R.M. (1999). A meta-analytic review of experiments examining the effects of extrinsic rewards on intrinsic motivation. *Psychological Bulletin, 125*, 627–668.

De Dreu, C.K.W. & De Vries, N.K. (1993). Numerical support, information processing and attitude change. *European Journal of Social Psychology, 23*, 647–663.

De Hoog, N., Stroebe, W. & de Wit, J. (2005). The impact of fear appeals on the processing and acceptance of action recommendations. *Personality and Social Psychology Bulletin, 31*, 24–33.

DeHouwer, J., Baeyens, F. & Eelen, P. (1994). Verbal evaluative conditioning with undetected US presentations. *Behavior Research and Therapy, 32*, 629–633.

DeLongis, A., Folkman, S. & Lazarus, R.S. (1988). The impact of daily stress on health and mood: Psychological and social resources as mediators. *Journal of Personality and Social Psychology, 54*, 486–495.

Dennis, A.R. (1996). Information exchange and use in small group decision making. *Small Group Research*, 27, 532–550.

Dennis, A.R. & Valacich, J.S. (1993). Computer brainstorms: More heads are better than one. *Journal of Applied Psychology*, 78, 531–537.

DeShon, R.P., Kozlowski, S.W.J., Schmidt, A.M., Milner, K.R. & Wiechmann, D. (2004). A multiple-goal, multilevel model of feedback effects on the regulation of individual and team performance. *Journal of Applied Psychology*, 89, 1035–1056.

Deutsch, M. & Gerard, H.B. (1955). A study of normative and informational influence upon individual judgment. *Journal of Abnormal and Social Psychology*, 51, 629–636.

Devine, P.G. (1989). Stereotypes and prejudice: Their automatic and controlled components. *Journal of Personality and Social Psychology*, 56, 5–18.

Devine, P.G. & Monteith, M.J. (1999). Automaticity and control in stereotyping. In S. Chaiken & Y. Trope (Eds.), *Dual process theories in social psychology* (pp. 339–360). New York: Guilford Press.

Devine, P.G., Hamilton, D.L. & Ostrom, T.M. (Eds.) (1994). *Social cognition: Impact on social psychology*. San Diego, CA: Academic Press.

De Vries, N.K., De Dreu, C.K.W., Gordijn, E. & Schuurman, M. (1996). Majority and minority influence: A dual interpretation. In W. Stroebe & M. Hewstone (Eds.), *European review of social psychology* (Vol. 7, pp. 145–172). Chichester: Wiley.

De Waal, F. (1983). *Chimpanzee politics: Power and sex among apes*. New York: Harper & Row.

De Waal, F. (1996). *Good Natured: The Origins of Right and Wrong in Humans and Other Animals*. Cambridge, MA: Harvard University Press.

Diehl, M. & Stroebe, W. (1987). Productivity loss in brainstorming groups: Toward the solution of a riddle. *Journal of Personality and Social Psychology*, 53, 497–509.

Dijksterhuis, A. & Bargh, J.A. (2001). The perception–behaviour expressway: Automatic effects of social perception on social behaviour. In M. Zanna (Ed.), *Advances in experimental social psychology* (Vol. 33, pp. 1–40). San Diego, CA: Academic Press.

Dijksterhuis, A. & van Knippenberg, A. (1998). The relation between perception and behavior or how to win a game of trivial pursuit. *Journal of Personality and Social Psychology*, 74, 865–877.

Dijksterhuis, A. & van Knippenberg, A. (2000). Behavioral indecision: Effects of self-focus on automatic behavior. *Social Cognition*, 18, 55–74.

Dijksterhuis, A., Aarts, H., Bargh, J.A. & van Knippenberg, A. (2000). On the relation between associative strength and automatic behavior. *Journal of Experimental Social Psychology*, 36, 531–544.

Dijksterhuis, A., Bargh, J.A. & Miedema, J. (2000). Of men and mackerels: Attention and automatic behavior. In H. Bless & J.P. Forgas (Eds.), *Subjective experience in social cognition and behavior* (pp. 36–51). Philadelphia: Psychology Press.

Dijksterhuis, A., Spears, R., Postmes, T., Stapel, D.A., Koomen, W., van Knippenberg, A. & Scheppers, D. (1998). Seeing one thing and doing another: Contrast effects in automatic behaviour. *Journal of Personality and Social Psychology*, 75, 862–871.

Dijkstra, P. & Buunk, B.P. (1998). Jealousy as a function of rival characteristics: An evolutionary perspective. *Personality and Social Psychology Bulletin*, 24, 1158–1166.

Dijkstra, P. & Buunk, B.P. (2001). Sex differences in the jealousy-evoking nature of a rival's body build. *Evolution and Human Behavior*, 22, 335–341.

Dill, K.E., Anderson, C.A., Anderson, K.B. & Deuser, W.E. (1997). Effects of aggressive personality on social expectations and social perceptions. *Journal of Research in Personality*, 31, 272–292.

Dirks, K.T. (1999). The effects of interpersonal trust on work group performance. *Journal of Applied Psychology*, 84, 445–455.

Dodge, K.A. (1980). Social cognition and children's aggressive behavior. *Child Development*, 51, 162–170.

Doise, W. (1969). Intergroup relations and polarization of individual and collective judgements. *Journal of Personality and Social Psychology*, 12, 136–143.

Doise, W. (2002). *Human rights as social representations*. London: Routledge.

Dollard, J., Doob, L.W., Miller, N.E., Mowrer, O.H. & Sears, R.R. (1939). *Frustration and aggression*. New Haven, CT: Yale University Press.

Dovidio, J.F., Kawakami, K., Johnson, C., Johnson, B. & Howard, A. (1997). The nature of prejudice: Automatic and controlled processes. *Journal of Experimental Social Psychology*, 33, 510–540.

Drigotas, S.M., Safstrom, C.A. & Gentilia, T. (1999). An investment model prediction of dating infidelity. *Journal of Personality and Social Psychology*, 77, 509–524.

Driskell, J.E. & Mullen, B. (1990). Status, expectations, and behaviour: A meta-analytic review and test of the theory. *Personality and Social Psychology Bulletin*, 16, 541–553.

Dröge, C. (1989). Shaping the route to attitude change: Central processing through comparative versus noncomparative advertising. *Journal of Marketing Research*, 26, 193–204.

Dryer, D.C. & Horowitz, L.M. (1997). When do opposites attract? Interpersonal complementarity versus similarity. *Journal of Personality and Social Psychology*, 72, 592–603.

Duncan, B.L. (1976). Differential social perception and attribution of intergroup violence: Testing the lower limits of stereotyping of blacks. *Journal of Personality and Social Psychology*, 34, 590–598.

Dunkel-Schetter, C., Blasband, D.E., Feinstein, L.G. & Bennett, H.T. (1992). Elements of supportive interactions: When are attempts to help effective? In S. Spacapan & S. Oskamp (Eds.), *Helping and being helped: Naturalistic studies* (pp. 83–114). Newbury Park, CA: Sage.

Dutton, D.G. & Aron, A.P. (1974). Some evidence for heightened sexual attraction under conditions of high anxiety. *Journal of Personality and Social Psychology*, 28, 510–517.

Dutton, D.G. & Lake, R.A. (1973). Threat of own prejudice and reverse discrimination in interracial situations. *Journal of Personality and Social Psychology*, 28, 94–100.

Duval, S. & Wicklund, R.A. (1972). *A theory of objective self-awareness*. New York: Academic Press.

Eagly, A.H., Ashmore, R.D. & Longo, L.C. (1992). What is beautiful is good, but . . . : A meta-analytic study on the physical attractiveness stereotype. *Psychological Bulletin*, 110, 109–128.

Eagly, A.H. & Chaiken, S. (1993). *The psychology of attitudes*. Fort Worth, TX: Harcourt Brace Jovanovich.

Eagly, A.H. & Chaiken, S. (1998). Attitude structure and function. In D.T. Gilbert, S.T. Fiske & G. Lindzey (Eds.), *The handbook of social psychology* (4th edn, Vol. 1, pp. 269–322). New York: McGraw-Hill.

Eagly, A.H. & Steffen, F.J. (1986). Gender and aggressive behavior: A meta-analytic review of the social psychological literature. *Psychological Bulletin*, 100, 309–330.

Ebbesen, E.B., Kjos, G.L. & Konecni, V.J. (1976). Spatial ecology: Its effects on the choice of friends and enemies. *Journal of Experimental Social Psychology*, 12, 505–518.

Eberhardt, J.S. (2005). Imaging race. *American Psychologist*, 60, 181–190.

Edwards, D. & Potter, J. (1993). Language and causation: A discursive action model of description and attribution. *Psychological Review*, 100, 23–41.

Edwards, J.R., Caplan, R.D. & van Harrison, R. (2000). Person–environment fit theory. In C.L. Cooper (Ed.), *Theories of organizational stress* (pp. 28–67). Oxford: Oxford University Press.

Eisenberg, N. & Fabes, R.A. (1991). Prosocial behaviour and empathy: A multimethod developmental perspective. In M.S. Clark (Ed.), *Prosocial behaviour* (pp. 34–61). Newbury Park, CA: Sage.

Eisenberg, N. & Shell, R. (1986). Prosocial moral judgment and behaviour in children: The mediating role of cost. *Personality and Social Psychology Bulletin*, 12, 426–433.

Eisenberg, N., Fabes, R.A., Carlo, G., Speer, A.L., Switzer, G., Karbon, M. & Troyer, D. (1993). The relations of empathy-related emotions and maternal practices to children's comforting behaviour. *Journal of Experimental Child Psychology*, 55, 131–150.

Eisenberger, N.I., Lieberman, M.D. & Williams, K.D. (2003). Does rejection hurt? An fMRI study of social exclusion. *Science*, 302, 290–292.

Eisenberger, R., Armeli, S., Rexwinkel, B., Lynch, P.D. & Rhoades, L. (2001). Reciprocation of perceived organizational support. *Journal of Applied Psychology*, 86, 42–51.

Eisenberger, R., Cummings, J., Armeli, S. & Lynch, P. (1997). Perceived organizational support, discretionary treatment, and job satisfaction. *Journal of Applied Psychology*, 82, 812–820.

Ellemers, N. (1993). The influence of socio-structural variables on identity management strategies. In W. Stroebe & M. Hewstone (Eds.), *European review of social psychology* (Vol. 4, pp. 27–57). Chichester: Wiley.

Ellemers, N., Kortekaas, P. & Ouwerkerk, J.W. (1999). Self-categorization, commitment to the group and group self-esteem as related but distinct aspects of social identity. *European Journal of Social Psychology*, 29, 371–389.

Elms, A.C. & Milgram, S. (1966). Personality characteristics associated with obedience and defiance toward authoritative command. *Journal of Experimental Research in Personality*, 1, 282–289.

Elovainio, M., Kivimäki, M. & Vahtera, J. (2002). Organizational justice: Evidence of a new psychosocial predictor of health. *American Journal of Public Health*, 92, 105–108.

Ensari, N. & Miller, N. (2002). The out-group must not be so bad after all: The effects of disclosure, typicality, and salience on intergroup bias. *Journal of Personality and Social Psychology*, 83, 313–329.

Epping-Jordan, J.E., Compas, B.E. & Howell, D.C. (1994). Predictors of cancer progression in young adult men and women: Avoidance, intrusive thoughts, and psychological symptoms. *Health Psychology*, 13, 373–383.

Erdmann, G. & Janke, W. (1978). Interaction between physiological and cognitive determinants of emotions: Experimental studies on Schachter's theory of emotions. *Biological Psychology*, 6, 61–74.

Erez, M. & Somech, A. (1996). Is group productivity loss the rule or the exception? Effects of culture and group-based motivation. *Academy of Management Journal*, 39, 1513–1537.

Erez, A., Lepine, J.A. & Elms, H. (2002). Effects of rotated leadership and peer evaluation on the functioning and effectiveness of self-managed teams: A quasi experiment. *Personnel Psychology*, 55, 929–948.

Esser, J.K. (1998). Alive and well after 25 years: A review of groupthink research. *Organizational Behavior and Human Decision Processes*, 73, 116–141.

Esser, J.K. & Lindoerfer, J.S. (1989). Groupthink and the space shuttle *Challenger* accident: Toward a quantitative case analysis. *Journal of Behavioral Decision Making*, 2, 167–177.

Esses, V.M., Haddock, G. & Zanna, M.P. (1993). Values, stereotypes, and emotions as determinants of intergroup attitudes. In D.M. Mackie & D.L. Hamilton (Eds.), *Affect, cognition, and stereotyping: Interactive processes in group perception* (pp. 137–166). New York: Academic Press.

Estrada-Hollenbeck, M. & Heatherton, T.F. (1998). Avoiding and alleviating guilt through prosocial behaviour. In J. Bybee (Ed.), *Guilt and children* (pp. 215–231). San Diego, CA: Academic Press.

Fantz, R.L. (1963). Pattern vision in newborn infants. *Science*, 140, 296–297.

Farr, R.M. (1996). *The roots of modern social psychology*. Oxford: Blackwell.

Farr, R.M. & Moscovici, S. (Eds.) (1984). *Social representations*. Cambridge: Cambridge University Press.

Fazio, R.H. (1990). Multiple processes by which attitudes guide behavior: The MODE model as an integrative framework. In M.P. Zanna (Ed.), *Advances in experimental social psychology* (Vol. 23, pp. 75–109). San Diego, CA: Academic Press.

Fazio, R.H. (1995). Attitudes as object-evaluation associations: Determinants, consequences, and correlates of attitude accessibility. In R.E. Petty & J.A. Krosnick (Eds.), *Attitude strength: Antecedents and consequences* (pp. 247–282). Hillsdale, NJ: Lawrence Erlbaum.

Fazio, R.H. (2000). Accessible attitudes as tools for object appraisal: Their costs and benefits. In G.R. Maio & J.M. Olson (Eds.), *Why we evaluate: Functions of attitudes* (pp. 1–36). Mahwah, NJ: Lawrence Erlbaum.

Fazio, R.H. & Dunton, B.C. (1997). Categorization by race: The impact of automatic and controlled components of racial prejudice. *Journal of Experimental Social Psychology*, 33, 451–470.

Fazio, R.H. & Olson, M.A. (2003). Implicit measures in social cognition research: Their meaning and use. *Annual Review of Psychology*, 54, 297–327.

Fazio, R.H. & Williams, C.J. (1986). Attitude accessibility as a moderator of the attitude–perception and attitude–behavior relations: An investigation of the 1984 presidential election. *Journal of Personality and Social Psychology*, 51, 505–514.

Fazio, R.H. & Zanna, M.P. (1971). Direct experience and attitude–behavior consistency. In L. Berkowitz (Ed.), *Advances in experimental social psychology* (Vol. 14, pp. 161–202). Orlando, FL: Academic Press.

Fazio, R.H., Chen, J., McDonel, E.C. & Sherman, S.J. (1982). Attitude accessibility, attitude–behavior consistency, and the strength of the object-evaluation association. *Journal of Experimental Social Psychology*, 18, 339–357.

Fazio, R.H., Jackson, J.R., Dunton, B.C. & Williams, C.J. (1995). Variability in automatic activation as an unobtrusive measure of racial attitudes: A bona fide pipeline? *Journal of Personality and Social Psychology*, 69, 1013–1027.

Fazio, R.H., Zanna, M.P. & Cooper, J. (1977). Dissonance versus self-perception: An integrative view of each theory's proper domain of application. *Journal of Experimental Social Psychology*, 13, 464–479.

Feeney, A. (2002). Attachment, marital interaction, and relationship satisfaction: A diary study. *Personal Relationships*, 9, 39–55.

Fehr, B. (2004). Intimacy expectations in same-sex friendships: A prototype interaction-pattern model. *Journal of Personality and Social Psychology*, 86, 265–284.

Feingold, A. (1992). Good-looking people are not what we think. *Psychological Bulletin*, 111, 304–341.

Fenigstein, A., Scheier, M.F. & Buss, A.H. (1975). Public and private self-consciousness: Assessment and theory. *Journal of Consulting and Clinical Psychology*, 43, 522–527.

Ferguson, C.K. & Kelley, H.H. (1964). Significant factors in overevaluation of own-group's product. *Journal of Abnormal and Social Psychology*, 69, 223–228.

Festinger, L. (1950). Informal social communication. *Psychological Review*, 57, 271–282.

Festinger, L. (1954). A theory of social comparison processes. *Human Relations*, 7, 117–140.

Festinger, L. (1957). *A theory of cognitive dissonance*. Stanford, CA: Stanford University Press.

Festinger, L. (Ed.) (1980). *Retrospections on social psychology*. New York: Oxford University Press.

Festinger, L. & Carlsmith, J.M. (1959). Cognitive consequences of forced compliance. *Journal of Abnormal and Social Psychology*, 58, 203–210.

Festinger, L. & Maccoby, N. (1964). On resistance to persuasive communications. *Journal of Abnormal and Social Psychology*, 68, 359–366.

Festinger, L., Riecken, H.W. & Schachter, S. (1956). *When prophecy fails*. Minneapolis: University of Minnesota Press.

Festinger, L., Schachter, S. & Back, K. (1950). *Social pressures in informal groups: A study of human factors in housing*. New York: Harper.

Fhanér, G. & Hane, M. (1979). Seat belts: Opinion effects of law-induced use. *Journal of Applied Psychology*, 64, 205–212.

Fincham, F.D. & Bradbury, T.H. (1991). Cognition in marriage: A program of research on attributions. In W.H. Jones & D. Perlman (Eds.), *Advances in personal relationships* (Vol. 2, pp. 159–204). London: Jessica Kingsley.

Fincham, F.D., Paleari, F.G. & Regalia, C. (2002). Forgiveness in marriage: The role of relationship quality, attributions, and empathy. *Personal Relationships*, 9, 27–37.

Finkel, E.J., Rusbult, C.E., Kumashiro, M. & Hannon, P.A. (2002). Dealing with betrayal in close relationships: Does commitment promote forgiveness? *Journal of Personality and Social Psychology*, 82, 956–974.

Fishbein, M. & Ajzen, I. (1975). *Belief, attitude, intention, and behavior: An introduction to theory and research*. Reading, MA: Addison-Wesley.

Fiske, S.T. (1989). Examining the role of intent: Toward understanding its role in stereotyping and prejudice. In J.S. Uleman & J.A. Bargh (Eds.), *Unintended thought* (pp. 253–283). New York: Guilford Press.

Fiske, S.T. (1998). Stereotyping, prejudice, and discrimination. In D.T. Gilbert, S.T. Fiske & G. Lindzey (Eds.), *The handbook of social psychology* (Vol. 2, 4th edn, pp. 357–411). New York: McGraw-Hill.

Fiske, S.T. (2004). *Social beings: A core motives approach to social psychology.* Chichester: Wiley.

Fiske, S.T. & Neuberg, S.L. (1990). A continuum of impression formation, from category-based to individuating processes: Influences of information and motivation on attention and interpretation. In M.P. Zanna (Ed.), *Advances in experimental social psychology* (Vol. 23, pp. 1–74). New York: Academic Press.

Fiske, S.T. & Taylor, S.E. (1991). *Social cognition* (2nd edn). New York: McGraw-Hill.

Fiske, S.T., Cuddy, A.J.C., Glick, P. & Xu, J. (2002). A model of (often mixed) stereotype content: Competence and warmth respectively follow from perceived status and competition. *Journal of Personality and Social Psychology, 82,* 878–902.

Flanagan, O. (1994). *Consciousness reconsidered.* Cambridge, MA: MIT Press.

Flowers, M.L. (1977). A laboratory test of some implications of Janis's groupthink hypothesis. *Journal of Personality and Social Psychology, 35,* 888–896.

Foa, E.B. & Rothbaum, B.O. (1998). *Treating the trauma of rape.* New York: Guilford Press.

Folkman, S., Lazarus, R.S., Dunkel-Schetter, C., DeLongis, A. & Gruen, R.J. (1986). The dynamics of a stressful encounter. *Journal of Personality and Social Psychology, 50,* 992–1003.

Forgas, J.P. (2000). Affect and information processing strategies: An interactive relationship. In J.P. Forgas (Ed.), *Feeling and thinking: The role of affect in social cognition* (pp. 253–280). Cambridge: Cambridge University Press.

Forgas, J.P., Bower, G.H. & Moylan, S.J. (1990). Praise or blame? Affective influences on attributions for achievement. *Journal of Personality and Social Psychology, 59,* 809–819.

Försterling, F. (2001). *Attribution: An introduction to theories, research, and applications.* Hove: Psychology Press.

Forsyth, D.R. (1995). Norms. In A.S.R. Manstead & M. Hewstone (Eds.), *Blackwell encyclopedia of social psychology* (pp. 412–417). Oxford: Blackwell.

Foster, C.A., Witcher, B.S., Campbell, W.K. & Green, J.D. (1998). Arousal and attraction: Evidence for automatic and controlled processes. *Journal of Personality and Social Psychology, 74,* 86–101.

Fox, S. (1980). Situational determinants in affiliation. *European Journal of Social Psychology, 10,* 303–307.

Frazier, P.A., Byer, A.L., Fischer, A.R., Wright, D.M. & DeBord, K.A. (1996). Adult attachment style and partner choice: Correlational and experimental findings. *Personal Relationships, 3,* 117–136.

Freedman, J.L. & Fraser, S.C. (1966). Compliance without pressure: The foot-in-the-door technique. *Journal of Personality and Social Psychology, 4,* 195–203.

Freedman, J.L., Wallington, S.A. & Bless, E. (1967). Compliance without pressure: The effect of guilt. *Journal of Personality and Social Psychology, 7,* 117–124.

Freese, L. & Cohen, B.P. (1973). Eliminating status generalization. *Sociometry, 36,* 177–193.

Freud, S. (1920). *Beyond the pleasure principle.* New York: Bantam Books.

Fried, Y. (1991). Meta-analytic comparison of the Job Diagnostic Survey and Job Characteristics Inventory as correlates of work satisfaction and performance. *Journal of Applied Psychology, 76,* 690–697.

Fried, Y. & Ferris, G.R. (1987). The validity of the job characteristics model: A review and meta-analysis. *Personnel Psychology, 40,* 287–322.

Frieze, I.H. (2000). Violence in close relationships: Development of a research area. Comment on Archer (2000). *Psychological Bulletin, 126,* 681–684.

Frieze, I.H. & Davis, K.E. (Eds.) (2002). *Stalking: Perspectives on victims and perpetrators.* New York: Springer.

Frijda, N. (1986). *The emotions.* New York: Cambridge University Press.

Gaertner, S.L. (1975). The role of racial attitudes in helping behavior. *Journal of Social Psychology, 97,* 95–101.

Gaertner, S.L. (1976). Nonreactive measures in racial attitude research. A focus on 'Liberals'. In P. Katz (Ed.), *Toward the elimination of racism.* New York: Pergamon Press.

Gaertner, S.L. & Bickman, L. (1971). Effects of race on the elicitation of helping behavior: The wrong number technique. *Journal of Personality and Social Psychology, 20,* 218–222.

Gaertner, S.L. & Dovidio, J.F. (1977). The subtlety of white racism, arousal, and helping behavior. *Journal of Personality and Social Psychology, 35,* 691–707.

Gaertner, S.L. & Dovidio, J.F. (1986). The aversive form of racism. In J.F. Dovidio & S.L. Gaertner (Eds.), *Prejudice, discrimination, and racism* (pp. 61–89). New York: Academic Press.

Gaertner, S.L. & Dovidio, J.F. (2000). *Reducing intergroup bias: The common ingroup identity model.* Philadelphia: Psychology Press.

Gaertner, S.L. & McLaughlin, J.P. (1983). Racial stereotypes: Associations and ascriptions of positive and negative characteristics. *Social Psychology Quarterly, 46,* 23–30.

Gaertner, S.L., Dovidio, J.F., Nier, J.A., Ward, C.M. & Banker, B. (1999). Across cultural divides: The value of a superordinate identity. In D.A. Prentice & D.T. Miller (Eds.), *Cultural divides: Understanding and overcoming group conflict* (pp. 173–212). New York: Russell Sage Foundation.

Gaertner, S.L., Mann, J.A., Murrell, A. & Dovidio, J.F. (1989). Reducing intergroup bias: The benefits of recategorization. *Journal of Personality and Social Psychology, 57,* 239–249.

Gaines, S.O. & Henderson, M.C. (2002). Impact of attachment style on responses to accommodative dilemmas among same-sex couples. *Personal Relationships, 9,* 89–93.

Gaines, S.O., Reis, H.T., Summers, S., Rusbult, C.E., Cox, C.L., Wexler, M.O., Marelich, W.D. & Kurland, G.J. (1997). Impact of attachment style on reactions to accomodative dilemmas in close relationships. *Personal Relationships, 4,* 93–113.

Gallo, L.C., Smith, T.W. & Ruiz, J.M. (2003). An interpersonal analysis of adult attachment style: Circumplex descriptions, recalled developmental experiences, self-representations, and interpersonal functioning in adulthood. *Journal of Personality, 71,* 141–182.

Ganong, L.H. & Coleman, M. (1994). *Remarried family relationships.* Thousand Oaks, CA: Sage.

Gardner, M.P. (1985). Does attitude toward the ad affect brand attitude under a brand evaluation set? *Journal of Marketing Research, 22,* 192–198.

Gardner, W.L., Gabriel, S. & Lee, A.Y. (1999). 'I' value freedom but 'we' value relationships: Self-construal priming mirrors cultural differences in judgment. *Psychological Science, 10,* 321–326.

Gawronski, B. (2005). Theory-based bias correction in dispositional inference: The fundamental attribution error is dead, long live the correspondence bias. In W. Stroebe & M. Hewstone (Eds.), *European review of social psychology* (vol. 11, pp. 183–217). Hove: Psychology Press.

Geen, R.G. (2001). *Human aggression* (2nd edn). Buckingham: Open University Press.

Gentile, D.A., Lynch, P.J., Linder, J.L. & Walsh, D.A. (2004). The effects of violent video game habits on adolescent hostility, aggressive behaviors, and school performance. *Journal of Adolescence, 27,* 5–22.

George, J.M. (1990). Personality, affect, and behavior in groups. *Journal of Applied Psychology, 75,* 107–116.

Gerard, H.B. (1963). Emotional uncertainty and social comparison. *Journal of Abnormal and Social Psychology, 66,* 568–573.

Gerard, H.B., Wilhelmy, R.A. & Connolley, E.S. (1968). Conformity and group size. *Journal of Personality and Social Psychology, 8,* 79–82.

Gergen, K.J. (1973). Social psychology as history. *Journal of Personality and Social Psychology, 26,* 309–320.

Gergen, K.J. (1978). Experimentation in social psychology: A reappraisal. *European Journal of Social Psychology, 8,* 507–527.

Gergen, K.J. (1999). *An invitation to social construction.* London: Sage.

Giancola, P.R. (2003). The moderating effects of dispositional empathy on alcohol-related aggression in men and women. *Journal of Abnormal Psychology, 112,* 275–281.

Gibbons, F.X. & Buunk, B.P. (1999). Individual differences in social comparison: Development of a scale of social comparison orientation. *Journal of Personality and Social Psychology, 76,* 129–142.

Gibson, J.J. (1979). *The ecological approach to visual perception.* Boston: Houghton Mifflin.

Giddens, A. (1982). *Profiles and critiques in social theory.* London: Macmillan.

Gigone, D. & Hastie, R. (1993). The common knowledge effect: Information sharing and group judgment. *Journal of Personality and Social Psychology, 65,* 959–974.

Gilbert, D.T. & Hixon, J.G. (1991). The trouble of thinking: Activation and application of stereotypic beliefs. *Journal of Personality and Social Psychology, 60,* 509–517.

Gilbert, D.T. & Malone, P.S. (1995). The correspondence bias. *Psychological Bulletin, 117,* 21–38.

Gilbert, D.T., Pelham, B.W. & Krull, D.S. (1988). On cognitive busyness: When person perceivers meet persons perceived. *Journal of Personality and Social Psychology, 54,* 733–740.

Glaser, B.G. & Strauss, A.L. (1967). *The discovery of grounded theory: Strategies for qualitative research.* Chicago, IL: Aldine.

Glazer, M.P. & Glazer, P.M. (1989). *The whistle-blowers: Exposing corruption in government and industry.* New York: Basic Books.

Gleason, M.E.J., Iida, M., Bolger, N. & Shrout, P.E. (2003). Daily supportive equity in close relationships. *Personality and Social Psychology Bulletin, 29,* 1036–1045.

Gleicher, F. & Petty, R.E. (1992). Expectations of reassurance influence the nature of fear-stimulated attitude change. *Journal of Experimental Social Psychology, 28,* 86–100.

Goethals, G.R. & Zanna, M.P. (1979). The role of social comparison in choice shifts. *Journal of Personality and Social Psychology, 37,* 1469–1476.

Goffman, E. (1963). *Behavior in public places.* New York: Free Press.

Goldhagen, D.J. (1996). *Hitler's willing executioners: Ordinary Germans and the Holocaust.* New York: Alfred A. Knopf.

Goldie, J., Schwartz, L., McConnachie, A. & Morrison, J. (2003). Students' attitudes and potential behaviour with regard to whistle blowing as they pass through a modern medical curriculum. *Medical Education, 37,* 368–375.

Gollwitzer, P.M. (1999). Implementation intentions: Strong effects of simple plans. *American Psychologist, 54,* 493–503.

Gollwitzer, P.M. & Brandstätter, V. (1997). Implementation intentions and effective goal pursuit. *Journal of Personality and Social Psychology, 73,* 186–199.

Gonzales, M.H. & Meyers, S.A. (1993). 'Your mother would like me': Self-presentation in the personal ads of heterosexual and homosexual men and women. *Personality and Social Psychology Bulletin, 19,* 131–142.

González, R. & Brown, R. (2006). Dual identities in intergroup contact: Group status and size moderate the generalization of positive attitude change. *Journal of Experimental and Social Psychology.*

Gordijn, E., Postmes, T. & de Vries, N.K. (2001). Devil's advocate or advocate of oneself: Effects of numerical support on pro- and counterattitudinal self-persuasion. *Personality and Social Psychology Bulletin, 27,* 395–407.

Gouldner, A.W. (1960). The norm of reciprocity: A preliminary statement. *American Sociological Review, 25,* 161–178.

Greenberg, J. (1990). Employee theft as a reaction to underpayment inequity: The hidden cost of pay cuts. *Journal of Applied Psychology, 75,* 561–568.

Greenberg, J. (1994). Using socially fair treatment to promote acceptance of a work site smoking ban. *Journal of Applied Psychology, 79,* 288–297.

Greenberg, J., Solomon, S. & Pyszczynski, T. (1997). Terror management theory of self-esteem and cultural worldviews: Empirical assessments and conceptual refinements. In M. Zanna (Ed.), *Advances in experimental social psychology* (Vol. 29, pp. 61–139). New York: Academic Press.

Greenberg, K.J. & Dratel, J.L. (2005). *The torture papers: The road to Abu Ghraib.* Cambridge: Cambridge University Press.

Greene, C.N. (1975). The reciprocal nature of influence between leader and subordinate. *Journal of Applied Psychology, 60,* 187–193.

Greenland, K. & Brown, R. (1999). Categorization and intergroup anxiety in contact between British and Japanese nationals. *European Journal of Social Psychology, 29,* 503–522.

Greenwald, A.G. (1968). Cognitive learning, cognitive response to persuasion, and attitude change. In A.G. Greenwald, T.C. Brock & T.M. Ostrom (Eds.), *Psychological foundations of attitudes* (pp. 147–170). New York: Academic Press.

Greenwald, A.G. (1975). On the inconclusiveness of 'crucial' tests of dissonance versus self-perception theories. *Journal of Experimental Social Psychology, 11,* 490–499.

Greenwald, A.G. & Banaji, M.R. (1995). Implicit social cognition: Attitudes, self-esteem, and stereotypes. *Psychological Review, 102,* 4–27.

Greenwald, A.G. & Pratkanis, A.R. (1984). The self. In R.S. Wyer & T.K. Srull (Eds.), *Handbook of social cognition* (pp. 129–178). Hillsdale, NJ: Lawrence Erlbaum.

Greenwald, A.G., McGhee, D. & Schwartz, J. (1998). Measuring individual differences in implicit cognition: The Implicit Association Test. *Journal of Personality and Social Psychology, 74,* 1464–1480.

Greenwald, A.G., Nosek, B.A. & Banaji, M.R. (2003). Understanding and using the Implicit Association Test: I. An improved scoring algorithm. *Journal of Personality and Social Psychology, 85,* 197–216.

Greenwald, A.G., McGhee, D. & Schwartz, J.L.K. (1998). Measuring individual differences in implicit cognition: The Implicit Association Test. *Journal of Personality and Social Psychology, 74,* 1464–1480.

Greenwald, A.G., Spangenberg, E.R., Pratkanis, A.R. & Eskenazi, J. (1991). Double-blind tests of subliminal self-help audiotapes. *Psychological Science, 28,* 191–194.

Greitemeyer, T. & Schulz-Hardt, S. (2003). Preference-consistent evaluation of information in the hidden profile paradigm: Beyond group-level explanations for the dominance of shared information in group decisions. *Journal of Personality and Social Psychology, 84,* 322–339.

Grice, H.P. (1975). Logic and conversation. In P. Cole & J. Morgan (Eds.), *Syntax and semantics 3: Speech acts* (pp. 41–58). San Diego, CA: Academic Press.

Grieve, P.G. & Hogg, M.A. (1999). Subjective uncertainty and intergroup discrimination in the minimal group paradigm. *Personality and Social Psychology Bulletin, 25,* 926–940.

Griffeth, R.W., Hom, P.W. & Gaertner, S. (2000). A meta-analysis of antecedents and correlates of employee turnover: Update, moderator tests, and research implications for the next millennium. *Journal of Management, 26,* 463–488.

Griffin, R.S. & Gross, A.M. (2004). Childhood bullying: Current empirical findings and future directions for research. *Aggression and Violent Behavior, 9,* 379–400.

Griffit, W. & Veitch, R. (1974). Preacquaintance attitude similarity and attraction revisited: Ten days in a fall-out shelter. *Sociometry, 37,* 163–173.

Grossman, R.P. & Till, B.D. (1998). The persistence of classically conditioned brand attitudes. *Journal of Advertising, 27,* 23–31.

Grove, T. (1998). *The juryman's tale.* London: Bloomsbury.

Guerin, B. (1993). *Social facilitation.* Cambridge: Cambridge University Press.

Guinote, A. (2004). Group size, outcome dependency, and power: Effects on perceived and actual group variability. In V. Yzerbyt, C.M. Judd & O. Corneille (Eds.), *The psychology of group perception: Perceived variability, entitativity, and essentialism* (pp. 221–236). New York and Hove: Psychology Press.

Guinote, A., Judd, C.M. & Brauer, M. (2002). Effects of power on perceived and objective group variability: Evidence that more powerful groups are more variable. *Journal of Personality and Social Psychology, 82,* 708–721.

Gump, B.B. & Kulik, J.A. (1997). Stress, affiliation, and emotional contagion. *Journal of Personality and Social Psychology, 72,* 305–319.

Haaland, G.A. & Venkatesan, M. (1968). Resistance to persuasive communication: An examination of the distraction hypotheses. *Journal of Personality and Social Psychology, 9,* 167–170.

Hackman, J.R. & Morris, C.G. (1975). Group tasks, group interaction process and group performance effectiveness: A review and proposed integration. In L. Berkowitz (Ed.), *Advances in experimental social psychology* (Vol. 8, pp. 47–99). New York: Academic Press.

Hackman, J.R. & Oldham, G.R. (1976). Motivation through the design of work: Test of a theory. *Organizational Behavior and Human Performance, 16*, 250–279.

Haddock, G. & Carrick, R. (1999). How to make a politician more likeable and effective: Framing political judgments through the numeric values of a rating scale. *Social Cognition, 17*, 298–311.

Haddock, G. & Maio, G.R. (Eds.) (2004). *Contemporary perspectives on the psychology of attitudes.* Hove: Psychology Press.

Haddock, G., Rothman, A.J., Reber, R. & Schwarz, N. (1999). Forming judgments of attitude certainty, intensity, and importance: The role of subjective experiences. *Personality and Social Psychology Bulletin, 25*, 770–781.

Haddock, G., Zanna, M.P. & Esses, V.M. (1993). Assessing the structure of prejudicial attitudes: The case of attitudes toward homosexuals. *Journal of Personality and Social Psychology, 65*, 1105–1118.

Hafer, C.L. (2000). Do innocent victims threaten the belief in a just world? Evidence from a modified Stroop test. *Journal of Personality and Social Psychology, 79*, 165–173.

Hafer, C.L. & Bègue, L. (2005). Experimental research on just-world theory: Problems, developments, and future challenges. *Psychological Bulletin, 131*, 128–167.

Haines, H. & Vaughan, G.M. (1979). Was 1898 a great date in the history of social psychology? *Journal for the History of the Behavioural Sciences, 15*, 323–332.

Haines, M.P. & Barker, G.P. (2003). The Northern Illinois University experiment: A longitudinal case study of the social norms approach. In H.W. Perkins (Ed.), *The social norms approach to preventing school and college age substance abuse: A handbook for educators, counselors, and clinicians* (pp. 21–34). San Francisco: Jossey-Bass.

Haines, M.P. & Spear, A.F. (1996). Changing the perception of the norm: A strategy to decrease binge drinking among college students. *Journal of American College Health, 45*, 134–140.

Hamilton, D.L., Sherman, S.J. & Ruvolo, C.M. (1990). Stereotype-based expectancies: Effects on information processing and social behavior. *Journal of Social Issues, 46*, 35–60.

Hamilton, V.L. (1980). Intuitive scientist or intuitive lawyer: Alternative models of the attribution process. *Journal of Personality and Social Psychology, 39*, 767–772.

Hamilton, W.D. (1964). The genetical evolution of social behaviour, part I and II. *Journal of Theoretical Biology, 7*, 1–52.

Haney, C., Banks, W.C. & Zimbardo, P.G. (1973). Interpersonal dynamics in a simulated prison. *International Journal of Criminology and Penology, 1*, 69–97.

Harari, H., Mohr, D. & Hosey, K. (1980). Faculty helpfulness to students: A comparison of compliance techniques. *Personality and Social Psychology Bulletin, 6*, 373–377.

Harmon-Jones, E., Greenberg, J., Solomon, S. & Simon, L. (1996). The effects of mortality salience on intergroup bias between minimal groups. *European Journal of Social Psychology, 25*, 677–681.

Hartup, W.W. & Stevens, N. (1997). Friendships and adaptation in the life course. *Psychological Bulletin, 121*, 355–370.

Harvey, O.J. (1989). Obituary of Muzafer Sherif (1906–1988). *American Psychologist, 44*, 1325–1326.

Harwood, J., Hewstone, M., Paolini, S. & Voci, A. (2005). Grandparent–grandchild contact and attitudes towards older adults: Moderator and mediator effects. *Personality and Social Psychology Bulletin, 31*, 393–406.

Haslam, S.A. (2001). *Psychology in organisations: The social identity approach.* London: Sage.

Hastie, R. (1993). *Inside the juror.* New York: Cambridge University Press.

Hastie, R. & Kumar, A.P. (1979). Person memory: Personality traits as organizing principles in memory for behaviours. *Journal of Personality and Social Psychology, 37*, 25–38.

Hastie, R., Penrod, S.D. & Pennington, N. (1983). *Inside the jury.* Cambridge, MA: Harvard University Press.

Hatala, M.N. & Prehodka, J. (1996). Content analysis of gay male and lesbian personal advertisements. *Psychological Reports, 78*, 371–374.

Hatfield, E. (1988). Passionate and companionate love. In R.J. Sternberg & M.L. Barnes (Eds.), *The psychology of love* (pp. 191–217). New Haven, CT: Yale University Press.

Hatfield, E. & Sprecher, S. (1986). *Mirror, mirror . . . : The importance of looks in everyday life.* New York: SUNY Press.

Haugtvedt, C.P. & Petty, R.E. (1992). Personality and persuasion: Need for cognition moderates the persistence and resistance of attitude change. *Journal of Personality and Social Psychology, 63*, 308–319.

Hays, R.B. (1988). Friendship. In S. Duck (Ed.), *Handbook of personal relationships.* Chichester: Wiley.

Hazan, C. & Shaver, P. (1987). Romantic love conceptualized as an attachment process. *Journal of Personality and Social Psychology, 52*, 511–524.

Hechter, M. & Opp, K.D. (Eds.) (2001). *Social norms.* New York: Russell Sage Foundation.

Hedges, L.V. & Olkin, I. (1985). *Statistical methods for meta-analysis.* New York: Academic Press.

Heider, F. (1944). Social perception and phenomenal causality. *Psychological Review, 51*, 358–374.

Heider, F. (1946). Attitudes and cognitive organization. *Journal of Psychology, 21*, 107–112.

Heider, F. (1958). *The psychology of interpersonal relations.* New York: Wiley.

Heider, F. & Simmel, M. (1944). An experimental study of apparent behavior. *American Journal of Psychology, 57*, 243–259.

Hemingway, H. & Marmot, M. (1999). Psychosocial factors in the aetiology and prognosis of coronary heart disease: Systematic review of prospective cohort studies. *British Medical Journal, 318*, 1460–1467.

Hemingway, H., Shipley, M.J., Stansfield, S. & Marmot, M. (1997). Sickness absence from back pain, psychosocial work characteristics and employment grade among office workers. *Scandinavian Journal of Work, Environment and Health, 23*, 121–129.

Henchy, T. & Glass, D.C. (1968). Evaluation apprehension and the social facilitation of dominant and subordinate responses. *Journal of Personality and Social Psychology, 10*, 446–454.

Hendrick, C., Hendrick, S.S. & Dicke, A. (1998). The love attitude scale: Short form. *Journal of Social and Personal Relationships, 15*, 147–159.

Henry, R.A., Strickland, O.J., Yorges, S.L. & Ladd, D. (1996). Helping groups determine their most accurate member: The role of outcome feedback. *Journal of Applied Social Psychology, 26*, 1153–1170.

Henwood, K.L. (1996). Qualitative inquiry: Perspectives, methods and psychology. In J.T.E. Richardson (Ed.), *Handbook of qualitative research methods for psychology and the social sciences* (pp. 25–40). Leicester: BPS Books.

Herek, G.M. (1986). The instrumentality of attitudes: Toward a neofunctional theory. *Journal of Social Issues, 42*, 99–114.

Herek, G.M., Janis, I. & Huth, P. (1987). Decision making during international crises: Is the quality of process related to outcomes? *Journal of Conflict Resolution, 31*, 203–226.

Hersh, S.M. (2004). *Chain of command.* London: Penguin.

Hertel, G., Kerr, N.L. & Messé, L.A. (2000). Motivation gains in performance groups: Paradigmatic and theoretical developments on the Köhler effect. *Journal of Personality and Social Psychology, 79*, 580–601.

Hewstone, M. (1989). *Causal attribution: From cognitive processes to collective beliefs.* Oxford: Blackwell.

Hewstone, M. (1994). Revision and change of stereotypic beliefs: In search of the elusive subtyping model. In W. Stroebe & M. Hewstone (Eds.), *European review of social psychology* (Vol. 5, pp. 69–110). Chichester: Wiley.

Hewstone, M. (2003). Intergroup contact: Panacea for prejudice? *The Psychologist, 16*, 352–355.

Hewstone, M. & Brown, R. (1986). Contact is not enough: An intergroup perspective on the contact hypothesis. In M. Hewstone & R. Brown

(Eds.), *Contact and conflict in intergroup encounters* (pp. 1–44). Oxford: Blackwell.

Hewstone, M., Fincham, F.D. & Jaspars, J. (1981). Social categorization and similarity in intergroup behaviour: A replication with 'penalties'. *European Journal of Social Psychology, 11,* 101–107.

Hewstone, M., Rubin, M. & Willis, H. (2002). Intergroup bias. *Annual Review of Psychology, 53,* 575–604.

Higgins, E.T. (1987). Self-discrepancy: A theory relating self and affect. *Psychological Review, 94,* 319–340.

Higgins, E.T. (1989). Continuities and discontinuities in self-regulatory and self-evaluative processes: A developmental theory relating self and affect. *Journal of Personality, 57,* 407–444.

Higgins, E.T. (1996). Knowledge activation: Accessibility, applicability, and salience. In E.T. Higgins & A.W. Kruglanski (Eds.), *Social psychology: Handbook of basic principles* (pp. 133–168). New York: Guilford Press.

Higgins, E.T. (1997). Beyond pleasure and pain. *American Psychologist, 52,* 1280–1300.

Higgins, E.T. (1999). Promotion and prevention as a motivational duality: Implications for evaluative processes. In S. Chaiken & Y. Trope (Eds.), *Dual-process theories in social psychology* (pp. 503–525). New York: Guilford Press.

Higgins, E.T., Bargh, J.A. & Lombardi, W. (1985). Nature of priming effects on categorization. *Journal of Experimental Psychology: Learning, Memory and Cognition, 11,* 59–69.

Hilton, D.J. (1988). Logic and causal attribution. In D.J. Hilton (Ed.), *Contemporary science and natural explanation: Commonsense conceptions of causality* (pp. 33–65). Brighton: Harvester.

Hilton, D.J. (1990). Conversational processes and causal explanation. *Psychological Bulletin, 107,* 65–81.

Hilton, D.J. & Slugoski, B.R. (1986). Knowledge-based causal attribution: The abnormal conditions focus model. *Psychological Review, 93,* 75–88.

Hoeksema-van Orden, C.Y.D., Gaillard, A.W.K. & Buunk, B.P. (1998). Social loafing under fatigue. *Journal of Personality and Social Psychology, 75,* 1179–1190.

Hoel, H., Rayner, C. & Cooper, C.L. (1999). Workplace bullying. In C.L. Cooper & I.T. Robertson (Eds.), *International review of industrial and organizational psychology* (Vol. 14, pp. 195–230). New York: Wiley.

Hoffman, M.L. (2000). *Empathy and moral development: Implications for caring and justice.* Cambridge: Cambridge University Press.

Hofling, C.K., Brotzman, E., Dairymple, S., Graves, N. & Pierce, C.M. (1966). An experimental study in nurse–physician relationships. *Journal of Nervous and Mental Disease, 143,* 171–180.

Hogg, M.A. (2000). Subjective uncertainty reduction through self-categorization: A motivational theory of social identity processes. In W. Stroebe & M. Hewstone (Eds.), *European review of social psychology* (Vol. 11, pp. 223–255). London: Wiley.

Hogg, M.A. & Abrams, D. (1988). Comments on the motivational status of self-esteem in social identity and intergroup discrimination. *European Journal of Social Psychology, 18,* 317–334.

Hogg, M.A. & Abrams, D. (1993). Towards a single process uncertainty reduction model of social motivation in groups. In M.A. Hogg & D. Abrams (Eds.), *Group motivation: Social psychological perspectives* (pp. 173–190). New York: Harvester-Wheatsheaf.

Hogg, M.A. & Turner, J.C. (1987). Intergroup behaviour, self stereotyping and the salience of social categories. *British Journal of Social Psychology, 26,* 325–340.

Hogg, M.A., Turner, J.C. & Davidson, B. (1990). Polarized norms and social frames of reference: A test of the self-categorization theory of group polarization. *Basic and Applied Social Psychology, 11,* 77–100.

Holland, R.W., Meertens, R.M. & van Vugt, M. (2002). Dissonance on the road: Self-esteem as a moderator of internal and external self-justification strategies. *Personality and Social Psychology Bulletin, 28,* 1713–1724.

Holland, R.W., Verplanken, B. & van Knippenberg, A. (2002). On the nature of attitude–behavior relations: The strong guide, the weak follow. *European Journal of Social Psychology, 32,* 869–876.

Hollander, E.P. (1958). Conformity, status, and idiosyncracy credit. *Psychological Review, 65,* 117–127.

Holmes, J.G., Miller, D.T. & Lerner, M.J. (2002). Committing altruism under the cloak of self-interest: The exchange fiction. *Journal of Experimental and Social Psychology, 38,* 144–151.

Holmes, T.H. & Rahe, R.H. (1967). The social readjustment rating-scale. *Journal of Psychosomatic Research, 11,* 213–218.

Homans, G.C. (1950). *The human group.* New York: Harcourt.

Homans, G.C. (1961). *Social behavior: Its elementary forms.* New York: Harcourt, Brace & World.

Homans, G.C. (1964). *Social behaviour: Its elementary forms.* New York: Harcourt.

Hood, W.R. & Sherif, M. (1962). Verbal report and judgment of an unstructured stimulus. *Journal of Psychology, 54,* 121–130.

Hornsey, M.J. (2005). Why being right is not enough: Predicting defensiveness in the face of group criticism. In W. Stroebe & M. Hewstone (Eds.), *European review of social psychology* (Vol. 16, pp. 301–334). Hove: Psychology Press.

House, J.S. (1981). *Work stress and social support.* Reading, MA: Addison-Wesley.

House, R.J. (1971). A path-goal theory of leader effectiveness. *Administrative Science Quarterly, 16,* 321–328.

House, R.J. (1996). Path-goal theory of leadership: Lessons, legacy, and a reformulated theory. *Leadership Quarterly, 7,* 323–352.

House, R.J. & Mitchell, T.R. (1974). Path-goal theory of leadership. *Contemporary Business, 3,* 81–98.

House, R.J., Hanges, P.J., Javidan, M., Dorfman, P. & Gupta, V. with GLOBE Associates (Eds.) (2004). *Leadership, culture, and organizations: The GLOBE study of 62 societies.* Thousand Oaks, CA: Sage.

Houston, D.A. & Fazio, R.H. (1989). Biased processing as a function of attitude accessibility: Making objective judgments subjectively. *Social Cognition, 7,* 51–66.

Hovland, C.I. (1951). Changes in attitude through communication. *Journal of Abnormal and Social Psychology, 46,* 424–437.

Hovland, C.I. (Ed.) (1957). *The order of presentation in persuasion.* New Haven, CT: Yale University Press.

Hovland, C.I. & Janis, I.L. (Eds.) (1959). *Personality and persuasibility.* New Haven, CT: Yale University Press.

Hovland, C.I. & Weiss, W. (1951). The influence of source credibility on communication effectiveness. *Public Opinion Quarterly, 15,* 635–650.

Hovland, C.I., Janis, I.L. & Kelley, H.H. (1953). *Communication and persuasion: Psychological studies of opinion change.* New Haven, CT: Yale University Press.

Hovland, C.I., Lumsdaine, A.A. & Sheffield, F.D. (1949). *Experiments in mass communication.* Princeton, NJ: Princeton University Press.

Hoyle, R.H., Kernis, M.H., Leary, M.R. & Baldwin, M.W. (1999). *Selfhood: Identity, esteem, regulation.* Boulder, CO: Westview Press.

Huesmann, L.R. (1998). The role of information processing and cognitive schema in the acquisition and maintenance of habitual aggressive behavior. In R.G. Geen & E. Donnerstein (Eds.), *Human aggression: Theories, research and implications for social policy* (pp. 73–109). San Diego, CA: Academic Press.

Huesmann, L.R. & Eron, L.D. (Eds.) (1986). *Television and the aggressive child: A cross-national comparison.* Hillsdale, NJ: Lawrence Erlbaum.

Huesmann, L.R. & Guerra, N.G. (1997). Children's normative beliefs about aggression and aggressive behavior. *Journal of Personality and Social Psychology, 72,* 408–419.

Huesmann, L.R. & Miller, L.S. (1994). Long-term effects of the repeated exposure to media violence in childhood. In L.R. Huesmann (Ed.), *Aggressive behavior: Current perspectives* (pp. 153–186). New York: Plenum Press.

Huesmann, L.R., Moise-Titus, J., Podolski, C.L. & Eron, L.D. (2003). Longitudinal relations between children's exposure to TV violence and their aggressive and violent behavior in young adulthood. *Developmental Psychology, 39,* 201–229.

Hulin, C.L. & Judge, T.A. (2003). Job attitudes. In W.C. Borman, D.R. Ilgen & R.J. Klimoski (Eds.), *Handbook of psychology* (pp. 255–276). Hoboken, NJ: Wiley.

Huskinson, T.L. & Haddock, G. (2004). Individual differences in attitude structure: Variance in the chronic reliance on affective and cognitive information. *Journal of Experimental Social Psychology*, *40*, 83–90.

Iaffaldano, M.T. & Muchinsky, P.M. (1985). Job satisfaction and job performance: A meta-analysis. *Psychological Bulletin*, *97*, 251–273.

Ilgen, D.R. & Pulakos, E.D. (1999). Introduction: Employee performance in today's organizations. In D.R. Ilgen & E.D. Pulakos (Eds.), *The changing nature of performance* (pp. 1–20). San Francisco: Jossey-Bass.

Ingham, A.G., Levinger, G., Graves, J. & Peckham, V. (1974). The Ringelmann effect: Studies of group size and group performance. *Journal of Experimental Social Psychology*, *10*, 371–384.

Isen, A.M., Clark, M. & Schwartz, M.F. (1976). Duration of the effect of good mood on helping: 'Footprints on the sands of time'. *Journal of Personality and Social Psychology*, *34*, 385–393.

Isenberg, D.J. (1986). Group polarization: A critical review and meta-analysis. *Journal of Personality and Social Psychology*, *50*, 1141–1151.

Islam, M.R. & Hewstone, M. (1993). Intergroup attributions and affective consequences in majority and minority groups. *Journal of Personality and Social Psychology*, *64*, 936–950.

Ito, T.A., Miller, N. & Pollock, V.E. (1996). Alcohol and aggression: A meta-analysis of the moderating effects of inhibitory cues, triggering cues, and self-focused attention. *Psychological Bulletin*, *120*, 60–82.

Jacobs, K.C. & Campbell, D.T. (1961). The perpetuation of an arbitrary tradition through several generations of a laboratory microculture. *Journal of Abnormal and Social Psychology*, *62*, 649–658.

James, K. & Greenberg, J. (1989). In-group salience, intergroup comparison, and individual performance and self-esteem. *Personality and Social Psychology Bulletin*, *15*, 604–616.

James, W. (1884). What is an emotion? *Mind*, *9*, 188–205.

James, W. (1950). *The principles of psychology* (Vol. 1). Cambridge, MA: Harvard University Press. (Original work published 1890.)

Janis, I.L. (1982). *Victims of groupthink* (2nd edn). Boston: Houghton Mifflin.

Janis, I.L. & Mann, L. (1977). *Decision making: A psychological analysis of conflict, choice and commitment*. New York: Free Press.

Jaramillo, F., Mulki, J.P. & Marshall, G.W. (2005). A meta-analysis of the relationship between organizational commitment and salesperson job performance: 25 years of research. *Journal of Business Research*, *58*, 705–714.

Johnson, B.T. & Eagly, A.H. (2000). Quantitative synthesis of social psychological research. In H.T. Reis & C.M. Judd (Eds.), *Handbook of research methods in social and personality psychology* (pp. 496–528). New York: Cambridge University Press.

Johnson, D.J. & Rusbult, C.E. (1989). Resisting temptation: Devaluation of alternative partners as a means of maintaining commitment. *Journal of Personality and Social Psychology*, *57*, 967–980.

Johnson, E. & Reuband, K.-H. (2005). *What we knew: Terror, mass murder and everyday life in Nazi Germany*. London: John Murray.

Johnson, J.T., Jemmott, J.B. & Pettigrew, T.F. (1984). Causal attribution and dispositional inference: Evidence of inconsistent judgments. *Journal of Experimental Social Psychology*, *20*, 567–585.

Johnson, J., Trawalter, S. & Dovidio, J. (2000). Converging interracial consequences to exposure to violent rap music. *Journal of Experimental Social Psychology*, *36*, 233–251.

Johnson, M.H. & Morton, J. (1991). *Biology and cognitive development: The case of face recognition*. Oxford: Blackwell.

Johnson, R.C. et al. (1989). Cross-cultural assessment of altruism and its correlates. *Personality and Individual Differences*, *10*, 855–868.

Johnson, T.J., Feigenbaum, R. & Weiby, M. (1964). Some determinants and consequences of teachers' perceptions of causation. *Journal of Educational Psychology*, *55*, 237–246.

Johnston, J.J., Hendricks, S.A. & Fike, J.M. (1994). The effectiveness of behavioural safety belt interventions. *Accident Analysis and Prevention*, *26*, 315–323.

Johnston, L. & Hewstone, M. (1992). Cognitive models of stereotype change: (3) Subtyping and the perceived typicality of disconfirming group members. *Journal of Experimental Social Psychology*, *28*, 360–386.

Joinson, A. (2003). *Understanding the psychology of Internet behaviour*. Basingstoke: Palgrave.

Jones, E.E. (1998). Major developments in five decades of social psychology. In D.T. Gilbert, S.T. Fiske & G. Lindzey (Eds.), *Handbook of social psychology* (4th ed., Vol. 1, pp. 3–57). Boston: McGraw-Hill.

Jones, E.E. & Davis, K.E. (1965). From acts to dispositions: The attribution process in person perception. In L. Berkowitz (Ed.), *Advances in experimental social psychology* (Vol. 2, pp. 219–266). New York: Academic Press.

Jones, E.E. & Harris, V.A. (1967). The attribution of attitudes. *Journal of Experimental Social Psychology*, *3*, 1–24.

Jones, E.E. & Nisbett, R.E. (1972). The actor and the observer: Divergent perceptions of the causes of behavior. In E.E. Jones et al. (Eds.), *Attribution: Perceiving the causes of behavior*. Morristown, NJ: General Learning Press.

Jones, W. & Hebb, L. (2003). Rise in loneliness: Objective and subjective factors. *International Scope Review*, *9*, 41–68.

Joule, R.V. (1987). Tobacco deprivation: The foot-in-the-door technique versus the low-ball technique. *European Journal of Social Psychology*, *17*, 361–365.

Judd, C.M. & Kenny, D.A. (1981a). *Estimating the effects of social interventions*. New York: Cambridge University Press.

Judd, C.M. & Kenny, D.A. (1981b). Process analysis: Estimating mediation in treatment evaluations. *Evaluation Review*, *5*, 602–619.

Judd, C.M. & Park, B. (1988). Out-group homogeneity: Judgments of variability at the individual and group levels. *Journal of Personality and Social Psychology*, *54*, 778–788.

Judge, T.A. & Piccolo, R.F. (2004). Transformational and transactional leadership: A meta-analytic test of their relative validity. *Journal of Applied Psychology*, *89*, 755–768.

Judge, T.A., Bono, J.I., Ilies, R. & Gerhard, M.W. (2002). Personality and leadership: A qualitative and quantitative review. *Journal of Applied Psychology*, *87*, 765–780.

Judge, T.A., Bono, J.E. & Locke, E.A. (2000). Personality and job satisfaction: The mediating role of job characteristics. *Journal of Applied Psychology*, *85*, 237–249.

Judge, T.A., Colbert, A.I. & Ilies, R. (2004). Intelligence and leadership: A quantitative review and test of theoretical propositions. *Journal of Applied Psychology*, *89*, 542–552.

Judge, T.A., Piccolo, R.F. & Ilies, R. (2004). The forgotten ones? The validity of consideration and initiating structure in leadership research. *Journal of Applied Psychology*, *89*, 36–51.

Judge, T.A., Thoresen, C.J., Bono, J.E. & Patton, G.K. (2001). The job satisfaction–job performance relationship: A qualitative and quantitative review. *Psychological Bulletin*, *127*, 376–407.

Kalven, H. & Zeisel, H. (1966). *The American jury*. Boston: Little, Brown.

Kanner, A.D., Coyne, J.C., Schaefer, C. & Lazarus, R.S. (1981). Comparison of two modes of stress measurement: Daily hassles and uplifts versus major life events. *Journal of Behavioral Medicine*, *4*, 1–39.

Kant, I. (1997). *Critique of pure reason*. Cambridge: Cambridge University Press. (Original work published 1781.)

Kaplan, K.J. (1972). On the ambivalence–indifference problem in attitude theory and measurement: A suggested modification of the semantic differential technique. *Psychological Bulletin*, *77*, 361–372.

Kaplan, M.F. (1987). The influencing process in group decision making. In C. Hendrick (Ed.), *Review of personality and social psychology* (Vol. 8, pp. 189–212). Newbury Park, CA: Sage.

Kaplan, M.F. & Miller, C.E. (1977). Judgments and group discussion: Effect of presentation and memory factors on polarization. *Sociometry*, *40*, 337–343.

Kaplan, M.F. & Miller, C.E. (1987). Group decision making and normative versus informational influence: Effects of type of issue and assigned decision rule. *Journal of Personality and Social Psychology*, *53*, 306–313.

Karasek, R.A. & Theorell, T. (1990). *Healthy work: Stress, productivity, and the reconstruction of working life*. New York: Basic Books.

Karlin, W.A., Brondolo, E. & Schwartz, J. (2003). Workplace social support and ambulatory cardiovascular activity in New York City traffic agents. *Psychosomatic Medicine, 65*, 167–176.

Karpinski, A. & Hilton, J.L. (2001). Attitudes and the Implicit Association Test. *Journal of Personality and Social Psychology, 81*, 774–788.

Karremans, J.C., Stroebe, W. & Claus, J. (2006). Beyond Vicary's fantasies: The impact of subliminal priming on brand choice. *Journal of Experimental Social Psychology, 42*, 292–306.

Kashima, Y., Kashima, E. & Aldridge, J. (2001). Toward cultural dynamics of self-conceptions. In C. Sedikides & M.B. Brewer (Eds.), *Individual self, relational self, collective self* (pp. 277–298). Philadelphia: Psychology Press.

Kassin, S.M. (1979). Consensus information, prediction, and causal attribution: A review of the literature and issues. *Journal of Personality and Social Psychology, 37*, 1966–1981.

Katz, D. (1960). The functional approach to the study of attitudes. *Public Opinion Quarterly, 24*, 163–204.

Katz, I. & Hass, R.G. (1988). Racial ambivalence and American value conflict: Correlational and priming studies of dual cognitive structures. *Journal of Personality and Social Psychology, 55*, 893–905.

Katz, D. & Stotland, E. (1959). A preliminary statement to a theory of attitude structure and change. In S. Koch (Ed.), *Psychology: A study of science* (Vol. 3, pp. 433–475). New York: McGraw-Hill.

Katzenstein, G. (1996). The debate on structured debate: Toward a unified theory. *Organizational Behavior and Human Decision Processes, 66*, 316–332.

Kawakami, K., Dion, K.L. & Dovidio, J.F. (1998). Racial prejudice and stereotype activation. *Personality and Social Psychology Bulletin, 24*, 407–416.

Keating, C.F. (1985). Gender and the physiognomy of dominance and attractiveness. *Social Psychology Quarterly, 48*, 61–70.

Kelley, H.H. (1950). The warm–cold variable in first impressions of persons. *Journal of Personality, 18*, 431–439.

Kelley, H.H. (1967). Attribution theory in social psychology. In D. Levine (Ed.), *Nebraska symposium on motivation* (Vol. 15, pp. 192–240). Lincoln: University of Nebraska Press.

Kelley, H.H. (1972). Causal schemata and the attribution process. In E.E. Jones et al. (Eds.), *Attribution: Perceiving the causes of behavior* (pp. 151–174). Morristown, NJ: General Learning Press.

Kelloway, E.K., Sivanathan, N., Francis, L. & Barling, J. (2005). Poor leadership. In J. Barling, E.K. Kelloway & M. Frone (Eds.), *Handbook of work stress* (pp. 89–112). Thousand Oaks, CA: Sage.

Kelly, C. (1989). Political identity and perceived intragroup homogeneity. *British Journal of Social Psychology, 28*, 239–250.

Kelman, H.C. & Hamilton, V.L. (1989). *Crimes of obedience: Toward a social psychology of authority and responsibility*. New Haven, CT: Yale University Press.

Keltner, D., Gruenfeld, D.H. & Anderson, C. (2003). Power, approach, and inhibition. *Psychological Review, 110*, 265–284.

Kenny, D.A., Kashy, D.A. & Bolger, N. (1998). Data analysis in social psychology. In D.T. Gilbert, S.T. Fiske & G. Lindzey (Eds.), *Handbook of social psychology* (Vol. 1, pp. 233–265). New York: McGraw-Hill.

Kenrick, D.T. & Trost, M.R. (1989). A reproductive exchange model of heterosexual relationships: Putting proximate economics in ultimate perspective. In C. Hendrick (Ed.), *Close relationships*. Newbury Park, CA: Sage.

Kerr, N.L. (1983). Motivation losses in small groups: A social dilemma analysis. *Journal of Personality and Social Psychology, 45*, 819–828.

Kerr, N.L. (1995). Juries. In A.S.R. Manstead & M. Hewstone (Eds.), *Blackwell encyclopedia of social psychology* (pp. 343–345). Oxford: Blackwell.

Kerr, N.L. & Bruun, S. (1983). The dispensability of member effort and group motivation losses: Free rider effects. *Journal of Personality and Social Psychology, 44*, 78–94.

Kerr, N.L. & MacCoun, R.J. (1985). The effects of jury size and polling method on the process and product of jury deliberation. *Journal of Personality and Social Psychology, 48*, 349–363.

Kessler, T. & Mummendey, A. (2001). Is there any scapegoat around? Determinants of intergroup conflict at different categorization levels. *Journal of Personality and Social Psychology, 81*, 1090–1102.

Kiesler, C.A. & Kiesler, S.B. (1969). *Conformity*. Reading, MA: Addison-Wesley.

Kim, J., Lim, J. & Bargava, M. (1998). The role of affect in attitude formation: A classical conditioning approach. *Journal of the Academy of Marketing Science, 26*, 143–152.

Kim, W.C. & Mauborgne, R.A. (1993). Procedural justice, attitudes, and subsidiary top management compliance with multinationals' corporate strategic decisions. *Academy of Management Journal, 36*, 502–526.

Kirsh, S.J. (1998). Seeing the world through Mortal Kombat-colored glasses: Violent video games and the development of a short-term hostile attribution bias. *Childhood, 5*, 177–184.

Kitson, G.C. (1982). Attachment to the spouse in divorce: A scale and its applications. *Journal of Marriage and the Family, 44*, 379–393.

Klandermans, B. (1997). *The social psychology of protest*. Oxford: Blackwell.

Klauer, K.C. & Wegener, I. (1998). Unraveling social categorization in the 'Who said what?' paradigm. *Journal of Personality and Social Psychology, 75*, 1155–1178.

Klein, S.B. (2001). A self to remember: A cognitive neuropsychological perspective on how self creates memory and memory creates self. In C. Sedikides & M.B. Brewer (Eds.), *Individual self, relational self, collective self* (pp. 25–46). Philadelphia: Psychology Press.

Klohnen, E.C. & Luo, S. (2003). Interpersonal attraction and personality: What is attractive: self similarity, ideal similarity, complementarity, or attachment security? *Journal of Personality and Social Psychology, 85*, 706–722.

Kochanska, G. & Thompson, R.A. (1997). The emergence and development of conscience in toddlerhood and early childhood. In J.E. Grusec & L. Kuczynski (Eds.), *Parenting and children's internalization of values* (pp. 53–77). New York: Wiley.

Kohlberg, L. (1976). Moral stages and moralization: The cognitive-developmental approach. In T. Lickona (Ed.), *Moral development and behavoir* (pp. 31–53). New York: Holt, Rinehart & Winston.

Köhler, O. (1926). Kraftleistungen bei Einzel- und Gruppenarbeit [Physical performance in individual and group situations]. *Industrielle Psychotechnik, 3*, 274–282.

Koss, M.P. & Oros, C.J. (1982). Sexual experiences survey: A research instrument investigating sexual aggression and victimization. *Journal of Consulting and Clinical Psychology, 50*, 455–457.

Krahé, B. (1991). Social psychological issues in the study of rape. In W. Stroebe & M. Hewstone (Eds.), *European review of social psychology* (Vol. 2, pp. 279–309). Chichester: Wiley.

Krahé, B. (1992). *Personality and social psychology: Towards a synthesis*. London: Sage.

Krahé, B. (2001). *The social psychology of aggression*. Hove: Psychology Press.

Krahé, B. & Möller, I. (2004). Playing violent electronic games, hostile attribution bias, and aggression-related norms in German adolescents. *Journal of Adolescence, 27*, 53–69.

Krahé, B., Bieneck, S. & Möller, I. (2005). Gender and intimate partner violence from an international perspective. *Sex Roles, 52*, 807–827.

Krahé, B., Schütze, S., Fritsche, I. & Waizenhöfer, E. (2000). The prevalence of sexual aggression and victimization among homosexual men. *Journal of Sex Research, 37*, 142–150.

Krahé, B., Waizenhöfer, E. & Möller, I. (2003). Women's sexual aggression against men: Prevalence and predictors. *Sex Roles, 49*, 219–232.

Kramer, R.M. (1999). Trust and distrust in organizations: Emerging perspectives, enduring questions. *Annual Review of Psychology, 50*, 569–598.

Kramer, R.M., Hanna, B.A., Su, S. & Wei, J. (2001). Collective identity, collective trust, and social capital: Linking group identification and group cooperation. In M.E. Turner (Ed.), *Groups at work: Theory and research*. Mahwah, NJ: Lawrence Erlbaum.

Krantz, J.H. & Dalal, R. (2000). Validity of web-based psychological research. In M.H. Birnbaum (Ed.), *Psychological experiments on the Internet* (pp. 35–60). San Diego, CA: Academic Press.

Kraus, S.J. (1995). Attitudes and the prediction of behavior: A meta-analysis of the empirical literature. *Personality and Social Psychology Bulletin, 21,* 58–75.

Kravitz, D.A. & Martin, B. (1986). Ringelmann rediscovered: The original article. *Journal of Personality and Social Psychology, 50,* 936–941.

Krosnick, J.A. & Petty, R.E. (1995). Attitude strength: An overview. In R.E. Petty & J.A. Krosnick (Eds.), *Attitude strength: Antecedents and consequences* (pp. 1–24). Hillsdale, NJ: Lawrence Erlbaum.

Krosnick, J.A., Betz, A.L., Jussim, L.J. & Lynn, A.R. (1992). Subliminal conditioning of attitudes. *Personality and Social Psychology Bulletin, 18,* 152–162.

Krosnick, J.A., Boninger, D.S., Chuang, Y.C., Berent, M.K. & Carnot, C. (1993). Attitude strength: One construct or many related constructs? *Journal of Personality and Social Psychology, 65,* 1132–1151.

Krueger, J. & Clement, R.W. (1994). Memory-based judgments about multiple categories: A revision and extension of Tajfel's accentuation theory. *Journal of Personality and Social Psychology, 67,* 35–47.

Krug, E.G., Dahlberg, L.L., Mercy, J.A., Zwi, A.B. & Lozano, R. (2002). *World report on violence and health.* Geneva: World Health Organization. Available online at: whqlibdoc.who.int/hq/2002/9241545615.pdf; retrieved 4 May 2005.

Kruglanski, A.W. (1989). *Lay epistemics and human knowledge: Cognitive and motivational bases.* New York: Plenum Press.

Kruglanski, A.W. & Freund, T. (1983). The freezing and unfreezing of lay inferences: Effects on impressional primacy, ethnic stereotyping, and numerical anchoring. *Journal of Experimental Social Psychology, 19,* 448–468.

Kruglanski, A.W., Webster, D.M. & Klem, A. (1993). Motivated resistance and openness to persuasion in the presence or absence of prior information. *Journal of Personality and Social Psychology, 65,* 861–876.

Krugman, H.E. (1965). The impact of television advertising: Learning without involvement. *Public Opinion Quarterly, 29,* 349–356.

Krull, D.S. (1993). Does the grist change the mill? The effect of the perceiver's inferential goal on the process of social inference. *Personality and Social Psychology Bulletin, 19,* 340–348.

Kühnen, U., Hannover, B. & Schubert, B. (2001). The semantic–procedural interface model of the self: The role of self-knowledge for context-bounded versus context-independent modes of thinking. *Journal of Personality and Social Psychology, 80,* 397–409.

Kulik, J.A., Mahler, H.I.M. & Moore, P.J. (2003). Social comparison affiliation under threat: Effects on recovery from major surgery. In P. Salovey & A. Rothman (Eds.), *Social psychology of health: Key readings in social psychology* (pp. 199–226). New York: Psychology Press.

Kunda, Z. (1999). *Social cognition: Making sense of people.* Cambridge, MA: MIT Press.

Kunst-Wilson, W.R. & Zajonc, R.B. (1980). Affective discrimination of stimuli that cannot be recognized. *Science, 207,* 557–558.

Lalljee, M. & Abelson, R.P. (1983). The organization of explanations. In M. Hewstone (Ed.), *Attribution theory: Social and functional extensions* (pp. 65–80). Oxford: Blackwell.

Lalljee, M., Lamb, R., Furnham, A. & Jaspars, J. (1984). Explanations and information search: Inductive and hypothesis-testing approaches to arriving at an explanation. *British Journal of Social Psychology, 23,* 201–212.

Lamm, H. & Myers, D.G. (1978). Group-induced polarization of attitudes and behaviour. In L. Berkowitz (Ed.), *Advances in experimental social psychology* (Vol. 11, pp. 145–195). New York: Academic Press.

Langer, E.J., Blank, A. & Chanowitz, B. (1978). The mindlessness of ostensibly thoughtful action. *Journal of Personality and Social Psychology, 36,* 635–642.

LaPiere, R. (1934). Attitudes versus actions. *Social Forces, 13,* 230–237.

Laplace, A., Chermack, S.T. & Taylor, S.P. (1994). Effects of alcohol and drinking experience on human physical aggression. *Personality and Social Psychology Bulletin, 20,* 439–444.

Larson, J.R., Jr. & Christensen, C. (1993). Groups as problem-solving units: Toward a new meaning of social cognition. *British Journal of Social Psychology, 32,* 5–30.

Larson, J.R., Jr, Christensen, C., Abbott, A.S. & Franz, T.M. (1996). Diagnosing groups: Charting the flow of information in medical decision-making teams. *Journal of Personality and Social Psychology, 71,* 315–330.

Larson, J.R., Jr, Christensen, C., Franz, T.M. & Abbott, A.S. (1998). Diagnosing groups: The pooling, management, and impact of shared and unshared case information in team-based medical decision making. *Journal of Personality and Social Psychology, 75,* 93–108.

Larson, J.R., Jr, Foster-Fishman, P.G. & Franz, T.M. (1998). Leadership style and the discussion of shared and unshared information in decision-making groups. *Personality and Social Psychology Bulletin, 24,* 482–495.

Larson, J.R., Jr, Foster-Fishman, P.G. & Keys, C.B. (1994). Discussion of shared and unshared information in decision-making groups. *Journal of Personality and Social Psychology, 67,* 446–461.

Latané, B. & Darley, J.M. (1969). Bystander 'apathy'. *American Scientist, 57,* 244–268.

Latané, B. & Darley, J.M. (1970). *The unresponsive bystander: Why doesn't he help?* New York: Apple Century Crofts.

Latané, B. & Darley, J.M. (1976). *Help in a crisis: Bystander response to an emergency.* Morristown, NJ: General Learning Press.

Latané, B. & Nida, S. (1981). Ten years of research on group size and helping. *Psychological Bulletin, 89,* 308–324.

Latané, B. & Rodin, A. (1969). A lady in distress: Inhibiting effects of friends and strangers on bystander intervention. *Journal of Experimental Social Psychology, 5,* 189–202.

Latané, B., Williams, K. & Harkins, S. (1979). Many hands make light work: The causes and consequences of social loafing. *Journal of Personality and Social Psychology, 37,* 822–832.

Laughlin, P.R. & Hollingshead, A.B. (1995). A theory of collective induction. *Organizational Behavior and Human Decision Processes, 61,* 94–107.

Laughlin, P.R. & Sweeney, J.D. (1977). Individual-to-group and group-to-individual transfer in problem solving. *Journal of Experimental Psychology: Human Learning and Memory, 3,* 246–254.

Lavidge, R.J. & Steiner, G.A. (1961). A model for predictive measurements of advertising effectiveness. *Journal of Marketing, 25,* 59–62.

Lazarus, R.S. (1966). *Psychological stress and the coping process.* New York: McGraw-Hill.

Lazarus, R.S. (1991). *Emotion and adaptation.* New York: Oxford University Press.

Lazarus, R.S. & Folkman, S. (1984). *Stress, appraisal, and coping.* New York: Springer.

Le, B. & Agnew, C.R. (2003). Commitment and its theorized determinants: A meta-analysis of the investment model. *Personal Relationships, 10,* 37–57.

Leana, C.R. (1985). A partial test of Janis's groupthink model: Effects of group cohesiveness and leader behavior on defective decision making. *Journal of Management, 11,* 5–17.

Leary, M.R. & Baumeister, R.F. (2000). The nature and function of self-esteem: Sociometer theory. In M. Zanna (Ed.), *Advances in experimental social psychology* (Vol. 32, pp. 1–62). San Diego, CA: Academic Press.

Leary, M.R., Tambor, E.S., Terdal, S.K. & Downs, D.L. (1995). Self-esteem as an interpersonal monitor: The sociometer hypothesis. *Journal of Personality and Social Psychology, 68,* 518–530.

Lee, A.Y., Aaker, J.L. & Gardner, W.L. (2000). The pleasure and pain of distinct self-construals: The role of interdependence in regulatory focus. *Journal of Personality and Social Psychology, 78,* 1122–1134.

Lee Toffler, B. & Reingold, J. (2003). *Final accounting: Ambition, greed, and the fall of Arthur Andersen.* New York: Broadway Books.

Lefkowitz, M.M., Eron, L.D., Walder, L.O. & Huesmann, L.R. (1977). *Growing up to be violent.* New York: Pergamon.

Leonardelli, G.J. & Brewer, M.B. (2001). Minority and majority discrimination: When and why. *Journal of Experimental Social Psychology, 37,* 468–485.

Lepore, L. & Brown, R. (1997). Category and stereotype activation: Is prejudice inevitable? *Journal of Personality and Social Psychology, 72,* 275–287.

Lepper, M.R. & Greene, D. (Eds.) (1978). *The hidden costs of reward.* Hillsdale, NJ: Lawrence Erlbaum.

Lepper, M.R., Greene, D. & Nisbett, R.E. (1973). Undermining children's intrinsic interest with extrinsic reward: A test of the 'overjustification' hypothesis. *Journal of Personality and Social Psychology, 28,* 129–137.

Lerner, M.J. (1980). *The belief in a just world: A fundamental delusion.* New York: Plenum Press.

Leventhal, H. (1970). Findings and theory in the study of fear communication. In L. Berkowitz (Ed.), *Advances in experimental social psychology* (Vol. 5, pp. 120–186). New York: Academic Press.

Levin, S., van Laar, C. & Sidanius, J. (2003). The effects of ingroup and outgroup friendship on ethnic attitudes in college: A longitudinal study. *Group Processes and Intergroup Relations, 6,* 76–92.

Levine, J.M. (1989). Reaction to opinion deviance in small groups. In P.B. Paulus (Ed.), *The psychology of group influence* (2nd edn, pp. 187–231). Hillsdale, NJ: Lawrence Erlbaum.

Levine, J.M. (1999). Solomon Asch's legacy for group research. *Personality and Social Psychology Review, 3,* 358–364.

Levine, J.M. & Moreland, R.L. (1998). Small groups. In D.T. Gilbert, S.T. Fiske & G. Lindzey (Eds.), *The handbook of social psychology* (4th edn, Vol. 2, pp. 415–469). New York: McGraw-Hill.

Levy, L. (1960). Studies in conformity behaviour: A methodological note. *Journal of Psychology, 50,* 39–41.

Lewin, K. (1948). *Resolving social conflicts.* New York: Harper & Row.

Lewin, K. (1951). *Field theory in social science.* New York: Harper & Row.

Lewin, K., Lippitt, R. & White, R.K. (1939). Patterns of aggressive behavior in experimentally created 'social climates'. *Journal of Social Psychology, 10,* 271–299.

Lewinsohn, P.M., Mischel, W., Chaplin, W. & Barton, R. (1980). Social competence and depression: The role of illusory self-perceptions. *Journal of Abnormal Psychology, 89,* 203–212.

Lewinsohn, P.M., Steinmetz, J.L., Larson, D.W. & Franklin, J. (1981). Depression-related cognitions: Antecedent or consequence? *Journal of Abnormal Psychology, 90,* 213–219.

Leyens, J.-P. & Corneille, O. (1999). Asch's social psychology: Not as social as you may think. *Personality and Social Psychology Review, 3,* 345–357.

Liang, D.W., Moreland, R. & Argote, L. (1995). Group versus individual training and group performance: The mediating role of transactive memory. *Personality and Social Psychology Bulletin, 21,* 384–393.

Liberman, A. & Chaiken, S. (1992). Defensive processing of personally relevant health messages. *Personality and Social Psychology Bulletin, 18,* 669–679.

Lickel, B., Hamilton, D.L., Wieczorkowska, G., Lewis, A., Sherman, S.J. & Uhles, A.N. (2000). Varieties of groups and the perception of group entitativity. *Journal of Personality and Social Psychology, 78,* 223–246.

Lieberman, J.D., Solomon, S., Greenberg, J. & McGregor, H.A. (1999). A hot new way to measure aggression: Hot sauce allocation. *Aggressive Behavior, 25,* 331–348.

Liebert, R.N. & Baron, R.A. (1972). Some immediate effects of televised violence on children's behavior. *Developmental Psychology, 6,* 469–478.

Liebkind, K. & McAlister, A.L. (1999). Extended contact through peer modelling to promote tolerance in Finland. *European Journal of Social Psychology, 29,* 765–780.

Likert, R. (1932). A technique for the measurement of attitudes. *Archives of Psychology, 140,* 5–53.

Linder, D.E., Cooper, J. & Jones, E.E. (1967). Decision freedom as a determinant of the role of incentive magnitude in attitude change. *Journal of Personality and Social Psychology, 6,* 245–254.

Lindsay, J.A. & Anderson, C.A. (2000). From antecedent conditions to violent actions: A general affective aggression model. *Personality and Social Psychology Bulletin, 26,* 533–547.

Linville, P.W. (1985). Self-complexity and affective extremity: Don't put all your eggs in one cognitive basket. *Social Cognition, 3,* 94–120.

Linville, P.W. (1987). Self-complexity as a cognitive buffer against stress-related illness and depression. *Journal of Personality and Social Psychology, 52,* 663–676.

Linville, P.W., Fischer, F.W. & Salovey, P. (1989). Perceived distributions of characteristics of ingroup and outgroup members: Empirical evidence and a computer simulation. *Journal of Personality and Social Psychology, 42,* 193–211.

Locke, E.A. & Latham, G.P. (2002). Building a practically useful theory of goal setting and task motivation: A 35-year Odyssey. *American Psychologist, 57,* 705–717.

Lodewijkx, H.F.M. & Syroit, J.E.M.M. (1997). Severity of initiation revisited: Does severity of initiation increase the attractiveness of real groups? *European Journal of Social Psychology, 27,* 275–300.

Loher, B.T., Noe, R.A., Moeller, N.L. & Fitzgerald, M.P. (1985). A meta-analysis of the relation of job characteristics to job satisfaction. *Journal of Applied Psychology, 70,* 280–289.

Loken, B. (2006). Consumer psychology: Categorization, inferences, affect, and persuasion. *Annual Review of Psychology, 57,* 453–485.

Lorenz, K. (1974). *Civilized world's eight deadly sins.* New York: Harcourt, Brace, Jovanovich.

Lücken, M. & Simon, B. (2005). Cognitive and affective experiences of minority and majority members: The role of group size, status, and power. *Journal of Experimental Social Psychology, 41,* 396–413.

Luepker, R.V., Murray, D.M., Jacobs, D.R. et al. (1994). Community education for cardiovascular disease prevention: Risk factor change in the Minnesota Heart Health Program. *American Journal of Public Health, 84,* 1383–1393.

Lundgren, S. & Prislin, R. (1998). Motivated cognitive processing and attitude change. *Personality and Social Psychology Bulletin, 24,* 715–726.

Maass, A. (1999). Linguistic intergroup bias: Stereotype perpetuation through language. In M. Zanna (Ed.), *Advances in experimental social psychology* (Vol. 31, pp. 79–121). San Diego, CA: Academic Press.

Maass, A. & Clark III, R.D. (1983). Internalization versus compliance: Differential processes underlying minority influence and conformity. *European Journal of Social Psychology, 13,* 197–215.

Maass, A. & Clark III, R.D. (1984). Hidden impact of minorities: Fifteen years of minority influence research. *Psychological Bulletin, 95,* 428–450.

Maass, A. & Volpato, C. (1994). Theoretical perspectives on minority influence: Conversion versus divergence? In S. Moscovici, A. Mucchi-Faina & A. Maass (Eds.), *Minority influence* (pp. 135–147). Chicago: Nelson-Hall.

MacBrayer, E.K., Milich, R. & Hundley, M. (2003). Attributional bias in aggressive children and their mothers. *Journal of Abnormal Psychology, 112,* 698–708.

MacDonald, T.K. & Zanna, M.P. (1998). Cross-dimension ambivalence toward social groups: Can ambivalence affect intentions to hire feminists? *Personality and Social Psychology Bulletin, 24,* 427–441.

MacKenzie, S.B., Lutz, R.J. & Belch, G.E. (1986). The role of attitude toward the ad as a mediator of advertising effectiveness: A test of competing explanations. *Journal of Marketing Research, 23,* 130–143.

MacKenzie, S.B., Podsakoff, P.M. & Fetter, R. (1991). Organizational citizenship behaviour and objective productivity as determinants of managerial evaluations of salespersons' performance. *Organizational Behavior and Human Decision Processes, 50,* 123–150.

Mackie, D.M. (1986). Social identification effects in group polarization. *Journal of Personality and Social Psychology, 50,* 41–52.

Mackie, D.M. (1987). Systematic and nonsystematic processing of majority and minority persuasive communications. *Journal of Personality and Social Psychology, 53,* 41–52.

Mackie, D.M. & Cooper, J. (1984). Attitude polarization: Effects of group membership. *Journal of Personality and Social Psychology, 46,* 575–585.

Mackie, D.M., Devos, T. & Smith, E.R. (2000). Intergroup emotions: Explaining offensive action tendencies in an intergroup context. *Journal of Personality and Social Psychology, 79,* 602–616.

Mackie, D.M., Hamilton, D.L., Susskind, J. & Rosselli, F. (1996). Social psychological foundations of stereotype formation. In C.N. Macrae, C. Stangor & M. Hewstone (Eds.), *Stereotypes and stereotyping* (pp. 41–78). New York: Guilford Press.

MacNamara, D.E.J. (1991). The victimization of whistle-blowers in the public and private sectors. In R.J. Kelly & D.E.J. MacNamara (Eds.), *Perspectives on deviance: Dominance, degradation and denigration* (pp. 121–134). Cincinnati, OH: Anderson.

MacNeil, M. & Sherif, M. (1976). Norm change over subject generations as a function of arbitrariness of prescribed norms. *Journal of Abnormal and Social Psychology, 62,* 408–412.

Macrae, C.N. & Bodenhausen, G.V. (2000). Social cognition: Thinking categorically about others. *Annual Review of Psychology, 51,* 93–120.

Macrae, C.N. & Johnston, L. (1998). Help, I need somebody: Automatic action and inaction. *Social Cognition, 16,* 400–417.

Macrae, C.N., Bodenhausen, G.V. & Milne, A.B. (1998). Saying no to unwanted thoughts: Self-focus and the regulation of mental life. *Journal of Personality and Social Psychology, 74,* 578–589.

Macrae, C.N., Bodenhausen, G.V., Milne, A.B. & Jetten, J. (1994). Out of mind but back in sight: Stereotypes on the rebound. *Journal of Personality and Social Psychology, 67,* 808–817.

Macrae, C.N., Bodenhausen, G.V., Milne, A.B., Thorn, T.M.J. & Castelli, L. (1997). On the activation of social stereotypes: The moderating role of processing objectives. *Journal of Experimental Social Psychology, 33,* 471–489.

Macrae, C.N., Milne, A.B. & Bodenhausen, G.V. (1994). Stereotypes as energy-saving devices: A peek inside the cognitive toolbox. *Journal of Personality and Social Psychology, 66,* 37–47.

Maier, N.R.F. (1967). Assets and liabilities in group problem solving: The need for an integrative function. *Psychological Review, 74,* 239–249.

Maio, G.R. & Haddock, G. (2004). Theories of attitude: Creating a witches' brew. In G. Haddock & G.R. Maio (Eds.), *Contemporary perspectives on the psychology of attitudes.* Hove: Psychology Press.

Maio, G.R. & Olson, J.M. (2000). What *is* a value-expressive attitude? In G.R. Maio & J.M. Olson (Eds.), *Why we evaluate: Functions of attitudes* (pp. 249–269). Mahwah, NJ: Lawrence Erlbaum.

Maio, G.R., Esses, V.M., Arnold, K. & Olson, J.M. (2004). The function-structure model of attitudes: Incorporating the need for affect. In G. Haddock & G.R. Maio (Eds.), *Contemporary perspectives on the psychology of attitudes.* Hove: Psychology Press.

Mantell, D.M. (1971). The potential for violence in Germany. *Journal of Social Issues, 27,* 101–112.

Mantell, D.M. & Panzarella, R. (1976). Obedience and responsibility. *British Journal of Social and Clinical Psychology, 15,* 239–245.

Marcus-Newhall, A., Pedersen, W.C., Carlson, M. & Miller, N. (2000). Displaced aggression is alive and well: A meta-analytic review. *Journal of Personality and Social Psychology, 78,* 670–689.

Markus, H.R. (1977). Self-schemata and processing information about the self. *Journal of Personality and Social Psychology, 35,* 63–78.

Markus, H.R. (1978). The effect of mere presence on social facilitation: An unobtrusive test. *Journal of Experimental Social Psychology, 14,* 389–397.

Markus, H.R. & Kitayama, S. (1991). Culture and the self: Implications for cognition, emotion, and motivation. *Psychological Review, 98,* 224–253.

Markus, H.R. & Kitayama, S. (1994). A collective fear of the collective: Implications for selves and theories of selves. *Personality and Social Psychology Bulletin, 20,* 568–579.

Markus, H.R. & Nurius, P. (1986). Possible selves. *American Psychologist, 41,* 954–969.

Markus, H.R. & Wurf, E. (1987). The dynamic self-concept: A social psychological perspective. *Annual Review of Psychology, 38,* 299–337.

Markus, H.R., Smith, J. & Moreland, R.L. (1985). Role of the self-concept in the perception of others. *Journal of Personality and Social Psychology, 49,* 1494–1512.

Marrow, A.J. (1969). *The practical theorist: The life and work of Kurt Lewin.* New York: Basic Books.

Marshall, G. & Zimbardo, P.G. (1979). Affective consequences of inadequately explained physiological arousal. *Journal of Personality and Social Psychology, 37,* 970–988.

Martin, R. & Hewstone, M. (2001a). Afterthoughts on afterimages: A review of the afterimage paradigm in majority and minority influence research. In C.K.W. De Dreu & N.K. De Vries (Eds.), *Group consensus and minority influence: Implications for innovation* (pp. 15–39). Oxford: Blackwell.

Martin, R. & Hewstone, M. (2001b). Conformity and independence in groups: Majorities and minorities. In M.A. Hogg & R.S. Tindale (Eds.), *Blackwell handbook of social psychology,* Vol. 1: *Group processes* (pp. 209–234). Oxford: Blackwell.

Martin, R. & Hewstone, M. (2003). Majority versus minority influence: When, not whether, source status instigates heuristic or systematic processing. *European Journal of Social Psychology, 33,* 313–330.

Martin, R., Hewstone, M. & Martin, P.Y. (2003). Resistance to persuasive messages as a function of majority and minority source status. *Journal of Experimental Social Psychology, 39,* 585–593.

Martin, R., Hewstone, M. & Martin, P.Y. (2007). Systematic and heuristic processing of majority- and minority-endorsed messages: The effects of varying outcome relevance and 'levels of orientation' on attitude and message processing. *Personality and Social Psychology Bulletin, 33,* 43–56.

Martin, R., Hewstone, M. & Martin, P.Y. (in press). Majority versus minority influence: The role of message processing in determining resistance to counter-persuasion. *European Journal of Social Psychology.*

Martin, R., Martin, P.Y., Smith, J.R. & Hewstone, M. (2007). Majority versus minority influence and prediction of behavioral intentions and behavior. *Journal of Experimental Social Psychology, 43,* 763–771.

Maslach, C. (1979). Negative emotional biasing of unexplained arousal. *Journal of Personality and Social Psychology, 37,* 953–969.

Maslow, A. (1970). *Motivation and personality* (Rev. edn). New York: Harper & Row.

Mayer, A. (1903). Über Einzel- und Gesamtleistung des Schulkindes. *Archiv für die Gesamt Psychologie, 1,* 276–416.

Mayle, P. (1993). *Hotel Pastis.* London: Hamish Hamilton.

McArthur, L. A. (1972). The how and what of why: Some determinants and consequences of causal attribution. *Journal of Personality and Social Psychology, 22,* 171–193.

McConahay, J.B., Hardee, B.B. & Batts, V. (1981). Has racism declined? It depends upon who's asking and what is being asked. *Journal of Conflict Resolution, 25,* 563–579.

McDougall, W. (1908). *An introduction to social psychology.* London: Methuen.

McGill, A.L. (1989). Context effects in causal judgement. *Journal of Personality and Social Psychology, 57,* 189–200.

McGrath, J.E. (1984). *Groups: Interaction and performance.* Englewood Cliffs, NJ: Prentice-Hall.

McGuire, W.J. (1968). Personality and susceptibility to social influence. In E.F. Borgatta & W.W. Lambert (Eds.), *Handbook of personality theory and research* (pp. 1130–1187). Chicago: Rand McNally.

McGuire, W.J. (1969). The nature of attitudes and attitude change. In G. Lindzey & E. Aronson (Eds.), *Handbook of social psychology* (2nd edn, Vol. 3, pp. 136–314). Reading, MA: Addison-Wesley.

McGuire, W.J. (1985). Attitudes and attitude change. In G. Lindzey & E. Aronson (Eds.), *Handbook of social psychology* (3rd edn, Vol. 2, pp. 233–346). New York: Random House.

McNulty, J., Karney, B.R. & McNulty, J.K. (2004). Positive expectations in the early years of marriage: Should couples expect the best or brace for the worst? *Journal of Personality and Social Psychology, 86,* 729–743.

Meeus, W.H.J. & Raaijmakers, Q.A.W. (1986). Administrative obedience: Carrying out orders to use psychological-administrative violence. *European Journal of Social Psychology, 16,* 311–324.

Meeus, W.H.J. & Raaijmakers, Q.A.W. (1995). Obedience in modern society: The Utrecht studies. *Journal of Social Issues, 51,* 155–175.

Messé, L.A., Hertel, G., Kerr, N.L., Lount, R.B., Jr. & Park, E.S. (2002). Knowledge of partner's ability as a moderator of group motivation gains: An exploration of the Köhler discrepancy effect. *Journal of Personality and Social Psychology, 82,* 935–946.

Messick, D.M. (2000). Context, norms and cooperation in modern society: A postscript. In M. van Vugt, M. Snyder, T.R. Tyler & A. Biel (Eds.), *Cooperation in modern society* (pp. 231–240). London: Routledge.

Messick, D.M., Wilke, H., Brewer, M.B., Kramer, R.M., Zemke, P.E. & Lui, L. (1983). Individual adaptations and structural change as solutions to social dilemmas. *Journal of Personality and Social Psychology, 44,* 294–309.

Meyer, J.P. (1997). Organizational commitment. In C.L. Cooper & L.T. Robertson (Eds.), *International review of industrial and organizational psychology* (Vol. 12, pp. 175–228). Chichester: Wiley.

Meyer, J.P., Stanley, D.J., Herscovitsch, L. & Topolnytsky, L. (2002). Affective, continuance, and normative commitment to the organization: A meta-analysis of antecedents, correlates, and consequences. *Journal of Vocational Behavior, 61,* 20–52.

Miceli, M.P. & Near, J.P. (1992). *Blowing the whistle: The organizational and legal implications for companies and employees.* New York: Lexington.

Mikelson, K.D., Kessler, R.C. & Shaver, P.R. (1997). Adult attachment in a nationally representative sample. *Journal of Personality and Social Psychology, 73,* 1092–1106.

Mikulincer, M. (1998). Attachment working models and the sense of trust: An exploration of interaction goals and affect regulation. *Journal of Personality and Social Psychology, 74,* 1209–1224.

Miles, D.R. & Carey, G. (1997). Genetic and environmental architecture of aggression. *Journal of Personality and Social Psychology, 72,* 207–217.

Milgram, S. (1963). Behavioral study of obedience. *Journal of Abnormal and Social Psychology, 67,* 371–378.

Milgram, S. (1965). Some conditions of obedience and disobedience to authority. *Human Relations, 18,* 57–76.

Milgram, S. (1974). *Obedience to authority.* New York: Harper & Row.

Milgram, S., Liberty, H.J., Toledo, R. & Wackenhut, J. (1986). Response to intrusion into waiting lines. *Journal of Personality and Social Psychology, 51,* 683–689.

Miller, A.G. (1986). *The obedience experiments: A case study of controversy in social science.* New York: Praeger.

Miller, A.G. (1995). Obedience. In A.S.R. Manstead & M. Hewstone (Eds.), *Blackwell encyclopedia of social psychology* (pp. 418–423). Oxford: Blackwell.

Miller, A.G., Collins, B.E. & Brief, D.E. (Eds.) (1995). Perspectives on obedience to authority: The legacy of the Milgram experiments. *Journal of Social Issues, 51,* 1–212.

Miller, A.G., Gordon, A.K. & Buddie, A.M. (1999). Accounting for evil and cruelty: Is to explain to condone? *Personality and Social Psychology Review, 3,* 254–268.

Miller, D.T. (1977a). Altruism and threat to a belief in a just world. *Journal of Experimental Social Psychology, 13,* 113–124.

Miller, D.T. (1977b). Personal deserving versus justice for others: An exploration of the justice motive. *Journal of Experimental Social Psychology, 13,* 1–13.

Miller, D.T. (1999). The norm of self-interest. *American Psychologist, 54,* 1053–1060.

Miller, D.T. & Ross, M. (1975). Self-serving bias in the attribution of causality. Fact or fiction? *Psychological Bulletin, 82,* 213–225.

Miller, G. (2001). *The mating mind: How sexual choice shaped the evolution of human nature.* London: Vintage.

Miller, J.G. (1984). Culture and the development of everyday social explanation. *Journal of Personality and Social Psychology, 46,* 961–978.

Miller, N.E. (1941). The frustration-aggression hypothesis. *Psychological Review, 48,* 337–342.

Miller, N.E. & Carlson, M. (1990). Valid theory-testing meta-analyses further question the negative state relief model of helping. *Psychological Bulletin, 107,* 215–225.

Miller, N., Pedersen, W.C., Earleywine, M. & Pollock, V.E. (2003). A theoretical model of triggered displaced aggression. *Personality and Social Psychology Review, 7,* 75–97.

Millikan, R.G. (1998). A common structure for concepts of individuals, stuffs, and real kinds: More Mama, more milk, and more mouse. *Behavioural and Brain Sciences, 21,* 55–100.

Milne, S., Sheeran, P. & Orbell, S. (2000). Prediction and intervention in health-related behavior: A meta-analytic review of protection motivation theory. *Journal of Applied Social Psychology, 30,* 106–143.

Mirrlees-Black, C. (1999). Domestic violence: Findings from a new British Crime Survey self-completion questionnaire. *Home Office Research Study 191.* London: Home Office. Available online at: www.homeoffice.gov.uk/rds/pdfs/hors191.pdf; retrieved 23 September 2004.

Mischel, W. (1977). On the future of personality measurement. *American Psychologist, 32,* 246–254.

Moede, W. (1920). *Experimentelle Massenpsychologie.* Leipzig: Hirzel.

Mohammed, S. & Dumville, B.C. (2001). Team mental models in a team knowledge framework: Expanding theory and measurement across disciplinary boundaries. *Journal of Organizational Behavior, 22,* 89–106.

Mojzisch, A. & Schulz-Hardt, S. (2006). Information sampling in group decision making: Sampling biases and their consequences. In K. Fiedler & P. Juslin (Eds.), *Information sampling and adaptive cognition* (pp. 299–325). Cambridge: Cambridge University Press.

Molleman, E., Pruyn, J. & van Knippenberg, A. (1986). Social comparison processes among cancer patients. *British Journal of Social Psychology, 25,* 1–13.

Monteith, M.J. (1993). Self-regulation of prejudiced responses: Implications for progress in prejudice reduction efforts. *Journal of Personality and Social Psychology, 65,* 469–485.

Monteith, M.J., Sherman, J.W. & Devine, P.G. (1998). Suppression as a stereotype control strategy. *Personality and Social Psychology Review, 2,* 63–82.

Monteith, M.J., Spicer, C.V. & Tooman, G.D. (1998). Consequences of stereotype suppression: Stereotypes on AND not on the rebound. *Journal of Experimental Social Psychology, 34,* 355–377.

Montepare, J.M. & Zebrowitz-McArthur, L. (1988). Impressions of people created by age-related qualities of their gaits. *Journal of Personality and Social Psychology, 55,* 547–556.

Moorman, R.H., Blakely, G.L. & Niehoff, B.P. (1998). Does perceived organizational support mediate the relationship between procedural justice and organizational citizenship behavior. *Academy of Management Journal, 41,* 351–357.

Moreland, R.L. & Levine, J.M. (1982). Socialization in small groups: Temporal changes in individual-group relations. In L. Berkowitz (Ed.), *Advances in experimental social psychology* (Vol. 15, pp. 137–192). New York: Academic Press.

Moreland, R.L., Argote, L. & Krishnan, R. (1996). Socially shared cognition at work: Transactive memory and group performance. In J.L. Nye & A.M. Brower (Eds.), *What's social about social cognition? Research on socially shared cognition in small groups* (pp. 57–84). Thousand Oaks, CA: Sage.

Morgan, H.J. & Janoff-Bulman, R. (1994). Positive and negative self-complexity: Patterns of adjustment following traumatic versus non-traumatic life experiences. *Journal of Social and Clinical Psychology, 13,* 63–85.

Moscovici, S. (1976). *Social influence and social change.* London: Academic Press.

Moscovici, S. (1980). Toward a theory of conversion behavior. In L. Berkowitz (Ed.), *Advances in experimental social psychology* (Vol. 13, pp. 209–239). New York: Academic Press.

Moscovici, S. & Personnaz, B. (1980). Studies in social influence: V. Minority influence and conversion behavior in a perceptual task. *Journal of Experimental Social Psychology, 16,* 270–282.

Moscovici, S. & Zavalloni, M. (1969). The group as a polarizer of attitudes. *Journal of Personality and Social Psychology, 12,* 125–135.

Moscovici, S., Lage, E. & Naffrechoux, M. (1969). Influence of a consistent minority on the responses of a majority in a color perception task. *Sociometry, 32,* 365–380.

Moskowitz, G.B. (2005). *Social cognition: Understanding self and others.* New York: Guilford Press.

Moskowitz, G.B., Gollwitzer, P.M., Wasel, W. & Schaal, B. (1999). Preconscious control of stereotype activation through chronic egalitarian goals. *Journal of Personality and Social Psychology, 77*, 167–184.

Mowday, R.T., Porter, L.W. & Steers, R.M. (1982). *Employee–organizational linkages: The psychology of commitment, absenteeism and turnover.* New York: Academic Press.

Mucchi-Faina, A., Maass, A. & Volpato, C. (1991). Social influence: The role of originality. *European Journal of Social Psychology, 21*, 183–197.

Mugny, G. (1975). Negotiations, image of the other and the process of minority influence. *European Journal of Social Psychology, 5*, 209–228.

Mugny, G. (1982). *The power of minorities.* London: Academic Press.

Mugny, G. & Pérez, J. (1991). *The social psychology of minority influence.* Cambridge: Cambridge University Press.

Mullen, B. & Copper, C. (1994). The relation between group cohesiveness and performance: An integration. *Psychological Bulletin, 115*, 210–227.

Mullen, B., Anthony, T., Salas, E. & Driskell, J.E. (1994). Group cohesiveness and quality of decision making: An integration of tests of the Groupthink hypothesis. *Small Group Research, 25*, 189–204.

Mullen, B., Johnson, C. & Salas, E. (1991). Productivity loss in brainstorming groups: A meta-analytic integration. *Basic and Applied Social Psychology, 12*, 3–24.

Mummendey, A. & Otten, S. (1998). Positive–negative asymmetry in social discrimination. In W. Stroebe & M. Hewstone (Eds.), *European review of social psychology* (Vol. 9, pp. 107–143). Chichester: Wiley.

Mummendey, A. & Schreiber, H.-J. (1983). Better or just different? Positive social identity by discrimination against, or by differentiation from outgroups. *European Journal of Social Psychology, 13*, 389–397.

Mummendey, A. & Simon, B. (1989). Better or different? III. The impact of importance of comparison dimension and relative in-group size upon intergroup discrimination. *British Journal of Social Psychology, 28*, 1–16.

Mummendey, A., Kessler, T., Klink, A. & Mielke, R. (1999). Strategies to cope with negative social identity: Predictions by social identity theory and relative deprivation theory. *Journal of Personality and Social Psychology, 76*, 229–245.

Murchison, C. (Ed.) (1935). *Handbook of social psychology.* Worcester, MA: Clark University Press.

Murphy, S.T. & Zajonc, R.B. (1993). Affect, cognition, and awareness: Affective priming with optimal and suboptimal stimulus exposures. *Journal of Personality and Social Psychology, 64*, 723–739.

Murray, S.L. & Holmes, J.G. (1997). A leap of faith? Positive illusions in romantic relationships. *Personality and Social Psychology, 23*, 586–604.

Murray, S.L., Haddock, G. & Zanna, M.P. (1996). On creating value-expressive attitudes: An experimental approach. In C. Seligman, J.M. Olson & M.P. Zanna (Eds.), *The psychology of values: The Ontario symposium* (Vol. 8, pp. 107–133). Hillsdale, NJ: Lawrence Erlbaum.

Murray, S.L., Holmes, J.G. & Griffin, D.W. (1996). The benefits of positive illusions: Idealization and the construction of satisfaction in close relationships. *Journal of Personality and Social Psychology, 70*, 79–98.

Myers, D.G. (1978). Polarizing effects of social comparison. *Journal of Experimental Social Psychology, 14*, 554–563.

Myers, D.G. & Kaplan, M.F. (1976). Group-induced polarization in simulated juries. *Personality and Social Psychology Bulletin, 2*, 63–66.

Myers, D.G. & Lamm, H. (1976). The group polarization phenomenon. *Psychological Bulletin, 83*, 602–627.

Myers, D.G., Bach, P.J. & Schreiber, F.B. (1974). Normative and informational effects of group interaction. *Sociometry, 37*, 275–286.

Neely, J. (1977). Semantic priming and retrieval from lexical memory: Roles of inhibitionless spreaded activation and limited capacity attention. *Journal of Experimental Psychology: General, 106*, 226–254.

Nemeth, C.J. (1986). Differential contributions of majority and minority influence. *Psychological Review, 93*, 23–32.

Nemeth, C.J. (1995). Dissent as driving cognition, attitudes and judgements. *Social Cognition, 13*, 273–291.

Nemeth, C.J. & Kwan, J. (1985). Originality of word associations as a function of majority and minority influence. *Social Psychology Quarterly, 48*, 277–282.

Nemeth, C.J., Mosier, K. & Chiles, C. (1992). When convergent thought improves performance: Majority vs. minority influence. *Personality and Social Psychology Bulletin, 18*, 139–144.

Nemeth, C.J., Swedlund, M. & Kanki, B. (1974). Patterning of the minority's response and their influence on the majority. *European Journal of Social Psychology, 4*, 53–64.

Neuberg, S.L. & Fiske, S.T. (1987). Motivational influences on impression formation: Outcome dependency, accuracy-driven attention, and individuating processes. *Journal of Personality and Social Psychology, 53*, 431–444.

Newcomb, T.M. (1943). *Personality and social change: Attitude formation in a student community.* New York: Dryden Press.

Newcomb, T.M. (1961). *The acquaintance process.* New York: Holt, Rinehart, & Winston.

Newman, L.S. & Erber, R. (Eds.) (2002). *Understanding genocide: The social psychology of the Holocaust.* Oxford and New York: Oxford University Press.

Nijstad, B.A., Stroebe, W. & Lodewijkx, H.F.M. (2002). Cognitive stimulation and interference in groups: Exposure effects in an idea generation task. *Journal of Experimental Social Psychology, 38*, 535–544.

Nisbett, R.E. & Wilson, T.D. (1977). Telling more than we know: Verbal reports on mental processes. *Psychological Review, 84*, 231–259.

Nisbett, R.E., Caputo, C., Legant, P. & Maracek, J. (1973). Behavior as seen by the actor and as seen by the observer. *Journal of Personality and Social Psychology, 27*, 154–164.

Nisbett, R.E. & Ross, L. (1980). *Human inference: Strategies and shortcomings of social judgment.* Englewood Cliffs, NJ: Prentice-Hall.

Nissani, M. (1990). A cognitive reinterpretation of Stanley Milgram's observations on obedience to authority. *American Psychologist, 45*, 1384–1385.

Noller, P. & Fitzpatrick, M.A. (1990). Marital communication in the eighties. *Journal of Marriage and the Family, 52*, 832–843.

Norman, P., Boer, H. & Seydel, E.R. (2005). Protection motivation theory. In M. Conner & P. Norman (Eds.), *Predicting health behaviour* (2nd edn, pp. 81–126). Maidenhead: Open University Press.

Nosek, B.A, Banaji, M. & Greenwald, A.G. (2002). E-research: Ethics, design, security, and control in psychological research on the Internet. *Journal of Social Issues, 58*, 161–176.

Novotny, T.E., Romano, R.A., Davis, R.M. & Mills, S.L. (1992). The public health practice of tobacco control: Lessons learned and direction for the States in the 1990s. *Annual Review of Public Health, 13*, 287–318.

Nuttin, J.M., Jr. (1990). In memoriam: John T. Lanzetta. *European Journal of Social Psychology*, 363–367.

Oakes, P.J. (1987). The salience of social categories. In J.C. Turner, M.A. Hogg, P.J. Oakes, S.D. Reicher & M.S. Wetherell (Eds.), *Rediscovering the social group: A self-categorization theory.* Oxford: Blackwell.

Oakes, P.J., Haslam, S.J. & Turner, J.C. (1994). *Stereotyping and social reality.* Oxford: Blackwell.

Obermiller, C. & Spangenberg, E.R. (1998). Development of a scale to measure consumer skepticism toward advertising. *Journal of Consumer Psychology, 7*, 159–186.

Ochsner, K.N. & Lieberman, M.D. (2001). The emergence of social cognitive neuroscience. *American Psychologist, 56*, 717–734.

O'Connor, S.C. & Rosenblood, L.K. (1996). Affiliation motivation in everyday experience: A theoretical comparison. *Journal of Personality and Social Psychology, 70*, 513–522.

Oliner, S.P. & Oliner, P.M. (1988). *The altruistic personality: Rescuers of Jews in Nazi Europe.* New York: Free Press.

Olson, J.M. & Stone, J. (2005). The influence of behavior on attitudes. In D. Albarracin, B.T. Johnson & M.P. Zanna (Eds.), *The handbook of attitudes* (pp. 223–271). Mahwah, NJ: Lawrence Erlbaum.

Olson, M.A. & Fazio, R.H. (2004). Reducing the influence of extra-personal associations on the Implicit Association Test: Personalizing the IAT. *Journal of Personality and Social Psychology, 86,* 653–667.

Olweus, D. (1979). Stability of aggressive reaction patterns in males: A review. *Psychological Bulletin, 86,* 852–875.

Olweus, D. (1994). Bullying at school: Long-term outcomes for the victims and an effective school-based intervention program. In L.R. Huesmann (Ed.), *Aggressive behavior: Current perspectives* (pp. 97–130). New York: Plenum Press.

Omoto, A.M. & Snyder, M. (1995). Sustained helping without obligation: Motivation, longevity of service and perceived attitude change. *Journal of Personality and Social Psychology, 68,* 671–686.

Onorato, R.S. & Turner, J.C. (2001). The 'I', the 'me', and the 'us': The psychological group and self-concept maintenance and change. In C. Sedikides & M.B. Brewer (Eds.), *Individual self, relational self, and collective self.* Philadelphia: Taylor & Francis.

Onorato, R.S. & Turner, J.C. (2004). Fluidity in the self-concept: The shift from personal to social identity. *European Journal of Social Psychology, 34,* 257–278.

Oppenheim, A.N. (1992). *Questionnaire design, interviewing and attitude measurement.* London: Pinter.

Orbell, S., Hodgkins, S. & Sheeran, P. (1997). Implementation intentions and the theory of planned behavior. *Personality and Social Psychology Bulletin, 23,* 953–962.

Organ, D.W. (1988). *Organizational citizenship behavior: The good soldier syndrome.* Lexington, MA: Lexington Books.

Organ, D.W. & Ryan, K. (1995). A meta-analytic review of attitudinal and dispositional predictors of organizational citizenship behavior. *Personnel Psychology, 48,* 775–801.

Orne, M.T. (1962). On the social psychology of the psychological experiment: With particular reference to demand characteristics and their implications. *American Psychologist, 17,* 776–783.

Orne, M.T. (1969). Demand characteristics and the concept of quasi-controls. In R. Rosenthal & R.L. Rosnow (Eds.), *Artifact in behavioral research* (pp. 143–179). New York: Academic Press.

Orpinas, P. & Frankowski, R. (2001). The aggression scale: A self-report measure of aggressive behavior for young adults. *Journal of Early Adolescence, 21,* 50–76.

Orwell, G. (1949). *Nineteen eighty-four.* London: Secker & Warburg.

Osborn, A.F. (1957). *Applied imaginations.* New York: Scribner.

Osgood, C.E., Suci, G.J. & Tannenbaum, P.H. (1957). *The measurement of meaning.* Urbana: University of Illinois Press.

Osterhouse, R.A. & Brock, T.C. (1970). Distraction increases yielding to propaganda by inhibiting counterarguing. *Journal of Personality and Social Psychology, 15,* 344–358.

Österman, K., Björkqvist, K., Lagerspetz, K.M.J., Kaukiainen, A., Landau, S.F., Fraczek, A. & Caprara, G.V. (1998). Cross-cultural evidence of female indirect aggression. *Aggressive Behavior, 1,* 1–8.

Ouellette, J.A. & Wood, W. (1998). Habit and intention in everyday life: The multiple processes by which past behavior predicts future behavior. *Psychological Bulletin, 124,* 54–74.

Paolini, S., Hewstone, M., Cairns, E. & Voci, A. (2004). Effects of direct and indirect cross-group friendships on judgments of Catholics and Protestants in Northern Ireland: The mediating role of an anxiety-reduction mechanism. *Personality and Social Psychology Bulletin, 30,* 770–786.

Papastamou, S. (1986). Psychologization and processes of minority and majority influence. *European Journal of Social Psychology, 16,* 165–180.

Park, C.W. & Young, S.M. (1986). Consumer response to television commercials: The impact of involvement and background music on brand attitude formation. *Journal of Marketing Research, 23,* 11–24.

Parker, K. (1988). Speaking turns in small group interaction: A context-sensitive event sequence model. *Journal of Personality and Social Psychology, 54,* 965–971.

Parker, R.N. & Auerhahn, K. (1999). Drugs, alcohol, and homicide. In M.D. Smith & M.A. Zahn (Eds.), *Homicide: A sourcebook of social research* (pp. 176–191). Thousand Oaks, CA: Sage.

Paulhus, D.L. & John, O.P. (1998). Egoistic and moralistic biases in self-perception: The interplay of self-deceptive styles with basic traits and motives. *Journal of Personality, 66,* 1025–1060.

Paulus, P.B. & Yang, H.-C. (2000). Idea generation in groups: A basis for creativity in organizations. *Organizational Behavior and Human Decision Processes, 82,* 76–87.

Pearce, C.L. & Sims, H.P. (2000). Shared leadership: Toward a multi-level theory of leadership. *Team Development, 7,* 115–139.

Pechmann, C. & Esteban, G. (1994). Persuasion processes associated with direct comparative and noncomparative advertising and implications for advertising effectiveness. *Journal of Consumer Psychology, 2,* 403–432.

Pendry, L.F. (1998). When the mind is otherwise engaged: Resource depletion and social stereotyping. *European Journal of Social Psychology, 28,* 293–299.

Pendry, L.F. & Macrae, C.N. (1994). Stereotypes and mental life: The case of the motivated but thwarted tactician. *Journal of Experimental Social Psychology, 30,* 303–325.

Pendry, L.F. & Macrae, C.N. (1999). Cognitive load and person memory: The role of perceived variability. *European Journal of Social Psychology, 29,* 925–942.

Penner, L.A. & Finkelstein, M.A. (1998). Dispositional and structural determinants of volunteerism. *Journal of Personality and Social Psychology, 74,* 525–537.

Penner, L.A., Dovidio, J.F., Piliavin, J.A. & Schroeder, D.A. (2005). Prosocial behaviour: Multiple perspectives. *Annual Review of Psychology, 56,* 365–392.

Penner, L.A., Fritzsche, B.A., Craiger, J.P. & Freifeld, T.S. (1995). Measuring the prosocial personality. In J. Butcher & C.D. Spielberger (Eds.), *Advances in personality assessment* (Vol. 10, pp. 147–163). Hillsdale, NJ: Lawrence Erlbaum.

Perdue, C.W. & Gurtman, M.B. (1990). Evidence for the automaticity of ageism. *Journal of Experimental Social Psychology, 26,* 199–216.

Pérez, J.A. & Mugny, G. (1987). Paradoxical effects of categorization in minority influence: When being an outgroup is an advantage. *European Journal of Social Psychology, 17,* 157–169.

Pérez, J.A. & Mugny, G. (1998). Categorization and social influence. In S. Worchel, J. F. Morales, D. Paez & J. Deschamps (Eds.), *Social identity: International perspectives* (pp. 142–153). Thousand Oaks, CA: Sage.

Perkins, H.W. & Berkowitz, A.D. (1986). Perceiving the community norms of alcohol use among students: Some research implications of campus alcohol education programming. *International Journal of Addictions, 21,* 961–974.

Pettigrew, T.F. (1958). Personality and sociocultural factors in intergroup attitudes. *Journal of Conflict Resolution, 2,* 29–42.

Pettigrew, T.F. (1996). *How to think like a social scientist.* New York: HarperCollins.

Pettigrew, T.F. (1997). Generalized intergroup contact effects on prejudice. *Personality and Social Psychology Bulletin, 23,* 173–185.

Pettigrew, T.F. (1998). Intergroup contact theory. *Annual Review of Psychology, 49,* 65–85.

Pettigrew, T.F. & Martin, J. (1987). Shaping the organizational context for black American inclusion. *Journal of Social Issues, 43,* 41–78.

Pettigrew, T.F. & Tropp, L.R. (2000). Does intergroup contact reduce prejudice? Recent meta-analytic findings. In S. Oskamp (Ed.), *Reducing prejudice and discrimination: The Claremont symposium on applied social psychology* (pp. 93–114). Mahwah, NJ: Lawrence Erlbaum.

Pettigrew, T.F. & Tropp, L.R. (2006). A meta-analytic test of intergroup contact theory. *Journal of Personality and Social Psychology, 90,* 751–783.

Petty, R.E. & Cacioppo, J.T. (1986a). The elaboration likelihood model of persuasion. In L. Berkowitz (Ed.), *Advances in experimental social psychology* (Vol. 19, pp. 123–205). New York: Academic Press.

Petty, R.E. & Cacioppo, J.T. (1986b). *Communication and persuasion: Central and peripheral routes to attitude change.* New York: Springer.

Petty, R.E. & Wegener, D.T. (1998a). Attitude change: Multiple roles for persuasion variables. In D.T. Gilbert, S.T. Fiske & G. Lindzey (Eds.), *Handbook of social psychology* (4th edn, Vol. 1, pp. 323–390). New York: McGraw-Hill.

Petty, R.E. & Wegener, D.T. (1998b). Matching versus mismatching attitude functions: Implications for scrutiny of persuasive messages. *Personality and Social Psychology Bulletin, 24,* 227–240.

Petty, R.E. & Wegener, D.T. (1999). The elaboration likelihood model: Current status and controversies. In S. Chaiken & Y. Trope (Eds.), *Dual-process theories in social psychology* (pp. 41–72). New York: Guilford Press.

Petty, R.E., Cacioppo, J.T. & Goldman, R. (1981). Personal involvement as a determinant of argument-based persuasion. *Journal of Personality and Social Psychology, 41,* 847–855.

Petty, R.E., Cacioppo, J.T. & Schumann, D. (1983). Central and peripheral routes to advertising effectiveness: The moderating role of involvement. *Journal of Consumer Research, 10,* 134–148.

Petty, R.E., Cacioppo, J.T., Sedikides, C. & Strathman, A.J. (1988). Affect and persuasion: A contemporary perspective. *American Behavioral Scientist, 31,* 355–371.

Petty, R.E., Haugtvedt, C. & Smith, S.M. (1995). Elaboration as a determinant of attitude strength: Creating attitudes that are persistent, resistant, and predictive of behavior. In R.E. Petty & J.A. Krosnick (Eds.), *Attitude strength: Antecedents and consequences* (pp. 93–130). Hillsdale, NJ: Lawrence Erlbaum.

Petty, R.E., Ostrom, T.M. & Brock, T.C. (Eds.). (1981). *Cognitive responses in persuasion.* Hillsdale, NJ: Lawrence Erlbaum.

Petty, R.E., Wells, G.L. & Brock, T.C. (1976). Distraction can enhance or reduce yielding to propaganda: Thought disruption versus effort justification. *Journal of Personality and Social Psychology, 34,* 874–884.

Pfeffer, J. & Langton, N. (1993). The effects of wage dispersion on satisfaction, productivity, and working collaboratively: Evidence from college and university faculty. *Administrative Science Quarterly, 38,* 382–407.

Phelps, E.A. & Thomas, L.A. (2003). Race, behavior, and the brain: The role of neuroimaging in understanding complex social behaviors. *Political Psychology, 24,* 747–758.

Phelps, E.A., O'Connor, K.J., Cunningham, W.A., Funayama, E.S., Gatenby, J.C., Gore, J.C., & Banaji, M.R. (2000). Performance on indirect measures of race evaluation predicts amygdala activation. *Journal of Cognitive Neuroscience, 12,* 729–738.

Pierce, J.L. & Newstrom, J.W. (2003). *Leaders and the leadership process: Readings, self-assessments and applications.* Boston: McGraw-Hill Irwin.

Piliavin, J.A., Dovidio, J.F., Gaertner, S.L. & Clark, R.D. (1981). *Emergency intervention.* New York: Academic Press.

Pliner, P.H., Hart, H., Kohl, J. & Saari, D. (1974). Compliance without pressure: Some further data on the foot-in-the-door technique. *Journal of Experimental Social Psychology, 10,* 17–22.

Plomin, R., Nitz, K. & Rowe, D.C. (1990). Behavior genetics and aggressive behavior in childhood. In M. Lewis & S. Miller (Eds.), *Handbook of developmental psychopathology* (pp. 119–133). New York: Plenum Press.

Podsakoff, P.M., Ahearne, M. & MacKenzie, S.B. (1997). Organizational citizenship behavior and the quantity and quality of work group performance. *Journal of Applied Psychology, 82,* 262–270.

Podsakoff, P.M., MacKenzie, S.B. & Ahearne, M. (1997). Moderating effects of goal acceptance on the relation between group cohesiveness and productivity. *Journal of Applied Psychology, 82,* 974–983.

Polizeiliche Kriminalstatistik 2003 (2003). Available online at: www.bka.de/pks/pks2003/index2.html. Retrieved 4 May 2005.

Posner, M. & Snyder, C.R.R. (1975). Attention and cognitive control. In R.L. Solso (Ed.), *Information processing and cognition: The Loyola symposium* (pp. 55–85). Hillsdale, NJ: Lawrence Erlbaum.

Potter, J. (1996). Discourse analysis and constructionist approaches: Theoretical background. In J.T.E. Richardson (Ed.), *Handbook of qualitative research methods for psychology and the social sciences* (pp. 125–140). Leicester: BPS Books.

Potter, J. & Wetherell, M. (1987). *Discourse and social psychology: Beyond attitudes and behavior.* London: Sage.

Pratkanis, A. & Aronson, E., (2001). *The age of propaganda.* New York: Freeman.

Pratto, F. (1999). The puzzle of continuing group inequality: Piecing together psychological, social, and cultural forces in social dominance theory. In M. Zanna (Ed.), *Advances in experimental social psychology* (Vol. 31, pp. 191–263). San Diego, CA: Academic Press.

Pratto, F., Sidanius, J., Stallworth, L.M. & Malle, B.F. (1994). Social dominance orientation: A personality variable predicting social and political attitudes. *Journal of Personality and Social Psychology, 67,* 741–763.

Prentice, D.A. (1987). Psychological correspondence of possessions, attitudes, and values. *Journal of Personality and Social Psychology, 53,* 993–1003.

Price-Bonham, S., Wright, D.W. & Pittman, J.F. (1983). A frequent 'alternative' in the 1970s. In E. Macklin & R.H. Rubin (Eds.), *Contemporary families and alternative lifestyles* (pp. 125–146). Beverly Hills, CA: Sage.

Priester, J.R. & Petty, R.E. (2003). The influence of spokesperson trustworthiness on message elaboration, attitude strength, and advertising effectiveness. *Journal of Consumer Psychology, 13,* 408–421.

Priester, J.R., Godek, J., Nayakankuppum, D.J. & Park, K. (2004). Brand congruity and comparative advertising: When and why comparative advertisements lead to greater elaboration. *Journal of Consumer Psychology, 14,* 115–123.

Prins, K.S., Buunk, A.P. & VanYperen, N.W. (1992). Equity, normative disapproval and extramarital sex. *Journal of Social and Personal Relationships, 10,* 39–53.

Prislin, R. & Wood, W. (2005). Social influence in attitudes and attitude change. In D. Albarracin, B.T. Johnson & M.P. Zanna (Eds.), *The handbook of attitudes* (pp. 671–706). Mahwah, NJ: Lawrence Erlbaum.

Prochaska, J.O., DiClemente, C.C. & Norcross, J.C. (1992). In search of how people change: Applications to addictive behaviors. *American Psychologist, 47,* 1102–1114.

Prochaska, J.O., Redding, C.A. & Evers, K.E. (2002). The transtheoretical model and stages of change. In K. Glanz, B.K. Rimer & F.M. Lewis (Eds.), *Health behavior and health education: Theory, research, and practice* (3rd edn, pp. 99–120). San Francisco: Jossey-Bass.

Pugh, M. & Wahrman, R. (1983). Neutralizing sexism in mixed groups: Do women have to be better than men? *American Journal of Sociology, 88,* 746–762.

Quattrone, G.A. & Jones, E.E. (1980). The perception of variability within ingroups and outgroups. *Journal of Personality and Social Psychology, 38,* 141–152.

Rabbie, J.M. (1963). Differential preference for companionship under threat. *Journal of Abnormal and Social Psychology, 67,* 643–648.

Rabbie, J.M. & de Brey, J.H. (1971). The anticipation of intergroup cooperation and competition under private and public conditions. *International Journal of Group Tensions, 1,* 230–251.

Rabbie, J.M. & Horowitz, M. (1969). Arousal of ingroup–outgroup bias by a chance to win or lose. *Journal of Personality and Social Psychology, 13,* 269–277.

Rabbie, J.M. & Wilkins, G. (1971). Intergroup competition and its effect on intragroup and intergroup relations. *European Journal of Social Psychology, 1,* 215–234.

Ramirez, J.M. (2003). Hormones and aggression in childhood and adolescence. *Aggression and Violent Behavior, 8,* 621–644.

Randall, P. (1997). *Adult bullying.* London: Routledge.

Rank, S.G. & Jacobson, C.K. (1977). Hospital nurses' compliance with medication overdose orders: A failure to replicate. *Journal of Health and Social Behavior, 18,* 188–193.

Raven, B.H. (1974). The Nixon group. *Journal of Social Issues, 30,* 297–320.

Ray, M.L. (1973). Marketing communication and the hierarchy-of-effects. In P. Clarke (Ed.), *New models for mass communication research* (Vol. 5, pp. 147–176). Beverly Hills, CA: Sage.

Ray, M.L. (1982). *Advertising and communication management.* Englewood Cliffs, NJ: Prentice-Hall.

Read, S.J. (1987). Constructing causal scenarios: A knowledge-structure approach to causal reasoning. *Journal of Personality and Social Psychology, 52,* 288–302.

Reed II, A., Wooten, D.B. & Bolton, L.E. (2002). The temporary construction of consumer attitudes. *Journal of Consumer Psychology, 12,* 375–388.

Regan, D.T. & Fazio, R.H. (1977). On the consistency between attitudes and behaviour: Look to the method of attitude formation. *Journal of Experimental Social Psychology, 13,* 28–45.

Regan, L. & Kelly, L. (2003). *Rape: Still a forgotten issue.* Briefing document for the Rape Crisis Network Europe. Available online at: www.rcne.com/. Retrieved 4 May 2005.

Reicher, S. & Haslam, S.A. (2006). Rethinking the psychology of tyranny: The BBC prison study. *British Journal of Social Psychology, 45,* 1–40.

Reingen, P.H. (1978). On inducing compliance with requests. *Journal of Consumer Reports, 5,* 96–102.

Reips, U.-D. (2002). Internet-based psychological experimenting: Five do's and five don't's. *Social Science Computer Review, 20,* 241–249.

Reis, H.T. & Patrick, B.C. (1996). Attachment and intimacy: Component processes. In E.T. Higgins & A.W. Kruglanski (Eds.), *Social psychology: Handbook of basic principles* (pp. 523–563). New York: Guilford Press.

Reis, H.T., Earing, B., Kent, A. & Nezlek, J. (1976). The tyranny of numbers: Does group size affect petition signing? *Journal of Applied Social Psychology, 6,* 228–234.

Reis, H.T., Senchak, M. & Solomon, B. (1985). Sex differences in the intimacy of social interaction: Further examination of potential explanations. *Journal of Personality and Social Psychology, 48,* 1204–1217.

Reisenzein, R. (1983). The Schachter theory of emotion: Two decades later. *Psychological Bulletin, 94,* 239–264.

Rennison, C.M. & Welchans, S. (2000). *Intimate partner violence.* Bureau of Justice Statistics Special Report, May 2000. Available online at: www.ojp.usdoj.gov/bjs/cvict.htm. Retrieved 20 December 2003.

Rhee, E., Uleman, J.S., Lee, H.K. & Roman, R.J. (1995). Spontaneous self-description and ethnic identities in individualistic and collectivistic cultures. *Journal of Personality and Social Psychology, 69,* 142–152.

Rhee, S.H. & Waldman, I.H. (2002). Genetic and environmental influences on antisocial behavior: A meta-analysis of twin and adoption studies. *Psychological Bulletin, 128,* 490–529.

Rhoades, L. & Eisenberger, R. (2002). Perceived organizational support: A review of the literature. *Journal of Applied Psychology, 87,* 698–714.

Rhoades, L., Eisenberger, R. & Armeli, S. (2001). Affective commitment to the organization: The contribution of perceived organizational support. *Journal of Applied Psychology, 86,* 825–836.

Richards, Z. & Hewstone, M. (2001). Subtyping and subgrouping: Processes for the prevention and promotion of stereotype change. *Personality and Social Psychology Review, 5,* 52–73.

Ridgeway, C.L. (2001). Social status and group structure. In M.A. Hogg & S. Tindale (Eds.), *Blackwell handbook of social psychology: Group processes* (pp. 352–375). Oxford: Blackwell.

Ring, K. (1967). Experimental social psychology: Some sober questions about some frivolous values. *Journal of Experimental Social Psychology, 3,* 113–123.

Ringelmann, M. (1913). Recherches sur les moteurs animés: Travail de l'homme [Research on animate sources of power: The work of man]. *Annales de l'Institut National Agronomique,* 2ᵉ série, tome XII, 1–40.

Rioux, S.M. & Penner, L.A. (2001). The causes of organizational citizenship behavior: A motivational analysis. *Journal of Applied Psychology, 86,* 1306–1314.

Rippetoe, P.A. & Rogers, R.W. (1987). Effects of components of protection-motivation theory on adaptive and maladaptive coping with a health threat. *Journal of Personality and Social Psychology, 52,* 596–604.

Robertson, L.S. (1986). Behavioral and environmental interventions for reducing motor vehicle trauma. *Annual Review of Public Health, 7,* 13–34.

Robinson, J.P., Shaver, P.R. & Wrightsman, L.S. (Eds.) (1991). *Measures of personality and social psychological attitudes.* San Diego, CA: Academic Press.

Robinson, T.W., Smith, S.W., Miller, M.D. & Brownell, M.T. (1999). Cognitive behavior modification of hyperactivity-impulsivity and aggression: A meta-analysis of school-based studies. *Journal of Educational Psychology, 91,* 195–203.

Robinson-Staveley, K. & Cooper, J. (1990). Mere presence, gender, and reactions to computers: Studying human–computer interaction in the social context. *Journal of Experimental Social Psychology, 26,* 168–183.

Rochat, F. & Modigliani, A. (1995). The ordinary quality of resistance: From Milgram's laboratory to the village of Le Chambon. *Journal of Social Issues, 51,* 195–210.

Roethlisberger, F.J. & Dickson, W.J. (1939). *Management and the worker.* Cambridge, MA: Harvard University Press.

Rogers, C.R. (1959). A theory of therapy, personality and interpersonal relationships, as developed in the client-centered framework. In S. Koch (Ed.), *Psychology: A study of a science* (Vol. 3, pp. 184–256). Toronto: McGraw-Hill.

Rogers, R.W. (1983). Cognitive and physiological processes in fear appeals and attitude change: A revised theory of protection motivation. In J.T. Cacioppo & R.E. Petty (Eds.), *Social psychophysiology: A source book* (pp. 153–176). New York: Guilford Press.

Rogers, R.W. & Mewborn, C.R. (1976). Fear appeals and attitude change: Effects of anxiousness, probability of occurrence, and the efficacy of coping responses. *Journal of Personality and Social Psychology, 34,* 54–61.

Rohrer, J.H., Baron, S.H., Hoffman, E.L. & Swander, D.V. (1954). The stability of autokinetic judgments. *Journal of Abnormal and Social Psychology, 49,* 595–597.

Römkens, R. (1997). Prevalence of wife abuse in the Netherlands: Combining quantitative and qualitative methods in survey research. *Journal of Interpersonal Violence, 12,* 99–125.

Rosenbaum, M.E. (1986). The repulsion hypothesis: On the nondevelopment of relationships. *Journal of Personality and Social Psychology, 51,* 1156–1166.

Rosenberg, M.J., Hovland, C.I., McGuire, W.J., Abelson, R.P. & Brehm, J.W. (1960). *Attitude organization and change.* New Haven, CT: Yale University Press.

Rosenhan, D.L., Underwood, B. & Moore, B. (1974). Affect moderates self-gratification and altruism. *Journal of Personality and Social Psychology, 30,* 546–552.

Rosenthal, A.M. (1964). *Thirty-eight witnesses.* New York: McGraw-Hill.

Rosenthal, R. (1966). *Experimenter effects in behavioral research.* New York: Appleton-Century-Crofts.

Rosenthal, R. & Fode, K.L. (1963). Three experiments in experimenter bias. *Psychological Reports, 12,* 491–511.

Rosenthal, R. & Rosnow, R.L. (1975). *The volunteer subject.* New York: Wiley.

Rospenda, K.M. & Richman, J.A. (2005). Harassment and discrimination. In J. Barling, E.K. Kelloway & M.R. Frone (Eds.), *Handbook of work stress* (pp. 149–188). Thousand Oaks, CA: Sage.

Ross, E.A. (1908) *Social psychology.* New York: Macmillan.

Ross, L.D. (1977). The intuitive psychologist and his shortcomings. *Advances in Experimental Social Psychology, 10,* 174–221.

Ross, L.D., Amabile, T.M. & Steinmetz, J.L. (1977). Social roles, social control, and biases in social-perception processes. *Journal of Personality and Social Psychology, 35,* 483–494.

Ross, L.D., Rodin, J. & Zimbardo, P.G. (1969). Toward an attribution therapy: The reduction of fear through induced cognitive-emotional misattribution. *Journal of Personality and Social Psychology, 12,* 279–288.

Roth, S. & Cohen, L.J. (1986). Approach, avoidance, and coping with stress. *American Psychologist, 41,* 813–819.

Rothbart, M. & John, O.P. (1985). Social categorization and behavioural episodes: A cognitive analysis of the effects of intergroup contact. *Journal of Social Issues, 41,* 81–104.

Rotter, J.B. (1966). Generalized expectancies of internal versus external control of reinforcement. *Psychological Monographs, 80*, whole issue no. 609.

Rotundo, M. & Sackett, P.R. (2002). Citizenship and counterproductive performance to global ratings of job performance: A policy-capturing approach. *Journal of Applied Psychology, 87*, 66–80.

Rubin, M. & Hewstone, M. (1998). Social identity theory's self-esteem hypothesis: A review and some suggestions for clarification. *Personality and Social Psychology Review, 2*, 40–62.

Rude, S.S., Valdez, C.R., Odom, S. & Ebrahimi, A. (2003). Negative cognitive biases predict subsequent depression. *Cognitive Therapy and Research, 27*, 415–429.

Rusbult, C.E. (1983). A longitudinal test of the investment model: The development (and deterioration) of satisfaction and commitment in heterosexual involvements. *Journal of Personality and Social Psychology, 45*, 101–117.

Rusbult, C.E. & Buunk, A.P. (1993). Commitment processes in close relationships: An interdependence analysis. *Journal of Social and Personal Relationships, 10*, 175–204.

Rusbult, C.E. & Farrell, D. (1983). A longitudinal test of the investment model: The impact on job satisfaction, job commitment, and turnover of variations in rewards, costs, alternatives, and investments. *Journal of Applied Psychology, 68*, 429–438.

Rusbult, C.E. & Martz, J.M. (1995). Remaining in an abusive relationship: An investment model analysis of nonvoluntary dependence. *Personality and Social Psychology Bulletin, 21*, 558–571.

Rusbult, C.E., Lange, P.A.M., Wildschut, T., Yovetich, N.A. & Verette, J. (2000). Perceived superiority in close relationships: Why it exists and persists. *Journal of Personality and Social Psychology, 79*, 521–545.

Russell, G.W. (2004). Sport riots: A social-psychological review. *Aggression and Violent Behavior, 9*, 353–378.

Rutledge, T., Matthews, K., Lui, L., Stone, K.L. & Cauley, J.A. (2003). Social networks and marital status predict mortality in older women: Prospective evidence from the study of osteoporotic fractures. *Psychosomatic Medicine, 65*, 688–694.

Sadalla, E.K., Kenrick, D.T. & Vershure, B. (1987). Dominance and interpersonal attraction. *Journal of Personality and Social Psychology, 52*, 730–738.

Saegert, S., Swap, W. & Zajonc, R. (1973). Exposure, context and interpersonal attraction. *Journal of Personality and Social Psychology, 25*, 234–242.

Sanbonmatsu, D.M. & Fazio, R.H. (1990). The role of attitudes in memory-based decision making. *Journal of Personality and Social Psychology, 59*, 614–622.

Sanders, G.S. (1981). Driven by distraction: An integrative review of social facilitation theory and research. *Journal of Experimental Social Psychology, 13*, 303–314.

Sanders, G.S., Baron, R.S. & Moore, D.L. (1978). Distraction and social comparison as mediators of social facilitation effects. *Journal of Experimental Social Psychology, 14*, 291–303.

Sanna, L.J. (1992). Self-efficacy theory: Implications for social facilitation and social loafing. *Journal of Personality and Social Psychology, 62*, 774–786.

Sanna, L.J. & Shotland, R.L. (1990). Valence of anticipated evaluation and social facilitation. *Journal of Experimental Social Psychology, 26*, 82–92.

Sarason, I.G. & Sarason, B.R. (1986). Experimentally provided social support. *Journal of Personality and Social Psychology, 50*, 1222–1225.

Sasfy, J. & Okun, M. (1974). Form of evaluation and audience expertness as joint determinants of audience effects. *Journal of Experimental Social Psychology, 10*, 461–467.

Sassenberg, K., Kessler, T. & Mummendey, A. (2003). Less negative = more positive? Social discrimination as avoidance or approach. *Journal of Experimental Social Psychology, 39*, 48–58.

Schaap, C., Buunk, B. & Kerkstra, A. (1988). Marital conflict resolution. In P. Noller & M.A. Fitzpatrick (Eds.), *Perspectives on marital interaction* (pp. 203–244). Clevedon/Philadelphia: Multilingual Matters.

Schachter, S. (1951). Deviation, rejection, and communication. *Journal of Abnormal and Social Psychology, 46*, 190–207.

Schachter, S. (1959). *The psychology of affiliation.* Stanford, CA: Stanford University Press.

Schachter, S. (1964). The interaction of cognitive and physiological determinants of emotional state. In L. Berkowitz (Ed.), *Advances in experimental social psychology* (Vol. 1, pp. 49–80). New York: Academic Press.

Schachter, S. (1994). Leon Festinger. Biographical Memoirs V. 64. The National Academies Press. Retrieved October 2005, from books.nap.edu.books/0309049784/html/98.html.

Schachter, S. & Singer, J.E. (1962). Cognitive, social, and physiological determinants of emotional state. *Psychological Review, 69*, 379–399.

Schacter, D.L. & Tulving, E. (Eds.) (1994). *Memory systems.* Cambridge, MA: MIT Press.

Scharlott, B.W. & Christ, W.G. (1995). Overcoming relationship-initation barriers: The impact of a computer-dating system on sex role, shyness and appearance inhibitions. *Computers in Human Behavior, 11*, 191–204.

Schat, A.C. & Kelloway, E.K. (2005). Workplace aggression. In J. Barling, E.K. Kelloway & M.R. Frone (Eds.), *Handbook of work stress* (pp. 189–218). Thousand Oaks, CA: Sage.

Scheier, M.F. & Carver, C.S. (1980). Private and public attention, resistance to change, and dissonance reduction. *Journal of Personality and Social Psychology, 39*, 390–405.

Scheier, M.F. & Carver, C.S. (1985). Optimism, coping, and health: Assessment and implications of generalized outcome expectancies. *Health Psychology, 4*, 219–247.

Scheier, M.F. & Carver, C.S. (1987). Dispositional optimism and physical well-being: The influence of generalized outcome expectancies on health. *Journal of Personality, 55*, 169–210.

Scheier, M.F., Carver, C.S. & Bridges, M.W. (1994). Distinguishing optimism from neuroticism (and trait anxiety, self-mastery, and self-esteem): A reevaluation of the life orientation test. *Journal of Personality and Social Psychology, 67*, 1063–1178.

Scheier, M.F., Matthews, K.A., Owens, J. et al. (1989). Dispositional optimism and recovery from coronary artery bypass surgery: The beneficial effects on physical and psychological well-being. *Journal of Personality and Social Psychology, 57*, 1024–1040.

Scherer, K.R. & Scherer, U. (1981). Speech behavior and personality. In J.K. Darby, Jr. (Ed.), *Speech evaluation in psychiatry.* New York: Grune & Stratton.

Schlenker, B.R. (1974). Social psychology and science. *Journal of Personality and Social Psychology, 29*, 1–15.

Schneider, M.E., Major, B., Luthanen, R. & Crocker, J. (1996). Social stigma and the potential costs of assumptive help. *Personality and Social Psychology Bulletin, 22*, 201–209.

Schopenhauer, A. (1995). *The world as will and idea.* London: Everyman. (Original work published 1819.)

Schuette, R.A. & Fazio, R.H. (1995). Attitude accessibility and motivation as determinants of biased processing: A test of the MODE model. *Personality and Social Psychology Bulletin, 21*, 704–710.

Schulz-Hardt, S., Brodbeck, F., Mojzisch, A., Kerschreiter, R. & Frey, D. (2006). Group decision making in hidden profile situations: Dissent as a facilitator for decision quality. *Journal of Personality and Social Psychology, 91*, 1080–1093.

Schulz-Hardt, S., Frey, D., Lüthgens, C. & Moscovici, S. (2000). Biased information search in group decision making. *Journal of Personality and Social Psychology, 78*, 655–669.

Schulz-Hardt, S., Hertel, G. & Brodbeck, F.C. (in press). Gruppenleistung und Leistungsförderung [Group performance and its facilitation]. In H. Schuler & K.-H. Sonntag (Eds.), *Handbuch der Arbeits- und Organisationspsychologie* [Handbook of Industrial and Organizational Psychology]. Göttingen: Hogrefe.

Schuster, E. & Elderton, E.M. (1906). The inheritance of psychical characters. *Biometrika, 5*, 460–469.

Schwartz, S.H. (1977). Normative influences on altruism. In L. Berkowitz (Ed.), *Advances in experimental social psychology* (Vol. 10, pp. 221–279). New York: Academic Press.

Schwartz, S.H. (1994). Are there universal aspects in the structure and contents of human values? *Journal of Social Issues, 50,* 19–45.

Schwartz, S.H. & Gottlieb, A. (1976). Bystander reactions to a violent theft: Crime in Jerusalem. *Journal of Personality and Social Psychology, 34,* 1188–1199.

Schwartz, S.H. & Howard, J.A. (1981). A normative decision-making model of altruism. In J.P. Rushton & R.M. Sorrentino (Eds.), *Altruism and helping behaviour* (pp. 189–211). Hillsdale, NJ: Lawrence Erlbaum.

Schwarz, N. (1990). Feelings as information: Informational and motivational functions of affective states. In E.T. Higgins & R.M. Sorrentino (Eds.), *Handbook of motivation and cognition* (Vol. 2, pp. 527–561). New York: Guilford Press.

Schwarz, N. (1994). Judgment in a social context: Biases, shortcomings, and the logic of conversation. In L. Berkowitz (Ed.), *Advances in experimental social psychology* (Vol. 26, pp. 123–162). New York: Academic Press.

Schwarz, N. (1999). Self-reports: How the questions shape the answers. *American Psychologist, 54,* 93–105.

Schwarz, N. & Clore, G.L. (1983). Mood, misattribution and judgments of well-being: Informative and directive functions of affective states. *Journal of Personality and Social Psychology, 45,* 513–523.

Schwarz, N., Groves, R.M. & Schuman, H. (1998). Survey methods. In D.T. Gilbert, S.T. Fiske & G. Lindzey (Eds.), *Handbook of Social Psychology,* 4th edn. (Vol. 1, pp. 143–179). New York: McGraw-Hill.

Schwarzwald, J., Raz, M. & Zvibel, M. (1979). The application of the door-in-the-face technique when established behavioural customs exist. *Journal of Applied Social Psychology, 9,* 576–586.

Sears, D.O. (1986). College sophomores in the laboratory: Influences of a narrow data base on social psychology's view of human nature. *Journal of Personality and Social Psychology, 51,* 515–530.

Sears, D.O. (1988). Symbolic racism. In P.A. Katz & D.A. Taylor (Eds.), *Eliminating racism: Profiles in controversy* (pp. 53–84). New York: Plenum Press.

Sears, D.O. & Henry, P.J. (2003). The origins of symbolic racism. *Journal of Personality and Social Psychology, 85,* 259–275.

Segal, M.W. (1974). Alphabet and attraction: An unobtrusive measure of the effect of propinquity in a field setting. *Journal of Personality and Social Psychology, 30,* 654–657.

Segerstrom, S.C., Taylor, S.E., Kemeny, M.E. & Fahey, J.L. (1998). Optimism is associated with mood, coping, and immune change in response to stress. *Journal of Personality and Social Psychology, 74,* 1646–1655.

Seligman, M.E.P. (1975). *Helplessness: On depression, development, and death.* San Francisco: Freeman.

Selye, H. (1956). *The stress of life* (2nd edn). New York: McGraw-Hill.

Sergios, P. & Cody, J. (1985/6). Importance of physical attractiveness and social assertiveness skills in male homosexual dating behavior and partner selection. *Journal of Homosexuality, 12,* 71–84.

Shallice, T. (1988). *From neuropsychology to mental structure.* New York: Cambridge University Press.

Shanab, M.E. & Yahya, K.A. (1978). A cross-cultural study of obedience. *Bulletin of the Psychometric Society, 11,* 267–269.

Shaver, P. & Klinnert, M. (1982). Schachter's theories of affiliation and emotion: Implications of developmental research. In L. Wheeler (Ed.), *Review of personality and social psychology* (Vol. 3, pp. 37–72). Beverly Hills, CA: Sage.

Shavitt, S. (1990). The role of attitude objects in attitude functions. *Journal of Experimental Social Psychology, 26,* 124–148.

Shavitt, S. & Wänke, M. (2004). Consumer behavior. In M.B. Brewer & M. Hewstone (Eds.), *Applied social psychology* (pp. 245–267). Oxford: Blackwell.

Sheeran, P. (2002). Intention–behavior relations: A conceptual and empirical review. In W. Stroebe & M. Hewstone (Eds.), *European Review of Social Psychology* (Vol. 12, pp. 1–36). Chicester: Wiley.

Sheeran, P., Milne, S., Webb, T.L. & Gollwitzer, P.M. (2005). Implementation intentions and health behaviors. In M. Conner & P. Norman (Eds.), *Predicting health behavior: Research and practice with social cognition models* (Vol. 2, pp. 267–323). Buckingham: Open University Press.

Shepard, R.N. (undated). Carl Iver Hovland. Biographical Memoirs V. 73. The National Academies Press. Retrieved October 2005 from books.nap.edu./html/bio73h/hovland.html.

Sherif, M. (1935). A study of some social factors in perception. *Archives of Psychology,* No. 187.

Sherif, M. (1936). *The psychology of social norms.* New York: Harper.

Sherif, M. (1966). *In common predicament: Social psychology of intergroup conflict and cooperation.* Boston: Houghton Mifflin.

Sherif, M. (1967). *Group conflict and co-operation.* London: Routledge & Kegan Paul.

Sherif, M. & Hovland, C.I. (1961). *Social judgment.* New Haven, CT: Yale University Press.

Sherif, M. & Sherif, C.W. (1953). *Groups in harmony and tension.* New York: Harper.

Sherif, M. & Sherif, C.W. (1969). *Social psychology.* New York: Harper & Row.

Sherif, M., Harvey, O.J., White, B.J., Hood, W.R. & Sherif, C.W. (1961). *Intergroup conflict and cooperation: The Robbers Cave Experiment.* Norman: University of Oklahoma.

Sherif, M., White, B.J. & Harvey, O.J. (1955). Status in experimentally produced groups. *American Journal of Sociology, 60,* 370–379.

Sherrod, D. (1989). The influence of gender on same-sex friendships. In C. Hendrick (Ed.), *Review of personality and social psychology: Close relationships* (pp. 164–186). Newbury Park, CA: Sage.

Shiffrin, R.M. & Schneider, W. (1977). Controlled and automatic information processing II: Perceptual learning, automatic attending, and a general theory. *Psychological Review, 84,* 127–190.

Sidanius, J. & Pratto, F. (1999). *Social dominance: An intergroup theory of social hierarchy and oppression.* New York: Cambridge University Press.

Sidanius, J., Pratto, F. & Bobo, L. (1996). Racism, conservatism, affirmative action, and intellectual sophistication: A matter of principled conservatism or group dominance? *Journal of Personality and Social Psychology, 70,* 476–490.

Siegrist, J. (1996). Adverse health effects of high effort/low reward conditions. *Journal of Occupational Health Psychology, 1,* 27–41.

Simon, B. (1992). The perception of ingroup and outgroup homogeneity: Re-introducing the intergroup context. In W. Stroebe & M. Hewstone (Eds.), *European review of social psychology* (Vol. 3, pp. 1–30). Chichester: Wiley.

Simon, B. (2004). *Identity in modern society: A social psychological perspective.* Oxford: Blackwell.

Simon, B. & Brown, R. (1987). Perceived intragroup homogeneity in minority–majority contexts. *Journal of Personality and Social Psychology, 22,* 407–413.

Simon, B. & Klandermans, B. (2001). Politicized collective identity: A social psychological analysis. *American Psychologist, 56,* 319–331.

Simonton, D.K. (1981). The library laboratory: Archival data in personality and social psychology. In L. Wheeler (Ed.), *Review of personality and social psychology* (Vol. 2, pp. 217–243). Beverly Hills, CA: Sage.

Simpson, J.A. (1990). Influence of attachment style on romantic relationships. *Journal of Personality and Social Psychology, 59,* 971–980.

Simpson, J.A., Rholes, W.S. & Nelligan, J.S. (1992). Support seeking and support giving within couples in an anxiety-provoking situation: The role of attachment styles. *Journal of Personality and Social Psychology, 62,* 434–446.

Singh, D. (1993). Adaptive significance of female physical attractiveness: Role of waist-to-hip ratio. *Journal of Personality and Social Psychology, 65,* 293–307.

Singh, D. (2004). Mating strategies of young women: Role of physical attractiveness. *Journal of Sex Research, 41,* 43–54.

Singh, R. & Ho, S.Y. (2000). Attitudes and attraction: A new test of the attraction, repulsion and similarity–dissimilarity asymmetry hypotheses. *British Journal of Social Psychology, 39,* 197–211.

Sivasubramaniam, N., Murry, W.D., Avolio, B.J. & Jung, D.I. (2002). A longitudinal model of the effects of team leadership and group potency on group performance. *Group and Organization Management, 27,* 66–96.

Slater, P.E. (1955). Role differentiation in small groups. *American Sociological Review, 20,* 300–310.

Smith, C.M. & Tindale, R.S. (in press). Direct and indirect minority influence in groups. In R. Martin & M. Hewstone (Eds.), *Minority influence and innovation: Antecedents, processes and consequences.* Hove: Psychology Press.

Smith, C.M., Tindale, S.R. & Steiner, L. (1998). Investment decisions by individuals and groups in 'sunk cost' situations: The potential impact of shared representations. *Group Processes and Intergroup Relations, 1,* 175–189.

Smith, C.A., Organ, D.W. & Near, J.P. (1983). Organizational citizenship behaviour: Its nature and antecedents. *Journal of Applied Psychology, 68,* 653–663.

Smith, E.E. & Medin, D.L. (1981). *Categories and concepts.* Cambridge, MA: Harvard University Press.

Smith, E.R. (1993). Social identity and social emotions: Toward new conceptualizations of prejudice. In D.M. Mackie & D.L. Hamilton (Eds.), *Affect, cognition, and stereotyping: Interactive processes in group perception* (pp. 297–315). San Diego, CA: Academic Press.

Smith, E.R. & Miller, F.D. (1983). Mediation among attributional inferences and comprehension processes: Initial findings and a general method. *Journal of Personality and Social Psychology, 44,* 492–505.

Smith, M.B., Bruner, J.S. & White, R.W. (1956). *Opinions and personality.* New York: Wiley.

Smith, P.B. & Bond, M.H. (1998). *Social psychology across cultures.* London: Prentice-Hall.

Smith, P.K. & Brain, P. (2000). Bullying in schools: Lessons from two decades of research. *Aggressive Behavior, 26,* 1–9.

Smith, P.K., Ananiadou, K. & Cowie, H. (2003). Interventions to reduce school bullying. *Canadian Journal of Psychiatry, 48,* 591–599.

Smith, P.K., Morita, Y., Junger-Tas, J., Olweus, D., Catalano, R. & Slee, P. (1999). *The nature of school bullying: A cross-national perspective.* London: Routledge.

Smith, P.K., Singer, M., Hoel, H. & Cooper, C.L. (2003). Victimization in the school and the workplace: Are there any links? *British Journal of Psychology, 94,* 175–188.

Smith, P.M. (1995). Leadership. In A.S.R. Manstead & M. Hewstone (Eds.), *Blackwell encyclopaedia of social psychology.* Oxford: Blackwell.

Smith, R.E. & Swinyard, W.R. (1982). Information response models: An integrated approach. *Journal of Marketing, 46,* 81–93.

Snyder, M. (1974). Self-monitoring of expressive behavior. *Journal of Personality and Social Psychology, 30,* 526–537.

Snyder, M. (1984). When belief creates reality. In L. Berkowitz (Ed.), *Advances in experimental social psychology* (Vol. 18, pp. 247–305). New York: Academic Press.

Snyder, M. (1987). *Public appearances/private realities: The psychology of self-monitoring.* New York: Freeman.

Snyder, M. & Cunningham, M.R. (1975). To comply or not to comply: Testing the self-perception explanation of the foot-in-the-door phenomenon. *Journal of Personality and Social Psychology, 31,* 64–67.

Snyder, M. & DeBono, K.G. (1985). Appeals to image and claims about quality: Understanding the psychology of advertising. *Journal of Personality and Social Psychology, 49,* 586–597.

Snyder, M. & Kendzierski, D. (1982). Acting on one's attitudes: Procedures for linking attitudes and behavior. *Journal of Experimental Social Psychology, 18,* 165–183.

Snyder, M., Tanke, E.D. & Berscheid, E. (1977). Social perception and interpersonal behavior: On the self-fulfilling nature of the social stereotype. *Journal of Personality and Social Psychology, 35,* 656–666.

Solomon, M.R. (2004). *Consumer behaviour: Buying, having, and being.* Upper Saddle River, NJ: Pearson.

Sparks, G.G. & Sparks, C.W. (2002). Effects of media violence. In J. Bryant & D. Zillmann (Eds.), *Media effects: Advances in theory and research* (2nd edn, pp. 269–285). Mahwah, NJ: Lawrence Erlbaum.

Spence, K.W. (1956). *Behavior theory and conditioning.* New Haven, CT: Yale University Press.

Spitzberg, B.H. (1999). An analysis of empirical estimates of sexual aggression victimization and perpetration. *Violence and Victims, 14,* 241–260.

Sprecher, S. (2001). Equity and social exchange in dating couples: Associations with satisfaction, commitment, and stability. *Journal of Marriage and the Family, 63,* 599–613.

Sprecher, S. & Schwartz, P. (1994). Equity and balance in the exchange of contributions in close relationships. In M.J. Lerner & G. Mikula (Eds.), *Entitlement and the affectional bond: Justice in close relationships. Critical issues in social justice.* (pp. 11–41). New York, NY: Plenum Press.

Srull, T.K. & Wyer, R.S., Jr. (1979). Category accessibility and social perception: Some implications for the study of person memory and interpersonal judgments. *Journal of Personality and Social Psychology, 38,* 841–856.

Stangor, C. & McMillan, D. (1992). Memory for expectancy-congruent and expectancy-incongruent information: A review of the social and social developmental literatures. *Psychological Bulletin, 11,* 42–61.

Stangor, C., Lynch, L., Duan, C. & Glass, B. (1992). Categorization of individuals on the basis of multiple social features. *Journal of Personality and Social Psychology, 62,* 207–218.

Stanton, A.L. & Snider, P.R. (1993). Coping with a breast cancer diagnosis: A prospective study. *Health Psychology, 12,* 16–23.

Stanton, A.L., Danoff-Burg, S., Cameron, C.L., Snider, P.R. & Kirk, S.B. (1999). Social comparison and adjustment to breast cancer: An experimental examination of upward affiliation and downward evaluation. *Health Psychology, 18,* 151–158.

Starbuck, W.H. & Farjoun, M. (Eds.) (2005). *Organization at the limit: Lessons from the 'Columbia' disaster.* Malden, MA and Oxford: Blackwell.

Stasser, G. & Birchmeier, Z. (2003). Group creativity and collective choice. In P.B. Paulus & B. Nijstad (Eds.), *Group creativity* (pp. 132–172). New York: Oxford University Press.

Stasser, G. & Titus, W. (1985). Pooling of unshared information in group decision making: Biased information sampling during discussion. *Journal of Personality and Social Psychology, 48,* 1467–1478.

Stasser, G., Kerr, N.L. & Bray, R.M. (1982). The social psychology of jury deliberations: Structure, process, and product. In N.L. Kerr & R.M. Bray (Eds.), *The psychology of the courtroom* (pp. 221–256). New York: Academic Press.

Staub, E. (1974). Helping a distressed person: Social, personality, and stimulus determinants. In L. Berkowitz (Ed.), *Advances in experimental social psychology* (Vol. 7, pp. 293–341). New York: Academic Press.

Staub, E. (1989). *The roots of evil: The origins of genocide and other group violence.* Cambridge: Cambridge University Press.

Steele, C.M. (1988). The psychology of self-affirmation: Sustaining the integrity of the self. In L. Berkowitz (Ed.), *Advances in experimental social psychology* (Vol. 21, pp. 261–302). New York: Academic Press.

Steiner, I.D. (1972). *Group processes and productivity.* New York: Academic Press.

Stephan, F.F. & Mischler, E.G. (1952). The relative rate of communication between members of small groups. *American Sociological Review, 17,* 482–486.

Stephan, W.G. & Stephan, C. (1985). Intergroup anxiety. *Journal of Social Issues, 41,* 157–175.

Steptoe, A. (2001). Psychophysiological bases of disease. In D.W. Johnston & M. Johnston (Eds.), *Health psychology* (Vol. 8, pp. 39–78). Amsterdam: Elsevier.

Sternberg, R.J. & Barnes, M.L. (Eds.) (1988). *The psychology of love.* New Haven, CT: Yale University Press.

Storms, M.D. (1973). Videotape and the attribution process: Reversing actors' and observers' points of view. *Journal of Personality and Social Psychology, 27,* 165–175.

Storms, M.D. & Nisbett, R.E. (1970). Insomnia and the attribution process. *Journal of Personality and Social Psychology, 16,* 319–328.

Strahan, E.J., Spencer, S.J. & Zanna, M.P. (2002). Subliminal priming and persuasion: Striking while the iron is hot. *Journal of Experimental Social Psychology,* 556–568.

Straus, M.A. (1979). Measuring intrafamily conflict and violence: The Conflict Tactics (CT) Scales. *Journal of Marriage and the Family, 41,* 75–88.

Straus, M.A., Hamby, S.L., Boney-McCoy, S. & Sugarman, D.B. (1996). The revised Conflict Tactics Scales (CTS 2): Development and preliminary psychometric data. *Journal of Family Issues, 17,* 283–316.

Strickland, L.H., Aboud, F. & Gergen, K. (Eds.) (1976). *Social psychology in transition.* New York: Plenum Press.

Stroebe, W. (2001). *Social psychology and health* (2nd edn). Buckingham: Open University Press.

Stroebe, W. & Diehl, M. (1988). When social support fails: Supporter characteristics in compliance-induced attitude change. *Personality and Social Psychology Bulletin, 14,* 136–144.

Stroebe, W. & Stroebe, M.S. (1986). Beyond marriage: The impact of partner loss on health. In R. Gilmour & S. Duck (Eds.), *The emerging field of personal relationships* (pp. 203–224). Hillsdale, NJ: Lawrence Erlbaum.

Stroebe, W. & Stroebe, M.S. (1996). The social psychology of social support. In E.T. Higgins & A.W. Kruglanski (Eds.), *Social psychology: Handbook of basic principles* (pp. 597–621). New York: Guilford Press.

Stroebe, W., Diehl, M. & Abakoumkin, G. (1996). Social compensation and the Köhler effect: Toward a theoretical explanation of motivation gains in group productivity. In E.H. Witte & J.H. Davis (Eds.), *Understanding group behaviour,* Vol. 2: *Small group processes and interpersonal relations* (pp. 37–65). Hillsdale, NJ: Lawrence Erlbaum.

Stroebe, W., Insko, C.A., Thompson, V.D. & Layton, B.D. (1971). Effects of physical attractiveness, attitude similarity, and sex on various aspects of interpersonal attraction. *Journal of Personality and Social Psychology, 18,* 79–91.

Stroebe, W., Stroebe, M.S. & Domittner, G. (1988). Individual and situational differences in recovery from bereavement: A risk group identified. *Journal of Social Issues, 44,* 143–158.

Stroebe, W., Stroebe, M., Abakoumkin, G. & Schut, H. (1996). The role of loneliness and social support in adjustment to loss: A test of attachment versus stress theory. *Journal of Personality and Social Psychology, 70,* 1241–1249.

Struch, N. & Schwartz, S.H. (1989). Intergroup aggression: Its predictors and distinctness from in-group bias. *Journal of Personality and Social Psychology, 56,* 364–373.

Suh, E.J., Moskowitz, D.S., Fournier, M.A. & Zuroff, D.C. (2004). Gender and relationships: Influences on agentic and communal behaviors. *Personal Relationships, 11,* 41–59.

Sumpton, R. & Gregson, M. (1981). The fundamental attribution error: An investigation of sensitivity to role-conferred advantages in self-presentation. *British Journal of Social Psychology, 20,* 7–11.

Sutton, G. & Griffin, M.A. (2004). Integrating expectations, experiences, and psychological contract violations: A longitudinal study of new professionals. *Journal of Occupational and Organizational Psychology, 77,* 493–514.

Sutton, S. (1982). Fear-arousing communications: A critical examination of theory and research. In J.R. Eiser (Ed.), *Social psychology and behavioral medicine* (pp. 303–337). New York: Wiley.

Sutton, S. (2005). Stage theories of health behaviour. In M. Conner & P. Norman (Eds.), *Predicting health behaviour* (2nd edn, pp. 223–275). Maidenhead: Open University Press.

Swann, W.B., Jr. (1984). Quest for accuracy in person perception: A matter of pragmatics. *Psychological Review, 91,* 457–477.

Swann, W.B., de la Ronde, C. & Hixon, J.G. (1994). Authenticity and positivity strivings in marriage and courtship. *Journal of Personality and Social Psychology, 66,* 857–869.

Swartz, M. & Watkins, S. (2003). *Power failure: The inside story of the collapse of Enron.* New York: Doubleday.

Sy, T., Coté, S. & Saavedra, R. (2005). The contagious leader: Impact of leader's mood on the mood of group members, group affective tone, and group processes. *Journal of Applied Psychology, 90,* 295–305.

Taarnby, M. (2002). *Motivational parameters in Islamic terrorism. Arbejdspapirer fra Center for Kulturforskning.* Århus, Denmark: Center for Kulturforskning.

Tajfel, H. (1978). Social categorization, social identity and social comparison. In H. Tajfel (Ed.), *Differentiation between social groups: Studies in the social psychology of intergroup relations* (pp. 61–76). London: Academic Press.

Tajfel, H. (1981). *Human groups and social categories: Studies in social psychology.* Cambridge: Cambridge University Press.

Tajfel, H. & Turner, J.C. (1979). An integrative theory of intergroup conflict. In W.G. Austin & S. Worchel (Eds.), *The social psychology of intergroup relations* (pp. 33–47). Monterey, CA: Brooks Cole.

Tajfel, H. & Turner, J.C. (1986). The social identity theory of intergroup behavior. In S. Worchel & W.G. Austin (Eds.), *Psychology of intergroup relations* (pp. 7–24). Chicago: Nelson-Hall.

Tajfel, H. & Wilkes, A.L. (1963). Classification and quantitative judgement. *British Journal of Psychology, 54,* 101–114.

Tajfel, H., Billig, M.B., Bundy, R.P. & Flament, C. (1971). Social categorization and intergroup behaviour. *European Journal of Social Psychology, 1,* 149–178.

Tashiro, T. & Frazier, P. (2003). 'I'll never be in a relationship like that again': Personal growth following romantic relationship breakups. *Personal Relationships, 10,* 113–128.

Taylor, S.E. (1981). A categorization approach to stereotyping. In D.L. Hamilton (Ed.), *Cognitive process in stereotyping and intergroup behavior* (pp. 88–114). Hillsdale, NJ: Lawrence Erlbaum.

Taylor, S.E. (2005). *Health psychology* (6th edn). New York: McGraw-Hill.

Taylor, S.E. & Brown, J.D. (1988). Illusion and well-being: A social psychological perspective on mental health. *Psychological Bulletin, 103,* 193–210.

Taylor, S.E. & Fiske, S.T. (1978). Salience, attention, and attribution: Top of the head phenomena. *Advances in Experimental Social Psychology, 11,* 249–288.

Taylor, S.E., Fiske, S.T., Etcoff, N.L. & Ruderman, A.J. (1978). Categorical and contextual bases of person memory and stereotyping. *Journal of Personality and Social Psychology, 36,* 778–793.

Taylor, S.P. (1967). Aggressive behavior and physiological arousal as a function of provocation and the tendency to inhibit aggression. *Journal of Personality and Social Psychology, 35,* 297–310.

Tekleab, A.G., Takeuchi, R. & Taylor, M.S. (2005). Extending the chain of relationships among organizational justice, social exchange, and employee reactions: The role of contract violations. *Academy of Management Journal, 48,* 146–157.

Tellis, G.J. (2004). *Effective advertising.* Thousand Oaks, CA: Sage.

Temkin, J. & Krahé, B. (2007). *Sexual assault and the justice gap: A question of attitude.* Oxford: Hart Publishing.

Tepper, B.J. (2000). Consequences of abusive supervision. *Academy of Management Journal, 43,* 178–190.

Tesser, A. (1988). Toward a self-evaluation maintenance model of social behavior. In L. Berkowitz (Ed.), *Advances in experimental social psychology* (Vol. 21, pp. 181–227). New York: Academic Press.

Tesser, A., Campbell, J. & Mickler, S. (1983). The role of social pressure, attention to the stimulus, and self-doubt in conformity. *European Journal of Social Psychology, 13,* 217–233.

Tetlock, P.E. (1979). Identifying victims of groupthink from public statements of decision makers. *Journal of Personality and Social Psychology, 37,* 1314–1324.

Tetlock, P.E. (1983). Accountability and complexity of thought. *Journal of Personality and Social Psychology, 45*, 74–83.

Tetlock, P.E. (1998). Social psychology and world politics. In D.T. Gilbert, S.T., Fiske & G. Lindzey (Eds.), *The handbook of social psychology* (4th edn, Vol. 2, pp. 868–912). New York: McGraw-Hill.

Tetlock, P.E. (2002). Social functionalist frameworks for judgment and choice: Intuitive politicians, theologians, and prosecutors. *Psychological Review, 109*, 451–471.

Tetlock, P.E. & Levi, A. (1982). Attribution bias: On the inconclusiveness of the cognition–motivation debate. *Journal of Experimental Social Psychology, 18*, 68–88.

Tetlock, P.E. & Manstead, A.S.R. (1985). Impression management versus intrapsychic explanations in social psychology: A useful dichotomy? *Psychological Review, 92*, 59–77.

't Hart, P. (1990). *Groupthink in government: A study of small groups and policy failure.* Amsterdam: Swets & Zeitlinger.

't Hart, P., Stern, E. & Sundelius, B. (Eds.) (1995). *Beyond groupthink.* Stockholm: Stockholm Center for Organizational Research.

Thibaut, J.W. & Kelley, H.H. (1959). *The social psychology of groups.* New York: Wiley.

Thibaut, J.W. & Walker, L. (1978). A theory of procedure. *California Law Review, 66*, 541–566.

Thompson, S.C. & Kelley, H.H. (1981). Judgments of responsibility in close relationships. *Journal of Personality and Social Psychology, 41*, 469–477.

Thompson, S.C., Levine, J.M. & Messick, D.M. (Eds.) (1999). *Shared cognition in organizations.* Mahwah, NJ: Lawrence Erlbaum.

Thompson, W.C., Cowan, C.L. & Rosenhan, D.L. (1980). Focus of attention mediates the impact of negative affect on altruism. *Journal of Personality and Social Psychology, 38*, 291–300.

Thurstone, L.L. (1928) Attitudes can be measured. *Journal of Sociology, 33*, 529–554.

Tindale, R.S. & Davis, J.H. (1983). Group decision making and jury verdicts. In H.H. Blumberg, A.P. Hare, V. Kent & M.F. Davies (Eds.), *Small groups and social interaction* (Vol. 2, pp. 9–38). Chichester: Wiley.

Tindale, R.S. & Kameda, T. (2000). 'Social sharedness' as a unifying theme for information processing in groups. *Group Processes and Intergroup Relations, 3*, 123–140.

Tindale, R.S., Davis, J.H., Vollrath, D.A., Nagao, D.H. & Hinsz, V.B. (1990). Asymmetrical social influence in freely interacting groups: A test of three models. *Journal of Personality and Social Psychology, 58*, 438–449.

Toi, M. & Batson, C.D. (1982). More evidence that empathy is a source of altruistic motivation. *Journal of Personality and Social Psychology, 43*, 281–293.

Torrance, E.P. (1954). The behavior of small groups under the stress of conditions of survival. *American Sociological Review, 19*, 751–755.

Totterdell, P. (2005). Work schedules. In J. Barling, E.K. Kelloway & M.R. Frone (Eds.), *Handbook of work stress* (pp. 35–62). Thousand Oaks, CA: Sage.

Triandis, H.C. (1995). *Individualism and collectivism.* Boulder, CO: Westview Press.

Triplett, N.D. (1898). The dynamogenic factor in pacemaking and competition. *American Journal of Psychology, 9*, 507–533.

Trivers, R.L. (1971). The evolution of reciprocal altruism. *Quarterly Review of Biology, 46*, 35–57.

Tschan, F., Semmer, N.K., Gautschi, D., Spychiger, M., Hunziker, P.R. & Marsch, S.U. (2006). Leading to recovery: Group performance and coordinating activities in Medical Emergency-Driven Groups. *Human Performance, 19*, 277–304.

Tuckman, B.W. (1965). Developmental sequence in small groups. *Psychological Bulletin, 63*, 384–399.

Tuckman, B.W. & Jensen, M.A.C. (1977). Stages of small group development reconsidered. *Group and Organizational Studies, 2*, 419–427.

Tulving, E. (1993). What is episodic memory? *Current Directions in Psychological Science, 2*, 67–70.

Turner, J.C. (1982). Towards a cognitive redefinition of the social group. In H. Tajfel (Ed.), *Social identity and intergroup relations* (pp. 15–40). Cambridge: Cambridge University Press.

Turner, J.C. (1991). *Social influence.* Buckingham: Open University Press.

Turner, J.C. & Reynolds, K.J. (2001). The social identity perspective in intergroup relations: Theories, themes, and controversies. In R. Brown & S. Gaertner (Eds.), *Blackwell handbook of social psychology: Intergroup processes* (pp. 133–152). Malden, MA: Blackwell.

Turner, J.C., Hogg, M.A., Oakes, P.J., Reicher, S.D. & Wetherell, M.S. (1987). *Rediscovering the social group: A self-categorization theory.* Oxford: Blackwell.

Turner, J.C., Wetherell, M.S. & Hogg, M.A. (1989). Referent informational influence and group polarization. *British Journal of Social Psychology, 28*, 135–147.

Turner, M., Pratkanis, A.R., Probasco, P. & Love, C. (1992). Threat, cohesion, and group effectiveness: Testing a social identity maintenance perspective on groupthink. *Journal of Personality and Social Psychology, 63*, 781–796.

Tyler, T.R. & Lind, E.A. (1992). A relational model of authority in groups. In M. Zanna (Ed.), *Advances in experimental social psychology* (Vol. 25, pp. 115–192). New York: Academic Press.

Underwood, B., Froming, W.J. & Moore, B.S. (1977). Mood, attention, and altruism: A search for mediating variables. *Developmental Psychology, 13*, 541–542.

USDHEW (US Department of Health, Education and Welfare) (1964). *Smoking and health: A report of the Surgeon General.* Washington, DC: US Government Printing Office.

Van de Vliert, E., Huang, X. & Levine. R.L. (2004). National wealth and thermal climate as predictors of motives for volunteer work. *Journal of Cross-Cultural Psychology, 35*, 62–73.

Van den Bos, K. (2005). What is responsible for the fair process effect? In J. Greenberg & J.A. Colquitt (Eds.), *Handbook of organizational justice: Fundamental questions about fairness in the workplace* (pp. 273–300). Mahwah, NJ: Lawrence Erlbaum.

Van den Bos, K. & Lind, E.A. (2001). The psychology of own versus others' treatment: Self-oriented and other-oriented effects on perceptions of procedural justice. *Personality and Social Psychology Bulletin, 27*, 1324–1333.

Van den Bos, K. & Lind, E.A. (2002). Uncertainty management by means of fairness. In M. Zanna (Ed.), *Advances in experimental social psychology* (Vol. 34, pp. 1–60). San Diego, CA: Academic Press.

Van den Bos, K., Lind, E.A., Vermunt, R. & Wilke, H.A. (1997). How do I judge my outcome when I do not know the outcome of others? The psychology of the fair process effect. *Journal of Personality and Social Psychology, 72*, 1034–1046.

Van Knippenberg, A., van Twuyver, M. & Pepels, J. (1994). Factors affecting social categorization processes in memory. *British Journal of Social Psychology, 33*, 419–431.

Van Knippenberg, D. (2000). Work motivation and performance: A social identity perspective. *Applied Psychology: An International Review, 49*, 357–371.

Van Knippenberg, D. & Ellemers, N. (2003). Social identity and group performance: Identification as the key to group-oriented efforts. In S.A. Haslam, D. van Knippenberg, M.J. Platow & N. Ellemers (Eds.), *Social identity at work: Developing theory for organizational practice* (pp. 29–42). New York and Hove: Psychology Press.

Van Knippenberg, D. & van Knippenberg, A. (1994). Social categorization, focus of attention and judgements of group opinions. *British Journal of Social Psychology, 33*, 477–489.

Van Knippenberg, D., Lossie, N. & Wilke, H. (1994). Ingroup prototypicality and persuasion: Determinants of heuristic and systematic message processing. *British Journal of Social Psychology, 33*, 289–300.

Van Lange, P.A.M., Rusbult, C.E., Drigotas, S.M., Arriaga, X.B., Witcher, B.S. & Cox, C.L. (1997). Willingness to sacrifice in close relationships. *Journal of Personality and Social Psychology, 72*, 1373–1395.

Van Scotter, J.R. (2000). Relationships of task performance and contextual performance with turnover, job satisfaction, and affective commitment. *Human Resource Management Review, 10*, 79–85.

Van Vugt, M. & Hart, C. (2004). Social identity as social glue: The origins of group loyalty. *Journal of Personality and Social Psychology, 86*, 585–598.

Vanberg, V. (1975). *Die zwei Soziologien*. Tübingen: Mohr.

Vandenberghe, C., Bentein, K. & Stinglhamber, F. (2004). Affective commitment to the organization, supervisor, and work group: Antecedents and outcomes. *Journal of Vocational Behavior, 64*, 47–71.

VanYperen, N.W. & Buunk, B.P. (1991). Sex-role attitudes, social comparison, and satisfaction with relationships. *Social Psychology Quarterly, 54*, 169–180.

Vasquez, E.A., Denson, T.F., Pedersen, W.C., Stenstrom, D.M. & Miller, N. (2005). The moderating effect of trigger intensity on triggered displaced aggression. *Journal of Experimental Social Psychology, 41*, 61–67.

Verplanken, B. & Aarts, H. (1999). Habit, attitude, planned behavior: Is habit an empty construct or an interesting case of goal directed automaticity? In W. Stroebe & M. Hewstone (Eds.), *European review of social psychology* (Vol. 10, pp. 100–134). Chichester: Wiley.

Viney, L. (1969). Self: The history of a concept. *Journal of the History of the Behavioral Sciences, 5*, 349–359.

Vinokur, A. & Burnstein, E. (1974). The effects of partially shared persuasive arguments on group-induced shifts: A problem solving approach. *Journal of Personality and Social Psychology, 29*, 305–315.

Visser, P. & Krosnick, J.A. (1998). Development of attitude strength over the life cycle: Surge and decline. *Journal of Personality and Social Psychology, 75*, 1389–1410.

Voci, A. & Hewstone, M. (2003). Intergroup contact and prejudice towards immigrants in Italy: The mediational role of anxiety and the moderational role of group salience. *Group Processes and Intergroup Relations, 6*, 37–54.

Von Hippel, W., Sekaquaptewa, D. & Vargas, P. (1997). The linguistic intergroup bias as an implicit indicator of prejudice. *Journal of Experimental Social Psychology, 33*, 490–509.

Vroom, V.H. & Jago, A.G. (1988). *The new leadership*. Englewood Cliffs, NJ: Prentice-Hall.

Wageman, R. (2001). How leaders foster self-managing team effectiveness: Design choices versus hands-on coaching. *Organization Science, 12*, 559–577.

Wagner, N., Fieldman, G. & Hussey, T. (2003). The effect on ambulatory blood pressure of working under favourably and unfavourably perceived supervisors. *Occupational and Environmental Medicine, 60*, 468–474.

Waller, J. (2002). *Becoming evil: How ordinary people commit genocide and mass killing*. Oxford and New York: Oxford University Press.

Waller, P.F. (2002). Challenges in motor vehicle safety. *Annual Review of Public Health, 23*, 93–113.

Walster, E., Aronson, V., Abrahams, D. & Rottmann, L. (1966). The importance of physical attractiveness in dating behavior. *Journal of Personality and Social Psychology, 4*, 508–516.

Walster, E., Walster, G.W. & Berscheid, E. (1978). *Equity: Theory and research*. Boston: Allyn & Bacon.

Walz, S.M. & Niehoff, B.P. (1996). Organizational citizenship behaviors and their relationship with indicators of organizational effectiveness in limited menu restaurants. In J.B. Keys & L.N. Dosier (Eds.), *Academy of Management Best Papers Proceedings* (pp. 307–311). Statesboro, GA: George Southern University.

Wänke, M. (1998). Markenmanagement als Kategorisierungsproblem [Brand management as a problem of categorization]. *Zeitschrift für Sozialpsychologie, 29*, 117–123.

Wänke, M., Bless, H. & Schwarz, N. (1998). Contrast and assimilation in product line extensions: Context is not destiny. *Journal of Consumer Psychology, 7*, 299–322.

Watson, D. (1982). The actor and the observer: How are their perceptions of causality different? *Psychological Bulletin, 92*, 682–700.

Watt, B.D. & Howells, K. (1999). Skills training for aggression control: Evaluation of an anger management programme for violent offenders. *Legal and Criminological Psychology, 4*, 285–300.

Weary, G., Harvey, J.H., Schwieger, P., Olson, C.T., Perloff, R. & Pritchard, S. (1982). Self-presentation and the moderation of self-serving attributional biases. *Social Cognition, 1*, 140–159.

Webb, E.J., Campbell, D.T., Schwartz, R.D. & Sechrest, L. (2000). *Unobtrusive measures* (rev. edn). Thousand Oaks, CA: Sage.

Weber, R. & Crocker, J. (1983). Cognitive processes in the revision of stereotypic beliefs. *Journal of Personality and Social Psychology, 45*, 961–977.

Wechsler, H., Lee, J.E., Kuo, M., Seibring, M., Nelson, T.F. & Lee, H. (2002). Trends in college binge drinking during a period of increased prevention efforts: Findings from 4 Harvard School of Public Health College Alcohol Study Surveys 1993–2001. *Journal of American College Health, 50*, 203–217.

Wegener, D.T., Petty, R.E. & Smith, S.M. (1995). Positive mood can increase or decrease message scrutiny: The hedonic contingency view of mood and message processing. *Journal of Personality and Social Psychology, 69*, 5–15.

Wegner, D.M. (1986). Transactive memory: A contemporary analysis of the group mind. In B. Mullen & G.R. Goethals (Eds.), *Theories of group behavior* (pp. 185–208). New York: Springer.

Wegner, D.M. (1987). Transactive memory: A contemporary analysis of the group mind. In B. Mullen & G.R. Goethals (Eds.), *Theories of group behaviour* (pp. 185–208). New York: Springer.

Wegner, D.M. (1994). Ironic processes of mental control. *Psychological Review, 101*, 34–52.

Weick, K.E. (1985). Systematic observational methods. In G. Lindzey & E. Aronson (Eds.), *Handbook of social psychology* (3rd edn, Vol. 1, pp. 567–634). New York: Random House.

Weiner, B. (1979). A theory of motivation for some classroom experiences. *Journal of Educational Psychology, 71*, 1–29.

Weiner, B. (1985). An attributional theory of achievement motivation and emotion. *Psychological Review, 92*, 548–573.

Weiner, B. (1986). *An attributional theory of motivation and emotion*. New York: Springer.

Weisband, S. (2002). Maintaining awareness in distributed team collaboration: Implications for leadership and performance. In P. Hinds & S. Kiesler (Eds.), *Distributed work* (pp. 311–333). Cambridge, MA: MIT Press.

Weiss, R.S. (1975). *Marital separation*. New York: Basic Books.

Wells, G.L. & Petty, R.E. (1980). The effects of overt head movements on persuasion: Compatibility and incompatibility of responses. *Basic and Applied Social Psychology, 1*, 219–230.

Werner, C. & Parmelee, P. (1979). Similarity of activity preferences among friends: Those who play together stay together. *Social Psychology Quarterly, 42*, 62–66.

West, S.G., Biesanz, J.C. & Pitts, S.C. (2000). Causal inference and generalization in field settings: Experimental and quasi-experimental designs. In H.T. Reis & C.M. Judd (Eds.), *Handbook of research methods in social and personality psychology* (pp. 40–84). New York: Cambridge University Press.

Wetherell, M.S., Stiven, H. & Potter, J. (1987). Unequal egalitarianism: A preliminary study of discourses concerning gender and employment opportunities. *British Journal of Social Psychology, 26*, 59–71.

Wheelan, S.A., Davidson, B. & Tilin, F. (2003). Group development across time: Reality or illusion? *Small Group Research, 34*, 223–245.

White, G.L., Fishbein, S. & Rutstein, J. (1981). Passionate love and the misattribution of arousal. *Journal of Personality and Social Psychology, 41*, 56–62.

White, J.W. & Kowalski, R.M. (1994). Deconstructing the myth of the nonaggressive woman. *Psychology of Women Quarterly, 18*, 487–508.

White, P.A. (1984). A model of the layperson as pragmatist. *Personality and Social Psychology Bulletin, 10*, 333–348.

White, P.A. (1989). A theory of causal processing. *British Journal of Psychology, 80*, 431–454.

White, R. & Lippitt, R. (1976). Leader behavior and member reaction in three 'social climates'. In D. Cartwright & A. Zander (Eds.), *Group dynamics: Research and theory* (3rd edn, pp. 318–335). New York: Harper & Row.

Wicker, A.W. (1969). Attitude versus action: The relationship of verbal and overt behavioral responses to attitude objects. *Journal of Social Issues, 25*, 41–78.

Wiehe, V.R. (1998). *Understanding family violence.* Thousand Oaks, CA: Sage.

Wilder, D.A. (1977). Perceptions of groups, size of opposition, and influence. *Journal of Experimental Social Psychology, 13*, 253–268.

Wilder, D.A. (1986). Social categorization: Implications for creation and reduction of intergroup bias. In L. Berkowitz (Ed.), *Advances in experimental social psychology* (Vol. 19, pp. 293–355). New York: Academic Press.

Williams, K.D. (2001). *Ostracism: The power of silence.* Philadelphia: Psychology Press.

Williams, K.D. & Karau, S.J. (1991). Social loafing and social compensation: The effects of co-worker performance. *Journal of Personality and Social Psychology, 61*, 570–581.

Wills, T.A. (1981). Downward comparison principles in social psychology. *Psychological Bulletin, 90*, 245–271.

Wills, T.A. (1991). Social support and interpersonal relationships. In M.S. Clark (Ed.), *Prosocial behavior* (pp. 265–289). Newbury Park, CA: Sage.

Wilson, T.D. & Brekke, N. (1994). Mental contamination and mental correction: Unwanted influences on judgments and evaluations. *Psychological Bulletin, 116*, 117–142.

Wilson, T.D. & Dunn, E.W. (2004). Self-knowledge: Its limits, value, and potential for improvement. *Annual Review of Psychology, 55*, 493–518.

Wilson, T.D. & LaFleur, S.J. (1995). Knowing what you'll do: Effects of analyzing reasons on self-prediction. *Journal of Personality and Social Psychology, 68*, 21–35.

Wilson, T.D., Lindzey, S. & Schooler, T.Y. (2000). A model for dual attitudes. *Psychological Review, 107*, 101–126.

Winnubst, J.A., Marcelissen, F.H. & Kleber, R.J. (1982). Effects of social support in the stressor–strain relationship: A Dutch sample. *Social Science and Medicine, 16*, 475–482.

Witte, E.H. (1989). Köhler rediscovered: The anti-Ringelmann effect. *European Journal of Social Psychology, 19*, 147–154.

Wittenbaum, G.M., Hubbell, A.P. & Zuckerman, C. (1999). Mutual enhancement: Toward an understanding of the collective preference for shared information. *Journal of Personality and Social Psychology, 77*, 967–978.

Wittenbrink, B., Judd, C.M. & Park, B. (1997). Evidence for racial prejudice at the implicit level and its relationship with questionnaire measures. *Journal of Personality and Social Psychology, 72*, 262–274.

Wofford, J.C. & Liska, L.Z. (1993). Path-goal theories of leadership: A meta-analysis. *Journal of Management, 19*, 857–876.

Wood, W., Lundgren, S., Ouellette, J.A., Busceme, S. & Blackstone, T. (1994). Minority influence: A meta-analytic review of social influence processes. *Psychological Bulletin, 115*, 323–345.

Woolfolk, R.L., Novalany, J., Gara, M.A., Allen, L.A. & Polino, M. (1995). Self-complexity, self-evaluation, and depression: An examination of form and content within the self-schema. *Journal of Personality and Social Psychology, 68*, 1108–1120.

Wright, E.F. & Wells, G.L. (1988). Is the attitude-attribution paradigm suitable for investigating the dispositional bias? *Personality and Social Psychology Bulletin, 14*, 183–190.

Wright, S.C., Aron, A., McLaughlin-Volpe, T. & Ropp, S.A. (1997). The extended contact effect: Knowledge of cross-group friendships and prejudice. *Journal of Personality and Social Psychology, 73*, 73–90.

Yamagishi, T. (1986). The provision of a sanctioning system as a public good. *Journal of Personality and Social Psychology, 51*, 110–116.

Yela, C. & Sangrador, J.L. (2001). Perception of physical attractiveness throughout loving relationships. *Current Research in Social Psychology, 6*, 57–75.

Yoo, C. & MacInnis, D. (2005). The brand attitude formation process of emotional and informational ads. *Journal of Business Research, 58*, 1397–1406.

Yoshida, T., Kojo, K. & Kaku, H. (1982). A study on the development of self-presentation in children. *Japanese Journal of Educational Psychology, 30*, 30–37.

Yukl, G. (2005). *Leadership in organizations* (6th edn). Upper Saddle River, NJ: Prentice-Hall.

Zaccaro, S.J., Rittman, A.L. & Marks, M.A. (2001). Team leadership. *Leadership Quarterly, 12*, 451–483.

Zajonc, R.B. (1965). Social facilitation. *Science, 149*, 269–274.

Zajonc, R.B. (1968). Attitudinal effects of mere exposure. *Journal of Personality and Social Psychology, 9*, Monograph Supplement No. 2, Part 2.

Zajonc, R.B. (1980). Compresence. In P.B. Paulus (Ed.), *Psychology of group influence* (pp. 35–60). Hillsdale, NJ: Lawrence Erlbaum.

Zajonc, R.B., Heingartner, A. & Herman, E.M. (1969). Social enhancement and impairment of performance in the cockroach. *Journal of Personality and Social Psychology, 13*, 83–92.

Zanna, M.P. & Cooper, J. (1974). Dissonance and the pill: An attribution approach to studying the arousal properties of dissonance. *Journal of Personality and Social Psychology, 29*, 703–709.

Zanna, M.P. & Hamilton, D.L. (1972). Attribute dimensions and patterns of trait inferences. *Psychonomic Science, 27*, 353–354.

Zanna, M.P. & Rempel, J.K. (1988). Attitudes: A new look at an old concept. In D. Bar-Tal & A.W. Kruglanski (Eds.), *The social psychology of knowledge* (pp. 315–334). Cambridge: Cambridge University Press.

Zanna, M.P., Higgins, E.T. & Taves, P.A. (1976). Is dissonance phenomenologically aversive? *Journal of Experimental Social Psychology, 12*, 530–538.

Ziegler, R., Diehl, M. & Zijlstra, G. (2000). Idea production in nominal and virtual groups: Does computer-mediated communication improve group brainstorming? *Group Processes and Intergroup Relations, 3*, 141–158.

Zillmann, D. (1978). Attribution and misattribution of excitatory reactions. In J.H. Harvey, W.J. Ickes & R.F. Kidd (Eds.), *New directions in attribution theory and research* (Vol. 2, pp. 335–368). Hillsdale, NJ: Lawrence Erlbaum.

Zimbardo, P.G. (1970). The human choice: Individuation, reason, and order versus deindividuation, impulse, and chaos. In W.J. Arnold & D. Levine (Eds.), *Nebraska symposium on motivation 1969* (Vol. 17, pp. 237–307). Lincoln: University of Nebraska Press.

Zimbardo, P.G. (2006). Commentary. Tyranny, freedom and social structure: The BBC prison study. *British Journal of Social Psychology, 45*, 47–54.

Zimbardo, P.G., Ebbesen, E.B. & Maslach, C. (1977). *Influencing attitudes and changing behavior* (2nd edn). Reading, MA: Addison-Wesley.

Zimbardo, P.G., Maslach, C. & Haney, C. (2000). Reflections on the Stanford Prison Experiment: Genesis, transformations, consequences. In T. Blass (Ed.), *Obedience to authority: Current perspectives on the Milgram paradigm* (pp. 193–238). Mahwah, NJ: Lawrence Erlbaum.

Zuckerman, M. (1979). Attribution of success and failure revisited, or: The motivational bias is alive and well in attribution theory. *Journal of Personality, 47*, 245–287.

Illustration Sources and Credits

The editors and publisher gratefully acknowledge the permission granted to reproduce the copyright material in this book:

318	Plate 15.1	© Mike Powell / Getty Images / Stone.
319	Plate 15.2a	© Getty Images.
319	Plate 15.2b	© ACE STOCK LIMITED / Alamy.
321	Plate 15.3	akg-images / ullstein bild.
323	Plate 15.4	© Jeff Greenberg / Alamy.

326	Plate 15.5	Courtesy of the Advertising Archives.
327	Plate 15.6	Courtesy of the Advertising Archives.
329	Plate 15.7	© Ryan McVay / Getty Images.
		Pioneer photo, p. 330, courtesy of Timothy A. Judge.
		Pioneer photo, p. 341, courtesy of Susan Folkman.

Name Index

Henningsen, D.D.   286
Henri, V.   9
Henry, P.J.   303, 304
Henry, R.A.   277
Henwood, K.L.   28
Herek, G.M.   121–122, 238
Herman, E.M.   218
Herscovitsch, L.   330
Hersh, S.M.   225
Hertel, G.   272, 274, 276
Hewstone, M.   3–19, 49, 61, 84, 217–243,
   231, 232–233, 292, 308, 310, 311, 312, 313
Heyman, R.E.   206, 207
Higgins, E.T.   70, 99, 117, 300–301, 308
Hilton, D.J.   48, 49, 51, 55, 62
Hilton, J.L.   128
Hinsz, V.B.   235
Hixon, J.G.   82, 211
Ho, S.Y.   203
Hoberman, H.M.   199–200
Hodgkins, S.   132
Hoeksema-van Orden, C.Y.D.   277
Hoel, H.   172
Hoffman, E.L.   221
Hoffman, M.L.   193
Hofling, C.K.   242
Hogg, M.A.   90, 103, 104, 106, 234, 236, 237,
   247, 260, 261, 301, 306, 308
Holland, R.W.   117, 124, 125
Hollander, E.P.   256
Holmes, J.G.   192, 211
Holmes, T.H.   340
Holt, R.   235
Hom, P.W.   330
Homans, G.C.   8
Hood, W.R.   221, 295–296
Hornsey, M.J.   241
Horowitz, L.M.   203, 208
Horowitz, M.   296, 297
House, J.S.   199
House, R.J.   280, 283
Houston, D.A.   124
Hovland, C.I.   11–12, 18, 136, 137, 338
Howard, A.   304
Howard, J.A.   179
Howell, D.C.   341
Howells, K.   173–174
Hoyle, R.H.   98
Huang, X.   188
Hubbell, A.P.   276
Huesmann, L.R.   159, 163–164, 168, 169
Hulin, C.L.   330
Hundley, M.   165–166
Hunziker, P.R.   318
Huskinson, T.L.   128
Hussey, T.   342
Huth, P.   238

Iaffaldano, M.T.   330

Iida, M.   212
Ilgen, D.R.   328
Ilies, R.   281, 282
Ingerman, C.   308
Ingham, A.G.   269
Insko, C.A.   209
Isen, A.M.   186
Isenberg, D.J.   237
Islam, M.R.   61, 311, 313
Ito, T.A.   166

Jaccard, J.J.   130
Jackson, J.R.   126, 127
Jacobs, D.R.   320–321
Jacobs, K.C.   221, 222–223
Jacobson, C.K.   242
Jago, A.G.   286
James, K.   260–261
James, W.   54, 90–91
Janis, I.L.   12, 21, 22, 23, 237, 238, 338
Janke, W.   55
Janoff-Bulman, R.   74
Jaramillo, F.   330
Jarvis, B.   142
Jaspars, J.   50–51
Javidan, M.   280
Jemmott, J.B.   57
Jensen, M.A.C.   254–255
Jetten, J.   4, 5, 6, 79, 81
John, O.P.   127, 313
Johnson, B.   304
Johnson, B.T.   35, 132
Johnson, C.   271, 304
Johnson, D.J.   212
Johnson, E.   242
Johnson, J.   84
Johnson, J.D.   168
Johnson, J.J.   339
Johnson, J.T.   57
Johnson, L.   84
Johnson, M.H.   64
Johnson, M.K.   72
Johnson, R.C.   185
Johnson, T.J.   61
Johnston, L.   83–84, 184
Joinson, A.   45
Jonas, K.   3–19, 317–344
Jones, E.E.   12, 14, 17, 47–49, 57, 59, 63, 102,
   152, 303
Joule, R.V.   227
Judd, C.M.   28, 35, 236, 300, 303, 304
Judge, T.A.   281, 282, 284, 330, 332
Jung, D.I.   285
Junger-Tas, J.   172
Jussim, L.J.   115, 148

Kaku, H.   109
Kallgren, C.A.   220, 223
Kalven, H.   235

Kameda, T.   257
Kanki, B.   230
Kanner, A.D.   340
Kant, I.   90
Kanungo, R.N.   283, 284
Kaplan, K.J.   118
Kaplan, M.F.   235, 236, 237
Karasek, R.A.   340
Karau, S.J.   272
Karbon, M.   191
Karlin, W.A.   199, 342
Karney, B.R.   211
Karpinski, A.   101–102, 103, 128
Karremans, J.C.   148, 322
Kashima, E.   108
Kashima, Y.   108
Kashy, D.A.   35
Kassin, S.M.   49
Katz, D.   120, 123, 188
Katz, I.   303, 304
Katzenstein, G.   277
Kaukiainen, A.   166
Kawakami, K.   116, 304
Kelley, H.H.   8, 12, 14, 44, 47, 49, 50, 211,
   247, 296, 338
Kelloway, E.K.   342
Kelly, C.   303
Kelly, L.   171
Kelman, H.C.   241
Keltner, D.   303
Kemeny, M.E.   341, 342
Kendzierski, D.   8, 131
Kenny, D.A.   28, 35
Kenrick, D.T.   17, 186, 207, 208, 209
Kent, A.   229
Kerkstra, A.   211
Kernis, M.H.   98
Kerr, N.L.   235, 246, 271, 272, 276
Kerschreiter, R.   275, 276, 277
Kessler, R.C.   199, 208, 340
Kessler, T.   291–314, 299, 308, 311
Keys, C.B.   276
Kiesler, C.A.   230
Kiesler, S.B.   230
Kim, W.C.   333
Kirk, S.B.   198
Kirsh, S.J.   168
Kitayama, S.   108–109, 185, 225
Kitson, G.C.   213
Kivimäki, M.   342
Kjos, G.L.   201
Klandermans, B.   8, 303
Klauer, K.C.   301
Kleber, R.J.   199
Klein, O.   300
Klein, R.   187, 191
Klein, S.B.   96
Klem, A.   121, 122
Klentz, B.   183, 227

Subject Index